Uruk Mesopotamia
& Its Neighbors

M000274421

**Publication of the Advanced Seminar Series
is made possible by generous support from
The Brown Foundation, Inc., of Houston, Texas.**

**School of American Research
Advanced Seminar Series**

Douglas W. Schwartz
General Editor

Uruk Mesopotamia
& Its Neighbors

Contributors

Guillermo Algaze
Department of Anthropology, University of California, San Diego

Terence N. D'Altroy
Department of Anthropology, Columbia University

Marcella Frangipane
*Dipartmento di Scienze Storiche Archeologiche e Antropologiche
dell'Antichità, Università di Roma, "La Sapienza"*

Hans J. Nissen
*Seminar für vorderasiatische Altertumskunde,
Freie Universität Berlin*

Holly Pittman
Department of the History of Art, University of Pennsylvania

Susan Pollock
*Department of Anthropology,
State University of New York, Binghamton*

Mitchell S. Rothman
Social Science Division, Widener University

Glenn M. Schwartz
Department of Near Eastern Studies, Johns Hopkins University

Gil J. Stein
Department of Anthropology, Northeastern University

Henry T. Wright
Museum of Anthropology, University of Michigan, Ann Arbor

Uruk Mesopotamia
& Its Neighbors

*Cross-Cultural Interactions
in the Era of State Formation*

Edited by Mitchell S. Rothman

School of American Research Press
Santa Fe

James Currey
Oxford

School of American Research Press

Post Office Box 2188
Santa Fe, New Mexico 87504-2188

James Currey Ltd

73 Botley Road
Oxford OX2 0BS

Acting Director: Cynthia Welch
Copy Editor: June-el Piper
Series Design: Context, Inc.
Indexer: Pilar Wyman
Printer: Sheridan Books, USA

Library of Congress Cataloging-in-Publication Data:

Uruk Mesopotamia & its neighbors : cross-cultural interactions in the era of state
formation / edited by Mitchell S. Rothman.—1st ed.
    p. cm.
  Includes bibliographical references and index.
    ISBN 1-930618-02-6 (alk. paper) — ISBN 1-930618-03-4 (pbk.: alk. paper)
    1. Middle East—Civilization—To 622. 2. Erech (Extinct city) I. Title: Uruk Mesopotamia
and its neighbors. II. Rothman, Mitchell S., 1952–
DS62.23 .U78 2001
935—dc21   2001049321

British Library Cataloguing in Publication Data:

Uruk Mesopotamia & its neighbors : cross-cultural interactions in the era of state
    formation. - (School of American Research advanced seminar series)
    1. Iraq - Civilization - To 634 2. Iraq - Antiquities 3. Iraq - History - To 634
    I. Rothman, Mitchell S., 1952–
    935
    ISBN 0-85255-461-3 (James Currey cloth) 0-85255-460-5 (James Currey paper)

Cover illustration: the period VI A temple-palace complex at Arslantepe, with artifacts.

Contents

Illustrations

Tables

Dedicated to Robert McCormick Adams

Preface

A volume such as this by its very nature reflects a collaborative process. Its success depends on the cooperation and to some degree passion of the participants for their subject. As an editor and the organizer of the advanced seminar from which this volume evolved, I have been blessed with the cooperation and enthusiasm of this set of participants. The days we spent in Santa Fe on the campus of the School of American Research were among the most gratifying and intellectually enlivening I have ever spent as an academic. The staff of SAR often expected us to rest in the evenings after a long day of discussion, but none of us wanted to stop exploring and reviewing what has become a passionate quest to understand Greater Mesopotamia in the late fifth and fourth millennia B.C., a most revolutionary place and time in human experience. In many ways this period, although fundamentally different from the present, presaged some of the trends that would lead to our modern world: the evolution of urbanism, administrative forms of social organization (complex chiefdoms and states), trade, and economic interdependence over a large region.

The cooperation of this group did not stop after we left Santa Fe. Many of the participants continued to correspond not just with me as an editor but also with each other, suggesting ways to improve their final chapters. Hans Nissen and Glenn Schwartz took it on themselves to work out some of the problems of the bibliography. Rarely did I have to push very hard for deadlines or changes, and the few times I did, the participants were gracious in their responses. My name is listed as editor of the book, but in fact we all contributed more than just individual articles to make this volume as good as it could be.

Of course, none of this would have happened without the programs of the School of American Research, its president and CEO, Douglas Schwartz, and its staff. The idea for the advanced seminars is a brilliant one. To give ten scholars the chance to meet and spend such quality academic time to work out problems in a new or developing topic is a model for other research-sponsoring organizations to follow. It did not hurt that the participants found themselves in a uniquely beautiful setting, treated with care by an always gracious and accommodating staff. I am sure we all forgive the cook for the pound or two we gained at SAR.

This volume comes out at a time of transition for SAR. Douglas Schwartz is stepping down as president; the School's vice president when we were there, Duane Anderson, has since taken up a position elsewhere; and the director of the SAR Press, Joan O'Donnell, has moved on to seek new ways to explore her talents. We thank them all for making our experience so fulfilling. We especially marvel at the energy, enthusiasm, and broad intellectual interests of Doug Schwartz, who joined our discussion more than once and who peppered me with insightful questions in private and at the public program. We wish also to thank Cecile Stein and her staff for helping us with arrangements of all kinds.

The current SAR Press staff was unendingly helpful in producing this volume. Cynthia Welch, acting press director, put up with my many queries and demands. Our copy editor, June-el Piper, dealt with a large and complex manuscript. She held her ground, making the volume as stylistically perfect as she could, although any fault lies with us. Jane Kepp came on at the end to clear up some of those final, important, and irritating minutiae that speak quality to the reader. Thanks to all.

Last, this volume is dedicated to Robert McCormick Adams, former professor and academic leader at the University of Chicago and secretary of the Smithsonian Institution. Dr. Adams was the teacher of two of our participants, Henry Wright and Guillermo Algaze. You can see his influence on both in their broad knowledge and ability to think and write on broad intellectual themes. Adams was an early collaborator with another participant, Hans Nissen, and together they researched and wrote *The Uruk Countryside.* Many of the remaining participants were students of Adams's students or were influenced in their intellectual development by Adams's writings. We hope this volume represents a small token of our thanks to one of the great scholars of our field, who opened new vistas on this place and time for us to see into and through.

Mitchell S. Rothman

Dedication

To Robert McCormick Adams

Henry T. Wright

If the authors of this book share one thing, it is that we have learned from Robert McCormick Adams. Many of us have known Adams for more than three decades, and he has taught us much, not only about ancient Mesopotamia but also about how to conceptualize civilizations. In particular, his contributions to the study of Uruk civilizations have been exceptional. We have learned and continue to learn much from him, as is evident in the pages of this volume.

Adams began his archaeological career under the tutelage of Robert Braidwood, when he was a fieldworker at the early village site of Jarmo in Iraqi Kurdistan. He wrote a broadly synthetic thesis on earliest Mesopotamian civilization, challenged by the insights of such great scholars at Chicago's Oriental Institute as Henri Frankfort, John Wilson, Carl Kraeling, and Thorkild Jacobsen and by such Chicago anthropologists as Robert Redfield. This study, leavened by insights gained from his first surveys in Mesopotamia and from archaeological research in the University of Chicago's interdisciplinary Chiapas project in southern Mexico, informed his Lewis Henry Morgan lectures at the University of Rochester, published as *The Evolution of Urban Society* (1966). This slim volume still sets the agenda for much of our discussion of early urbanism in Mesopotamia. In it, Adams presents a total and coherent view of culture. In that view ordinary farmers and craftsmen are as important as urban scribes and priests, religion cannot be understood without politics, and nothing can be understood without knowledge of its broader natural context.

He was inspired to begin his now-famous series of surveys by Jacobsen's mapping of ancient sites on the alluvium of southern Iraq in order to locate former watercourses and by Gordon Willey's pioneering demonstration of the power of archaeological survey to define successive patterns of human settlement in Peru (1953). In 1957, Adams began the archaeological survey of the northern alluvial plains of Lower Mesopotamia. This research was begun in the regions near Baghdad scheduled for new irrigation projects and was integrated with the work of soil scientists, biologists, and agronomists who were attached to these same projects. In the field, Adams used aerial photographs to define and map settlements and traces of irrigation systems, coring techniques to establish the thickness of the alluvium perhaps covering smaller sites, and small-scale excavation to date irrigation works. The major study resulting from these surveys was *Land Behind Baghdad* (1965), an eloquently written introduction to the ecological history of alluvial Mesopotamia, still frequently consulted for its discussion of the strengths and limitations of archaeological survey, its presentation of the cultural ecology of traditional irrigation communities, and its analysis of the great Sasanian and early Islamic irrigation systems in the region of Ctesiphon and Baghdad.

Adams took a brief respite from his work in Iraq to survey, in less than two months, the central Susiana Plain in southwestern Iran, an area about to be covered by extensive new irrigation works. He reported this in the journal *Science* in "Agriculture and Urban Life in Early Southwestern Iran" (Adams 1962). Using the data and maps Adams generously provided, other archaeologists resurveyed the region around Susa at least five successive times during the late 1960s and the 1970s (Carter 1971; Hole 1985; Johnson 1973; Miroschedji 1981; Schacht 1976; Wenke 1975–76). Though more precise chronological ascription of sites was used to answer new questions, few if any of the general historical inferences in his overview article were found to be inaccurate.

It was in these early years that Adams developed the extensive full-coverage survey technique that remains the method of choice for primary regional studies in arid alluvial valleys everywhere. In these studies, one traversed every square kilometer of a topographically defined region. This required a strong four-wheel-drive vehicle, whose purpose, as Adams put it, "was to be run into the ground." This also required aerial photographs, not only because maps were poor but also because the photos showed sites, canal traces, and other cultural features. Without photos, one could not get half the story. In addition, Adams was assiduous in seeking, both locally and afar, such resources as soil studies, agronomic studies, historical texts, and ethnographic studies (even supporting ethnographic fieldwork in key areas [Fernea 1970] when necessary). When I started my own work in southwestern Iran, a decade after his survey, Adams was well remembered at the engineering settlement of the Khuzistan Water and Power Authority. He returned late each day and laid out his aerial photos on a table in the engineers' modest "club," and then added sites to his base maps, aided by little more than a cold bottle of "ab-i jo." It was no accident that the "club" was not far from the largest archive of soils, hydrological, and agronomic studies for the region and that Adams developed good relations with the best specialists in these fields. If surveyors in recent years have developed more intensive techniques for answering different questions (Wilkinson and Tucker 1995), the broad contextual perspective provided by extensive surveys is still needed. One need only note the disagreements that arise in some of the papers that follow, because we do not have extensive full-coverage surveys published for the Mosul, Khabur, Harran, and other plains in Upper Mesopotamia.

In his syntheses, and in the studies based on his first surveys, the cultures of the fourth millennium B.C. were not emphasized. Archaeologists working with the evidence from excavations at Uruk-Warka, Eridu, and other sites recognized the importance of transformations of the arts and crafts and the development of writing during this time, but in the absence of a regional perspective, the period was viewed as one of small, temple-centered settlements lacking a broader organization. In the northern alluvium of lower Iraq, Adams found that settlements prior to the third millennium were deeply buried. On the plains of southwestern Iran, fourth millennium land surfaces were less obscured. However, the key to interpreting them, a detailed chronology of local ceramics, could not be inferred from the extant publications on the important site of Susa. Adams nonetheless urged us to look more closely at this period whenever research opportunities presented themselves. It was Adams himself, however, working with Hans Nissen, who was to provide the evidence that would shatter our inadequate ideas about the events and achievements of the fourth millennium.

After several years as director of the University of Chicago's Oriental Institute, Adams returned to Mesopotamia in 1967 to apply his survey approach on the southern alluvium to the central and most populous part of ancient Sumer, around the great cities of Uruk-Warka, Larsa, and Umma. Adams was able to live at Uruk-Warka with the archaeologists of the Deutches Archäologisches Institut, who had labored for decades at the long-abandoned city. With Hans Nissen, Adams mapped sites and traces of watercourses, dating recovered ceramics using the fine-scale chronological distinctions established by Nissen during his studies at Uruk-Warka (Nissen 1970). The work provided a picture of the extraordinarily rapid emergence of a dense network of smaller urban centers and rural dependencies around the regional center of Uruk-Warka during the fourth millennium B.C. It also uncovered their surprising coalescence into a few very large urban centers during the third millennium. Adams and Nissen rapidly brought out their research in *The Uruk Countryside* (1972), a study that has formed the basis for many subsequent reanalyses related to the questions of state and urban origins.

In 1968, Adams initiated survey in northern Sumer around the ancient city of Nippur, but local conditions made fieldwork in Iraq difficult. Adams spent several years as dean and then provost of the University of Chicago. The Nippur-Adab survey was brought to a conclusion in 1976. In the course of these seasons, Adams sharpened his methods, introducing systematic surface collection so that the densities of economically important debris could be assessed. He also used satellite images for the first time to detect larger environmental features not evident on conventional aerial photographs. This study documented a cycle of settlement growth centuries before the emergence of Uruk-Warka on a short-lived river channel east of Nippur, one so large that it was thought to be a conjoined channel of the Tigris and Euphrates.

This study and a complete reanalysis of his earlier surveys, answering many criticisms of his earlier analyses, appeared as the magisterial *Heartland of Cities* (1981).

Beginning in 1981, Adams began a long period of national service, first as a Councilor of the National Academy of Sciences and then as the Secretary of the Smithsonian Institution. Even with the heavy burdens of these offices, he continued to write, laying the groundwork of his social history of technology from the cylinder seal to the computer chip, *Paths of Fire* (1996).

Now, at a time of life when many might continue to write in a more contemplative vein, especially given the tragic effects of the Gulf War and subsequent events in the region that have devastated his primary area of field research, Adams is in the midst of exciting new research on Mesopotamian landscapes, using a new approach. The declassification of cold war satellite imagery has given us the possibility of mapping the entirety of Lower Mesopotamia, of pinpointing every tell that still rises above the alluvium and revising our understanding of the changing patterns of natural watercourses and canals. While only some sites on the two-thirds of the alluvium not surveyed in detail can be precisely dated, one can connect traces of watercourses to others already dated. At this moment, Adams is forging ahead on a synthesis and publication of the human use of the entire landscape from 4000 B.C. to A.D. 1900.

During this very active career of field research, writing, and both university and national service, Adams has always been a teacher. His generosity to students in all areas of archaeology has been exemplary. He has worked not only with those who come with impressive credentials but also with others who his intuition told him might make unusual and exceptional contributions. He is the master of the searching question that makes a student completely rethink an issue and is adept at making available just enough resources so that each can find his or her own way. We and many others have profited from his generosity, and we dedicate this volume to him in recognition of his decades of inspiring work in the "Heartland of Cities."

Uruk Mesopotamia & Its Neighbors

1

The Local and the Regional

An Introduction

Mitchell S. Rothman

The volume you are holding is the product of a School of American Research advanced seminar entitled "Greater Mesopotamia in the Era of State Formation." The ten participants whose individual contributions make up this volume were brought together to evaluate current interpretations of and new data concerning the Greater Mesopotamian region during the late fifth and fourth millennia B.C. Nine of the participants are field archaeologists who have been generating data relevant to our topic. They represent various schools of thought on these matters. As a group, these ten bring a variety of intellectual traditions to this volume, representing the European culture-historical and the American anthropological archaeology schools. The last participant, Terry D'Altroy, brings useful and innovative perspectives on this topic from his work on New World complex societies.

Intensive effort has been expended on the Mesopotamian case by these authors and many others because of its central importance for understanding the origin of both the first truly urban settlement systems—cities—and the first state-level societies. As D'Altroy comments, "Uruk Mesopotamia has stood as *the* model for the study of the rise of state society for several decades. It provides both the conceptual and the organizational standards against which we most often compare the developments in the other areas where we work" (chapter 12, this volume). As the age of Boasian particularism faded and new evolutionary theories emerged, ancient Mesopotamia became one of the most often cited cases for theorists such as Julian Steward (1955, 1973) in their models of the evolution of complex societies. Periodically reviewing the state of our knowledge and interpretations of the Mesopotamia case therefore takes on an importance beyond the culture history of this particular region for the fields of anthropology, history, and more recently political science (Cioffi-Revilla 2000).

This is especially so since the speed with which new data relevant to fourth millennium B.C. Mesopotamia have been accruing is quite astonishing. Ironically, as Nissen comments below, field research over the last twenty years of the twentieth century has mostly been conducted in areas outside of what Robert Adams, the intellectual pioneer to whom we dedicate this volume, calls the Heartland of Cities, the southern alluvium of Mesopotamia. This research indicates that there were systematic connections between this heartland and the rest of the region.

Guillermo Algaze, whose essay follows this one, has had a profound effect on Mesopotamian research because he recognized the importance of this fact. Starting with his dissertation (1986a), he has reinterpreted older ideas on Mesopotamian society in a way that redirected the questions scholars asked and the field research they did. He asserted that the connections among the different subregions of Greater Mesopotamia not only were symptomatic of the changes that were taking place, but were the catalyst for development and change. The systematic nature of the economic, political, and social relationships that crossed cultural boundaries determined the course of the region's evolutionary trajectory for millennia to come. As you will read, not all those who study this region agree with his interpretation, but most acknowledge the explanatory model he learned from Adams and also from Wright, and later built upon.

As often happens when dramatic new ideas are matched by a generation of new fieldwork, the field becomes overwhelmed by the need to analyze all the new material. Older "common knowledge," which gives scholars a framework for reducing detail and understanding larger patterns and trends, becomes entrenched. I would submit that this is what has been happening in Near East studies. Our advanced seminar, as well as a recent gathering of scholars in Europe,[1] was an attempt to step back and look anew at the data and interpretations we have been utilizing. In the words of Hans Nissen (this volume), we wanted to see if it was necessary "to shuffle the deck."

An explanation of terminology is required here. The term "Uruk" has been applied, often very imprecisely, to three distinctly different things. First, it is a time period roughly coterminous with the fourth millennium B.C. Second, it is applied to the cultures of the societies that occupied the southern alluvium of modern Iraq. Third, it is the name of the city after which the period was named. To minimize confusion here, the city will always be referred to as Uruk-Warka or simply Warka. The period name will always be specified as the "Uruk period," most often followed by the appropriate chronological subdivision. When appropriate, the cultural aspects of the Uruk will be referred to as "southern Mesopotamian" or "southern," or the context will make it clear that various aspects of, for example, the "Uruk *network*," "Uruk *administrative system*," "Uruk *culture*," or "Uruk *stylistic corpus*" are being discussed.

GOALS OF THE VOLUME

Chronology

In order to reassess our interpretations, we attempt to accomplish three interrelated goals. The first is to reassess the chronological framework for the Greater Mesopotamian region (fig. 1.1). Until recently, scholars believed that the dramatic changes in Mesopotamia occurred during the last part of the fourth millennium, the Late Uruk (LC 5) period from 3300 to 3100 B.C. (Porada 1965: chronology table 2). Since the so-called expansion of southern Mesopotamian culture—whether via colonists, emulation, or exchange networks—into the areas outside the heartland was thought to be a phenomenon of the Late Uruk, most researchers assumed that the Uruk expansion was a rapid and short-term phenomenon.

As more and more sites were excavated and more and more dates were added, this view became untenable. What would replace it? A

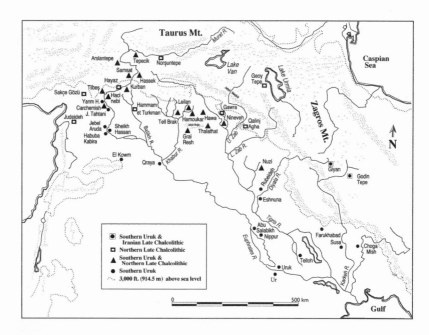

FIGURE 1.1

Greater Mesopotamia in the Late Chalcolithic/Uruk period.

chronology that showed which levels of sites throughout Greater
Mesopotamia were roughly coterminous would have to be a first step.
Since we are talking about cause and effect, obviously various developments have to be put into proper chronological order. For example, in
his earlier presentations, Algaze asserted that all increases in complexity among indigenous societies of the north were catalyzed by contact
with the south. The north covers the steppes of Assyria in modern Iraq
and Syria (Jazira and Jezirah),[2] the piedmont of northeastern Iraq, and
the hills and intermontane zones of eastern Turkey and western Iran.
New analyses from Arslantepe (Frangipane and Palmieri 1983b;
Frangipane 1997b and this volume), Hacınebi (Stein, ed., 1999), and
Tepe Gawra (Rothman and Peasnall 1999; Rothman n.d.) indicate that
sophisticated control mechanisms and indicators of rank were evident
long before any *increased* cross-cultural contact with the south was evident. As Wright states in chapter 4, the so-called Uruk Expansion must
now be dated much earlier than previously thought. It now seems to
have lasted for more than 600 years and to have definable stages.

TABLE 1.1

New Chronological Framework for Greater Mesopotamia in the Late Chalcolithic/Uruk Period

Date B.C.		South	Iran	Syria	Upper Euphrates	Tigris	Southern Mesopotamia
3000	LC 5 / Late	IVA Eanna IVB V; Eanna VI	Early 17 Susa Acropole; Godin V	Habuba Kabira Jebel Aruda; Sheikh Hassan 4; Brak TW 12	Arslantepe VIA; Hassek Höyük	Nineveh (Gut) Spätüruk Ninevite 4 L: 31–20; Mohammad Arab Late Uruk	Late Uruk
3400	LC 4	Abu Salabikh *Uruk Mound*; Nippur XV–XVII; Eanna VII; Nippur XVIII hiatus?	Late 18 Susa; Early 18 Sharafabad	Sheikh Hassan 5–7; Brak TW 13	Arslantepe VII; Hacinebi B2; Hacinebi B1	Norduruk B L: 37–31	Late Middle Uruk
3600	LC 3	Eanna IX–VIII; Nippur XX–XIX; Eanna XI–X	Susa 19–22; Susa Acropolis 23–27	Sheikh Hassan 8–10/13; Brak TW 14–17; Leilan V; Qraya	Hacinebi A	Norduruk A L: 45–37; Tepe Gawra VIII; Tepe Gawra IX–X	Early Middle Uruk
3800 / 4000	Late / LC 2 / Early	Eanna XII	Geoy Tepe M; hiatus?	Hammam et Turkman VB; Brak TW 18–19; Leilan hiatus?	Arslantepe VIII	Gawra B; Tepe Gawra IX–X; Gawra A; Tepe Gawra XI/XA L: 59–45	Early Uruk
4200	LC 1	Eanna XVI–XIV	Susa Acropolis 23–27; Hammam et Turkman VA; Hammam et Turkman IVD	Leilan late VIb	Arslantepe VIII	Tepe Gawra XIA/B hiatus?; Tepe Gawra XII L: 60	Ubaid transitional Ubaid 4?
	Term. Ubaid					XIIA–XIII	

As a result of this need to build a regional chronology, the participants spent the first full day in Santa Fe reviewing those issues. Each of the participants was asked to review the chronology of the particular subregion he or she knew best with an eye to connecting them. The key to this new regional chronology was to be the only absolute scale that we have available, radiocarbon dating. Henry Wright, with the technical help of Eric Rupley, brought together and assessed the most reliable carbon date material (see chapter 3). Beginning with the radiocarbon skeleton, we then tried to find a way to flesh out the regional chronology by correlating the radiocarbon dates with the more traditional relative chronologies. The result is presented in table 1.1.

One might ask why we chose to add yet another set of terminologies, that of the LC 1–5 dates, in constructing this new chronology. The problem has been the accretion of so many terminologies using the same terms in different ways. The Early, early Middle, late Middle, and Late Uruk temporal scale pretty much approximates our own. However, the introduction of the northern Uruk terminology by David and Joan Oates (1997) and the Gawran A and B and Uruk A, B, and C by Renata Gut (1995) has, in our opinion, confused the existing southern chronological nomenclature. Gut (1995) has argued that fine-tooled chronologies can be worked out only for local areas and particular sites. She is right to a degree, but our intent was to create a new, overarching chronology for the region. To separate ours from the many *different* Uruk terminologies, we decided to give the periods a new name. Many suggestions were offered from SAR 1–5 to GM (Greater Mesopotamia) 1–5. I suggested that we jettison the names altogether in favor of purely temporal designations: 4200–3900 B.C., 3900–3700 B.C., etc. This would better reflect our wish to emulate our colleagues in Classical Studies, who refer to the late-seventh-century Phrygians, for example. However, we are still talking about periods hundreds of years long. In the end, we simply settled on "LC" (Late Chalcolithic, but to be used only as LC) as a term that had historical connections to the literature on this period but had not been so manipulated that it had lost its clear meaning.

The chapters in this volume also include references to a number of other time periods. Table 1.2 gives these period names and approximate, uncalibrated dates.

TABLE 1.2

Time Periods Mentioned in Text

Date B.C., Uncalibrated	North	South	LC
2000	↑ Khabur ware Middle Bronze EB IV Leilan IIa ↑ Ninevite V	Old Babylonian Isin Larsa Ur III Akkadian ↑	
3000	▼ Early Bronze 1 ↑	Early Dynastic Jemdet Nasr Late Uruk	LC 5 LC 4
	Amuq F	Middle Uruk	LC 3
		Early Uruk	
4000	Late Chalcolithic ↑		LC 2 LC 1
		Terminal Ubaid ↑	
5000	Ubaid ↓	Ubaid ↓	
	Late Halaf	Choga Mami transitional	
6000	Early Halaf Hassuna-Samarra	Sawwan III	

New Data and Interpretation of the Local and the Regional

The second charge to the participants, that is, the second goal for this volume, was to pull together the basic data sets for the areas or sub-regions in which each was working.[3] As I have already said, the amount of new material that has been discovered or more fully published in the last decade of the twentieth century is staggering. A focus on the local and the regional simultaneously is a position that we all have taken in building each of our interpretations, no matter how different they are. Our first focus is always continuity and, more so, change in the particular societies of antiquity. The importance of studying the so-called Uruk Expansion is in part to put local patterns and dynamics into their widest, regional context (see below). What sense we make of the regional patterns depends on how we understand first the local conditions and social arrangements and second the role of interactions among the different groupings. Most of the essays therefore concentrate on only one area. Nissen discusses the Uruk-Warka area, Pollock the northern part of the southern alluvium near Nippur and Adab, Schwartz the Syrian Plains, Stein the piedmont plains to their north, Frangipane the northern hilly areas of the Upper Euphrates Basin, and I deal with the eastern Jazira and foothills of the Tigris Basin with reference to highland western Iran. The only subregions that lack explicit data coverage are the Susiana Plains and the Diyala Basin. A recent article on the Susiana by Wright (1998) provides just the sort of summary each author includes here, and there seems little sense in reprinting it here. The hilly country along the Diyala River and its tributaries in the Hamrin has not been systematically studied since the Oriental Institute's work in the 1930s (Delougaz and Lloyd 1942; Delougaz et al. 1967) with the exception of sites like Rubeidheh (Killick 1988) and the Ubaid sites of Abade and Madhur (Moon and Roaf 1984; Roaf 1984, 1990). Therefore, the most critical areas involved in the various Uruk interaction spheres are reviewed here or have been recently summarized elsewhere.

The primary goal of this volume and the seminar, however, was interpretation and synthesis. Each of the authors has reviewed the data from all the subregions. We have worked together on the regional chronology. We have each constructed a model of how a regional system, if there was one, would have worked, and focused on one aspect of that model. What were the basic economic and political patterns in what all of us saw as two contrasting spheres within the larger region, the north and the south? What was the nature of the interaction between them, and what effects did that interaction have?

The model that Algaze constructed has been very influential in research on Uruk Mesopotamia and its neighbors. His latest synthesis of this model is presented in chapter 2. As Algaze envisions it, the basic regional pattern of late fifth and fourth millennia B.C. Mesopotamia is fairly easy to describe. During the first half of the fourth millennium B.C., polities in the southern alluvium of Mesopotamia (modern southern Iraq) developed enough societal complexity to warrant classifying them as states (Johnson 1973; Wright 1977b; Wright and Johnson 1975, 1985). This classification was based on a number of factors, including:

- the development of higher-level administrative systems that controlled decision making and some activities through an essentially urban enclave with a clear central site and its outlying, dependent sites (manifested in site size hierarchies).

- a marked increase in economic specialization and the probable encumbering of a significant labor pool, supported through surplus production that was controlled by state leaders on their own estates and/or through tribute or taxation. In Algaze's formulation, the key element is trade.

- centralization of some key activities, among which may have been religious ritual, military action, policing, and production and/or distribution of foodstuffs and other goods.

- increasing social stratification in which elite elements were members or clients of newly established leadership organizations.

The cultures that were part of these emerging states shared a common symbolic language and ideology in which certain exotic goods were designated as elite signifiers and in which a corpus of common styles in utilitarian products like pottery was shared. Outside the alluvium, polities in the hills of western Iran and in the steppes and hills of southeastern Turkey, northern Iraq, and northern Syria were also developing increasingly complex societal systems, but not to the same degree as those of southern Mesopotamia. Certainly, cities were developing in the south. The period of widespread urbanization in the north would not come until the mid-third millennium. However, some would argue that sites such as Tell Brak, which reached 45 to 100 hectares before 3500 B.C., were in fact equal in size and complexity to contemporaneous LC 3 southern cities (although we know incredibly little about that period in the south). These northern areas also shared one of a number of common stylistic symbol systems, quite distinct from those of the south. In the second half of the fourth millennium B.C., stylistic elements of a distinctly southern type began appearing in significant numbers at some sites in the north. By the last quarter of the millennium, sites in previously sparsely occupied areas, especially along the Euphrates River, were occupied by southern immigrants using distinctly southern-styled artifacts, eating southern foods prepared in traditional ways, using southern tools, and employing typical southern methods of administration. At the end of the fourth millennium, these southern colonies were abandoned, and the people who remained, presumably representing the pre-expansion local population, experienced new challenges and developed new solutions. This dramatic readaptation spawned the idea of the Uruk collapse.

Algaze's argument also points to other elements in this cross-cultural interaction. First, he believes that the expansion of Uruk culture out of the south was inevitable. He argues that it is the nature of state societies to expand and encompass their neighbors because of the need of elite organizations to maintain and expand their control over resources for state economies to grow and thrive. These necessary resources were available only in the peripheries. He further sees the presence of southern elements in the north as indicators of a planned, state-controlled emplacement of trading colonies. As he states in chapter 2, "the locations of both the earliest and, eventually, the largest Uruk sites around historical fording points of the river...suggest that control of the focal nodes along the river where east-west overland routes and north-to-south water transport came together was both the earlier and the more important motivation." This planned emplacement is evident because "at those same locations, the [southern] Mesopotamian outposts were embedded within culturally alien hinterlands but were, at the same time, at the head of dendritically arranged settlement networks within those hinterlands" (Algaze, this volume). Such a regional plan, according to Algaze, could only be developed by a sophisticated, urban, administratively elaborate society. Originally, he saw the city of Uruk-Warka as the center of the expansion plan, but now he sees the south as a balkanized land of competing city centers. Algaze visualizes the trading networks that developed as the first *economic* empire or world system in Greater Mesopotamia. This empire was not built by military force, but by economic domination. He now acknowledges that some of the societies in the "periphery," the north, were more economically and politically complex than he had originally proposed. Algaze asserts, however, that the tremendous differences in scale between southern states and what he describes as northern complex chiefdoms mean that both the control of the trading networks and the resulting economic gains favored the south. The effect of the southern intrusion into the periphery was to catalyze social, political, and economic developments until the system collapsed, stunting development in the north.

THE LOCAL AND THE REGIONAL

The model proposed by Algaze raises a number of issues that are discussed in the essays that follow. One of those questions involves the unit of analysis. Certainly, all the authors in this volume agree that the Uruk expansion represents the creation of cross-cultural interaction spheres of some kind. The nature of these interactions must be investigated and understood. Nissen argues that the social, economic, and political structures of societies were based on a series of overlapping networks of interaction that lend themselves to the sorts of network analysis done by social scientists (for example, Knoke and Kuklinski 1982:10).

According to the tenets of network analysis, a state is a network in which leaders establish certain kinds of interactions with the individuals and groups who are their subjects. These interactions are not open-ended, because leaders have the authority to control them depending on the basis of their rule. Those bases could include storing food for later redistribution, guaranteeing trade, controlling the production of goods, defending their territory, positioning themselves as the surrogate for the divine, or other ideological posturing. Based on the needs and potentials of the system, and leaders' interference in its functioning, people's behaviors are to some degree limited and directed, institutions arise as the concrete entities through which activities are carried out, and so forth.

Algaze's specific reference to World Systems Theory and his idea of the cause of state origins imply that the unit of analysis is the region. Wallerstein's (1974) key insight in analyzing the economic systems of Europe and their less economically and politically complex trading partners was that the unit of analysis was not the local system, the society, but the world system. In that light, "the fundamental unit of social change is the world-system and not the society" (Hall and Chase-Dunn 1996:11–12). In Wallerstein's conception, those world systems were almost always constructed with a highly economically and politically developed core and a less developed periphery. The role of the periphery in this world system was to provide raw materials and other products processed by unskilled workers. The core societies sent goods made using highly technical manufacturing skills, often using the raw materials derived from the periphery. Given my description of the Mesopotamian scene in the mid-fourth millennium B.C., it is easy to see why a world systems model, beautifully explained by Algaze (1993a) for the Mesopotamian case, is so attractive.

An alternative unit of analysis is the society or polity. Frangipane (chapter 9) writes that the best approach to understanding north-south relations in the Uruk period is to view the phenomena from the north. This approach emphasizes the characteristics and trajectories of development in the north and then reconstructs "the historical roots of their external relations." This represents a different approach, one shared explicitly in the articles by Frangipane, Stein, Nissen, and myself. Nissen emphasizes that change always occurs in response to a particular set of needs, which come out of the local situation. He explicitly asserts that the appearance of Uruk cultural elements, especially administrative ones, represents the adoption by local populations of some innovation that is of use to them rather than an imposition by an outside force. It is in fact the nature of local development that determines the degree and kind of interaction outside of the local area. Blanton and Peregrine adopt a similar approach to analyzing the local and the regional in the same heuristic framework. They write, "The main shared assumption of economic analyses beyond the local system is that some features of any social formation may be the result of interactions across local-system boundaries." "This is not to imply that extra-local interaction is necessarily always the major source of socio-cultural change" (Blanton and Peregrine 1997:5–6). A second assumption they make is that the regional system is not just an expansion of a local system, even a dominant one. The various networks on a regional scale take on their own dynamics.

Within the purview of these two theoretical approaches the details of interaction in Greater Mesopotamia in the fourth millennium B.C. have been investigated. In the next section, I will review some of the specific issues discussed by the authors in this volume. All references will be to the authors' contributions to this volume unless otherwise specified.

SPECIFIC ISSUES

Wright in his essay on the Uruk world sets the stage for the essays that follow. He first points out what our chronology chart (table 1.1) makes clear. The period of the so-called Uruk Expansion was hundreds of years longer than earlier scholars had thought. The period as a whole lasted more than a thousand years, the same time span as that from the Crusades to World War I. In spatial terms, Wright notes the size and diversity of the region. He states, however, that during this period travel time had shrunk to some extent because of more masterful use of the rivers and because of the domestication of the donkey. In his discussion of raw materials, he somewhat contradicts Algaze's model by showing that the resources of the alluvium were greater than Algaze implies. He then reviews some areas that need further study in terms of the material record: food production, craft organization, tribute, and control. In his concluding section, "The Uruk World in Historical Perspective," he sketches a long transition from small, scattered agricultural villages to cities, and increasing political and economic elaboration and competition.

In chapter 5 Nissen describes one of the greatest problems in the interpretation of events and trends in the Greater Mesopotamian region in the fourth millennium B.C., the Uruk period. Despite a century of excavation by German teams, Uruk-Warka, the site for which the period was named, is surprisingly mute on chronological issues. The earlier Uruk period is represented only in one small trench, and Late Uruk horizons have been excavated only in large-scale, architectural units rather than finer stratigraphic units. Despite these problems, the cultural information from Uruk-Warka conveys both its amazing size and internal complexity. To Nissen the evidence from Uruk-Warka IVa at the very end of the period, especially the accounting texts and the Professions List, portrays a society that was extremely formalized in its hierarchical organization. This hierarchy, built upon control of the city's hinterland and its labor potential, was unparalleled in the Uruk period. In terms of the relations between cities like Uruk-Warka and areas to its north and east, Nissen sees a complete dominance by the southern Mesopotamian city-states over Khuzistan throughout most of the LC 2–5 periods, a position not subscribed to by Wright. Perhaps his most critical insight is that he does not see a dramatic Uruk expansion.

He asserts that if one looks at the era from the Ubaid period of the fifth millennium through the end of the fourth millennium, one sees a continuous movement of people and ideas across the whole of the region. This movement tends to be represented by a series of overlapping interaction spheres or networks. For example, he discusses the seeming homogeneity of the so-called Ubaid ceramic design corpus. It is, according to Nissen, the invention and spread of the technology of the slow wheel and its potential for faster throwing and decoration that cover a multitude of local variations. He sees the spread of various techniques as fulfilling the local needs of people who are constantly in flux geographically. He asks, for example, why none of the northern societies adopted the technology of writing, if they are all southern migrants. In conclusion, he writes, "The necessity for southern Mesopotamians to guarantee the flow of imported raw materials and goods must be recognized as one of the prime movers. In particular, the observation that the 'Uruk expansion' not only spread over a longer period of time, but dissolved into various stages or waves, opens the opportunity of seeing this phenomenon not as a short-term, single stimulus affair. Rather it probably was a mixture of adaptations to new situations and deliberate moves by individuals and groups."

In chapter 6 Pollock focuses on one subregion in the south, the Nippur-Adab area north of Uruk-Warka. The Uruk-Warka area is, of course, the model for the south, as Nissen has written. The images of the Nippur-Adab region that Pollock paints are in sharp contrast to the image of the south as intensely centralized, specialized, and hierarchical. For example, she sees the larger settlements in the Nippur-Adab area as "agricultural towns," in which most of the citizenry are farmers. The need for tribute was low, according to Pollock, and their interference in or control of neighboring sites was minimal. Pollock argues that, to the contrary, most households were engaged in a full range of subsistence production activities. This echoes D'Altroy's concern (voiced in chapter 12) about the overemphasis on elites and centralized administrative control.

One of the claims made about the cities of the south is that they were all drawing immigrants from the surrounding subregions, creating an unsettled and rapidly changing demographic situation everywhere in the south. Using a corrective proposed by Dewar, Pollock reaches a contrary conclusion. She writes, "The Nippur-Adab area appears to have been more stable both demographically and in terms of settlement longevity than the area around Uruk-Warka. Its towns were less dependent on tribute extractions to sustain their residents, and it was characterized throughout the fourth millennium by a number of large communities. There are also fewer indications that the population was controlled by repressive means in comparison with the Uruk-Warka area. In contrast, the Uruk-Warka area was highly volatile both demographically and in terms of settlement locations." She further concludes that if the "periphery" was peopled by Southerners, they would most likely have been drawn from the Uruk-Warka area with its very large and shifting population. Evidence of the glyptic, according to Pollock, suggests a repressive, tribute-hungry leadership, which might impel segments of the population to "vote with their feet" (and with their donkeys).

In general, Pollock questions whether the evidence of Uruk cultural expansion was primarily a result of people from the south settling in the north. She sees a long-term, gradual movement and interchange of population in the Mesopotamian region rather than a major displacement of people south to north.

In the model proposed by Algaze, the impetus for development in both north and south is contact between the more advanced societies of the south and the less developed societies of the north through southern expansion north and eastward. The essay by Frangipane stands as a clear counter example to this idea based on her analysis of the remains from Arslantepe. In her vision of Greater Mesopotamia at this period, there were large and *constant* population movements. This is a view shared by Nissen. She does not believe that long-distance trade was very significant in the dynamics certainly of the north. She writes, "As I have already pointed out, there are no archaeological remains that suggest the existence of significant trade activities either in the colonies or in other sites where the possible presence of southern groups is attested. Even the soaring development of metallurgy at Arslantepe, while probably involved in trade with the southern Mesopotamian areas, was mainly important to meet the strong demand from the internal elites, as shown from the type of objects produced there (weapons, ornaments, luxury household items) and their plentiful remains in the public buildings. Their limited circulation in the Malatya and neighboring regions suggests that the main object of trade was probably raw materials, thus confirming that the great development of metallurgical technology may have been stimulated by the local demand." She sees in the development of centralized authority at various places the need to define the area of territorial control, in part as a process of integrating various distinct populations and different economic specializations. In my own essay, I point to the integrative power of religious ritual as a major source of polity building, as the temples at Gawra and also the temple districts at Arslantepe VII and VIA exemplify. According to Frangipane, newly instituted leadership organizations emerged from the households of earlier days. Depending on the modes of production, competition among households and the need to integrate various segments of society led to centralization. In this model, the responsibility of the central authorities becomes the feeding, literally with food and also with goods, of various segments of the population to harness labor for integrative activities. However, because of the lower agricultural productivity in the north, the potential for local centralization was always less than that of societies in the south.

As do Stein and Rothman in their essays, Frangipane rejects the proposition that southern leaders were capable of exerting tight control over trade or colonies, even if the volume of trade was as large as Algaze asserts. Stein specifically argues that there is a measurable decline in the ability of leaders to control activities as the distances from the centers increase. The friction of distance becomes simply too great for such control to succeed. Frangipane goes a step beyond. She argues in chapter 9 "that the public sector of the economy, despite the fact that it was certainly expanding all the time, was not able to exercise any real and widespread control over the circulation of staple goods in its own hinterland. Therefore, it must have been even less capable of influencing the management of economic activities over large distances, and certainly of provoking the physical movement of large segments of the population in distant areas to meet its own operational requirements." Added to these arguments, I question in my article the possibility of such control without the application of significant military force.

Schwartz in chapter 7 has similar doubts that the Uruk expansion was based purely or even largely on trade. After a very detailed analysis of the evidence from each of the LC periods in Syria, he assesses Algaze's thesis. The only large cities in his area that were apparently occupied by Southerners were in the Euphrates Basin of north Syria. Following the logic of the trade model, these sites—Habuba Kabira South, Jebel Aruda, and the earlier Sheikh Hassan—should yield overwhelming evidence of trade-related activities. Schwartz argues to the contrary that there was no reason to locate trade colonies in the Middle Euphrates. The sites are quite far from the primary resource extraction areas. The trade relations of later historical north Syria were always directed toward the Mediterranean Sea. In the fourth millennium B.C., areas to the west of the north Syrian sites on the Euphrates do not yield foreign, southern Mesopotamian artifacts. Since trade does not seem to explain the establishment of large, southern cities in north Syria, Schwartz proposes that they were occupied by colonists looking for a new place to live. The sites were located near sufficient land and water for successful irrigation agriculture as well as large tracts of pastureland. Schwartz therefore questions the attribution of Habuba Kabira and Jebel Aruda to the Uruk trading network. The new LC chronology indicates that the so-called expansion might be a multistage process. Schwartz suggests that perhaps the earliest stage of southern penetration into the north, represented by Sheikh Hassan and Hacınebi, may have been for trade. As the Southerners became more familiar with this great open area, they saw it as a place to set up a new home beyond the control of leaders back home.

Stein in chapter 8 addresses the same issue of contact and change. He first demonstrates that societies in the north had been developing increasingly sophisticated economic and political organizations long before the supposed Uruk expansion. From his excavation at Hacınebi, he shows that in the A and B1 phases (LC 2–early 3) the site was already a center with monumental architecture, ample evidence of administrative sophistication (seal and sealing use), and economic specialization. He describes the site as a "subregional center for a small-scale complex polity, perhaps something we could call a simple chiefdom, with hereditary elites, a complex administrative technology, advanced metallurgy, socioeconomic differentiation, long-distance exchange of raw materials and/or prestige goods, and a craft economy that combined household production with small-scale specialization by independent producers of ceramics, and copper ornaments." At the same time evidence from phase B2 (LC 3–4) indicates that a colony of Southerners was established in an already existing local Late Chalcolithic community. Stein provides us with a clear set of criteria to judge whether we are observing a colony of actual southern immigrants or a case of emulation (see below). Unlike Frangipane's, Stein's case confirms Algaze's proposition to a degree by arguing that there was a colony at Hacınebi. It is hard to imagine that Southerners would migrate over a thousand kilometers northward to the Upper Euphrates if they were not drawn by the prospect of trade at a site with a long history of specialized metal production. At the same time, the evidence from Hacınebi indicates that the interactions between the native and migrant communities were not characterized by domination, but rather by at least tacit cooperation. Although Stein accepts the possibility of southern colonies in the north, he questions whether the south was a single unified area, a point with which most participants, including Algaze, now agree.

In chapter 10, I take a position close to that of Stein. Now properly dated, Gawra was occupied before the increase in the intraregional contact in LC 4 and 5. Like Hacınebi, Gawra appears to have been a small center in its heyday. Evidence of specialized production and distribution systems with much higher production than the residents of the mound would need indicates a greater degree of complexity than has previously been imagined. These levels saw violent competition, marked by large burned areas and the skeletons of murdered people lying in the streets. The early LC 2 occupations demonstrate a surprising degree of specialized production in weaving, woodworking, bead and seal making, and figurine firing, and also the development of administrative buildings—the "Fortress"—and specialized temples. As the site of Gawra developed over the next few hundred years, craft production became more decentralized, but religious ritual took on more of a central role with separate administrative or social buildings continuing to be prominent. It was at the beginning of the LC 3 that the two types of emphases—religion and craft production—came together. The production of obsidian blade blanks increased tremendously. Bead or seal carving, including the first experiments with cylinder seals (see Pittman, below), became a specialized craft. Most striking is a central warehouse, similar to a later Sheikh Hassan building (Boese 1995–96), which was full of manufactured goods. A new level of hierarchy is demonstrated by a group's apparent control of this warehouse. The individuals involved seem to be provisioning each of the institutions/buildings on the Gawra mound. The lack of domiciles on the mound also indicates an increasingly central role for Gawra. D'Altroy emphasizes in chapter 12 that we must search for evidence of a more heterarchical (rather than hierarchical) development—that is, development based on competition and cooperation among multiple groupings and institutions. Using goods that should represent prestige items, I attempt to show the development of such units from extended kin groups to more centralized groupings.

In chapter 10 I emphasize the importance of the subregion of the Iraqi Jazira and the Tigris piedmont for studying the Uruk expansion. Except for a possible colony at Nineveh in the LC 3, parallel in time to Hacınebi, the influence of southern culture is relatively small. Centers like Tell al-Hawa continue to grow and carve out a central place in the Jazira Plain well into the *third* millennium without evidence of much southern influence. Like the Karababa subregion where Samsat is located, the Jazira does not develop like a periphery, as Algaze proposes it does. The continued, if not increased, supply of northern metals after the supposed collapse belies the very idea of a suspension of trade or an economic downturn in the north after the Uruk period.

D'Altroy calls the idea of the temple-state one of the major intellectual insights from Mesopotamian studies. In my article, I briefly look at the uses of religion. I see three major uses: as a way to regulate economic activity when cooperation or forced labor is necessary, as a form of sanctification through which the newly instituted leaders claim legitimacy, and as a way to integrate an ethnically and occupationally diverse population.

One of the first indicators of the Uruk expansion was the presence of southern-styled artifacts and technologies. Frangipane, Stein, Pittman, and I all look at the process of adoption, asking whether the appearance of these artifacts represents colonization by Southerners, trade, or emulation. Using an example from nineteenth-century America, I propose that in LC 3 the presence of goods foreign to the north may have served as prestige or elite markers. They would have been few in number and confined to elite areas. As time went on, these formerly elite markers become adopted more generally. As occurred with the Brooklyn accent, which began as an upper-class affectation but has now spread throughout an entire community and is more a geographic than a status marker, the meaning and symbolic utility of adopted elements can change over time. The increase in Uruk-styled artifacts may not mean the widespread presence of Southerners in the north. All the participants see the need for more work on this issue.

Chapter 11 by Pittman takes us into a uniquely Near Eastern data set, one probably too informally and peripherally dealt with by dirt archaeologists—seals and sealings. After a detailed review of the relevant corpus for each period, Pittman is able to draw a number of conclusions. As the earlier uses of glyptic and glyptic style show, no subregion was more advanced than any other in the common Mesopotamian tradition. In addition, she notes that the various subregional traditions were never "eradicated." Further, only northern societies emulated southern designs. Northern seal types are, however, found in the south. To the degree that sealing represents administrative technology, much more refinement and elaboration occurred in the south than in the north. She sees in the process of emulation distinct changes in the favored routes of interaction, the Euphrates route having been most active in the LC 3 period, the Tigris route in the LC 4, and again the Euphrates route in the LC 5.

Glyptic plays a unique role as markers of identity along a number of axes. As Pittman writes in chapter 11, "Probably the most important contribution that the glyptic makes to a more refined understanding of the era of state formation in Greater Mesopotamia is establishing the existence of nodes where both traditions were equally strong."

ENVIRONMENTAL RECONSTRUCTION

The careful reader will note a fairly wide discrepancy between the reconstruction of the Greater Mesopotamian natural environment and climate in these pages. Certainly, Wright's and Nissen's sources disagree. The issue of how to reconstruct an ancient environment is a technical and difficult one.

Our interest as students of antiquity tends to be in terms of conditions for agriculture and pastoralism—in other words, basic subsistence. A number of ways have been developed to approach this reconstruction. The first is through the products whose remains we can find in archaeological sediments. Miller (1991) in her review of paleobotanical research in the Middle East illustrates how the kinds of plants found—an example is the relative frequency of drought-resistant barley versus wheat—and equally important the kinds that are missing can give the researcher a general indicator of growing conditions. In addition to agricultural remains, wild plants may be recoverable. Most Near Eastern villagers (then as now) used dung for heating fuel. Seeds from many of the grasses sheep and goats ate can therefore be recovered by flotation. Phytolith analysis, when combined with more traditional seed identification, can give further detail (Pearsall and Piperno 1993). Analysis of animal bone can also be used effectively (e.g., Zeder 1991). In some cases erosion processes can expose ancient land surfaces (Adams 1981).

However, most reconstructions, including the ones cited here, are based on the analysis of ancient climate patterns, which are much harder to detect. As Frenzel (1966) writes, even if a perfectly accurate measurement of regional climate were possible, the plants of interest grow close to the ground. Regional climate assays cannot hope to monitor these microenvironments in antiquity. Current tools are also problematic. Lake corings can be a significant distance from the areas of interest, and they are not always accurate in terms of dating because they rely on micro-carbon samples. Other measurements suffer from similar problems.

Further, as Adams writes, "we have too frequently approached ancient agriculture from the misleading viewpoint of average yields and requirements. Fields are not irrigated with average stream flow, nor families fed and debts paid with average harvests" (1974b:11).

I feel I lack the expertise to choose among the different readings represented in this volume. I recommend that the reader go to the cited sources and make his or her own evaluation.

COMMON THREADS, DISAGREEMENTS, AND PROSPECTS

The reader will find in these essays a very complex set of arguments, using wide and sometimes not fully integrated sets of data. Clearly our work on this period in this region is not done. There are, however, certain areas of agreement and disagreement. We all agree that the theorized increase in contact between Uruk and the other local Late Chalcolithic societies, the creation of new regional economic networks, and the possible migration of Southerners into the north and east cannot be explained by any single factor or cause. Different patterns of interaction should be in evidence in different areas, depending on such elements as ease of transport, distance, nature of preexisting societies, basis of the interaction and formation of new networks, and of course local conditions. We agree that the data paint a very complex picture of interactions over a long span of time and a great distance. We further agree that patterns emerged in this region in the fourth millennium that would last for millennia to come.

The authors do not agree on the following points. Perhaps most fundamentally, we disagree on the role of southern state administrators in sponsoring and controlling those who went northward to settle. Some even see little population movement and much less trade than Algaze's model suggests. While some of us see direct control of immigrant groups sent for the purpose of trade, whose proceeds went directly to elites in the south, others see a much more entrepreneurial effort of those who came north for goods and raw materials. Some do not believe that the largest of the southern-occupied settlements, for example, Habuba Kabira South, were intended primarily as trade stations at all. Whether or not they engaged in exchange, some of us believe that they were migrants of another sort entirely, seeking a new life and a new place to live far from the intrusive rulers of their southern homelands. We do not agree on the full consequences of long-distance trade and immigration for the trajectories of development of both northern and southern societies. We see the imports, exotic and utilitarian, as catalyzing changes in local economic structure in different ways, and we therefore attribute to them different effects on local and regional development. We especially disagree on the role of exports in the elaboration of leadership organizations.

Despite our disagreements on interpretation of the data, we are confident that answers can be found. One of our chief problems has been a lack of complete publication of the newer projects. As this information becomes available, the necessary details will be easier to agree upon and the number of possible interpretations should be reduced. We especially need a better understanding of the relations of LC 1–3 sites in the north and east and LC 4–5 sites in the south and north. We have had a tendency to concentrate on larger, more spectacular sites, but ultimately the picture will not be clear without a more complete picture of the relations of the residents of smaller and larger sites in each polity. In terms of the cross-cultural connections, we need further work on the degree to which intercultural contact between Late Chalcolithic and Uruk cultures affected the trajectory of development in the north. Would, for example, Arslantepe be different without the presence of Uruk people in the north? To answer this question we need a better understanding of individual, local polities in southeastern Turkey, Syria, the Jazira of Iraq, and western Iran. We especially need to focus on sites that had a long history of local development and of contact with southern Mesopotamians—for example, Tell Brak. Not enough information is available from critical levels at Brak to assess its significance. We also need more data on the early third millennium aftermath of the Uruk expansion in order to contrast it with the peak of Uruk contact and theorized regional economic reintegration of the LC 5. In particular, we want to know what caused the apparent withdrawal of Southerners at places like Jebel Aruda, Habuba Kabira, and other smaller sites. We need to ask, does this withdrawal imply a collapse of the regional economic and, perhaps, political system or a reorientation? What effect did this withdrawal have on local polities in the north and on north-south economic exchange? The eleven chapters that follow were written with these questions in mind.

Notes

1. This conference, called "Artefacts of Complexity," was organized by Nicholas Postgate and Stuart Campbell at the University of Manchester (and was slated for publication in 2001).

2. A lot of confusion surrounds the spelling and use of the term Jazira. Traditionally, it referred to the plains of northern Iraq, as reflected in the British military handbooks (British Naval 1944). The term, usually spelled Jezirah, has also been used for a broader area including the Khabur River basin and in a recent chronological review by Lebeau (2000) for the eastern steppe as well. The

confusion is unfortunately now set in the literature. We will try to distinguish the traditional usage, Jazira, from the broader definition, Jezirah, by their spelling.

3. The term "region" has also been a source of confusion. In the early drafts of the papers, many referred to smaller areas as regions—for example, the Uruk-Warka region, the Jazira region. As I wrote in the introduction to *Chiefdoms and Early States in the Near East* (1994:6), "Functional definitions [of a region] emphasize greater frequency of demographic, economic, or political interactions among subregions within one region as contrasted with neighboring geographical zones." The essence of the issue discussed here is this very interaction. The Levant and Egypt, for example, were not included explicitly because their level of interaction with areas in the basins of the Tigris and Euphrates and their tributaries, the Karun, Karkeh, Ab-i-Diz, Diyala, Greater and Lower Zab, Khabur, and Balikh, are considerably less frequent. Because Greater Mesopotamia is, by definition, the area of this expansion and interaction, the region is Greater Mesopotamia. All smaller units within that unit are subregions or areas.

2

The Prehistory of Imperialism

The Case of Uruk Period Mesopotamia

Guillermo Algaze

...when dominions are acquired in a province differing in language, laws, and customs, the difficulties to be overcome are great and it requires great fortune as well as great industry to retain them.... One of the best and most certain ways of doing so...is to plant colonies in one or two of those places which form as it were the keys of the land; for it is necessary either to do this or to maintain a large force of armed men. These colonies will cost the prince little.... But by maintaining a garrison instead of colonists, one will spend much more, and consume all the revenues of that state in guarding it, so that the acquisition will result in a loss.

—Niccolo Machiavelli, *The Prince*, 1532

INTRODUCTION AND DEFINITIONS

In his book *In Search of the Primitive,* Stanley Diamond (1974:5) noted that "Imperialism and colonialism are as old as the State; they define the political process." This chapter uses Diamond's insight as its point of departure, arguing that cases of pristine state formation, by their very nature, involve processes of external expansion that can be characterized as early examples of economic imperialism. Further, it contends that these early examples differ from modern examples of the same phenomenon only in degree and intensity, not in essence. To illustrate these points, I will review data concerning the emergence of early Mesopotamian civilization in the alluvial lowlands of the Tigris and Euphrates Rivers, in what is today southern Iraq, during the fourth millennium B.C., and I will show how that emergence affected areas immediately surrounding the Mesopotamian core area. In so doing, I will attempt to explain:

1. Why pristine civilizations require access to resources drawn from areas they do not directly control.

2. Why the required access leads to vigorous processes of cross-cultural contact and exchange and, eventually, to outright external expansion.

3. Why, in faraway areas, the expansion of pristine states typically gets operationalized by the establishment of variously configured outposts (ranging from outright colonial enclaves to smaller trade diasporas embedded within important preexisting settlements) that function as collection points for peripheral commodities and distribution points for core manufactures.

4. Why, typically, the outposts eventually collapse or are withdrawn.

5. Why, in the aggregate, the outposts can be characterized as cases of economic imperialism.

Before turning to a discussion of archaeological data that support these contentions, it is necessary to make explicit what is meant here by imperialism. It is probably fair to say that many social scientists view economic imperialism as a phenomenon that is characteristic only of the modern age and the rise of capitalism and have, therefore, failed to take proper account of comparable phenomena in antiquity—much less in pre- and protohistoric times! They would argue that premodern imperial processes are different in quality from those of the modern era by noting that in the former the boundaries of political and economic hegemony are coterminous whereas in the latter the extent of economic hegemony commonly far outreaches the boundaries of direct territorial control (Wallerstein 1974, 1995). For those who subscribe to this view, the truly revolutionary feature of modern imperialism is the profoundly destabilizing effect of both asymmetrical exchange and economic dependency, factors that are taken as the root causes of unequal development.

In my opinion, however, views that emphasize the essential difference between modern and ancient imperialism are rooted in two crucial misunderstandings about the nature of cross-cultural interactions at the dawn of history. The first is failure to understand how profoundly asymmetrical and destabilizing ancient trade was for the societies exposed to it, even if that trade was based largely on the exchange of low-bulk, high-value preciosities (Adams 1974a; Ekholm 1977). The second is a tendency to overemphasize the political aspects of formal institutionalized extension of territorial and political dominion over previously independent polities as the key characteristic of imperial relationships. In defining imperialism, I follow the work of the British historians Ronald Gallagher and Jack Robinson (1953), who see asymmetrical relationships of dependency as the root of imperial phenomena. The actual form that those relationships of dependency take, whether political or economic, is for them of secondary importance (on this point, see also Landes 1961). Formal political rule and territorial dominion are only the most specific and easily defined modes of imperialistic dependency, but not the only, or even the most common, ones. In fact, formal political ties need not necessarily develop in all cases, and when those ties do develop, they generally do so only after a process of "informal" economic penetration, which is also a mode of imperialistic domination.

We can better visualize the various forms that attempts at initial colonial penetration may have taken at the dawn of history by looking at relatively well-documented cases of the modern era. Two particularly instructive cases are the initial stages of the Portuguese intrusion into Senegambia (West Africa) in the sixteenth and seventeenth centuries A.D. (Curtin 1975) and the early stages of British and French colonial penetration of eastern Canada and the American Midwest (Ray 1978) in the seventeenth and eighteenth centuries A.D. Although the institutions responsible for these colonial efforts varied dramatically within Portuguese, French, and British societies, and although the level of organization of the colonial enterprises also varied considerably, in each case we see initial contacts being primarily economic in nature, taking the form of variously configured intrusive core outposts implanted within resource-rich peripheral hinterlands. Historical records show that these outposts served to mediate exchange between the intruding groups and preexisting societies, ensuring to the intruding societies privileged access to coveted commodities, principally fur in the French and British cases in North America and slaves, gold, ivory, and spices in the Portuguese case in West Africa. Depending on the nature of the varied societies encountered, geographic constraints, and transport logistics, the outposts were commonly established at natural passage points between distinct cultural or ecological subregions. More specifically, they were usually placed at locations of transportational significance where long-distance and local trade routes would naturally intersect, or astride preexisting trade routes, near concentrations of coveted resources, or in the midst of centrally positioned and locally powerful native communities already exploiting those resources and willing to trade.

When did colonial outposts such as those described come into existence? Archaeological data now suggest that such outposts are not limited to the modern era and the rise of capital imperialism. On the contrary, they are an instrument of expansion common even to the earliest pristine states, and by inference, so too is the essentially asymmetrical resource procurement strategy that the outposts entail (Algaze 1993b; Ekholm and Friedman 1979). These points will become clearer when we review the processes whereby Mesopotamian civilization—the earliest state-level society in the world—emerged and expanded.

SOUTHERN MESOPOTAMIA: SOCIAL TRANSFORMATIONS

Cultural Ecology

Mesopotamian civilization arose in the alluvial lowlands of the Tigris and Euphrates Rivers during the Uruk period, roughly dating between 3800 and 3100 B.C. (see Wright and Rupley, chapter 3, this volume, for the absolute chronology of the process). Neither the roots nor the tempo of the process is particularly well understood, principally because of the lack of exposures of sites and levels dating to the earliest phase of the period (Early Uruk [LC 2]). What seems indisputable, however, is that by the later part of the Uruk period, Mesopotamian civilization was already fully formed (i.e., ca. 3500–3100, encompassing what are commonly termed the Middle [ca. Eanna VIII/VII–VI and Susa, Acropolis I sounding, levels 21/20–19] and Late [ca. Eanna V–IV and Susa, Acropolis I sounding, levels 18–17] phases of the Uruk period). This entailed a profound restructuring of social relationships and human settlement across the alluvial landscape of southern Mesopotamia. Evidence for these processes is provided by the long-term excavations of German teams at the ancient city of Uruk-Warka and by the pioneering and extensive archaeological surveys of Robert McC. Adams (1981; Adams and Nissen 1972), which document the explosive growth of multiple cities across the southern Mesopotamian alluvium through the Uruk period and the emergence of clear, four-tiered hierarchies in settlement size. This growth was not the result of natural population growth, since Adams's research clearly shows that overall population levels across the Mesopotamian alluvium barely changed over the 700- to 800-year span of the Uruk period (see also Pollock, chapter 6, this volume). Rather, the survey data clearly indicate that Uruk cities grew largely by absorbing rural populations from the surrounding countryside (Adams 1981).

Adams's work also documents the shifting fortunes of these preco-cious urban centers in different sectors of the Mesopotamian alluvium through the Uruk period. Prior to the advent of heavy machinery, urban fortunes in the alluvial environment of southern Iraq had always been partly dependent on unpredictable shifts in the Tigris and Euphrates river channels crisscrossing the plain (Adams 1978). However, the later part of the Uruk period was a time when the chronic instability of the Mesopotamian alluvial landscape would have been magnified. A combination of recent paleoenvironmental data from var-ious Near Eastern locales (see Hole 1994 for an overview) and increas-ingly sophisticated computer simulations of global paleoclimatic change resulting from orbitally induced variations in the amount of solar radiation reaching the earth (e.g., de Noblet et al. 1996; Harrison et al. 1998) shows that climate across large portions of the Near East would have been warmer and wetter at about 4000 B.C. than at present and, further, that parts of southern Mesopotamia that today receive no summer precipitation whatsoever would have been within the areas affected by Indian Ocean summer monsoon rains at that time. This started to change by the second half of the fourth millennium, as cli-mate became increasingly drier, more seasonal, and more variable across large portions of the Near East and as summer monsoons regained the more southerly track they follow at present, which skips southern Mesopotamia altogether (Hole 1994). The conjuncture of increasing aridity and more sharply marked seasonality that characterized the later portion of the Uruk period created conditions in which spring floods would have been increasingly abrupt and, therefore, more likely to cause substantial river channel meanders in the alluvium. Striking without warning, such shifts must have been an important factor promoting social instability, regional competition and conflict, and population agglomeration across the alluvium through the later part of the Uruk period—just at the time that Mesopotamian civilization was crystallizing.

The Urban Revolution

The best understood Mesopotamian city of the Uruk period is the site of Uruk itself, modern Warka, which has been explored by German teams for the better part of the twentieth century (Eichmann 1989). New surveys conducted just before the Gulf War show that the city grew exponentially through the fourth millennium and achieved the extraordinary size of about 250 hectares by the end of the period (Finkbeiner 1991). This reassessment means that by the Late Uruk (LC 5) period, Uruk-Warka had become four to five times larger than any competing center in the Tigris-Euphrates alluvial lowlands (Adams 1981). Although no direct architectural evidence exists, Uruk-Warka was almost certainly fortified at this time: a recently published Uruk period seal impression from the site depicts a crenellated city wall (Boehmer 1991: fig. 5).

The emergence of Uruk-Warka as the preeminent demographic center of southern Mesopotamia in the Middle and Late Uruk (LC 3–5) periods went hand in hand with the growth of its religious institutions and their ideological prestige. In fact, Steinkeller (1999) has recently argued that Uruk-Warka functioned as the religious capital of Sumer through the Uruk and the succeeding Jemdet Nasr periods. This assessment is based on a handful of Jemdet Nasr period tablets (Uruk III script) from Jemdet Nasr, Uqair, and Uruk-Warka that show that individual Sumerian cities were sending resources (including various types of foodstuffs and slave women) to Uruk-Warka as ritual offerings to Inanna, one of the city's chief deities. Steinkeller suggests, plausibly, that this situation reflects a continuation of conditions that must have started in the Uruk period and that it represents, in turn, the precursor of the well-documented BALA distribution system that would later keep the religious institutions of Nippur supplied with necessary offerings and resources during the Ur III period.

The growth of Uruk-Warka through the second half of the fourth millennium was accompanied by an audacious building program at the very center of the city, based on the separate precincts of Eanna and Kullab dedicated to Inanna and Enlil, respectively (Eichmann 1989; Nissen 1988). Religion must have been quite central to social control within the city at this time, since many of the structures in these central precincts have offering tables that clearly mark them as temples (Heinrich 1982). In this, the public structures at the very center of Uruk-Warka are not much different from those at the core of much smaller Ubaid period towns that preceded the Uruk explosion, as seen most clearly at the site of Eridu (Safar, Mustafa, and Lloyd 1981). However, the Uruk period structures were an order of magnitude larger than their prehistoric predecessors, as may be observed at Uruk-Warka itself when we compare the Ubaid period temples found at the base of the Anu Ziggurat with their much larger but similarly shaped Uruk period counterparts at the site (Eichmann 1989). A more important difference is that not all of the monumental structures at the core of Uruk-Warka were temples, as had been the case at Eridu. In fact, a good number of the Late Uruk (LC 5) period structures cleared in the Eanna Precinct (Eanna V–IV) lack offering tables and, therefore, almost certainly were not temples. Unfortunately, we cannot be more specific as to the exact nature of the activities conducted within these latter structures owing to the general lack of in situ remains within these structures because almost all of the Uruk-Warka buildings uncovered in the Eanna Precinct had been carefully cleaned out in antiquity, dismantled, and filled. Equally regrettable is the fact that for the Uruk period we know almost nothing about the nature of the city beyond the extensive exposures at its very center (Nissen 1998).

Nonetheless, however unrepresentative they may be, existing exposures and surveys leave no doubt that human settlement in the Mesopotamian alluvium was profoundly restructured through the Uruk period. This went hand in hand with the appearance of new forms of political, social, economic, and cultural arrangements within alluvial societies that, in effect, represent the earliest instantiation of Mesopotamian (Sumerian) civilization. Putting together inferences from a variety of pertinent archaeological, representational, and textual evidence, during the Uruk period we may deduce the emergence of the following developments:

1. Institutionalized rulers whose power was based on religious, political, and military roles. This may be inferred from the iconography of the period, which commonly depicts a muscular and bearded male figure sporting a net skirt, a cap, and his hair arranged in a chignon. This character can be recognized in *(a)* numerous seals and seal impressions (e.g., Amiet 1980: pls. 43–47; Delougaz and Kantor 1996:146), *(b)* stelae (Becker 1993: pl. 38: nos. 783–84), *(c)* sculptures in the round (e.g., Becker 1993: pls. 35, 58–59), *(d)* carved stone vases (Lindemeyer and Martin 1993: pls. 19–25), *(e)* furniture inlays (Schmandt-Besserat 1993: figs. 7–8), and *(f)* a small obelisk and matching plaque that record a poorly understood sale or transfer of land (i.e., the so-called Blau Monuments, cf. Gelb, Steinkeller, and Whiting 1991:39–43, pls. 11–12).[1] Typically, this central character is depicted as a warrior, dispenser of justice, hunter and master of animals, and as a source of fertility (feeding domestic herds). Less commonly, as is the case in the famous Warka vase, he is portrayed officiating in rituals connected with the goddess Inanna, possibly acting as her consort. Comparison with inscribed statues of later Sumerian rulers in strikingly similar poses leaves no doubt that the analogous Uruk-period images are stylized and standardized representations of kings (Schmandt-Besserat 1993).

2. A state role in the collection and distribution of strategic commodities. This may be inferred from a variety of textual, pictorial, and archaeological evidence. Some of the earliest pictographic tablets that appear by the end of the Uruk period (the difficult-to-read Archaic Texts), for instance, deal either with the disbursement of commodities, such as metals, finished textiles, and grain, or with the acquisition of raw agricultural resources, principally wool and dairy products (Nissen 1986b). A group of these early tablets studied by Green (1980) attests to the existence and economic importance of state-managed flocks. Depictions in Uruk period glyptic can also be interpreted as providing evidence for state involvement in important subsistence and productive

activities. Pittman, for instance, has recently discussed a number of scenes that illustrate what she interprets as scribes monitoring grain being bagged and sealed and collected in (central) granaries (Amiet 1980: nos. 267–69; Pittman 1993: figs. 3–4) and flocks of hoofed animals (Pittman 1993: fig. 6), presumably the same flocks documented in the tablets noted above. Finally, public sector involvement in the accumulation (and acquisition?) of nonlocal strategic commodities can also be deduced from actual finds in religious/administrative quarters of Uruk cities, such as Warka. Most instructive in this respect is the body of materials found within the subterranean foundations of the Riemchengebäude, an enigmatic structure of Eanna, level IV date that may represent either a temple (Forest 1999) or a storehouse for a nearby temple (Nissen 1988). Burnt in antiquity, the building was literally brimming with imported exotic goods, including several wooden chests with elaborate inlays of precious and semiprecious stones; small fragments of what would have been life-size stone and copper statues; vessels and vases made of alabaster as well as various exotic stones and copper; mirrors and other implements made of copper; fragments of jewelry made of copper, silver, and gold; and various tools and weapons made of copper, copper-silver alloys, obsidian, and rock crystal (Lenzen 1958; Forest 1999:67–73).

3. Craft and occupational specialization on an industrial scale. Archaeologically, this may be inferred from the mass production of standardized ceramics (Nissen 1974) and from evidence for metalworking installations in Uruk cities, as found at Warka for instance (Nissen 1970). More direct and detailed information about the nature of social and occupational specialization characteristic of southern Mesopotamian societies by the Late Uruk (LC 5) period is provided by the Archaic Texts. The Titles and Professions List, for instance, was already being produced and copied by the end of the Uruk period (Uruk IV script) and almost certainly reflects a standardized system that had been in place for some time. This scribal exercise lists some 130 categories of specialized personnel in some sort of rank order. Entries start with an obscure official (NÁM-ESHDA), who, on the basis of lexical texts of much later date, can be identified as the king, and are followed by the titles of administrators in charge of various state offices or departments. On occasion, several ranks of lesser officials within an

individual department are also listed. These are followed by the titles of religious functionaries, whose relationship with state activities is uncertain, and by a listing of other specialized personnel engaged in a variety of more lowly professions (e.g., gardener, baker) (Nissen, Damerow, and Englund 1993:110–11).

4. Some measure of state control over dependent labor (Zagarell 1986). This can be inferred, most directly, from many of the Archaic Texts. A number of these tablets (Uruk IV script) are accounts of rations of barley given by state officials to female (SAL) and male (KUR) workers. The status of these individuals as both captives and fully encumbered workers is clarified in some of the later and more complex Uruk III script texts, where these same individuals are sometimes further qualified with the ideograms ERIM or SAG+MA, visually indicating that they represented some sort of yoked or shackled class of people (Englund 1998). Presumably these captives included slaves of foreign or local origin, prisoners of war, and other persons in temporary or permanent captivity (Nissen, Damerow, and Englund 1993:74). These fully dependent laborers would have represented only a portion of the available labor force in southern cities, which in later historical periods also included laborers in various categories of temporary (but recurring) state service receiving rations and a difficult-to-quantify number of free peasants and craftsmen (Gelb 1979). Nonetheless, if Nissen (1974, 1988) is correct in believing that beveled-rim bowls were used to disburse grain rations, then the massive quantities of these bowls commonly found in individual Uruk sites corroborate the importance of fully or semi-encumbered workers receiving state rations to the overall political economy of Uruk city-states.

Art historical evidence also points to the importance of dependent labor to the political economy of Uruk societies. Many Uruk period pictorial representations illustrate diverse individuals performing various productive tasks under the supervision of record keepers, seemingly at the service of the state (Pittman 1994a). Activities illustrated include weaving, threshing, grain storage, herding, hoeing fields, and the transport of goods. A case in point are depictions of workers attending horizontal looms on seals and sealings found at a variety of sites, including Susa (Amiet 1972: nos. 673–74) and Ur (Amiet 1980: nos. 319–20). In almost all cases, the workers depicted as loom attendants are clearly female (i.e., wear their hair in pigtails). Two factors combine to make these images particularly relevant to the issue at hand. The first is that weaving scenes are associated with seals, which were instruments of administration used in institutional contexts (Nissen 1977; Dittmann 1986a; but see Wright, this volume, for a cautionary note). The second is that we know that state-controlled weaving establishments staffed by dependent women and their children were an important component in the industrial production of textiles (both for local consumption and export) in third millennium Sumerian city-states (Waetzoldt 1972; Maekawa 1980).

5. New forms of symbolic representations needed to validate the economic and sociopolitical changes discussed earlier. This had two principal manifestations. The first was writing, which, in Mesopotamia, served primarily as a tool of social and economic control in its initial stages (Nissen, Damerow, and Englund 1993). Also connected to social control, but more subtle, was the creation of an artistic tradition that served to legitimate the newly institutionalized rulers by emphasizing their purported role as intermediaries with the gods and by generally portraying them in a heroic, larger-than-life manner (Schmandt-Besserat 1993). As Helene Kantor perceptively noted, the iconographic repertoire that first appeared in the Uruk period effectively set the framework for pictorial representation in Mesopotamia for millennia to come (Kantor 1984; Delougaz and Kantor, 1996:146–47).

THE URUK EXPANSION

The momentous social transformations that took place in the Mesopotamian alluvium during the Uruk period could not—and did not—occur in a vacuum. The alluvial environment of southern Mesopotamia lacked many of the resources necessary for the maintenance of complex social organizations, most notably metals and roofing-grade timber (discussed below; but see Wright, this volume, and Potts 1997:91–121 for cautionary notes). Of equal importance, it also lacked exotic commodities that could be manipulated by emerging elites to legitimize and enhance their status. From this, it follows that the emergence of civilization in southern Mesopotamia during the Uruk period can only be understood in the context of a wider system of interaction tying together the nascent state polities of the Mesopotamian alluvium and contemporary communities in the surrounding highland areas, where the resources necessary to satisfy the needs of rapidly growing alluvial cities and rapidly differentiating Uruk societies were obtainable (Algaze 1993a).

Only in the past twenty years or so, principally as a result of archaeological salvage programs associated with the construction of dams along the Euphrates, Tigris, and Khabur Rivers, has it become clear that relations and exchange between the emerging Uruk polities of the south and communities in surrounding areas were mediated by the establishment of a number of intrusive Uruk outposts at locations far from the Mesopotamian alluvium. Recognizing such outposts is not always simple because some elements of Uruk material culture are found in many otherwise indigenous sites across the northern Mesopotamian periphery (for a full discussion, see Algaze 1993a: 63–73). As a rule, however, the outposts are characterized by a wide variety of cultural traits of southern origin, including architectural plans and building techniques of southern type, Uruk ceramics, iconographic motifs, and administrative procedures. Nonetheless, varying proportions of indigenous materials are also typically found in all of the Uruk outposts. Presumably, differences in their assemblages are related to (a) the nature and frequency of relations between the outposts and the Uruk world; (b) distance from the alluvium or from other Uruk outposts; (c) the nature of social relations between the intruding Uruk groups and surrounding indigenous cultures; (d) the demographic composition, number, and gender ratio of Uruk settlers at any one outpost; and (e) the degree of intermarriage between Uruk colonists and local populations. Given sufficient archaeological data, indigenous sites are easily distinguished from the outposts because Uruk materials are found only as isolated imports within larger local assemblages or as a result of emulation of specific aspects of Uruk culture by local populations and elites, as both Wattenmaker (1990) and Pollock (1994) have correctly noted. In reality, however, the often meager and incompatibly recorded archaeological data at our disposal make figuring out which sites were intrusive Uruk settlements and which were indigenous occupations in contact with, and affected by, those settlements less straightforward than researchers would like. Drawing a clear line between the two types of settlements remains one of the most important tasks at hand for scholars seeking to elucidate the nature of the Uruk expansion.

Leaving aside for the moment problems of identification, it is clear that there is substantial variability within those sites that can be safely recognized as outposts. In areas where a local settlement hierarchy was already in place, outposts were commonly relatively small and were situated in the midst of preexisting indigenous centers already exploiting coveted resources or controlling access to those resources. However, in areas where no such preexisting occupation had to be reckoned with, Uruk penetration could, and in some cases did, become a process of urban implantation, as Schwartz (this volume) has rightly emphasized in connection with some of the Euphrates data discussed below. The locational circumstances of the outposts, in turn, were determined by geographical imperatives. They were commonly emplaced at strategic locations of transportational significance within the Mesopotamian periphery, either *(a)* in the midst of preexisting indigenous societies controlling natural trade routes across the resource-rich highland areas of Anatolia and Iran or *(b)* at fording places where historical east-west overland routes across the well-watered plains of northern Syria, northern Iraq, and southeastern Turkey intersected the south-flowing Euphrates, Tigris, and upper Khabur Rivers (for the routes, see Dillemann 1962). Since I have described many of the Uruk outposts and their locational circumstances at greater length elsewhere (Algaze 1993a), here I only briefly summarize some of the most representative evidence and outline recent changes in my interpretation of that evidence made necessary by new research.

Of outposts situated in the midst of preexisting indigenous societies in control of resources or routes, the best known are Hacınebi Tepe, located along the Euphrates River in Turkey just north of the historical ford at Birecik, and Godin Tepe, situated in the Kangavar Valley of the Zagros Mountains of western Iran. Excavated only recently, Hacınebi is the clearest case and appears to have consisted of a small group of resident southern Mesopotamian settlers/traders living at the edge of a larger and thriving preexisting indigenous site. However, because the site is discussed in detail by G. Stein in this volume, I will focus instead on Godin Tepe, which appears to represent a similar occupation. Located in the center of the Kangavar Valley, Godin sits astride the historical route (the Khorasan Road) from southern Mesopotamia into the Iranian Plateau. Here, a fortified structure containing a broad variety of Mesopotamian material culture (Godin V) was found at a commanding position within a larger preexisting Chalcolithic center (Godin VI) that was characterized by an indigenous material culture with a long in situ tradition. Many of the artifacts found within the structure were typically Uruk in style and included various common forms of (locally made?) Uruk ceramic types and typical glyptic, iconography, and accounting devices. These last are crucial for the identification of Godin as an outpost since they include a number of numerical notation tablets, one of which bears a sign commonly found in the earliest Archaic Texts from Warka (Young 1986). It may therefore be surmised that the small but strategically situated fort at the top of Godin housed a small delegation of Mesopotamian individuals, more likely than not an isolated group of male traders (Badler 1998).

Outposts at river fording places existed along the upper Euphrates River within modern-day northern Syria and southeastern Turkey, and, almost certainly, along the upper Khabur and Tigris Rivers of northern Syria and Iraq as well (below). The Upper Euphrates cases are by far the clearest. The northernmost Uruk outpost along that river thus far identified is a small (ca. 1 hectare) fortified settlement at Hassek Höyük, located just south of the Anti-Taurus Mountains in Turkey and immediately adjacent to a historical ford of the river. The Uruk settlement at this location consisted of a typical "Mittelsaal" house attached to a more massive, equally typical, but poorly preserved tripartite structure decorated with clay mosaic cones of presumed administrative/religious function. Surrounding these central structures were several monocellular reception rooms, work and storage structures, and a granary (Behm-Blancke 1992b). Associated artifacts found within the Hassek enclosure are largely of Uruk type, although the ceramic assemblage also includes a substantial component of indigenous types and wares and of Uruk forms made in local wares (Helwing 1999). Hassek is unusual in terms of the Uruk presence along the Euphrates in that it was an isolated settlement. The site was situated more than 120 kilometers north of what appears to have been the core area of Uruk settlement along the Upper Euphrates (below).

More typical were a small number of town-sized outposts commanding the historical Euphrates fording points near Meskene in Syria and Carchemish in Turkey. These outposts were commonly surrounded by clusters of much smaller Uruk villages, which may have served to supply the larger sites with agricultural and pastoral products (although this remains untested). The best understood examples are the excavated sites of Habuba Kabira-süd (Kohlmeyer 1996, 1997; Strommenger 1980; Sürenhagen 1986a) and the nearby settlement of Jebel Aruda (Van Driel and Van Driel-Murray 1979, 1983), both along the Euphrates in the Tabqa Dam area of Syria near Meskene. As both sites have been the subject of thorough recent reassessments (Vallet 1997, 1998), only brief remarks are needed. The Uruk settlement at Jebel Aruda was founded over virgin soil on top of an easily defensible hilltop overlooking the Euphrates Valley and may have constituted the administrative center of the cluster. Its Dutch excavators were able to expose about 10,000 square meters of the settlement, representing about 30% of the total occupation (which covers slightly more than 3 hectares). Their exposures revealed several phases of construction and reconstruction, all dating to the Late Uruk (LC 5) period. Throughout the period, however, the essential character of the settlement remained unchanged and consisted of a number of large domestic structures, apparently representing elite housing, surrounding a central raised platform where first one and later two massive tripartite structures of presumable administrative/religious function stood.

Some 8 kilometers to the south and bordering directly on the ancient Euphrates floodplain was the larger, contemporaneous, and, no doubt, associated urban settlement of Habuba Kabira. This settlement was excavated jointly by a German team in the lower parts of the site (Habuba Kabira-süd) and a Belgian team in the associated acropolis (Tell Qannas). As the site was largely unoccupied after the Uruk period, extensive horizontal exposures of Uruk levels were practicable, totaling well over 20,000 square meters. A recent reassessment of pertinent data by Regis Vallet (1998) indicates that the Habuba/Qannas settlement grew in three stages, all datable to the Late Uruk (LC 5) period. The earliest settlement was about 6 hectares in extent and was founded on virgin soil. Unfortunately, this early emplacement was hardly touched by the excavators, and we can say little in detail about its nature save that it appears to have been unfortified. This initial

settlement was soon thoroughly remodeled and converted into a fortified town, about 12 hectares in extent, with carefully laid-out streets
and well-differentiated residential, industrial, and administrative quarters, all apparently constructed as part of a single master plan. At a later
date still, a further extramural area of habitations grew on the south
side of the settlement, accounting for a contiguously occupied area
totaling about 22 hectares at its floruit. It is clear, however, that the
extent of the Uruk occupation at Habuba was larger, possibly much
larger, than the contiguously occupied areas just described because
Uruk ceramics were also found across a 200-meter-wide band extending north of the walled settlement for an additional distance of about 1
kilometer. Vallet surmises that this area, which adds a further 20
hectares to the extent of the site, represents traces of less dense suburban occupations surrounding the walled enclave. There can be little
doubt that the planners and, almost certainly, a substantial proportion
of the inhabitants of Habuba Kabira and nearby sites were of southern
Mesopotamian origin. This is shown by the familiar southern
Mesopotamian architectural plans and construction techniques, diagnostic ceramics and ceramic production procedures, typical small
objects, characteristic glyptic practices and iconography, and, lastly, distinctive accounting and recording systems, including numerical notation tablets and impressed balls (Algaze 1993a).

Recent surveys along portions of the Euphrates in southeastern
Turkey to be flooded by the eventual construction of a dam just north
of Carchemish suggest that several intrusive Uruk outposts also existed
on or near the Carchemish ford, although, admittedly, this conclusion
remains somewhat speculative insofar as the sites in question are being
generally recognized only on the basis of the large number of typical
grit-tempered Uruk ceramics on their surface and the general absence
of the partly contemporary indigenous Amuq F assemblage.[2] One such
apparent outpost was Tiladir Tepe, which is about 12 hectares in extent
and is situated directly opposite Carchemish. A limited collection of
ceramics from this site suggests a Middle Uruk (LC 3–4) date (Algaze,
Breuninger, and Knudstad 1994: site 82). Another potential outpost is
formed by a cluster of three sites centered around a natural promon-
tory overlooking the Euphrates some 4 to 5 kilometers upstream of
Carchemish. The central site in the cluster, Sadi Tepe, enjoys a natu-

rally defensible situation not unlike that of Jebel Aruda in the Tabqa area and was about 7 hectares in extent, while the flanking sites on the river terrace, Komeçli and Kum Ocağı, add a further 9 hectares of occupied area. Ceramics from these sites, in turn, appear to be entirely of Late Uruk (LC 5) date, suggesting that Tiladir and the Şadı Tepe cluster were consecutive rather than contemporaneous (Algaze et al. 1994: sites 64, 76, 80).[3]

Earlier, I had interpreted the Uruk presence along the Upper Euphrates as consisting of urban-sized enclaves and associated clusters of supporting agricultural villages situated only near important river fords, such as the environs of Carchemish and Meskene (Algaze 1993a). New excavations in the Tishreen Dam of Syria, however, show that the intervening area (situated midway between the Carchemish and Meskene fords) also contains a number of small sites with Uruk period occupations. In fact, this new evidence brings the number of excavated or surveyed sites yielding varying collections of typical Uruk material culture between the Tabqa and Birecik Dam areas of the Upper Euphrates (a linear distance of some 110 km) up to 28.[4] Some of these sites, no doubt, will turn out to be indigenous occupations in contact with Uruk settlements nearby. However, the number of both certain and possible Uruk sites now attested along the Upper Euphrates is such that an actual colonization of portions of the Upper Euphrates Basin by settlers from southern Mesopotamia has to be considered a distinct possibility, as Johnson (1988–89) had previously argued. Nonetheless, the existence of a thriving indigenous Late Chalcolithic community north of Birecik at Hacınebi that both predates the Uruk intrusion into the Upper Euphrates and was certainly contemporary with some of the larger Uruk outposts downstream (discussed below) suggests that the preexisting inhabitants were not entirely displaced from the Euphrates and, moreover, that contacts between the local and the intrusive groups were commonplace (Stein, this volume; Stein, Bernbeck et al. 1996; Stein, Edens et al. 1996).

A substantial Uruk presence also existed at other strategic fording places along the Euphrates and the other principal waterways criss-crossing Upper Mesopotamia. However, much of the pertinent evidence is derived from less reliable older excavations and is therefore more ambiguous than the Euphrates data already discussed. In earlier publications (Algaze 1986c, 1989b, 1993a) I argued that Uruk outposts comparable to those uncovered in the Tabqa Dam had been implanted, almost certainly by force, at a small number of other historical fords across northern Mesopotamia where important indigenous regional centers already existed, such as *(a)* Samsat along the northern Euphrates in Turkey, *(b)* Tell Brak on the Jaghjagh branch of the upper Khabur, and *(c)* Nineveh on the Tigris. Save perhaps for Tell Brak (below), this view now needs to be modified. Recent research at Hacınebi (Stein, this volume) shows that the Godin model of contact (small enclaves of Uruk intruders existing within larger preexisting centers with the consent of local populations) was far from unique. This raises the possibility that Uruk interaction with preexisting Late Chalcolithic settlements in command of known river fords across Upper Mesopotamia was closer to the Godin or Hacınebi model than it was to the Habuba model (large population movements) that I had previously espoused, a point already noted by Wattenmaker (1990).

Nonetheless, a precise understanding of the nature of the Uruk emplacements at some of the regional centers commanding river fords across northern Mesopotamia continues to elude us. Since my original views first appeared, much hitherto unknown material from earlier excavations at Nineveh (Gut 1995) and some of the Uruk materials from recent excavations at Samsat (Özgüç 1992) have been published. These new data leave no doubt that both indigenous and intrusive Uruk assemblages existed at each of the two sites, but available evidence from either site continues to be insufficient to clarify the cultural context of the materials, their spatial relationships, or their relative frequency. Because of these caveats, I now think that Wattenmaker's (1990) suggestion that Samsat may represent an indigenous settlement, perhaps not unlike Arslantepe (below), in contact with the Uruk world and where some elements of Uruk material culture were consumed or emulated by local elites is more likely to be correct than my earlier suggestion. However, I still think that some sort of an Uruk outpost existed at Nineveh. The reason for this is that Nineveh, unlike Samsat, has yielded a variety of categories of characteristic Uruk material culture. This includes a full range of typical Uruk ceramics found in widely separated squares at the very center of the mound (Gut 1995) and, more importantly, Uruk glyptic practices and accounting procedures (numerical notation tablets), which were used at the site in a typical southern Mesopotamian fashion (Collon and Reade 1983).[5] The latter finds are strong evidence for an actual Uruk presence at Nineveh (of an undetermined type, but presumably closer to Hacınebi than to Habuba) because while Uruk glyptic practices and iconography were widely imitated in indigenous Late Chalcolithic sites across the northern periphery of Mesopotamia, such emulations were always used in the context of recording systems that were both simpler and different than those employed in actual Uruk sites or outposts (Algaze 2001).

New research at Brak is similarly inconclusive but is likewise suggestive of some sort of an Uruk presence at the site. To some degree, existing uncertainties result from the fact that the excavators at Brak (Oates and Oates 1993a, 1994, 1997; Matthews 1995, 1996) and the surveyors of its hinterland (Eidem and Warburton 1996) have used the term "Uruk" to refer to both indigenous Late Chalcolithic Amuq F type materials and intrusive Uruk materials of direct southern Mesopotamian derivation. While this usage makes sense on chronological grounds, its lack of precision in terms of material culture makes it almost impossible to elucidate the temporal and spatial relationships between the two contemporaneous but distinct assemblages, either at the site itself or in immediately surrounding settlements. Nonetheless, recent excavations in area TW at Brak (levels 11–13) provide evidence for long-term interaction between Brak and the Uruk world and show that Uruk materials at Brak were introduced at the end of a long indigenous sequence (Emberling et al. 1999; Oates and Oates 1993a, 1994, 1997). An earlier episode of that interaction (of a still undetermined nature) is visible in TW 13, with its mixed Uruk and indigenous assemblages. This appears to have led eventually to some sort of an Uruk outpost at the site. This is discernible in TW 11–12, where all architectural plans and artifacts thus far published appear to be of southern Mesopotamian Late Uruk type (Oates and Oates 1993a, 1994). However, because of the reduced exposures that have been practicable at TW thus far, it is not yet clear whether the Uruk occupation at Brak took the form of an isolated enclave within a larger indigenous site or whether Brak as a whole was taken over by intruding Uruk populations that displaced the preexisting populations. On account of Brak's later historical role as the southern Mesopotamian gateway to the north in the Akkadian and Ur III periods, the latter alternative is the more likely one. Further, for the same reason, I expect that future excavations and pertinent ^{14}C data (Matthews 2000) will show that Brak was one of the earliest sites in the north affected by the Uruk expansion.

Because many areas at the northern and northwestern periphery of Mesopotamia have yet to be surveyed systematically, it is possible—indeed likely—that other Uruk outposts will be recognized in the near future. However, the survey data we do have (Algaze et al. 1991, 1992, 1994; Eidem and Warburton 1996; Levine and Young 1987; Lyonnet 1997; Meijer 1986; Özdogan 1977; Stein and Wattenmaker 1990; Whallon 1979; Wilkinson 1990a; Wilkinson and Tucker 1995) indicate that the hinterlands away from the strategic focal nodes where Uruk settlements were established remained under the control of the preexisting Late Chalcolithic communities.

CHRONOLOGICAL PARAMETERS FOR THE EXPANSION

Duration

Ever since the first reports about the excavations at Tell Sheik Hassan in Syria appeared (Boese 1995, 1995–96), it has been apparent that the Uruk penetration of selected portions of Upper Mesopotamia and the surrounding highlands was a relatively long-lived phenomenon (Algaze 1993a:56–57). However, only now as a result of a thorough reanalysis of available radiocarbon dates by Henry Wright and Eric Rupley (this volume) has it become clear that the expansionary process may have lasted as long as 400 to 500 years (equivalent to LC 3–5 in the chronological scheme used in this volume; see chapter 1). This conclusion follows from a comparison of available radiocarbon dates from Middle Uruk (LC 3–4) period levels at the site of Hacınebi with dates from Late Uruk (LC 5) period levels at both Hassek Höyük and Jebel Aruda. Supporting evidence is provided by both excavations and surveys. Sites such as Brak (Oates and Oates 1993a, 1997), Sheikh Hassan (Boese 1995, 1995–96), and, to a lesser extent, Tell 'Abr (Hammade and Yamazaki 1993; Yamazaki 1999), all in Syria, and the site of Nineveh (Gut 1995) exhibit long stratigraphic sequences with superimposed Middle and Late Uruk (LC 5) period materials. However, not all of the Uruk outposts thus far recognized were occupied simultaneously. This is clear on the basis of both excavations and surveys along the Euphrates. Habuba Kabira and Jebel Aruda, for instance, were only established at the end of a long sequence of settlement in the Tabqa area that had started with the much more modest implantation of Tell Sheikh Hassan. A similar case can be made for the Carchemish area. As already noted, surface ceramics from Tiladir Tepe and the Şadı Tepe cluster suggest that the two outposts in that area were consecutive rather than contemporary. In short, the Uruk expansion across the northern periphery is best conceived as a dynamic and probably uneven process that varied through time, even in a single area, and that affected various areas of the Mesopotamian periphery differently at different times.

Collapse

At least along the Euphrates, the end of the Uruk expansion can be correlated with the archaeological sequence of southern Mesopotamia with some precision. The absence of Archaic Texts in the northern outposts suggests that most Uruk settlements in the north were abandoned or collapsed just before level IVa of the Eanna sequence at Warka (Nissen, this volume). However, the presence of one tablet with an archaic sign at the Godin V fort suggests that at least some of the smaller outposts continued to operate until the very end of the Uruk period (Algaze 1993a:56–57). Some potential reasons for the collapse or withdrawal of the Uruk outposts are discussed in the concluding section of this chapter.

THE FUNCTION OF THE OUTPOSTS

What was the motivation behind the large influx of Uruk settlers into the Upper Euphrates area, and, further, what was the function of the variously configured Uruk outposts across the northern periphery of Mesopotamia? In answer to the first question, Johnson (1988–89), Schwartz (this volume), and Wright (this volume) would see Uruk settlements in the Upper Euphrates as refugee communities established as a result of population displacements in the Mesopotamian alluvium or in the at this time closely related Susiana Plain of Khuzistan.

Although plausible in light of environmental and social dislocations taking place in the Mesopotamian alluvium during the second half of the Uruk period (discussed above), I would argue that lust for land is unlikely to have been the *initial* motivation for the intrusion because the number of known Middle Uruk (LC 3–4) sites along the Upper Euphrates remains small.[6] Rather, the locations of both the earliest and, eventually, the largest Uruk sites around historical fording points of the river, outlined earlier, suggest that control of the focal nodes along the river where east-west overland routes and north-to-south water transport came together was both the earlier and the more important motivation. The evidence from Habuba Kabira clearly shows that the large-scale movement of southern Mesopotamian populations into the Upper Euphrates occurred only toward the final phase of the Uruk expansion (Late Uruk [LC 5]). Thus, whatever territorial control is implied by these movements was a consequence of an intrusion that was initially focused on the river fords rather than the cause of the intrusion in the first place (i.e., the flag followed the trade).

Addressing the second question, the function of the outposts, forces us to look beyond the Euphrates and consider the patterns of Uruk settlement across the northern Mesopotamian periphery as a whole. Presuming that a correlation exists between settlement location, marketing structure, and modes of regional economic articulation (Smith 1974), it is possible to derive clues about the function of the variously configured Uruk outposts by looking at their locational circumstances. Irrespective of their type and location, the outposts are generally not centrally situated in relationship to available prime agricultural land—as would be expected if the extraction of surplus agricultural resources were a primary consideration. Instead, the locations of small outposts, such as Godin, astride historical trade routes across the highlands, and of other outposts in Upper Mesopotamia along natural fording places of the principal waterways, suggest that access to lines of communication (and hence to trade routes) across the northern periphery of Mesopotamia was a primary rationale. A complementary rationale is that proposed originally by Rita Wright (1989) and now defended in more detail by Nicholas Kouchoukos (1998). They see the location of some of the Uruk outposts in Upper Mesopotamia at the watered edges of wide steppe lands as also ideal to ensure access to the considerable pastoral resources of the area—resources that would have been of strategic value to the textile industries of growing Uruk cities. This last suggestion has the advantage of explaining the otherwise puzzling presence of Uruk artifacts in the context of what must have been ephemeral pastoral encampments in the Syrian Jezira (e.g., in the Wadi Ajij area; cf. Pfälzner 1984). In either case, however, whether the outposts were ideally positioned in relationship to trade routes, pastoral resources, or, as is more likely, in relationship to both, their function was to engage in exchange with the variously configured societies that already existed in the areas into which they intruded, ranging from pastoral nomads to fully settled polities already well on their way to complexity (see below). The fords, in particular, represent natural junctures where long-distance and local trade networks come together. At those locations, the Mesopotamian outposts were embedded within culturally alien hinterlands but were, at the same time, at the head of dendritically arranged settlement networks within those hinterlands.

This settlement configuration not only provides strong support for believing that the outposts functioned as mediators of exchange between Uruk and peripheral societies but yields clues as to how the exchange was organized as well. Economic geographers note that dendritic settlement structures limit the ability of hinterland producers to find alternate markets for their production and maximize the ability of eccentric, but strategically located, urban centers to control and secure information and resources from the surrounding hinterlands (Smith 1974). For this reason, dendritic mercantile systems are typically monopolistic systems whereby urban elites can stipulate the terms of trade with hinterland communities (Santley and Alexander 1992). According to Carol Smith (1974), dendritic settlement configurations are typical for "colonial or recently colonial societies where marketing is...imposed by an outside group involved in the international market and import-export trade."

To argue, on the basis of the locational circumstances of the Uruk outposts, that exchange was a primary motivation for the Uruk expansion should not be taken to mean, however, that we understand the nature of political relations between specific Uruk outposts in the north and specific Uruk city-states. We do not. In fact, we cannot yet tackle this question because much of the pertinent data from excavated northern outposts are not fully published, and, regrettably, we still lack representative and well-excavated data from most of the larger Uruk urban sites in the south. Nonetheless, we can model, for future testing, the range of possible ways in which relations between southern cities and northern outposts may have been structured by looking at comparative material from presumably related and well-documented phenomena. A useful study is that of Philip Curtin (1984), a historian who explores the forms cross-cultural exchange has taken through history, the ways in which it has been organized, and the impact such contacts have had on the societies exposed to it. He argues that the most common institutional form of cross-cultural exchange after the emergence of cities was the "trade diaspora," a term that is applicable to the Uruk outposts insofar as it is defined broadly as any community or communities set up for the specific purpose of mediating contacts between areas with different but complementary resource endowments. Historically, asserts Curtin, trade diasporas have taken diverse forms. These range from small groups of male commercial specialists removing themselves from their own society and settling as aliens in a foreign community (Hacınebi, Godin?) to the diametrically opposed case of trade diasporas staffed by a larger cross-section of colonists and founded as political entities from the beginning (Habuba?), with the founding power or powers retaining some sort of control over the trading settlements. Between these extremes are myriad possibilities in terms of the relationship between the trade diaspora settlements and their host communities, the relationship among the diaspora settlements themselves, and their relationship, if any, with their original homeland.

Arguments about the primacy of trade as a motivating factor for the Uruk intrusion should also not be understood as implying that economic imperatives can in and of themselves fully explain the complex web of motivations and events that originally set in motion and eventually sustained that expansion over a period of 400 to 500 years. On the contrary, historically, expansion and colonization are always as closely interwoven with the self-aggrandizing political and religious ideologies of ruling elites as they are with the desire to obtain coveted resources, as Lamberg-Karlovsky (1995, 1996) and Adams (1992) have repeatedly and correctly argued. This was no doubt also the case in Uruk times, but, having taken place at the dawn of history, the precise ideological underpinnings of the Uruk expansion still elude us.

THE NATURE OF THE TRADE

The need for resources as an important motivating factor in the Uruk expansion, deduced from the locational circumstances of the outposts, is corroborated further by available archaeological evidence from Uruk sites, such as Warka, which shows that Uruk societies in the Mesopotamian alluvium were importing a much wider variety of commodities than was the case in the preceding Ubaid period and were doing so in amounts that, though difficult to quantify, far surpassed those typical for the earlier period. These would have included commodities that leave few traces in the archaeological record, such as timber and other wood products, slaves, and, if Wright and Kouchoukos are correct, wool and goat hair, as well as commodities more easily traced in the archaeological record of Uruk sites, such as precious and utilitarian metals, bitumen, and various exotic, semiprecious, and utilitarian stones (see Algaze 1993a:74–84, and Wright, this volume, for a fuller discussion). In terms of volume and ideological value (to judge from later royal inscriptions), one of the most important resources brought in at the time would have been timber, which was necessary for roofing. Margueron (1992) estimated that somewhere between 3,000 and 6,000 linear meters of roofing-grade timber would have been necessary to roof the Limestone Temple at Warka, dated to the Late Uruk period (Eanna V).[7] Margueron's estimate of the substantial amounts of timber required for a single monumental building leaves no doubt as to the massive amounts of roofing-grade timber that would have been necessary to satisfy the explosive growth of cities in the southern Mesopotamian alluvium during the Uruk period. Other commodities imported in the Uruk period are more difficult to quantify because many would have been exotics, which, by their very nature, are recycled and reused in later times. More importantly, our understanding of the scale of the flow of imported exotic commodities into the alluvium in Uruk times is crippled by the general lack of mortuary data for the period. However, finds of substantial amounts of precious and semiprecious stones and metals, such as those recovered within the Riemchengebäude structure (see above), suggest that significant amounts of imports were indeed making their way into the alluvium in the Late Uruk (LC 5) period. It is also very likely that many of the exotics contained in the so-called Sammelfund Hoard at Warka, which was discovered in a Jemdet Nasr period level, represent heirlooms of Uruk date (Heinrich 1936).

Save for the metals, most of the commodities imported into southern Mesopotamia in the Uruk period would have been acquired in their raw, unprocessed state. Because metal technology was more advanced in northern societies, which had exploited highland ore sources for centuries prior to the Uruk period, early metal imports into the alluvium would have consisted principally of semiprocessed ingots and, perhaps, even some finished products (Yener 2000). Nonetheless, it is certain that some processing of imported metal ores still took place in some of the Uruk outposts across the north and in some Uruk cities in the south. For instance, in addition to numerous finished copper objects, several litharge cakes were found in the excavations at Habuba-süd (Kohlmeyer 1997). Found in various contexts in the northeastern quarter of the city, these cakes represent the remains of a fairly elaborate cupellation process whereby silver and lead were extracted, separated, and refined from imported polymetallic ores (Pernicka et al. 1998). Various metallurgical activities are also attested within the Uruk *karum* at Hacınebi (Stein, this volume). Uruk levels at Warka, in turn, yielded both raw copper ores (Heinrich 1938:25) and the metallurgical installations to smelt and process them (Nissen 1970:114). It is likely that a number of knowledgeable northern smiths may have accompanied the flow of metal products southwards (Helms 1993).[8]

The nature of exports from the Mesopotamian alluvium in the Uruk period is less clear than that of imports into the area at the time. New chemical characterization studies of raw bitumen lumps and finished bitumen artifacts from Hacınebi (Stein, this volume) and Tell Sheikh Hassan (Boese 1995–96) suggest that bitumen obtained from central Iraqi sources near modern Hit was a common southern Mesopotamian export (possibly used as packing material for other, as-yet-undetermined commodities). Most exports from the alluvium, however, would have consisted of perishable commodities that left few traces in the archaeological record (Crawford 1973). The most important of these would have been dyed woolen textiles, which had started to replace linen as the basic surplus textile fiber in southern Mesopotamia by the fourth millennium B.C. (McCorriston 1997). Such elaborately crafted woolen textiles constituted the bulk of exports from southern Mesopotamia in the third and second millennia (Foster 1997; Larsen 1987). Admittedly, because of the lack of preservation, we do not have direct quantifiable evidence for the export of dyed woolen textiles from the Mesopotamian alluvium in the Uruk period. However, it should be clear from previous discussions that, historically, textiles were central to the international trade of southern Mesopotamian societies and, further, all of the necessary preconditions for the existence of an export-oriented textile industry were in place within Uruk cities: horizontal looms, state access to raw resources (wool), the dependent (female) labor needed to process the wool and operate the looms, and the bureaucratic apparatus needed to record, store, and redistribute that production. Also available to Uruk societies, as noted by Wright (this volume), were the donkeys needed to transport the finished woolen products upriver.

In addition to textiles, a small variety of other low-bulk, high-value processed agricultural commodities appear to have been exported from the Mesopotamian alluvium at this time. This is suggested by a variety of specialized Uruk vessels commonly found within local sites at various locations across the Mesopotamian periphery. Best documented are small four-lugged jars with nose lugs and several types of narrow-necked bottles with drooping spouts (for specific references and sites, see Algaze 1993a:63–74). A case in point is provided by several Late Uruk (LC 5) jars found in storerooms and within ritual structures at the site of Arslantepe (period VIA). Although chemical characterization analyses have yet to be made, these jars (e.g., Palmieri 1989: figs. 3.4–3.7; Frangipane 1997b: figs. 10–11), and some of the stoppers that once sealed them (e.g., Palmieri and Frangipane 1989: fig. 3a), are almost certainly imports into the site. If so, they unequivocally indicate southern Mesopotamian involvement in the long-distance movement of valuable liquids. Possible candidates include wine (Badler, McGovern, and Glusker 1996), resins, utilitarian and aromatic oils, aromatic or medicinal unguents (Algaze 1995), or various types of animal fats (Englund 1998:161–69). Save for the aromatics and the fats, historically most of the commodities noted were neither produced in nor exported from the Mesopotamian alluvium (Pettinato 1972). Thus, it is likely that at least some of the prized liquids exported in Uruk vessels consisted of commodities acquired by Uruk outposts in Upper Mesopotamia and repackaged at the outposts for export to peripheral societies. This raises the possibility that some outpost-based Uruk merchants succeeded in interposing themselves as participants (no doubt for profit!) in intraregional trade in some areas of the periphery in which they were located—a pattern that strongly recalls the activities of Old Assyrian merchants in some of the same areas a millennium and a half later (Dercksen 1996; Larsen 1976).

THE URUK EXPANSION: ISSUES OF CAUSATION

What was the historical setting within which the Uruk colonial enterprise, the earliest in the world, came to be, and why did the Uruk expansion take the form of isolated enclaves implanted within alien hinterlands? We can only speculate about the answers to these questions because of limitations inherent in the evidence at our disposal. However, it is certain that any attempt to approach them must explore, first, the relationship between the Uruk expansion and the political framework of the Mesopotamian alluvium in the Uruk period; second, the various internal and external social and economic factors that made the expansion necessary in the first place and helped propel it once underway; and, third, the geographical and transportational constraints that selected for strategically located outposts embedded within alien hinterlands as the principal mechanism for managing cross-cultural contacts and exchange between southern Mesopotamian and peripheral societies.

Political Factors in the Uruk Expansion

In my initial attempt to explore the possible role that Mesopotamian political configurations of the Uruk period may have had on the Uruk expansion (Algaze 1986c), I drew a broad parallel between the impact of Uruk societies on Upper Mesopotamia and the historically attested territorial expansion of the Akkadian Empire into the same area a millennium or so later. From this, albeit with some trepidation, I went on to infer that the Uruk expansion could not be conceived under conditions of chronic city-state fractionation such as those prevalent in southern Mesopotamia through the Early Dynastic period (for a similar view see Flannery 1995 and Marcus 1998). Although left largely unstated at the time, the implications of this view were that *(a)* a large territorial state or empire already existed in the Uruk period; *(b)* Uruk itself, being four to five times larger than its closest competitor by the Late Uruk (LC 5) period, must have been the center of that primordial empire; and *(c)* the multiple Uruk outposts in the Mesopotamian periphery could be understood as a conscious and systematic act of policy of a single political entity—similar in function to the outposts of the later Akkadian Empire over much of the same area.

Upon further reflection, however, it became clear to me that my initial characterization of the Uruk phenomenon was implausible (Algaze 1989b, 1993a). Two reasons led me to this conclusion. The first is that later Mesopotamian literary and historical traditions make no reference whatsoever to such a commanding primordial empire—as I would expect to have been the case if one had existed.[9] The second is that available surveys of the Mesopotamian alluvium (Adams 1981) and the Susiana Plain show that processes of urban growth in both areas through the Uruk period resulted in the creation of buffer zones between the emerging urban polities of the time. These uninhabited areas suggest competition and strife rather than an overarching political unity. Such buffer areas have been noted in the southern Mesopotamian alluvium around Uruk itself (Adams and Nissen 1972) but are most clearly delineated in Susiana, where Johnson (1973) was able to document by the Late Uruk (LC 5) period the abandonment of all villages along a 15-kilometer-wide arc separating what appear to have been two rival states centered, respectively, at Susa and Chogha Mish. Significantly, armed conflict is often portrayed in Uruk iconography. A common scene in cylinder seal impressions of the time depicts various military activities, the siege of cities or buildings, and the taking of prisoners (Amiet 1972; Brandes 1979; Delougaz and Kantor 1996).

In light of the above, it seems more profitable to visualize the political environment of the Uruk core subregions as characterized by a small number of competitive peer polities, each surrounded by a hinterland of immediately dependent settlements providing both labor and essential agricultural and pastoral resources. Uruk, with its larger size and more extensive hinterland, is clearly a *primus inter pares* within the political landscape of southern Mesopotamia at the end of the fourth millennium, but not more than that.[10] The fragmented political configuration of the Mesopotamian alluvium through the Uruk period is very relevant to our understanding of the Uruk colonial enterprise. Scholars studying the dynamics of later colonial phenomena elsewhere have often documented the crucial role that competition between individual core polities, cities, and even semiautonomous commercial companies has in spurring the initial foundation of colonies away from core subregions and in determining the later tempo, direction, and dynamics of the colonial enterprise itself. Two particularly clear examples of this dynamic are provided by the aggressive expansion of rival European nation states in the modern era (Scammell 1989:67) and the competitive expansion of Greek city-states across the Mediterranean and the Black Sea in the Classical Age (Boardman 1980). These later historical parallels buttress the likelihood that intercity competition within the equally balkanized Mesopotamian alluvium also played a key role in unleashing the expansionary processes of Uruk societies and in magnifying those processes after their onset. More specifically, I would argue that the existence of multiple urban-sized polities in the Mesopotamian alluvium already by the Early Uruk (LC 2) period (Adams 1981) must have been a necessary precondition for the Uruk expansion because this fragmentation would have encouraged both conflict and exchange between individual alluvial centers. Both of these activities, but particularly the latter, must have been instrumental in providing Uruk urban elites with the managerial skills and material surpluses that they would eventually need in order to operate successfully in the external commercial arena opened by the Uruk expansion.

The political balkanization of the Mesopotamian alluvium through the Uruk period, in turn, would have had a further, and more direct, impact on the Uruk expansion. Although precise evidence is lacking, I consider it likely that the various Uruk colonies across the Mesopotamian periphery can be seen as an extension of the preexisting subregional rivalry of Uruk states into a transregional arena. If indeed so, the establishment of faraway colonies can be conceived as part of an organic process of action and counteraction, with individual Uruk city-states scrambling to found specific enclaves or outposts in order to secure access to the critical lines of communication through which resources were obtainable and, equally important, to deny their local rivals such access. Specific states would have been oriented toward particular portions of the periphery and trade routes into that periphery, by virtue of their location within the alluvium and their history of cross-cultural contacts and trade. A later historical parallel is available from Mesopotamia for the sort of hypothetical situation envisioned here for the Uruk period. Late in the Isin-Larsa period (first quarter of the second millennium B.C.), after the collapse of the empire of the Third Dynasty of Ur and before the unification of the alluvium under the emerging power of Hammurabi of Babylon, documents indicate that specific states controlled particular segments of the trade routes—whether overland alongside either the Tigris or Euphrates or maritime towards the Persian Gulf. The city of Ur in the southern edge of the alluvium, for example, seems to have been intimately connected with gulf trade, whereas Larsa, its neighbor to the northeast, was more closely associated with land routes eastwards into southwestern Iran via the Diyala subregion. Similarly, Sippar, in the northern edge of the alluvium, appears more closely tied with trade routes alongside the Tigris toward Assur and the north, while Babylon, on one of the main branches of the Euphrates in the central alluvium, was oriented mainly toward routes in the direction of northern Syria and the northwest (Larsen 1987; Leemans 1960).

Social and Economic Factors in the Uruk Expansion

The political framework of the Mesopotamian alluvium in the Uruk period represents a necessary but not a sufficient condition for the Uruk expansion. If we are to understand why Mesopotamian societies would want to expand in the first place and why that expansion was successful, at least initially, we must also explore social and economic factors within Uruk and peripheral societies that selected for the expansion.

Starting with Uruk societies, an important spur for expansion came from the social consequences of a pattern of trade that was inherently asymmetrical in both its nature and impact. As noted earlier, save for metals, the outpost-mediated trade patterns of the Uruk period generally involved the exchange of unprocessed commodities from the periphery, both exotic and essential, for processed or semiprocessed goods from the Mesopotamian alluvium that required a substantial amount of labor to produce. This pattern of trade would have had important economic, social, and political "multiplier effects" on Uruk polities. The economic consequences of such patterns of trade have been explored by Jane Jacobs (1969) and Donald Kurtz (1987). They note that the exchange of raw resources for finished goods would have substantially strengthened the economic base of the core societies involved in the exchange (i.e., those exporting largely processed goods) because *(a)* a large proportion of the imports had to be processed before they could be incorporated into the economy, thus creating a significant amount of down-the-line employment, and *(b)* under premodern conditions, the production of an exportable surplus of finished goods would also have required a sizable investment in labor. In the Uruk case, all of this would naturally lead to the diversification and expansion of preexisting bureaucratic superstructures because of *(a)* the need to oversee and maintain the semi- or fully dependent laborers that were involved in the processing of imports and, more importantly, in the production of exported commodities such as textiles; *(b)* the need to supply workshops with raw materials in a timely manner; and *(c)* the need to record and distribute the resulting commodities for local consumption and to record, store, package, and transport exportable surpluses.

Once underway, the beneficial economic impact of the exchange would have acted as a powerful spur for Early Uruk (LC 2) administrators, both secular and religious, to involve themselves directly in the production of local commodities for export by extending their authority over the countryside and to take any steps necessary to regularize and institutionalize the mechanisms whereby peripheral resources were acquired (i.e., the establishment of outposts). The reasons for this are rooted in the social and political impact of the exchange on core societies. Ethnographic studies show how the acquisition, display, and distribution of exotic goods buttress vertical ties of dependency within social systems (Ekholm 1977; Helms 1988) as elites who are able to monopolize the acquisition of those goods typically use them *(a)* to cement alliances with equals, *(b)* to attract and maintain the acolytes they need in order to compete more effectively against their peers (Clark and Blake 1994), and *(c)* to legitimize their right to demand and receive surplus production from peasants and other laborers. Since surpluses, in turn, can be exchanged for further exotics, a feedback loop is thereby initiated that expands the ability of emerging elites to attract ever larger numbers of dependents (Adams 1974a).

A further social impact of the exchange patterns described for Uruk societies was that, once started, the continued import of exotic commodities would have become a strategic necessity for those institutions and individuals engaged in the trade. The reasons for this have been explained by Mary Helms (1988, 1993), who uses a variety of ethnographic, historic, and literary evidence to show how, in traditional societies, exotic resources attesting to contacts with geographically and culturally alien cultures are commonly imbued with ritual meaning and typically come to be seen as a direct demonstration of a leader's fitness to rule. Thus, the ability to acquire, display, and distribute exotic imports becomes crucial to the success of self-aggrandizing leaders in legitimizing their unequal access to resources and power. Those imports become, in short, central to the very reproduction of the social order. More specifically, in the Uruk case the flow of status-validating imports had to be maintained at all costs since an interruption would have led to a loss—no doubt unacceptable—of legitimacy for Uruk urban elites. Furthermore, an interruption in the flow of imports would also have led to a cessation of production for export and, given the large number of laborers commonly involved under Mesopotamian conditions, this too would soon have resulted in unacceptable social dislocations.

It is clear why access to nonlocal resources became a strategic necessity for Uruk societies and why Uruk urban elites would seek to expand in order to secure such access. However, why did peripheral societies allow the Uruk expansion to take place? To be sure, the massive city walls at Habuba and Sheikh Hassan, and the defensible positions of Jebel Aruda and Şadı Tepe, suggest that, at least in some areas, coercion may have been a factor in the implantation of colonies. However, situated more than 1,000 kilometers from the Mesopotamian alluvium, such settlements could not have survived for long in the face of active and systematic local opposition, in spite of their mighty walls or hilltop locations. Thus, at least initially, the Uruk expansion makes sense only if the intruders were generally assured of a substantial measure of indigenous acceptance and cooperation.

The reason such cooperation could be expected has to do with the short-term effects of the exchange on peripheral polities. In the long term, of course, the impact of the inherently asymmetric trade would have been prejudicial to the economies of peripheral societies *(a)* because of overspecialization in the production of only a limited number of resources for export to a single market capable of exercising monopolistic control over the terms of trade and *(b)* because for peripheral communities the exchange commonly only involved the extraction of preexisting resources and, save for the metals, did not create much down-the-line processing employment (Galtung 1971). However, it is unlikely that peripheral elites would have understood the long-term systemic drawbacks of the exchange at the onset of the contacts. On the contrary, those elites surely would have seen the start of an exchange relationship with the Uruk world in an overwhelmingly favorable light because the trade would have had an immediate and obvious beneficial impact on their narrow class interests. This is explained by a variety of reasons, each representing a powerful motivation for initial peripheral acquiescence to the Uruk intrusion. First, the natural role of local chieftains as mediators and facilitators of the trade, and as organizers of the extraction of resources for export, would have allowed those leaders to expand and consolidate their already asymmetrical economic and political positions, both within their own society and vis-à-vis local and subregional rivals. Second, for reasons already discussed, the core-manufactured items that peripheral elites would have acquired as mediators of exchange would have served to mark and validate their growing status within their own societies. And, third, as Mary Helms (1988, 1993) has noted, evidence for the capacity to cope ably with particularly powerful foreigners would have been taken as a measure of the prowess and capabilities of the leaders of the less complex society involved in the contacts, so that substantial prestige would have accrued to peripheral elites mediating contacts with Uruk colonies in their midst.

Geographical Factors in the Uruk Expansion

The preceding discussions explain why the emerging southern Mesopotamian city-states of the Uruk period would have expanded and why local elites of less-developed areas into which they intruded would initially have welcomed that expansion. However, we must still explain why the expansion so often took the form of strategically positioned outposts implanted within otherwise alien hinterlands. This is explained, in turn, by what the economic historian Paul Bairoch (1988:11–12) has termed the "tyranny of distance." The primitive transportational technologies common to premodern societies meant that on the whole direct exploitation of distant resources would have been prohibitively expensive and time-consuming. Under such conditions, coveted commodities were much more efficiently and cheaply obtained by allowing indigenous communities already exploiting them (e.g., Arslantepe) to continue, provided they could (directly or through middlemen) be persuaded or coerced into trade at terms favorable to core polities. The latter is actually the function of the strategically situated Uruk outposts positioned, as they were, at focal nodes astride trade routes and at the head of dendritic settlement networks. Studies by economic geographers show that when long-distance exchange is of primary importance, and where relatively undeveloped transportation networks are the norm, an efficient way of channeling regular trade between distant societies is via "gateway communities" that serve as collection and transshipment points for commodities from less-developed areas and as distribution nodes for manufactures from more highly organized polities. Such gateway communities are always created by the more complex of the societies involved in the exchange and commonly develop at the natural passage point between subregions with contrasting resource endowments, or in situations where there are abrupt discontinuities in the efficiency of transport (Burghardt 1971), such as railheads, seaports, or, in the Uruk case, river fords.

RELATIONS BETWEEN THE URUK OUTPOSTS AND PREEXISTING SOCIETIES

How did the various types of Uruk outposts articulate with preexisting societies in the areas into which they intruded? This issue is particularly difficult to address because any answer requires regionally representative exposures of contemporary (Late Chalcolithic) indigenous communities at *every* level of the local settlement hierarchy, both in the immediate vicinity of Uruk outposts and at varying distances from them. While the recent excavations at indigenous sites such as

Hacınebi Tepe and Arslantepe are starting to fill this gap, we are still far from achieving the necessary critical mass of representative data needed to address the articulation issue properly.

Nevertheless, clues as to the nature of relations between the intruders and preexisting groups may be obtained by drawing parallels to pertinent historically attested cases of "trading post" empires. A case in point is that of the French and British fur trading outposts in North America in the seventeenth and eighteenth centuries A.D. Ray's study (1978) of that intrusion shows a complex system of interaction composed of *(a)* a zone of direct influence or, on occasion, even outright control in the immediate environs of the larger outposts where trade between indigenous populations and the intruders was essentially asymmetrical and directly controlled by outpost traders; *(b)* an intermediate zone where the terms of trade became increasingly more symmetrical and the trade was controlled mostly by local middlemen (either actual producers themselves, such as pastoral nomads, or specialized traders who marshaled regional resources for exchange); and *(c)* a final, more distant zone where no direct or mediated trade links existed but where intrusive trade goods still penetrated through wholly indigenous (down-the-line) trade networks.

What makes Ray's model important for the generation of testable hypotheses about the ways in which Uruk and indigenous societies may have articulated is the realization that, under premodern transportation constraints, the nature of potential interactions between competing groups, the frequency of contacts, and the level of asymmetry in those contacts are all factors critically shaped by distance, as Stein has argued (Stein, Bernbeck et al. 1996; Stein 1998, 1999, and this volume). Nonetheless, Ray's model needs to be amended for use in the Uruk case because it assumes an even distribution for the coveted resource (i.e., fur was obtainable anywhere forests were to be found, which was almost everywhere in the American Midwest and eastern Canada in the seventeenth and eighteenth centuries). In the Uruk case, however, some of the coveted resources (metals, exotic stones, timber, etc.) would have been unevenly distributed and highly concentrated. Given this difference, it is possible to envision a further pathway for the interaction between Uruk outposts and faraway polities: *(d)* small groups of traders sent out from existing outposts in Upper

Mesopotamia take up residence in, or periodically visit, well-positioned indigenous centers controlling desired resources in order to engage in symmetrical and mutually beneficial exchange relations with preexisting elites willing to trade.

The latter scenario appears to fit best a case such as Arslantepe, a site situated well outside the orbit of any known Uruk outpost either along the upper Euphrates or the upper Khabur but located near several substantial deposits of copper in the Malatya area (Palmieri and Sertok 1993; Palmieri et al. 1995) and within easy access to the nearby and even richer polymetallic deposits of the Altınova and Ergani maden areas (de Jesus 1980; Seeliger et al. 1985). Hacınebi, closer to some of the major Uruk outposts near Carchemish (ca. 20 km north of the contemporary [Middle Uruk (LC 3–4)] outpost at Tiladir) but farther from any source of coveted resources, on the other hand, can be interpreted in light of Ray's model as a specialized indigenous polity acting as a middleman between indigenous producers elsewhere and the nearby Uruk outposts (which were represented at that indigenous site by a small group of resident traders; see Stein, this volume). Copper may represent one example of the sorts of nonlocal commodities assembled and processed at Hacınebi by local middlemen, both for local consumption and, almost certainly, for export to the Uruk world. Excavations in both the precontact and Uruk contact phases at the site have produced ample evidence (slag, crucibles, artifacts) for the import and smelting of copper ores (Stein, Edens et al. 1996; Stein et al. 1997, 1998) by the indigenous inhabitants of the site. Chemical characterization analyses suggest that the ores processed at Hacınebi were obtained from mines in the Malatya/Altınova and Ergani areas (Stein et al. 1997, 1998).

THE IMPACT OF THE URUK EXPANSION ON PREEXISTING SOCIETIES

When societies at different levels of sociopolitical and economic integration come into close economic contact, a certain amount of institutional restructuring in the social texture of each polity is inevitable. Invariably, however, the effect of the contacts is far greater on the less complex society involved in the interaction—particularly if that society was already on the verge of a social evolutionary process fueled by internal pressures (Paynter 1981). Available evidence (discussed below) indicates that Late Chalcolithic communities in the Mesopotamian periphery were just at a take-off point at the time that the Uruk intrusion took place. Thus, it is to be expected that the outpost-mediated trade between the Uruk world and communities at its northern periphery would have significantly affected the developmental trajectories of societies in the latter area. We now turn to an examination of this assumption.

Late Chalcolithic Complexity

Any assessment of the impact of the Uruk intrusion on Late Chalcolithic societies must start by defining the nature of the Late Chalcolithic societies that existed prior to the intrusion. In an earlier attempt to do this, I had concluded (albeit with reservations; see Algaze 1993a:104, 135, n. 6) that the Uruk outposts across the Upper Mesopotamian plains were generally larger, and therefore organizationally more complex, than the Late Chalcolithic communities that already existed in the areas into which they intruded. From this, I had argued that the evolution of complex indigenous societies across Upper Mesopotamia in the final phase of the Late Chalcolithic period could be understood as a reaction to the Uruk intrusion and a consequence of the onset of outpost-mediated contacts with the Uruk world.

Recent archaeological work in southeastern Turkey, northern Syria, and northern Iraq now requires these views to be modified. First, it is now clear that indigenous Late Chalcolithic sites of substantial size existed in at least some portions of the northern periphery of Mesopotamia. One example is the already discussed site of Tell Brak. Recent excavations at the site (area TW, levels 18–19) have revealed small portions of what appear to be a casemate-type fortification wall, which, if continuous, would have encircled what no doubt would have been a substantial indigenous Late Chalcolithic settlement (possibly between 40 and 65 hectares in extent) that predated the Uruk intrusion into the Upper Khabur area (Emberling et al. 1999; Oates and Oates 1997). Another example is Tell al-Hawa in the Sinjar plains of northern Iraq, surveyed by Tony Wilkinson and David Tucker (1995). Although the surveyors were not able to discern the extent of the settlement prior to the Uruk intrusion, their results do indicate that al-

Hawa encompassed somewhere between 33 and 50 hectares during parts of the Late Chalcolithic period—a substantial extent that is roughly comparable to that of the largest known Uruk outposts in the Tabqa area.

Second, it is now also clear that substantial sociopolitical complexity existed within some Late Chalcolithic polities in the north prior to the Uruk intrusion. A case in point is the site of Arslantepe (Frangipane, this volume). Earlier, I had viewed the emergence of Arslantepe VIA as an indigenous subregional redistributive center that arose in response to the onset of commercial contacts with the more advanced urban and state polities of Late Uruk (LC 5) period Mesopotamia. However, the scale of the newly uncovered Late Chalcolithic (period VII) architecture at Arslantepe (Frangipane 1997a, 1997b), and the association of string-cut mass-produced bowls and 70 or so sealings in the recently excavated period VII–VI transitional level at the site (Frangipane, this volume), now makes it more likely that the excavators are correct in seeing the emergence of specialized elite institutions at Arslantepe VIA in control of the subregional economy of the Malatya area as the culmination of indigenous development that was underway before the onset of intense contacts between the area and the Uruk world.[11] This inference is in line with the results of recent excavations at Hacınebi Tepe and Tell Brak revealing the substantial complexity that existed at both sites well before any evidence for contacts with the Uruk world. At Hacınebi evidence is provided by a series of massive storage structures and two monumental stone platforms uncovered in the precontact phases (A–B1) at the site. Associated with these remains was an indigenous accounting tradition based on stamp seals similar to that of Arslantepe. Also associated with these early levels at Hacınebi is evidence for the import and smelting of copper ores, an activity that continues, as already noted, in the Uruk period levels of the site (Stein, Edens et al. 1996; Stein et al. 1997, 1998; and Stein, this volume). Similarly, at Tell Brak recent excavations have revealed the presence of substantial architecture in indigenous Late Chalcolithic levels (i.e., TW 14–19) that clearly predates the establishment of an Uruk presence at the site (Emberling et al. 1999).

The evidence just outlined suggests that Uruk traders and colonists may have naturally gravitated toward important preexisting indigenous regional centers. Thus, such centers clearly helped shape the nature and direction of the Uruk intrusion. It does not follow, however, that indigenous societies should be construed either as unaffected by the intrusion or as being at an equal level of organizational complexity. In fact, Late Chalcolithic societies in the north should hardly be conceived as being comparable in scale to Uruk polities in the south or to have possessed an equivalent level of organizational complexity (Algaze 2001). No unequivocal regional survey or excavation data from the north have yet appeared that requires us to interpret the precontact societies in the area as anything other than complex chiefdoms (but see Frangipane 1997a, 1997b, and this volume, chapter 9, for a contrary argument), although this view may well change once additional data become available for the indigenous Late Chalcolithic settlement at Tell Brak (Emberling, personal communication 2000). In contrast, it is clear that the Uruk outposts were appendages of state-level societies and must themselves have been organized at a similar level. More to the point, although individual Late Chalcolithic sites in the north could have been larger than even the largest of the Uruk outposts established in their midst (Habuba/Qannas/Aruda), Late Chalcolithic polities as a group were no match for contemporary Uruk societies in the Mesopotamian alluvium. There is nothing in the Mesopotamian periphery that comes even close to matching the extent of the urban agglomeration at Warka in the Late Uruk (LC 5) period or the scale and monumentality of its central administrative district at the time. Equally unparalleled in any area of the periphery is the density of interacting urban agglomerations that existed in the southern Mesopotamian alluvium throughout the various phases of the Uruk period (LC 2–5) (Adams 1981).

Scholars who minimize the existence of significant developmental asymmetries between southern Mesopotamian and peripheral polities in the Uruk period generally start from the premise that there were no essential differences in the material technologies available to both groups at that time (e.g., Kohl 1987b; Lamberg-Karlovsky 1996:92; Stein 1990, 1999, and this volume). This premise is correct only in the narrow sense that the transportational and craft technologies available to them throughout the fourth millennium were comparable,[12] but it misses the mark in several important respects. First, the premise is flawed in that it does not take into account the fact that societies in the alluvial lowlands of the Tigris-Euphrates system during the fourth millennium held several environmentally and geographically determined advantages that helped accelerate the tempo of processes of social evolution in the alluvium vis-à-vis comparable processes in neighboring regions. These were (a) a more varied concentration of exploitable subsistence resources, (b) higher and more reliable agricultural yields, and (c) a naturally more efficient distribution system based on water transport. By the end of the Uruk period, differential growth rates fueled by these various advantages had led to more concentrated populations in the Mesopotamian alluvium than those characteristic for neighboring areas at that time. This, in turn, gave Uruk elites much greater access to labor than that possessed by their peers elsewhere, and it made possible economies of scale, efficiencies in communication and transportation, and levels of interaction and competition within and between alluvial polities that, again, were not achievable by contemporary peripheral communities.

Second, and perhaps most important, the premise fails to take account of the fact that differences in ideologies of social organization are as capable of creating significant developmental asymmetries between different societies as imbalances in material technology.

More specifically, I am suggesting that by the fourth millennium B.C. southern societies possessed a variety of organizational advantages unparalleled in the periphery, which fall in the realm of what Jack Goody (2000) has termed "ideational" technologies. A case in point is provided by the greater ability of Uruk societies to process socially useful information. Bluntly put: no peripheral site has yet provided any evidence for the existence of formal reckoning and writing systems comparable in their complexity to those that had emerged in southern Mesopotamia and Khuzistan by the Middle and Late Uruk (LC 3–5) periods. The thousands of sealings discarded at various locations within the period VIA complex at Arslantepe, for instance, commonly bear the impression or impressions of but a single seal. A similar case obtains in the Late Chalcolithic levels of Tepe Gawra. At both sites, impressions of more than one seal on a single sealing surface are exceptional (Fiandra 1994:168; M. Frangipane, personal communication 1999; M. Rothman, personal communication 1999). In contrast, contemporary procedures in Uruk cities in the south and in Uruk out-posts in the north regularly exhibit the imprints of multiple seals, par-ticularly in the case of balls and bullae (Delougaz and Kantor 1996). The greater frequency of complex devices with multiple, often super-imposed impressions of different seals in the south can be taken as a proxy for the greater number of levels of bureaucratic control and accountability that existed within Uruk centers as compared to those characteristic of the much smaller northern sites (Nissen 1977; Pittman 1993; but see Wright's cautionary remarks in this volume about the pre-sumption that the use of seals is restricted to state bureaucrats). The northern counterpart to the impressed balls and numerical notation tablets of the south is but a few tallying slabs at Arslantepe VIA with evenly sized indentations on their surfaces (presumably representing numbers), which appear to have served as mnemonic devices (Liverani 1983 [1988]: figs. 1–4). These devices could only convey a fraction of the information that could be transmitted by the more elaborate reck-oning systems of southern societies at this time, which relied on com-plex combinations of numbers and images (seal impressions). Moreover, unlike the more complex southern systems, which were capable of conveying information at a distance and across time, the mnemonic devices of the north were inherently incapable of commu-nicating any information beyond their immediate institutional and temporal context. The disparity in efficiency and in the recording sys-tems of the two areas became even more marked by the very end of the Uruk period with the appearance of the earliest Archaic Texts in the south (Uruk IV script). These new pictographic tablets allowed south-ern administrators to record nuances of time, location, persons involved, and action effected, and to abstract and summarize detailed data about collections and disbursements of goods and labor in a form usable by themselves at a later time, by higher-level supervisory officials at any time, and by later generations of similarly trained bureaucrats. Indigenous systems of administrative control equivalent in their sophis-tication to those already being used in southern Mesopotamia in the final centuries of the fourth millennium would not be attested in Upper Mesopotamia for at least 600 years or so after the end of the Uruk period (Postgate 1988).

The Uruk Impact on Preexisting Societies

Because the site has been excavated and published in such exemplary fashion, it is possible to address the issue of the impact of the Uruk intrusion on preexisting societies by turning again to the evidence provided by Arslantepe. As already noted, new evidence from periods VII and VII/VI shows that Arslantepe was well on the way to achieving some measure of complexity on its own prior to the Uruk intrusion. However, it is still fair to ask whether Arslantepe would have developed the way it did in period VIA if contacts with the Uruk world had not existed. This question is, of course, unanswerable given the uncertainties inherent in the interpretation of archaeological data. However, clues as to the potential impact that contacts with Uruk polities had on Arslantepe VIA do exist. One set of clues is provided by the ceramic repertoire found within the period VIA administrative/religious complex. Elites at the site were consuming a large proportion of locally made vessels in wares and styles that imitated what must have been more prestigious Uruk prototypes (Frangipane 1997b:70). While the meaning of this emulation cannot be untangled without knowing what commodities were contained within those vessels, it may be possible to monitor the ideological consequences that contacts with the Uruk world had on elite behavior at Arslantepe by looking at the glyptic tradition in use at the site at the same time. It is clear that Arslantepe elites adopted some glyptic practices that are of unmistakable southern Mesopotamian (Uruk) origin. These include the use of cylinder seals, which are capable of conveying more information than the stamp seals typical of the local glyptic tradition, and selected Uruk iconographic themes (Ferioli and Fiandra 1983 [1988]; Frangipane 1997b:67–69).[13] Of the various themes that they chose to emulate, one stands out as particularly important because it was reproduced at the site not only in glyptic media (Frangipane 1997b: fig. 16:1) but in much larger wall frescoes (Frangipane 1997b: fig. 15) as well. This was a depiction of a presumably royal or chiefly figure on a cattle-driven sledge surrounded by attending personnel. Particularly in its glyptic rendition, this theme finds very close parallels in the iconography of the Uruk world where the figure at issue is commonly depicted in a variety of media (above) and is unquestionably that of a city ruler (Schmandt-Besserat 1993).

The prominent use of this Uruk-derived iconography at Arslantepe can be interpreted as evidence for the partial adoption at that local site of explicitly Mesopotamian ideas of the social order (i.e., "symbolic entrainment" in Renfrew's [1986:8–9] terminology). This makes sense only if the society adopting the iconography was itself on the verge of parallel social transformations. While the adoption of Uruk-derived notions about the nature of social order and rulership by the emerging elites of Arslantepe did not change the general direction of preexisting trends toward social complexity in the Malatya area, I suspect that the southern ideologies being emulated may well have affected the tempo and intensity of those trends and that, almost certainly, the borrowed ideologies helped shape and legitimize the specific strategies pursued by the early rulers at Arslantepe in their quest for power.

CONCLUSION

Uruk Civilization

The carefully selected locational circumstances of the Uruk outposts at focal nodes of the network of preexisting trade routes across Upper Mesopotamia and the surrounding highlands indicate that they represent the world's first colonial enterprise. The necessary precondition that made this enterprise possible was the imbalance that had developed by the second half of the fourth millennium in the abilities of southern polities to amass and control information, labor, and surpluses vis-à-vis those of their immediate neighbors. With disparity in organizational complexity came disparities in power, both real and perceived, and with that came opportunities for Sumerian expansion. That expansion was intrinsically different from the later territorial (direct political dominion) or hegemonic (tribute-paying) empires that are more familiar to students of both ancient and modern imperial systems (for definitions, see D'Altroy 1992; Doyle 1986; Santley and Alexander 1992; Stark 1990). What made it different was the initial acquiescence of elites in the intruded areas to the onset of systemic contacts with the Uruk world that, initially, they would have seen as beneficial to their class/factional interests. Although this acquiescence would ultimately prove ephemeral, it explains why the Uruk intrusion was more variegated, geographically more extensive, and, in places, locally more intense than many of its later counterparts, a fact that still puzzles some authors (e.g., Lamberg-Karlovsky 1996:85). In part as a consequence of the long-term impact that the Uruk intrusion must have had on the further development of indigenous societies in the Mesopotamian periphery, later attempts to expand into some of the same areas, such as those of individual Late Early Dynastic rulers or of the early kings of the Akkadian Empire, were met by mature northern polities whose power, on occasion, rivaled that of the southern intruders (Larsen 1979; Liverani, ed. 1993; Westenholz 1979). It should come as no surprise, therefore, that the later alluvial intrusions into the northern periphery of Mesopotamia—intrusions that were explicitly motivated, in part, by the need to secure access to northern resources—never matched the geographical extent of the earlier Uruk phenomenon and never succeeded in the implantation of populous colonies such as those found along the Euphrates in the Uruk period. Moreover, the later Mesopotamian intruders had to rely on expensive military garrisons to achieve what their Uruk predecessors had largely achieved by less expensive and more informal means; to a large degree coercion and tribute came to replace the cooperation and exchange that had sufficed before.

Because of the political balkanization that characterized southern Mesopotamia through the Uruk period, it is likely that the Uruk colonial enterprise in areas to the north and northwest was the result of a long organic process of action and counteraction, as individual Uruk states scrambled to lay claims to portions of the lines of communication through which needed resources were acquired and simultaneously attempted to deny such access to their local rivals by founding variously configured trading outposts at focal nodes in the network of preexisting trade routes across Upper Mesopotamia and the surrounding highlands. The nature of the outposts, in turn, appears to have been largely determined by two factors: (1) distance away from the alluvium and (2) the nature of the preexisting societies in the areas into which they intruded. In largely uninhabited areas, Uruk outposts amounted to cases of urban implantation exhibiting such evidence of planning and centralized organization in their construction (i.e., the second building phase at Habuba/Qannas) that, in my opinion, it is difficult to visualize them as anything other than the

implementation of conscious acts of policy by specific but still uniden-
tified Mesopotamian state(s)—whatever the nature of the subsequent
political relationships between such colonies and their founding states
may have been. If so, because of the massive outlay of resources and
labor needed to found such urban outposts in the first place, it must
be concluded that for the most part it was the public sector (temple
and palace) that took an active role in ensuring the procurement of
resources in the Uruk period (but see below). Smaller outposts in the
vicinity of the larger outposts along the Upper Euphrates may have
been immediately dependent offshoots of the larger intrusive settlements and may have consisted of specialized personnel sent out either
to deal with important preexisting indigenous centers (Hacınebi) or
to control trade routes at locations of transportational significance
where no significant preexisting occupations existed (Hassek). In
areas far away from the Mesopotamian alluvium and away from the
bulk-transport advantages offered by the rivers, however, Uruk outposts were much smaller and consisted of spatially discrete occupations embedded within preexisting indigenous centers already
exploiting coveted resources or controlling access to those resources
(Godin)—a situation akin to the trade diasporas established by Hausa
traders within larger Yoruba communities in West Africa (Cohen 1971;
Stein 1999) or, more to the point, similar to the Old Assyrian trading
colonies established in the shadow of powerful Anatolian kingdoms in
the early second millennium B.C. (Larsen 1976). No doubt, an important strategy in securing the consent of preexisting populations in
these faraway areas to the Uruk presence would have been trade
alliances with indigenous elites, alliances cemented in part through
marriage with local women.

If the general outlines of the foregoing scenario are correct, the
proportion of foreign resources brought to Mesopotamia in the Uruk
period through institutionally organized commerce would have been
notably higher than the proportion of resources brought in by those
same means later on in the third millennium, when more coercive
mechanisms (tribute and booty) and noninstitutional modes of
exchange (merchant families) appear to have become increasingly
more common (Foster 1977). However, it does not follow from this that
we should view all Uruk traders as acting only in an official capacity, or

all fourth millennium trade as funneled only through state-founded outposts. In fact, what evidence we do have can be interpreted as reflecting a more flexible resource procurement effort whereby larger state-founded colonial outposts and their offshoots tapped into the most crucial nodes of preexisting trade networks across the plains of northern Mesopotamia, allowing locals to bring in desired commodities, while smaller (and more flexible) kin-based entrepreneurial groups operated on their own to secure desired resources in areas far from the larger outposts. Such hypothesized independent traders could even have founded small outposts in areas where distance would have made it uneconomical for alluvial states to maintain a regular presence or in areas where there was no need for an "official" presence to begin with because preexisting contacts and alliances had already assured Uruk merchants privileged access to resources controlled by local populations (Godin?). A third millennium parallel for the sort of complementary institutional and private resource procurement strategies just described is available. Benjamin Foster (1993) has recently discussed a small group of Akkadian period texts from Susa that reveal the long-term presence at that site of a merchant colony from Umma, which apparently operated in the shadow of the Sargonic administration of the site but independently from it (i.e., they had their own land and access to agricultural resources).

Similarly, it is not necessary to see all Uruk trade as "official" exchange geared toward fulfilling the strategic needs of the controlling institutions of distant Mesopotamian states. Evidence, noted earlier, of valuable liquids in Uruk containers suggests that Uruk merchants also peddled peripheral commodities to peripheral polities, perhaps acting, in part, in search of personal or familial profit, again much like their better-documented Old Assyrian successors would do a millennium and a half later (Steinkeller 1993). Admittedly, the Old Assyrian case is unusual in the context of Mesopotamian history as a whole in that Assyrian merchants were operating entirely outside the governmental sphere (Larsen 1976), but third and second millennia textual documentation from Babylonia clearly shows that it was quite common for merchants working in the public sector to take advantage of their position in order to engage in personal entrepreneurial activities at the same time that they fulfilled their resource procurement obligations to the state (Foster 1977; Leemans 1960; Neumann 1999).

From the above, it may be concluded that, in the aggregate, the variegated Uruk outposts functioned like the "informal" or "trading post" empires (Gallagher and Robinson 1953) typical of the initial stages of colonial penetration by many modern European states in relatively less-developed areas of the world, empires created as a result of varying combinations of complementary (though not necessarily coordinated!) institutional and private efforts and based not on political dominion but rather on asymmetrical economic influence mediated through variously configured trading outposts. More likely than not, this conclusion will not be generally accepted, principally because it is hard to demonstrate asymmetric economic influence when, owing to the unrepresentative nature of the archaeological data at our disposal, we cannot quantify in any meaningful way the extent of the trade between northern resource-producing communities and the resource-consuming polities of the Mesopotamian alluvium—much less the varying degrees of employment and economic activity created in each of the two areas as a result of the exchange. Nonetheless, estimates based on architectural reconstructions of Uruk period architecture coupled with chance archaeological discoveries at Warka (discussed above) provide us with clues for both the substantial scale of the exchange that was taking place between southern Mesopotamian cities and peripheral polities in the Uruk period and the centrality of that exchange for the internal transformations of the process that we commonly refer to as the rise of civilization within southern Mesopotamia.

Additionally, but more indirectly, we may gain both an appreciation for the extent of the trade between the alluvium and resource-rich areas at its periphery, and the impact that trade had on peripheral communities, by considering what happened to Late Chalcolithic societies in the north after the Uruk outposts in the subregion were abandoned. In those areas of the northern periphery of Mesopotamia where detailed surveys are available, a coherent pattern may be observed: from the Euphrates to the Tigris the transition from the Late Chalcolithic to the earliest phase of the Early Bronze Age (which directly follows the Uruk collapse or withdrawal from the north) sees a reduction in the number of settlements and their average extent, and a

parallel decline in the level of complexity of regional settlement structures (Schwartz, this volume; Wilkinson 1990a; Wilkinson in Algaze et
al. 1992; Algaze et al. 1991, 1994; Eidem and Warburton 1996; Stein
and Wattenmaker 1990). The same appears to have been the case in
some portions of the highlands, at least to judge from the Malatya area
evidence revealed at Arslantepe (period VI B1–B2; see Frangipane and
Palmieri 1983c [1988]). The broad geographical extent of the northern areas affected by sociopolitical devolution just after the end of the
Uruk expansion argues against localized explanations for the phenomenon as a whole, whether historical or environmental. The common
denominator, however, is that all of the areas affected had been part of
the previously flourishing trade network uniting the various disparate
subregions of the north and Uruk-period Mesopotamia. This network
was disrupted in a late but not final phase of the Late Uruk (LC 5)
period (above), which helps account for the loss of social complexity
observable in so many areas across the northern periphery of
Mesopotamia at the end of fourth millennium. The disruption meant
the end, at least temporarily, of the highland–lowlands trade which in
part had come to underpin the prosperity of many northern societies at
the end of the Chalcolithic period.[14]

The reasons for the disruption of the Uruk trade network still
elude us, but they are as likely to be related to events in the northern
areas where the Uruk outposts had intruded as they are to still-not-well-
understood events in the Mesopotamian core area itself at the end of
the Uruk period. Beginning with the former, it is possible to understand the collapse of the Uruk expansion as related in part to the emergence of northern polities that, partly as a result of trade with the Uruk
world, had become expansive in their own right and were thus becoming increasingly unwilling to cede a portion of the profits of intraregional trade to the intruders in their midst. The short-term result of
the Uruk intrusion, therefore, would have been increased competition
across the Mesopotamian periphery as local groups jockeyed among
themselves for control of trade routes feeding into the outposts and as
increasingly powerful local polities eventually started to challenge individual Uruk outposts that, after a while, would come to be seen as
unwanted rivals. Thus, the impact of the Uruk expansion on societies
in the various areas where they intruded inevitably ensured the end of

the initial acquiescence that had made the intrusion possible in the first place. This would have taken place at slightly varying rates and times in the different areas where Uruk outposts intruded, but in the end growth of peripheral resistance meant, in effect, the demise of the intrusion itself because of the naturally higher costs (and declining returns) of conducting trade in increasingly hostile environments and because transportational constraints inherent in overland transport between the alluvium and its northern periphery would have made it almost impossible for individual Uruk polities in a balkanized political environment to mount an effective military response above and beyond that which could be mounted from the specific outposts already in place.

Some scholars see the widespread movement of populations of eastern Anatolian, Armenian, and Georgian origin (Early Trans-caucasian cultures) as contributing to the collapse or abandonment of the outposts by first severing and then taking over the highland trade routes on which the outposts ultimately depended (e.g., Kelly-Buccellati 1990:120–21; Lyonnet 1997). This is plausible. It is not diffi-cult to visualize a scenario in which the complex settled northern polities that initially benefited from inclusion in the wider exchange network opened by the Uruk outposts would have eventually come to contest the presence of the outposts in their midst at the same time that, unwittingly, they were themselves becoming targets for previously less-sophisticated local competitors that were also becoming increas-ingly complex and expansive as the impact of the highland exchange with the Uruk world trickled out to the farther reaches of the system of interaction. Early Transcaucasian societies, purveyors of metals to inter-mediary Late Chalcolithic polities in contact with the Uruk world (e.g., Arslantepe), could well be seen as one of the latter groups. The Early Transcaucasian irruption into the Zagros-Taurus piedmont can thus be understood at the same time as one of the long-term consequences of the Uruk expansion and as another of the proximate exogenous causes contributing to the collapse of the expansion. This suggestion has the virtue of explaining why Mesopotamian trade shifted its focus south-wards toward the Persian Gulf immediately after the Uruk period, a shift revealed by references to Dilmun in 11 economic texts of Uruk III date from Warka (Englund 1983) and by the presence of Jemdet Nasr style ceramics in numerous local tombs throughout coastal Oman, an area rich in metals which became a major exporter of copper to Mesopotamia throughout the third and early second millennia (Potts 1990[I]:72–76).

The impact of the Uruk outposts on social evolutionary trends within the southern Mesopotamian core area would have been no less important. The need to acquire external resources, common to all state-level societies, was particularly acute for societies in the resource-starved alluvial environment of southern Mesopotamia. Efforts to secure such resources by means of outposts, some of which must have been expensive to found, must therefore have contributed significantly to social and political competition within and between emerging Uruk polities. Whether or not this competition, in turn, eventually became a factor contributing to the collapse of the outposts is unclear. However, the abandonment of many of the public structures at the very core of Uruk itself at the transition from levels IV to III (Eichmann 1989) and the substantial shifts in rural settlement documented across the surrounding alluvial plain at this time (Postgate 1986) do suggest that political instability and intercity competition (open warfare?) marked the end of the Uruk period in southern Mesopotamia.

Cross-Cultural Implications

The central role that external resources and outright colonial expansion had in the emergence of Mesopotamian civilization in the Uruk period has important implications for our conceptualization of both historical process as a whole and, more specifically, processes of early state formation across the world. Starting with the former, it would seem to me that we need to abandon or at least substantially modify the generally accepted view of the rise of capital-driven imperialism in the modern era as a watershed that defines historical process in the modern world and separates those processes from phenomena in the premodern era that are presumed to be different in essence (Wallerstein 1974, 1995; Polanyi 1957). Changes resulting from the emergence of modern capitalism may have greatly intensified imperialistic processes, both economic and political, and may have brought into much sharper focus relationships of asymmetrical exchange, economic dependency, and unequal development, but by no means created those processes or relationships (Algaze 1993a; Ekholm and Friedman 1979). This is clearly shown by the Uruk expansion with its inherently asymmetric mixture of implanted colonies at strategic locations, institutional trade, and entrepreneurial commercial activities, all serving to institutionalize and regularize privileged access by competing alluvial polities to needed external resources. Thus, the real disjuncture that forever altered the nature of historical process in the human career was not the emergence of capital-driven imperialism 500 years ago but rather the rise of the state 5,000 years prior to that.

Further, the Uruk case forces us to revise our conceptualization of the meaning of the term "pristine," a term that is commonly applied to a small number of the earliest regionally organized urban civilizations that arose in the world—civilizations that cannot be said to be derived or diffused from elsewhere, precisely because they were the earliest in their respective geographic localities. Often, this has (mistakenly!) been taken to mean that pristine civilizations are wholly the result of varying combinations of mutually reinforcing endogenous factors (e.g., class conflict, warfare, economic redistribution, agricultural intensification fueled by population growth, managerial requirements arising from water management or intraregional trade, the adoption of risk-abatement strategies in stochastically unstable environments, and aggrandizing behaviors of self-conscious elites). However crucial these various forces may have been in the different areas where pristine civilizations first emerged, they are not in themselves sufficient to explain that emergence. The fact remains that complex social systems neither exist nor evolve in isolation, as many historians (e.g., Lüthy 1961:484) and anthropologists (e.g., Adams 1974a:249; Kohl 1987a) have repeatedly (and correctly!) warned us. A case in point is provided by the Uruk colonies in the north and northwestern periphery of Mesopotamia, which clearly show that processes of initial state formation always involve contacts between areas with complementary resources and societies at different levels of social evolution. The characteristic condition for the rise of civilization, therefore, as Kajsa Ekholm (1981) has already perceptively noted, is the creation of a supraregional economic structure allowing elites in increasingly urbanized societies privileged access to resources controlled by less-developed communities at their periphery. The ways in which this was effected in the Uruk period were far from unique. As I have argued elsewhere (Algaze 1993b), expansionary dynamics based on strategically located gateway communities embedded within preexisting alien centers or within alien peripheries are typical for many early pristine civilizations across the world.

While all states are inherently predatory organizations, as Diamond insightfully noted (on this point, see now also Spencer 1998), pristine states are typically able to expand beyond their original geographical, ethnic, linguistic, and cultural boundaries more rapidly and more efficiently (in relative terms) than later states in the same areas (Marcus 1992, 1998; Algaze 1993b). Two reasons account for this. The first is that emerging elites in pristine states have a greater need to validate their transformed social position and to consolidate their newly found power over rapidly burgeoning urban populations than more established elites in second or third generation states, who are naturally born in more stable demographic conditions and into by-then-well-established and largely uncontested social statuses.[15] The second is that, for reasons already explained, indigenous chieftains in areas surrounding pristine states would not be likely to contest the initial attempts of those states to acquire economically and ideologically important resources. Thus, when considered as a whole, contacts between pristine states and surrounding polities will always be inherently asymmetric, although the degree of asymmetry will level off toward the outer edges of the system of interaction, as Stein has correctly noted (1998, 1999, and this volume), and will eventually disappear with time as indigenous societies in the intruded areas themselves become more complex as a result of the interaction (Curtin 1984).

Although outpost-based intrusions are a particularly common mode of cross-cultural interaction between distant societies at times of pristine state formation, such intrusions are also commonplace in any situation of cross-cultural contacts over long distances in which substantial developmental, technological, and organizational asymmetries exist. This is why strategically situated but isolated colonial outposts again become such a common contact strategy in the modern world just after the rise of capitalism; not because they are a modern invention, but because technological and organizational leaps in Europe over much of the rest of the world by the start of the modern era (Landes 1998; but see Frank 1998 for a diametrically opposing view), and particularly over the areas where competing European polities intruded, had ensured that the substantial organizational asymmetries that are required for the outposts to flourish were in place at that time. One notable difference, however, is that as indigenous social systems in colonized parts of the modern world started to collapse as a result of the relentless asymmetries of unequal exchange made systematic by efficient sea transport, the outposts that had generally spearheaded the early European intrusions eventually gave way to territorial annexation and direct political control. These latter outcomes are not typical for the outpost-based intrusions associated with pristine states. This was so not because those earlier intrusions were of an intrinsically different nature than their modern counterparts (contra Wallerstein 1995), but rather because the inherent inefficiencies of premodern transportational technologies meant that the intrusions of pristine states into distant peripheries would be necessarily more episodic and less well integrated than those of their modern equivalents and, consequently, that early core societies would naturally be less successful than their later counterparts in reacting to threats and exploiting opportunities in the areas into which they intruded. As a result, a common characteristic of the early intrusions was a tendency to collapse before the pernicious realities of long-term unequal exchange could have a chance to assert themselves in the affected peripheries.

Differences of degree aside, in the final analysis, the observable commonalities in how state-level societies interact with polities in their periphery from the time such societies first emerged until modern times are perhaps most succinctly explained by the historian David Landes (1961:510), who notes that imperialism (economic and otherwise) is "a multifarious response to a common opportunity that consists simply in disparity of power. Whenever and wherever such disparity has existed people and groups have been ready to take advantage of it. It is, one notes with regret, in the nature of the human beast."

Notes

Earlier drafts of this article were read and criticized by all of the members of the SAR symposium, and particularly by Gil Stein and Mitchell Rothman. Additional substantive criticism, important editorial comments, and crucial missing references have been offered by R. McC. Adams (UCSD), V. Badler

(University of Toronto), R. Englund (UCLA), B. Foster (Yale University), E. Rupley (University of Michigan), P. Steinkeller (Harvard University), D. Tuzin (UCSD), P. Wattenmaker (University of Virginia) and T. Wilkinson (University of Chicago). Their valuable contributions are acknowledged with gratitude, but remaining errors of omission and interpretation are entirely my own.

1. However, although the Blau Monuments belong to the group in terms of their iconography, the associated inscriptions would seem to date (on paleographic grounds) to the succeeding Jemdet Nasr (Gelb, Steinkeller, and Whiting 1991:39–43) or Early Dynastic I (Englund 1994:12, n. 7) periods.

2. See Rothman et al. 1998 for recent excavations at Yarım Tepe, a small village-sized site north of Carchemish that spans the Uruk/Early Bronze Age transition.

3. The low terraces where Kum Ocağı and Komeçli were located are now being intensively cropped with cotton and irrigated with water from the Hancağız Dam. As a result, many of the sites have been partially or totally destroyed in recent years. Kum Ocağı was being bulldozed even as we were surveying it. Komeçli appears to have been destroyed sometime between 1989 and 1994. As of summer 1999, Şadı Tepe is still in place, although large portions of the site have been destroyed by stone quarrying operations for the construction of the Carchemish Dam.

4. Excavations and surveys allow us to identify at least nine sites of various sizes with Uruk materials in the Tabqa Reservoir area. Details and references for these sites are provided in Algaze 1993a:25–29 and Boese 1995–96. At least four sites with Uruk materials, all apparently small village-sized sites, are known from ongoing excavations in the Tishreen Dam area. The Tishreen data are still largely unpublished but references follow: Tell 'Abr (Hammade and Yamazaki 1993; Yamazaki 1999), Tell Kosak Shamali (Nishiaki 1999), Tell Jerablus Tahtani (Peltenburg et al. 1996), and Tell Siyuh Fauqani (Dr. D. M. Bonacossi, personal communication 1998). In addition, the site of Tell Siyuh Tahtani has produced evidence for beveled-rim bowls, but the context of those finds is still unclear (Falsone 1999). Finally, 16 sites of various sizes with surface Uruk materials were recorded in the Carchemish and Birecik Dam areas of the Euphrates in southeastern Turkey (Algaze et al. 1994:10–12, fig. 15B).

5. Renata Gut's (1995) thorough reassessment and republication of the full range of stratigraphic and artifactual evidence from Kuyunjik, the larger mound of Nineveh, shows that typical Uruk ceramics were common across squares MM (the deep sounding), BB, H, G, F, and E of the Ishtar Temple excavation area.

Although the context and associations of these finds are no longer reconstructable, these squares spanned a linear area of 50 x 350 feet (ca. 15.4 x 107.7 meters) (Gut 1995:277, 282, fig. 5).

6. From south to north: Tell Sheikh Hassan (Boese 1995), Tell 'Abr (Hammade and Yamazaki 1993, Yamazaki 1999), Tiladır Tepe (Algaze et al. 1994), and the isolated Middle Uruk (LC3-4) outpost at the edge of Hacınebi (Stein 1999 and this volume).

7. The large range in the estimate is due to the various ways in which the building could be reconstructed (i.e., number of levels, whether or not the courtyard was roofed, and differences in beam interval).

8. This was certainly the case later on in the third millennium. The Lugalbanda and Enmerkar epic poem, for instance, clearly states that the Iranian city of Aratta supplied Uruk's rulers with stone and metal workers.

9. In fact, later literary traditions (e.g., the Sumerian King List [Jacobsen 1939]) explicitly conceptualize the earliest Mesopotamian political configurations as composed of independent cities, each with its own ruler. Admittedly, the passage in question, which refers to five antediluvian cities, is almost certainly entirely fanciful, but the fact remains that the Ur III and Isin-Larsa period scribes that compiled the King List explicitly presumed that the pattern of competing city-states characteristic of the Mesopotamian alluvium for much of the third and the earlier part of the second millennia had not changed from the very beginnings of urbanism and kingship in the area.

10. Even if, as noted above, Warka may have served as the religious capital of Sumer in the fourth millennium (Steinkeller 1999), this need not be automatically interpreted as a reflection of political paramountcy at that time. Warka's successor in that role throughout the third millennium, Nippur, was never a key political player within the Mesopotamian alluvium—in spite of its central position as a pan-Sumerian religious center (or perhaps because of it).

11. The prevalence of public architecture over a large portion of the 4 hectare or so mound of Arslantepe in periods VII and VIA, highlighted by Frangipane (1997a, 1997b, and this volume), raises the question of exactly where domestic habitations would have been located at that site. Is it possible that the mound of Arslantepe as presently understood is in fact only the acropolis of a larger contemporary and as-yet-undefined settlement?

12. Although wheeled vehicles are first attested (and may have been invented) in southern Mesopotamia during the Uruk period (Bakker et al. 1999), such vehicles would not have given southern societies a significant trans-

portational advantage over their neighbors, as early wagons were hitched to oxen or onagers and would have been usable only for short-distance transport. Such vehicles would thus have had greater ceremonial than practical import. In any event, wheeled transportation appears to have diffused very quickly since model wheels are attested in indigenous societies in the Mesopotamian periphery already by the later phases of the Uruk expansion into the area (Bakker et al. 1999).

13. A related phenomenon can be observed at the indigenous Late Chalcolithic site of Tepe Gawra, near Mosul (Rothman, this volume). Though cylinder seals were never adopted at Gawra, as they were at Arslantepe, a small number of isolated Uruk iconographic themes was incorporated into the stamp seal glyptic tradition of the site (for discussion and specific references, see Pittman, this volume).

14. This disruption, of course, would prove to be only temporary, because substantial amounts of imported resources continued to make their way into southern Mesopotamia throughout the third millennium (Foster 1977; Yoffee 1981). What changed after the Uruk period was the way the trade was organized, the terms of the trade itself, the sources of traded items, and, depending on the degree of political centralization in the alluvium at any one time, the relative proportions of commodities that were acquired as a result of tribute and booty instead of exchange.

15. As noted by Sabloff (1990:139–40), this same reason also explains why so many pristine states typically start with an initial burst of monumental construction on a scale that is seldom matched by later generations.

3

Calibrated Radiocarbon Age Determinations of Uruk-Related Assemblages

Henry T. Wright and E. S. A. Rupley

The absolute chronology of the key time span for the emergence of complex cultural formations in Southwest Asia, the fourth millennium B.C., remains imprecise. For many years, few absolute dates were available, and many of those were isolated individual dates from dubious contexts. Finally, however, enough series of ^{14}C determinations have been made on well-excavated samples by laboratories whose performance is well-documented that the latest pooling and calibration techniques can be used to make a first attempt at sorting out the relation between different developments in the greater Uruk world.

METHOD
We have grouped suites of calibrated ^{14}C determinations within a Bayesian framework in which additional constraining information is taken into account. We incorporate where possible chronologically relevant archaeological information, such as stratigraphy or cultural association (for discussion of the methods and rationale of Bayesian methods in the interpretation of radiocarbon analyses, see Buck 1996; on the dangers of improper modeling assumptions, see Steier and Rom 2000).

All ^{14}C determinations were calibrated and combined using OxCal (Bronk Ramsey 1995).[1]

In this study, we do not rely upon radiocarbon determinations where the direct cultural association is unclear—for example, samples removed from the eroded sections of old excavations at Tepe Gawra or samples from large pits containing pottery of various Uruk and pre-Uruk phases at Susa or samples from buildings without associated cultural material as at Uruk-Warka. We have also not considered cases where there were only one or two determinations from an excavation. In addition, we have screened our series of determinations for outliers, under the assumption that the making and decay of mud brick, the digging of pits, and the reuse of old beams in arid Southwest Asian sites are likely to introduce earlier charcoal into later layers, and that outlying earlier dates may be screened out before calibration. We have considered the possibility of intrusive newer material but have noted few cases of later outliers. Once outlying dates have been eliminated, the calibrated dates could only depart from the actual dates if there was some general factor affecting the series of dates. There may be some general problem with the site contexts—for example, pervasive contamination with ancient carbon from bitumen—making whole suites of dates earlier than we would expect (cf. Venkatesan et al. 1982). We consider such possibilities where appropriate.

Alternatively, there may be systematic errors in particular laboratories. Such problems can be recognized through study of larger sample series from related sites, or of dates run on the same samples by different labs. We have chosen not to follow the practice of multiplying a given determination's error by a correction factor, or increasing it to a preset large number (Clark 1975). In the determinations reported here, the recovery of which spans several decades in time and crosses different counting technologies, error terms are surely not of equivalent accuracy across the data set. However, to increase error terms globally by a large factor would blur more precise determinations that exist in the data. On the assumption that inaccurate error terms will be common to a suite of dates produced together by the same lab, we have chosen to retain the original, reported errors. Where error terms are underreported, a site may be incorrectly placed in the overall sequence, but suites of dates that have more accurate error estimation will remain in place, and in proper relation. Definitive resolution of these various problems will only come when methods of absolute dating completely independent of ^{14}C dating are applied.

We present this chronological study in several parts. For each site, we report in a table the uncalibrated ^{14}C determinations, applicable provenience information, and the 95.4% confidence interval of the calibrated date range. We have reported this interval as a single range for the sake of brevity, but this single range should not be confused with the OxCal option to generate single-range "floruits" (Aitchison, Ottaway, and Al-Ruzaiza 1991). Rather, our range begins with the earliest date from the 95.4% probability interval and ends with the latest date of that interval; thus, in some cases our 95.4% range in fact represents an interval of slightly greater confidence. In addition, for each date we also present the calibrated probability histogram generated by OxCal. We feel this is important information to present since our screening for outliers includes the visual review of each suite of related calibrated probability histograms (but see Christen 1994:497 for an alternative approach to outlier detection).

Calibrated ^{14}C probability histograms are multimodal, reflecting the nonlinear "wiggles" and measurement error in dendrochonological calibration curves; within archaeology, a generally accepted method of presenting summaries of these dates remains to be worked out (see Waterbolk 1971 on graphical methods). In this paper, we present summaries of suites of dates in alternative ways, by taking either the sum or the product. We always report these ranges as a 95.4% interval of the resulting probability distribution. Summation of probability distributions has a benefit of maintaining in the result the maximum range among the summands. Alternatively, taking the product emphasizes areas of probability overlap between the individual dates. Neither result, when taken alone, effectively represents a suite of calibrated determinations; rather, we consider the sum and the product of suites of calibrated dates as separate windows on the same underlying archaeological event. However, both should be considered together as a primary baseline in sorting out chronological relations between sites and phases. In this paper, we follow OxCal in terming sums of dates as "summed," while products of dates are "combined." OxCal provides an "agreement index," A, for combinations of dates. This index is a measure of the

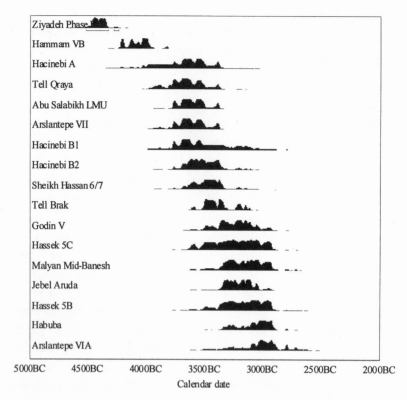

FIGURE 3.1

Summed probability distributions of calibrated dates for Uruk-related sites.

average overlap of individual dates with the group combination; it is reported that when this index falls *below* a rejection threshold, An, dependant on the degrees of freedom within the sample, this approximates exceeding a rejection value in a chi-squared test at 5% significance (Bronk Ramsey, personal communication 1998; for mathematical definition of the index, see "Agreement" in Bronk Ramsey 1998). We report this agreement index and its rejection threshold for groups of associated dates. The uncritical use of this statistic in the rejection of determinations made on deposits formed over a long period is problematic. We do not expect to observe close agreement between dates stratified across a long duration of time ("long" with respect to the error associated with the underlying determinations, cf. Bronk Ramsey 1998: manual, discussion of combination of dates). In such situations, summed (rather than

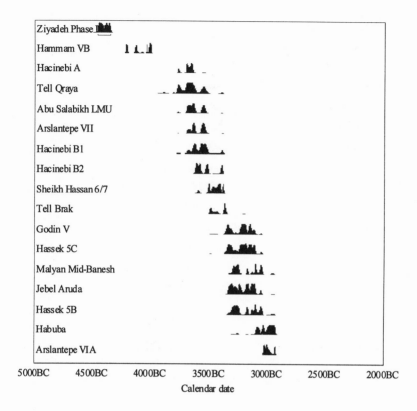

FIGURE 3.2

Combined probability distributions of calibrated dates for Uruk-related sites.

combined or overlap-derived) ranges are a more appropriate description of the chronological distribution of the group. Figures 3.1 and 3.2 compare, respectively, suites of dates summed and combined without regard to the stratigraphic relations within each reported phase.

In addition, we have applied OxCal's Bayesian modeling capabilities to generate an alternate set of chronological range estimates that reflect the stratigraphic relations between samples. These stratigraphic relations may be used to produce constrained probability distributions of the calibrated dates, and these constrained distributions may be treated and displayed in a variety of ways. We present the results of these models in figure 3.3 as the probability distribution of the approximate interval that bounds the dated samples. In interpreting this illustration, one should bear in mind the following caveats.

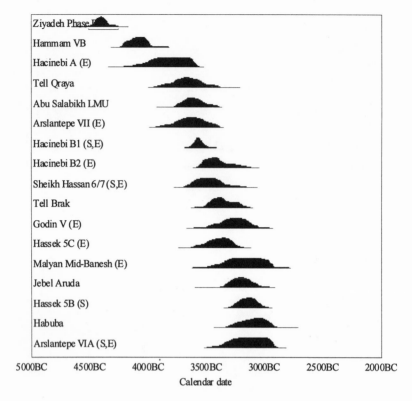

FIGURE 3.3

Probability distributions of the intervals encompassing the dates associated with the labeled phases, modeled to include available stratigraphic information as described in the text. "S" indicates a constrained start to the phase; "E" indicates a constrained end.

First, we caution the reader that while some of these distributions appear almost Gaussian, they are *not*. They do not have a "mean" date. Rather, they represent the probability that an interval of time will bracket a suite of calibrated radiocarbon determinations, given the stratigraphic constraints imposed. The specifics of this form of display within OxCal were devised by Bronk Ramsey and can be observed in the program's example file `mult.14i` (Bronk Ramsey 1998; the intervals thus produced are generally somewhat longer than the ranges reported by the OxCal "span" command). We additionally report a fiftieth percentile midpoint, or median, of the normalized probability distribution. In most cases, it is *incorrect* to take this value as an "average" description of the group. Rather, the interval that encloses the dated events has its approximate center at this year.

Second, by being able to constrain a group of dates with additional information, we improve our estimation of the duration of the underlying archaeological events. Where we lack such constraining information, however, the tails of the resulting probability distributions are drawn out, and our interval estimations are likewise expanded. We feel that it is important to take these differences between models into account when comparing the distributions and therefore have noted in figure 3.3 where a distribution is constrained at its start (S) and at its end (E).

Third, the inclusion of stratigraphic information allows us to differentiate chronologically between groups that otherwise have overlapping date ranges; the results achieved for Hassek 5C/5B and Hacınebi B1/B2 highlight this potential. However, the degree to which results represent archaeological phases depends on the sampling of the dates from the full duration of phases. In many cases, an assumption of sample adequacy is unreasonable.

Last, the accuracy of our modeled estimates is contingent on other factors, including the underlying accuracy of the reported stratigraphic relations and the current authors' successful understanding of these relations. Recognizing that the search for methods of data reduction in working with large sets of ^{14}C determinations is far from over, we hope that the reader will use these estimates as tools to improve our interpretations of the baseline summaries discussed above, and not in preference to them. We further hope that any inaccuracies in our models will elicit corrections from the original excavators, leading to the improvement of the chronology.

The samples are discussed more or less in geographical order, beginning in Lower Mesopotamia, going to Iran, and then proceeding up the Euphrates into Anatolia.

URUK-WARKA

Three dates have been determined for charcoal samples excavated in 1962–63 from the floor of the Mittelraum of Temple C in the Eanna precinct at Uruk-Warka (fig. 3.4). This context is conventionally ascribed to architectural phase IVa, dated to the end of the Late Uruk period. These samples were thought by the excavator to be burned roof beams

Lab No.	^{14}C Yrs. B.P.	B.C. Range (95.4%)	Material
HD 13041-12713	4660 ± 35	3610–3350	Charcoal
HD 13042-12731	4690 ± 35	3620–3360	Charcoal
HD 13043-12732	4670 ± 35	3610–3360	Charcoal

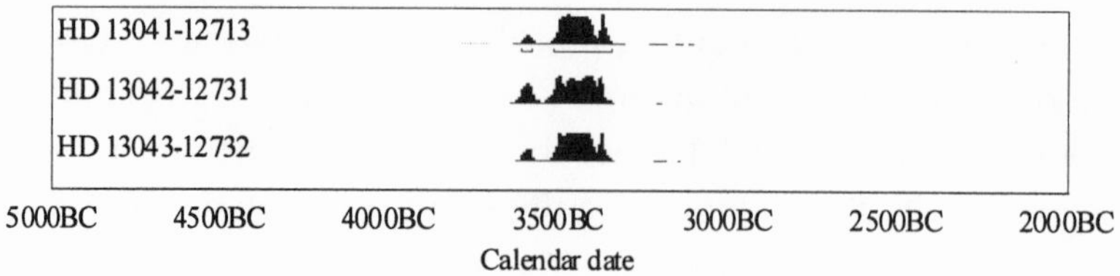

FIGURE 3.4

Dates from Eanna Precinct, Uruk-Warka.

and were identified as cedar (H. Lenzen, personal communication 1966). The dates were run at the Heidelberg laboratory (Boehmer, Dreyer, and Kromer 1993). Heidelberg is an established laboratory with a good record, and these determinations cluster well. Unfortunately, for two reasons they are not helpful in building a chronology for fourth millennium B.C. assemblages.

First, slow-growing, long-lived genera such as cedar begin laying down tissue centuries before they can be cut for use as roof beams. In a dry climate, these beams may be in good condition when the building is rebuilt and may be reused. We have no way of knowing how much earlier than a building's phase of use the dated charcoal from beams may be. This issue also arises with Hassek and Arslantepe VIA, discussed below. However, in contrast to Uruk-Warka, the other two sites have yielded many dates from different contexts and it is possible to account for the problem.

Second, there seems to be very little on the floors of Temple C or stratigraphically associated with its use. Thus, even if these dates were on short-lived material such as twigs or grain, they would probably not help us to date specific cultural assemblages.

For what it is worth, these dates have a combined range of 3510–3370 B.C. (expressing 95.4% of the combined probability distributions), which suggests important construction in the Eanna after 3500 B.C., and their very existence emphasizes the need for a future program of stratigraphic excavation at Uruk-Warka using the best available dat-

Lab No.	^{14}C Yrs. B.P.	B.C. Range (95.4%)	Material	Sample No.	Context
AA.10170	4760 ± 50	3690–3370	Charcoal	U2064	Oven
AA.10169R	5005 ± 60	3970–3690	Barley	U2010	Surface

AA.10170						
AA.10169R						
5000BC	4500BC	4000BC	3500BC	3000BC	2500BC	2000BC

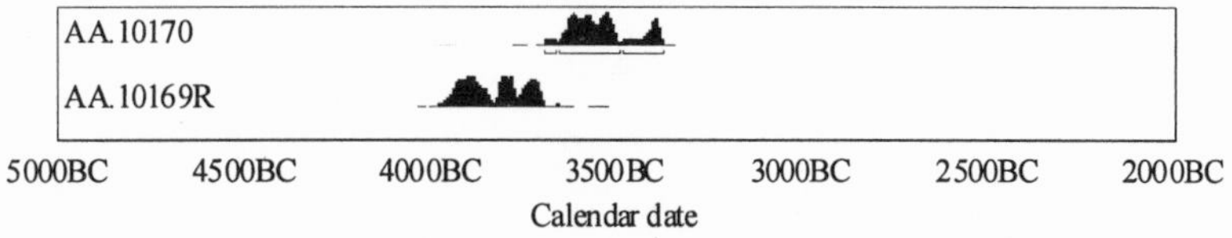

Calendar date

FIGURE 3.5

Dates from Abu Salabikh, early Middle Uruk.

ing techniques. In the meantime, if additional pieces of these beams survive, it would be helpful if they were submitted for dendrochrono-logical study (cf. Kuniholm 1996).

ABU SALABIKH

New dates from stratified contexts at the town site of Abu Salabikh in the northwestern portion of the Lower Euphrates alluvium, associated with Middle Uruk ceramics, have been made available by the excavator, Susan Pollock. In general, the Middle Uruk contexts at Abu Salabikh have high densities of beveled-rim bowls; open bowls with round and flat rims; a few spherical or hole-mouth jars lacking necks but having plain or ledge rims; heavy round-rim and expanded-rim jars; flared round-rim and expanded-rim jars, ledge-rim jars, thickened round-rim jars with a broad interior groove on the inside of the rim, and straight-neck, round-rim jars, often with grooved shoulder decoration and strap handles. Straight spouts and nose lugs occur on jars. Other forms of surface decoration include red wash, reserve slip, combing, punctate decoration, and crosshatch-incised bands. The earlier Middle Uruk contexts are distinguished by significant proportions of a markedly everted variant of the standard beveled-rim bowls and a few of the tapered "proto-beveled-rim" bowls more common in Early Uruk assemblages. The more richly represented later Middle Uruk contexts are distinguished by high-necked, round-rim jars; jars with low band rims; a proliferation of conical spouts; and a few bottles with droop spouts (Pollock, personal communication 1994).

Lab No.	^{14}C Yrs. B.P.	B.C. Range (95.4%)	Material	Sample No.	Context
AA. 5289	4785 ± 65	3700–3370	Seeds and chaff	U1043	Surface
AA. 5288	4790 ± 60	3710–3370	Plant remains	U1063	Surface
AA.10168	4900 ± 50	3790–3530	Seeds	U1074	Kiln

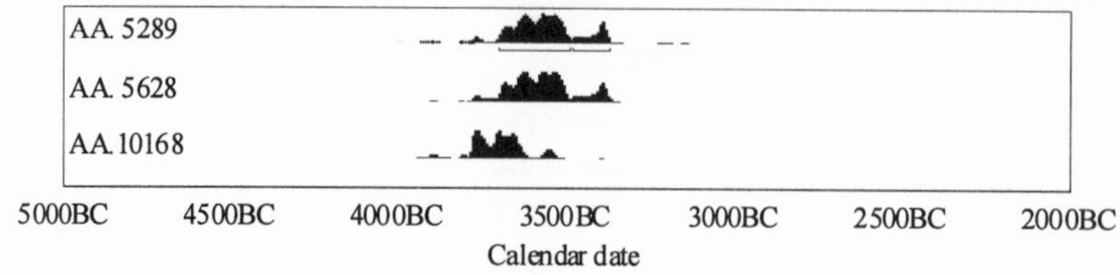

FIGURE 3.6

Dates from Abu Salabikh, late Middle Uruk.

Two dates are on samples associated with earlier Middle Uruk ceramics (fig. 3.5): OxCal reports these as statistically different (A = 13.8%; An = 50%, n = 2). There are no grounds for combining these determinations, and setting either of them aside would leave only a single unverifiable determination. The prudent policy would seem to be to await further determinations on earlier Middle Uruk samples from this site.

Five dates are on samples associated with later Middle Uruk ceramics (fig. 3.6). Two of these are reruns of determinations that yielded early and stratigraphically reversed dates. Here, the most recent assessments of these samples are used. These samples are statistically the same (A = 86.9%; An = 40.8%, n = 3). The summed range of the dates runs from 3790 B.C. to 3370 B.C. The combined range is 3700–3520 B.C. These results are shown in figures 3.1 and 3.2, respectively.

In modeling these dates, presented in figure 3.3, we have not assumed any constraining stratigraphic relations. An interval from 3770 B.C. to 3410 B.C. encloses these dates; the fiftieth percentile midpoint of this probability distribution falls at about 3610 B.C.

GODIN V

The samples discussed here are from the period V "oval complex" on the summit of the large mound of Godin near Kermanshah, on the High Road from Mesopotamia to Central Asia, excavated by T. Cuyler Young, Jr. The associated materials include beveled-rim bowls,

Lab No.	¹⁴C Yrs. B.P.	B.C. Range (95.4%)	Operation	Locus	Room
SI-2673	4580 ± 75	3550–3000	A01	44	18: Main
SI-2678	4465 ± 75	3360–2920	A01	50	17: Main
SI-2671	4520 ± 80	3500–2900	A01	41	17: Later
SI-2672	4570 ± 80	3650–3000	A01	43	18: Later
SI-2681	4570 ± 55	3510–3090	B01	56	18: Later

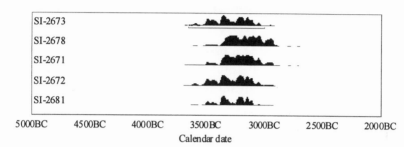

FIGURE 3.7

Dates from Godin V.

expanded-rim jars with nose lugs and incised crosshatched triangles and painted decoration, and sealed numerical tablets, one having a sign (Young 1986). Figure 3.7 depicts the determinations done by Robert Stuckenrath at the Smithsonian lab, as published by Elizabeth Henrickson (1983) and discussed by Robert Dyson (1987). We have not included determinations by the Gakashuin laboratory, simply because it is not advised to pool dates from different labs. These dates are similar (A = 139.7%; An = 31.6%, $n = 5$). They have a summed range from 3550 B.C. to 2900 B.C., combined from 3370 B.C. to 3100 B.C. These results are shown in figures 3.1 and 3.2.

We can constrain these dates *terminus anti quem* using a series of determinations run on samples recovered from loci characterized as "terminal" and "intrusive" (Dyson 1987:677, table 2). For our interval model, we have created a sequence in which sample subgroups are ordered from "Main" as the earliest through "Later" samples, constrained by more recent "Terminal" and "Intrusive" samples (table 3.1). Within these subgroups, no stratigraphic relations are imposed. From the constrained individual dates that result from this model, we have constructed a probability distribution for the duration of the main and

TABLE 3.1

Dates from Later Godin V and IV

Lab No.	^{14}C Yrs. B.P. (95.4%)	B.C. Range	Operation	Locus	Room
SI-2677	4290 ± 75	3300–2600	A01	47	17: Terminal
SI-2682	4350 ± 85	3350–2700	B01	52	18: Terminal
SI-2674	4180 ± 80	2930–2500	A01	44	18: Intrusive
SI-2676	4080 ± 75	2890–2470	A01	45	18: Intrusive

later floors (shown in fig. 3.3). Based on this model, the interval from 3490 B.C. to 3050 B.C. (95.4% of the resulting probability distribution, with a fiftieth percentile midpoint at about 3260 B.C.) encloses the dated Godin V events.

TAL-I MALYAN

Excavations at the ancient city of Anshan in the highlands of southern Iran under William Sumner provide an important point of reference for efforts to devise an absolute chronology for the fourth millennium B.C. in Mesopotamia proper. The reason for this is that layers with ceramics, tablets, and sealings identical to those of the Middle Banesh phase of Malyan are found immediately above Late Uruk materials in layer 17 of the Acropole I sounding in the lowland center of Susa (Le Brun 1971). While we do not yet have radiocarbon dates from these layers at Susa, we can take the extensive series of dates from Malyan as a proxy for dates from post-Uruk layers 14b–16 in the Acropole I sounding. We here use the dates reported by Dyson (1987), eliminating two samples with standard deviations greater than 200 years (fig. 3.8).

The samples from ABC Building 4A and TUV Building 3A show good agreement (A = 77.8%; An = 21.3%, n = 11). The summed range for these dates is 3400–2850 B.C.; the combined range is much shorter, 3330–3020 B.C. These results are graphed in figures 3.1 and 3.2.

Using OxCal we can model these dates as a single phase, without specifying internal stratigraphic relations, but using a Late Banesh date (P-2982, 4260 ± 70 B.P., 3090–2610 B.C. at 95.4% of the probability distribution; Dyson 1987:678) to constrain the end of the phase. We thus derive an interval of 3450–2900 B.C. (with a fiftieth percentile midpoint of the probability distribution at about 3165 B.C.), shown in figure 3.3.

Lab No.	¹⁴C Yrs. B.P.	B.C. Range (95.4%)	Context
P-2187	4370 ± 60	3310–2890	Bldg. 4A
P-2334	4460 ± 70	3350–2920	Bldg. 4A
P-2335	4390 ± 90	3350–2850	Bldg. 4A
P-2985	4450 ± 60	3340–2920	Bldg. 3A
P-2986	4590 ± 70	3650–3000	Bldg. 3A
P-3050	4500 ± 60	3370–2920	Bldg. 3A
P-3063	4430 ± 70	3340–2910	Bldg. 3A
P-3061	4490 ± 70	3370–2920	Bldg. 3A
P-3266	4410 ± 60	3340–2910	Bldg. 3A
P-3268	4520 ± 70	3500–2900	Bldg. 3A
P-3269	4480 ± 50	3350–2930	Bldg. 3A

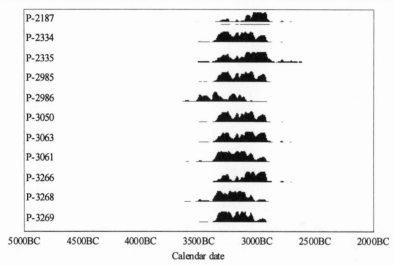

FIGURE 3.8

Dates from Middle Banesh, Tal-i Malyan.

The Pennsylvania lab was of high quality and these dates are consistent. The above calibrations imply that the Late Uruk at Susa could have terminated before 3450 B.C. and probably terminated before 2900 B.C.

We now turn from the few useful date series from Lower Mesopotamia and southwestern Iran to consideration of dates from Upper Mesopotamia.

ZIYADEH PHASE III

At Tell Ziyadeh in the Khabur drainage of eastern Syria, fifth millennium layers have been a special focus of recent work of the Yale University

Lab No.	¹⁴C Yrs. B.P.	B.C. Range (95.4%)	Material	Exc. Unit
AZ-739	5540 ± 55	4500–4250	Charred plants	X 019
AZ-740	5555 ± 55	4500–4250	Charred plants	X 012
AZ-741	5535 ± 55	4500–4250	Charred plants	X 009

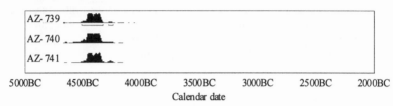

| 5000BC | 4500BC | 4000BC | 3500BC | 3000BC | 2500BC | 2000BC |

Calendar date

FIGURE 3.9

Dates from Ziyadeh phase III.

Project directed by Frank Hole. Dates run at the University of Arizona AMS facility have been made available by Frank Hole (personal communication, 1998) (fig. 3.9). Dates on Ziyadeh phase III are associated with a "post-Ubaid" cultural assemblage, in which bowl and jar forms of Ubaid wares continue, but with little painted decoration. There is no reported similarity to Early Uruk ceramic assemblages or to related assemblages from the north, such as Hammam et-Turkman VB or Gawra XI.

These dates are apparently on short-lived materials. They exhibit close agreement (A = 134%; An = 40.8%, *n* = 3) and have a summed range between 4500 B.C. and 4250 B.C. and a combined range of 4460 B.C. to 4330 B.C. These distributions are displayed in figures 3.1 and 3.2.

As graphed in figure 3.3, we have modeled these dates using their stratigraphic sequence (X 009 as the youngest, X 019 as the oldest) to obtain an estimated phase interval of 4480 B.C. to 4260 B.C. (with the fiftieth percentile of this probability distribution at about 4385 B.C.). The suite as a whole suggests that ceramics with early Uruk affinities developed in northern Mesopotamia sometime after 4250 B.C.

HAMMAM ET-TURKMAN VB

The large center of Hammam et-Turkman in the Balikh valley of Syria was excavated by a Dutch team under the direction of Maurits Van Loon (1988, dates from p. 704) (fig. 3.10). Of prime concern in this chronological study are samples associated with an elaborate building with recessed pilasters, associated solely with local Late Chalcolithic

Lab No.	[14]C Yrs. B.P.	B.C. Range (95.4%)	Material	Layer
GrN 11909	5185 ± 35	4220–3940	Charcoal	7
GrN 11910	5290 ± 35	4240–4000	Charcoal	7
GrN 11911	5270 ± 35	4230–3990	Charred beam	7
GrN 11912	5235 ± 35	4230–3980	Charred beam	7
GrN 11913	5235 ± 40	4230–3980	Charred beam	7

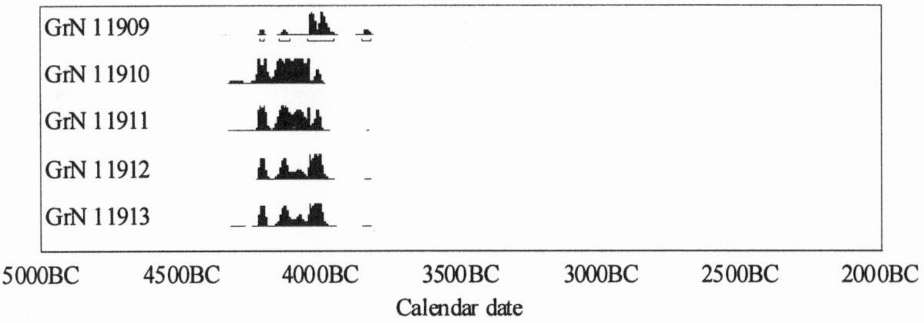

FIGURE 3.10

Dates from Hammam et-Turkman.

ceramics of Amuq F affinity (Braidwood and Braidwood 1960), including carinated bowls with plain rims, open bowls with inner ledge rims, open bowls with beaded rims, small fine jars, flared-neck jars with thickened rims, and various heavy jars. The only vessels with Uruk ceramic affinities are neckless ledge-rim jars on a very coarse ware, widely known in the Early Uruk period (Van Loon 1988, pls. 107:101, 108:101–4).

These dates are well clustered (A = 80.3%; An = 31.6%, n = 5). They sum to a range of 4230–3970 B.C. and combine to a range of 4220–3990 B.C. These results are displayed in figures 3.1 and 3.2.

We have modeled these dates as an unconstrained phase without imposing stratigraphic relations, which gives us an interval from 4230 B.C. to 3940 B.C. with a fiftieth percentile midpoint at about 4090 B.C. These results are presented in figure 3.3. Since the beam dates would be older than the building's use, we can infer that the building was probably used after 4100 B.C. We have considered the possibility that the pairs of dates Grn-11910 and Grn-11911, and Grn-11912 and Grn-11913, could be sampled respectively from two beams. This would allow the combination of these pairs of dates before calibration. Results from this alternative model are almost identical to those just presented.

Lab No.	¹⁴C Yrs. B.P.	B.C. Range (95.4%)	Locus	Layer
LJ 5759	4830 ± 100	3800–3350	22	11
LJ 5760	4880 ± 100	3950–3350	3	10
LJ 5762	4900 ± 100	3950–3350	1	11

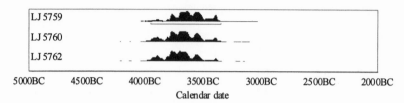

FIGURE 3.11

Dates from Tell Qraya.

Groningen is an excellent lab, and these dates are highly consistent. Two age determinations (Grn-11908 and GrN-11149) run at about the same time on Hammam et-Turkman VIIB, a later layer with well-known Middle Bronze Age ceramics similar to Old Babylonian ceramics, yield a combined date of 1890–1690 B.C. (A = 104.3%; An = 50%, n = 2), which is what we would expect given currently accepted textually based dynastic chronologies. These results give us grounds for accepting the calibrated dates for the Hammam et-Turkman VB building and the associated ceramics.

TELL QRAYA

Stephen Reimer kindly made available the dates from Qraya on the Middle Euphrates, excavated under the direction of Giorgio Buccellati. Daniel Shimubuku was in charge of the 1981 season at Qraya when the samples were recovered. Reimer was on the team and reports the samples were mostly from the latest phase of Uruk occupation at the site. The pottery appears similar to the Middle Uruk ceramics of Abu Salabikh, but a detailed reporting is not yet available. The dates are as follows (fig. 3.11).

The dates cluster tightly (A = 146.5%; An = 40.8%, n = 3). Their summed range extends from 3959 B.C. to 3350 B.C., with a combined range from 3780 B.C. to 3520 B.C. These results are graphed in figures 3.1 and 3.2.

We have modeled these dates in simple stratigraphic order; the layer 11 dates are taken as a group, followed by the date from layer 10.

Lab No.	^{14}C Yrs. B.P.	B.C. Range (95.4%)	Material
BM-2900	4660 ± 35	3610–3350	Charred grain
BM-2901	4570 ± 35	3500–3100	Charred grain
BM-2914	5670 ± 60	4720–4360	Wooden bowl
BM-2915	4650 ± 50	3630–3340	Charcoal

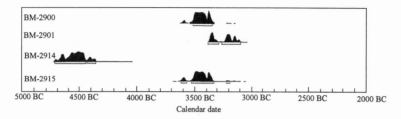

FIGURE 3.12

Uruk dates from Tell Brak.

In practical terms, however, the results from this model are very close to simpler models that assume no stratigraphic relations between the dates. The interval from 3900 B.C. to 3420 B.C. encompasses the activities that produced these samples. The fiftieth percentile midpoint of this distribution is about 3670 B.C. This result is graphed in figure 3.3.

La Jolla is no longer an operational radiocarbon lab, and so far we have not been able to find any lab records. However, there is independent confirmation of the accuracy of the lab from three determinations made not long before the Qraya determinations (LJ-4824, 5054, and 5055; see Linick 1984) on samples from layers of later date excavated by the same team at nearby Terqa, which have tablets dated between 1720 and 1680 B.C. The determinations are in close agreement (A = 131.5%; An = 40.8%, n = 3) and yield a combined range between 1910 and 1680 B.C. The agreement between the dates based on dynastic chronologies and these calibrated radiocarbon dates provides grounds for accepting the Uruk dates from Qraya.

BRAK

At the large early town of Tell Brak, on the Khabur plains of eastern Syria, fourth millennium layers have been a special focus of recent work directed by David and Joan Oates. Soon, a long and well-dated sequence of fourth millennium layers will be available from Brak. We

Lab No.	[14]C Yrs. B.P.	B.C. Range (95.4%)	Context
Bln 3881	4400 ± 50	3310–2910	Habuba-Süd
Bln 3880	4330 ± 50	3100–2870	Habuba-Süd
Bln 3886	4480 ± 60	3360–2920	Tell Habuba

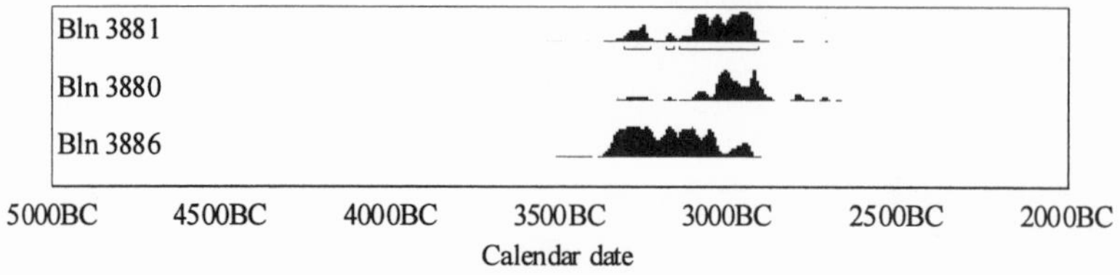

FIGURE 3.13

Dates from Habuba Kabira.

present here (fig. 3.12) a series of dates from excavation TW, level 16 (Oates 1994:171–84), and a date on a comparable layer in excavation CH (Oates 1982:203), made available by Joan Oates (personal communication, 1995). These contexts have some standard beveled-rim bowls, but most of the ceramics are "chaff-faced" in-curved, beaded-rim ("hammerhead") bowls; carinated pots ("casseroles") and flared-neck, thickened-rim jars; and fine ware small bowls and ledge-rim jars (Oates and Oates 1993a:178–97). This assemblage is broadly similar to that from nearby Leilan V, and from Kurban VI and Hacınebi B1 on the Turkish Middle Euphrates.

The very early outlier is on an artifact that may well have been an antique when it was destroyed. The dates on the other three samples overlap strongly, passing OxCal's agreement index (A = 71.9%; An = 40.8%, $n = 3$). They produce a summed range of 3650–3100 B.C. and a combined range of 3500–3340 B.C.

As graphed in figure 3.3, we have modeled these dates as an unconstrained group, without internal stratigraphic relations, which results in an interval of 3540–3140 B.C. with a fiftieth percentile midpoint at about 3370 B.C.

HABUBA KABIRA

The major town of Habuba Kabira on the Syrian Middle Euphrates has well-documented architecture (Strommenger 1980), ceramics (Sürenhagen 1974–75), and other materials. The ceramic corpus includes standard beveled-rim bowls; conical cups; open bowls with round or obliquely flattened rims; a wide range of bottles, often having band rims and droop spouts; jars with flattened or low band rims, nose lugs, and crosshatch-incised bands and triangles; jars with ledge rims; and jars with straight round rims, grooved or grooved and oblique incised shoulders, and strap or twist handles.

Four dates have been determined for fourth millennium deposits at Habuba Kabira and Habuba Süd (fig. 3.13). One date is incompletely documented and cannot be used. Three were run by G. Kohl and J. Görsdorf at the Berlin laboratory (Kohlmeyer 1993:48, n. 75 and 76). Further remarks on the context or materials dated are not yet available.

These samples cluster moderately well (A = 67.1%; An = 40.8%, n = 3), although the date from Tell Habuba seems a bit earlier. The group summed range is 3340 B.C. to 2890 B.C., and the combined range is 3100 B.C. to 2920 B.C., graphed in figures 3.1 and 3.2. In figure 3.3, we have modeled the dates as an unconstrained phase with an interval from 3300 to 2910 B.C. and a fiftieth percentile midpoint at 3090 B.C.

JEBEL ARUDA

Several dates have been determined on samples excavated under the direction of Govert Van Driel from Jebel Aruda, a briefly occupied center with both residential and ceremonial architecture located in the Syrian Middle Euphrates (Van Driel and Van Driel-Murray 1979, 1983). The site has Uruk ceramics similar to those of Habuba Kabira, but they have not yet been reported in detail. The dates presented (fig. 3.14) are from Oates (1983:272, fig. 9).

As noted above, Groningen has a good record. These samples cluster well (A = 88.6%; An = 40.8%, n = 3). They have a summed range of 3370–3010 B.C. and a combined range of 3350–3090 B.C. These results are presented in figures 3.1 and 3.2.

We have modeled this group as an unconstrained phase with no stratigraphic relations imposed, resulting in a period of 3360–2970 B.C. This probability distribution is graphed in figure 3.3. The fiftieth percentile midpoint falls at about 3200 B.C. There are no grounds to reject this radiocarbon evidence. It would be helpful, however, to know the exact contexts for these samples and to have more dates from Jebel Aruda and Habuba Kabira.

Lab No.	^{14}C Yrs. B.P.	B.C. Range (95.4%)	Material
Grn-7989	4495 ± 35	3350–3040	Charred small branches
Grn-8463	4490 ± 45	3350–3040	Charred small branches
Grn-8464	4510 ± 80	3500–2900	Charcoal

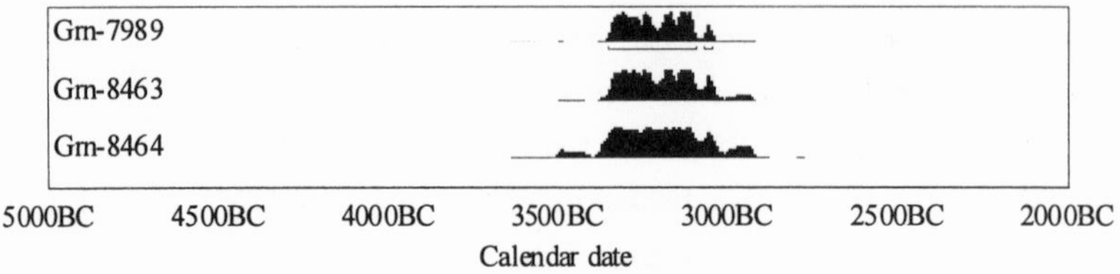

FIGURE 3.14

Dates from Jebel Aruda.

SHEIKH HASSAN

Excavations at the center of Sheikh Hassan on the Syrian Middle Euphrates are under the direction of Johannes Boese. The site has a long and well-stratified sequence of fourth-millennium layers, but the dates detailed below are primarily from layers 6 and 7, which share a coherent series of ceramics with layer 5 above and layers 8 to 10 below (Boese 1995:160–74, 212–30). Common in layers 6 and 7 are standard beveled-rim bowls, including a strongly everted variant; fine conical cups, often with lip spouts; open round-lip and band-rim bowls; and small jars with straight round rims, grooved shoulder decoration, and strap handles. Also attested are small carinated cups; high-neck jars with round rims; ledge-rim jars; both high- and low-band-rim jars, the latter often with reserve-slip shoulder decoration and conical spouts; and a striking series of out-turned expanded-rim jars with four lugs and shoulder decorations, some with crosshatch-incised bands and triangles, and some with bands of punctate impressions and round appliques.

Twenty-seven carbon samples from Uruk contexts have been processed (Boese 1995:272, fig. 15). Details are available on nine dates from the Kiel lab (Boese 1995:240–41) (fig. 3.15). The seven samples from layer 6 and 7, with ceramics of later Middle Uruk affinity (Boese 1995:253–72), cluster well (A = 62.4%; An = 26.7%, *n* = 7). The group has a summed range of 3750–3100 B.C. and a combined range of 3610–3370 B.C., graphed in figures 3.1 and 3.2, respectively.

In figure 3.3, we have modeled the layer 6 and 7 dates as a phase,

Lab No.	¹⁴C Yrs. B.P.	B.C. Range (95.4%)	Material	Sample No.	Locus	Layer
KI-2332	4430 ± 90	3350–2910	Charcoal	N-3	4 Z 27	5–6
KI-3789	4670 ± 40	3620–3350	Charcoal	N-76	3 V 46	6–7
KI-3790	4780 ± 65	3700–3370	Charcoal	N-77	3 V 55	6–7
KI-3791	4650 ± 50	3630–3340	Charcoal	N-78	3 R 118	6–7
KI-3792	4620 ± 55	3650–3100	Charcoal	N-79	3 R 122	6–7
KI-3298	4640 ± 75	3650–3100	Charcoal in hearth	N-33	0 S 21	7
KI-3285	4810 ± 80	3780–3370	Charcoal	N-29	0 M 11	7
KI-3492	4750 ± 65	3690–3370	Charcoal	N-39	0 M 13	7
KI-3014	4900 ± 80	3950–3500	Charred grain	N-13	7 O 33	10

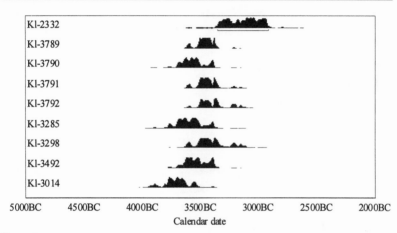

FIGURE 3.15

Dates from Sheikh Hassan 5–10.

without internal stratigraphic relations but constrained by the dates from layers 10 and 5. This results in a period range from 3680 to 3200 B.C. with a fiftieth percentile midpoint at 3475 B.C.

HACINEBI

Excavations at the site of Hacınebi, overlooking the Middle Euphrates valley in southeastern Turkey, began in 1993 under the direction of Gil Stein (Stein, Bernbeck et al. 1996; Stein, Edens et al. 1996; Stein et al. 1997). A large number of fourth millennium samples have been processed at the Beta Analytic laboratory (Stein, personal communication 1998). In the illustrations that follow, we have excluded dates that have a reported error of greater than 110 years,

Lab. No.	14C Yrs. B.P.	B.C. Range (95.4%)	HN No.	Oper- ation	Locus	Lot	Stratum	Context
B 113714	4690 ± 80	3650–3100	15691	4	276	522	4c	Pit with stamp seal
B 113710	4940 ± 80	3960–3530	14963	4	249	484	4c	Roof collapse
B 113708	4840 ± 60	3780–3380	14917	4	242	474	4d	Brick collapse
B 80945	4780 ± 80	3780–3370	6673	4	192	448	4d	Hearth
B 80944	5150 ± 80	4250–3700	6588	5	138	271		Trash deposit
B 113717	4770 ± 60	3700–3370	16035	12	265	525	12g	Smelting pit fill
B 113716	5130 ± 100	4250–3700	16004	12	258	516	12g	Pit fill
B 113718	4850 ± 60	3780–3380	16348	14	199	387	14g2	Ash deposit in central house
B 113712	5050 ± 80	4000–3690	15237	16	170			
B 113713	4800 ± 80	3720–3360	15238	16	170			
B 88312	5280 ± 110	4400–3800	8382	17	82		17d	Trash deposit

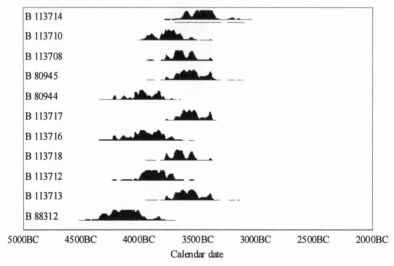

FIGURE 3.16

Dates from Hacınebi phase A.

and samples from contexts for which phase ascriptions have not yet been made.

Figure 3.16 illustrates determinations on samples from Late

Chalcolithic phase A contexts with ceramics of Amuq F affinity similar to those of Hammam et-Turkman VB, including carinated bowls with plain rims, open bowls with inner ledge rims, open bowls with beaded rims, hole-mouth jars with ledge rims, small fine jars, and flared-neck jars with plain or thickened rims (Pollock and Coursey 1995).

As a group, these samples have a summed range of 4250–3350 B.C. and a combined range of 3780–3640 B.C.; they do not pass OxCal's agreement index (A = 0.50%; An = 21.3%, n = 11). If we remove a possible outlier, B 88312, the summed range becomes 4050–3350 B.C., while the combined range remains 3700–3640 B.C. The agreement test still fails (A = 2.1%; An = 22.4%, n = 10). It is this group, without B 88312, that is graphed in figures 3.1 and 3.2. These ranges are generally robust even when other possible outliers such as B 113714, which appears to have a late date in possible conflict with its stratigraphic position, are removed. It is unreasonable, however, to seek close agreement among the entire suite of determinations from Hacınebi A, since it includes several series of dates from separate areas of excavation. It is possible that there would be little total overlap between dates sampled from a sequence that spans several centuries.

Hacınebi phase B, with distinctive later Late Chalcolithic ceramics of Amuq F affinity, particularly its "chaff-faced" in-curved beaded-rim ("hammerhead") bowls; carinated pots ("casseroles"); flared-neck, thickened-rim jars; and fine ware small bowls and ledge-rim jars (Pollock and Coursey 1995), is better known. Recently excavated stratigraphy allows a division into earlier (B1) and later (B2) subphases (Pearce 1996). The former is characterized by later local Late Chalcolithic ceramics but without Uruk-related ceramics or sealings. The latter is associated with ceramics of Uruk affinity, including beveled-rim bowls, fine conical cups with lip spouts, jars with straight round rims and grooved shoulders, heavy round-rim jars, thickened round-rim jars with a broad interior groove on the inside of the rim, flared round-rim jars, high-neck round-rim jars, ledge-rim jars, heavy expanded-rim jars, and low-band-rim jars. Among the appendages are conical spouts and strap handles. Bottles with droop spouts and twist handles occur but are rare. The assemblage is similar to that of the later Middle Uruk of Abu Salabikh, noted above, and to those of related sites (Pollock and Coursey 1995), but with a few later features.

Lab No.	^{14}C Yrs. B.P	B.C. Range (95.4%)	HN No.	Operation	Locus	Lot	Stratum	Context
B 113709	4890 ± 70	3940–3510	14923	4	237	476	4e	Foundation trench
B 113707	4840 ± 60	3780–3380	14905	4	230	469	4e	Floor
B 113705	5300 ± 70	4340–3990	14256	11	176	318	11j	Ashy lens
B 113704	4580 ± 100	3650–2900	11824	14	146	263	14l	Trash deposit
B 88320	4670 ± 110	3700–3000	9134	14	101	143	14b2	Court Surface
B 113706	5370 ± 80	4360–4000	14443	16	133	196	16e5	Trash with stamp seal

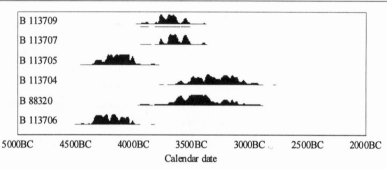

FIGURE 3.17

Dates from Hacınebi phase B1.

Phase B1 dates have much variability as a suite (fig. 3.17). At this writing, B 113706 is assigned only preliminarily to B1, and we exclude it from analysis. In addition, we eliminate B 113705 as a possible early outlier. The four remaining dates have a summed range of 3900–3000 B.C. and a combined range of 3690–3380 B.C. Agreement fails, principally because B 113704 has a comparatively late date (A = 33.9%; An = 35.4%, n = 4). The probability distributions of these ranges are displayed in figures 3.1 and 3.2.

Phase B2 dates cluster well (fig. 3.18). These dates sum to give a range of 3750–3300 B.C. and combine to give a range of 3630–3380 B.C. (passing agreement: A = 77.1%; An = 25.0%, n = 8); they are graphed in figures 3.1 and 3.2.

Based on the samples discussed here, phases B1 and B2 are so close in time as to be indistinguishable. This may be due in part to the grouping of samples from stratigraphically unrelated units on the basis

Lab No.	^{14}C Yrs. B.P.	B.C. Range (95.4%)	HN No.	Oper-ation	Locus	Lot	Stratum	Context
B 67919	4660 ± 80	3650–3100	4000	4	97	220	4j	Wall collapse
B 67916	4810 ± 90	3790–3370	3221	4	53	153	4k	Trash pit
B 80939	4660 ± 60	3640–3330	4869	5	75			Pit fill
B 80940	4820 ± 60	3780–3370	5834	10	54		10i	Pit [a]
B 80943	4750 ± 60	3690–3370	6114	11	40	67	11t	Pit fill
B 88311	4670 ± 80	3650–3100	8200	14	28		14o	Pit fill
B 88322	4810 ± 60	3710–3370	9277	16	51		16g	Pit fill
B 88316	4740 ± 60	3650–3360	8653	16	51		16g	Pit fill

[a] Pit contained a cylinder-seal-impressed tablet and stoppers.

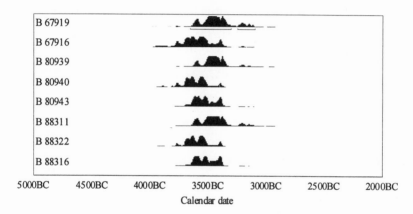

FIGURE 3.18

Dates from Hacınebi phase B2.

of ceramic similarities. Alternatively, our difficulties in resolving the transition with radiocarbon determinations may arise from gross differences in phase length or the nature of the transition. The relative lack of variability in the B2 dates, if not due to sample bias, may indicate a short duration for this phase, in contrast to the variability observed in the B1 and A dates.

We can use OxCal's modeling potential to gain further insight into the Hacınebi sequence. We have modeled the phases as a sequence, without regard for stratigraphic relations internal to each phase. This model gives results that are close to those obtained by alternate models that take into account the stratigraphy internal to each phase, as we know it at this writing. The derived 95.4% probability distribution for phase A runs from 4100 B.C. to 3550 B.C. (fiftieth percentile midpoint at 3800 B.C.), phase B1 from 3640 B.C. to 3480 B.C. (fiftieth percentile midpoint at 3570 B.C.), and phase B2 from 3570 B.C. to 3180 B.C. (fiftieth percentile midpoint at 3420 B.C.). These results are graphed in figure 3.3.

Additionally, we can derive from OxCal's iterative sampling capabilities an estimate of the period in which those transitions bounded by sets of dates occurred. Use of this feature of OxCal indicates the A/B1 transition occurred sometime between 3660 B.C. and 3450 B.C., with the fiftieth percentile of the probability distribution around 3600 B.C., and the B1/B2 transition occurred somewhere between 3600 B.C. and 3440 B.C., with a fiftieth percentile midpoint of the probability distribution at about 3530 B.C. The model suggests that the duration of phase B1 is about a century, surprisingly brief given an accumulation of at least four architectural rebuilding phases in some areas. Estimates for the duration of phases A and B2 would be difficult because phase A is not bounded by earlier dates and phase B2 is not bounded by later dates. A more accurate picture of the relative length of phases A and B2 could be obtained if samples that bracket the sequence were available for analysis. Again, it is important to note that the results of this modeling are presented as examples of what can be done when larger date series are available. Ongoing analysis of the Hacınebi samples is certain to improve our understanding of the duration of these phases.

HASSEK HÖYÜK

Twelve dates from Uruk contexts at Hassek Höyük are reported by Willkomm (1992:135–39) and discussed in detail by the excavator (Behm-Blancke 1992a:10–18). One of these is from midden fill, which is earlier than the structures with copious amounts of ceramics upon their floors; four are from an ash-filled pit actually sealed by one of these structures, Haus 1. All are assigned to Hassek phase 5C, typified by exclusively local Late Chalcolithic ceramics similar to Hacınebi B1 (Helwing 1999:94).

The Hassek Höyük 5C samples (fig. 3.19) pass OxCal's agreement index test (A = 33.6%; An = 31.6%, n = 5). These samples have a summed range of 3650–2900 B.C. and a combined range of 3360–3090 B.C. and are graphed in figures 3.1 and 3.2. Note that, as far as we now know, these samples were not in architectural context and may repre-

Lab No.	14C Yrs. B.P.	B.C. Range (95.4%)	Material	Layer	Context
KI-2353	4490 ± 100	3500–2900	Charcoal	5C	Under Haus 1
KI-2354	4680 ± 70	3650–3330	Charcoal	5C	Under Haus 1
KI-2355	4430 ± 70	3340–2910	Charcoal	5C	Under Haus 1
KI-2963.03	4600 ± 110	3650–2900	Charcoal	5C	Under Haus 1
KI-2965	4440 ± 80	3340–2920	Charcoal	5C	General

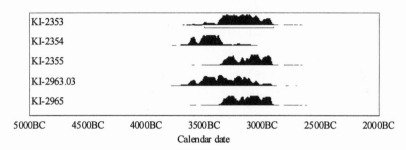

FIGURE 3.19

Dates from Hassek Höyük 5C.

sent a long sequence of unrelated incidents that occurred before the Uruk-associated complex was constructed at Hassek Höyük.

Seven of the dated samples are variously associated with the floors of rooms having both local and Late Uruk–related ceramics (Helwing 1999:95–96). Mass-produced, beveled-rim bowls and conical cups comprise one third of the assemblage. The Uruk-related ceramics include heavy round-lip and flared round-lip jars, four-lugged jars (some with red slip), ledge-rim jars, band-rim bottles (some with reserve slip and/or droop spouts), and other forms. The local Late Chalcolithic ceramics include beaded-rim ("hammerhead") bowls (some on high pedestal bases), "casseroles," flared-rim jars, and other forms. There are also hybrid forms, combining the two traditions. These rooms are assigned to Hassek 5B.

The first three of these dates come from Haus 3; the last four dates come from Haus 1 (fig. 3.20). The last three dates were run at the Berlin lab, whereas the first four were run at Kiel. As a group, these dates do not pass OxCal's agreement index (A = 21.7%; An = 26.7%, n = 7). There are several possibilities for screening these dates predicated on different assumptions concerning error sources: intrusive carbon, differences between labs, or a lack of synchrony between Haus 1 and Haus 3 may all be considered. The more parsimonious solution, eliminating the relatively late determination of KI-2964.01, brings the remaining dates into a passable degree of total overlap (A = 52.5%; An = 28.9%, n = 6). The date range for this group is 3500–2900 B.C. summed, or 3330–3030 B.C. combined. Alternatively, the excavator gives 3100–2940 B.C. as the span of 5B (Behm-Blancke 1992a:15). The substantially later starting date for the excavator's range (by 170 years) is a result of using only the Haus 1 samples, including KI-2964.01 (Behm-Blancke 1992a:13, table 1). Using this group with OxCal, we replicate Behm-Blancke's results with a combined range of 3100–2920 B.C. (A = 60%; An = 35.4%, n = 4). However, the single date KI-2964.01 from the Haus 1 group is responsible for moving the start of the group's combined range forward by 190 years. For the current analysis, we have thus chosen to follow the original excavator in his exclusion of Haus 3 dates and, in addition, have excluded the possible outlier KI-2964.01. The summed range of this minimal suite is 3340–2910 B.C., and its combined range is 3310–2920 B.C. (A = 94.1%; An = 40.8%, n = 3). Until more is known about the excavation contexts of each sample, this latter screening procedure seems more defensible. It is these ranges we present in figures 3.1 and 3.2.

In addition to these dates on Uruk contexts, there are five radio-carbon assays on stratigraphically higher and more recent Early Bronze Age contexts (Willkomm 1992: KI-2352.01, KI-2961, KI-2959, KI-2960, Bl-2733). Except for one later outlier (Bln-2733), run by the Berlin lab on charred grain and assigned by the excavators to phases 3–2 (Behm-Blancke 1992a:13, table 1), these phase 4 dates fall within the cluster of Uruk dates (as they have a summed range of 3370–2900 B.C. and a combined range of 3340–2920 B.C.; A = 115.8%; An = 35.4%, n = 4).

We can use OxCal to develop a model that places stratigraphic constraints upon the overlapping probability distributions of the date series and allows us to explore the consequences of various underlying assumptions involved in the analysis of these dates. For example, if we were to assume that the Haus 3 dates were later than the strata from

Lab No.	¹⁴C Yrs. B.P.	B.C. Range (95.4%)	Material	Layer	Context
KI-2352.02	4560 ± 110	3650–2900	Grain	5B	Haus 3
KI-2352.03	4580 ± 60	3510–3090	Grain	5B	Haus 3
KI-2962	4470 ± 110	3500–2850	Charcoal	5B	Haus 3
KI-2964.01	4300 ± 50	3090–2700	Charcoal	5B	Haus 1
Bl-2730	4470 ± 50	3350–2930	Charcoal	5B	Haus 1
Bl-2731	4390 ± 50	3310–2910	Charcoal	5B	Haus 1
Bl-2732	4400 ± 60	3330–2910	Grain	5B	Haus 1

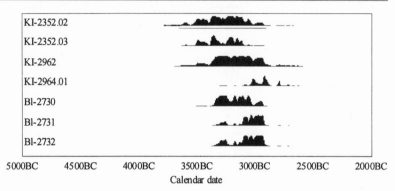

FIGURE 3.20

Dates from Hassek Höyük 5B.

which the 5C dates were sampled, regardless of any other stratigraphic
relations it may—or may not—share with Haus 1, and also to accept the
excavator's use of the phase 4 dates as a *terminus ante quem*, we constrain
both the intervals of phase 5C and phase 5B (5C: 3600–3210 B.C., fiftieth percentile midpoint at 3385 B.C.; 5B: 3280–3010 B.C., fiftieth percentile midpoint at 3145 B.C.). However, to take a stricter approach, if
we instead follow the excavator in disregarding the Haus 3 dates and
yet also entertain the possibility that timbers from ruined Uruk buildings were being burned by Early Bronze Age squatters (thus disregarding the phase 4 group), we have changed the constraints upon the
Hassek dates. Phase 5C ends its 95.4% interval 130 years later, and 5B
begins its interval 90 years later (5C: 3580–3080 B.C., fiftieth percentile
midpoint at 3320 B.C.; 5B: 3170–2920 B.C., fiftieth percentile midpoint
at 3030 B.C.). We note that this result, presented graphically in figure
3.3, is similar to that achieved by the excavator using a somewhat different argument (Behm-Blancke 1992a:11–15).

ARSLANTEPE

The important center of Arslantepe in southeastern Anatolia has been excavated under the direction of Alba Palmieri and Marcella Frangipane (Alessio et al. 1983, dates published in Alessio et al. 1976 and Calderoni et al. 1994; additional information from Di Nocera 1998; Frangipane, personal communication 1998, 1999). Samples have been dated by the experienced Rome lab, both before and after major equipment renovations in 1989. Determinations on historical buildings of known date, made by the Rome laboratory before its renovation and about the time these Arslantepe samples were processed, allow an independent assessment of these dates. For example, determinations run on construction timbers of the Roman Coliseum, historically dated between A.D. 70 and 80, and dendrochronologically shown to have cutting dates between A.D. 73 and 84, agree with these expected dates (R-953a and R-1002a: Alessio et al. 1976:329–30).

Figure 3.21 presents the available dates from Arslantepe VII, a phase with a local Late Chalcolithic assemblage with plain shallow bowls with shaved bases, open plain bowls with rounded or beaded rims, and jars with flared necks and rounded rims, all on chaff-faced plain and red-slipped wares. The first three samples from the west sector of the site were run after the major equipment renovations; the second three from the northeast sectors of the site were run before these changes.

With the possible exception of R-933a, these determinations cluster well (A = 79.6%; An = 28.9%, n = 6). They sum to a range of 3800–3350 B.C. and combine to a range of 3690–3520 B.C. These results are presented in figures 3.1 and 3.2.

Arslantepe VIA is a phase dominated by a later local assemblage in which there are many small conical bowls; high stemmed or footed cups; and jars with flared round rims, often thickened, and sometimes with reserve slip decoration (all typically on a chaff-faced ware). There are also a few standard beveled-rim bowls and sandy ware band- and ledge-rim bottles; jars with flared round and ledge rims with such elaborations as incised crosshatch bands, reserve slip, and nose lugs; and tall jars with high necks and flattened or rounded rims, all familiar from Late Uruk assemblages from lowland sites. This is the most thoroughly dated fourth millennium assemblage in Southwest Asia. Two

Lab No.	¹⁴C Yrs. B.P.	B.C. Range (95.4%)	Room	Phase	Period	Context
Rome-164	4840 ± 80	3800–3350	A580	VII	L. Chalc	On floor
Rome-165	4930 ± 80	3960–3520	A582	VII	L. Chalc	On floor
Rome-166	4840 ± 80	3800–3350	A617	VII	L. Chalc	In room fill
R-932a	4790 ± 60	3710–3370	A21	VIIe	L. Chalc	In room fill
R-933a	4730 ± 50	3640–3370	A21	VIIe	L. Chalc	In room fill
R-931a	4860 ± 50	3780–3520	A11	VIId	L. Chalc	On floor

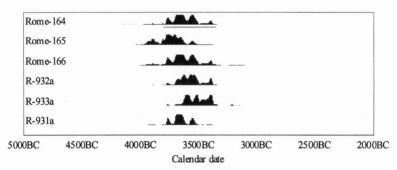

FIGURE 3.21

Dates from Arslantepe VII.

large suites of determinations are available, and these are considered separately. We first present the suite of samples from the southwest part of the site processed prior to renovation of the Rome laboratory. We have as well included one determination (Rome-173) from the vicinity of the Temple B complex, which compares well with these dates (fig. 3.22). When pairs of determinations have been reported for the same sample, we have pooled these dates before calibration (R-1017a, R-1018a, R-1562a, where "a" indicates a second determination made after additional preparatory treatments).

These 21 samples appear to have several outliers. As a group, they show little total overlap. As discussed in regard to Hacınebi, there is no reason to expect such a large set of dates to have much mutual overlap, as they were recovered from several buildings, perhaps including old timber reused from earlier buildings, and may also represent a considerable period of debris accumulation in different times and places across the site. However, determinations from samples found upon the same surfaces, within the same room, should show less variability than the across-site group. Thus, we have screened the Arslantepe dates for

KEY TO FIGURE 3.22, ARSLANTEPE VIA

Lab No.	14C Yrs. B.P.	B.C. Range (95.4%)	Room	Phase	Period	Context
R-1010	4420 ± 50	3330–2910	A28	VIA	EB IA	Bldg. I, grain from floor
R-1013	4860 ± 50	3780–3520	A36	VIA	EB IA	From Pot 9, floor Bldg. I
R-1014	4270 ± 50	3040–2690	A36	VIA	EB IA	Bldg. I, floor
R-1015	4310 ± 50	3090–2770	A36	VIA	EB IA	From Pot 3, floor Bldg. I
R-1017	4360 ± 50	3300–2890	A46	VIA	EB IA	Bench 44, Bldg. I
R-1017a	4360 ± 50	3300–2890	A46	VIA	EB IA	Bench 44, Bldg. I
R-1018	4350 ± 50	3270–2280	A46	VIA	EB IA	Bldg. I, floor
R-1018a	4410 ± 50	3320–2910	A46	VIA	EB IA	Bldg. I, floor
R-1019a	4570 ± 60	3510–3090	A46	VIA	EB IA	Bldg. I, floor
R-1455	4600 ± 70	3650–3050	A51	VIA	EB IA	Bldg. II
R-1474	4380 ± 80	3350–2850	A113	VIA	EB IA	Bldg. III
R-1488	4380 ± 80	3350–2850	A127	VIA	EB IA	Bldg. III
R-1468	4270 ± 80	3100–2600	A132	VIA	EB IA	Bldg. IV, early
R-1467a	4340 ± 80	3350–2700	A134	VIA	EB IA	Bldg. IV, early
R-1464	4240 ± 80	3040–2590	A135	VIA	EB IA	Bldg. IV, late
R-1562	4360 ± 80	3350–2700	A135	VIA	EB IA	Bldg. IV, late
R-1562a	4360 ± 80	3350–2700	A135	VIA	EB IA	Bldg. IV, late
R-1563	4460 ± 80	3350–2920	A135	VIA	EB IA	Bldg. IV, late
R-1486	4300 ± 80	3350–2600	A181	VIA	EB IA	Bldg. IV, late
R-1564	4370 ± 80	3350–2870	A181	VIA	EB IA	Bldg. IV, late
Rome-173	4350 ± 75	3350–2700	A650	VIA	EB IA	Overlies Late Chalc.

outliers on a room-by-room basis. Of the suite, we remove only two from our analysis: R-1013 and R-1019a. Other possible outliers include R-1014, R-1455, and R-1464, but we have chosen to include them in the present analysis. The suite, excluding R-1013 and R-1019a, sums to 3400–2600 B.C. and combines to 3040–2910 B.C. (A = 34.7%; An = 17.7%, n = 16); these results are presented in figures 3.1 and 3.2. The inclusion of R-1019a does not substantially alter these ranges, although it does reduce OxCal's agreement index (A = 11.8%, An = 17.1%, n = 15).

The other suite of Arslantepe VIA determinations is on samples processed in the renovated laboratory (Calderoni et al. 1994, extensively considered by Di Nocera 1998). All are from burned wood,

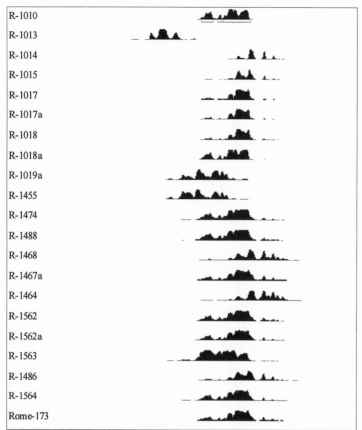

| | 5000CalBC | 4500CalBC | 4000CalBC | 3500CalBC | 3000CalBC | 2500CalBC | 2000CalBC |

Calibrated date

FIGURE 3.22

Dates from Arslantepe VIA.

mostly beams, in or near Temple B (fig. 3.23). The first dendrochrono-
logical sequence for a Mesopotamian fourth millennium site has been
constructed with charred beams from Temple B (Kuniholm 1996).

As discussed by Di Nocera (1998), these samples appear to be from
two separate harvesting events, involving species that are locally available. The later group, from the main room of the temple, provides a
dendrochronological cutting date for a Temple B beam of 3374 B.C. ±
30 (Kuniholm 1996:330–31). This may well be close to the beginning of
the Arslantepe VIA occupation (see below). Temple B currently

Lab No.	¹⁴C Yrs. B.P.	B.C. Range (95.4%)	Material	Room	Phase	Period	Context
Rome-752	4630 ± 65	3650–3100	Pine	A450	VIA	EB IA	Temple B
Rome-754	4530 ± 65	3500–2900	Ashes	A450	VIA	EB IA	Temple B
Rome-747	4580 ± 65	3520–3040	Alder	A480	VIA	EB IA	Temple B
Rome-748	4920 ± 65	3940–3530	Poplar	A796	VIA	EB IA	Temple B
Rome-753	4815 ± 65	3780–3370	Pine	A796	VIA	EB IA	Temple B
Rome-755	4900 ± 65	3940–3520	Pine	A796	VIA	EB IA	Temple B
Rome-749	4740 ± 65	3690–3360	Juniper	A800	VIA	EB IA	Temple B
Rome-751	4860 ± 65	3790–3380	Juniper	A800	VIA	EB IA	Temple B

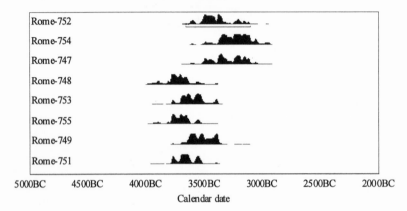

FIGURE 3.23

Dates from Arslantepe Temple B.

appears to belong to the final building phase of Arslantepe VIA, indicating the residents of the settlement recycled timber for a several-hundred-year period until destruction of the temple at the close of VIA.

In addition to these dates, we have from Arslantepe determinations on samples from contexts that continue into the earlier Iron Age (Arslantepe period III). We can use the dates from VIB (table 3.2) to constrain the upper range of the VIA occupation.

Within OxCal, we have modeled each sequential period, VII, VIA, and VIB, as a phase without internal stratigraphic ordering. We have considered alternative internal stratigraphic ordering for phase VIA (building I after buildings VI, III, II, VI, III, and II, taken as a group without ordering imposed), although our results changed little. Nor is it clear that imposition of a stratigraphic ordering of these dates within

TABLE 3.2

Dates from Arslantepe VIB

Lab No.	*^{14}C Yrs. B.P.* *(95.4%)*	*B.C. Range*	*Room*	*Phase*	*Period*
R-1009	4360 ± 50	3300–2890	A33	VIB1	EB IB
R-1489	4230 ± 80	3040–2580	A184	VIB1	EB IB
R-1482	4290 ± 80	3300–2600	A128	VIB2	EB IB
R-1482a	4360 ± 80	3350–2700	A128	VIB2	EB IB
R-1491	4330 ± 80	3350–2650	A151	VIB2	EB IB
R-1494	4240 ± 80	3040–2590	A166	VIB2	EB IB
R-1493	4090 ± 80	2890–2460	A199	VIB2	EB IB
R-1493a	4030 ± 80	2900–2350	A199	VIB2	EB IB
R-1454	4190 ± 60	2920–2600	A69	VIB2	EB IB
Rome-163	4060 ± 70	2880–2460	K759	VIB2	EB IB

phase VI is appropriate, as a number of the samples are from reused construction materials (Frangipane, personal communication 1999). We have excluded R-1013, R-1019a, and the Temple B dates from our VIA group. The 95.4% interval of the resulting probability distribution for VII is 3860–3400 B.C. (fiftieth percentile midpoint at 3630 B.C.), and for VIA it is 3380–2900 B.C. (fiftieth percentile midpoint at 3130 B.C.). We note that the beginning of the modeled interval for VIA falls within the range of dates from the Temple B beams. These results are graphed in figure 3.3.

The calibrated dates for Arslantepe VII and VIA merit discussion. The calibrations indicate a substantial chronological hiatus between the VII and VIA occupations; comparing the end of the combined range for VII with the beginning of the combined range for VIA, we note an interval of nearly 400 years. In recent excavations, however, the Arslantepe team found footings of period VIA buildings set directly on top of phase VII walls, and therefore argue that the hiatus was brief (Frangipane 1993:138). Frangipane notes that the dated Arslantepe VII samples are from relatively deep floors, while most dated Arslantepe VIA samples are from the latest destruction layer of Arslantepe VIA (personal communication 1995). The hiatus is thus probably illusory.

It appears the occupation of Arslantepe during phase VIA ended later than did Late Uruk occupations elsewhere. Since most items from Arslantepe VI are locally made, and there is other evidence for continuations of Uruk styles in this area (Trentin 1993), this is quite possible. If so, this would be evidence that a local Late Chalcolithic Anatolian tradition continued to flourish, and to develop some Uruk-related ceramic traditions, even after the nexus of Late Uruk societies on the plains declined.

GENERAL COMMENT

As noted above, the suggested dates for sites from which we have series of determinations are shown in figures 3.1, 3.2, and 3.3, generally ordered from older to younger. Examination of these charts permits the following general statements about the absolute chronology of cultural assemblages and phases in Greater Mesopotamia.

The beginning of Early Uruk—in ceramic terms, the addition to the simple bowls and jar forms of Terminal Ubaid assemblages of press-molded bowls, carinated and thickened-rim bowls, and various hole-mouth and flared-rim jars—is not well constrained, since few assemblages of the period are well-dated. For northern Mesopotamia, at least, the Ziyadeh Post-Ubaid dates indicate that it may have begun after 4250 B.C., whereas the dates from Hammam et-Turkman indicate it began before 4100 B.C.

The beginning of Middle Uruk—in ceramic terms, the appearance of assemblages dominated by standard beveled-rim bowls, and the basic Uruk cup, bowl, and jar forms with strap handles, reserve slip, and crosshatch incising—is also not well constrained because of the rarity of well-dated Early Uruk assemblages. We can say that Middle Uruk ceramic innovations were established before 3800 B.C. in Lower Mesopotamia, given the dates from Abu Salabikh and Qraya. These ceramic innovations are attested in Upper Mesopotamia before 3600 B.C. at Hacınebi B2 and Sheikh Hassan 6–7, both of which have a few features that become important in Late Uruk assemblages and are therefore perhaps relatively late Middle Uruk. At the same time, northern Late Chalcolithic assemblages—in ceramic terms those with the distinctive in-curved thickened-rim bowls, carinated "casseroles," and thickened-rim jars on chaff-faced wares—flourished on the Khabur plains, as is indicated by dated assemblages from Brak TW 16.

The transition to Late Uruk—in ceramic terms, the increasing predominance of wheel-made mass-produced cups, the diversification of a range of bottles, and the elaboration of incised decoration, handles, nose lugs, and spouts—is indirectly constrained in Lower Mesopotamia by dates on the Godin V assemblage of 3400 B.C. In Upper Mesopotamia this transition is constrained by dates on assemblages in which these innovations are absent or only presaged, such as Brak TW 16 and Sheikh Hassan 6–7, and those where they are well established, such as Jebel Aruda, Hassek Höyük 5B, Habuba Kabira, and Arslantepe VIA. It appears to have occurred about 3350 B.C.

Late Uruk assemblages appear to persist in northwestern Mesopotamia until 3000 B.C., given the excavator's interpretation of the series of dates from Hassek Höyük, even if the Habuba series is taken as problematic and Arslantepe VIA is taken to extend into post-Uruk times. On the other hand, given the dates on the Late Uruk assemblage at Godin, and on the supposedly post-Uruk Middle Banesh dates from Malyan, Late Uruk assemblages are unlikely to have persisted in southwestern Iran after 3100 B.C. A late persistence of Uruk styles in Syro-Anatolia is possible, but it requires confirmation with other evidence.

It is remarkable how many recent high-quality dating programs have been undertaken on Uruk-related assemblages, and it is remarkable how few contradictions there are among these data. However, problems still remain, and more dating programs would be useful. Unfortunately, the areas for which the need is greatest—southern Iraq and southwestern Iran, particularly such major deeply stratified sites as Uruk, Nippur, and Susa—are the least likely to be available for research in the immediate future.

Our experience with these fourth-millennium ^{14}C determinations points to a few simple principles, which, if respected by field archaeologists, will ensure much better dating in the future.

First, serious thought must be given to dating strategies. Where possible, deposits both earlier and later than the periods of interest should be dated. This allows analysts to take advantage of the most powerful features of Bayesian modeling, as one can do, for example, with extant series from Godin, Hassek Höyük, and Arslantepe.

Second, samples from features and burned material on building floors give more consistent results than dates from trash pits and other secondary and tertiary fills. In any event, it is important for the field archaeologist to report the exact context of each dated sample.

Third, it is important to establish the material being dated, not just wood versus bone, but if possible the genera of plant or animal that produced the material. Short-lived materials, such as seeds, have many advantages over long-lived materials.

Fourth, wherever possible, alternative methods of dating should be attempted. In particular, dendrochronology promises precise dates wholly independent of ^{14}C age determinations. Unfortunately, many of the carbonized wood samples found in lowland Mesopotamia prove to be of genera not amenable to tree-ring dating. Continued submission of samples will eventually provide enough datum points to provide a much more accurate chronology than is possible at present with radio-carbon measurements.

Note

1. As of press time, a new version of OxCal (3.5) has been released. Most of the calibrations in this paper were made with the 3.0 beta release. We have rerun all Uruk period dates and models in 3.5 and have found small differences in the reported 95.4% ranges; where these calibrations and pendant results are different by more than 50 years, we have updated this paper to reflect these changes (which are very few and do not impact our conclusions). The majority of our calibrations, however, are unchanged or changed by less than 50 years, and we have allowed these results to remain.

4

Cultural Action in the Uruk World

Henry T. Wright

This chapter is an effort to introduce a broader perspective on the larger cultural system of the fourth millennium B.C. in the Tigris-Euphrates-Karun watershed, both the plains of Mesopotamia proper and the valleys of the foothills and the Zagros and Anti-Taurus Mountains. It is stimulated by the challenges laid down in Guillermo Algaze's *The Uruk World System* (1993) and related writings. In Algaze's conception, complex societies emerge in the Lower Mesopotamian plain early in the fourth millennium B.C. The large and socially differentiated populations of this heartland, needing materials scarce on the alluvium but available in the Taurus and Zagros Mountains and the plateau lands beyond, placed enclaves in Upper Mesopotamia and outposts on the routes connecting these enclaves, drawing indigenous peoples of both the plains and the mountains into exchange relations. These relations led to prosperity and increased social complexity in the peripheries and emulation of Lower Mesopotamian styles in the indigenous communities. When southern Mesopotamia entered into a period of decline, exchange diminished, and northern Mesopotamian enclaves were abandoned. As a result, the dependent indigenous societies declined in prosperity and complexity. All Mesopotamianists are indebted to Algaze for proposing a comprehensive understanding that accounts for much of the evidence available in the 1980s and that has inspired much new research. Many critiques have been leveled against Algaze's construct, but none of the critics has proposed a construct that successfully accounts for the full range of evidence.

The critics have, however, pointed to many of the elements and relationships that must enter into a more comprehensive perspective. First, we have to consider the vast size of the network of communities. It includes not only southern Mesopotamia, but parts of southwestern Iran, the Persian Gulf, the valleys of the Zagros and the Iranian Plateau beyond, northern Mesopotamia, the valleys of the Taurus and Anti-Taurus and the Anatolian Plateau beyond, the Levant, and parts of Arabia as well. Second, we have to consider all kinds of resources used by these communities, both mundane agricultural, pastoral, and material resources as well as rare or exotic resources. Third, we have to consider all kinds of actors, individuals and groups, nomad and settled, ordinary villagers and townspeople and the leading elites. Fourth, we have to consider not only the peaceful movement and exchange of peoples and items, but also violent and destructive movements. Fifth and finally, the evolving relations between such elements and processes have to be understood in terms of the cultural conceptions of the participants.

For practical purposes, I begin this brief essay by breaking down the complex and largely seamless web of interrelationships into topics:

- the time-space framework,

- the natural environments and subsistence systems,

- the present state of knowledge of the population and social mass of the component regions of the Uruk world,

- material production and its organization and exchange, and

- issues of political organization and conflict.

After this, a dynamic succession of models is proposed as a challenge to future research. The treatment cannot be comprehensive, but it should encourage discussion.

Throughout this chapter, I break the continuous development of the Uruk period into "Early," "Middle," and "Late Uruk" spans, modifying the scheme proposed by Gregory Johnson (1973). The absolute dates, discussed in chapter 3, are still tentative. Because these concepts are used in various ways by different specialists, let me briefly define what I mean (see table 1.1).

- "Early Uruk" or "LC 2" (ca. 4150–3800 B.C.) is a time period in which differentiated ceramic assemblages were made on local wares, but in which such forms as round-lip (Coba) bowls and tapered beveled-rim bowls, neckless ledge-rim jars, high-band-rim jars, and expanded-rim jars occur widely. Long, straight spouts are distinctive appendages on jars in Lower Mesopotamia and adjacent subregions.

- "Middle Uruk" or "LC 3–4" (3800–3350 B.C.) is a time period in which the conventional beveled-rim bowl becomes common everywhere, and two regional ceramic traditions developed from local ceramics of the earlier fourth millennium B.C. In the southeast, in Lower Mesopotamia and southwestern Iran, a full range of small jars with straight or ledge rims and large jars with straight, expanded, and ledge rims were made on sand- or "grit"-tempered wares. These often have conical spouts and plain strap handles and are decorated with reserved slip, red slip, simple grooving, or simple crosshatch-incised bands. In the northwest, in Upper Mesopotamia, these forms occur on some sites, but a range of heavy bowls, open pots or "casseroles," and a range of jars, all with thickened rims and made on "chaff-faced" (probably dung-tempered) wares, predominated.

- "Late Uruk" or "LC 5" (ca. 3350–3100 B.C.) is a time period in which the extant forms in the sand-tempered tradition are supplemented by band-rim bottles and other jars with markedly drooping spouts, groove-and-oblique and complex crosshatch-incised decoration, and twist handles. While twisted handles may appear first in Lower Mesopotamia, or complex incising may appear first in Upper Mesopotamia, these variants spread throughout the Uruk world, and the coalescent Late Uruk sand-tempered ceramic assemblage seems to replace the chaff-faced tradition throughout the lowlands.

TIME

The span in years of Uruk civilization was much longer than anyone thought even a few years ago. With the calibration of the radiocarbon chronology, and the wide use of thorough sample pretreatment on suites of samples, the evidence now indicates that the Uruk civilization endured for more than a millennium, from before 4100 until after 3100 B.C. (Evin 1995; Wright and Rupley, this volume). Setting aside the earlier span of local cultural developments and considering what is termed in this synthesis the Middle and Late Uruk periods (LC 3–5), the time of intense cultural interaction throughout much of the Tigris-Euphrates basin and beyond lasted for more than seven centuries, from before 3800 until after 3100 B.C.

In terms of human reproduction and socialization, this is at least 35 generations. In political terms, allowing an average of ten years for paramount political tenure in a world of relatively short life spans, this was at least 70 political generations. This is a time span equivalent to the period from the Crusades to the First World War. In terms closer in time and space to the Uruk world, this is the span from Ur-Nanshe of Lagash to Hammurabi of Babylon. The practical import of this is that there was sufficient time for many different phases of political and economic integration and disintegration during the long flourishing of Uruk civilization.

DISTANCE

Similarly, we now know that the Uruk world was much larger and more diverse than we previously thought. For more than half a century, it has been known that Late Predynastic lapis lazuli in Egypt was probably transported at least 4,000 kilometers from northeastern Afghanistan (Hermann 1968). Such valuables could have moved through linked spheres of exchange without Egyptians being aware of the people of the Hindu Kush, and vice versa. The actual limits within which people interacted (as indicated by the movement of skilled workers, discussed below), probably with some knowledge of each other (indicated by toponyms and by the earliest geographical sign lists, discussed by Nissen), extended from central Iran on the east to the Mediterranean on the west, from the Taurus on the northwest to the head of the gulf on the southeast, a distance of 1,500 kilometers. At 25 kilometers per day, over tracks sometimes mountainous and difficult, sometimes level and easy, an intrepid traveler on foot could go from the high valleys of Fars to the Levantine coast in little more than 60 days. From Ubaid times if not before, however, travel in Southwest Asia on one route would have been easier. From the Taurus toward lower Mesopotamia, travel by raft on the Tigris or Euphrates would enable one to cover 1,000 kilometers in only 20 days and with substantial cargo. By the Middle Uruk period, however, another means of travel, the donkey, had spread from the Levant, as demonstrated by the well-dated and firmly identified remains from Tell Rubeidheh in the middle Diyala valley (Payne 1988). A rider on a donkey could cover 45 kilometers a day. More important, however, is that donkeys can be organized into pack trains. One person on foot with several donkeys could move substantial loads. Thus, beasts of burden enabled families with their goods, craft workers with their tools, and traders with their wares to move throughout Southwest Asia much more easily than before.

Even with this increased facility in travel, it would be difficult to exert enduring control over settlements more than a day or two apart. At any time, the Uruk world probably contained scores if not hundreds of discrete polities, of different scales and organized in different ways.

BIOME

For several decades, it was assumed that the only major changes in natural conditions in Southwest Asia since the Holocene were those resulting from unwise cultivation and overgrazing. However, it has become increasingly apparent that there have been interrelated changes in climate, geological processes, vegetation, and potential for agriculture and herding throughout Southwest Asia during the Holocene. It is necessary to outline the general environmental conditions during the fourth millennium, while emphasizing that the immediate challenge for farmers and pastoralists has always been coping with intense and unpredictable variations in water supplies and crop yields and pasturage from year to year.

Current evidence indicates that climatic processes were somewhat different in the northwestern versus the southeastern portions of the Uruk world. The pollen evidence from the northwestern zone—the Taurus and northern Zagros Mountains and the Syro-Anatolian foothills and lowlands of Upper Mesopotamia, the region affected by air masses moving from the west and north—indicates that the Middle Holocene, from sometime before the sixth millennium until the early third millennium B.C., had a more lush vegetation with a denser oak forest in the mountains (Kuzucuoglu and Roberts 1997) and a heavier grass cover on a more extensive belt of steppe lands. To be sure, there were, within this span, periods of decreased rainfall (Hole 1997), which probably affected farmers and herders. In general, however, farmers in the Levant and Upper Mesopotamia could have exploited larger dry farming areas more reliably than in later times (Rosen 1989, 1997). The limited pollen evidence from the southeastern zone—the southern Zagros Mountains and the plains of Lower Mesopotamia affected by monsoons from the Indian Ocean—indicates that the Middle Holocene, from sometime in the seventh millennium until the mid-fourth millennium B.C., had a more lush vegetation with a denser oak forest in the mountains (Van Zeist and Bottema 1977) and grassy steppes where open deserts exist today (al-Moslimany 1994). After this time, the southeastern zone became less humid, and the climate more like today's. If in general there was increased rainfall in the Tigris-Euphrates watershed, it is not necessary to propose that the large earlier fourth millennium channel documented by Adams (1981:16–18, 61–63) on the lower alluvial plain was caused by a joining of the Tigris and Euphrates channels. The great magnitude of floods, implied by meander belt width, could have been a result of greater rainfall and larger floods. Uruk farmers would have benefited from greater rainfall (and thus less need for irrigation) but could have suffered from more devastating floods, particularly on the lower alluvium of the Euphrates, where floods tend to arrive around the time of harvest, when more water is not needed. Increased rainfall and ponded floodwaters, however, would have yielded better pasture, and herders would have been able to keep flocks closer to villages. Indeed, long-distance transhumant pastoralism may not have been the preferred strategy that it became in later Holocene times.

A largely unrelated environmental change affected the head of the gulf and the lowest part of the alluvium during the fourth millennium B.C. Postglacial melting of the ice caps raised sea level in the gulf above its present mean position during the fifth millennium (Larsen 1983), and higher sea level must have flooded the still undeveloped channel system of the Tigris, Euphrates, and Karun with brackish water, as is rightly emphasized by Nissen (1988:56), creating a mosaic of shifting channels, natural levees, and marshes (Sanlaville 1989).

While there is a need for much additional geoarchaeological and paleoenvironmental research—not only the study of local landscape patterns but of actual year-to-year variation, which can be gained from the dendrochronological or malacological records—it is a near certainty that resource structure and resource productivity of the component subregions of Greater Mesopotamia during the fourth millennium were very different from those of our era.

PEOPLE

The precise accounting of people remains among the more difficult tasks faced by regional archaeologists (Kramer 1980; Postgate 1994). This task is even harder for Uruk specialists, because we have almost no information from cemeteries. However, there are primarily two kinds of questions that demand precise estimates, those involving the approach of human population to the limits of subsistence productivity (Boserup 1965) and those involving the estimation of potential surplus production, and thus potential tribute, for particular areas (Steponaitis 1982). For other questions, general estimates of absolute numbers will suffice, and the key issue is often the number of elemental social units involved (Johnson 1987a:111).

For regional studies, a primary question is that of the number of communities occupied at any one time. The most promising approach to estimating the average number of settlements occupied at any point during a given period is that proposed by Dewar (1991) and now applied to several areas of Greater Mesopotamia (Neely and Wright 1994; Pollock 1999:55–72, this volume). Wherever they have been applied—and so far, this has been attempted only in Lower Mesopotamia and the foothill plains of southwestern Iran—these methods have resulted in a lowered estimate for the number of occupied settlements,

TABLE 4.1
Population Estimates for the Susiana Plain Using Devar's Model

| Period | Duration (Years) | Small to Medium-Size Sites | | Size of Centers (Hectares) | Total Site Size (Hectares) | Population Estimates (100–200 ha) |
		Mean No.	Mean Size (Hectares)			
Terminal Susa A (LC1)	150	10.5	1.1	10.0	21.5	2,150–4,250
Early Uruk (LC 2)	300	27.5	1.6	18.9	62.9	6,290–12,580
Middle Uruk (LC 3–4)	350	27.2	1.6	44.6	87.6	8,760–17,520
Late Uruk (LC 5)	200	6.1	1.7	35.2	45.6	4,560–9,120

Note: "Mean No." is the mean number of simultaneously occupied settlements.

implying lower population estimates. For example, at 200 people per hectare of settlement, the Middle Uruk period (LC 3–4) population of the 2,280-square-kilometer Susiana Plain would have been about 17,000 people (table 4.1) rather than the 25,000 conventionally estimated (Johnson 1973:101). The 940-square-kilometer Deh Luran Plain, an agriculturally marginal plain northwest of the Susiana, is estimated to have had 115 people per hectare on architectural grounds; thus the Middle Uruk (LC 3–4) period population would have been about 770 people (Dewar and Wright 1994:211) rather than the 1,100 people conventionally estimated.

Because the survey evidence from northern Mesopotamia has not generally been reported in terms of finer grained chronologies, it is difficult to estimate populations there. The areas in the northern Jazira carefully surveyed by Wilkinson and Tucker (1995) and the Altınova Plain in the Anti-Taurus carefully surveyed by Whallon (1979) could provide useful estimates. I suspect that such studies will show that the limits of agricultural and pastoral potential were rarely approached in the fourth millennium. This, however, is an issue for careful future study. The issue of surplus and tribute exaction is discussed below.

FOOD

It is surprising to discover that the number of careful studies of fourth millennium B.C. food remains can be counted on the fingers of two hands. With the circulation of the first Deh Luran monograph (Hole, Flannery, and Neely 1969) and its detailed studies of farming by Hans Helbaek and animal use by Kent Flannery, one had reason to hope that such studies would become widespread. Unfortunately, important fourth millennium sites have been excavated even in the last two decades of the twentieth century with little effort to save or analyze the relevant samples. Only recently have subsistence studies become standard.

In the few available paleoethnobotanical studies, barley generally predominates among the carbonized seeds—at Sharafabad (Wright, Redding, and Miller 1980) and Farukhabad (Miller 1981) in Khuzistan, Abu Salabikh in southern Mesopotamia (Pollock, personal communication 1998), Hacınebi (Miller 1996), and Kazane (Miller, personal communication 1997) in upper Mesopotamia. Only in the inner

Taurus Mountains, for example at Korucutepe (Van Ziest 1978) and at Fatmall-Kalecik (Van Zeist 1998), do wheat seeds predominate. However, burned seeds are frequently those found in dung burned as fuel and may tell us more about the diet of sheep and goats than of people (N. Miller 1984). A high density of wheat rachises from threshing at Sharafabad (Wright, Redding, and Miller 1980) and the predominance of wheat phytoliths at Kazane (A. M. Rosen, University College London, personal communication 1994) demonstrates that wheat may have been more important than the carbonized seeds indicate. A number of sites produced lentils and peas, important as a protein source. Grapes, figs, olives, and flax are also reported.

Paleoethnozoological studies must also take into account preservation and sampling bias in excavation. Sharafabad, Farukhabad, Godin, Abu Salabikh, Rubeidheh, Qseir, Hassek Höyük, Hacınebi, Kazane, Arslantepe, Yarım Höyük, and Fatmall-Kalecik have reported studies. The broad contrast between some sites with strong proportions of sheep and goat, others with strong proportions of pig and cow (emphasized by Stein and Nicola 1996), and yet others with more hunted animals (emphasized by Zeder 1994) argues for varying articulations between cultivators, herders, and hunters, or varying cultural preferences in diet. The taphonomic issue of the deposition of larger mammal bones on the edges of sites where we have been less likely to excavate must be addressed before the variation in the occurrences of cow remains can be resolved. Pollock raises the intriguing point that the increase in sheep and goat bone in food remains during the fourth millennium may be an epiphenomenon of the increased use of hair and wool in Uruk economies (Pollock 1999:106–10). Discussion of "cultural preference" raises the intertwined issues of food preferences that arise from social status and wealth discussed in detail for Anshan, a center of the post-Uruk times, by Zeder (1991) versus preferences that express ethnicity, recently discussed for Hacınebi by Stein (1999:71–72, 139–148, and this volume). Certainly, as Emberling (1997) shows, ethnicity will arise as a social strategy whenever states dominate weaker communities. The possibility, however, of high social status attached to cuisine with certain kinds of meat butchery and cooking and certain grain preparations has not been comprehensively addressed for any fourth millennium site.

MATERIAL

It is often said that Lower Mesopotamia lacks any resources other than mud, water, and human labor. Strictly speaking, this may be true, but it is surprising how many useful resources can be found within a few days travel of alluvial Mesopotamia.

- There are woody trees in both the gallery thickets and levees of the rivers (poplar, date palm, and tamarisk) and of the steppes (acacia and jujube), though these are either structurally weak or do not grow to a robust size. However, in the fourth millennium B.C., oak, juniper, and other trees were available in the Zagros and Anti-Taurus front ranges, only two or three days travel from major populations.

- Fine-grained stones useful for making flakes and blades are found as pebbles in the wadis draining the southern desert and in the Pliocene deposits of the Zagros foothills, but their density is low. Mesopotamians were able to make substitutes of ceramic, for example "clay sickles" (Benco 1992). However, concentrations of excellent fine mottled gray cherts and fine banded brown occur south of the Middle Euphrates in the Syrian Desert, and dense concentrations of medium-textured gray chert are found just northwest of Susa and northeast of Lower Mesopotamia (Wright ed. 1981:262–72). Both were imported to southern Mesopotamia in quantity during Uruk times (Pope and Pollock 1995).

- Bitumen, not only a useful adhesive but also essential for waterproofing boats and architectural elements, had three major source areas: Khuzistan, the Middle Euphrates, and the Middle Tigris (Marschner and Wright 1978; Conan and Deschesne 1996; Schwartz, Hollander, and Stein 1999). No major fourth millennium town was more than a few days from a bitumen source.

- Ground stone materials, cements, and other bulk materials could also be found not far from the alluvium.

In fact, the only class of utilitarian materials not found in quantity within a few days of the lowland plains was that of metal ores. It is debatable to what extent metal provided utilitarian items, as opposed to social luxuries, and what amounts were actually imported during the fourth millennium. In contrast to the working and use of stone tools, which leave measurable by-products as each step of the process diminishes the material, metal could be infinitely recycled, and it is difficult to infer the quantity imported from what remains. Certainly Early Uruk metalworking is well documented in Syro-Anatolia (Özbal, Adriaens, and Earl 1999; Hauptmann et al. 1998), but the organization and magnitude of exchange are difficult to determine. It is better to assess the amount removed from mines and smelted, but this is not easy since ancient mines were massively exploited subsequently, and slag heaps are difficult to date (see, however, Yener, Özbal, and Kaptan 1989; Yener and Vandiver 1993).

Given the relative proximity of materials actually moved in bulk and discarded in quantity, the negotiating and coordinating of exchange would not be so difficult. Indeed, many of these resources could have been obtained by direct visits of procurement groups to sources, rather than by exchange. The small quantities of precious materials moved over greater distances must have been relatively easy to transport, and their movement could have been negotiated as gift exchanges between individuals and institutions. What kind of agents engaged in which kinds of procurement and how transactions were negotiated is discussed below.

CRAFTS

The monotonous standardization over vast distances of later Uruk craft products is often noted, though rarely verified with detailed formal studies. Let us take a look at a few of the production activities requiring skills learned in long apprenticeships and special equipment.

- The potters' craft has produced countless tons of material for archaeological analysis, but only recently have archaeologists begun to look at this wealth of material as a craft product. It is critical to realize that this is not pottery produced in each individual household. Potters concentrated their activities in certain areas in larger settlements, such as Chogha Mish (Delougaz and Kantor 1996), Susa (Miroschedji 1976), Abu Salabikh (Pollock, Pope, and Coursey 1996), and Habuba Kabira (Sürenhagen 1974–75:45–50). Similarities in pottery do not imply "close cultural relations," but only close relations among a specialized group of potters. Many ceramic items were simply produced by press-molding, for example the beveled-rim bowl, made in a mold (A. Miller 1981) or pressed by hand (Karlsbeek 1980). Others were made by slab construction, for example the trays and drains (Van der Leeuw 1994:275, 277–79). Many individuals doubtless had the skill to produce such items. Most vessels were built with patches and fillets on a simple turntable, with only the rim formed by rotary motion. This requires considerable skill, but the equipment—a few scrapers and cutting tools, a turntable perhaps made from a broken sherd—is minimal and easily replaced (Roux and Courty 1997; Van der Leeuw 1994:276, 279–90). Some jars, bottles, smaller bowls, and cups were actually thrown on a rotating wheel, sometimes in several parts bonded together later (Van der Leeuw 1994:276, 290–93). Large fast wheels suitable for throwing multiple vessels "off the hump" by a team of potters seem to have been rare until post-Uruk times. The skill required for wheel throwing is similar to that needed for hand building on a tournette, but a wheel is a bulky and valuable piece of equipment. Vessels of standard sizes and forms were produced at least in the southeast portion of the Uruk world, as demonstrated by the measurements of features of three common Late Uruk vessel types (table 4.2). The degree of standardization is astonishing. Most differences in color and so forth are probably related to the different clays used in each subregion (Wright, ed. 1981:187–88). The significantly lower neck height in Susiana bottles is apparently a local style feature, visually noticeable in the large semi-complete series recently illustrated from Chogha Mish (Delougaz and Kantor 1996). Unfortunately, it has not been possible to measure the same types of ceramics in unselected samples from Upper Mesopotamia. The available evidence suggests a continuous circulation of potters throughout the Uruk world. In spite of such circulation, some innovations developed in one area and spread only slowly to others. For example, the thickened rim bowl (the so-called hammerhead bowl) that developed in the local Post-Ubaid Late Chalcolithic pottery industries of Upper Mesopotamia appears in Lower Mesopotamia early in Middle Uruk (LC 3) times (Nissen 1970: tafel 87:37/4, 93:39/27,

TABLE 4.2

Late Uruk Ceramic Variation in Lower Mesopotamia

	Location	N	Mean	s.d.	Significant?
Strap handle					
Width (cm)	All areas	104	3.70	0.88	No
	Warka area	16	3.53	0.98	
	Farukhabad	12	3.74	0.93	
	Susa area	76	3.72	0.86	
Thickness (cm)	All areas	104	1.00	0.22	No
	Warka area	16	0.99	0.20	
	Farukhabad	12	0.99	0.33	
	Susa area	76	1.01	0.21	
Crosshatch-incised bands					
Shoulder thickness (cm)	All areas	72	0.82	0.14	P = .996
	Warka area	10	0.80	0.12	
	Farukhabad	11	0.70	0.13	
	Susa area	51	0.86	0.12	
Diagonal line width (cm)	All areas	71	0.08	0.03	No
	Warka area	9	0.07	0.03	
	Farukhabad	11	0.10	0.05	
	Susa area	51	0.08	0.03	
Diagonal line intersection angle (degrees)	All areas	72	77	19	P = .985
	Warka area	10	66	12	
	Farukhabad	11	93	23	
	Susa area	51	76	18	

99:39/14; Killick 1988: fig. 29–27, type 21; Wright, ed. 1981: fig. 47d). Its roots in northern traditions are indicated by the retention of a dung temper. Conversely, bowls with an exterior band rim first occur in earlier Middle Uruk times in the south on a sandy buff paste as an imitation of a band rim stone bowl (Nissen 1970: tafel 88:38/14, 93:39/28; Wright, ed. 1981:158–59, figs. 46g, 77g–j). This bowl becomes common in northern Mesopotamia in later Middle Uruk (LC 4) times (Pollock and Coursey 1996) and is often red-slipped, unlike its stone antecedents.

- The builders' craft has received close attention from archaeological architects. Standardized brick sizes and bonding patterns are widespread. Differing levels of skill are indicated by the contrast between simple buildings and elaborate nondomestic buildings with niched facades. However, there are systematic variations in the canons of planning and construction. Some buildings, for

(Table 4.2 continued)

	Location	N	Mean	s.d.	Significant?
Bottle necks					
Rim diameter (cm)	All areas	37	5.08	0.72	No
	Warka area	14	5.21	0.59	
	Farukhabad	11	4.91	0.83	
	Susa area	12	5.08	0.79	
Inner rim angle (degrees)	All areas	37	72	11	No
	Warka area	14	75	7	
	Farukhabad	11	68	16	
	Susa area	12	70	8	
Rim top angle (degrees)	All areas	37	153	23	No
	Warka area	14	147	29	
	Farukhabad	11	155	18	
	Susa area	12	159	19	
Rim height (cm)	All areas	37	1.47	0.60	No
	Warka area	14	1.55	0.46	
	Farukhabad	11	1.11	0.58	
	Susa area	12	1.66	0.70	
Space (neck) height (cm)	All areas	33	1.22	0.50	P = .99
	Warka area	11	1.55	0.46	
	Farukhabad	11	1.37	0.42	
	Susa area	11	1.01	0.26	

Source: Adapted from the Farukhabad monograph (Wright ed. 1981: table 51).[1]

Note: The samples used from the Warka region were collected by Adams and Nissen (1972) in 1966 and are curated at the Oriental Institute of the University of Chicago. Those from the Susa area were collected by G. A. Johnson (1973) in 1970–71. The significance test used is the Kruskal-Wallace nonparametric one-way analysis of variance (Seigel 1956:184–93). The difference in shoulder thickness on crosshatch-incised bands probably results from the presence of more small sherds in the screened Farukhabad samples in comparison with the surface-collected Warka and Susa region samples. The diagonal line intersection of crosshatch-incised bands is time regressive (Johnson 1973), and the difference may result from a different chronological span for the Farukhabad sample. The difference in space height (height of neck below the rim) of bottles, however, is apparently a regional stylistic difference.

example at Susa, are laid out in a linear unit of 65 centimeters (Wright 1998:184). Other buildings, for example those at Habuba Kabira, are laid out in units of both 62 centimeters, divisible into two units of 31 centimeters, and about 75 centimeters, divisible into three units of about 25 centimeters (Kohlmeyer 1996). Detailed studies of the measurements of buildings at Jebel Aruda, Sheikh Hassan, and Hassek Höyük have yet to appear; however, their builders seem to have used similar units. This is an old specialization, with roots in the Ubaid (Kubba 1990), and it may already have given rise to diversified, guildlike corporate groupings in which divergent traditions were passed from master to apprentice.

• Another activity that can be viewed as an Uruk craft was that of record keeping. Every adult in the fourth millennium world must have been familiar with the use of seals and must have recognized the designs of those important to them. The routine of preparing counting technology, the actual counting of items, the recording of numbers of items with counters, the sealing of items with stamp and/or cylinder seal impressions, and the checking of incoming sealed items—both their impressions and their counts—all required specialized knowledge. We should not think of the individuals who practiced these skills as "bureaucrats," because there is no evidence of formal training, heritability, and nepotism among the record keepers, or social values protecting and exalting the skill. It is only with the first sign lists and practice texts at the very end of the Uruk period (LC 5) (Nissen 1988:80) that we can begin to detect prototypic bureaucracies. Nevertheless, the widespread use of similar counters, bullae, sealing practices, and (later) numbers and tablets argues for communication between record keepers throughout the Uruk world. The extent to which there were also local styles of seal use and of recording items (Frangipane and Palmieri 1983a, 1989; Frangipane 1993), as well as of seals (Pittman, this volume), and the extent to which there were patterns in the spread of innovations are subjects for future investigation.

That people actually conceived of the workers engaged in the activities noted above (and many others) as specified social categories or roles is indicated by the glyptic representations. Representations of record keepers (Pittman 1993) and potters (Sürenhagen 1974–75:91) have been explicitly discussed. Other occupations appear to be depicted as well. The canonization of the Standard Professions List in latest Uruk times (Nissen 1988:80–81) is an even more formalized indication of social categorization. A general point to keep in mind is that once a socially well-defined skill is established, its practitioners can move to wherever their services might be needed. One reason that they may do this is social, rather than economic. If skilled crafts have emerged as social categories guarding craft secrets, there will be a motivation for endogamous marriage. Since there may be relatively few families skilled in a given craft in any one community, young people seeking partners may have to look to distant communities. The increasingly broad homogenization of Uruk material styles may simply be a result of the changing social organization of the crafts, facilitated by the greater transport capacities of donkeys (relative to humans on foot).

The mobility of workers does not imply wholesale migration of communities. The latter may have occurred, as is discussed below, but it must be demonstrated by showing that an entire community system that developed in one area is implanted in an area where it has no local roots.

EXCHANGE

The specialization of labor implies some form of exchange. Exchange involves the movement of items from one social unit to another and a balancing reciprocal movement of other items back to the first unit. In prehistoric studies, actual exchange cannot be proven, but co-varying reciprocal movement can be shown, particularly with increasingly available physical or chemical techniques for establishing the sources of raw materials and products. Some evidence for the transport of material over varying distances has been noted above. We must now specify the contexts of transport and the social relations of exchange, neither of which can be assumed to be homogeneous given the spans of time, the different participating polities, and the differing varieties of goods in the Uruk world. Archaeological demonstration that exchange involves either administered exchange with equivalencies fixed for periods of time or marketing with equivalencies fluctuating in accordance with supply and demand is possible but has not yet been undertaken.

In general, if agents act independently, seeking transactions to their greatest advantage, we can expect supplies from different sources to vary in quantity over time and space. If we can document reciprocal movement of goods with discarded durable manufacturing by-products and consumed items, we would expect a relative balance in the quantities of goods sent and received. On the local level, some of the stylistically distinct decorative styles on ceramics at Middle Uruk Sharafabad appear to be related to different towns (Wright and

Johnson 1975: fig. 4e, f). This suggests that these rural people were independent agents, who could obtain some of their consumer goods from the sources more convenient to them. On the regional level, the Middle Uruk inhabitants of Farukhabad on the Deh Luran Plain (Wright, ed. 1981:182–84, 262–77), intermediate between the Susa and Nippur areas, prepared and exported substantial quantities of bitumen, local coarse chert, and (perhaps) fabrics, judging from increases in manufacturing by-products without comparable increases in consumption. In return, they received and discarded exotic cherts, metal items, and marine shell. The Deh Luran communities seem to have been independent agents in a larger economic network.

Conversely, if agents are bound by fixed relations, we expect supply from one source and in more uniform amounts. If we can document the movement of goods with durable traces, we may find evidence of extraction with very little reciprocity. On the local level, some of the stylistically distinct decorated ceramics at Late Uruk KS 54 on the southern Susiana appear to be in the style of only one town (Johnson and Wright 1986), as noted above. This suggests that these rural people could obtain some of their consumer goods from only one source. On the regional level, the Late Uruk (LC 5) period inhabitants of Farukhabad (Wright, ed. 1981:188, 262–77) exported even greater quantities of bitumen, local coarse chert, and fiber for fabric production than in Middle Uruk times, judging from increases in processing by-products without comparable increases in consumption. During this period, however, they received little in return. They seem to have been exploited dependents within a larger economic network, providing tribute to more powerful centers with little tangible return.

It will be interesting to see what statistical study of ceramics, stone debris, spinning and weaving gear, bitumen, metal slag, and other goods indicates about the social relations of exchange in other well-excavated sites such as Godin, Habuba Kabira, Jebel Aruda, Hacınebi, Hassek Höyük, and Arslantepe. If the actual densities are sufficiently well recorded to assess rates of discard, we may find that some of these sites participated in little or only local exchange, while others were in either bound tributary relations or more independent and open reciprocal relations of various types.

TRIBUTE

If there is some evidence for more balanced forms of exchange, there is also evidence that important economic sectors were administered as command economies, in which mass labor was organized and sustained with rations, and in which goods were exacted as tribute from producers. The evidence for this is multiple.

First, some towns are so closely surrounded by smaller communities that they themselves could not have subsisted with their own fields. This has been most carefully modeled for the Early and Middle Uruk (LC 2–4) period town of Susa (Johnson 1973:96–98, 137–39). Because Uruk land surfaces south and west of Uruk-Warka no longer exist and cannot be surveyed, a similar study cannot be done for the much larger city of Uruk-Warka. The apparently subsidiary 24 hectare Late Uruk (LC 5) period town of KS-125, 30 kilometers north of Uruk-Warka, had nearby villages on all sides (Adams and Nissen 1972) and would probably prove incapable of feeding itself with its own fields. Study of Tell al-Hawa, Brak, and other large centers on the Jazira in northern Mesopotamia (Wilkinson 1994) may indicate a similar situation. These towns, and no doubt others, must have obtained food from the rural settlements.

Second, there are communities without evidence of participation in balanced exchange and without evidence of detailed accounting of transactions, such as Late Uruk (LC 5) period KS-54 and Farukhabad noted above. It is reasonable to infer that their products were taken as tribute with little or no reciprocity.

Third, the mass-produced bowls—the earlier Coba bowls, the tapered rim bowls or "proto-beveled-rim" bowls, the true beveled-rim bowls, and the later conical cups and bowls—are still best understood as containers for rations in systems of mass labor, as Nissen has repeatedly argued with great elegance (see Nissen 1988:83–85 for a recent statement). Whether such rations were grain, gruel, groats, or bread, and whether these bowls were also used or reused in other ways, is beside the point. Their increased discard at the time of bountiful harvest at Sharafabad near Susa suggests that such labor had been used, among other ends, to bring in crops. The increased preparation of bullae in this year of bounty, coupled with the lack of finished and sealed bullae at Sharafabad, further implies that goods left the site accompanied by invoice records (Wright, Redding, and Miller 1981; Wright,

Redding, and Pollock 1989). Some portion of the all-important grain supply thus seems to have been under the control of administrative hierarchies. Whether animals were also taken as tribute remains to be demonstrated.

CONTROL

Both administered economies and entrepreneurial economies require some level of political order to guarantee future action and transaction. Early Uruk information technologies seem to involve primarily the sealing of goods. Although counters that could aggregate and store numbers existed, it is not apparent how they were used. The appearance of the information-storing technology of the counters in sealed bullae during the Middle Uruk (LC 3–4) period implies the rise of information processing hierarchies that could control the movement of goods and information in space and time. Detailed studies of the quantities of such artifacts in different sites, the clays used to make them, and the styles of seals used to impress them, are giving us a more nuanced view of the processes of control in fourth millennium economies. In administered economies where the bullae could serve as invoices (Wright, Redding, and Miller 1981), this technology implies, at the least, four levels: aggregation, storage and/or transport, receipt and verification, and adjudication. In entrepreneurial economies where the bullae could mark agreements for future repayment (Le Brun and Vallat 1978), the use of bullae implies at least three levels: aggregation, loan and repayment, and adjudication. In addition, during the Middle Uruk (LC 3–4) period, objects with a single clear impression, which must have been used for identifying a messenger or authenticating a message, appear to have been sent over great distances (Blackman 1999). Many more analyses, however, are required to map the extent of the different types of activities implied by bullae and messenger sealings in various times and places.

Control of production, procurement, and distribution is only one aspect of control in the Uruk world. The iconography of the sealings and other representations show commanding figures in charge of ritual, judgment, battle, and other aspects of life (Schmandt-Besserat 1993). The larger residences of important people are known from sites such as Jebel Aruda (Van Driel and Van Driel-Murray 1979, 1983) and

Habuba Kabira (Strommenger 1980; Vallet 1997). What, beyond the elaboration of lifestyles and proclamation of their self-defined importance, did members of the fourth millennium elite do? Finding the durable evidence of how fourth millennium polities actually operated should be a priority. The range of enigmatic, nondomestic buildings from the Eanna IVa of Uruk, Gawra VIII, and Sheikh Hassan 6–10 may be the context of the core control activities in fourth millennium polities. Unfortunately, these well-maintained buildings had little associated contemporary debris, or at least little that has been reported. Rothman's useful restudies (Rothman 1994a, n.d., and this volume) of Gawra buildings and their contents give an indication of what can be learned if we persevere. Only when research teams diligently seek out the debris of activities performed in these buildings (wherever it was dumped), as the Arslantepe team has so impressively done (Frangipane and Palmieri 1983a, 1989; Frangipane 1997b), will we begin to understand the nuances of central control in its cultural context.

In contrast, the results of the exercising of central control are quite evident. The construction of mud brick platforms and terraces at Early Uruk Eridu (Safar, Mustafa, and Lloyd 1981), Middle and Late Uruk Uruk-Warka, Middle Uruk Brak, and other sites required massed corvée labor. The massive wall of relatively modest Late Uruk Abu Salabikh (Pollock 1999:178; Pollock, Steele, and Pope 1991:63) was similarly demanding. The emplacement of a planned urban settlement at Late Uruk Habuba Kabira, with construction of its fortifications—a system of bastions and gates that would demand careful staffing in time of crisis—is unlikely to have been done without central planning and multilevel hierarchies for the control of labor.

BREAKDOWN AND CONFLICT

Aggrandizing rulers with control over tribute and labor—over thousands of men and women in smaller states such as Middle Uruk period Susa, and over tens of thousands in larger states such as Uruk-Warka in the Late Uruk (LC 5) period—are likely to move against their neighbors. The walls noted above are indications that, at least by Late Uruk times, elites were planning to face such moves. Walls without evidence of actual attack and defense can be symbols of the capacity to control people. There is, however, evidence of actual breakdown and conflict.

Some of the best evidence of breakdown is in settlement pattern changes. Settlement evidence shows progressive abandonment of the foothill plains west of Susa in Middle Uruk (LC 4) times (Wright 1987:146–48). For the Susiana Plain, Johnson has made a cogent argument for the breakdown of the Middle Uruk state into two competing Late Uruk polities (Johnson 1973). Arguments for patterned abandonment require precise chronological assessments. Fine chronologies now exist for Upper Mesopotamia, but they have not yet been applied to the archaeological survey evidence. Once they are, interruptions in growth and actual abandonment will probably indicate breakdown at various periods in the Trans-Tigridian plains, the Khabur plain, and the Balikh and Euphrates valleys.

Direct evidence of settlement destruction at Gawra, Hassek Höyük, and other sites may be ambiguous, but the iconography of violence (Amiet 1972; Delougaz and Kantor 1996) leaves no doubt that rulers celebrated their victories with parades, the abuse of captives, and other all-too-familiar cruelties. It was perhaps in the context of military campaigns, whether as a result of deliberate stationing of outpost communities or the flight of communities seeking a better life far from areas of warfare (Johnson 1988–89; Schwartz, this volume), that sites ranging from such Early Uruk settlements as Sargarab in Deh Luran (Neely and Wright 1994) to Late Uruk enclaves such as Habuba Kabira (Strommenger 1980) were implanted.

THE URUK WORLD IN HISTORICAL PERSPECTIVE

The examples used above to exemplify various structures and processes are scattered in time and space. To attempt to view more than a millennium of cultural action in even the broadest developmental terms is premature. Nonetheless, there may be some value in proposing a series of dynamic models as bases for further discussion. These constructions are predicated on the assumption that, at the dawn of tyranny, the critical dynamic is that between would-be rulers and those whom they sought to dominate. In such systems, one cannot assume that political expansion was motivated by a desire for wealth in goods. On the contrary, the following constructions assume that wealth is acquired to manifest the control of people and to symbolize political dominance.

During the period from at least 4150 B.C. until about 3800 B.C., the proposed dynamic is one of widespread intraregional conflict and experimentation with new modes of political organization. Many smaller settlements and formerly inhabited areas are abandoned, and it is likely that the overall population of Greater Mesopotamia declines. Within each major area of productive agricultural soils, however, a number of evenly spaced centers of roughly the same size typically develops. This even spacing indicates rivalry and competition. Exceptional, emergent, large centers—centers such as Eridu, Brak, and others less well known were surprisingly large in this period—could expand rapidly, perhaps unifying their surrounding area and attacking areas in other subregions. This may be the context of experiments in which new strategies and technologies of control are developed, but they did not become widespread. Long-extant devices for the control of goods—seals, sealings, and simple counters—remain in use, and evidence for the sustenance of controlled labor is not yet common. There is little investment of symbolism on permanent objects, and such iconography of dominance as is known represents ancient themes. New and more stable modes of political control have not yet emerged. The acquisition of valuable goods is minimal, as befits a period in which polities and alliances are ephemeral. Materials commonly used in domestic contexts do move, however, perhaps via traditional mechanisms of direct procurement or reciprocal exchange.

From about 3800 B.C. until 3350 B.C., the dynamic is one of growth in all areas, competition and alliance between emergent regional states and epi-state polities, and the consolidation of organizational advances. Many smaller settlements are founded and formerly inhabited areas are reoccupied, and it is likely that the overall population of Greater Mesopotamia increased. Within major areas of agriculture, enduring settlement hierarchies develop. Emergent large centers expand and dominate their surrounding areas, bringing smaller centers, and large and small rural settlements of various types, into structured relations. More elaborate devices for the control of goods and information— sealed bullae and messenger sealings—come into use, and mass-produced "throwaway" vessels for the sustenance of controlled labor become very common. A new symbolism expressing different social and ritual orders is expressed on permanent objects, indicating the new and more stable modes of control. There is limited exchange of both valuable goods and materials used in domestic contexts. Competing polities reach out over great distances, making alliances, sharing symbols with more distant polities, and implanting outposts. However, no single center dominates Greater Mesopotamia, and different local cultural variants flourished.

From about 3350 B.C. until 3100 B.C., the predominant dynamic is one of differential growth, accelerating intraregional conflict, the emergence of very large polities, and their collapse. Many smaller settlements and formerly inhabited areas are abandoned. The Lower Mesopotamian heartland, however, shows evidence of growth (Adams 1981; Pollock 1999 and this volume); whether the overall settled population of Greater Mesopotamia once again decreases or whether the changes balance each other is not yet clear. However, there are indications of the increasing importance of nomadic and transhumant communities, particularly on the steppes of Upper Mesopotamia (Bernbeck 1993). In some areas, the Raqqa bend of the Middle Euphrates for example, hierarchical settlement clusters flourish for the first time. In others, the Susiana Plain of southwestern Iran for example, settlement hierarchies fragment. With the abandonment of older centers and peripheral subregions, the single great center of Uruk-Warka comes to dominate Lower Mesopotamia. Even more elaborate devices for the control of goods and information—complex tokens, numerical tablets, and written symbols—come into use, and evidence for controlled labor is elaborated in the first texts. A new iconography of violence and dominant political and ritual offices is expressed on permanent objects, indicating a new ideology of political control. There is evidence for the appropriation of both valuable goods and materials used in domestic contexts from distant source regions, and Uruk-Warka itself receives a wide diversity of tributary goods. Its intraregional span of dominance, however, is not long maintained. Outlying plains closely allied with Uruk-Warka are abandoned, distant populations are either wiped out or return to the Lower Euphrates, and new ethnic groups develop separate identities in areas formerly part of the broader Uruk world. The old Lower Mesopotamian heartland became only one among many different cultural and political areas, albeit a prosperous area, at the turn of the millennium.

FINAL REMARKS

This chapter has considered a range of processes that we know existed and that must have been central, unfolding an argument for an ever-changing and multicentric Uruk world in which growth, exchange, alliance, domination, conflict, and collapse all have a role. This construct is different from that presented in *The Uruk World System*, but it owes much to Algaze's work. If it leads to discussion that will motivate more and better research, then it has served its purpose.

5

Cultural and Political Networks in the Ancient Near East during the Fourth and Third Millennia B.C.

Hans J. Nissen

This chapter is intended to accomplish two goals. First, I will outline what I think happened in the Uruk period with the rise of urban societies and, particularly, with the so-called Uruk Expansion. I will argue that it should be studied within the framework of the much longer developments in the ancient Near East between the fifth and the third millennium, and not as an isolated phenomenon. Second, a collection of papers that carries "Uruk" in its title would, for obvious reasons, be incomplete without a presentation of at least the basic results from study of the site of Uruk-Warka.

It may indeed sound strange that our conference did not contain a paper on Uruk-Warka itself, although it probably was the most cited name in the course of the discussions. Yet, there is a reason for it. All of the relevant excavations at Uruk-Warka for the time range we are considering occurred in the years between 1928 and 1939 and again between 1954 and 1968. Thus, they came to an end before the wave of new discoveries of Uruk-related sites in the subregions neighboring southern Mesopotamia started, particularly the excavation of Habuba Kabira South in Syria in 1969. During all those years, Uruk-Warka was treated as a site from a unique culture with its own particular cultural material and its own set of problems to be solved, using field methods appropriate only to it. At the same time, it was the only site that had yielded substantial remains of the Uruk period and offered a long sequence of levels reaching back into Ubaid times. In particular, the pottery sequence gave the impression of representing a reliable and detailed chronological and cultural frame of reference.

The discussions inaugurated by the new Uruk-period excavations, first at Habuba Kabira, Jebel Aruda, and later at Tepecik, Arslantepe, Sheikh Hassan, Tell Brak, and so on, as a matter of course had to refer to Uruk-Warka as the key site. In particular they had to cite the evidence of the deep sounding in Eanna (Haller 1931). Although this sounding was already begun in 1931 the excavators never made an effort to reevaluate its results or to confirm them by putting them in a broader regional context with other ceramic evidence. As I have argued elsewhere (Nissen 1998), the deep sounding must be seen as a product of the kind of work done at that time, all with good intentions, but excavated and published by historians of architecture without the assistance of archaeologists. However, while on its own there was no motive to question the results from Uruk-Warka, the conclusions were questioned when they were used by the excavators of the new sites as the standard against which to measure their own pottery sequences. After all, it was partly the dissatisfaction with the southern Mesopotamian standard that led to the present conference with the goal of combining the available evidence without constantly referring to the Uruk-Warka deep sounding.

URUK-WARKA AND CHRONOLOGICAL ISSUES

For this presentation I will repeat only the most basic misconceptions about the excavations at Uruk-Warka. The deep sounding was started in one of the courtyards of the so-called Limestone Temple of Archaic level V (early LC 5). Thus, the actual sequence of layers and pottery of the sounding starts below level V, and only from level VI downwards do the levels form a continuous sequence. Consequently, the pottery labeled level V and later in the publication does not come from controlled contexts, but rather it represents a collection of sherds from trash layers distributed all over Eanna. Although they are from secondary contexts they nevertheless had been attributed to one of the Archaic levels. The deep sounding was begun in the third year of the excavation, and until then most work had been done on first millennium B.C. remains. The earlier pottery sequence was still virtually unknown. It is understandable, therefore, that Old Babylonian and Kassite sherds could slip in as earlier material.

Another danger for interpretations originated from the fact that none of the finds, whether sherds, sealings, or tablets, was found in situ, since they all originated from trash layers. Although lacking direct stratigraphic connection, these layers were nevertheless attributed to the time period of the building underneath. This is another major source of errors. Finally, the beveled-rim bowls are not mentioned once for levels IV to VI, neither in the text nor in drawings, in spite of their huge numbers in these very levels. The absence of reliable pottery assemblages for Archaic levels V–III proved to be especially problematic and explains the lengthy inability to assign the Habuba material to its proper date at the end of the Late Uruk period (LC 5) (contrary to Sürenhagen 1993). It is only rational, therefore, that Uruk-Warka should forfeit its role as a yardstick when it comes to fine-tuned chronological comparisons on the basis of pottery.

However, it fully retains its role as the yardstick for studying societal complexity. As I will demonstrate, despite the systematic incompleteness of the archaeological evidence and the questionable field methods sometimes employed, there remains more than enough evidence to make Uruk-Warka stand out as the most remarkable large site of the early urban phase (fig. 5.1). Still, a word of caution is necessary. According to the philosophy of H. J. Lenzen, the long-time director of the Uruk-Warka excavations, most of Eanna should be cleared down to Archaic level IVa with its magnificent ensemble of large buildings to enable the visitor to experience the architectural layout of Eanna for this period. Consequently, remains of older periods in Eanna are known only from work done in the years before Lenzen took over or when by chance a level IVa floor was missed. We therefore know very little about the preceding phases—or, to turn the argument around, nearly all we know of the Uruk period from Uruk-Warka originates from level IVa. The next level, IIIc, marks the beginning of the Jemdet Nasr period.

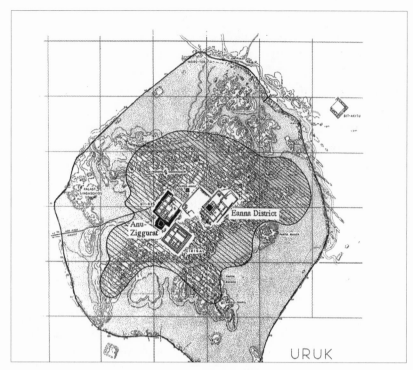

FIGURE 5.1

Uruk-Warka city plan. The hachured area indicates the extent of the late fourth millennium
B.C. occupation.

Some further discussion is necessary to understand Uruk-Warka chronologically in the Greater Mesopotamian context. For a number of years I had favored a 3200/3100 B.C. date for the end of the Late Uruk period (LC 5) because that seemed to go best with the chronology of early Egypt, connected to southern Mesopotamia through Mesopotamian finds in Egypt. When viewed in the light of radiocarbon dates, however, the end of the period seemed to shift 200 to 300 years earlier (Boehmer 1991; Ehrich 1992). Yet still more recent dates, especially from the Uruk period (LC 2–5) sites in southeast Anatolia and Syria, and a new method of calibration revive the old end date of 3200/3150 B.C. (Wright and Rupley, this volume).

A more serious change is provided by the new dates for the beginning of the Middle/Late Uruk range around 3800 B.C. (LC 2–3), since previously this phase had been estimated as encompassing a relatively short period, in spite of earlier suggestions in favor of a longer duration (Nissen 1987). The new dates, again primarily from southeastern Anatolian and Syrian sites, leave no doubt that the period covered in Uruk-Warka by Archaic levels VIII–IV (LC 3–5) extended over a period of 500 to 600 years. Thus the use of descriptors such as "sudden" or "short" in connection with the developments during the Uruk period is even less appropriate than it was before. These notions, however, retain their usefulness in comparisons with the slow pace of change during the preceding millennia.

A final remark on chronology concerns the discrepancy in the use of "Middle" and "Late" Uruk (LC 3–5). While I keep using "Late Uruk" for the entire time span of Uruk-Warka Archaic levels VIII–IV (LC 3–5), Johnson, Wright, and others would divide this period into early Middle, late Middle, and Late Uruk (LC 3, 4, and 5). It is true that subdividing this period makes it easier to place various sites temporally, but I have two objections. One is that within the Uruk period I see the only sharp cultural dividing line as one between levels IX and VIII, separating Early Uruk and Late Uruk. Differences within that later part are gradual ones, which are more quantitative than qualitative. My second point, connected to the first, is that there are too few "index fossils" or diagnostics for either Middle or Late Uruk to attribute surface pottery assemblages to either phase with complete certainty. At least, neither the Warka nor the Nippur survey could make that distinction. It would be inaccurate to use the differentiation between Middle and Late Uruk in any context involving the evidence of these surveys. There is no doubt that the extended period of Uruk-Warka Archaic levels VIII–IV calls for a subdivision, but I would much prefer talking about an early and a late part of the Late Uruk, or any other terminology emphasizing continuity, and avoiding coining new terms for the periods. As I will explain presently, seen from Uruk-Warka we are basically talking about the brief phase of level IVa at the very end of the Uruk period when we use the term "Uruk."

THE LATE URUK EVIDENCE FROM URUK-WARKA

To be sure, we can argue in quite a number of cases that the situation evidenced in level IVa should be taken as representative for preceding phases as well, but quite often these assumptions are not more than probabilities, however high. Naturally, we can be less certain about a similarity the further we go back in time. This word of caution should be kept in mind when I assert in the following discussion that during the final centuries of the fourth millennium Uruk-Warka was as powerful a center, both economically and politically, as we know of from that time period.

The importance of the site is revealed by the astonishing size of both the settlement and its central district. The area most densely covered by Late Uruk pottery and most probably settled in this period covers at least 250 hectares or 2.5 square kilometers, with the possibility of extending beyond that (Finkbeiner 1991). A city wall probably surrounded it. Since the area within a probable wall was smaller than the later one uncovered during the excavations (Nissen 1972), the course of the older wall presumably was covered by thick later deposits. In the middle of town we find two central districts next to each other. The eastern one probably extended over an area of approximately 300 by 300 meters, or 9 hectares, of which more than half is excavated. This area, called "Eanna" in later periods, was separated from the city by an enclosure wall of its own. It contained several large, freestanding buildings, probably rising to 10 meters or more from a surface already at least 2 meters above the level of the surrounding eastern part of the city. The western district, named the "Anu District" because of a sanctuary dedicated to the gods Anu and Antum in the third century B.C., was organized differently. It was centered around an 11-meter-high terrace with a temple on top, which may have measured 6 to 7 meters in height. Its full extent and whether there was an enclosure wall are unknown. Since the western part of the city was considerably lower than the eastern part, both this temple on a terrace and the large buildings of the eastern center may have reached the same height. They must have formed an impressive skyline and certainly could be seen from afar (Heinrich 1982).

The designation of the eastern center as Eanna, dedicated to Inanna, the city goddess of Uruk-Warka, probably originated in an older period. Yet there is no real evidence for its cultic character, since the only tangible proof was the initial excavators' identification of the large buildings as "temples," which is now rejected. Heinrich (1982:xiii) talks about "cult-houses," indicating that the buildings had multiple uses. Among its functions, Heinrich asserts that the cultic one was dominant. I would prefer to put the main emphasis on "assembly halls" without excluding their cultic functions. For instance, the central hall of "Temple C" would accommodate up to 300 seated people (based on the space required in mosques; see Schmid 1980:54, 57). In any case, there is no doubt that these buildings did serve public functions, although the exact criteria for defining cult centers remain unclear. Again, large, plazalike open spaces may have served to accommodate large numbers of people.

Apart from its assumed cultic/public function, Eanna is thought to have served as an economic center as well. On the one hand, this is indicated by spaces that served as workshops. Remains of kilns, which were interpreted as metal-working installations (Lenzen 1959), indicate their workshop function. On the other hand, this is suggested by the recovery in dump areas of thousands of sealed clay fasteners and inscribed clay tablets, both of which have been interpreted as means of controlling economic transactions.

Both cylinder seals (fig. 5.2) and writing are examples of the increasing attempts within the last phase of this tradition to enlarge the capacity of the methods of information storage. Clearly, this administrative elaboration resulted from the increasing needs of the economy for more encompassing means of control. This is obvious for the tablets, because about 80% of them contain data relating to a complex, centralized economic administration (fig. 5.3). The remaining ones belong to the genre of so-called Lexical Lists (Englund and Nissen 1993). We assume not only that Eanna was the area where these controls were administered, but that economic transactions took place there as well. However, one should be careful not to assume that writing was done only in Eanna, because little work has been done outside of the precinct. In fact, wherever Uruk period traces were found outside of Eanna, some Archaic tablets were discovered as well (OXI/XII: tablets W 14148 and W 14210 [Heinrich 1934:13; Green and Nissen 1987:142]; K/L XII: tablets W21755; W 21761a–c, W 21771 [Nissen 1970:151]; Archaische Siedlung: tablet W 20389 [Strommenger 1963:46]). A preliminary analysis of the textual evidence reveals that the economic administration not only controlled a vast set of resources (Nissen, Damerow, and Englund 1993:66–75) but also operated within

FIGURE 5.2

Cylinder seal and impression from Uruk-Warka.

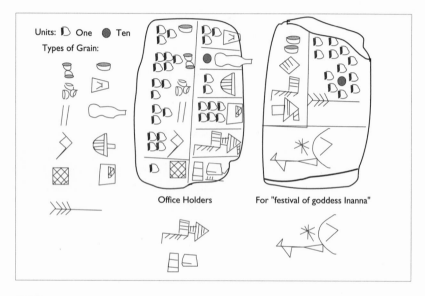

FIGURE 5.3

Archaic accounting tablet, obverse and reverse (Nissen et al. 1993: fig. 32).

a strictly ranked society.

Specifically, this is shown by one of the Lexical Lists, the so-called Titles and Professions List. In that series of tablets the entries for each occupation are apparently ordered by rank. After an opening title that later on is equated with "king," we find a number of titles that may be loosely translated as heads of departments. Among others, the fields of responsibility mentioned are law or justice, the city, barley, plough, and labor force. It seems that we are dealing with a ranked, well-organized administration (Nissen, Damerow, and Englund 1993: chap. 16). This hierarchy is reflected in a vase from Uruk-Warka (fig. 5.4) on which the

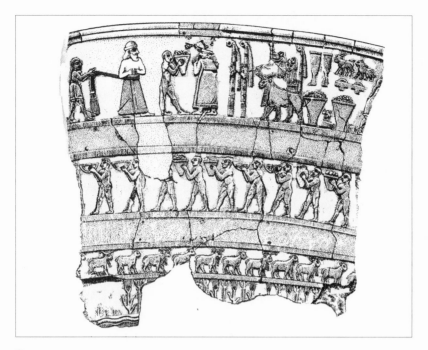

FIGURE 5.4

Detail of the Warka vase from Uruk-Warka.

world of the south is visualized by the artist as one ascending from the
basic foodstuffs, grain and animals, to human service to the gods (in
this case the goddess of Uruk-Warka, Inanna). The figure with a cap
and a beard on the Warka vase is interpreted (Nissen 1988:106, fig. 43)
as a king or "priest king" (Schmandt-Besserat 1993:208–9). He is
depicted in hunting scenes, as a warrior, on ships, in front of monumental buildings, as a supplicant to the gods, or as a master of animals.

Not surprisingly, the notion of hierarchy is not restricted to the
socioeconomic situation of the city and its inhabitants but applies also
to the relation between the city and its hinterland, as interpreted from
the spatial and rank-size distribution of contemporary settlements
in the surrounding region. In fact, there we find a settlement pattern
that corresponds to a multitiered system in the terms of geography
(Adams and Nissen 1972; Nissen 1993a). The erection of large central
buildings as well as the projected city wall furthermore presupposes the
existence of a strong political authority, if we accept the narrative of the

Gilgamesh epic, hinting at the use of forced labor (George 1999; Soden 1982:17). This leads to the conclusion that the political apparatus was as well organized as the economic one, if the two were not one and the same. Obviously, by the end of the fourth millennium B.C. Uruk-Warka was a center of enormous power, and its central authority controlled vast resources of all kinds, such as food supplies, raw materials, and labor. Its manpower can best be judged by the observation that the city of Uruk-Warka had at least 20,000 inhabitants, accepting the traditional (conservative) estimate of 100 inhabitants per hectare (Adams 1981:349–50). A large suburban or rural population inhabiting settlements outside the walls with an aggregated area of about half the size of the walled city augmented this number. The full relevance of these figures is revealed by a comparison with the conditions of the preceding Ubaid period, when the largest settlements, Susa and Chogha Mish in lowland Khuzistan, did not exceed 17 hectares (Nissen 1985b). The impact of this new urban density cannot be overestimated.

Uruk-Warka was not the only southern city of its time. We can be sure that other settlements known to have been inhabited during the late fourth millennium B.C., such as Kish, Nippur, Girsu (Telloh), and Ur, were similarly well organized. Although too little is known from these places, they probably would have been of equal importance to Uruk-Warka and would have acted as local centers. Given current knowledge, however, we can consider the entire southern Mesopotamia as having clearly been a single culture area. We are at a complete loss, however, when asked whether this cultural similarity generated any kind of politically coherent polity. Given the long way southern Mesopotamia still had to go until the first political unification in the second half of the third millennium, it is highly unlikely that a single political or economic entity with a single, central authority existed (Nissen 1993c). This is directly opposed to Algaze's proposal (1993a:5–6), which assumes that already in the fourth millennium the Late Uruk system was organized along the lines of the dynasty of Akkad of the late third millennium.

Unfortunately, as mentioned above, we know very little about the earlier stages, since nearly all information from Uruk-Warka pertains to the very end of the Uruk period, while older remains have been uncovered only to a very limited extent. The picture sketched above is therefore valid only for the time of the building phase of level IVa in Eanna.

Tracing things back into earlier phases is possible only for isolated elements like architecture or cylinder seals. The so-called Limestone Temple of Archaic level V and the temples of level IVa indicate the architectural similarities, as does cylinder seal design (for cylinder seals see Boehmer 1999). Writing, on the other hand, most probably did not antedate level IVa (Nissen in Green and Nissen 1987:50–51; Nissen 1995:476, n. 19). On the whole, therefore, too many pieces are missing to confirm more than that the general situation must have been very similar. Indeed, thus far the time of IVa has been described as a stage of such complexity and internal coherence that it is impossible to ignore the likelihood of a high degree of complexity preceding that of level IV. In fact, we should be able to argue for a rather long duration of such earlier developments (Nissen 1993b). There is no doubt that Uruk-Warka, like all of southern Mesopotamia, had attained a level of urbanity, of population density, and of economic power far in advance of its neighbors during the earlier phases of the Late Uruk (LC 3–4).

NEIGHBORING REGIONS DURING LATE URUK

In only a few areas of ancient Near Eastern studies has our knowledge been so expanded and our interpretations so altered as for the second half of the fourth millennium B.C., also known as the Uruk or LC 3–5 period in recent years. As recently as thirty years ago our knowledge was restricted to a notion that towards the end of the Uruk period the so-called Early High Civilization had appeared in southern Mesopotamia, defined by major art and architecture, cylinder seals, and the early writing system (Moortgat 1945). In addition, it was known that this culture had expanded into the eastern plain of lowland Khuzistan with almost identical features (Le Breton 1957), and cylinder seals found at various places in Syria and Egypt could be interpreted as witnesses for an otherwise undefined contact with southern Mesopotamia (Bittel 1939–41; Boehmer 1974; Joffe 2000).

Only a few years later, several settlements were found during salvage operations along the Euphrates accompanying the building of a dam in Syria. Totally unexpectedly, architecture and other finds exactly matched those artifacts that so far had been known only from the excavations in Uruk-Warka of the so-called Late Uruk period (for the southern and Khuzistan Late Uruk [LC 5] pottery corpus, see fig. 5.5). Excavations

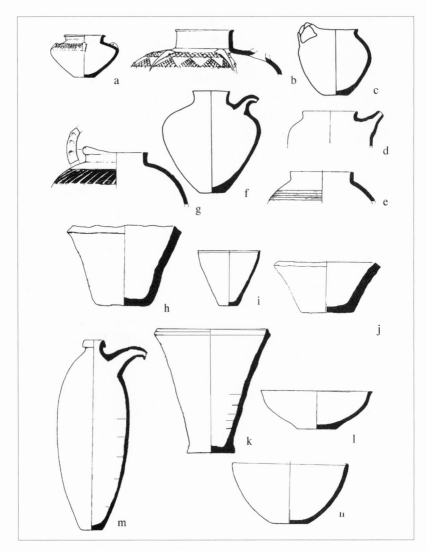

FIGURE 5.5

Repertoire of classic Late Uruk–style pottery.

at Habuba Kabira South (summarized in Strommenger 1980), Tell Qannas, and subsequently Jebel Aruda (Van Driel 1982, 1983; Van Driel and Van Driel-Murray 1979, 1983) provided new examples of Uruk-type settlements throughout Syria and southeastern Anatolia. The finds from these excavations either mirror the finds known from southern

Mesopotamia or show an unmistakable affinity (Algaze 1993a).

Thus the available archaeological information left no doubt as to the existence of strong ties between southern Mesopotamia and some of its neighboring subregions. This led to all kinds of interpretations. With southern Mesopotamia as the allegedly dominating power and the other regions seen as underdeveloped, the actors seemed to be defined. The interpretations ranged from the assumption of an early empire to colonies sent out from southern Mesopotamia to trade networks. This simplistic case of archaeological evidence for core-periphery relations was particularly attractive for those who focus their research on the early development of political institutions. In fact, this evidence was used to test various models (summarized in Algaze 1989b and accompanying comments). The more recent "common knowledge" seems to have settled on the explanation of the Uruk settlements outside southern Mesopotamia as colonies created to provide southern Mesopotamia with all kinds of raw materials that the alluvial area itself did not possess.

None of the existing explanations is satisfactory, including the most comprehensive one that explains this regional structure as a "world system" (Algaze 1993a). If nothing else, however, these discussions had the positive effect of initiating a period when scholars started to think in larger frameworks. Yet, this improved outlook basically concerns the larger spatial context; little consideration has been given to the temporal context. The aim here is to reintroduce this temporal aspect without neglecting the spatial aspect. Following is an attempt to develop a three-dimensional scenario in the hope that it will show to what extent the Uruk interaction sphere was an answer to earlier developments, and also convey a little of the dynamics that affected the fourth and third millennia in the Near East.

As indicated earlier, the term "Uruk period" has become synonymous with the phase in the ancient Near East of the early high civilization or early urban phase, as others prefer to call it. As outlined above, at Uruk-Warka within a short space of time around 3200 B.C. we find all those elements that from then on represent the salient and long-lasting features of southern Mesopotamian culture. These include major art and architecture, cylinder seals, writing, and a high degree of hierarchy in leadership, administration, social structure, and labor.

Lowland Khuzistan

The first area to be mentioned is the eastern neighbor of southern Mesopotamia, the plains of lowland Khuzistan. After a lengthy, more or less local development lasting into the beginning of the Uruk period in southern Mesopotamia (LC 2), this local development suddenly came to an end and was replaced by the entire set of southern Mesopotamian Uruk cultural innovations (Dittmann 1986b). Except for the themes depicted on cylinder seals (Dittmann 1986a; Pittman 1994b), lowland Khuzistan for a while developed as if it were an integral part of southern Mesopotamia. This parallelism was almost complete, in particular with regard to those developments that helped control the economy, such as the introduction of cylinder seals, sealed clay bullae (sealed hollow balls with counters inside; fig. 5.6), and finally sealed numerical clay tablets (Le Brun and Vallat 1978). These tools and techniques signify close similarities between the economic systems that were being administered in the two areas.

The surprise comes in the next stage, when, contrary to developments in southern Mesopotamia, writing was not introduced. Instead, after a short interval a uniquely Proto-Elamite writing system was created, which used different sign forms and ways of arranging the signs on the tablet, although some of the same principles used in southern Mesopotamian script were also utilized (Damerow and Englund 1989; Englund 1996). It is part of a development that in many respects shows a marked departure from southern Mesopotamia. To be sure, the cylinder seal continued to be used, but most conspicuously, the complex of mass-produced pottery did not continue, indicating a significant change in the administration of workers on public projects. Most important, however, is the evidence that political allies were sought among groups in the eastern highlands of modern Iran, not westward into southern Mesopotamia (Alden 1982; Dittmann 1986c, 1987).

Northern Mesopotamia

Unfortunately, developments in the region of northern Mesopotamia, which later became known as Assyria, are less well known. To be sure, the assemblages from places like Nineveh show a close relation with the Uruk period in southern Mesopotamia. Because of incomplete coverage of the region by archaeological surveys and limited informa-

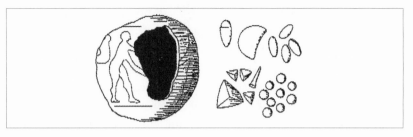

FIGURE 5.6

Bulla (sealed clay ball) with numerical counting tokens.

tion from sites themselves, we still do not have a firm grasp of either the temporal dimension or the scope and intensity of interaction (Abu al-Soof 1985; Algaze 1986b; Gut 1996; but see Rothman, this volume).

Middle Euphrates Valley and the Khabur Triangle

The picture is different as we follow the Euphrates route into Syria and Anatolia. Here we find places like Habuba Kabira South and its associated center, Tell Qannas, or Jebel Aruda. It was the recovery of information from these sites that started to expand our knowledge of fourth millennium B.C. Greater Mesopotamia in the first place. Apparently, they had been inhabited only for one or two generations, and they resembled the southern Mesopotamian material corpus in every respect. Among the common features were all forms of architecture as well as pottery. Most conspicuously, as in lowland Khuzistan, we also find all forms of early economic control devices such as cylinder seals, tokens, sealed bullae, and sealed numerical clay tablets (Strommenger 1980; Van Driel 1982, 1983). Again, as in lowland Khuzistan, we are disillusioned by not finding any traces of early writing. Here, however, the end of the parallelism to southern Mesopotamia is marked not by continuing cultural development but by the abandonment of the sites, presumably before Uruk-Warka IVa (Sürenhagen 1986a, 1993). Habuba Kabira and Jebel Aruda had been interpreted as examples of a short-term expansion into the area of modern Syria (Nissen 1974; Sürenhagen 1974–75; Strommenger 1980). New findings from the excavations of Tell Sheikh Hassan and Tell Brak in Syria show that southern influence on this area had begun much earlier than originally thought (Boese 1986–87).

Tell Sheikh Hassan is a good example of how the accidental course of archaeological discovery can change the overall interpretation of the past. Had, for example, Tell Sheikh Hassan (or Hacınebi) been found prior to Habuba and Aruda, the discussion most probably would have taken another direction, since it was mainly the sudden and short-lived existence of Habuba Kabira, seemingly confirmed by Jebel Aruda, that prompted the use of terms such as "colonies" or "outposts." The new general picture has changed, however, since those Uruk settlements seem not to be alien to the local cultural environment; instead, the entire region appears to be under the same influence.

It seems that here again we find a close parallelism to lowland Khuzistan, as Syria in its entirety appears to have adopted the southern Mesopotamian Uruk-Warka set of artifacts and ideas. There is a difference, however; in Syria, in addition to the settlements founded earlier during the Uruk period sequence, new ones like Habuba Kabira or Jebel Aruda were founded during the latest phase of the Uruk period. With few exceptions, like Tell Brak, these Uruk-related settlements all seem to have come to an end at approximately the same time, whether they belonged to the older group or to the sites founded in LC 5. Wherever our chronological information is sufficiently sensitive, we find that the site occupations ended just before the advent of writing in southern Mesopotamia. This conclusion is based on the observation that all earlier means of information technology were used, indicating that these settlements took part in the same system of administrative control, but no writing was found. It would be strange if they did not adopt the next stage as well.

Southeastern Anatolia

So far, I have considered only sites in the steppes and open plains of Syria, southeast Anatolia, and lowland Khuzistan. However, these boundaries do not mark the limits of southern Mesopotamian influence: it extended into the foothills and mountains of Anatolia and western Iran. The nature of influence, however, is different in these ecological zones. The mountain ranges apparently acted as filters, observable in the fact that beyond these mountain fronts we find not one site whose residents totally adopted the southern Mesopotamian set of artifacts. Rather, what we find are a number of settlements, which in addition to local material culture display varying degrees of influence from the south (Frangipane 1993).

The sites of Arslantepe near Malatya, Tepecik, and Hassek Höyük represent three different types of settlements north of the Taurus Mountain range. The remains from Arslantepe show minor Uruk cultural influence, not in identical artifacts of any category but more in a vague similarity in pottery shapes and manufacture, and in the application of similar principles of administration (Frangipane and Palmieri 1983b). Interestingly, for a site of the same period and with clear signs of contact with southern traditions, the administrators of Arslantepe with few exceptions used stamp seals instead of cylinder seals (Frangipane and Palmieri 1983b; Frangipane 1993). On the other hand, a suburb at Tepecik yielded southern-influenced pottery (Esin 1975, 1987). Hassek Höyük cannot have been more than a farmstead, based on its size. The pottery resembles that from Tepecik's suburb (Behm-Blancke 1986; Behm-Blancke et al. 1981, 1984; but see Helwing 1999). Although we have little good evidence for dating the end of their occupations, we may speculate that it was the same temporal horizon as the abandonment of Habuba Kabira and Jebel Aruda, although all three sites north of the Taurus were reoccupied after that horizon, unlike the Syrian sites.

Another variation on this same theme is evident in the mountains of western Iran. Although the evidence from Iran is scant, it is sufficient to show that this phenomenon was not restricted to Anatolia. Godin Tepe (Young 1986) and Tell i-Ghazir (Caldwell 1968) within the Zagros Mountains, as well as Tal-i Iblis (Caldwell 1967) and Tepe Sialk (Amiet 1985b) in the intermontane valleys beyond the mountain front, testify to the presence of southern Mesopotamian influence in the Iranian highlands. It is again "filtered" by the mountain barrier. Only Godin Tepe, however, can be reliably dated. There within the area of an older settlement sits a walled complex at the top of the fourth millennium mound. This "Oval" shows nonlocal architecture and artifacts (Weiss and Young 1975). The regular, symmetrical plan of the main building is in obvious contrast to the local tradition; in fact, there are similarities with the buildings at Arslantepe. In addition to Uruk-related pottery and cylinder seals, clay tablets were found, one of which contains a southern Mesopotamian–type sign. The sign is certainly not one found in Proto-Elamite script. The southern advance to Godin seems to have been but a brief episode, the end of which may have occurred a bit later than the end of southern settlements in Syria and Anatolia. This I base on the presence of the sign on the tablet. Again, however, like elsewhere, the end came suddenly, without affecting the evolution of local traditions in succeeding levels.

Alternative Explanatory Frameworks

As mentioned above, the most frequently cited explanation for these phenomena seemed to be obvious. All the changes theoretically resulted from the invasion of southern Mesopotamians into foreign, even hostile territories, as indicated by the walls surrounding Habuba Kabira and Godin Tepe (Algaze 1989b with comments). The reason for an intrusion also seemed to be obvious, as alluvial southern Mesopotamia had to import all kinds of raw materials (for a cautionary remark see H. Weiss 1989). When the undisputed organizational superiority of southern Mesopotamia is added, it is easy to see how this interpretation emerged, involving terms like "expansion" or even "colonization." The proponents of an expansion theory attempted to demonstrate that southern Mesopotamians moved into the neighboring areas, but that this period ended with the migrants being repulsed by the formerly dominated populations. However, the idea of military expulsion by local populations proves to be especially unrealistic because it would have meant a concerted action throughout Syria, Anatolia, and Iran in order to expel the southern Mesopotamian invaders.

If not military expulsion, proponents of the Uruk Expansion theory seek to find the reason for abandonment in a collapse of demand for goods—that is, a collapse of the southern economy (Algaze 1993a:104–107; see also Johnson 1988–89). This is not plausible, either. For one thing, this hypothesis rests on incorrect basic assumptions. The development in the northern part of the southern alluvium apparently took a slightly different course from the area of Uruk-Warka, as the number of Early and Middle Uruk (LC 2–3) sites seems to be larger than in the south (Adams 1981:61–63). Even so, it is a gross exaggeration to state that the overall settled area remained the same between Early and Late Uruk (Algaze 1993a:105–6). Likewise, I see no material basis for the statement that the number of urban settlements was larger in the early phase. Even if some of these sites may have reached a size of 20 hectares, that is not comparable to Uruk-Warka with 250 hectares in the Late Uruk period. Again, I see no evidence for stating that the same number of settlements were founded in the Jemdet Nasr period as were abandoned by the end of Late Uruk (Algaze 1993a:106, referring to Postgate 1986). As I previously observed (Adams and Nissen 1972: 99–100, 103), it is almost impossible to determine from surface material whether a site has been occupied only during the Jemdet Nasr period or continued into the Early Dynastic. This is because common Jemdet Nasr period pottery is the same as Early Dynastic I pottery without Early Dynastic idiosyncrasies. It is therefore impossible to differentiate between settlements founded in Jemdet Nasr or Early Dynastic I. On the other hand, we have clear evidence from early written sources pointing to an uninterrupted continuity in southern Mesopotamia and even an internal expansion of economic activities (Nissen 1985c).

For lowland Khuzistan the explanation of purported economic decline cannot provide an answer because the southern Mesopotamian repertoire of artifacts and ideas had been adopted by the entire country, replacing traditional forms and leaving no local pockets of those older forms to reinterpret. The same explanatory scenario fits the Syrian case as well. It seems to me that we must look for a different explanation by readjusting the frame through which we view the events of the fourth millennium. In order to readjust our focus, we need a broader background to the events of the fourth millennium. I attempt to show here that the various phenomena coming under the heading of "expansion" in most cases are nothing but attempts to reorganize relations between the different subregions of Greater Mesopotamia. This reorganization was occurring at various levels of organization. In fact, I will argue that the events of the fourth millennium B.C. were nothing but more or less successful attempts to reconstitute older, fifth millennium Ubaid exchange networks that had been disrupted.

The Ubaid Interaction Sphere and Network

For the Ubaid period we encounter a similar basic problem as for the Uruk period, since some scholars also propose that there was an Ubaid expansion (Henrickson and Thuesen 1989). Just as the classical Uruk pottery can be seen to have evolved from the earlier Ubaid pottery, we can draw the line back from the Ubaid pottery to the older pottery groups of Hajji Mohammed and Eridu (Vertesálji 1984). Ubaid pottery is easily identified on the basis of its technique of manufacture, shapes, and decoration. Its characteristics include a simple range of shapes and decorative schemes, which consist of concentric bands and filled-in repeating patterns such as garlands and wavy lines (Oates 1960). The Ubaid ceramic style was first observed from the site of Ur in southern Mesopotamia in 1917. Thereafter, pottery groups of similar appearance were found in northern Mesopotamia, in Syria, and in Anatolia, where they invariably have been called "Northern Ubaid" or "Ubaid-like."

Scholars did not recognize at first that Ubaid pottery developed directly from older, local pottery styles, because in most places the beginning of this pottery and its relation to earlier levels had not been found in good stratigraphic context. Consequently, for the areas outside southern Mesopotamia the idea prevailed that the Ubaid styles were intrusive, the result of a movement of Ubaid-period southern Mesopotamians (Mallowan 1970). This concept only emerged because by pure chance at a number of excavated sites the transition from the earlier Halaf levels to the Ubaid levels could not be recognized (Tepe Gawra: Tobler 1950; Arpachiyah: Mallowan and Rose 1935), or because the pottery from post-Halaf layers was called "degenerated" and consequently disregarded (Tell Halaf: Schmidt 1943). In more recent days, either theoretical reasons have been put forward to explain the local transition to Ubaid styles (Rothman 1988) or analysis of pottery recognized stratigraphically as late Halaf has shown how the elaborate Halafian painted decoration was subsequently simplified. The resulting styles were seen as clearly pre- or early Ubaid designs (Arpachiyah: Hijara 1980; Kashkashok: Koizumi 1993). Consequently, the so-called Ubaid-like groups were finally understood as developments arising out of earlier local traditions.

What the potters shared across Greater Mesopotamia was a series of new techniques that, when used to elaborate older local designs, produced seemingly similar, homogenized local styles that looked more similar than they actually were. The key was the introduction of the tournette or slow wheel. This tool permits potters to produce standard shapes more quickly. Decoration is applied by holding the brush while the pot turns. This creates the repeating patterns around the pot. The tournette consists of a disk with a central pivot around which it can be turned. Unlike in the true potter's wheel, motion persists only as long as the wheel is turned (Rieth 1960:20–23). Yet this tool used in this way makes painting or shaping the vessel easier than before.

We do not know when the slow wheel appeared for the first time. An early example comes from an Ubaid context in Ur (Woolley 1955b:28, reproduced in Rieth 1960: fig. 22). The excavators suggested that it was used to produce Ubaid pottery, but an earlier appearance in the late Halaf period cannot be excluded. What matters here is that from a certain point on, the slow wheel changed the process of pottery decoration, as is apparent when the painting techniques on Halaf and Ubaid pottery are compared. The major difference is that before the introduction of this new tool, the delicate Halaf patterns were painted first on one side of the vessel and then on the other (Schmidt 1943; Mallowan and Rose 1935). Although concentric bands are also found in Halaf decoration, they do not constitute the main pattern. I argue that this near-uniformity in Ubaid-period artifact style should be seen as the result of a new technique in pottery manufacturing introduced by the end of the Halaf phase, rather than as the result of southern Mesopotamian migrations.

It is of minor importance, in this sense, to know where the tournette originated. It is more important that we can document its use over large areas of the Near East within a short space of time. Although in itself it is a phenomenon that might deserve further discussion, only one aspect concerns us here: no one adopts a new tool unless there is a need for it. Whatever may have led to the appearance of this new tool in the first place, there can be no doubt that it constituted an answer to a problem, whether in the context of speeding up the production of ceramics or in the organization of labor. At any rate, its adoption in other subregions indicates that it was found to meet an existing need (Nissen 1989).

To put it into a more general explanatory framework, we can assume that the problems were identical or similar in all those regions where this new tool was adopted. We may furthermore assume that these areas not only had attained a similar level of organization but also were part of a regional communications and exchange network. This network, which I assume operated on the basis of equal partners ("symmetric," as others would call it), would have been the basis and the context for swift exchanges of both information and goods.

Another common feature tying together the areas with Ubaid-like pottery was the so-called house with the central hall (Mittelsaalhaus). This house form had small rooms attached to both long sides of an elongated roofed space (Heinrich 1982:7–14). This pattern is found to predominate in the large buildings of the Late Uruk period at Uruk-Warka (Heinrich 1982:46–50), and it is known from the southern Mesopotamian Ubaid period sites such as Eridu, (Safar, Mustafa, and Lloyd 1981) and Tell Abade (Jasim 1989). In addition we find it as far north as Tepe Gawra (Tobler 1950), Değirmentepe (Esin and Harmankaya 1987), and possibly even in level XVI at Mersin (Garstang 1953), all of which belong to the Ubaid horizon. As Schmid (1992) has shown, because of the traffic pattern within this house type, these structures are too complicated to have been simple primary residential buildings for small families. Once again it must be an answer to particular organizational needs. Rothman (1988, n.d.) and Forest (1983) suggest that it is an extended family structure within the context of an evolving chiefly society. Since this specialized plan is unlikely to have developed independently in different places, its occurrence over such a large area cannot simply be by chance. Rather it suggests that organizational or functional commonalities were shared by these various groups over a large area.

Taking all these points of the argument together, we see that during the Ubaid period large parts of the Near East were tied into an active communications and exchange network. This is in sharp contrast to the situation during the Late Uruk period when there were quite a number of differences between southern Mesopotamia and its neighbors, although these differences were at the organizational level. It is this organizational difference, the reasons for it, and particularly its consequences on which I focus in the remainder of this chapter.

The Formation of the Uruk Network

Unfortunately, the intervening centuries between Ubaid and Late Uruk are among the least-well-documented phases of Near Eastern prehistory (Nissen 1993b, 1999). Yet it is exactly this period of time when the Ubaid network was thrown off balance. In order to get at least a notion of what may have happened we have to examine what little evidence we have. In our search for a reason that may have impelled southern Mesopotamia to develop differently from the other areas, an environmental phenomenon may prove critical. At about the end of the Ubaid period or during the Early Uruk, the southern Mesopotamian plain changed from a swamp- and flood-ridden zone into dry land, which could be occupied by large groups of new settlers (Nützel 1976). In fact, there is evidence for a slight climatic change leading to a decrease of surface water. Apparently as a result of this climatic change, settlement increased enormously over a large part of southern Mesopotamia around the middle of the fourth millennium B.C. The environmental changes climaxed within the time range of the Uruk period (LC 2–5). Within a relatively short span of time we encounter both settlements and settlement density of hitherto unknown dimensions (Adams and Nissen 1972; Nissen 1983). An increase in size, density, and agglomeration of population seems to have catalyzed conflicts and social problems. The end result of the process, its social and political resolution, can be deduced from the very complex structures of administration and control known from the first written sources appearing at the very end of the Late Uruk period (Nissen, Damerow, and Englund 1993; Nissen 1999).

Presumably, the interrelated structures of economic administration and political organization documented in the early written records resulted from increasing pressure and the necessity of finding satisfying solutions to organizational problems. Certainly, this climatic change did not only affect southern Mesopotamia; as it shifted the limits of rainfall agriculture it altered other areas as well. Such shifts probably never occurred in sufficient dimensions to leave traces that would be recognized archaeologically. As Adams argues, the shifts would be apparent in the minimum and maximum annual crop yields, which may be hard to document but which are critical catalysts for agricultural and social change (Adams 1981). It thus was primarily southern Mesopotamia where the quantitative changes were transformed into qualitative (and recognizable) ones. The restriction of this particular process to southern Mesopotamia threw the communication and exchange network off balance, affecting everyone who had participated in the former interaction sphere.

Although no details are known, we can be sure that these climatic and concomitant social changes had consequences on all levels. We have known for a long time of major changes that took place within the Uruk-period Near East; it is now appropriate to ask whether these might not be reactions, or at least linked, to the disturbance of the earlier system. The former network partners would presumably sense this disturbance as negative to their interests and would try to "heal" the system. Since calling back in time the renegade region was unrealistic, the most plausible way to restore the former partnership was to try to push oneself onto that new level. It was easiest for the lowland Khuzistan to overcome the difficulties involved, since the plains of Khuzistan come closest to the situation of southern Mesopotamia. In fact, during the later Ubaid this area seems to have been the most densely settled region of the Near East and probably had become relatively more advanced than others (Johnson 1987a). One may speculate whether or not lowland Khuzistan would have attained a similar level of organization given exactly the same external conditions and exposed to the same pressures. One may further speculate that because of the similarity in the problems they faced, lowland Khuzistan may have seen the southern Mesopotamian innovations as solutions to their own problems. Under these circumstances it makes sense that lowland Khuzistan would adopt the entire southern Mesopotamian set of organizational means (Nissen 1983).

This assumption presents a plausible explanation for why the Uruk culture flooded the entire region within a short period without leaving traditional pockets of material culture: if a system is to be adopted en masse there are only limited possibilities for local differentiation. If at all, these possibilities should lie in the area of "adornment," which coincides nicely with the observation that the only local traces retained are found in the themes depicted on cylinder seals (Dittmann 1986a). Given the new picture for Syria, which again indicates that not much local material survived, we should conclude for this area as well that we are dealing with a similar development to the one just described for lowland Khuzistan. Within a reasonably short period, a way would have been found to restore communication and exchange lines in both regions, enabling them to come close to the former relations—probably including northern Mesopotamia, although we have insufficient evidence to make a robust argument.

Though larger parts of the former network were left out, particularly those beyond the natural borders of the Taurus and Zagros mountain chains, the new arrangement could have been strong enough to remain a stabilizing factor for some time to come. However, southern Mesopotamia had embarked on a trajectory that called for rapid further development and could not be stopped. On the one hand, the continuous increase in the population of southern Mesopotamia inferred from the rising size and number of settlements called for additional increases in the level of organization. On the other hand, the wave of immigration or population shift responsible for the rapid settlement of the southern Mesopotamian plain in the Uruk period probably did not come to a sudden stop. We get an idea of the size of the problem if we see that the city of Uruk-Warka already covered 250 hectares by the Late Uruk period. It then doubled in size within the next 250 to 300 years to encompass close to 600 hectares within the city wall, and probably about 100 more outside the wall by 2900 B.C. (Nissen 1983). There can be no doubt that the sheer increase of population in southern Mesopotamia in relation to the neighboring regions made it impossible to achieve a stable balance among the societies in these subregions. Growth of the southern Mesopotamian population led to the emergence of even more complex forms of organization and increased demands for goods that southern Mesopotamia did not have. This is especially true for metals, which southern Mesopotamia imported on a large scale, to judge from their occurrence in the Archaic Texts from Uruk-Warka, and also for high-quality timber and stone, particularly those used for prestige items. To be sure, open systems like the networks we are talking about for the older periods can tolerate inequalities to some extent and thus would have been able to meet moderately increasing demands from the southern Mesopotamian side. But there is a limit to what a system based on equal partnership can provide. To remain operating, the area of the network would have to be extended. Not only would this have meant crossing natural borders, it would have failed because those areas were not on the same socioeconomic level as southern Mesopotamia and would not have found the set of organizational techniques in total or in part as solutions to their own problems. What happened instead of a new balance is that southern Mesopotamia started using its power and organizational superiority to settle the question in its own favor. It is only here that I see asymmetrical relations developing with the foundation of fortified colonies or stations like Habuba, populated by southern Mesopotamians, in addition to the older settlements. It is this conscious move that was finally strong enough to penetrate the mountain barriers and resulted in influencing the areas beyond, as we have seen from the evidence of Arslantepe, Tepecik, and Godin Tepe.

The End of the Uruk Network

As I argued above, most of the close ties to Uruk-period southern Mesopotamia seem to have come to an end at roughly the same time. Therefore the explanation must be found in the only region with which all the disparate subregions had relations—southern Mesopotamia. However, all explanations based on the assumption of a disruption of political and economic life in southern Mesopotamia, or of a deceleration in the pace of development, fail. To the contrary, southern Mesopotamia experienced a phase of further internal expansion, which led to the emergence of the first script. According to finds from southern Mesopotamia, the influx of foreign goods increased. To postulate a reduction in exchange would contradict every piece of information currently available. It would be hard to argue that this should have been the moment when southern Mesopotamia cut communication and exchange lines with its neighbors. Settlements such as Habuba Kabira ceased to exist. Only a few, such as Tell Brak, survived, although there may be others for which we lack evidence. Could the exchange system have undergone a complete reorganization, with new routes channeled through a few strong centers? That at least some rerouting had taken place is shown by the Jemdet Nasr artifacts found in the Umm en-Nar area of Oman. Strangely enough, for the Uruk period the Persian Gulf area has not yielded any evidence of contacts with southern Mesopotamia (Potts 1990).

Even if ties were maintained to guarantee the influx of goods into southern Mesopotamia, the large-scale abandonment at the end of the Uruk period marked the end not only of the Uruk network but also of the attempts to reestablish a far-flung network. It would be unreasonable to assume that the end of the Uruk network had no effect only because we find no traces in southern Mesopotamia. The most conspic-

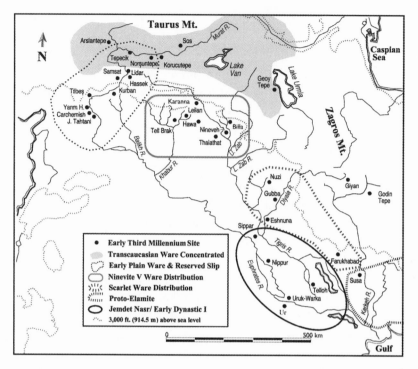

FIGURE 5.7

Distribution of pottery style areas in post-Uruk Mesopotamia, early third millennium B.C.

uous evidence for a reorientation of the political map of the Near East comes from lowland Khuzistan, as mentioned above. Again, this area had left the Uruk network before the advent of writing in southern Mesopotamia. In contrast to Syria and Anatolia, however, we know its subsequent development. After a brief hiatus we find lowland Khuzistan if not the center then certainly an integral part of a new social and political construct (fig. 5.7) known as Proto-Elam (Carter and Stolper 1984; Dittmann 1987; Pittman 1994b).

The Proto-Elamite Network

Evidence of the brief interval between the end of the Uruk network and the emergence of the new one derives from the observation that Proto-Elamite script paleographically connects not to the oldest stage of southern Mesopotamian writing, but to the second one (Englund 1994). While it follows the same principles, the organization of the script and shape of signs differ. The Proto-Elamite writing system thus probably is observer-induced rather than the result of an actual takeover. This new Proto-Elamite complex, consisting of a new kind of writing, cylinder seals with locally inspired patterns, and other parts of a local tradition, reveals lowland Khuzistan to be part of a new network encompassing the central and eastern parts of Iran. No more details are available because the only evidence we can go by is the fact that in lowland Khuzistan, at Tell Malyan (Sumner 1986) and Tepe Sialk (Amiet 1985b) on the eastern side of the Zagros, and at Tepe Yahya in central Iran (Potts 1975; Dittmann 1987), we are confronted with a homogeneous artifactual corpus. In addition to pottery we find seals and writing that indicate common administrative structures (Damerow and Englund 1989; Vallat 1986). Proto-Elamite seals and writing have been found as far east as Shahr i-Sokhta in Iranian Seistan (Amiet and Tosi 1978).

On a general level, there might have been differences between the Uruk and Proto-Elamite networks, as the former comprised a fairly homogeneous region, mainly consisting of the plains south and west of the Fertile Crescent. Therefore, the system was able to start from more or less common conditions, whereas the Proto-Elamite network in low-land Khuzistan, in the Zagros intermontane zone, and on the Marv Dasht plain on the eastern side of the Zagros covered very environmentally differentiated areas. A unification of those areas demanded much greater effort at both the initial stage and for maintenance. To put it more generally: it seems to be conceivable that the Proto-Elamite network had to be organized on much stricter lines than the Uruk network. Apparently this network existed only for a short period, as indicated by the virtual absence of evidence for internal development. This is most clear in the case of writing (Vallat 1986). In southern Mesopotamia within 300 years the semi-pictographic system of the Late Uruk changed into the totally abstract cuneiform system of the Archaic Texts from Ur. Since this change is seen as a response to the pressure for making the script easier to use, we should take the immobility of the Proto-Elamite system to indicate that it was subject to less pressure. At the same time, the assumed lessening of internal pressure could explain the short life of the Proto-Elamite phenomenon. Although in its eastern extent it ended as suddenly as it began, the end resembles more a fading out in Fars and lowland Khuzistan (to the west). In any case, in all parts of this former Proto-Elamite network the subsequent development has a local appearance. In the eastern portions this strictly local development continued for a long while, whereas lowland Khuzistan eventually returned to closer contacts with southern Mesopotamia. At least from the time of the dynasty of Akkad on, approximately 2300 B.C., lowland Khuzistan adopted the cuneiform system of writing from southern Mesopotamia and with it Akkadian as the language of written expression. Although nominally independent, from then on the rulers of Susa depended on the southern Mesopotamian rulers for some time to come.

The Nineveh V Network

Since the formation of the Proto-Elamite network was undoubtedly a response to the end of the Uruk network, it would be strange if this reaction were restricted to the areas east of southern Mesopotamia. Surely the end of the Uruk network would have affected the northern and northwestern regions of the former Uruk network at least as much as it affected lowland Khuzistan. However, we have less clear indications from those areas. With further research the Nineveh V phenomenon could emerge as another local network, but thus far it is known only by a common style of pottery (Schwartz 1987). Obviously, more information is needed to support this contention. The scarlet ware phenomenon in the Diyala region may represent another small network, operating between southern Mesopotamia and Proto-Elamite Iran. Also in the case of Nineveh V, the tradition fades out into local aspects. As with lowland Khuzistan we do not have good information until Early Dynastic II, or roughly the middle of the third millennium B.C., when we encounter evidence of closer links to southern Mesopotamia, exemplified by the Early Dynastic II statues and seals of Tell Chuera (Moortgat 1967:42–43), the Early Dynastic III finds from Assur (Andrae 1922), and the tablets from Ebla and Tell Beydar.

THIRD MILLENNIUM DEVELOPMENTS

By the second half of the third millennium, we see the Near East again tied into a larger network, though of a totally different character than in the Ubaid period, where we began our discussion. This new network is indisputably dominated by southern Mesopotamia, which we conclude not only from the adoption of southern Mesopotamian cuneiform as a means of controlling the economy in the neighboring areas but even more from the adoption of southern Mesopotamian literature and school texts (Matthiae 1977; Pettinato 1979). This adaptation of cuneiform writing systems offers an excellent counterargument to the uncritical view of a one-sided core-periphery relation where progress was restricted to the core. Had it not been for the necessity of adapting the southern Mesopotamian script for use with other languages, like the Semitic languages in Syria, the cuneiform system would probably not have been forced to change. Cuneiform was used for centuries to render the monosyllabic Sumerian language in written form, but it was the necessity of writing Semitic languages that promoted the use of the syllabic value of the written signs, thus enabling scribes to write Sumerian grammatical elements for the first time (Finkelstein 1963). This innovation of the middle of the third millennium B.C. enabled cuneiform to render spoken language. And only from this moment on was it possible to write coherent texts. This presents a good example of how something that seems to be the highlight of all southern Mesopotamian inventions—writing and literature—in fact has its background in the common and interlocking developments of the various regions of the Near East (Nissen 1988:138–39).

CONCLUSION

While this sketch cannot be more than a set of plausible propositions, the extent to which developments in the Near East from early times on resulted from interconnections among the various areas should be clear. Unless this regional context is considered, developments in particular subregions are hard to understand. This is especially true for the period when southern Mesopotamia appears to have followed its own path. Although I chose to begin with the Ubaid period, communication and exchange interconnections existed even earlier. In addition, to make the temporal and spatial entanglements for a limited span of time transparent, my idea was to show that the better-known dynamics of fourth and third millennia southern Mesopotamia in particular corresponded to less-well-known dynamics of the neighboring areas.

In order to understand the long-term trends at work in this region I have focused on the entanglements of southern Mesopotamia and its neighbors in temporal and spatial contexts. Much remains hypothetical, and I hope that new research will fill in the blanks and maybe even correct what I have said. However, no matter how much more research is conducted and how many new theories are proposed, we will not advance our understanding if we do not see the dynamics of any place in a broad temporal and spatial framework.

For the Uruk period, this proposal offers the opportunity to shuffle the cards. The necessity for southern Mesopotamians to guarantee the flow of imported raw materials and goods must be recognized as one of the prime movers. In particular, the observation that the "Uruk Expansion" not only spread over a longer period of time but dissolved into various stages or waves opens the door to seeing this phenomenon not as a short-term, single-stimulus affair but as a mixture of adaptations to new situations and deliberate moves by individuals and groups. After all, we saw that Uruk-Warka was governed by a well-organized group of leading figures. This pattern probably applies to other sites and areas as well. Within a relatively short period these people devised a social system that continued without radical changes and determined the course of Mesopotamia over the next couple of millennia. I see no reason why we should deny these Uruk leaders the capability of acting and reacting appropriately and also of having been farsighted.

6

The Uruk Period in Southern Mesopotamia

Susan Pollock

The alluvial plains of southern Mesopotamia are considered by most scholars to have been the heartland of Uruk-period social, political, and economic developments. During this time, states and urban societies emerged. A variety of technological innovations were adopted, and artifacts used in bureaucratized systems of accounting proliferated. There were major movements of people within the alluvial lowlands and, according to many authors, also north to the Upper Mesopotamian plains and foothills of the Taurus Mountains as well as east to the Zagros Mountains and beyond. Iconographic images show some of the first clear pictorial evidence of the taking of captives and killing of people. Many scholars have argued that major economic transformations occurred during the Uruk period, resulting in a more centralized, specialized, and administratively regulated economy (Johnson 1973, 1975, 1980a, 1987a; Nissen 1974, 1988, 1999; Wright 1977a, ed. 1981, 1998; Wright and Johnson 1975; Wright, Miller, and Redding 1980; cf. Adams 1981, Yoffee 1995). This increasingly complex economy and stratified sociopolitical organization, together with demographic growth and general prosperity, are often assumed to have underpinned rising demands for nonlocal resources. Some scholars have contended that these demands were a major impetus for Southerners to send traders to found outposts and colonies in resource-rich areas or at important nodes on trading networks (Weiss and Young 1975; Algaze 1989b, 1993a, this volume; Stein 1990, 1998, 1999, 2000, this volume; Stein and Mısır 1994; Stein, Bernbeck et al. 1996).

I suggest in this chapter that many general scenarios that seek to explain developments in the fourth millennium in Greater Mesopotamia are based on assumptions about the political economy of the southern alluvial lowlands that require reconsideration. I will argue that there were substantial differences in economic organization within southern Mesopotamia between the so-called Nippur-Adab and Warka areas, the latter where the city of Uruk-Warka is located (fig. 6.1). In contrast to conventional understandings, I suggest that the Nippur-Adab subregion was characterized by a collection of relatively autonomous polities and was in fact more stable than the Uruk-Warka area, albeit with a less integrated and less "complexly" organized economic system. Societies in the Uruk area seem to have relied more heavily on the extraction of tribute using repressive means and may have been dominated by a single powerful center, the city of Uruk-Warka itself. It is therefore not possible to speak about *the* economic organization of southern Mesopotamia; rather, the heartland was neither unified nor uniform (see also chapter by Algaze, Nissen, Schwartz, and Stein, this volume). In this chapter I also reevaluate data relevant to an assessment of demographic trends and argue that the results contradict the widely accepted scenario in which the Nippur-Adab area lost a substantial portion of its population to the Warka area in the Late Uruk (LC 5) period. Together these analyses have profound implications for an evaluation of the roles of southern Mesopotamian polities in any expansive moves into other subregions.

BACKGROUND ON THE POLITICAL ECONOMY OF SOUTHERN MESOPOTAMIA

I first present a brief review of some of the commonly accepted understandings or assumptions about the political economy of southern Mesopotamia in the Uruk period. I concentrate my remarks on two

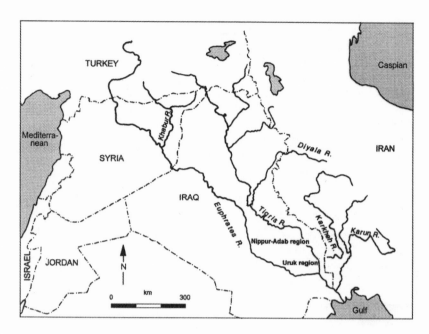

FIGURE 6.1

The Near East, showing the locations of the Nippur-Adab and Uruk regions.

main themes: first, the degree of specialization and centralized control
of economic activities, and second, political organization.

In their highly influential writings on the Uruk period based principally on research conducted in southwestern Iran, Wright and
Johnson (Wright 1977a, ed. 1981, 1987, 1998; Wright and Johnson
1975; Wright, Miller, and Redding 1980; Johnson 1973, 1975, 1980a,
1987a, 1988–89) have argued that Uruk states were characterized by
centralized and specialized production of mundane, utilitarian goods.
Production of at least some of these goods was concentrated at large,
centrally located settlements, with the result that people from surrounding smaller communities had to procure some of their necessities from these centers. This pattern of production went hand in hand
with an administered system of exchange. The result was a hierarchically organized political system in which political elites exerted substantial control over production and distribution of critical goods.

A rather different understanding of Uruk political economy has
been promoted by Adams (1974a, 1981), who has contended that there

is little evidence of a centralized, administered economic system during this period in the alluvial lowlands of southern Iraq. Instead, Adams suggests that economic organization was more loosely structured, with specialization primarily the result of localized differences in resource availability. For example, some areas may have been more suitable for agriculture, while others were better for pasturage. The production of many mundane goods, such as pottery or stone tools, was carried out in most communities regardless of size or centrality of location. Rather than seeing them as administrative and production centers, Adams views Uruk towns and cities as places that facilitated—but did not administer—exchange of goods and services, stored surplus products, sponsored long-distance trade, housed religious institutions and their attendant rituals, and contained defensive structures.

A related issue is whether southern Mesopotamia was organized into one integrated political entity—or at most a very few—during the later portions of the Uruk period or whether it was composed of numerous smaller, competitive states. This question of political organization has substantial relevance for our understanding of political and economic conditions, changes in southern Mesopotamia, and the capabilities of southern polities to influence events outside the alluvial lowlands. Few scholars in recent years have claimed that all of southern Mesopotamia was politically unified during the Uruk period. However, discussions of the south's influence on other subregions often seem to be predicated on the existence of an integrated political unit that had the capability of devoting substantial resources to (its attempts to) control access to distant trade routes. In the contributions to this volume, most authors agree that the south was not a single, integrated polity (see Algaze, Nissen, Schwartz, Stein, and Wright, this volume; also Baines and Yoffee 1998:215–16). Algaze proposes that the competitive and fractured nature of political organization in the southern lowlands was in fact a precondition for Uruk "colonization" of other areas, as each polity attempted to ensure its own access to imported goods. A logical extension of this position is that the people and/or goods from the south that are found in the northern and eastern "peripheries" could have come from different parts of southern Mesopotamia and not just from the cities of Uruk-Warka or Susa (Boehmer 1999:114–27; Schwartz, this volume).

With this brief review of some scholarly understandings of Uruk-period political economy and political organization in southern Mesopotamia as a background, I turn now to a discussion of the sources of data that are available for this period.

THE DATA

Despite the interpretive weight placed upon Uruk period developments in southern Mesopotamia, little new data have been published in the past fifteen years that are directly relevant to the subject, nor have there been sustained, critical reexaminations of existing interpretations (for an exception, see Johnson 1988–89). Much of the reason for this neglect of the "heartland" can be traced to the politics of archaeological research in the Middle East in the last several decades of the twentieth century. The cessation of foreign fieldwork in Iran in the late 1970s, and in Iraq in 1990,[1] coincided in part with new opportunities for excavations and surveys in Syria and southeastern Turkey, often related to dam-building projects. As a result, the focus of most recent fieldwork efforts has been on the latter areas, which have been traditionally labeled peripheral to the heartland of Uruk developments in southern Iraq.[2] As researchers have delved more deeply into investigations of the political economy of the "peripheries," it has become ever more apparent that our understanding of the political economy of the "core" is in need of fresh evaluation.

A reexamination of the political economy of southern Mesopotamia faces a number of serious obstacles. Most excavations of Uruk-period occupations in southern Iraq have been quite restricted in scale (Nippur: Hansen 1965; Wilson 1986; Uqair: Lloyd and Safar 1943; Jemdet Nasr: Matthews 1990; Rubeidheh: Killick 1988; Uruk Mound at Abu Salabikh: Pollock 1990; Pollock, Pope, and Coursey 1996; Pollock, Steele, and Pope 1991; Khafajah: Delougaz and Lloyd 1942; Delougaz, Hill, and Lloyd 1967; Eridu: Safar, Mustafa, and Lloyd 1981; Ur: Woolley 1955b). A single exception, Uruk-Warka, has been extensively excavated, but the excavated area was confined almost exclusively to the administrative/religious center of the city (see preliminary reports in *UVB [Uruk Vorläufige Berichte]* and final reports in *AUWE [Ausgrabungen in Uruk-Warka Endberichte]*). The restricted excavation focus, coupled with the unfortunate propensity of the ancient occupants to clean out buildings prior to their demolition and rebuilding, has resulted in excavation data that are often inappropriate for addressing the kinds of questions about economic and social organization posed by scholars in recent decades (see Nissen, this volume). Furthermore, much of the fieldwork was conducted without the benefit of today's standards for recovery and recording procedures.

The limitations of the available excavation evidence have encouraged a heavy reliance on settlement pattern studies based on regional surveys (Adams 1965, 1981; Adams and Nissen 1972; Gibson 1972; Johnson 1975, 1980a, 1988–89; Wright 1981). Surveys have covered substantial portions of the alluvial lowlands, documenting site size, periods of occupation, and, in some cases, artifact presence or frequency. Settlement pattern data are attractive in that they offer an overview of areal patterns of settlement in southern Mesopotamia over many millennia. They are not, however, without significant problems of their own. Severe deflation, heavy alluviation, dune movement, and mound formation have contributed to obscuring or destroying parts of sites. Modern political circumstances have often been less than favorable to regional studies and, in combination with the difficult terrain and size of areas to be covered, have dictated an extensive rather than intensive approach to survey work. Little of the artifactual material on which assessments of date and activities are based is available for restudy. Surface collections were usually not taken from the sites (Adams 1981:45) or are currently inaccessible, and the publication of surveys has rarely been accorded the same detailed attention that is customary for excavation reports (Bernbeck 1997–98).

In this chapter I rely principally on data obtained from settlement surveys, mostly regional in scope but supplemented by the surface collections and mapping carried out by a team that I directed at the Uruk Mound of Abu Salabikh (Pollock 1987, 1990; Pollock, Pope, and Coursey 1996; Pollock, Steele, and Pope 1991) and the comprehensive surface study of Uruk by Finkbeiner (1991). Much of the data has only a rather coarse chronological resolution, and it is not possible to distinguish Early (LC 2) from Middle Uruk (LC 3–4) occupations in many cases. For this reason, I refer throughout this chapter to "earlier Uruk" (LC 2–4) to mean Early (LC 2) and Middle Uruk (LC 3–4) combined.

In the following sections I will use settlement pattern and surface collection data to compare two subregions distinguished by Adams (1981:69), the Warka and Nippur-Adab subregions, in terms of settlement integration and distribution, tribute demands, distributions of activities among and within settlements, and changes in population (see the Appendix for the settlement survey data on which these analyses are based). It should be noted at the outset that the Warka and Nippur-Adab areas do not necessarily correspond in any simple or direct way to meaningful political or economic units in the fourth millennium. Although there does seem to be a boundary area with few settlements between them (illustrated below), their limits in other directions are determined only by the edges of the surveyed areas. Nonetheless, the two areas, as defined on these more or less arbitrary grounds, show a number of distinct features that suggest that they do bear some correspondence to actual subregional differences.

SETTLEMENT DIFFERENTIATION

Site size is widely regarded as a useful, if coarse, basis for categorizing settlements. Physical size is often presumed to bear a more or less direct relationship to population numbers and hence to a settlement's food requirements as well as to functional size (Adams 1981:69, 85–94; Johnson 1980a; Kramer 1980; on problems relating to functional size, see Bernbeck 1999a:159–71).

For southern Mesopotamia, Adams (1981:71–75) has differentiated two principal categories of sites based on size: those that are 10 hectares or larger (towns and cities) and those less than 10 hectares (villages). Johnson (1975), on the other hand, distinguishes four groups, two of which he considers villages (less than 3 hectares, 3 to 7 hectares) and two kinds of centers (8 to 15 hectares, 19 or more hectares). A reexamination of the histograms of site sizes has led me to propose a tripartite grouping: less than 8 hectares (small), 8 to 14 hectares (medium), and 20 hectares or more (large). Uruk-Warka, at 100 hectares in the earlier Uruk (LC 2–4) and 230 hectares by Late Uruk (LC 5) (Finkbeiner 1991; Bernbeck 1999b), may be in a fourth category of its own (fig. 6.2).

Adams (1981) has remarked upon the striking differences in settlement patterns in the Nippur-Adab and Warka areas of southern Mesopotamia during the Uruk period. From the beginning of the

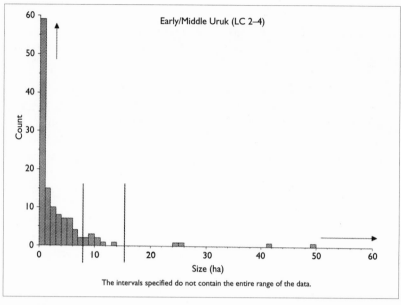

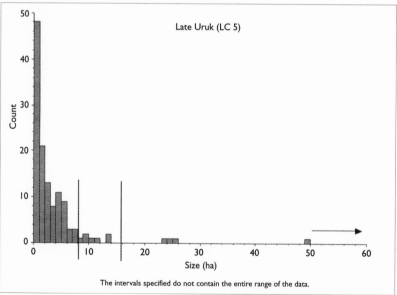

FIGURE 6.2

Histograms of settlement sizes, showing divisions between small, medium, and large categories for the Early/Middle Uruk (LC 2–4) period (top) *and the Late Uruk (LC 5) period* (bottom). *Note that the intervals specified do not contain the entire range of the data.*

TABLE 6.1

Medium-Size and Large Sites in the Nippur-Adab and Uruk Regions in Early/Middle (LC 2–4) and Late (LC 5) Uruk Times

	Early/Middle Uruk (LC 2–4)		Late Uruk (LC 5)	
Region	Medium-Size	Large	Medium-Size	Large
Nippur-Adab	678 (13.5 ha)	1172 (25.5 ha)	678 (13.5 ha)	1172 (25.5 ha)
	1020 (8.2 ha)	1237 (42 ha)	1194 (11.5 ha)	1306 (50 ha)
	1046 (8.6 ha)	1306 (50 ha)		Nippur (25 ha)
	1166 (10.6 ha)	Nippur (25 ha)		
	1194 (11.5 ha)			
	Abu Salabikh (10.0 ha)			
Uruk-Warka	4 (10 ha)	Uruk-Warka (100 ha)	4 (10 ha)	Uruk-Warka (230 ha)
	171 (10 ha)		110 (9 ha)	125 (24 ha)
	201 (11 ha)		201 (11 ha)	
			242 (10 ha)	
			260 (14 ha)	

TABLE 6.2

Rank-Size Indices, Using 0.5 Hectares as the "Lower-Limb" Cutoff

Region	Earlier Uruk (LC 2–4)	Late Uruk (LC 5)
All southern Mesopotamia	- .057	- .289
Nippur-Adab	+ .080	- .184
Uruk-Warka	- .488	- .400

Source: Calculated according to Johnson 1980a, 1980b.

fourth millennium, the Warka area was dominated by the extraordinarily large site of Uruk-Warka. Uruk-Warka seems to have prevented the growth of other large settlements: only in the Late Uruk (LC 5) period did one site (WS-125) attain a size to warrant its placement in the large category (table 6.1). Rank-size indices for the Uruk area in both the earlier (LC 2–4) and Late Uruk (LC 5) period are negative (table 6.2), indicating a political minimization of economic competition, with strongly developed vertical integration (Johnson 1980a:243, 1980b) and/or the articulation of Uruk with a larger, extra-areal system.

In contrast, several large settlements were already established in the Nippur-Adab area in the earlier Uruk (LC 2–4) period. None of the large sites stands out as paramount on the basis of size. The rank-size index for earlier Uruk (LC 2–4) is nearly log-normal (table 6.2). This result is, however, mainly attributable to the very small sites; most of those of 1 hectare or more are substantially larger than expected, producing a convex rank-size curve in its upper reaches. Johnson (1980a:253) and Voorrips (1981) have demonstrated that the lower ends of rank-size distributions often exhibit "lower limb fall-off"; hence, for interpretative purposes, the relative sizes of the larger sites are of principal importance. In Late Uruk (LC 5) the decrease in the number of medium-sized sites and disappearance of one of the large settlements (table 6.1) results in a rank-size distribution that appears log-normal in its upper reaches and then becomes somewhat concave, although markedly less so than in the Warka area.

The two subregions also exhibit quite different spatial patterning of sites. These distributions are visible on settlement pattern maps: in the earlier Uruk period (LC 2–4) there is a markedly denser concentration of sites in the Nippur-Adab area, whereas in Late Uruk (LC 5) the situation is reversed (figs. 6.3 and 6.4). Beyond this general pattern the distributions of larger settlements can be compared by a modified nearest-neighbor analysis in which the distances between each medium-size or large site and its five nearest neighbors are summed.[3] This calculation has the advantage of not relying on distance to a single nearest neighbor, which may be too dependent on the vagaries of archaeological sampling. The sum of the distances of the five nearest neighbors provides a measure of the degree to which larger settlements were isolated or, instead, were situated in the midst of densely occupied zones.

During the earlier Uruk (LC 2–4) period, medium-size and large sites in the Warka area were quite isolated, much more so than those in the Nippur-Adab area (table 6.3). There is, furthermore, a marked distinction in degree of isolation among the Nippur-Adab settlements: those that form an arc along the southern and western "borders" of the settled area are notably more isolated from their nearest neighbors

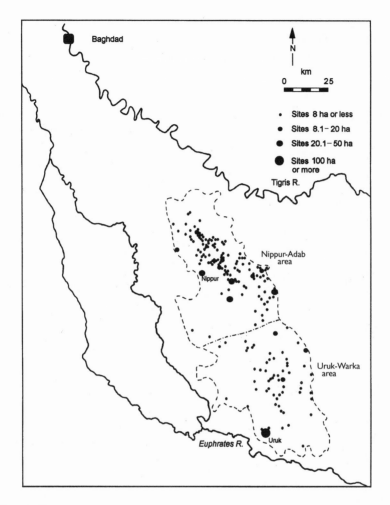

FIGURE 6.3

Earlier Uruk (LC 2–4) settlement patterns (after Adams 1981:fig. 12).

than those in the remainder of the region. In neither subregion does the degree of isolation correspond in any simple, direct way to settlement size.

In the Late Uruk (LC 5) period, medium-size and large settlements in the Nippur-Adab area top the list of most isolated sites, although the tendency remains for some to be markedly more isolated than others. All five of the medium-size and large sites in the Nippur-Adab area that had been occupied in the earlier Uruk (LC 2–4) period

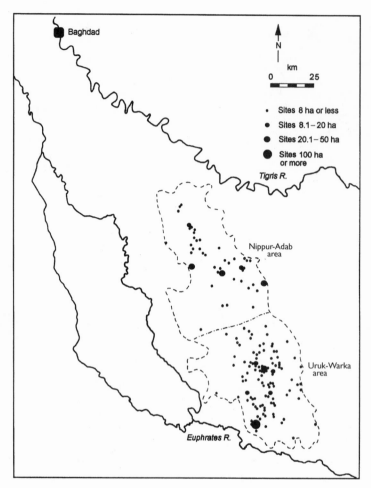

FIGURE 6.4

Late Uruk (LC 5) settlement patterns (after Adams 1981:fig. 13).

became more isolated (have greater sums of the five nearest neighbors) than previously. Continuously occupied settlements in the Warka area exhibit the opposite trend: all three have comparable or lower degrees of isolation in Late Uruk (LC 5) than earlier. These patterns suggest that larger settlements in the Warka area were increasingly able to keep (or draw) rural population nearby, preventing people from moving further away from the towns that may have been the source of heavy tribute demands (see below). In contrast, rural dwellers in the

TABLE 6.3

Sums of Distances from Medium-Size and Large Sites to Their Five Nearest Neighbors

Site	Region	Sum of Distances (km)	Site Size (ha)
Earlier Uruk (LC 2–4)			
Uruk-Warka	U	49.6	100.0
171	U	46.8	10.0
4	U	45.9	10.0
Abu Salabikh	N	44.8	10.0
Nippur	N	38.4	25.0
1237	N	35.1	42.0
201	U	28.6	11.0
1306	N	21.2	50.0
1172	N	15.3	25.5
1166	N	13.5	10.6
678	N	12.6	13.5
1046	N	11.4	8.6
1194	N	10.0	11.5
1020	N	8.9	8.2
Late Uruk (LC 5)			
Nippur	N	56.7	25.0
1306	N	52.2	50.0
678	N	48.2	13.5
4	U	45.1	10.0
1172	N	26.6	25.5
Uruk	U	21.5	200.0
1194	N	19.7	11.5
201	U	19.3	11.0
242	U	19.0	10.0
260	U	18.7	14.0
125	U	12.0	24.0
110	U	11.2	9.0

Key: U = Uruk-Warka area, N = Nippur-Adab area

Nippur-Adab area may have been better able to escape unacceptable demands imposed by town residents by "voting with their feet" (Johnson 1987a:126) and putting a greater distance between themselves and larger communities. Alternatively, some villagers may have moved *into* towns, based perhaps on their perceptions that town life offered more options for making a living or more material or other rewards. The longevity of Nippur-Adab towns is indicated by the fact that only one of the earlier ones in the subregion failed to be occupied into the Late Uruk (LC 5) period. This, together with the evidence that rural population was not or could not be compelled to reside near towns, may suggest that rural dwellers, their labor, and their products were not essential to the maintenance of towns in the Nippur-Adab area.

TRIBUTE DEMANDS

Integral to questions about the relationship between rural and town dwellers is the issue of how residents of larger communities were provisioned with food. To what degree did towns rely on tribute from rural communities to supply their subsistence needs?

There are several ways in which archaeologists have tried to assess the demand for and flow of tribute. I will use two complementary approaches to this problem here. First, I consider estimates of the probable size of sustaining areas of large and medium-size sites and the possibility or improbability that residents of those communities *could* have adequately provisioned themselves with food.[4] However, even if estimates suggest that a given settlement *could* have supplied itself with food, this does not mean that it necessarily *did* so. To obtain an indication of the kinds of activities in which community members engaged and a rough approximation of the extent of their participation, I examine the distribution of artifacts that could have been used in food and related subsistence production.

Calculations of sustaining areas available to settlements must be based on a series of assumptions and estimates of relevant variables. These include population size, land required per capita to meet subsistence needs, the amount of land that could be cultivated per capita, and the distance residents would have been willing to go to reach their fields (Flannery 1976; Johnson 1987a; Rossmann 1976; Steponaitis 1978, 1981; Vita-Finzi and Higgs 1970). Because of the uncertainty associated with many of these estimates, I present several figures for each parameter to illustrate some of the range of possible outcomes and errors (table 6.4). I have used two widely cited estimates for population density, 125 people per hectare and 200 people per hectare

(Adams 1981:69; Kramer 1980). Land requirements per capita, taking into consideration the possibility of fallowing, have been estimated as 0.5 hectares (cf. Kramer 1980:328, Johnson 1987a:112), 1.0 hectares (Oates and Oates 1976:120; Johnson 1987a:112), and 1.5 hectares (Adams 1981:86–87). The amount of land that could be cultivated per capita, using "traditional" techniques, has been calculated as approximately 2 hectares (Oates and Oates 1976:120; Johnson 1987a:112). This figure is substantially higher than any of the estimates for the amount of land required per capita, indicating that production of surplus food was well within the range of possibility. Finally, I have used estimates of 3, 4, and 5 kilometers for the distances people will travel to their fields on a daily basis.[5]

The resulting figures (table 6.4) show that already in the earlier Uruk (LC 2–4) period, the city of Uruk-Warka had exceeded the limits of its immediate sustaining area. In other words, Uruk-Warka's residents could not possibly have produced enough food to meet the needs of the city's population. Such a situation strongly suggests that tribute was exacted from the rural population as a significant source of provisions for urban residents. Other large sites (1172 and 1306) are borderline in terms of their ability to be self-sustaining: depending on the specific values chosen for the relevant variables, they may or may not have been able to feed themselves. Most likely these communities relied to at least some extent on the extraction of tribute from rural producers; otherwise, one would have to assume that nearly all of their resident population engaged in food production, an assumption that seems unlikely. Medium-size sites, however (represented in table 6.4 by the largest one, site 678), could probably have sustained themselves from the food produced by their residents, except under the most unfavorable assumptions or circumstances. These communities may not have *depended* upon tribute in the form of food to provision their population, although, once again, this does not mean that they did not extract any. If climate changes in the middle of the fourth millennium did indeed lead to drier conditions in the alluvial lowlands (see Wright, this volume), they may have resulted in lessened possibilities for communities to sustain themselves without tribute extractions from rural dwellers.

Another way to address the issue of local production and demand for tribute is to examine the evidence for production of specific kinds

TABLE 6.4

Estimates of Land Available to Feed Residents of Several Medium-Size or Large Early/Middle Uruk (LC 2–4) Period Sites

Site	Size (ha)	Population		Total land required (ha), if land needed per capita is:				Land (ha) available within radius of:		
		125/ha	200/ha	0.5 ha	1.0 ha	1.5 ha		3 km	4 km	5 km
Uruk	100.0	12,500	20,000	6,250–10,000	12,500–20,000	18,750–30,000		3,888	6,441	9,621
1306	50.0	6,250	10,000	3,125–5,000	6,250–10,000	9,375–15,000		3,578	6,026	9,103
1172	25.5	3,188	5,100	1,594–2,550	3,188–5,100	4,782–7,650		3,363	5,740	8,745
678	13.5	1,688	2,700	844–1,350	1,688–2,700	2,532–4,050		3,216	5,544	—

of goods in different communities. In particular, what kinds of differences, whether qualitative or quantitative, existed between large and medium-size sites on the one hand and small settlements on the other? Here I consider the production of ceramics and the production and use of clay sickles and chipped stone implements. I use the evidence provided by Adams (1981:118, table 9) from his intensive surface collections at selected sites, supplemented by data collected in intensive surveys of the Uruk Mound at Abu Salabikh (Pollock, Steele, and Pope 1991; Pollock, Pope, and Coursey 1996) and Uruk-Warka (Finkbeiner 1991).[6] Because of the unevenness of the available data, the discussion pertains primarily to the Nippur-Adab area,[7] and the sample of larger sites is quite limited. Furthermore, the uncertainty associated with assigning surface remains to phases of the Uruk period results in some ambiguities in comparing patterns from the earlier and later part of the period. However, in his sample of intensively surveyed sites, Adams (1981: table 9) was able to distinguish a substantial number of sites that in many cases were occupied only in the Uruk or Jemdet Nasr period.[8] Because of the limitations of the evidence, I have considered both the Uruk period as a whole as well as earlier (LC 2–4) and later Uruk (LC 5) occupations separately, where those can be distinguished. The use of obsidian blades appears to be confined principally to the earlier part of the Uruk period (LC 2–4), and therefore those items have been excluded for the segment of the analysis that considers Late Uruk (LC 5) occupations only.

Although Adams reports his intensive surface collections in terms of artifact counts—or frequencies—these figures should be understood as densities (table 6.5). Artifacts were collected from more or less similar-sized sample units (Adams 1981:45), and as such, they represent counts per unit area.[9] Although the use of densities for comparisons among sites of different sizes would be desirable, the relative rarity of several of the artifact categories considered renders the use of density figures misleading: a small change in the frequencies reported would result in the appearance of a significant change in density. For this reason, I have relied primarily on presence/absence data and divergence from the mean density values of particular artifact categories (table 6.6).

Clay sickles were used for harvesting reeds and/or grain (Anderson 1983; Anderson-Gerfaud and Formenti 1996). They are found at larger

TABLE 6.5

Densities per Collection Unit (78.5 m²) and Presence/Absence of Selected Artifact Categories from Intensive Surface Collections on Uruk Period Sites

Site	Date	Size (ha)	Clay Sickles
Uruk-Warka	E/MU, LU	100/230	+
1172	E/MU, LU	25.5	33.3
125	LU	24.0	0.0
1194	E/MU, LU	11.5	2.0
AbS UM	E/MU	10.0	7.1
1020	E/MU	8.2	57.0
1205	E/MU	7.9	60.0
792	E/MU	6.8	43.0
1124	E/MU, LU	6.8/1.0	101.0
245	E/MU, LU	6.0	18.5
975	E/MU, LU	5.8/0.6	39.0
790	E/MU, LU	5.5	20.0
AbS UM	LU	5.5	4.8
118	E/MU	5.3	73.0
1165	E/MU, LU	5.3	1.0
1159	E/MU	4.5	27.0
126	LU	4.0	14.0
1137	E/MU, LU	3.8	33.5
1198	E/MU	3.4	51.0
1072	E/MU, LU	3.4	28.0
1315	LU	2.8	9.0
1154	LU	2.6	1.0
128	LU	1.8	38.5
940	E/MU, LU	1.7	32.5
1432	E/MU, LU	1.7	27.0
804	E/MU	1.7	78.0
837	E/MU	1.4	78.0
574	E/MU, LU	1.0	10.0
573	E/MU, LU	1/0.2	38.0
1164	E/MU, LU	1/0.2	11.0
1448	E/MU, LU	0.9	19.5
1163	LU	0.9	2.0
1261	LU	0.8	38.0
1118	E/MU	0.6	36.0
1416	E/MU	0.6	20.0
805	LU	0.5	11.0
1312	E/MU	0.2	45.0
1375	E/MU, LU	0.2	15.0
1216	E/MU, LU	0.1/4.8	2.5

Sources: Adams 1981:118, table 9; Finkbeiner 1991; author's field notes from the Uruk Mound at Abu Salabikh.

Note: Where applicable, sizes are listed for each phase of occupation. E/MU = Early/Middle Uruk (LC 2–4); LU = Late Uruk (LC 5).

Chipped Stone Blades	Cores	Obsidian Blades	Kiln Debris
+	N.d.	+	N.d.
6.3	0.0	3.3	Sickles
2.5	0.5	0.0	+
6.0	1.0	2.0	BRB
7.1	0.3	0.8	Sickles, pottery
2.0	0.5	0.5	Sickles
3.0	0.0	1.0	Sickle, jar rim
0.0	0.0	0.0	+
2.0	0.0	0.0	Sickles
4.0	0.0	0.0	+
2.0	0.0	1.0	Sickles, BRB
2.0	0.0	0.0	Sickles
8.5	0.4	1.3	Sickles, pottery
2.0	0.0	0.0	+
1.0	0.0	0.0	+
1.0	0.0	0.0	+
3.0	0.0	0.0	0.0
1.0	0.0	0.0	Sickles
0.0	0.0	0.0	Sickles, jars, proto-BRBs, handle
4.3	0.0	1.3	Sickles, BRB
3.0	1.0	0.0	+
0.0	0.0	0.0	Sickles
1.5	0.0	0.0	+
3.0	0.0	1.0	Sickles
1.0	1.0	0.0	+
2.0	0.0	0.0	Sickles, bowls
2.0	0.0	1.0	0.0
7.0	0.0	0.0	Sickles
2.0	0.0	0.0	Sickles
0.0	0.0	0.0	Sickles
1.5	0.0	0.0	+
0.0	0.0	0.0	Sickles
3.0	0.0	0.0	0.0
0.0	0.0	0.0	0.0
0.0	0.0	1.0	0.0
1.0	0.0	0.0	Sickles, BRBs
1.0	1.0	0.0	Sickles
0.0	0.0	0.0	0.0
2.0	0.5	1.0	BRBs

TABLE 6.6

Comparisons of Densities and Presence/Absence Data for Selected Categories of Artifacts from Intensive Surface Collections (Derived from Table 6.5)

Artifact Category	Entire Uruk Period		Earlier Uruk (LC 2–4) Only		Late Uruk (LC 5) Only	
	Large Sites (7)	Small Sites (32)	Large Sites (3)	Small Sites (9)	Large Sites (1)	Small Sites (8)
Clay sickles	26.6 (σ = 25.1)	29.6 (σ = 21.6)	41.4 (σ = 24.3)	50.1 (σ = 14.2)	0	14.8 (σ = 20.5)
Clay sickles: > mean value	50%	42%	67%	44%	0%	38%
Chipped stone blades: presence	100%	75%	100%	56%	100%	75%
Chipped stone blades: > mean value	83%	27%	100%	33%	0%	50%
Obsidian blades: presence	83%	22%	100%	22%	N.A.	N.A.
Cores: presence	67%	16%	67%	11%	100%	25%
Ceramic wasters: presence	100%	81%	100%	67%	100%	75%

Note: Large sites are those of 8 hectares or more; small sites are less than 8 hectares. Percentages are based on the number of sites in each category; figures in parentheses represent the total number of sites in each category. "Entire Uruk period" refers to all Uruk period sites at which Adams reports intensive surface collections, plus the Uruk Mound at Abu Salabikh, regardless of occupational date within the Uruk period (except for obsidian blades, which do not occur in the intensively collected samples at "Late Uruk [LC 5] only" sites). "Earlier Uruk (LC 2–4) only" and "Late Uruk (LC 5) only" include only those sites with Uruk occupations that are restricted to one of those phases or where it is possible to differentiate collections from areas of the site that seem to have been occupied solely or at least predominantly in those phases.

and smaller settlements in approximately comparable densities, although in earlier Uruk (LC 2–4) proportionately more large sites had a higher than mean density of clay sickles.

Chipped stone blades are tools, or components of tools, used for agricultural and animal-processing activities (Pope and Pollock 1995). The stone used for making these tools had to be imported, owing to the absence of appropriate raw material in the alluvial lowlands. The presence of chipped stone blades at nearly all sites—with the occasional exception of small ones—indicates that almost all communities had access to imported stone and that agriculture and animal-processing activities in which blade tools were used were conducted in most communities (see also Wright 1998:183). Settlements with greater than the mean density of chipped stone blades are overwhelmingly larger sites, except in the Late Uruk (LC 5) period (however, there is only one large site). Obsidian blades—probably used for some of the same tasks as other chipped stone blades but made of a raw material that takes a particularly sharp edge, is easy to work, and has distinctive aesthetic qualities—were concentrated principally in larger sites. Interestingly, the locations of communities with access to obsidian seem to follow river channels (fig. 6.5). Settlements situated along the main northeastern channel apparently had little or no access to obsidian, whereas those settlements where obsidian was found are distributed in a more or less linear fashion along the central river channel. This pattern suggests not only that exchange networks tended to follow water routes but also that access to desired imported materials was not controlled exclusively by larger communities to the detriment of smaller ones.

Cores, which figure in the primary stages of lithic reduction, are present mostly on large sites in this sample, albeit in very low quantities. The small site WS-264 in the Uruk area, although not part of the intensively collected sample of sites, is said to have contained hundreds of cores on its surface (Adams and Nissen 1972:230). It would appear that core preparation, and perhaps some initial reduction, was concentrated to a substantial extent at one small community that, from its location, may have been under the control of the city of Uruk-Warka (Johnson 1975:332–34). Other communities, mostly larger ones, also participated in the first stages of chipped stone tool production, but to a limited degree.

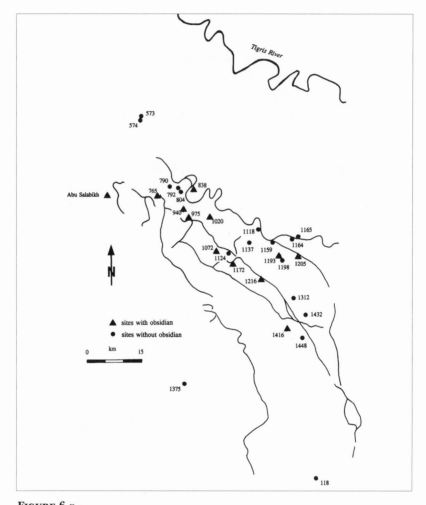

FIGURE 6.5

Locations of intensively collected sites at which obsidian was reported (channels drawn after Adams 1981:Base Map).

Ceramic wasters are an indication of the production—more specifi-cally, the firing—of ceramic artifacts. In most of the cases for which the types of wasters are specified, Adams identified them as clay sickles rather than pottery;[10] however, in many instances, we know only that some kind of ceramic artifacts were fired. Quantitative data on wasters are lacking, but based on presence/absence it appears that ceramic production took place in all larger communities and most smaller ones as well.

In summary, each of these indicators of production shows a similar pattern; they tend to occur in equal or higher densities or to be more ubiquitous in larger communities than in small ones. Taken together, this evidence suggests that residents of larger settlements engaged in subsistence production—of agricultural products, of the tools used in agricultural pursuits, and of ceramics—to a similar if not greater degree than rural dwellers. Assuming that the amount of work expended on subsistence production is directly related to tribute extraction, these data imply that the demand on town residents to produce surpluses for tribute was at least as high and probably higher than that on villagers. Unfortunately, the limitations of the samples permit only a very restricted evaluation of whether demands on town and village inhabitants changed during the course of the Uruk period. Based on the proportion of small communities with a higher than average density of chipped stone blades, it is possible to suggest that demands on rural dwellers increased in the Late Uruk (LC 5) period, much as Johnson (1987a:120–21, 124–25) has argued for the Susiana Plain. The decrease in proportion of small sites with a greater than mean density of clay sickles in Late Uruk (LC 5) does not support this conclusion. However, the drop (44% to 38%) is quite small and may be in part a function of the overall decline in clay sickle use at this time, as indicated by their densities (table 6.6).

That residents of larger communities in the Nippur-Adab area were involved to a substantial extent in subsistence pursuits, including agriculture, may make it more appropriate to envision these settlements as "agricultural towns" rather than "centers." By agricultural town I refer to communities that were concerned primarily with local production, whereas the notion of centers is generally taken to imply a significant degree of involvement in managerial functions over a larger area. Many agricultural towns may not—at least not initially—have depended upon a heavy extraction of tribute from rural neighbors; rather, they appear to have had ample land in their immediate vicinities and sufficient labor with which to work it. Furthermore, their greater densities of chipped stone implements and roughly similar quantities of clay sickles in comparison to smaller communities indicate that residents of agricultural towns did indeed engage in agricultural pursuits to at least as great and probably even a greater extent than villagers. In marked contrast to this situation, the dependence of the city of Uruk-Warka on the extraction from rural dwellers of food and labor in the form of tribute suggests that its internal organization—including the apparatus to extract and monitor tribute—as well as its relationships to other communities may have been markedly different than that of the larger Nippur-Adab settlements.

Intrasite distributions of artifacts from the Uruk Mound at Abu Salabikh lend further support to the contention that a substantial proportion of town residents in the Nippur-Adab area participated in subsistence-related productive activities (Pollock, Pope, and Coursey 1996; Pope and Pollock 1995). The Uruk Mound is a 10-hectare mound, of which approximately two-thirds was occupied during the Uruk period. The Uruk occupation seems to have reached its maximal extent in the Middle Uruk (LC 3–4) period, decreasing somewhat in size in Late Uruk (LC 5). Portions of the neighboring West Mound were also occupied during the Middle Uruk (LC 3–4) period (Postgate 1983; Postgate and Moon 1982), making the settlement approximately 10 hectares in total at this time and thus one of the medium-size communities in the Nippur-Adab area. On Adams's survey maps, Abu Salabikh appears to be one of the isolated towns (fig. 6.3). However, approximately 1 kilometer north of the principal mound cluster lies the Northwest Mound, a 4-hectare settlement that was inhabited during the Middle (LC 3–4) and Late (LC 5) Uruk periods.[11] Moreover, an intensive survey around Abu Salabikh, conducted by Wilkinson (1990b), located at least two other Uruk-period sites within an approximately 3-kilometer radius of Abu Salabikh, but their phases of occupation within the Uruk period could not be established.

Fieldwork at the Uruk Mound of Abu Salabikh included extensive, systematic surface mapping of artifacts covering nearly 40% of the mound's surface (see Pollock et al. 1991 and 1996 for additional information on the surface mapping).[12] These data were plotted on maps of the site, and, where the artifacts in question were sufficiently abundant, contour maps were created showing their densities across the mound's surface.[13] Here I consider distributions of four kinds of artifacts and their associated production activities: ceramic wasters; chipped stone, including both debitage and tools; clay sickles; and spindle whorls.

Ceramic wasters, both pottery and shapeless blobs, which may be

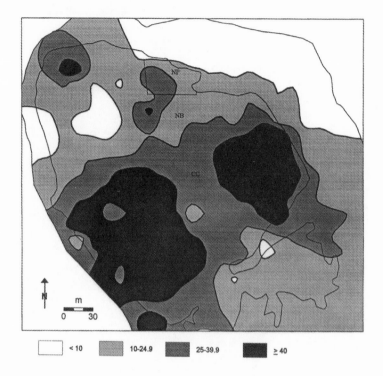

FIGURE 6.6

Distribution of nondiagnostic wasters on the surface of the Uruk Mound at Abu Salabikh.

melted parts of the inside of kilns, are widely dispersed across the mound with large areas of dense concentrations (fig. 6.6). The nearly ubiquitous distribution of wasters suggests that pottery manufacture was widely practiced within the community (see also Coursey 1997:171–76).

The Uruk Mound has yielded substantial evidence for all stages of chipped stone production except for primary core reduction. Blades and flakes were struck from prepared cores and then modified (often very minimally), used, and discarded. The near absence of evidence for the very first stages of lithic reduction—preparing cores from cobbles—fits the pattern already observed for southern Mesopotamia as a whole, in which one community seems to have borne the primary responsibility for first-stage lithic reduction.[14] Chipped stone debitage is widely distributed across the Uruk Mound, although there are definite concentrations in certain areas (fig. 6.7). Tools—including any used or retouched pieces—exhibit a similar pattern, although there

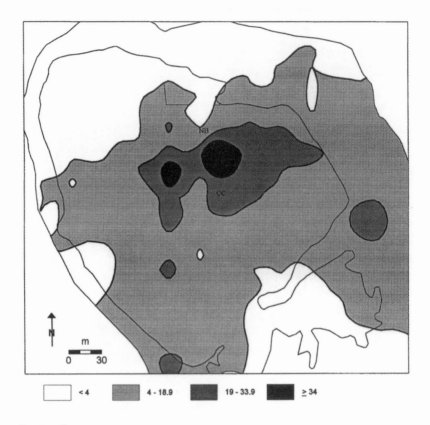

| | < 4 | | 4 - 18.9 | | 19 - 33.9 | | ≥ 34 |

FIGURE 6.7

Distribution of chipped stone debitage of fine mottled tan and grey chert on the surface of the Uruk Mound at Abu Salabikh.

tend to be more areas of concentration (fig. 6.8). These patterns suggest that many households produced, used, and maintained their own chipped stone implements. The tools were used in various activities, most of which, based on microwear analysis, seem to have involved plant and animal processing (Pope and Pollock 1995).

Clay sickles were also widely dispersed across the mound with some areas of marked concentration (fig. 6.9) (Benco 1992). Most households seem to have engaged in activities using these tools, including cutting reeds and perhaps also cereal harvesting.

Spindle whorls are present in low numbers at the Uruk Mound. Their surface distribution is dispersed (fig. 6.10), with some minor

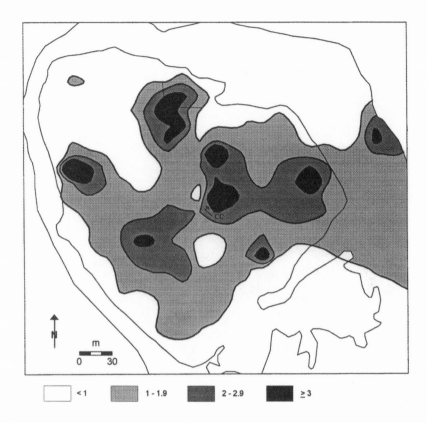

FIGURE 6.8

Distribution of chipped stone blades of fine mottled tan and grey chert on the surface of the Uruk Mound at Abu Salabikh.

clusters but no evidence of any single large concentration of spinning.

Taken together, these indicators of production at the Uruk Mound are all quite widely distributed, although with notably denser clusters evident in a number of locations. I have argued that such patterns indicate that many households were engaged in all or most of these types of production, although some households may have participated more heavily than others in certain activities (Pope and Pollock 1995; Pollock, Pope, and Coursey 1996).[15] Stated differently, the Uruk Mound data support the idea that many residents in larger communities in the Nippur-Adab area engaged in subsistence production. This is not to deny the existence of specialists: surely not every individual

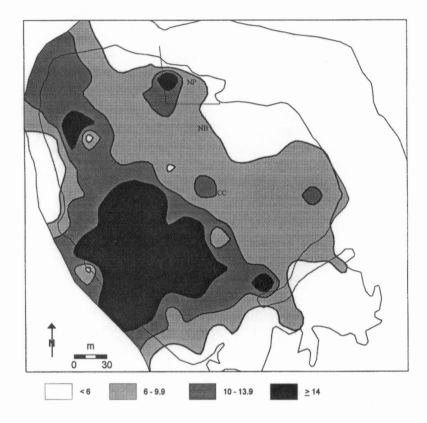

FIGURE 6.9

Distribution of clay sickles on the surface of the Uruk Mound at Abu Salabikh.

performed every kind of subsistence production. Rather, I envision a situation in which many households endeavored to produce a substantial portion of what they required for daily activities. In order to acquire those goods that they did not themselves produce, they may in many cases have turned to other people in their neighborhoods rather than to a centrally controlled workshop.

In summary, various lines of evidence—albeit all limited in scope and requiring additional support when it is again possible to carry out fieldwork in southern Iraq—suggest that the Nippur-Adab area in the earlier Uruk (LC 2–4) period was *not* characterized by a highly integrated economy. The implication is, on the one hand, that larger communities in this subregion had considerably less power to influence the

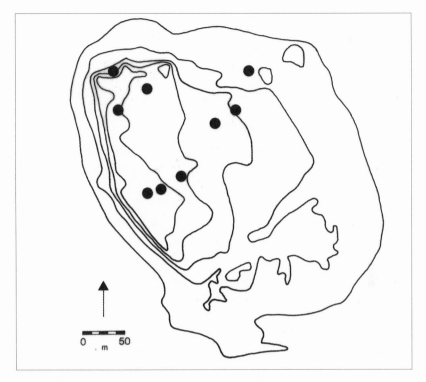

FIGURE 6.10

Distribution of spindle whorls (represented by dots) on the surface of the Uruk Mound at Abu Salabikh.

movements and productive activities of their village neighbors than did the city of Uruk-Warka in its area. On the other hand, the lower degree of integration may also have resulted in a more stable set of relationships, in that communities were less directly dependent on their ability to extract tribute from others and required a lesser degree of repression to continue to function. Negative evidence must be treated with caution. However, the limited indications of the use of accounting technology from the Nippur-Adab area, and especially the absence of images of violence and repression seen in later Uruk (LC 5) sealings from the Warka subregion and the Susiana Plain, may stem from the lesser dependence on threats of force to compel people's compliance. This suggestion may seem to be contradicted by the appearance of a massive wall around the Uruk Mound at Abu Salabikh in the Late Uruk

(LC 5) period (Pollock, Pope, and Coursey 1996:688–89). Such a wall could, however, be a sign of intraregional unrest rather than internal coercion and associated threats of force or, as Frangipane (this volume) suggests, a marking of urban spaces as distinct political entities.

The suggestion that the Nippur-Adab area formed a more stable configuration of local systems than the Warka area contrasts with conventional interpretations of the relationship between these areas. Reconsideration of the demographic patterns in southern Mesopotamia during the Uruk period lends additional support to this interpretation.

DEMOGRAPHY

As part of the evaluation of his survey evidence, Adams has argued that the Nippur-Adab area lost substantial proportions of its population over the course of the fourth millennium, whereas the Warka area increased by almost exactly the same amount (Adams 1981:60–81). Adams attributed these trends to migration of people from north to south,[16] occasioned by ecological factors (especially the drying up of at least one major channel in the Nippur-Adab area) and possibly political ones as well.

Although these arguments for population movement and, by extension, the magnetic attraction of the Warka area appear compelling, they fail to take into consideration a problem that plagues many settlement pattern studies, the so-called contemporaneity problem (Dewar 1991; Schacht 1981, 1984; Weiss 1977). This problem arises from treating a site that yields artifacts diagnostic of a particular period as if it were occupied throughout the entire period. So, for example, a southern Mesopotamian site with diagnostic Early Uruk (LC 2) ceramics is assumed to have been occupied for the full duration of that period and hence to be contemporary with all other sites that also contain Early Uruk (LC 2) artifacts. The result is that site distribution maps tend to be "overfilled," producing inflated estimates of numbers of sites and population.

The contemporaneity problem is most severe in situations in which archaeological periods are relatively long and where frequent population movement resulted in the abandonment of old settlements and formation of new ones (or reoccupation of previously abandoned ones) (Dewar 1991:605). Unfortunately, this describes precisely the situation for fourth millennium southern Mesopotamia. Especially with the relatively coarse resolution offered by surface collections, we are dealing with period lengths of at least 200 (Jemdet Nasr) to as much as 750 (Early/Middle Uruk [LC 2–4]) years (Wright and Rupley, this volume). The visual impression offered by the settlement pattern maps (figs. 6.3 and 6.4) also suggests strongly that fourth millennium sites were abandoned frequently and new ones founded (contra Johnson 1980a:239).

Robert Dewar (1991) has proposed a simple, yet elegant method for "correcting" conventional settlement pattern data to account for the contemporaneity problem. His method is based on a model that estimates the rates at which sites were founded and abandoned and, from these, the average number of contemporary occupations. The model works on the conservative assumption that a site with diagnostic artifacts indicating occupation during period Q was occupied only for a *portion* of period Q *unless* the site also contains diagnostics indicating occupation during preceding phase P and succeeding phase R. Put differently, it is unreasonable to assume that a site that has evidence of occupation during a particular period was *necessarily* occupied during the full length of that period.

To apply Dewar's method, one must be able to identify whether sites of the period(s) of interest were occupied in the preceding and succeeding periods and to estimate the length of the period(s) in question. The annual rate of settlement abandonment is calculated as the number of sites abandoned during a given period (those with no indications of occupation in the succeeding period) divided by the length of the period in years. The annual rate of site founding is calculated as the number of sites newly established (those with no indications of occupation in the preceding period) divided by the length of the period in years. The abandonment and founding rates serve as input data for a simulation that estimates how many sites were occupied at any one time, based on an assumption of constant rates of settlement abandonment and establishment. The method cannot, however, tell us which specific sites were occupied at the same time (Dewar 1991).[17]

Dewar's model includes at least two assumptions that are oversimplifications: that rates of settlement abandonment and founding are constant and that only those sites with evidence of occupation in the

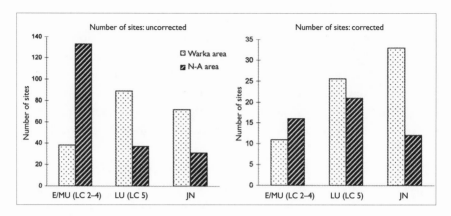

FIGURE 6.11

Numbers of sites in the Warka and Nippur-Adab areas, based on Adams's data and adjusted using Dewar's method.

preceding and succeeding period were occupied throughout the entire period in question. Nonetheless, the model offers a useful corrective for "raw" data and may at least approximate a more accurate pattern of settlement activity.

When Dewar's method is applied to the southern Mesopotamian settlement data, a number of striking and subtle differences appear, as compared with the uncorrected data. The corrected figures result in far fewer sites and hence total hectares occupied than conventional observations would suggest (figs. 6.11 and 6.12).[18] Of greater interest, however, is that patterns of growth and decline differ significantly in some cases from those that one sees using the uncorrected data. The Nippur-Adab area ceases to exhibit a decline in the Late Uruk (LC 5) period and instead appears to have witnessed modest growth, followed by a leveling off in occupied area but a marked decrease in numbers of settlements in the Jemdet Nasr period. The Uruk area exhibits a continual increase in total settled area, regardless of whether conventional or "corrected" observations are used. These figures do not show the direct reversal from earlier (LC 2–4) to later Uruk (LC 5) in population and settlement trends in the two subregions that has underpinned many interpretations of fourth millennium dynamics in southern Mesopotamia. The high levels of growth in the Uruk area nonetheless require explanation. One possibility, albeit without any direct support,

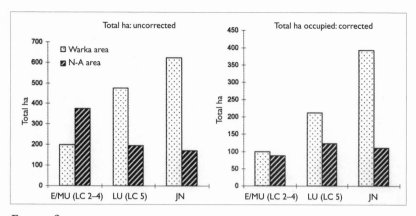

FIGURE 6.12

Total hectares of settlement in the Warka and Nippur-Adab areas, based on Adams's data and adjusted using Dewar's method.

is that the rate of biological reproduction was substantially higher there than in the Nippur-Adab area. Alternatively, people from elsewhere, including from outside the alluvial lowlands, in addition, perhaps, to modest numbers from the Nippur-Adab area, immigrated to the Warka area. A combination of these two factors—immigration and greater biological increase—might also have been responsible.

Estimated annual rates of settlement establishment and abandonment provide relative indications of volatility or stability in settlement (fig. 6.13). The absolute differences in rates between the Warka and Nippur-Adab areas are probably related to total numbers of settlements. More interesting, however, is the relationship between founding and abandonment rates within each area. Despite the major growth in settlement in the Warka area in the Late Uruk (LC 5) period, there is a precipitous rise in *both* abandonment and founding rates. Conversely, both rates drop sharply at the same time in the Nippur-Adab area. Together these figures suggest that there was far more settlement volatility—characterized by frequent establishment *and* abandonment of settlements—in the Warka area in the Late Uruk (LC 5) period than in the Nippur-Adab area.[19] The volatility in the Warka area may be a kind of intraregional "voting with the feet," a strategy to try to avoid the demands of the tax collector, albeit one that does not seem to have been very successful, as the nearest-neighbor distances suggest (table

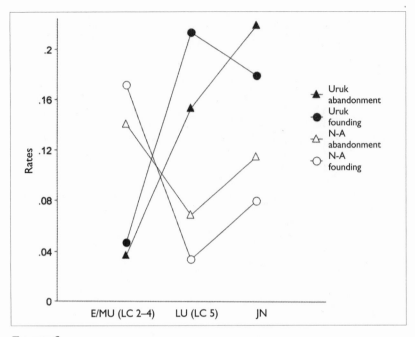

FIGURE 6.13

Annual rates of settlement abandonment and founding in the Nippur-Adab and Uruk areas.

6.3). One can argue for instability in the Warka area even if a substantial portion of the population growth was attributable to biological increase: demographic growth is not necessarily a "normal" phenomenon. Volatility remained relatively high in the Warka area during the Jemdet Nasr period, although it was substantially less than in Late Uruk (LC 5). Overall, rates of establishment and abandonment rose and fell hand-in-hand, indicating that frequent establishment of new settlements was accompanied by abandonment of old ones and vice versa. This is especially interesting in light of van de Mieroop's (1997:52–61) contention that continuity and tradition were most commonly emphasized in Mesopotamian accounts of their cities—as mound formation itself would also suggest—rather than innovation and founding of new communities.

It is also instructive to consider variations in settlement dynamics by settlement size. For this purpose, I consider medium-size and large sites together as one category ("large") and all other sites as small. Growth in the Uruk area in Late Uruk (LC 5) was high among both small and large settlements, with, however, a greater emphasis on the former (table 6.7, fig. 6.14). In the Jemdet Nasr period the increase in numbers of sites and total occupied area was due almost entirely to growth of large settlements. These observations bear out Adams's (1981:70) conclusions that rural settlement proliferated in the Warka area in the Late Uruk (LC 5) period, but that this trend began to reverse itself in the Jemdet Nasr period (compare Adams and Nissen 1972:27). In the Nippur-Adab area during the Late Uruk (LC 5) period growth occurred primarily in the rural sector, whereas in the Jemdet Nasr period larger settlements grew and smaller ones declined. If total settled area is a reasonable guide to population, there seems to have been no substantial difference between the two subregions in the proportion of the population living in large ("urban") versus small ("rural") settlements in any of the three periods (table 6.7). This conclusion contrasts with conventional interpretations that suggest that the proportion of population living in towns and cities in the Nippur-Adab area by Late Uruk (LC 5) times was substantially greater than in the Warka area (Adams 1981:75, table 4).

In summary, adjustment of settlement patterns to take into account the contemporaneity problem results in a picture of relative stability in the Nippur-Adab area during the Uruk period, especially among larger communities, in marked contrast to the more volatile situation in the Warka area. The extraordinary growth in settled population in the Warka area between earlier (LC 2–4) and later (LC 5) Uruk periods may indeed have drawn in part on people from the Nippur-Adab area. The demographic stability in the latter area hints strongly that the situation was far more complex than a simple north-to-south migration would suggest. It is also possible that some people from the Nippur-Adab area moved further to the north or east, into some of the "peripheral" areas associated with the "Uruk expansion." However, this revised evaluation of the settlement data does not bear out the contention that the Nippur-Adab area lost a substantial portion of its settled population, probably to emigration, by Late Uruk (LC 5).

CONCLUSION

Like so many others who have written about the Uruk period, I have presented in this chapter a very normative view of the "populations"

TABLE 6.7

Estimates of Numbers of Small and Large Settlements and Total Occupied Area, Based on Dewar's Method

	Warka Area				Nippur-Adab Area			
	≤ 8.0 ha		> 8.0 ha		≤ 8.0 ha		> 8.0 ha	
	No. Sites	Total Hectares	No. Sites	Total Hectares	No. Sites	Total Hectares	No. Sites	Total Hectares
Early/ Middle Uruk	9.2	17.6 [18%]	2.5	82.2 [82%]	13.1	16.6 [19%]	3.9	71.8 [81%]
Late Uruk	20.3	47.0 [22%]	5.51	64.8 [78%]	17.6	36.5 [30%]	3.5	87.1 [70%]
Jemdet Nasr	22.6	49.7 [13%]	10.4	343.6 [87%]	7.7	7.5 [7%]	5.0	103.3 [93%]

Note: Small settlements are ≤ 8 hectares in extent; large settlements are > 8 hectares. Lengths of periods are estimated as 750 years (Early/Middle Uruk [LC 2–4]), 350 years (Late Uruk [LC 5]), and 200 years (Jemdet Nasr), respectively. The simulation was run through 1,000 iterations. Figures in brackets are row percentages, showing the proportion of settlement—and, by inference, popula- tion—in the form of small and large communities.

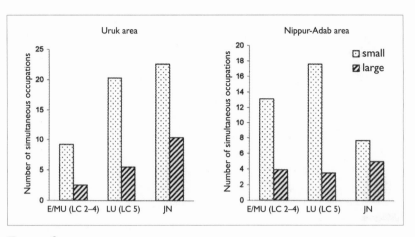

FIGURE 6.14

Estimated numbers of simultaneous occupations of small and large settlements in the Uruk and Nippur-Adab areas.

who resided in southern Mesopotamia at that time. This approach is useful only insofar as it represents a first stage in our interpretations. A normative perspective allows us to establish variables and possibilities— for example, whether communities could or could not have produced enough food to sustain themselves. Such an approach does not, however, encourage us to examine the true complexity and richness of life in the fourth millennium. To do so, we need to incorporate "insider" perspectives, which explore the varying standpoints and circumstances of different interest groups—distinguished by class, gender, age, and so forth—and their contributions and responses to the larger-scale changes with which our studies have been preoccupied. In this concluding section, I first summarize the main results of my reexamination of southern Mesopotamian political economy and then touch in a very preliminary way on some issues related to the different circumstances in which people in the Uruk period in southern Mesopotamia found themselves.

The reexamination undertaken in this chapter shows that southern Mesopotamia cannot be regarded during any part of the Uruk period as a homogenous entity, with a single overarching political, economic, or social organization. Instead, this analysis suggests—despite the numerous problems with and holes in the existing data—that there are significant, potentially far-reaching differences between the Nippur-Adab and Warka areas. If additional data were available, we might find considerable variation within these areas as well; as pointed out earlier in this chapter, they are to some extent analytical conveniences.

The Nippur-Adab area appears to have been more stable both demographically and in terms of settlement longevity than the area around Uruk-Warka. Its towns were less dependent on tribute extractions to sustain their residents, and it was characterized throughout the fourth millennium by a number of large communities. There are also fewer indications that the population was controlled by repressive means as opposed to the Warka area. In contrast, the Uruk area was highly volatile both demographically and in terms of settlement locations. This volatility may be related to the extraordinary growth of settlement in the area, to repressive measures exerted to control the population, or both. Repression is evident not only indirectly in the increasing requirements for tribute, but also in visual representations, most especially those in which a dominant figure *("Mann im Netzrock")* —generally thought to be a political leader—is portrayed supervising the killing of bound individuals. There is every reason to think that these images may be depictions of the state-directed murder of members of the local population. Finally, unlike the Nippur-Adab area, the Uruk area seems to have been dominated by a single major city, Uruk-Warka, in the earlier part of the fourth millennium. Even in Late Uruk (LC 5), when a number of other sizable towns emerged, none came close to approaching the size of Uruk-Warka itself.

In addition to these distinguishing features, evidence from both areas—albeit skewed toward the Nippur-Adab area—indicates that production of a variety of mundane goods continued to take place at most settlements. Elsewhere I have analyzed production activities in excavated buildings from several fourth millennium sites and have argued that many people in "ordinary" household contexts continued to produce a range of goods to meet their subsistence needs (Pollock 1999:100–101). At the same time, there are also indications that by Late Uruk (LC 5) hierarchically organized households had emerged that employed large, specialized workforces (Nissen 1988, this volume; Charvát 1997:7–22). The evidence for these large households comes principally from the so-called Archaic Texts and seal motifs that show repetitive, hierarchically organized labor (Pollock and Bernbeck 2000). Both the texts and the sealings bearing these motifs come principally from Uruk-Warka (and, in the case of the sealings, also from the two major towns in the Susiana Plain, Susa and Chogha Mish). Their much more limited presence in the Nippur-Adab area may indicate that these kinds of households were less common in that area.[20] Even in the Warka area, however, I see little sign that these large households dominated economically during this period to the exclusion of smaller households, presumably structured along lines of kinship. Similarly, I would argue that southern Mesopotamia, and especially the Nippur-Adab area, was not characterized by highly specialized and centrally controlled production, as argued by Nissen for the Late Uruk (LC 5) period and Wright and Johnson for the Susiana Plain by Middle Uruk (LC 3–4).

This is not to suggest that the Uruk economy was unchanged from earlier periods. Rather, I contend that there has been a tendency to overemphasize the degree and pervasiveness of economic control in the form of administration, centralization, and specialization. As I have suggested elsewhere (Pollock 1999:93–116), the weight of the available evidence points toward a complex, interdigitated economy. A similar position is taken by Frangipane (1996:198–205, this volume), who maintains that although Late Uruk (LC 5) politico-religious leaders were able to mobilize resources and exert control over some kinds of production, this did not preclude the continued importance of household production and management of labor or the relative autonomy of smaller communities in terms of subsistence production. D'Altroy (this volume) also cautions us against assuming that the emergence of states brought about a radical change in all aspects of daily life.

The significance of these conclusions extends beyond the internal organization and relationships within the south, impacting our understandings of the broader Uruk phenomenon of the later fourth millennium that has loomed so large in recent debates on the Uruk period. Many scholars are convinced that the "Uruk expansion" involved the movement of substantial numbers of people from southern Mesopotamia into "peripheral" subregions (for example, Algaze 1993a, this volume; Stein 1999). Dramatic changes in settled population in the Warka area as well as in the Susiana Plain in both the Early (LC 2) and

Late (LC 5) Uruk (Wright, this volume) make it clear that substantial movements of people were not unprecedented (see also Wright 1998:174). The critical questions are *who* moved, and *why*.[21] For those people benefiting from the increasingly stratified social, political, and economic conditions in the Warka area, there would be little incentive to leave their homes to undertake an arduous trip to a foreign land. Instead, I wish to make a case that many of the people who emigrated were probably disaffected members of lower classes who had the least to lose by abandoning their homes and moving elsewhere (see Cancian 1980:167).

Both the demographic and political economic data can be used to support the argument that if people from southern Mesopotamia moved out of the alluvial lowlands into the "peripheral" subregions of the Zagros Mountains, Upper Mesopotamian plains, or piedmont zone of southeastern Anatolia, it is more likely that they—or at least most of them—originated in the Warka rather than in the Nippur-Adab area.[22] With its substantially larger settled population, the Warka area had more people to lose; on the other hand, one could argue that the apparent lesser growth in the Nippur-Adab area is indicative of a loss of people there by Late Uruk (LC 5). More telling are the indications that the Warka area, with its greater tribute demands, more repressive conditions, and alienating new forms of socioeconomic organization (large hierarchical households), was not, for many people, a pleasant place to live. The area's far greater settlement volatility substantiates the readiness of the local population to move frequently. This volatility was due principally to the frequent establishment and abandonment of small settlements (Pollock 1999: table 3.3) that were home to rural dwellers who were subjected to heavy demands for their labor and products. The extraordinary growth of the city of Uruk-Warka from 100 hectares in the earlier Uruk (LC 2–4) to 230 hectares by Late Uruk (LC 5) argues against the idea that substantial numbers of emigrants came from there, unless there was a rapid cycling of people into and out of the city.

This scenario is similar to Johnson's (1988–89) suggestion that the people leaving southern Mesopotamia were essentially refugees.[23] The situation in the Susiana Plain seems to have been similar: the Late Uruk (LC 5) period witnessed a breakdown of earlier polities and a substantial depopulation of the plain (Johnson 1973).

Emigrants from southern Mesopotamia quite likely included peasants with a variety of skills as well as artisans of various sorts, few of whom enjoyed privileged positions in Uruk society (Nissen 1986b:329). It would have been these people who had the skills to reproduce Uruk-style material goods—whether pottery, seals, chipped stone tools, or buildings—in their new environment, not the "specialized merchant groups" who are said to have composed the trade diaspora (Stein 1999:47).

Some of the people who left southern Mesopotamia as quasi-refugees may well have taken the opportunity to engage in trade. Opportunistic participation in trading ventures is, however, very different from a scenario in which southern Mesopotamian cities—or specific groups within them—organized colonial expeditions to secure their access to trade routes or in which groups of entrepreneurs scrambled to set up outposts in critical locations in faraway places. As Schwartz observes (this volume), it may have been the very vacancy of the Euphrates Valley in Syria that was appealing to immigrants, many of whom, if my proposals have any merit, may have been more than glad to be out of reach of predatory political elites back home.

APPENDIX
SITES USED IN THE SETTLEMENT PATTERN ANALYSES IN THIS CHAPTER

Site	Region	L Ubaid	E Uruk	M Uruk	E/M Uruk	L Uruk	Jemdet Nasr
4	U	P			10.0	10.0	
6	U					0.3	
9	U					4.7	
12	U					7.8	
18	U					5.8	1.0
20	U					5.0	
22	U		2.5		2.5		
23	U		1.0		1.0		
24	U		1.0		1.0		
28	U					2.9	
34	U				4.2		
42	U	P			P	3.0	
44	U					0.8	0.8
47	U						2.0
48	U					0.5	1.0

Site	Region	L Ubaid	E Uruk	M Uruk	E/M Uruk	L Uruk	Jemdet Nasr
51	U	P				3.6	
60	U					1.8	0.5
68	U						4.0
71	U			6.7	6.7	6.7	
76	U					2.0	2.0
82	U					0.5	
86	U					4.2	1.0
87	U					7.8	7.8
91	U						2.9
95	U					0.1	0.6
101	U						19.0
102	U						6.0
103	U				1.0		
105	U					0.6	0.6
106	U					1.7	
107	U			2.6	2.6		0.1
108	U					1.0	
109	U					5.2	
110	U				P	9.0	
112	U					1.0	
114	U					2.9	2.9
115	U					1.7	
118	U		5.3		5.3		
125	U					24.0	18.0
126	U	P				4.0	
127	U					4.0	4.0
128	U					1.8	
129	U				1.0		
130	U						12.0
132	U						2.6
133	U					0.2	
137	U	P				1.5	
139	U						1.0
144	U					2.0	0.5
152	U					6.6	
153	U					2.0	2.0
156	U				0.1		
160	U	P				0.4	0.4
162	U					6.0	6.0
163	U				4.0	4.0	1.6
164	U					1.0	
166	U					4.0	4.0
168	U			5.0	5.0	5.0	

Site	Region	L Ubaid	E Uruk	M Uruk	E/M Uruk	L Uruk	Jemdet Nasr
169	U			2.0	2.0		
170	U						< 0.01
171	U				10.0		
173	U					2.6	2.6
174	U						9.0
177	U						4.6
178	U	P	0.7	0.7	0.7		0.1
179	U						3.0
181	U				5.8	5.8	5.8
185	U					4.4	
187	U					0.6	
190	U					3.0	
191	U					4.0	
193	U					3.0	
199	U						4.8
201	U		11.0	11.0	11.0	11.0	11.0
203	U					0.6	
209	U				1.0		
212	U						6.8
215	U		0.1		0.1		
218	U	P	6.5	6.5	6.5	6.5	
219	U					1.4	0.5
220	U						2.6
229	U				0.1		
230	U						53.0
232	U						7.4
233	U						13.6
234	U						4.8
236	U					4.8	
237	U				0.9	0.9	
242	U					10.0	65.0
245	U	P	6.0	6.0	6.0	6.0	17.0
256	U						1.9
258	U				0.5		
260	U					14.0	14.0
262	U						2.0
264	U				1.9	1.9	1.9
267	U					0.3	0.1
272	U					0.5	1.7
273	U						0.1
274	U					1.1	
276	U					0.5	3.0
277	U						0.6

Site	Region	L Ubaid	E Uruk	M Uruk	E/M Uruk	L Uruk	Jemdet Nasr
281	U						23.0
282	U					2.6	2.6
285	U					0.9	0.3
286	U					0.5	
288	U						6.0
289	U						0.6
292	U					1.9	1.0
293	U					1.7	1.7
297	U						1.6
309	U					0.6	
310	U					0.9	0.9
312	U						4.1
314	U					0.6	
317	U				0.1		
318	U				1.1		
325	U					0.1	
327	U						2.2
328	U						0.4
330	U				1.2		
331	U					0.9	
334	U					0.4	
338	U					2.6	
347	U						1.0
350	U					0.8	
367	U					2.0	
373	U					0.5	
376	U					4.8	
386	U				P	1.5	
387	U					1.0	
402	U				0.5		
406	U					0.8	
407	U					6.0	
409	U				0.1		
410	U				0.2		
417	U				.	0.3	
418	U					0.4	
453	U					4.9	
460	U	10.0			1.0	1.0	
462	U						2.8
539	N					2.0	
573	N	< 0.01			1.0	0.2	
574	N				1.0	1.0	

Site	Region	L Ubaid	E Uruk	M Uruk	E/M Uruk	L Uruk	Jemdet Nasr
639	N				0.1		
655	N				0.1		
662	N						0.2
667	N				0.1		
671	N				0.5		
677	N				0.3		
678	N		13.5	13.5	13.5	13.5	
680	N	P	0.1		0.1		
706	N				0.1		
711	N				0.1		
722	N				0.2		1.0
743	N		2.0		2.0		
744	N				3.6		
748	N						0.4
749	N				0.1		
765	N				5.3		
781	N				5.0		0.5
782	N				0.1		
783	N				0.1		
786	N					0.6	< 0.01
790	N			5.5	5.5	5.5	
792	N		6.8		6.8		
793	N		0.4		0.4		
802	N				0.2		
804	N		1.7		1.7		
805	N					0.5	
818	N				0.5		
821	N				0.1		
824	N				1.4		
826	N				0.5		
829	N				0.3		
831	N		5.0		5.0		
832	N		3.0		3.0		
835	N				2.9		
837	N		1.4		1.4		
838	N				0.1		
845	N		8.0		8.0		
853	N				4.0		
854	N				0.2		
912	N		3.0		3.0		
935	N		0.8		0.8		
936	N		0.2		0.2		

Site	Region	L Ubaid	E Uruk	M Uruk	E/M Uruk	L Uruk	Jemdet Nasr
939	N		2.4		2.4		
940	N				1.7	1.7	
945	N						0.1
952	N		0.2		0.2		0.2
964	N				0.7		
975	N		5.8		5.8	0.6	
976	N				0.2		
977	N		0.6		0.6	0.2	0.2
979	N						0.8
980	N				0.8		
981	N		1.5		1.5		
982	N				0.1		
1019	N		1.4		1.4		
1020	N		8.2		8.2		
1021	N				1.0		
1024	N		1.3		1.3		
1027	N				0.1		
1031	N					< 0.01	
1032	N				3.0		29.0
1034	N				2.6		
1044	N				1.0		
1046	N		8.6		8.6		
1054	N				0.1		
1059	N						3.7
1067	N				0.1		
1069	N				0.5		
1070	N				0.1		
1071	N				0.1		
1072	N		3.4	3.4	3.4	3.4	
1096	N			2.0	2.0	2.0	11.5
1100	N						1.8
1103	N				5.0		
1109	N				0.5		
1112	N				0.1		
1113	N		4.0		4.0		
1114	N				4.0		
1115	N				0.5		
1118	N		0.6		0.6		
1124	N		6.8	6.8	6.8	1.0	
1129	N		2.4	2.4	2.4	2.4	2.4
1131	N					3.0	
1135	N				0.1		
1137	N		3.8	3.8	3.8	3.8	0.1

Site	Region	L Ubaid	E Uruk	M Uruk	E/M Uruk	L Uruk	Jemdet Nasr
1152	N				0.1		
1154	N					2.6	
1159	N		4.5		4.5		
1163	N					0.9	
1164	N		1.0	1.0	1.0	0.2	
1165	N			5.3	5.3	5.3	
1166	N				10.6		10.6
1168	N						0.1
1169	N				0.5		
1170	N				0.5		
1172	N		25.5	25.5	25.5	25.5	
1174	N				0.1		
1178	N				0.1		
1180	N				0.1		
1194	N		11.5	11.5	11.5	11.5	
1195	N				0.1		
1196	N		0.5	0.5	0.5	0.5	
1197	N					1.1	0.1
1198	N		3.4		3.4		0.1
1199	N				1.0		
1205	N		7.9	7.9	7.9		2.0
1208	N				0.1		
1210	N				0.1		
1216	N				0.1	4.8	0.5
1217	N				0.1		
1230	N				0.5		
1237	N				42.0		42.0
1247	N				0.1		
1261	N					0.8	
1271	N				0.5		
1278	N				0.1		
1284	N				0.5		
1293	N					5.0	
1294	N				0.8		
1304	N				0.1		
1306	N		50.0	50.0	50.0	50.0	20.0
1312	N		0.2	0.2	0.2		
1315	N					2.8	0.5
1316	N				0.1		
1318	N				0.1		
1337	N				0.1		
1353	N			4.2	4.2	4.2	4.2
1355	N			3.0	3.0	3.0	3.0

Site	Region	L Ubaid	E Uruk	M Uruk	E/M Uruk	L Uruk	Jemdet Nasr
1356	N						0.1
1357	N					1.2	1.2
1375	N			0.2	0.2	0.2	
1383	U				1.0		
1386	U				0.1		0.5
1394	U					7.7	7.7
1416	N		0.6		0.6		
1428	N				0.5		
1432	N		1.7	1.7	1.7	1.7	
1434	N				0.1		
1437	N				0.1		
1440	N				1.0		
1443	N				0.1		
1448	N			0.9	0.9	0.9	0.9
1451	N				1.4		
1460	N				0.1		
1465	N				0.1		
1471	N				0.1		0.1
1615	U			0.6	0.6	0.6	0.2
A221	N				1.0		
A259	N				0.2		
A261	N				0.1		
A264	N				0.1		
AbS	N		X	10.0	10.0	5.5	8.0
Deheshiya	U				0.5		
Fara	U				1.0		25.0
Nippur	N	P	25.0	25.0	25.0	25.0	25.0
Raidu Sharqi	U	P			0.5		
Uruk	U	P	100.0	100.0	100.0	200.0	200.0

Source: Adams 1981.

Note: Numbers in the columns designating periods are the size of the sites in hectares.
P = occupation present but size unknown.

Notes

I would like to thank the other members of the Santa Fe conference for stimulating discussions and the staff of SAR for making the setting so congenial and productive. I also thank Reinhard Bernbeck for comments and invaluable suggestions.

1. In Iran and Iraq, fieldwork by Iranian and Iraqi archaeologists, respectively, has continued, albeit on a reduced scale. However, publications have been difficult to access in the West. This situation seems poised to change, but it will certainly be some years before substantial new data are available.

2. Some scholars have considered southwestern Iran, especially the Susiana Plain, to be closely related and in effect a part of the "core" area of Uruk development (Johnson 1973; Wright 1998:195; Wright and Johnson 1975; cf. Boehmer 1999). Others have viewed the Susiana as an early colonial venture (Algaze 1993a:11–18). My view is that the Susiana experienced parallel but by no means the same developments during the fourth millennium, that is, it formed another "core" along with the Nippur-Adab and Warka areas.

3. Distances were measured as straight lines between two points (sites).

4. Food is, of course, not the only kind of good that people need. It is, however, one of the most basic necessities, and provisioning of food thus provides a baseline measurement.

5. These estimates of distance from home to field are minimal ones, because I have measured distance from the *edge* of each settlement. Distance to fields for those who happened to live in the center of the community would have been even greater. Under certain circumstances, people may be willing—or compelled—to live farther from their fields, as seems to have occurred in Mesopotamia in the Early Dynastic period (Adams 1981:87, cf. 70; Pollock 1999:72). In such cases, however, there were probably other means of compensating for the distance that had to be traveled, such as temporary houses or encampments in fields.

6. To calculate a density for each of the artifact categories from the Uruk Mound at Abu Salabikh that would, as far as possible, be comparable to those from Adams's work, I randomly chose five sample areas from each temporal component of the site. For each artifact category I then determined the mean densities per 78.5 square meters, i.e., the area of a circle of 5-meter radius, which was Adams's (1981:45) usual collection unit. Following the same procedure for Uruk yielded extraordinarily low densities for all of the artifact types reported (clay sickles, chipped stone blades, and obsidian). I assume that collection procedures must have been sufficiently different from those used elsewhere to result in these differences, and I have therefore used only presence/absence data for Uruk. Given the large size of the site and of the collection units (10,000 square meters), it is hardly surprising that procedures were less intensive.

7. Only five of the Uruk period sites at which Adams made intensive surface

collections are from the Warka area, in contrast to 31 from the Nippur-Adab area.

8. Of the 36 sites, 25 were occupied only during the Uruk period; four others have only Uruk and Jemdet Nasr occupations, and their Jemdet Nasr sizes are often much reduced from those of their Uruk occupations. With one exception, the remaining sites were settled in Uruk, Jemdet Nasr, and Early Dynastic I times; again the sites tended to be much smaller in the later periods compared with their Uruk occupations.

9. The importance of this point for the present discussion is that finding more artifacts at larger sites *in the same size collection units* implies a higher density of those items, that is, more *per capita* than at smaller sites, *not* necessarily the presence of more people.

10. This is not surprising since, in order to make them durable tools, clay sickles were intentionally overfired.

11. Dating of the Northwest Mound at Abu Salabikh is based on my observations on the surface ceramics.

12. I refer only to the portion of the mound that was occupied during the Uruk period.

13. Contour maps were created using SURFER (Version 4, Golden Software).

14. It is, of course, possible that one or more communities in the unsurveyed areas to the north and west of the Nippur-Adab region engaged in core production for that area.

15. Future analysis will use quantitative measures to examine the extent of clustering or dispersal of artifact classes.

16. Johnson (1988–89) has attempted to show that population growth alone could have accounted for the increase in population in the Warka area in the Late Uruk (LC 5) period. Much depends, however, on estimates of "reasonable" annual population growth rates.

17. The inability to specify which sites were occupied simultaneously has repercussions for many commonly used methods for evaluating settlement pattern data, including those used in the previous sections of this chapter. In the absence of more precise chronologies that would permit us to assign sites to shorter time periods, there is no clear solution to this problem. One could, however, create "minimal" settlement pattern maps that contain only those sites that were occupied in the preceding and succeeding periods as well as in the one in question.

18. I have estimated total hectares occupied by determining the mean site size (using Adams's size estimates) of small (≤8 hectares) and larger (>8 hectares) sites for a given period and multiplying that by the estimated number of sites of each size category.

19. In evaluating relative changes in abandonment and founding rates, it is imperative to keep in mind that increases or decreases depend upon the rates calculated for the previous period. Because the identification of Ubaid settlements is especially problematic owing to heavy alluviation and frequent burial under debris from many centuries or millennia of subsequent occupation, it is quite possible that the Early/Middle Uruk (LC 2–4) rates are substantially skewed. This, in turn, would affect our perception of whether settlement abandonment and founding rates were relatively higher, lower, or similar in the Late Uruk (LC 5) period. However, if, as a hypothetical case, one assumes that 10% of the settlements in each region were occupied during the Ubaid period but not identified as such, founding rates for the earlier Uruk (LC 2–4) change, but not enough to result in a marked change in the relative founding rates for earlier (LC 2–4) and Late (LC 5) Uruk (Nippur-Adab: founding rate for earlier Uruk would be .155 as opposed to .172, Uruk region: .041 as opposed to .047).

20. The limited amount of excavation conducted at the larger settlements in the Nippur-Adab region must, of course, be borne in mind.

21. Although I do not doubt that some people from the southern lowlands moved to other regions, I remain unconvinced by many of the arguments based on material culture similarities that claim to document the presence of "ethnically" southern people in other regions. Similarities in any material culture—regardless of kind or quantity—can be attributable to a host of factors (see Wright, this volume, for some suggestions), only some of which can be convincingly ruled out with archaeological evidence.

22. For the purposes of this discussion, I leave aside the Susiana Plain (cf. Boehmer 1999; Pittman, this volume).

23. I do not think, however, that Johnson's demographic argument can be sustained, especially in light of revised figures for the growth of the city of Uruk-Warka.

7

Syria and the Uruk Expansion

Glenn M. Schwartz

This chapter reviews some of the basic issues currently under debate with respect to Syria in the fourth millennium B.C. and its involvement in the southern Mesopotamian Uruk "expansion." No effort at exhaustiveness is implied, but I attempt a consideration of some of the more conspicuous themes. Among these are the temporal and geographical distribution of the Uruk expansion, its explanation, and the circumstances of its termination. Since the first two sections of the chapter include detailed discussions of regional material culture, a brief summary of the main points is provided at the end of those sections.

My assignment to review the current data on the Uruk expansion in Syria is timely since Syria, along with Turkey, has seen a plethora of recent fieldwork, in contrast to Iraq and Iran. Not only has Syria generated an impressive body of data in recent years, it has also supplied the largest excavated samples from Mesopotamian Uruk "colony" sites, namely Habuba Kabira South, Jebel Aruda, and Sheikh Hassan in the Tabqa Dam Euphrates salvage area (fig. 7.1). As a result, I place particular emphasis on these sites and offer some remarks on their function and character.

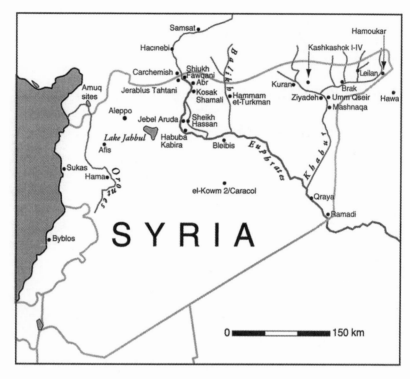

FIGURE 7.1

Map of Syria, with relevant sites indicated.

What is meant by the Uruk expansion in Syria? In the fourth millennium B.C., the material culture of numerous sites manifests, to varying degrees, stylistic traits characteristic of southern Mesopotamia in the Uruk period. In some cases, most of the material culture present is of southern Mesopotamian Uruk style, including architecture, administrative technology, and pottery. In others, southern Mesopotamia–style objects are relatively rare within an otherwise "local" assemblage. The meaning of these distributions has been debated extensively and discussed within the contexts of colonialism, informal empire, migration, and elite emulation, among others (e.g., Algaze 1989b; Johnson 1988–89; J. Oates 1993; Schwartz 1988b). Although Uruk-Warka is the best-known site from southern Mesopotamia in this period and thus gives its name both to the period and its associated artifact styles, there is no reason to assume that Uruk-Warka was the only major center of southern Mesopotamia, much less the only source of the Uruk expansion (contra Marcus 1998).

An important point to emphasize is that the Uruk expansion is not the first occasion of southern Mesopotamian material culture styles appearing in Syria (J. Oates 1993). In the fifth millennium, the pottery of Syria takes on many characteristics of the ceramics of the Ubaid period in southern Mesopotamia. As with the Uruk case, the explanation of this phenomenon has been much debated, but it is necessary to recall, in any event, that Mesopotamian "contacts" with Syria did not commence with the Uruk episode.

One further caveat: much of the Syrian evidence is derived from relatively small excavated exposures, with the exception of the Tabqa Dam sites of Habuba Kabira South, Sheikh Hassan, and Jebel Aruda as well as Hama on the Orontes. As a result, we are often dependent on results from deep soundings or step trenches of limited extent. While these excavations are restricted in terms of horizontal area, they often provide evidence of long-term occupational changes useful for diachronic analysis. Among the most important of such sequences are, in the Upper Khabur plains, Tell Brak areas TW and CH and Tell Leilan operation 1; in the Middle Khabur salvage area, the sequence from Mashnaqa still to be comprehensively published; in the Balikh Valley, the Hammam et-Turkman step trench; and in the Amuq plain, the soundings at Judeideh, Dhahab, and Chatal Hüyük.

Despite the limited nature of our sample from fourth millennium Syria, the size, character, and availability of data from southern Mesopotamia are of an even smaller scale. It is one of the ironies of this era of the world's first cities that our most extensive evidence for an Uruk Mesopotamian urban center is derived not from southern Mesopotamia itself but from colony sites like Habuba Kabira South. In southern Mesopotamia, the evidence from the site of Uruk-Warka is primarily limited to monumental architecture, and the available data from other sites derive from small samples or are poorly reported. Until further fieldwork is conducted in southern Iraq, the "tail" of the peripheries will continue to "wag the dog" of the southern Mesopotamian heartland.

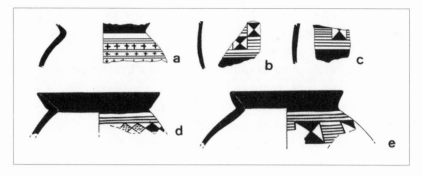

FIGURE 7.2

LC 1 black-on-red pottery: a–c, Leilan VIb; d–e, Brak area CH (Oates 1987). Scale = 1:5.

CHRONOLOGY

A tentative outline of the chronology of Post-Ubaid and fourth-millennium Syria can be attempted, but its preliminary nature must be emphasized. Especially problematic is the temporal relationship between sites with local as opposed to southern Mesopotamian material culture. Is an occupation with purely local material to be interpreted as a community existing prior to the Uruk expansion, or should it be considered contemporaneous to the expansion but without close connections to southern-influenced communities? Similarly, are occupations with local material accompanied by only a few southern ceramic types to be interpreted as contemporaneous with, but marginal to, the Uruk expansion, or should they be dated to a period before or after the full thrust of the expansion? Given recent progress in the relative chronology of local Syrian material culture, these issues have become somewhat less problematic, but further research is necessary.[1]

In the periodization suggested in this volume, the Syrian data might be organized as follows.

Late Chalcolithic 1 (Terminal Ubaid), ca. 4400–4200 B.C.

LC 1 represents the latest phase of Ubaid-related painted pottery in Syria, a period in which painted pottery is still being produced but in smaller proportions than before. Characteristic painted types are black-on-red ware (fig. 7.2) and Sprig Ware (Oates and Oates 1994:170), each with parallels to Gawra XII in northern Iraq. The period also sees the early appearance of Coba bowls—crude, incompletely oxidized, flat-based, simple-rim vessels with evidence of scraping on the lower body, first identified at Coba Höyük (Sakçe Gözü) in southeastern Anatolia.

In Syria, LC 1 material can be recognized in the Upper Khabur at Leilan (late Leilan VIB, stratum 52a pit) and in the Brak CH sounding from deposits now interpreted as unstratified leveling fill (Oates and Oates 1994:170), as well as at Hammam et-Turkman in the Balikh (period IVd). A comparable assemblage in the Middle Khabur salvage area has been reported in association with a tripartite house excavated at Mashnaqa (Beyer 1998a) and from Ziyadeh (Hole et al. 1998).

Late Chalcolithic 2, ca. 4200–3900 B.C.

The traditions characterized by painted Ubaid-style pottery in Syria disappear sometime in the later fifth millennium B.C. and are replaced by ceramic assemblages dominated by undecorated, vegetal-tempered, often incompletely oxidized vessels. Akkermans (1988a:292) has suggested that this shift represents a trend toward mass-production, with vegetal temper favored owing to the relatively short firing time and low firing temperature required.

Coba bowls are common in such LC 2 contexts as Hammam et-Turkman period VA, where they constitute 50% of the ceramic sample (fig. 7.3a–d); angle-neck jars and hole-mouth pots are also typical constituents of this assemblage. In the subsequent Hammam et-Turkman period VB, Coba bowls lose popularity and are replaced by bead-rim bowls and an increasing tendency toward the use of mineral temper. In western Syria, Coba bowls have been reported from Tell Afis southwest of Aleppo (Cecchini and Mazzoni 1998) and are said to be very common in the Qoueiq Valley survey area (Aleppo vicinity) (Mellaart 1981). An assemblage from this phase is also reported from Kosak Shamali in the Tishrin salvage subregion of the Middle Euphrates (Nishiaki et al. 2000:fig. 13).

To the east in the Upper Khabur, Brak area TW levels 18–19 (Oates and Oates 1997) are apparently datable to this phase, as are Kuran area D (Hole et al. 1991) and Leilan early Post-Ubaid strata (early V) (Schwartz 1988a). Relevant material in the Middle Khabur is attested from domestic contexts at Mashnaqa, where Coba bowls were associated with a phase subsequent to the aforementioned tripartite house, from

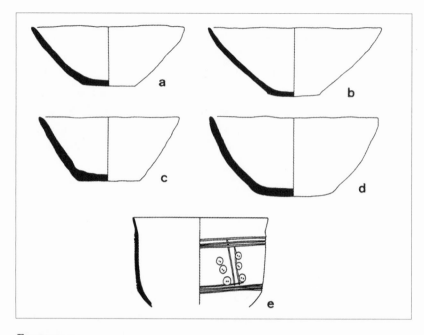

FIGURE 7.3

LC 2 pottery: a–d, Coba bowls from Hammam et-Turkman VA (Akkermans 1988a); e, fine incised-impressed vessel from Brak, area CH (Oates 1987). Scale = 1:5.

pits at Umm Qseir (Tomita 1998a), from Ziyadeh (Hole et al. 1998), and from unstratified contexts at Mulla Matar (Sürenhagen 1990).

Also diagnostic of LC 2 are ceramic types known from Tepe Gawra levels XIA–IX in northern Iraq. Gawra-style fine incised-impressed pottery (fig. 7.3e), perhaps a status marker (Lupton 1996:15), has been reported from Brak area CH (Oates 1987; Oates and Oates 1994) and other sites in the Upper Khabur such as Ailun (Moortgat 1957: fig. 11, top right) and site K-107 (Hole et al. 1990). Double-rim pots related to Gawra XIA are also attested at Umm Qseir (Tomita 1998a). Relevant radiocarbon evidence for this phase is primarily available from Hammam et-Turkman VB.

Late Chalcolithic 3, ca. 3900–3600 B.C.

In LC 3, a "chaff-faced" assemblage (Braidwood and Braidwood 1960) recognizable in a broad area extending from the Turkish Euphrates to the Upper Khabur and the Iraqi north Jazira is typified by

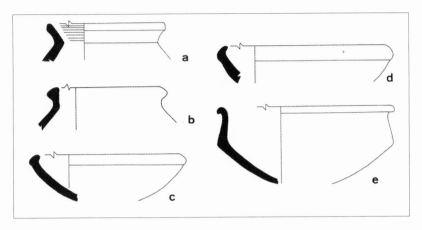

FIGURE 7.4

LC 3 chaff-faced pottery, Leilan V. Scale = 1:5.

carinated "casseroles" (fig. 7.4e) and hammerhead bowls (fig. 7.4c, d) as well as large jars with short, triangular-section rims (fig. 7.4b) and simple ware jars whose necks are corrugated on the interior (fig. 7.4a). Rather than a homogeneous tradition, the chaff-faced assemblage comprises several stylistic subgroups that may have regional or chronological significance (or both). Pollock and Coursey (1995) have recently made a pioneering effort to recognize chronological developments in this assemblage; their early types may be assigned to early LC 3 or perhaps later LC 2, while the later types may extend from LC 3 to 5.

In the Upper Khabur, this assemblage predominates in period V at Leilan (Schwartz 1988a), layer 1 at Kashkashok II (Matsutani 1991: fig. 93-4), and appears in poorly stratified circumstances at Tell Halaf and Mulla Matar. Brak area TW levels 14–17 are characterized by a chaff-faced assemblage that includes a few beveled-rim bowl fragments and other sherds of southern Mesopotamian Uruk type; it is not unlikely that Brak, with its characteristically close ties to the south, manifested southern Uruk traits earlier than other settlements in eastern Syria (for a hypothesized early appearance of beveled-rim bowls at selected sites like Brak and Nineveh, see Gut 1995:250; beveled-rim bowls are illustrated in figs. 7.5d and 7.6c).

The casserole and hammerhead bowl assemblage is distinctly underrepresented in western Syria, where other shapes predominate in

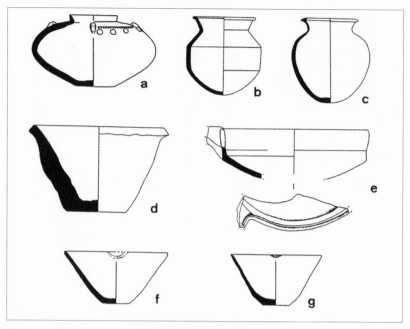

FIGURE 7.5

LC 4 southern Mesopotamian Middle Uruk pottery from Sheikh Hassan (Boese 1995). Scale = 1:5.

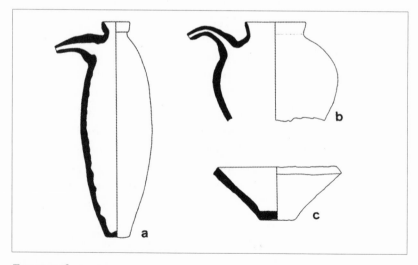

FIGURE 7.6

LC 5 southern Mesopotamian Late Uruk pottery from Habuba Kabira South (Sürenhagen 1974–75). Scale = 1:5.

chaff-faced ware. Given the presence of Mesopotamian Uruk-style beveled-rim bowls in late Amuq F contexts, it seems appropriate to assign much of Amuq F and related assemblages (e.g., Abou Danne VII, Tabara el-Akrad VI-V, Afis Late Chalcolithic post-Coba bowls) to LC 3, with possible extensions into LC 2 or 4. Three samples of carbonized grain from the Brak area TW level 16 burned building yielded mid-fourth-millennium radiocarbon dates, but their overlap with LC 4 dates requires clarification.

Late Chalcolithic 4 (Southern Middle Uruk), ca. 3600–3400 B.C.

After a period of local material culture in Syria, southern Mesopotamian–style Uruk pottery makes its first major appearance. In many cases, these ceramics are found together with local chaff-faced ware, while in others indigenous pottery is absent or rare.

An important recent development has been the recognition of a lengthy duration for the presence of Mesopotamian Uruk material culture in Syria, with two phases, Middle and Late, equivalent to LC 4 and 5, contrary to earlier assumptions of a short-lived episode restricted to some part of the Late Uruk period. The most useful Middle Uruk material has been retrieved from levels 6–13 (or, following Bachmann 1998a, levels 15/13–6/5) at Sheikh Hassan on the middle Euphrates (Boese 1995). In this assemblage, ceramic diagnostics include thin-walled conical bowls with pouring lips (fig. 7.5f, g), carinated bowls with spouted rims (fig. 7.5e), incised four-lugged squat jars with red slip and applied pellets (fig. 7.5a), and tall-necked thin-walled jars ("aryballoi") with everted ledge or bead rims, sometimes with an inner bead or ledge (fig. 7.5b, c). Examples of bowls with pouring lips have also been cited from Qraya, el-Kowm 2/Caracol, and the lowest Post-Ubaid deposit at Tell 'Abr (Tishreen Dam Euphrates subregion), and Middle Uruk ceramics have also been identified at Tell Bleibis west of Raqqa on the Euphrates, from surface finds (Finkbeiner 1995), and at Umm Qseir on the middle Khabur, from a "flood layer" (Tomita 1998a). At Brak area TW level 13, a comparable assemblage was found together with local chaff-faced pottery. Radiocarbon dates for later middle Uruk levels 6–10 at Sheikh Hassan help to estimate an absolute chronological time span for this phase (see Wright and Rupley, this volume).

Late Chalcolithic 5 (Southern Late Uruk), ca. 3400–3000 B.C.

The Late Uruk phase is well represented in the large excavated exposures from the Middle Euphrates (Tabqa) sites of Habuba Kabira-South/Tell Qannas, Jebel Aruda, and Sheikh Hassan levels 4–5 (redefined as "level 4" by Bachmann 1998a), and a comparable assemblage has been identified at Tell Brak area TW level 12. Among the southern Mesopotamian–style, Late Uruk diagnostics peculiar to this phase are tall bottles and drooping spouts (fig. 7.6a, b). Current opinion assigns the corpus to earlier in the Late Uruk period, in other words, Eanna VI–IVb; since the tablets from Habuba Kabira South and Jebel Aruda were numerical and not logographic/pictographic, a pre–Uruk IVa date appears to be appropriate. A mid- to late-fourth-millennium date is suggested by the radiocarbon evidence from Sheikh Hassan and from Habuba Kabira South (Kohlmeyer 1996).

Southern and Local Material Culture in Association (Late Chalcolithic 3–5)

Sites where both local chaff-faced pottery and southern Uruk ceramics were found in association are numerous. However, apart from Brak area TW level 13, the dating of the southern materials (i.e., Middle or Late Uruk) is usually not clarified, and a LC designation can be difficult to assign.[2] Mixed assemblages in the Khabur aside from Brak TW 13 include Brak TW 14–17 and Leilan IV (in both cases, beveled-rim bowls together with chaff-faced ware), Brak area CH 9–12 (beveled-rim bowls, flowerpots, and chaff-faced ware), Kuran area E, and perhaps Kashkashok III (Suleiman and Taraqji 1993). Uruk materials identified at Nustell in the Upper Khabur are said to be conspicuously lacking in beveled-rim bowls, but further details are not provided (Seeden 1991). At Mashnaqa, a chaff-faced assemblage associated with domestic architecture from an occupation subsequent to the Coba bowl phase (see above, LC 2) is also said to include southern Mesopotamian ceramic types (Beyer 1998a).

In western Syria, beveled-rim bowls are associated with local pottery at Hama K, but these results are compromised by stratigraphic mixing and poor control of provenience (Thuesen 1988). Beveled-rim bowl fragments were also found in the Amuq sites in late phase F, together with a local chaff-faced assemblage, and in early phase G, when chaff-faced ware was displaced by a plain simple mineral-tempered ware. Finally, mixed assemblages of Uruk and local chaff-faced LC 3–type pottery have recently been identified at Shiukh Fawqani and Kosak Shamali in the Tishrin salvage area of the Middle Euphrates (Morandi Bonacossi 1998; Nishiaki et al. 2000: fig. 14).

Post-LC Chronology

I append a discussion of the chronology of the period after the Uruk expansion to provide a framework for understanding the end of the phenomenon.

Khabur Region

In the period following the Uruk expansion, the material culture of Syria becomes regionalized and almost completely devoid of connections to contemporaneous southern Mesopotamia. The major exception to this pattern occurs at Tell Brak, area TW levels 9–11 (or 9–10), where two southern Mesopotamian–style Jemdet Nasr painted polychrome sherds were reported alongside Jemdet Nasr–type tall flowerpots and beveled-rim conical bowls (see also Schwartz 1988b:8, n. 40). Painted sherds from Umm Qseir identified as Jemdet Nasr remain to be clarified. Otherwise, there is no evidence of a southern Mesopotamian Jemdet Nasr–style material culture presence in Syria. It is likely that Brak's characteristically close ties with the south, in its role as "gateway" to the Khabur plains, are responsible for its Jemdet Nasr connections (Rova 1996:20).

The major material culture assemblage subsequent to Uruk in the Khabur Valley and northern Iraq is Ninevite V, which includes painted, incised, and plain pottery with distinctive shapes (e.g., inverted-rim cups with pointed bases, pedestal-base bowls) as well as hole-mouth cooking pots with crescentic lugs. Work remains to be done on elucidating the transition from Uruk to Ninevite V and on the internal periodization of Ninevite V. In the Eski Mosul (Saddam Dam) salvage operations on the upper Tigris in northern Iraq, a five-phase sequence has been proposed (Numoto 1991, 1993): (1) a post-Uruk "transitional" phase with a distinctive painted pottery style, followed by (2) the appearance of Ninevite V painted pottery (Numoto's "intermediate" phase), (3) painted and early incised Ninevite V, (4) early excised

Ninevite V (i.e., combinations of thick grooves and thin incisions), and (5) late incised and excised Ninevite V.

In the Khabur, the situation requires further investigation. Following the Jemdet Nasr–related strata at Brak in the area TW sequence are levels 2–8, characterized by undecorated pottery with shapes of Ninevite V character (pedestal-base bowls, carinated ribbed cups, pointed-base cups, hole-mouth cooking pots with crescent lugs) associated with grill architecture. The latest stratum, TW level 1, originally said to contain no Ninevite V pottery (Oates and Oates 1991:139), has more recently been associated with Ninevite V plain and painted ware (Oates and Oates 1993a:168). In the Leilan operation 1 step trench, the chaff-faced ware and beveled-rim bowls of period IV are succeeded by period IIIa strata including Ninevite V painted sherds and early incised varieties (Mayo and Weiss 1998; Schwartz 1988a); Leilan IIIb and IIIc include incised and painted pottery together (Schwartz 1988a), while IIId includes the Khabur variant of excised pottery, and painted ware disappears (Weiss 1989; Calderone and Weiss 1988). The period III sequence has been radiocarbon-dated to ca. 3000–2500 (Weiss et al. 1993). No transitional level showing a gradual displacement of Uruk types by Ninevite V types has been noted at Leilan, indicating a possible break in the sequence.

There is a similar absence of a gradual Uruk–Ninevite V transition in the Middle Khabur salvage area, where many sites were founded or reoccupied after the end of the Uruk period. The earliest post-Uruk levels in Middle Khabur sites are dominated by a crude handmade ware with extremely few, if any, examples of Ninevite V incised or painted pottery, although a variety of painted pottery distinct from Ninevite V is employed (Schwartz and Curvers 1992; Klengel-Brandt et al. 1997).[3] At 'Atij (Fortin 1995) and Raqa'i levels 5–7, these contexts are associated with grill architecture like that of Brak TW levels 2–8. Raqa'i 4 has incised pottery comparable to Leilan IIIb–c, and the excised pottery of Raqa'i 3 parallels Leilan IIId (Curvers and Schwartz 1990; Schwartz and Curvers 1992). In the periodizations recently suggested by Pfälzner (1997) and Lebeau (2000), Raqa'i 4–7 and Leilan IIIa–c are dated to Early Jezirah I; Raqa'i 3 and Leilan IIId date to Early Jezirah II. Given the available evidence from sequences in the Khabur and in the Upper Tigris, it appears that Ninevite V decorated pottery was first manufactured in the Tigris area and achieved popularity comparatively late in the Khabur area (Rova 1988:159).

Western Syria

As in the Khabur, the post-LC material culture of western Syria is a regional phenomenon with no significant connections to contemporaneous southern Mesopotamia. A post-LC chronology can be reconstructed from the Amuq sequence, the Middle Euphrates salvage sites, and Hammam et-Turkman, but a continuous transition is difficult to document. West of the Euphrates and in the Turkish Lower Euphrates, the earliest post-Uruk phase in this region is characterized by sinuous-sided bowls and by what Jamieson (1993) and others have termed "Late Reserved Slip Ware," a successor to Uruk Reserved Slip pottery. Amuq G, whose earliest floor at Judeideh contained a beveled-rim bowl rim, might otherwise be considered post-LC, with a Late Reserved Slip component. Late Reserved Slip seems to be absent from the Tabqa area and the Balikh.

Other common west Syrian ceramic types in the post-LC period (Curvers 1989) include hemispherical bowls with simple rims and jars with everted rims, both occasionally incised with "potter's marks" (cf. Hammam VIA, Halawa, Sweyhat), and "champagne" cups or bowls with tall pedestal bases, well-attested in graves at Carchemish. In the later phase exemplified by Amuq phase H, green, high-fired, "cyma recta" bowls with small ring bases are popular, a type found in approximately the same subregions as Late Reserved Slip. Red-Black Burnished Transcaucasian–style pottery appears in the coastal areas and the upper Orontes Valley.

Chronological Summary

The Uruk expansion in Syria is preceded by several material culture phases characterized by undecorated, often mass-produced pottery types (Late Chalcolithic 2–3). Contrary to earlier opinions, the intrusion of southern Mesopotamian Uruk material culture can be assigned to a relatively long Middle and Late Uruk period that includes much of the middle and late fourth millennium B.C. (Late Chalcolithic 4–5). Some manifestations of southern Mesopotamian Uruk material culture in Syria may predate LC 4 (see, for example, the early radiocarbon dates for the Middle Uruk assemblage at Qraya cited by Wright and Rupley, this volume). By the end of the millennium, the material culture of Syria becomes regionalized and displays few connections to southern Mesopotamia.

LATE CHALCOLITHIC SYRIA: LOCAL DEVELOPMENTS AND FOREIGN MANIFESTATIONS

Before the Uruk Expansion: Indigenous Complexity?

I next attempt to outline the current state of Syrian evidence relevant to our understanding of the Uruk expansion in Syria and the period preceding it. One of the most important recent developments has been the recognition of societal complexity *prior* to the Uruk expansion, in a pattern echoed by recent results from southeastern Anatolia (see Stein, Frangipane, this volume). While these data are still relatively minimal, they are suggestive. Particularly important is the evidence from Brak, undoubtedly one of the major communities of the Upper Khabur in this period. In the 1997 excavations, an early fourth millennium (LC 2) monumental gateway and a possible casemate enclosure wall were discovered in area TW levels 18–19 (fig. 7.7). The feature is tentatively identified as the northern gate of the community. In the succeeding period (LC 3, area TW levels 17–14), prior to major Uruk contact, Brak is thought to have achieved its maximum dimensions. According to David and Joan Oates (1997:290), the entire 43-hectare tell was occupied, in addition to a set of smaller satellite settlements, perhaps indicating an urban agglomeration of as much as 100 hectares. The earliest phases of the monumental Eye Temple are also dated to this period (Oates and Oates 1997:291; see below). In general, Oates and Oates's recent publications (1993b, 1997) emphasize the local nature of Brak's urbanization, prior to the period of southern influence.

Also dated to the fourth millennium is a pronounced upswing in the number and density of sites in Brak's hinterland, observed in the recent survey of the lower Jaghjagh drainage (Eidem and Warburton 1996). It is not yet clear, however, if this phenomenon is to be assigned to a period before the Uruk expansion or contemporaneous with it. The surrounding sites are small (5 ha maximum), implying a primate

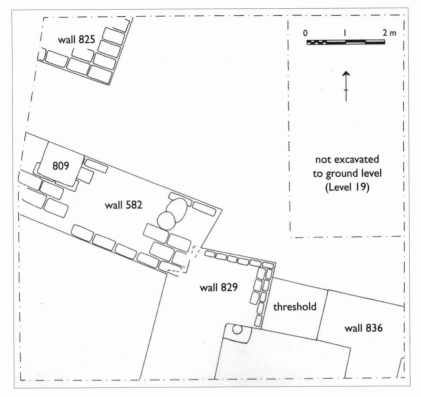

FIGURE 7.7

Tell Brak monumental gateway and associated walls, area TW levels 18–19 (Oates and Oates 1997).

system in which Brak exercised inordinate political and economic dominance over its hinterland.

Precontact urbanization is also implied by the vast extent of the site of Hamoukar (100+ ha) east of Brak near the Iraqi border, covered with local chaff-faced sherds (Oates and Oates 1991:140, n. 1; Schwartz 1994a:168, n. 19).[4] Similarly, Tell al-Hawa in the Iraqi northern Jazira southeast of Hamoukar, also with chaff-faced ware, is estimated at 33 to 50 hectares in this period (Wilkinson and Tucker 1995).

To the west, indications of large-scale or monumental public architecture have been noted at Hammam et-Turkman period VB, where a tripartite-plan monumental building with recessed buttresses and triple niches was built atop a mud brick terrace (van Loon 1988).[5]

Contact Period: Uruk Colonies

I define Uruk colonies as those sites where southern Mesopotamian material culture is predominant and manifested in a wide variety of architectural and artifactual types (see Stein, this volume). Communities fitting this description are primarily found in the Euphrates Valley, where two clusters of sites and several isolated examples can be identified. The best-known cluster is located in the Tabqa Dam (Thawra) salvage area at the great bend of the Euphrates, including Habuba Kabira South/Tell Qannas, Tell el-Hajj, Jebel Aruda, and Hadidi on the right bank and Mureybit, Sheikh Hassan, and Tannira (Boese 1995–96:171) on the left bank. Habuba Kabira South/Tell Qannas, one of the few colony sites where a large horizontal area has been excavated, had a maximum of three building levels and thus a short occupation of no more than a century or two. With a walled area of 10 hectares, an extramural mound of 8 hectares, and possible additional occupation area, the site has been identified as a large-scale, urban community of at least 18 hectares and possibly as much as 40 hectares, with a population of many thousands (Strommenger 1980; Sürenhagen 1986a). The central planning evident from the street and drainage system is particularly striking, as is the impressive fortification system with multiple walls, towers, and at least two gates (fig. 7.8). The architecture of the community, both the domestic tripartite Mittelsaal houses and the larger-scale "temples" on Qannas, reveals an emphasis on standardization (tripartite plans, southern Mesopotamian–style small *riemchen* bricks that are square in section) and labor specialization.

Jebel Aruda, on an imposing natural hill 8 kilometers north of Habuba Kabira, was a small settlement dominated by two monumental niched and buttressed tripartite buildings, the "red temple" and "gray temple," surrounded by large and well-constructed houses (fig. 7.9) (van Driel and van Driel-Murray 1983). The site has been interpreted as an administrative and religious center for the Uruk enclave. Across the river is the small (1 ha or more) site of Sheikh Hassan, notable for its long sequence of Uruk colonial occupation with domestic and specialized architecture and a city wall whose towers and niches compare to those of the Habuba fortifications (Boese 1995).

To the north, a cluster of Uruk colony sites is located in the Tishrin subregion, probably centered on Carchemish. Sites here include

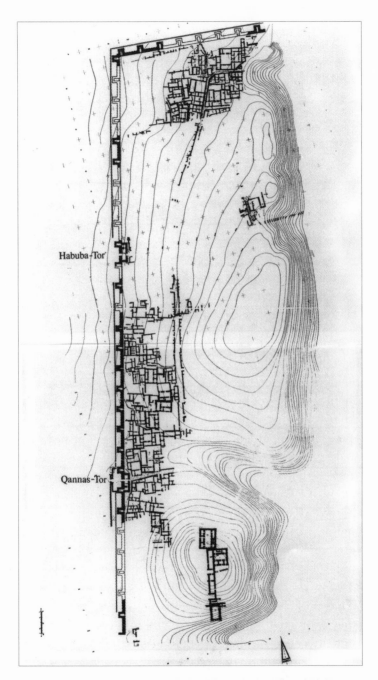

FIGURE 7.8

Habuba Kabira South/Tell Qannas (Strommenger 1980).

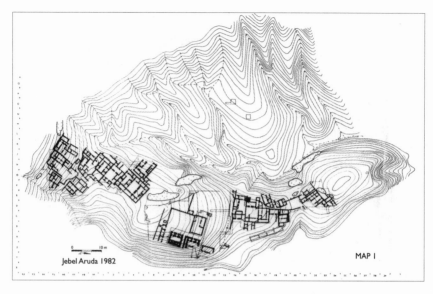

FIGURE 7.9

Jebel Aruda (van Driel and van Driel-Murray 1983).

Jerablus Tahtani (Peltenburg et al. 1995), where abundant southern Mesopotamian pottery, often containing bitumen residues, has been found in pits, and Tell 'Abr (Hammade and Yamazaki 1993), with *riemchen* architecture and Middle to Late Uruk pottery, stratified on top of an Ubaid-period tell. A third, northernmost cluster of colony sites has been suggested in the Turkish lower Euphrates Valley, in the Samsat vicinity (Algaze 1993a; but see Algaze, this volume, for a different assessment).

Two other colony sites can be noted in Syria, each in apparent isolation. Qraya, located just downstream from the Euphrates' confluence with the Khabur, included numerous pyrotechnic installations and has been interpreted as a salt-processing center (Buccellati 1990); the excavated sample was highly productive but small. El Kowm 2/Caracol in the Syrian Desert oasis of el-Kowm northeast of Palmyra evinced no significant architectural remains but yielded Uruk ceramics in pits and midden deposits. Also well attested in these deposits were numerous gazelle bones as well as domestic sheep/goat (Cauvin and Stordeur 1985). The data from this oasis outpost suggest a specialized, perhaps seasonal community concentrating on the exploitation of a single wild species.

Other colony sites may have existed in Syria, and survey results have raised possibilities yet to be corroborated. Sites with Uruk materials have been mentioned, but it is usually not clear if they are predominantly southern Mesopotamian in character (and thus "colonial") or contain a mixture of local and southern material. A survey of the Euphrates Valley between the Tabqa/Thawra Dam and Halabiya, for example, noted five small Uruk sites, but the presence or absence of local material culture was not mentioned (Finkbeiner 1995; Kohlmeyer 1984). Similarly, the west Jezirah survey between the Balikh and Euphrates reported a rarity of Uruk materials at any site except for the largest tell in the area, Tell Hajib, at which a high concentration of Uruk pottery including beveled-rim bowl fragments was found at the base of the high mound (Einwag 1993). The survey of the Balikh Valley identified three small sites with southern Uruk–type pottery (Curvers 1991), but no such material was identified on the larger tells of the area such as Hammam et-Turkman.

In the Upper Khabur, Uruk-type ceramics such as beveled-rim bowls have been noted on site surfaces (Stein and Wattenmaker 1990; Meijer 1986) but without the diversity of types that would suggest a colony (Bertille Lyonnet, CNRS, personal communication 1998; Wilkinson 1998). To the south, Uruk pottery has been identified in soundings at Ramadi near Mari in the Euphrates Valley (Geyer and Monchambert 1987; Beyer 1991–92) and on the surface of Fadgami in the lower Khabur Valley (Röllig and Kühne 1977–78:126) and Anaiat-ash-Sharqi III in the Wadi Ajij on the Syro-Iraqi border (Bernbeck 1993); not enough evidence is available to determine if these are colony sites.

Contact Period: Uruk-Related Sites

By Uruk-related, I refer to sites with significant amounts of both local and southern Mesopotamian Uruk material culture in association. Perhaps the best-documented site of this type in Syria is Tell Brak. In the area TW sequence, level 13, without significant architecture, yielded Middle Uruk pottery alongside chaff-faced local ceramics. Cylinder seal impressions from this level are among the earliest examples from stratified proveniences in the Near East (see also Sheikh Hassan level 10). Possibly contemporaneous if not slightly earlier are a group of cylinder seal impressions excavated in area HS 1, a 10-by-10-meter trench in the northwest part of the tell (Matthews 1996). Level 12 in area TW contained domestic architecture with "*riemchen*-like" bricks, abandoned with its contents in situ, including lithic manufacturing debris in a courtyard and abundant Late Uruk pottery comparable to that of Habuba Kabira South. A western extension of the TW exposure revealed more domestic architecture with pear-shaped fireplaces like those of Habuba. Oates and Oates (1997) compare the disquietingly peaceful abandonment of this occupation with that of Habuba and Jebel Aruda.

Elsewhere at Brak, area CH levels 9–12 yielded beveled-rim bowls, numerical tablets, tokens, and chaff-faced ware, but from insecure contexts. Other problematic contexts at Brak have produced painted clay wall cones, sealed bullae, and two small unbaked clay tablets with unusual pictographic symbols.

Most prominent of the Uruk-related discoveries at Brak is the sequence of Eye Temples excavated by Mallowan (1947) in the 1930s. While the Eye Temple proper (fig. 7.10), with its tripartite plan, niches and buttresses, and cone mosaic decoration, implies southern Mesopotamian influence, local or northern characteristics include the eastern wing with its narrow storage rooms and the large, central, cruciform room (cf. Ubaid Gawra, Hamrin). Below this building were three earlier constructions, the white, gray, and red Eye Temples. Thousands of the famous limestone eye plaquettes ("eye idols") were found in the gray temple layer, as well as vast quantities of "spectacle idols" (with perforations instead of engraved eyes), amulets, and beads, interpreted as votive deposits. The dating of the Eye Temples has been a persistent problem since their excavation, particularly given Mallowan's failure to publish any associated pottery. Oates and Oates (1993a) conclude that the gray temple layer is contemporaneous with area TW level 16 because of the discovery of eye idols in the latter occupation. Area TW level 16, with chaff-faced pottery, is stratigraphically prior to the large-scale appearance of southern Mesopotamian middle Uruk pottery in level 13 of the TW sequence. According to this interpretation, therefore, the earliest phases of the Eye Temple, including the eye idol phase, were constructed prior to the major onset of the Uruk expansion.[6]

In addition to Brak, other Upper Khabur sites with a mixture of

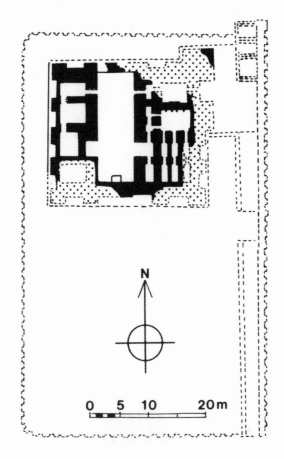

FIGURE 7.10

Tell Brak, Eye Temple (Algaze 1993a).

local and southern Uruk material culture include Kuran, Leilan, and perhaps Nustell and Kashkashok III. In the Middle Khabur, Mesopotamian-style Uruk pottery has been reported from a number of sites, but its association with or without local material culture is still to be clarified. At Mashnaqa, an "Uruk" level stratigraphically overlying domestic architecture with local chaff-faced ware contains an enigmatic circular building with regular gaps in its 3.5-meter-thick round wall and a bastionlike feature to the northwest, tentatively interpreted as a small fort (fig. 7.11) (Beyer 1998b). Uruk pottery is also reported, likewise with few details provided, from the Middle Khabur site of Bderi, from a

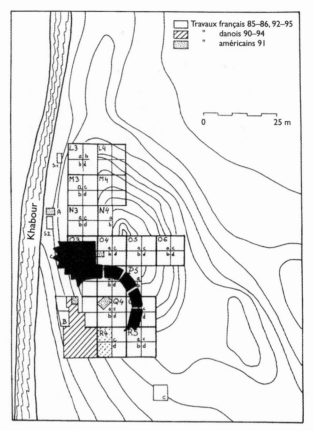

FIGURE 7.11

Tell Mashnaqa, "Uruk" circular building (Beyer 1998b).

kiln in the fields outside the tell (Pfälzner 1990), and from domestic contexts at Ziyadeh (Buccellati, Buia, and Reimer 1991), where spouted jars and conical bowls were found but no beveled-rim bowls. At Umm Qseir, two expeditions have retrieved Middle and Late Uruk pottery whose association with local material culture is ambiguous (Hole and Johnson 1986–87; Tsuneki and Miyake 1998). No architecture was recovered at this site, perhaps a seasonal encampment.[7]

To the west, mixed indigenous and Mesopotamian-style assemblages have been found at Shiukh Fawqani on the Euphrates and at Hama K and Amuq F/G.

Summary: Spatial and Functional Patterns

An important recent development is the recognition of significant societal complexity in Syria in the period prior to the Uruk expansion, indicating that the Mesopotamians encountered societies of some sophistication. Once the expansion occurs, we can observe a pronounced dichotomy in the geographical distribution of colonial and Uruk-related sites: colonial sites are located in a southern zone largely restricted to the Euphrates Valley, while Uruk-related sites are found in a northern band extending from the Upper Euphrates to the Upper Khabur and northern Iraq.[8] In western Syria, the Euphrates appears to serve as the limit of the Uruk expansion, with only occasional beveled-rim bowl sherds found at selected sites west of the river. A similar boundary may be identified in the Upper Tigris beyond the Iraqi-Turkish border (Algaze et al. 1991).

Colony sites in Syria include two clusters of settlements in the Euphrates Valley as well as isolated communities such as el-Kowm 2/Caracol, apparently exploiting specific local Syrian resources. In the case of Habuba Kabira and Jebel Aruda, at the least, the sites were founded as completely new communities on virgin soil. Their overwhelmingly southern material culture—pots, architecture, tablets, sealings, and iconography—convincingly points to the establishment and occupation of these communities by *people* from southern Mesopotamia rather than to a diffusion of ideas or objects.

Uruk-related sites with a mixture of local and southern material culture, on the other hand, are not clearly identifiable as "colonies." Brak, for example, was not founded *ex nihilo* and has numerous local as well as southern characteristics in its material culture. While Brak has been interpreted as a local center appropriated by southern colonialists (Algaze 1993a), a more persuasive interpretation might identify the site as a local center whose elites emulated the "high culture" of the southern Mesopotamians to legitimize their own status (Wattenmaker 1990). Also possible is the existence of an Uruk quarter within an otherwise local community, as proposed for Godin in Iran and Hacınebi in Turkey (see Stein, this volume). Sites like Leilan and Kuran with mixtures of local and southern material culture may be seen as local communities exposed to ideas and goods of the Southerners.

Since Middle and Late Uruk assemblages are both represented in the same subregions (e.g., Euphrates Valley, Middle Khabur, Brak), it appears at this preliminary stage that the geographical distribution of the Uruk expansion remained relatively constant throughout its history.

EXPLAINING THE URUK EXPANSION IN SYRIA

The most influential explanation of the Uruk expansion has been the core-periphery world systems model proposed by Algaze (1993a). Algaze interprets the Uruk expansion in terms of an asymmetric economic relationship between the newly emergent complex societies of southern Mesopotamia and less politically developed societies in adjacent subregions. The motivation for the enterprise is said to come from the emerging elites of southern Mesopotamia, concerned with acquiring the raw materials of Anatolia and Iran. In this model, sites with significant amounts of southern Uruk material culture are interpreted as strategically situated control points for the collection of peripheral raw materials and for the distribution of finished goods manufactured in the southern Mesopotamian core.

Problems observed with this model include: *(a)* evidence of economic and societal complexity in the periphery and thus the improbability of an asymmetric relationship between southern Mesopotamia and its neighbors (Rothman 1993; Stein, Bernbeck et al. 1996), *(b)* little evidence of peripheral raw materials in the core or of Mesopotamian finished goods in the periphery (Algaze 1989b and comments; J. Oates 1993), and *(c)* the likelihood that some sites interpreted as colonies (e.g., Brak, Nineveh) were local centers emulating southern Mesopotamian elite culture (Lupton 1996:68; Schwartz 1989; Stronach 1994; Wattenmaker 1990).

Given these issues, I would like to consider the best-known Syrian colonial enclave, that of the Tabqa/Thawra salvage area, with respect to its location and its putative function. Why was it appropriate to establish a set of urban and smaller communities with many thousands of people here?

In the models focused on long-distance exchange, the enclave is seen as a control point for the collection of peripheral raw materials. Let us first consider whether there were any raw materials in the vicinity of the enclave to justify such an imposing colonial establishment.

Although access to the salt resources of the Jabbul lake to the west has been put forward as a possible rationale for the enclave (Buccellati 1990), research in the Jabbul has revealed no evidence of any fourth millennium site with southern Mesopotamian–related material culture (Maxwell-Hyslop et al. 1942–43; Schwartz et al. 2000). Otherwise, desired raw materials in this subregion were ostensibly scarce.

If there were no resources to tap into in the immediate vicinity, then the Habuba enclave could be interpreted as a control point providing access to more distant raw materials. In one suggestion, the enclave, positioned at the juncture of the Euphrates Valley and a westward route to the Mediterranean, served as a "hinge" to the Syrian coast and, ultimately, Egypt (Forest 1996:145). A Mediterranean extension of the Uruk international enterprise has become of particular interest since the discovery of Syrian Amuq F–style pottery and Uruk-style clay cones at Buto in the Nile Delta (von der Way 1987). The presence of Mesopotamian artistic motifs and architectural elements in late Predynastic Egypt has bemused scholars for generations, not least because of the distance between the two regions. Given the discoveries at Habuba Kabira South and at Buto, a Mesopotamian-Egyptian connection has been suggested via Syria, leading from the Euphrates to the Syrian coast, with maritime travel thence to the delta (Moorey 1990). The discovery of a Nile Valley black incised ware potsherd at Habuba Kabira South (Sürenhagen 1986a) would seem to add further weight to this proposal.[9]

However, the material culture from areas west of the Habuba enclave reveals no evidence of Uruk colonial activity. Indeed, there is remarkably little Uruk-related material from western Syria.[10] No southern Mesopotamian Uruk-style pottery has been reported from any surface materials at sites in the Qoueiq drainage near Aleppo (Mellaart 1981), from sites in the Sajour survey area west of the Euphrates Valley (de Contenson 1985), or from the Jabbul plain east of Aleppo (Maxwell-Hyslop et al. 1942–43; Schwartz et al. 2000). Similarly, the soundings at Sukas on the coast (Oldenburg 1991) and at Tabara el-Akrad on the Amuq plain (Hood 1951) revealed only local-style Amuq F-G–related pottery without southern Uruk characteristics. Thus, evidence of southern Uruk material culture in Syria west of the Euphrates primarily consists of beveled-rim bowls in select sites, probably important centers with interregional contacts. As a result, it seems unlikely that the main function of the Habuba enclave was to provide a link to an important western route.[11]

If the Habuba enclave cannot be convincingly interpreted as the control point for a western route, one might suggest that it served as a node along the Euphrates route to southeastern Anatolia. However, why establish such a formidable presence in a region so far removed from the desired resources? Lupton's proposal (1996:56) that Habuba Kabira served as a gateway city between northern local polities and southern Mesopotamians fails to account for the existence of at least one if not two populous Uruk enclaves upstream.

According to Algaze, the Habuba enclave must have been established as a trading control point because the area had no other inducement for settlement: "that control of neither territory nor agricultural resources were primary factors behind Uruk emplacements in the north is underscored by the location of the Habuba/Qannas/Aruda enclave in the Tabqa, an area where average annual rainfall is at best marginal (150–250 mm) and where river incision precludes irrigation outside of the Euphrates floodplain" (Algaze 1993a:62). Given the presumed agricultural limitations of the region, both Algaze (1993a:62) and Sürenhagen (1986a) propose that the inhabitants of Habuba were dependent on local Syrian farmers for their subsistence. In support of this argument, Sürenhagen notes the pronounced absence of flint blades with sickle sheen at Jebel Aruda (Hanbury Tenison 1983), an apparent scarcity of agricultural implements and large-scale storage facilities at Habuba Kabira-South, and the discovery of several Amuq F–style chaff-faced globular jars containing grain at Habuba.

The above arguments can be refuted on a number of grounds. The paucity of agricultural implements in Habuba Kabira's excavated exposures might simply imply that much of the agricultural labor was being performed either by residents of unexcavated parts of the city or by residents of smaller communities in the enclave.[12] Similarly, one would expect Jebel Aruda, a small, specialized ridgetop site, to have been provisioned by other sites of the enclave. As for the absence of large-scale storage facilities, the same pattern may be observed at other large-scale urban exposures in Mesopotamia from later periods (e.g., Khafaje, Abu Salabikh, and Ur) without assuming long-distance transport of grain. Such facilities may not have been located in the sampled area (Algaze 1993a:133, n. 2).

Contrary to Algaze's and Sürenhagen's arguments, the unquestionably large population of the Habuba enclave need not have depended on agricultural supplies from distant sources. In the mid- to late third millennium, the same area sustained a string of urban centers along the Euphrates ranging from 15 to as much as 60 hectares in area (Hadidi, Selenkahiye, Halawa, Sweyhat, Banat, and the unexcavated Emar), as well as a profusion of smaller sites (Habuba Kabira North, Tell Qannas, Munbaqa, Tell al-'Abd). The evidence indicates local cultivation and, indeed, in the case of Sweyhat and Hadidi, a dry-farming strategy that supported the large and dense populations of the area (Wilkinson 1994; van Zeist 1994). It may be important to note, therefore, that both clusters of Uruk settlement in the Syrian Euphrates were located north of the great bend of the river near Meskene, which might have formed the southern limit of the dry-farming zone in this period (Wilkinson n.d.b).

In the second millennium, urban populations continued to prosper in this subregion, and the textual sources available from Emar, Hadidi, and Munbaqa in the Late Bronze Age reveal little concern with international exchange. While these sites, like those of the Uruk period, were well-situated with respect to long-distance trade routes, control of trade need not have served as their primary raison d'être. Important and prosperous communities throughout Syrian history tend to be located along major routes, whether or not trade was their principal concern.

Not only were the Middle Euphrates colony sites perfectly capable of sustaining themselves, there is an intriguing scarcity of "locals" who could support them agriculturally or otherwise interact with them. In contrast to the Turkish Lower Euphrates, there is almost no evidence of local material culture in the period of the Uruk expansion in the Syrian Euphrates Valley.[13] Outside the valley, the relevant surveys noted a few sites with local chaff-faced pottery to the west of the Euphrates in the Sajour and Jabbul subregions, but the number and size of these sites are decidedly small. Evidence from east of the river is even more minimal. Certainly, there is little indication of a local rural population large enough to service the urban conglomeration of Habuba!

Considering the above evidence, one might question whether the large population and multitiered settlement hierarchy of the Habuba enclave could be interpreted solely within the framework of the long-distance exchange model. It would seem unnecessary to establish such a sizable population at this location for purposes of controlling the trade route, when there were almost no locals who could pose a threat or serve a useful economic purpose. I would suggest, therefore, that it was precisely the relative "vacancy" of the subregion that attracted the Southerners. Here was an area within the rainfall agriculture zone without significant local occupation, available for exploitation and the support of a large colonial population.

If we downplay the importance of long-distance exchange, what other motivations can we suggest for the colonial enterprise here? One approach has focused on social unrest in southern Mesopotamia precipitating large-scale emigration. Johnson (1988–89), viewing the Late Uruk period as one of interstate conflict and turmoil in southern Mesopotamia, has proposed that the Syrian colonies were refugee communities of displaced elites and their dependents. A parallel process can be cited from medieval Iceland, where Norwegian chiefs and their dependents initiated settlement on the uninhabited island rather than submit to the authority of the new state forged by Harald Fairhair (Byock 1988:53–55). In a similar vein, the archaic Greek colonization has been cited as a possible analogy, in which the dispossessed peasants of an emerging complex, hierarchical society were resettled in distant subregions (Schwartz 1988b). Although the latter case was invoked as a cautionary note against an exclusive focus on long-distance exchange, it may not be out of the question to consider a model of landless peasants settled in new and virgin territories.

Another approach has been suggested by Rita Wright (1989) and Joy McCorriston (1997), focusing on the advent of specialized pastoralism. In this perspective, the shift from flax to wool production necessitated large amounts of pastureland for sheep/goat grazing, for which the unexploited zones of the northern Mesopotamian steppe may have been well-suited: "the exponentially greater amount of pasture required to produce wool as a substitute for flax may have fueled northward expansion of Uruk populations already firmly committed to wool production or heightened north-south exchange" (McCorriston

1997:534). The pronounced importance of pastoralism, as opposed to agriculture, in the urban economies of the later third millennium Middle Euphrates at sites like Sweyhat and Banat has also been hypothesized, if not yet firmly documented (Zettler et al. 1996).

Perhaps these interpretive problems can be approached more effectively by considering the temporal dimension. Well-documented Middle Uruk (LC 4) colonial settlements are small (Sheikh Hassan) or consist of neighborhoods within local communities (Hacınebi), whereas the Late Uruk (LC 5) settlement of Habuba Kabira is a large urban community of many thousands. One might hypothesize, then, that the small, earlier colonial emplacements like Hacınebi and Sheikh Hassan, both with a focus on the import of bitumen (Stein, this volume; Boese 1995–96), were established for trading purposes, whereas later large-scale colonies like Habuba served broader needs. In the case of the archaic Greek colonization, voyages to acquire exotic raw materials for emerging elites preceded and facilitated the subsequent large-scale colonial ventures (Sherratt and Sherratt 1993:362). Whichever hypothesis one might favor, it is apparent that an explanation for the function of the Habuba Kabira enclave, our best-documented example of an Uruk colonial emplacement, is far from obvious, and that variables in addition to long-distance exchange might profitably be considered.

THE END OF THE EXPANSION

The collapse of the Uruk expansion presents us with one last problem to consider. Colony sites like Habuba Kabira South, Jebel Aruda, Sheikh Hassan, Qraya, and Tell 'Abr were abandoned. While occupation continued at Uruk-related sites like Brak, Leilan, and Hama, the material culture evinces little or no continued contact with southern Mesopotamia. Why did the episode come to an end?

Several explanations have been advanced, but little substantial evidence exists to corroborate any of them. Sürenhagen (1986a) proposed that the locals became hostile to the Southerners and cut off their agricultural supplies, but the dependence of the colonists on indigenous farmers seems unlikely, as discussed above. Still, some kind of local hostility could be suggested. The town walls at Habuba and Sheikh Hassan, constructed subsequent to the initial occupations of those communities (Boese 1995:94), indicate that the colonists were afraid of something—unless these constructions were simply symbolic demarcations of urban boundaries. But who were the enemies? Indigenous groups may have posed a threat, but there is no evidence of the emergence of powerful polities or local elites taking advantage of the Uruk withdrawal in Syria (Schwartz 1994a). The colonists, perhaps associated with differing and rival political or economic entities, may well have feared one another. Similarly, problems in southern Mesopotamia resulting from "overexpansion" can be reasonably implicated (Algaze 1993a; Yoffee 1995) but remain to be well documented. Climatic desiccation has also been raised as a possible factor (Weiss et al. 1993).

Despite Syria's encounter with southern Mesopotamian civilization, not to mention intimations of local complexity in the earlier fourth millennium, complex, urban societies do not reappear in Syria for another five hundred years or more (Schwartz 1994a). This pattern furnishes an interesting contrast to the Iranian case, where Proto-Elamite civilization emerged quickly in the wake of the Uruk phenomenon. The reasons for this development remain to be convincingly elucidated and will serve as yet another important research question for future fieldwork and interpretation.

Notes

I am grateful to Mitchell Rothman for inviting me to participate in a highly stimulating seminar and to Douglas Schwartz and the School of American Research for their superb hospitality. While writing this chapter, I greatly benefited from discussions with Tony Wilkinson, Elena Rova, Thomas McClellan, Kevin Smith, Anne Porter, Jerrold Cooper, and Betsy Bryan.

1. After preparing this chapter, I received copies of the valuable contributions of Franca Trufelli (1997) and Elena Rova (n.d.) on this subject. While there are some points still to be clarified, I am in agreement with many of their conclusions. Given these efforts and those of Tomita (1998b), it would appear that a consensus on fourth-millennium Syrian chronology is beginning to emerge.

2. In southeastern Anatolia, chaff-faced casserole and hammerhead bowl assemblages have been found in association with southern Mesopotamian Middle Uruk pottery at Hacınebi (see Stein, this volume) and with Late Uruk material at Hassek (Helwing 1998).

3. Although examples of this painted tradition bear formal and stylistic resemblance to the Karababa painted ware of southeastern Anatolia (Schwartz 1985:60; Marro and Helwing 1995), the two groups are not identical. Compare, for instance, the characteristic horizontal files of painted pendant triangles in the Khabur group with the upward-pointing triangles of the Karababa tradition.

4. Excavations at Hamoukar were initiated in 1999 under the direction of MacGuire Gibson and Muhammad Maktash.

5. A massive stone enclosure wall at Tell Afis south of Aleppo in western Syria originally attributed to an early Late Chalcolithic phase with Coba bowls (Mazzoni 1994) has more recently been redated to a later fourth millennium phase contemporaneous with, if unaffected by, the Uruk expansion (Cecchini and Mazzoni 1998; Giannessi 1998).

6. However, Holly Pittman (personal communication 1998) has noted many points of similarity between the stamp seals of the gray Eye Temple layer and those of Hacınebi B2, which dates to the period of Middle Uruk contact (LC 4). The gray temple layer may therefore belong in an early period of the Uruk expansion.

7. Zeder's study of the faunal remains at Umm Qseir revealed a focus on wild species, particularly onager and gazelle, a pattern also observed for Kuran (Zeder 1998) and for el-Kowm 2/Caracol. In contrast, domestic sheep and goat were prevalent at Kashkashok II and Brak. Other evidence of Uruk material in the Middle Khabur has been cited from Sheikh Othman, a small site just east of Umm Qseir, said to have Uruk ceramics on its surface (Peter Pfälzner, personal communication 1998), and Knedig, an early third millennium occupation further downstream that yielded a unique beveled-rim bowl sherd (Wartke 1997:126).

8. Lupton (1996:66) arrives at a similar conclusion and proposes a third zone in the highlands without significant evidence of southern Mesopotamian presence.

9. An appearance of similar motifs in west Syrian cylinder seal art (albeit of questionable provenance) and in the art of Egypt and Susiana (southwestern Iran) has been interpreted along similar lines (D. Matthews 1997:58–59). It might be objected that such motifs (e.g., the griffin) need not imply connections among all three subregions, since western Syria and Egypt might have been exposed to the Uruk expansion independently. However, if the evidence of an Uruk-influenced west Syrian cylinder seal style is accepted, we might hypothesize indigenous polities west of the Euphrates acting as intermediaries between the

Uruk Mesopotamians and Egypt. In such a scenario, the Habuba enclave could be interpreted as a "gateway" between the world of the Uruk expansion and local polities to the west. But the existence of such entities remains to be convincingly documented, and we would still need to explain why an urbanized colonial enclave with a population of many thousands was required in the Habuba vicinity.

10. In the Amuq plain, a few beveled-rim bowls and sherds were found on a late period F floor at Chatal Hüyük, and one rim sherd was recovered from an early period G floor at Judeideh (Braidwood and Braidwood 1960). At Alalakh, west of Judeideh, beveled-rim bowl sherds were found in Middle Bronze Age contexts (level XIV) (Woolley 1955a:308–9). Beveled-rim bowl sherds were also found at Tell Qarqur in the Ghab depression (Dornemann 1997), inside bricks at Ebla (S. Mazzoni, personal communication 1998), and in the sequence at Hama in the upper Orontes Valley (Thuesen 1988).

11. The discovery of Syrian-style sherds in the Nile Delta need not imply that Syria was the *primary* means of connection between southern Mesopotamia (or Susiana) and Egypt. With respect to Syrian maritime connections to Egypt in this period, it should be noted that the links between Egypt and Byblos posited by Prag (1986) do not survive close scrutiny.

12. Strommenger (1980:55) makes the same suggestion and notes the occasional recovery of clay sickles and flint sickle blade fragments at Habuba Kabira South. The archaeobotanical evidence from Jerablus Tahtani near the Syro-Turkish border indicates that the inhabitants of this small Uruk colonial settlement cultivated nearby fields (Peltenburg 1999:99–100).

13. Although it is conceivable that local sites in the floodplain have been covered by alluviation or destroyed by erosion (Wilkinson n.d.a; van Loon 1967:2), it is unlikely that all such sites would disappear while so many Uruk colonial sites survived.

8

Indigenous Social Complexity at Hacınebi (Turkey) and the Organization of Uruk Colonial Contact

Gil J. Stein

> ...this is an imperialism that weakens at its periphery. At the center are hands on the levers of power, but the cables have, in a sense, been badly frayed or even cut. It is a world system in which minor agents, allies, and even subjects at the periphery often guide the course of empires.
>
> —Richard White, *The Middle Ground: Indians, Empires, and Republics in the Great Lakes Region, 1650–1815*

The impact of Mesopotamian expansion during the Middle and Late Uruk periods (ca. 3700–3100 B.C.) on neighboring societies in Iran, Syria, and Anatolia has been the subject of considerable debate (Algaze 1989b, 1993a; Rothman 1993; Schwartz 1988b; Stein 1990, 1998; Wattenmaker 1990). Only recently, however, have researchers broadened their research focus away from the Uruk colonies themselves towards an examination of the indigenous societies with whom the Mesopotamians interacted (Frangipane 1993; Stein, Bernbeck et al. 1996). It is impossible to determine the degree of Uruk influence on the development of neighboring groups without establishing a baseline for comparison. We can do so by documenting indigenous social and political organization in southeast Anatolia, north Syria, and the Iraqi Jazira in the periods before intensive contact and Mesopotamian colonization began ca. 3700 B.C. At the same time, we can best understand the Uruk expansion by studying the organization of economic and political interaction between the Mesopotamians and indigenous polities in these zones of primary contact. In this chapter I examine the

Uruk expansion by looking at the evidence from Hacınebi Tepe, on the Euphrates River trade route in southeast Turkey.

This chapter has three parts. The first section presents evidence from Hacınebi indicating that the indigenous polities of this area were already complex before the Uruk expansion, so one cannot argue that contact with Mesopotamia was the primary influence on political development in the periphery. This preexisting, indigenous social complexity in areas such as southeast Anatolia structured the political economy of interaction between the Uruk colonies and their local host polities. In the second part, I present a definition of colonies and their archaeological correlates. Using these criteria, I show that a small colony of ethnically distinct Mesopotamians was present at Hacınebi for at least two centuries but did not dominate the local Anatolian population either politically or economically. Instead, the two groups seem to have engaged in symmetric exchange. Finally, I will explore the implications of this long-term, peaceful, symmetric exchange for the overall organization of the Uruk regional interaction network. In particular, I suggest that we need to recognize the existence of tremendous internal variation in power relations between the urbanized Uruk states and neighboring subregions. Consequently, Mesopotamian political and economic influence varied depending on the power of the indigenous polities and declined with distance from the southern alluvium.

THE INDIGENOUS SOCIETIES OF SYRO-ANATOLIA BEFORE THE URUK EXPANSION

In chronological terms, the late fifth and early fourth millennia B.C. indigenous cultures in north Syria and southeast Anatolia are contemporaneous with the terminal Ubaid and Early Uruk cultures of Mesopotamia. However, in cultural terms they were distinctive local entities. The social, cultural, and political organizations of these small-scale and heterogeneous northern polities are only now being clarified through excavations (or reanalyses) of sites such as Arslantepe in the Anatolian highlands (Frangipane 1993), Brak in the north Syrian plain (Oates and Oates 1997), Gawra in the Iraqi Jazira (Rothman 1988, 1994b), and Hacınebi in the piedmont zone between them (Stein, Bernbeck et al. 1996; Stein, Edens et al. 1996; Stein et al. 1997; Stein, ed. 1999). In the absence of a better term, researchers often refer to the indigenous groups of Syro-Anatolia in the fourth millennium B.C. as the "Local Late Chalcolithic" cultures, to distinguish them from the intrusive Uruk colonies of the mid- to late fourth millennium.

Although differing from one another in terms of local ceramic and architectural styles, the Local Late Chalcolithic polities of the eastern Taurus (Arslantepe), the Taurus piedmont (Hacınebi), the Khabur headwaters in north Syria (Brak, Hamoukar), and the north Iraqi Jazira (Gawra, Hawa) seem to exhibit a number of fundamental similarities in their economic, political, and ideological systems. The highland site of Arslantepe has a crucial location close to the principal copper, lead, and silver deposits of eastern Anatolia (Frangipane and Palmieri 1987:299; Palmieri 1985:196–202; Palmieri et al. 1993). Evidence for metallurgy and ceramic mass production suggests that local highland communities had already begun to develop a fairly complex, specialized economic organization in Arslantepe period VII, before the Uruk expansion (Palmieri 1985:196). In the piedmont and steppe zones, sites such as Hacınebi, Brak, Hamoukar, and Gawra show similar evidence for social complexity in the early fourth millennium, before Uruk contact.

During the following period of strong Mesopotamian influences (VIA), Arslantepe shows signs of increasing socioeconomic complexity. Seal impression motifs reflect both local traditions and Mesopotamian iconography. Door-lock sealings reflect centralized control over storage and disbursement of commodities (Palmieri 1985:202, 1989). Overall, the evidence suggests that Arslantepe VIA had developed a highly centralized administrative system controlling metallurgy, agricultural production, and the local exchange system (Frangipane and Palmieri 1987:299). There is virtually no evidence for the physical presence of Mesopotamians at Arslantepe; it is a completely local Anatolian site under the control of the local rulers. The highland sites would thus appear to be independent complex polities that traded with the Mesopotamians (whether directly or indirectly) while remaining *outside* the zone of actual Uruk colonization. Indigenous complex polities had developed also in the piedmont and steppe zones, at sites such as Hacınebi, Brak, and Gawra (and possibly Hamoukar and Hawa, if survey-based size measurements of these latter sites are accurate).

Although these Local Late Chalcolithic societies show a high degree of variability in material culture, they appear to share several key characteristics, among them two-level site-size hierarchies, regional centers with internal functional differentiation, monumental architecture, exotic raw materials obtained through long-distance exchange, advanced copper and silver metallurgy, mortuary evidence for hereditary elites, and complex administrative systems based on stamp seals whose broadly similar wild animal motifs suggest some kind of shared elite ideology across the Syro-Anatolian borderlands. Taken together, the limited available evidence suggests that these Local Late Chalcolithic polities had independently developed complex forms of political, social, and economic organization in the early fourth millennium B.C.

Excavations at Hacınebi afford a rare opportunity to make the broad-scale horizontal exposures necessary to clarify the organization of these polities in the period prior to the onset of intensive contact with Uruk southern Mesopotamia. At the same time, the presence of an Uruk enclave in the northeast corner of the site enables us to study Mesopotamian-Anatolian interaction at the micro level. Comparison of the earlier and later phases at Hacınebi allows us to determine the degree to which the Uruk expansion affected the indigenous political and economic systems of southeast Anatolia.

Hacınebi, Turkey: Indigenous Complexity in the Early Fourth Millennium

Hacınebi Tepe is a 3.3-hectare, roughly triangular mound on the limestone bluffs overlooking the east bank of the Euphrates River, 5 kilometers north of the modern town of Birecik in Şanlıurfa province, southeast Turkey. The site lies on the main north-south river trade route linking Anatolia with Syria and Mesopotamia. Hacınebi also commands a strategic location at the midpoint of the major east-west river crossing zone that extends from Zeugma (the location of the Hellenistic bridge) in the north down to Birecik, where the ford or bridge has been in more or less continuous use from the Roman/ Byzantine periods to the present. Six seasons of excavation (1992–97) at Hacınebi have investigated the Local Late Chalcolithic (LLC) indigenous societies in southeast Anatolia and the organization of their interaction with Uruk Mesopotamia during the fourth millennium B.C. (Stein 1998; Stein and Mısır 1994, 1995, 1996; Stein,

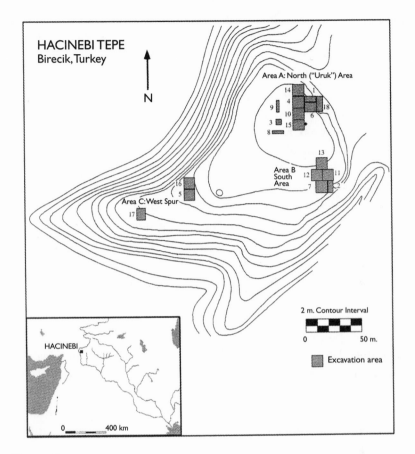

FIGURE 8.1

Site map of Hacınebi Tepe, Turkey.

Bernbeck et al. 1996; Stein, Boden et al. 1997; Stein, Edens et al. 1996, 1998). Eighteen trenches have exposed more than 1,400 square meters of Late Chalcolithic deposits in three separate excavation areas, providing a spatially representative sample of variation in architecture and activities at the site (fig. 8.1).

Three main occupations are attested at Hacınebi. Fifth- to second-century B.C. Achaemenid/Hellenistic deposits are present immediately below the plow zone and extend over the entire site. These overlie and often cut through a layer of erosional deposits that seals off two areas of Early Bronze I burials at the north and south ends of the site (Stein, Boden et al. 1997). These burials cut into a second erosion layer and the underlying Late Chalcolithic occupation, dating approximately 4100–3300 B.C., based on calibrated radiocarbon dates (Stein, Edens et al. 1996: fig. 14). Stratigraphy and associated ceramics allow us to subdivide the Late Chalcolithic occupation into an earlier phase A (equivalent to LC 2 in the chronological system of this volume), which has early forms of local Anatolian handmade, chaff-tempered ceramics, and a later phase B. Phase B1 (LC 3: ca. 3800–3700? B.C.) has late forms of local Anatolian ceramics (with beveled-rim bowls appearing at the end of the phase), while phase B2 (LC 4: ca. 3700–3300? B.C.) has both late local Anatolian and the full range of Mesopotamian Late Middle Uruk ceramics (Stein, Edens et al. 1996:96–97). Late Chalcolithic phase A marks the earliest occupation of Hacınebi and directly overlies sterile gravels or bedrock.

The Evidence for Social Complexity in Phases A and B1 (LC 2 and LC 3)

Social complexity is difficult to identify in the archaeological record for two main reasons. First, in prehistoric or nonliterate societies, the relationship between systems of meaning such as political ideologies and their material culture correlates is problematical and subject to serious interpretive ambiguities. In addition, theoretical critiques of evolutionary typologies have emphasized that the application of terms such as "chiefdom" as a unitary "type" of society can mislead researchers into lumping fundamentally different societies within a single conceptual framework that masks rather than clarifies variation (Kristiansen 1991; Yoffee 1993). Although one must always beware the perils of uncritical trait listing, there is a general consensus among archaeologists that co-occurrence of a number of locational, mortuary, architectural, and artifactual patterns provides reasonably secure evidence for the emergence of hierarchically organized complex societies that—for heuristic purposes—we can call "chiefdoms" in the broad, flexible sense that this term is now generally taken to mean (Creamer and Haas 1985; Earle 1991; Flannery 1972, 1995; Johnson 1987a; Peebles and Kus 1977; Snarskis 1987; Spencer 1987; Stein 1994b; Steponaitis 1981; Wright 1984; Wright, Miller, and Redding 1980). These lines of evidence include multilevel site-size hierarchies, differentiation in grave goods, high-status adult and/or children's burials,

architectural differentiation both within settlements and between centers and surrounding rural communities, long-term economic differentiation, concentrations of exotic and/or precious raw materials in
regional centers, high volumes of long-distance trade in prestige goods,
attached craft specialization, monumental public architecture, evidence for the centralized appropriation and storage of surpluses, and
complex administrative or decision-making hierarchies. On this basis,
locational, architectural, mortuary, administrative, and artifactual evidence argue for a relatively high degree of sociocultural complexity at
Hacınebi in the early fourth millennium phases A and B1, before the
beginnings of contact with Uruk Mesopotamia.

In this period, two-tiered settlement hierarchies of small regional
centers and dependent villages can be seen in a broad band across the
piedmont-steppe interface in southeast Anatolia, north Syria, and
northern Iraq (Lupton 1996; Whallon 1979; Wilkinson and Tucker
1995). In the Khabur headwaters subregion, survey data suggest that
some early fourth millennium indigenous centers such as Brak,
Hamoukar, and Hawa reached sizes of 12 to 33 hectares (for Hamoukar:
estimated size 12 hectares—Jason Ur, personal communication 1999;
Hawa: estimated size 33 to 50 hectares—Wilkinson and Tucker 1995:44;
for Brak site size estimates, see Schwartz, this volume). In the Euphrates
River valley, the phase A settlement at Hacınebi starts to show clear
signs of architectural differentiation and the construction of monumental stone architecture in all three main excavation areas. At the
west end of the site, a series of at least four narrow stone storerooms 7
meters long were constructed. These storerooms are associated with
evidence for metallurgy and with administrative activities. At the south
end of the site (area B), a monumental stone enclosure wall was constructed with 2-meter-wide niches and buttresses along its east face.
This 3-meter-wide wall is preserved to a height of over 3.3 meters and
extends at least 20 meters in the excavated exposures. Inside the
enclosed area, a stone and mud brick platform 3 meters high, at least 7
by 5 meters in area, was constructed (fig. 8.2). During phase B1, the
northeast end of the site was transformed into a special-purpose area
consisting of a monumental stone platform 2.8 meters high, measuring
at least 8 by 7 meters in trench exposures. A large open area was created to the east and northeast of the platform through the construction

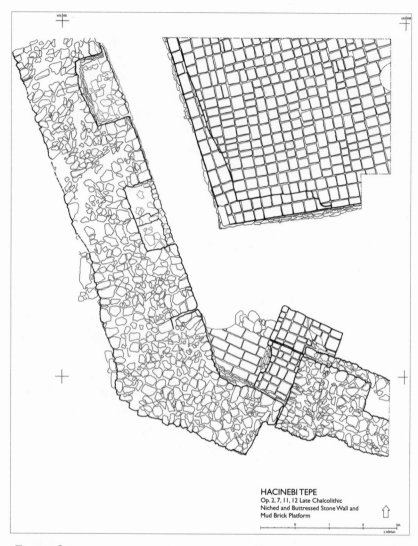

HACINEBI TEPE
Op. 2, 7, 11, 12 Late Chalcolithic
Niched and Buttressed Stone Wall and
Mud Brick Platform

FIGURE 8.2

Hacınebi Area B, enclosure wall and platform (phases A–B1).

of two massive stone terraces (fig. 8.3). The platform may have been either a ritual structure or possibly an elite residence; however, its function remains uncertain because it was remodeled and rebuilt, so that nothing remains from its original mud brick superstructure.

Mortuary practices provide additional evidence for emergent social complexity in the early fourth millennium occupation at Hacınebi.

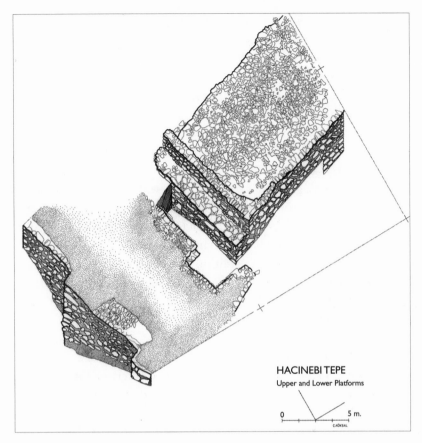

FIGURE 8.3

Hacınebi Area A, isometric projection of terrace and platform complex (phase B1).

The inhabitants of the phase A and B1 settlements continued the fifth millennium local southeast Anatolian tradition of jar burials of infants and small children. The burials are generally articulated, with no grave goods. An unusual phase A infant burial sealed beneath a room floor in operation 17 at the west end of the site provides important evidence for emerging social stratification and elite formation in the early fourth millennium. Inside the burial jar along with the skeleton were placed a miniature ceramic vessel, one copper ring, and two silver earrings as grave goods (Stein, Edens et al. 1996:96). This is significant for several reasons. First, the infant jar burials very rarely contain grave offerings of any sort. Second, the earrings are the earliest known silver artifacts from the site and would certainly be among the earliest silver pieces known from Anatolia (apparently predating the silver finds at Korucutepe by three to five hundred years—Brandt 1978; van Loon 1978:7–9; see also discussion in Prag 1978:39). The combination of silver's scarcity in general and its presence in an atypical mortuary context suggests that this was a highly valued prestige good. The deposition of the three metal rings in an infant burial provides good evidence for ascribed status—specifically the emergence of inherited elite identity in the early fourth millennium at Hacınebi.

Record-keeping artifacts such as stamp seals and seal impressions provide a third line of evidence for hierarchical administrative and social systems in phases A and B1 at Hacınebi. Stamp seals with a broadly similar repertoire of animal motifs are well known from fourth millennium Local Late Chalcolithic sites in the eastern Anatolian highlands (at sites such as Arslantepe and Değirmentepe—Esin 1990; Ferioli and Fiandra 1983; Frangipane 1993, 1994a), in the steppes of the northern Iraqi Jazira at Gawra (Rothman 1994a, 1994b; Tobler 1950), and at Hacınebi in the Taurus piedmont zone. Each stamp seal was carved with a unique design to identify its individual or institutional owner. Stamp seals in the north and cylinder seals in southern Mesopotamia served as extremely important administrative technologies that allowed individuals or centralized institutions to monitor the ownership, movement, receipt, storage, and disbursement of goods as trade items, rations, taxes, or tribute with remarkable accuracy even in the absence of a developed writing system. As such, the presence and spatial distribution of seals and seal impressions can serve as evidence for the operation of decision-making hierarchies and centralized control over economic activities (Dittmann 1986a; Ferioli and Fiandra 1983; Frangipane 1994a; Frangipane and Palmieri 1989; Johnson 1973, 1987a; Pittman 1994a; Rothman 1988; Wright and Johnson 1975; Wright, Miller, and Redding 1980; Wright, Redding, and Pollock 1989; Zettler 1987).

A number of stamp seals and seal impressions have been recovered from phases A and B1 at Hacınebi (fig. 8.4). This is not in itself conclusive evidence for complex bureaucratic systems, since stamp seals occur at Near Eastern sites as markers of personal ownership from Neolithic times onward (see, e.g., Akkermans and Duistermaat 1996). However,

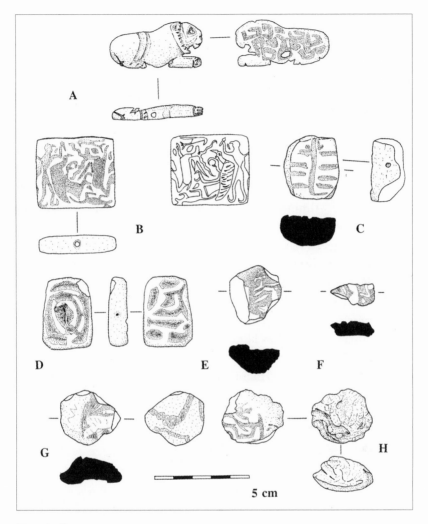

FIGURE 8.4

Hacınebi Local Late Chalcolithic stamp seals and seal impressions.

variation in seal design and the spatial distribution of the seals and sealings provide important evidence for administrative hierarchy. Hans
Nissen has argued that in late fourth millennium Mesopotamia one can
distinguish high-status individuals from lower-level temple functionaries based on the complexity and manufacturing technique of seal
designs (Nissen 1977). The early fourth millennium seals from
Hacınebi fall into two categories: baked clay or limestone seals with

crudely incised geometrical designs (Pittman 1996a) and one example of a rectangular seal carved from red siltstone bearing an elaborate design depicting deer, vultures, and a mace-carrying anthropomorphic figure (possibly a god or demon—Pittman 1998). The simple, crudely carved seals were found in domestic contexts, while the elaborate seal was recovered from a pit inside a niched, white-plastered mud brick building in area A at the north end of the site. Thus, the spatially patterned variation in seal quality and motifs is consistent with the other evidence suggesting a distinction between higher- and lower-status individuals at Hacınebi. The unbaked clay seal impressions support this interpretation. Although our evidence is still limited, the amount of variation in the design motifs on seal impressions from the north part of the site suggests that the individuals or institutions in this area were receiving goods from a variety of sources, a pattern consistent with the payment of tribute or taxes to a central authority of some sort. Taken together, the seals and seal impressions from the phase A and B1 settlement argue for the hierarchical ordering of the economic system and of individuals, and possibly larger-scale institutions.

Several independent lines of evidence indicate that the phase A and B1 settlement at Hacınebi was an active participant in long-distance exchange networks aimed at procuring exotic raw materials from the Mediterranean in the west, the Tigris-Euphrates headwaters to the north, and the Taurus piedmont to the east. Small amounts of exotic raw materials and finished items (possibly prestige goods) have been recovered from the early fourth millennium settlement. On the floor of a phase A room in the south end of the site, a small carved gray stone pendant was found, apparently made of chlorite, while a chlorite bowl fragment was found in the west area of the site. Since the nearest known chlorite sources are in the Diyarbakır area, almost 300 kilometers to the east (Philip Kohl, personal communication 1996), the Hacınebi pendant and bowl provide evidence for regional exchange of either exotic raw materials or finished prestige goods in the early fourth millennium B.C. (Stein, Edens et al. 1996:212). A second exotic raw material found in the early fourth millennium settlement is cowrie shell from the Mediterranean (170 km to the west), present in the form of three deliberately abraded shell beads. Obsidian was another import to Hacınebi. Instrumental Neutron Activation Analysis (INAA) results indicate that a surprisingly wide variety of sources was used in phases A and B1, including Nemrut and Bingöl Dağ in eastern Anatolia, Göllüdağ in central Anatolia, and the Gutansar source in Armenia just north of Yerevan (M. James Blackman, personal communication 1998).

Finally, metals—notably copper and silver—were the most important exotic raw materials obtained through long-distance exchange by the phase A and B1 inhabitants of Hacınebi. Neither metal occurs naturally anywhere near the site. We have already noted above the presence of two silver earrings in a phase A infant jar burial at the site. The most likely sources for the Hacınebi silver are either the Amanus Mountain range (the "Silver Mountain" of third-millennium Mesopotamian texts) to the west of Hacınebi on the route to the Mediterranean (Prag 1978) or (most probably) the Keban area, upstream on the Euphrates (Seeliger et al. 1985).

Copper and copper-processing artifacts are far more common than silver, occurring in phase A and B1 deposits in all three main excavation areas at the site (fig. 8.5). Not only are finished products such as small chisels, earrings, and pins present, but open-faced casting molds, crucibles, slags, a tuyere (blowpipe for copper smelting), and four actual smelting pit furnaces have been found as well, indicating that copper was brought to the site in raw form and worked locally (Özbal, Earl, and Adriaens 1998). Analyses of the phase A and B1 copper objects suggest that they were smelted from ores whose composition most closely matches the Ergani source (Özbal 1996, 1997), about 200 kilometers to the north of Hacınebi. Ergani has been one of the richest and most important copper sources in the Middle East since the Neolithic. Ores were presumably transported down the Euphrates by raft to Hacınebi for processing.

The available evidence does not permit us to determine whether the exchange system was monopolized by local elites or functioned in a more open, entrepreneurial fashion. However, the scarcity and exotic origins of the raw materials, combined with their use as ornaments, are consistent with their hypothesized social role as prestige goods materializing an elite ideology (DeMarrais, Castillo, and Earle 1996; Earle 1982). The long-distance exchange of copper, silver, marine shell, and chlorite, presumably as raw materials for prestige goods, supports the locational, architectural, administrative, and mortuary evidence for the

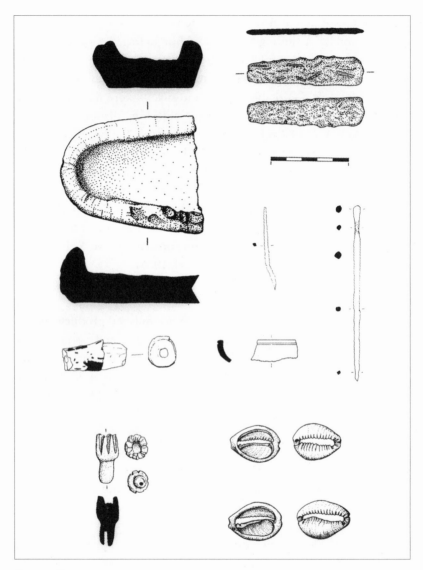

FIGURE 8.5

Hacınebi metallurgical artifacts and imported materials: oval mold fragment for open cast-ing of copper ingots, copper chisel, copper pins, tuyere (blowpipe), beaded-rim chlorite bowl fragment, blossom-shaped chlorite pendant, worked cowrie shells.

emergence of a small-scale hierarchical social system with hereditary elites in southeast Anatolia during phases A and B1 at Hacınebi.

Overview of Phases A and B1 at Hacınebi

The social, cultural, and political organizations of the phase A and B1 occupations at Hacınebi can be inferred indirectly from architectural, mortuary, administrative, and economic evidence. What we see is the regional center for a small-scale, complex polity, perhaps something we could call a simple chiefdom, with hereditary elites, a complex administrative technology, advanced metallurgy, socioeconomic differentiation, long-distance exchange of raw materials and/or prestige goods, and a craft economy that combined household production with small-scale specialization by independent producers of ceramics and copper ornaments. In general, the economy seems to have been largely geared toward local consumption (see Stein 1999:130–37), although some surplus production must have been taking place to support the limited importation of exotic raw materials for use as prestige goods legitimating the existing social hierarchy. The administrative technology of seals and sealings also suggests that the elites were mobilizing surplus subsistence or craft goods, although the scale of these exactions remains to be determined. The inferred sociopolitical organization of Hacınebi in the early fourth millennium matches the evidence from the centers of other small-scale northern polities such as Arslantepe in the Anatolian highlands (Frangipane 1993), Hamoukar and Brak in the north Syrian plain (Oates and Oates 1997), and Gawra in the Iraqi Jazira (Rothman 1988, 1993, 1994a, 1994b; Rothman and Blackman 1990). The commonalities between these polities in their administrative technology of stamp seals and the broad similarity of the wild animal motifs on the seals also suggest some kind of shared elite ideology across the Syro-Anatolian borderlands. These ideological links between different local elites were probably closely connected to the economic connections among the polities in this interaction network. The exotic raw materials at Hacınebi suggest that the major trade connections at the end of the fourth millennium were to the west, north, and east, linking the site with the other piedmont/steppe chiefdoms, rather than southward toward Mesopotamia.

Hacınebi Late Chalcolithic Phase B2

Phase B2 (LC 4 in the chronology used in this volume—ca. 3700–3300? B.C.) at Hacınebi shows complete continuity in the local material culture from the earlier phases A and B1. However, we now have the relatively sudden appearance of an Uruk Mesopotamian material culture component as a second, alien assemblage concentrated in the northeast corner of the site (although smaller amounts of Uruk material are present as well in other parts of the site). This material is both contemporaneous with and often separate from the continuing local Anatolian material culture tradition that predominates in all other excavated parts of the site. With about 1,400 square meters exposed in areas A, B, and C, phase B2 is the best-documented Late Chalcolithic occupation period at Hacınebi. Both radiocarbon dates and stylistic evidence indicate that this period of culture contact and interaction began at Hacınebi during the latter part of the Middle Uruk period (in terms of the Mesopotamian chronology; see Wright and Rupley, this volume). The Uruk material encompasses a full range of artifact categories, functions, and behavioral patterns that, taken together, provide strong evidence for the presence of a small Mesopotamian colony existing as an autonomous trade diaspora in this local Anatolian site.

COLONIES AND EMULATION AS FORMS OF INTERACTION

Colonies are a widespread cross-cultural phenomenon closely connected with the emergence of many early state societies in both the Old and New Worlds (Algaze 1993a, 1993b; Champion 1989; Dyson 1985). Archaeologically documented colonies were established by state societies such as Teotihuacan (Pool 1992; Santley, Yarborough, and Hall 1987), Oaxaca (Spence 1993, 1996), Tiwanaku (Goldstein 1993), the Inka (Pease 1982; Van Buren 1996); Uruk Mesopotamia (Sürenhagen 1986a), Egypt (W. Adams 1984), Assyria (Larsen 1976, 1987), Greece (Boardman 1980; Tsetskhladze and De Angelis 1994), the empire of Alexander the Great and his Hellenistic successors (Descoeudres 1990; Hopkins 1979; Rostovtzeff 1938), and Rome (Bartel 1989; Haselgrove 1987; Millett 1990).

A colony can be defined as an implanted settlement established by one society in either uninhabited territory or the territory of another society. The implanted settlement is established for long-term residence by all or part of the population and is both spatially and socially distinguishable from the communities of the host society. The settlement at least starts off with a distinct formal or informal corporate identity as a community with some level of cultural, economic, military, or political ties to its homeland, but the homeland need not politically dominate the implanted settlement.

Colonies can be established for a variety of purposes, many of them overlapping:

1. as military outposts connected with direct conquest—e.g., Roman provincial colonies;

2. as refuges—e.g., the Puritan Massachusetts Bay Colony;

3. as "safety valves" to resettle population or defuse social conflict—e.g., Greek colonies or Australia;

4. as outposts for the spread of a specific ideology—e.g., the Spanish missions in California;

5. as capital investments in agriculture—e.g., the early English colonies in Virginia;

6. as trade colonies—e.g., Old Assyrian colonies, Phoenician/Carthaginian colonies, Greek colonies such as Massalia, the Venetian or Genoese commercial enclaves, and the early stages of English colonialism in India.

Exchange, usually in conjunction with other purposes, is probably the single most common reason for the establishment of colonies.

Colonies are not the only form of interregional interaction. Emulation is another important way in which people, information, or physical materials can move across social boundaries. Emulation is a process of social identity negotiation in which one group attempts to raise or reinforce its own status by adopting the behavioral, material, or ideological attributes of another group of equal or higher status. Emulation can take place within a society when lower-ranked groups adopt markers of local elite status (see, e.g., Pollock 1983). Often, however, local elites in one area emulate the elites of other, higher-status polities as a way to redefine or reinforce their status relative to competitors or lower-ranked groups in their own society (e.g., Flannery 1968; Joyce 1993; Wells 1992; Winter 1977). This second form of emulation underlies prestige-goods economies but is not limited to the actual acquisition of foreign goods. Cross-cultural emulation can also occur through the copying in local media of foreign prestige markers (Marcus 1990a, 1990b; Winter 1977). Cross-cultural emulation often involves transformations of meaning, so the same item of material culture may have completely different meanings in its place of origin and in the emulating society (Rogers 1990; Sahlins 1990; Thomas 1991). Emulation is almost always selective, in the sense that some items or styles will be borrowed while others will not, depending on the degree to which they can be rationalized within the cultural system of the emulating group. For these reasons, it is important to emphasize that cross-cultural emulation cannot be taken as evidence for the control of one society over another, since ideological, political, economic, and military power do not necessarily coincide (Schortman and Urban 1994:402). The mere presence of Uruk material culture or Uruk stylistic "influences" cannot in and of themselves be used to prove Uruk control.

Archaeological evidence for cross-cultural emulation would consist of local imitations of the architecture, iconography, and material culture associated with foreign elites. As for portable items of material culture, one might find genuine imported prestige goods as well. These borrowings should be associated with the public buildings, residences, or burials of local elites. One would expect to see differences between local elites and commoners in the distribution of foreign or foreign-inspired material culture. Local elites would be expected to emulate foreign styles in those items of material culture associated with the highly visible "public" identity (e.g., architecture, personal ornamentation, clothing, or food serving and consumption), while continuing to use local styles of material culture in domestic contexts and activities (such as food preparation, child rearing, or subsistence). By contrast, commoners would be expected to retain the full range of local material culture for use in both "public" contexts and in more circumscribed social spheres. We would expect the evidence for emulation to appear gradually, selectively, and incrementally in the archaeological record.

In contrast with the archaeological signatures of emulation, one can identify colonies as those settlements whose architecture, site plan, and material culture assemblage are identical to those of another region but are located as spatially discrete occupations surrounded by settlements of the local culture. One would expect colonies to be founded as completely new settlements on previously unoccupied land. Alternatively, if founded in a preexisting settlement, a colony should show sharp architectural and artifactual discontinuities with earlier occupations. The foreign material should appear suddenly, and as a complete assemblage, rather than gradually and selectively limited to elite items. One could also imagine varying forms of contact through time in which there was first local emulation and later actual colonization, in which case the abruptness of the new assemblage in the archaeological record will be less pronounced, but still present. Artifactual similarities to the homeland should reflect a broad complex of material culture used in a variety of activities and social contexts.

In an analysis of the evidence for an intrusive Teotihuacan presence at the site of Matacapan on the Mexican gulf coast, Santley and his colleagues argue that the ethnic identity of the inhabitants in a colonial enclave should be expressed in the artifactual repertoire associated with two distinct levels of social inclusiveness—the enclave as a whole, and the more restricted domestic level (Santley, Yarborough, and Hall 1987:87). At the enclave level, the identity of the foreigners will be expressed through public rituals; these are often centered on a ceremonial structure such as a church, temple, or mosque, whose architecture generally incorporates the style or symbolic elements of the homeland. Common language, styles of dress, the wearing of particular badges or emblems, and burial customs are also enclave-wide ways to express the foreigners' separate identity. These practices are especially common because they provide highly visible identification of a person's ethnicity by others both within and outside the group (Santley et al. 1987:87).

At the domestic level, the members of a foreign colonial enclave generally live together in a contiguous area, distinct from other parts of the host community. In these households, ethnicity will be expressed principally through mortuary and culinary practices. Food preferences, preparation procedures, and the material culture associated with these practices should differ from local patterns in the host community while resembling the cultural practices of the homeland. The foreigners' distinctive ethnic identity can also often be seen in the use of raw materials or styles from the homeland (Santley et al. 1987:87–88). By virtue of its explicit focus on the ways that material culture is used differently in different social contexts, this model provides a rigorous, cross-culturally applicable set of general criteria for the identification of colonies in the archaeological record.

Uruk Colonies

In addition to the general criteria suggested by Santley and colleagues for the identification of colonies, the co-occurrence of several different forms of Uruk material culture—notably ceramics, architecture, and administrative technology—has been suggested as a way to identify Uruk colonies in specific instances, while distinguishing them from contemporaneous local settlements (Sürenhagen 1986a:9–13). Multiple criteria are necessary because ceramics alone are not a reliable indicator of ethnicity (Kramer 1977; Santley et al. 1987).

A limited range of Uruk ceramic types, notably beveled-rim bowls, occurs frequently at Late Chalcolithic sites in the central Zagros (Henrickson 1994; Weiss and Young 1975; Young 1986), north Syria (Algaze 1989b; Braidwood and Braidwood 1960; Fielden 1981; Schwartz 1988a; Wattenmaker and Stein 1989), and southeast Anatolia (Algaze 1989a; Algaze et al. 1991; Palmieri 1985; Wattenmaker and Stein 1989). At these sites, beveled-rim bowls invariably occur in association with a larger local chaff-faced ceramic assemblage, such as the characteristic "hammerhead bowls" of the Local Late Chalcolithic in southeast Anatolia and the Khabur headwaters region. By contrast, only a few sites in these areas have the *full* repertoire of Uruk ceramics such as beveled-rim bowls, bottles with droop spouts, four-handled jars, and ceramic elements such as string-cut bases, cross-hatched triangles, nose lugs, and diagonal "early" (Palmieri 1985:192) or "pseudo" (Sürenhagen 1986a:26) reserved-slip decoration. Local ceramics tend to be rare or absent from sites or parts of sites that have the full Uruk ceramic assemblage.

The sites with the full Uruk ceramic repertoire also have distinctive Uruk domestic or public/ritual architecture. The southern Mesopotamian tripartite "middle hall" house characterizes implanted Uruk settlements (Sürenhagen 1986a:10), although considerable variation exists within this overall house plan at Uruk colonies (see, e.g., Kohlmeyer 1996). Wall cone mosaic decoration is a second characteristic Uruk architectural element (Behm-Blancke 1989; Özten 1984).

Similarly, niched-façade tripartite temples are a distinctive Mesopotamian type of public building (Finet 1977; Van Driel and Van Driel-Murray 1979), although this architectural form was copied by some northern indigenous sites—e.g., at Gawra XIII and Hammam et-Turkman.

Perhaps the most important material signature of Uruk colonies is the presence of a full range of southern Mesopotamian administrative technology such as cylinder seals, hollow clay balls, bullae, tokens, and clay tablets with numerical inscriptions used to monitor the mobilization, transportation, storage, and disbursement of goods (Nissen 1985a; Schmandt-Besserat 1978, 1981; Van Driel 1982, 1983; Young 1986).

The Archaeological Evidence for an Uruk Colony at Hacinebi in Phase B2 (LC 4)

When evaluated by both the general and Uruk-specific sets of criteria for the identification of colonies, the Hacinebi data provide clear evidence for the establishment and long-term operation of a small Mesopotamian residential enclave inside the local Anatolian regional center at Hacinebi. Both Uruk and Anatolian artifacts are present in phase B2 contexts in markedly contrasting distributions. Mesopotamian artifacts are not just limited to ceramics, but rather represent the full range of Uruk material culture used in both public and domestic contexts. These different forms of Uruk material culture are found together and are spatially distinct from contemporaneous local Anatolian deposits. The south and west areas of the phase B2 settlement have predominantly Local Late Chalcolithic material culture (although Uruk materials are present in these areas as well). In contrast, the majority of the Uruk material is localized within area A. In other words, contemporaneous B2 deposits showed clear spatial differences between the distributions of local and Mesopotamian ceramics. Even when phase B2 is divided into finer stratigraphic units, distinct (and largely homogeneous) Uruk and local assemblages can be isolated as both contemporaneous and interstratified deposits.

The full range of late Middle Uruk ceramic forms and decorative techniques is present at Hacinebi (Pollock and Coursey 1996). Ceramic vessel form classes run the full gamut of functions, including food preparation (e.g., strap-handled cooking pots, ladles), serving

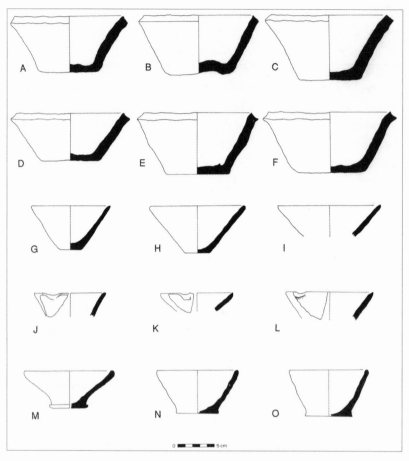

FIGURE 8.6

Hacınebi phase B2, Uruk ceramics: beveled-rim bowls, conical cups, crude conical cups.

(trays, conical cups, lip spouts, beveled-rim bowls, band-rim bowls), and storage (low expanded-band-rim jars, droop spouts) (figs. 8.6 and 8.7). Vessel forms closely match those of other Middle Uruk colonies such as Sheikh Hassan (e.g., Boese 1995:171–74, 200–201, 266–70) and sites in the southern Mesopotamian Uruk heartland (e.g., Sürenhagen 1986b). Ware types and manufacturing techniques such as the use of the fast wheel, throwing "from the hump," and string-cut bases are also identical to southern Mesopotamian practices. A few minor variations have been noted in the ways that stylistic motifs were combined on Uruk ceramics at Hacınebi; this would be consistent with the distance of Uruk potters

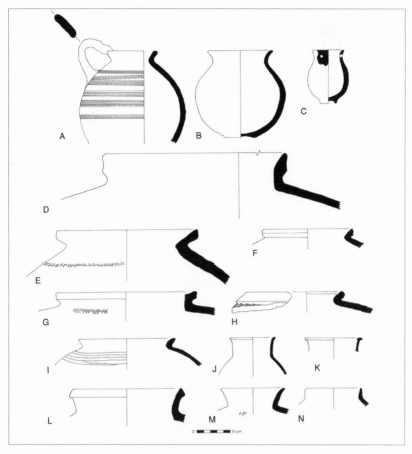

FIGURE 8.7

Hacınebi phase B2, Uruk ceramics: cooking pots with strap handles and comb-incised bands, storage jars.

at Hacınebi from their homeland 1,300 kilometers to the south. Finds of Uruk-style kiln wasters and the preliminary results of neutron activation analysis all indicate that the Uruk-style ceramics were manufactured on-site; the production of Uruk ceramics was contemporaneous with, but stylistically and technologically distinct from, the manufacture of the local Anatolian hand-built, chaff-tempered ceramic forms.

Other forms of Mesopotamian material culture occur as well. Uruk architecture is attested—albeit indirectly—at Hacınebi through the presence of ceramic wall cones, the uniquely Mesopotamian form

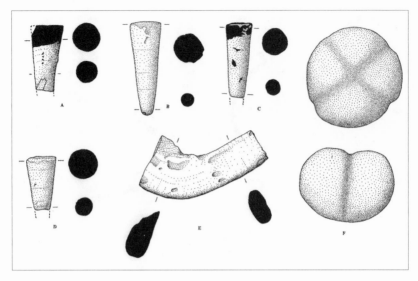

FIGURE 8.8

Hacınebi phase B2, selected items of Uruk material culture: A–D, *wall cones;* E, *baked clay sickle fragment;* F, *cruciform grooved stone weight.*

of building decoration, in secondary (trash) deposits at the site (Stein, Bernbeck et al. 1996:215–16) (fig. 8.8). Excavations in southern Mesopotamia at Uruk-Warka and at colonies such as Habuba Kabira, Jebel Aruda, and Hassek Höyük have shown that this architectural decoration was used on public buildings in the Uruk period (Behm-Blancke 1989).

An additional form of distinctively Mesopotamian material culture at Hacınebi is bitumen. Bitumen is a malleable, petroleum-based material that occurs as a tarlike substance in natural seeps. When temper is added (e.g., chaff or sand), bitumen can be used for a variety of purposes. Bitumen sources are common in southern Mesopotamia and southwestern Iran (Connan and Deschesne 1991, 1996), where in the Uruk period this material was ubiquitous as a construction material, sealant, and raw material for a variety of functional or decorative objects. Bitumen has also been identified at Uruk colonies in Syria (Boese 1995–96; Peltenburg et al. 1996). Although the local Anatolian population also imported and used small amounts of bitumen in phases A and B1, this material was obtained from non-Mesopotamian sources from the Batman area to the east and possibly from Samsat, on the Euphrates 100 kilometers upstream from Hacınebi; this latter source was well known at least as early as Classical times (Forbes 1955:3; Pliny 1931:35, 179; M. Schwartz et al. 1999) and was still mined by villagers in the area as recently as the 1970s (Necmi Yaşar, personal communication 1998). However, the volume of bitumen at Hacınebi increased markedly in phase B2, where it has been found concentrated in deposits associated with Uruk ceramics (Stein, Bernbeck et al. 1996). The bitumen in Uruk contexts at Hacınebi matches the chemical composition of the bitumen sources at Hit in southern Mesopotamia and in the Deh Luran plain (M. Schwartz et al. 1999), suggesting that this material was either a trade good imported to southeast Anatolia from Mesopotamia (or southwest Iran) or else the packaging within which some other trade good was transported.

Other distinctively Mesopotamian forms of material culture found at Hacınebi include personal ornaments, artifacts associated with commercial activities, and subsistence-related technology (fig. 8.8). A conical-headed copper pin found in Uruk deposits at Hacınebi has an exact parallel in the Uruk colony at Tell Sheikh Hassan (Boese 1995:224, pl. 10d) and at southern sites such as Telloh and Susa (Tallon 1987: numbers 934, 936, 937). Cruciform grooved stone weights, known from southern Uruk sites such as Uruk-Warka and Susa and from Uruk colonies at Habuba Kabira (Rouault and Masetti-Rouault 1993: pl. 148) and Sheikh Hassan (Boese 1995:175, pl. 13b), are also present at Hacınebi. Finally, two examples of high-fired clay sickles have been found at Hacınebi. These tools are characteristic of fourth millennium southern Mesopotamia in the Ubaid, Uruk, and Jemdet Nasr periods (Benco 1992) and are unknown in Local Late Chalcolithic settlements, where the easy availability of high-quality chert made the use of clay sickles unnecessary. The clay sickles are particularly important evidence of Uruk styles in subsistence technology at Hacınebi. This is entirely consistent with the presence of an actual Uruk working population at the site; one would not expect to find a humble item of this sort in a situation of elite emulation.

Most importantly, the north area of Hacınebi has yielded evidence for both Mesopotamian and Anatolian forms of administrative (sealing) technology. Mesopotamian record-keeping technology is easily recognizable in its use of cylinder seals as opposed to the Anatolian use of stamp seal technology. Local Anatolian-style stamp seals and seal impressions are present at Hacınebi in phases A and B1 and continue in use in phase B2. However, phase B2 deposits in the northeast area of Hacınebi have yielded an almost complete range of standard Uruk administrative artifacts, including jar sealings, jar stoppers, a hollow clay ball filled with tokens, and a fragmentary (numerical notation?) clay tablet, all bearing Uruk cylinder seal impressions and all found in association with Uruk ceramics (fig. 8.9). These record-keeping devices are common at southern Mesopotamian urban sites such as Uruk-Warka and at Uruk colonies such as Habuba Kabira, Jebel Aruda, Tell Sheikh Hassan, and Hassek Höyük (Behm-Blancke 1992b; Boese 1995; Nissen, Damerow, and Englund 1993; Sürenhagen 1986a; Van Driel 1983). Although the occasional Uruk cylinder seal impression or local imitations of Uruk cylinder seals have been found at wholly indigenous sites such as Arslantepe, the *full* assemblage of Uruk administrative technology *only* occurs in the Uruk homeland and in Uruk colonies.

Instrumental neutron activation analysis (INAA) of the sealing clays by M. James Blackman complements the glyptic studies to provide further evidence for the presence of a Mesopotamian trading enclave at Hacınebi (Blackman 1999). Blackman compared the chemical compositions of the clay artifacts bearing Anatolian stamp seal impressions with those bearing Uruk cylinder seal impressions. Two results are of particular importance. First, the Uruk-style sealings were chemically distinct from the contemporaneous Anatolian-style sealings. Second, the Uruk-style sealings could be divided into two subgroups. One consisted of sealings on local clays, indicating that the Uruk cylinder seals were being used on-site at Hacınebi. This subgroup included the cylinder seal–impressed hollow clay ball with tokens (fig. 8.9). The other subgroup consisted of Uruk-style sealings on nonlocal clays that most closely matched provenienced samples from the Susa area, one of the main urban centers in the Uruk heartland. This second subgroup included the cylinder seal–impressed tablet (fig. 8.9). These INAA results suggest the presence of two contemporaneous groups of people at the site, each using their own record-keeping system. The people using the Anatolian-style stamp seals used only local clays, presumably for local transactions (although we cannot exclude the possibility that they may also have been exporting goods from the site). The people

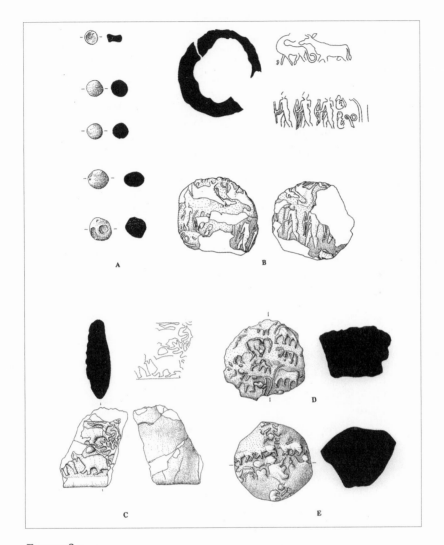

FIGURE 8.9

Hacinebi phase B2, Uruk administrative technology: A, tokens; B, hollow clay ball bearing the impressions of two cylinder seals; C, fragment of cylinder seal-impressed (numerical?) tablet; D–E, cylinder seal-impressed jar stoppers.

using the Uruk-style cylinder seals were both receiving sealed goods from southern Mesopotamia and also sealing containers and keeping records on local clays. This fits exactly with what one would expect for a trading colony that maintained close economic ties with its homeland.

291

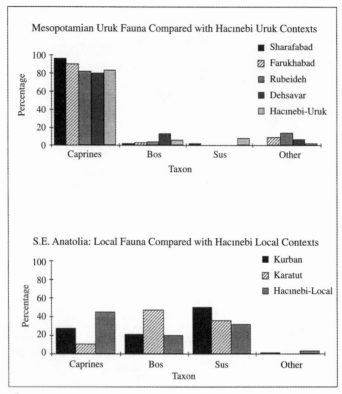

FIGURE 8.10

Hacınebi phase B2 fauna. Top: *Hacınebi Uruk contexts compared with Mesopotamian Uruk sites.* Bottom: *Hacınebi Local Late Chalcolithic contexts compared with southeast Anatolian (LLC) sites.*

Finally, behavioral patterning at Hacınebi is consistent with the artifacts in matching the expected profile of a Mesopotamian colony. Animal bone remains can provide particularly strong evidence for the presence of a Mesopotamian enclave at Hacınebi, since food preferences and food preparation procedures are often very culture-specific (Crabtree 1990; Emberling 1997). The presence of such an enclave should be reflected by clear differences in food preferences, food preparation procedures, and butchery practices. Preliminary analyses show that major differences exist in the relative frequencies of different animal species between those parts of Hacınebi with Uruk material culture and those where the local Anatolian assemblage predominates. A pilot study of the faunal remains associated with Uruk artifacts at Hacınebi showed that the relative abundance of the main taxa (sheep, goats, cattle, and pigs) closely matches known Mesopotamian food preferences and differs markedly from the animal bones associated with Anatolian contexts (fig. 8.10) (Stein and Nicola 1996). Subsequent analyses with larger samples and a more refined stratigraphic breakdown of the site sequence reinforce this conclusion. At the same time, a preliminary study of butchery patterns shows marked differences in the widths and locations of cut marks between the Uruk and local Anatolian parts of the phase B2 settlement (Stein 1997). Analyses of the Hacınebi fauna are ongoing (e.g., Bigelow 1999).

Taken together, the distinctively Mesopotamian ceramic, architectural, administrative, and other forms of material culture used in both public and domestic contexts at Hacınebi are completely consistent with both general criteria for the identification of colonies in the archaeological record and the specific complex of material characteristic of Uruk colonies and settlements in the southern Mesopotamian homeland (tables 8.1 and 8.2). Uruk ceramics in and of themselves are *not* sufficient evidence for the existence of a Mesopotamian enclave at Hacınebi. However, when we have Uruk wall cones, clay sickles, cruciform grooved stone weights, copper pin styles, administrative technology, trade goods (bitumen), and deposits of almost exclusively Uruk pottery occurring with faunal remains that exactly match Mesopotamian food preferences, then we can be fairly certain that the midden was deposited by a group of Mesopotamians living among the local people at the site. The food preferences are particularly telling because they suggest that these are actual Mesopotamians, not simply local elites who emulated southern Uruk styles of material culture. This does not mean that there was no emulation of Mesopotamians by Anatolians. On the contrary, sites such as Arslantepe suggest that at least some Anatolian elites in the major centers were emulating Mesopotamian iconography and possibly other aspects of material culture. At Hacınebi, local elites may well have been present in another part of the site, and these as-yet-unidentified elites may well have emulated certain aspects of Uruk material culture. However, the evidence from the northeast corner of Hacınebi represents actual Mesopotamians and not Anatolian imitators.

TABLE 8.1

General Criteria for the Archaeological Identification of Colonies

Criterion	Hacınebi
1. Homeland styles in public architecture	Uruk wall cone ornaments for public architecture
2. Homeland styles of	
a. dress	?
b. ornament	Uruk-style copper pin
c. burial customs	Absence of on-site adult burials in Hacınebi and Uruk Mesopotamia
3. Contiguous residence in a spatially distinct quarter	Concentration of Uruk material in northeast corner of site
4. Culinary practices distinct from local patterns while resembling the homeland's cultural practices	Differences between Uruk and local contexts in butchery and food preparation patterns
5. Use of homeland raw materials	Mesopotamian bitumen concentrated in Uruk areas; southern Mesopotamian sealing clays present

Source: Santley et al. 1987:87–88.

TABLE 8.2

Specific Criteria for the Archaeological Identification of Uruk Colonies

Criterion	Hacınebi
1. Full functional range of Uruk ceramic types	Full functional range of Uruk ceramic types
2. Uruk administrative technology of cylinder sealings, tablets, bullae, and tokens	Uruk administrative technology of cylinder seals, sealings, tablets, bullae, tokens
3. Copper production	Copper production
4. Use of clay wall cones to decorate public buildings	Clay wall cones present
5. Tripartite house with "middle hall" plan	
6. Sculpture in the round or in relief	
7. Uruk small objects	Uruk clay sickles, cruciform grooved weights, and copper pins present

Source: Sürenhagen 1986b:9–10.

The Organization of the Mesopotamian Colony in Hacınebi B2

How was this Mesopotamian colony or trade diaspora organized as an economic, social, and political entity? What was the nature of interaction between the foreigners and their indigenous host community? The most important point to emphasize is that we have absolutely no evidence for fortifications, weapons, warfare, or violent destruction in the phase B2 settlement. All indications are that the relations between the Mesopotamian trade diaspora and its local Anatolian host community were peaceful and long-lasting, for a period of at least 200, and possibly as long as 400, years (based on calibrated radiocarbon dates). A second key feature is that the Uruk colonists were a small minority at Hacınebi; the distributions of ceramics, administrative technology, and faunal remains suggest that the foreign enclave was located in the northeast corner of the site, while the local Anatolian population seems to have predominated in the other areas.

One of the most significant aspects of culture contact at Hacınebi is the evidence that the Uruk colony did not dominate the local Anatolian community either economically or politically. We can infer this from the absence of any evidence for tribute and from the fact that the Mesopotamians and Anatolians each maintained their own parallel record-keeping systems of seals and sealings (discussed below; also see Stein 1998). Comparative analyses of ceramics, chipped stone, fauna, and record-keeping (administrative) artifacts from Uruk and local contexts at Hacınebi suggest that the Mesopotamian enclave was a socially and economically autonomous diaspora whose members raised their own food, produced their own crafts, and administered their own encapsulated exchange system. The variety of artifact classes shows that the people who generated the trash in Uruk and local contexts were engaged in similar types of activities, suggesting low levels of intracommunity exchange and a high degree of socioeconomic autonomy in the Uruk enclave. This autonomy can be seen in the encapsulated nature of craft production, subsistence, and exchange-related administrative activities.

Patterns of chipped stone tool production and use suggest that the Uruk enclave at Hacınebi had been characterized by a high degree of economic autonomy in both craft production and subsistence. Uruk deposits show clear evidence for stone tool manufacturing. The frequency of secondary flakes with large areas of cortex reflects early stages in the manufacture of large "Canaanean blades" made from a distinctive medium-grained banded cream/tan chert. The presence of this raw material and of secondary flakes in Local Late Chalcolithic deposits as well suggests that blade tool manufacture took place concurrently in both Uruk and Anatolian parts of the site. Stone tool forms in the Uruk and Anatolian midden deposits suggest that occupants of both parts of the site were engaged in agricultural production (Wright and Bernbeck 1996; C. Edens 1996, 1997, 1998a, 1998b). Many of the Canaanean blades show traces of bitumen hafting in the typical locations for sickle blades. Similarly, silica gloss or "sickle sheen" is present on at least some blades from both areas. This is important because it suggests that the people who generated the midden on the Uruk side of the wall at Hacınebi were harvesting cereals. This stands in marked contrast to the near absence of sickle blades at the Uruk colony of Habuba Kabira in Syria; on this basis Dietrich Sürenhagen has suggested that the Uruk colonists were supplied with food by the local population (Sürenhagen 1986a:22).

The same forms of stone tools were produced by both the Mesopotamian and Anatolian communities, although Canaanean blades and simple blades from contexts with Mesopotamian material culture match the dimensions of these tool types in the Mesopotamian homeland while being significantly smaller than Canaanean and simple blades from Anatolian contexts (Edens 1996, 1997, 1998a, 1998b). These differences are consistent with ethnically specific contrasts in technological style (Lechtman 1977) between Mesopotamians and Anatolians at Hacınebi.

Overall, the lithic evidence suggests three conclusions. First, both Anatolians and Mesopotamians at Hacınebi had access to the same raw materials. Second, both the Uruk and Anatolian areas were independently manufacturing parallel tool forms although there may have been some ethnically distinctive differences in the technological styles they used to make particular blade types. Finally, both the Uruk and local areas were engaged in agricultural production and had some kind of regularized access to agricultural land.

Other craft activities were also practiced in parallel by the Uruk and Mesopotamian communities. Ceramic spindle whorls are present in both areas, suggesting that both groups were weaving their own textiles. Spindle whorls show no stylistic differences between Uruk and local contexts (Keith 1997). Similarly, finds of Uruk-style kiln wasters indicate that the foreign enclave was manufacturing its own pottery, following southern Mesopotamian technological practices and stylistic conventions. Copper manufacturing debris such as open-faced casting molds and crucible fragments have been found in both Uruk and Anatolian parts of the site. Most remarkably, a fragment of unprocessed raw malachite (a form of copper ore) was found adhering to the wall of a typical Uruk beveled-rim bowl. One intriguing suggestion is that the bowl was being used as a measuring scoop for the malachite ore (Özbal 1997). The presence of raw materials and manufacturing debris suggests that the Mesopotamians were directly engaged in copper working, perhaps in addition to obtaining finished copper ingots or objects from local trading partners. Thus, basic craft goods such as stone tools, ceramics, metals, and textiles were all produced in parallel by the Uruk and Anatolian communities.

The Uruk administrative technology coexists with, but is separate from, the local stamp seals and sealings. Unused sealing clays are found in both Uruk and local contexts, confirming that each group monitored the movement of commodities. The two sealing systems differ in technology, iconography, function, and pathways of economic circulation. The Mesopotamian record-keeping system used cylinder seals, which were rolled over the wet clay sealing medium to produce a long, narrow, continuous band of repeating images. Mesopotamian motifs stressed animal processions or work scenes depicting laborers engaged in agricultural or craft production. Uruk cylinder seals were impressed on hollow clay balls or bullae, on tablets, on mushroom-shaped clay jar stoppers, and most frequently on clay sealings affixed to the rim or exterior of ceramic vessels.

By contrast, the Anatolian system consisted of rectangular or round stamp seals, which created a single image each time the seal was pressed into the wet clay lumps affixed to the container closures. Phase B2 Anatolian seals almost always depicted lions and caprids in chase or hunt scenes (Pittman 1996b). The two systems were used for completely different functions. Anatolian stamp seal impressions at Hacınebi are found on sealings affixed to wooden boxes, packets of reed matting, leather bags, and cloth sacks; they never appear on ceramic vessels, tablets, jar stoppers, or bullae. Most telling of all, a comparison of the administrative artifacts with the distribution of other classes of material culture shows very low levels of interaction between the Uruk and local spheres of exchange. This is important, because if Anatolians were delivering supplies as trade goods or tribute to the Mesopotamians, then we would have expected to see the discarded local stamp sealings in Uruk Mesopotamian contexts. This is not the case. Instead, Uruk-style cylinder-sealed record-keeping artifacts occur exclusively with Uruk-style ceramics, while local-style stamp-sealed administrative artifacts are found almost always with local Anatolian ceramics. The few cases of Anatolian sealings in Uruk deposits are important because they confirm the contemporaneity of the two record-keeping systems while emphasizing that they were used to seal different goods that moved in separate economic spheres. The distribution of sealings suggests the operation of two autonomous, minimally interacting systems monitoring separate sets of economic transactions, rather than the kinds of commodity flows to be expected if the Uruk colony were exercising political or economic dominance over its Anatolian host community.

Analysis of faunal body part representation was used to determine whether the people in the Uruk enclave were being provided with meat by the local population. Generally, when a sheep or goat is butchered, elements with little meat value such as the head and foot bones are removed and discarded. By contrast, the body parts with the most meat on them, the forelimb and hind limb, are retained. If the people in the Uruk enclave were being provisioned with meat by their host community, then we would expect to see high proportions of limb bones in Uruk deposits, but few head or foot bones. However, since all of the main body parts are present, and there is no clear predominance of the meat-rich limb bones, the available evidence suggests that the people in both the Uruk and local contexts were raising and butchering their own animals.

Overview of Mesopotamian-Anatolian Interaction at Hacınebi

Excavations and artifact analyses thus indicate five important aspects of relations between the Uruk colony and its local host community at Hacınebi. First, the colonists were a small minority. Second, interaction between the Mesopotamians and the Anatolians was peaceful. Third, the colonists did not dominate the locals either economically or politically. Fourth, the colonists and the locals seem to have been members of economically autonomous, self-sufficient, encapsulated communities. Finally, calibrated radiocarbon dates and ceramic styles suggest that the colonists were present and retained a distinct foreign social identity at Hacınebi during the Middle Uruk and the first part of the Late Uruk periods, a time span from ca. 3700 to as late as 3300 B.C.—in other words, for up to 400 years. The economic evidence suggests that the Mesopotamians were engaged in the working of copper obtained through exchange—most likely with the local inhabitants at Hacınebi, but possibly with traders from the upstream source areas. Presumably, the colony had been established in order to tap into the preexisting southeast Anatolian copper exchange network and to extend it southward to Mesopotamia. The Mesopotamian enclave was economically autonomous in the sense that it produced its own crops, pastoral products, and crafts. The Mesopotamians appear to have been able to survive as a distinct social group with its own identity, while maintaining both economic autonomy and peaceful relations with the elites of the local polity for an extended period of time. In the absence of any evidence for political, military, or economic domination, the most reasonable conclusion is that the foreigners were able to survive and flourish only at the sufferance of the local rulers, most likely by forging strategic alliances with them through marriage or exchange relations (Stein 1997).

CONCLUSION: IMPLICATIONS FOR THE OVERALL STRUCTURE OF THE URUK EXPANSION

The evidence presented here has five main implications for our understanding of the organization of the Uruk expansion and its influence on indigenous polities in southeast Anatolia, north Syria, and northern Iraq. First, the data from Hacınebi, Arslantepe, Brak, and Gawra all indicate that the local societies of these areas were already complex, hierarchically organized polities before the Uruk expansion. These polities continued to exist as discrete entities during the Uruk expansion. For that reason, it is misleading and inaccurate to subsume these indigenous cultural traditions under broader terms such as

"Northern Uruk." We need to be careful not to conflate "Uruk" as a time period with "Uruk" as a material culture assemblage.

Second, the distribution of metals and other prestige goods indicates that the indigenous early fourth millennium polities of southeast Anatolia, north Syria, and the Iraqi Jazira had their own exchange networks, linking the Mediterranean, the Ergani copper source areas, and the eastern Taurus highland/steppe interface zones. Metals were widely traded among the early fourth millennium polities of these areas and were worked locally at regional centers such as Hacınebi. It is therefore reasonable to conclude that Mesopotamians were drawn to Hacınebi in order to gain access to both raw and processed copper.

Third, the functional range and behavioral patterning of Uruk material culture at Hacınebi cannot be explained as simply the products of emulation. Instead, numerous lines of evidence indicate that an ethnically distinct Uruk colony was present in one corner of the local settlement at Hacınebi. This colony engaged in exchange (to obtain copper), copper smelting and casting, and a full range of subsistence and craft activities.

Fourth, spatial and functional analyses of ceramics, lithics, faunal remains, and administrative artifacts show that this colony did not exert economic or political control over the indigenous host polity. Instead, the Mesopotamians lived as an economically autonomous diaspora community, trading with the Anatolians on equal, symmetric terms. This essential symmetry in Uruk-local political and economic relations at Hacınebi can be explained as the result of a distance-related decay in the Mesopotamian ability to project its power into the highland resource zones (Stein 1998). As a small, outnumbered minority more than 1,000 kilometers from home, in the midst of an already hierarchical, complex, and technologically advanced polity, the Uruk colonists at Hacınebi were in no position to obtain copper through either coercion or unequal exchange. Instead, we can reasonably infer that the Uruk colony at Hacınebi gained access to the Anatolian trade routes and Anatolian resources such as copper and lumber through strategies of economic and marriage alliances with local elites (Stein 1997, 1998). Presumably, these arrangements were profitable to local elites, although we still do not know what the Mesopotamians traded in return for metal.

Fifth, the Uruk colony at Hacınebi was founded quite early—in

Middle Uruk times, ca. 3700 B.C.—and interacted peacefully with the local polity at Hacınebi for at least 300 and possibly as long as 400 years. Both calibrated radiocarbon dates and ceramics from Hacınebi, Sheikh Hassan, and Tell Brak indicate that the Uruk expansion began in the latter portion of the Middle Uruk period (LC 4) and lasted well into the Late Uruk period (LC 5). In other words, we can no longer think of this regional interaction network as a short-lived phenomenon; instead, the period of colonization and intensive exchange relations between Mesopotamia and its neighbors lasted from 3700–3100 B.C. Over the course of this long period there appear to have been several shifts in the location of the Uruk enclaves, as some (e.g., Hacınebi) were apparently abandoned, some continued in use (Sheikh Hassan), and others were founded from scratch (Habuba, Jebel Aruda, and Hassek). The number of Uruk colonies also seems to have increased dramatically from the Middle to the Late Uruk period. This temporal variation suggests that there may well have been major changes in the organization of the network over the course of six centuries. Although there is some evidence for coercion and unequal exchange at the Late Uruk site of Habuba Kabira, the enormous spatial extent of this regional interaction network, its internal variation, and its six-century duration make it highly unlikely that Uruk Mesopotamia was able to dominate its trading partners, either economically or politically, everywhere and at all times. In fact, instances of Mesopotamian dominance (e.g., at sites such as Habuba Kabira) might possibly be the exception, rather than the rule, in the Uruk expansion.

Taken together, the longevity of the Uruk expansion and the differences between colonies such as Habuba Kabira and Hacınebi (or the analogous site of Godin) mean that we have to rethink our basic ideas concerning the political organization of this regional interaction network. Power relations and terms of trade varied considerably in space (and probably over time as well). The Uruk expansion can no longer be seen as a short-lived episode of colonial domination. Instead, we must recognize that this was a network characterized by long-term stability and balanced exchange relations with unexpectedly complex local polities in the resource-rich highland zones at the outer reaches of the Greater Mesopotamian world. However, this network was by no means homogeneous.

First of all, we have no reason to believe that Uruk Mesopotamia was a single state with one integrated trading system. Even though Uruk-Warka is the largest site of this period, settlement pattern data suggest multiple urban centers in the southern alluvium and the Susiana. The locational data are completely consistent with the idea of multiple competing urbanized polities in a pattern analogous to the Early Dynastic social landscape. Second, regardless of whether Uruk Mesopotamia was one or several competing states, we have no reason to believe that exchange and colonization were monopolies under centralized control. Certainly in later periods, there is ample evidence to suggest that Mesopotamian exchange was conducted by entrepreneurial individuals or groups either in tandem with state institutions or in place of these institutions (Adams 1974a; Foster 1977). As a result, one can reasonably hypothesize a fragmented political landscape in which several urbanized states competed for access to the raw materials of highland Anatolia and Iran. Each polity would have had its own colonies, in a pattern analogous to the competition between Genoa, Venice, and other city-states of medieval/Renaissance Italy (Lane 1966). In some cases the centralized institutions of the Uruk states might have organized trading settlements, while in others, entrepreneurial individuals and groups might have been the primary colonists and traders in a pattern similar to what we see later in the Old Assyrian trading system (Larsen 1976, 1987). In short, both the Uruk homeland and its exchange network were probably multicentric in character.

This type of heterogeneous nature was apparently characteristic of power relations within the interregional interaction network formed by the Uruk expansion. Fourth millennium Mesopotamian states seem to have been able to exert political and economic control over their immediate hinterlands (see, e.g., Wright, Miller, and Redding 1980; Wright, Redding, and Pollock 1989); however, Uruk power over other parts of the interaction network appears to have declined with increasing distance from the alluvium. I have suggested elsewhere that this spatial variation in power relations can be described through a "distance-parity" model of interregional interaction (Stein 1993, 1998). The model draws on the economics of transportation to specify a gradient in power and exchange relations between the different parts of an interaction network, so that within certain very specific parameters, one can expect to see a distance-related decay in the power of the core states, leading to increasingly equal relations with increasingly distant peripheries. Under conditions of technological/demographic superiority or ease of access between two areas of differential social complexity, areas close to the core would be characterized by asymmetric (i.e., unequal) exchange and the kind of core dominance hypothesized in world system models of world empires (Wallerstein 1974). However, when these conditions do *not* obtain, then we would expect to see increasing parity with distance in core-periphery relations at the outer reaches of such a network. In the latter case, the transportation costs involved in projecting economic or military power would offset the core's advantages and lead to symmetric or equal exchange.

Thus, for example, in fourth millennium B.C. Mesopotamia, a comparison of *(a)* the city of Uruk-Warka itself, *(b)* large colonies such as Habuba Kabira (or Sheikh Hassan), and *(c)* small, distant colonies such as Hacinebi shows a tremendous degree of variation in the social and economic organization of this earliest colonial network as one moves outward from the urban core to its periphery. In the Mesopotamian heartland, cities such as Uruk-Warka and Susa controlled their rural hinterlands, exacting taxes and sending out administrators to control the most basic activities, such as planting, harvesting, and collection of crop surpluses (Wright et al. 1980, 1989). In the "near periphery"—areas of Syria closest to southern Mesopotamia proper—Uruk colonies such as Habuba Kabira were large fortified settlements that apparently used coercion in a short-lived and ultimately unsuccessful effort to exert economic control over the surrounding local Syrian communities (Strommenger 1980; Sürenhagen 1986a). In more distant subregions, Uruk settlements such as Godin V in highland Iran (Weiss and Young 1975; Young 1986) and Hacinebi in southeast Turkey took the form of small "outposts" located inside the preexisting towns of local polities. We have no evidence to suggest that the outposts dominated local economies through asymmetric exchange or coercion. Instead, the small numbers and vulnerable position of the Mesopotamians at sites such as Hacinebi and Godin meant that they could only survive by remaining on good terms with their more powerful indigenous neighbors. The organization of these settlements and the ways they interacted with their local neighbors varied markedly, depending on the distance from Mesopotamia, the size of the local population, and the degree of preexisting social complexity in the indigenous polities.

I have argued here that the easy archaeological identifiability of Uruk Mesopotamian material culture has biased our interpretations of interregional interaction in the fourth millennium B.C. Near East. The presence of Uruk artifacts and even Uruk colonies does not necessarily mean that Uruk Mesopotamia dominated its periphery or that it determined the trajectory of political development in north Syria, southeast Anatolia, and western Iran.

Until recently, our reconstructions of the Uruk expansion have been able to postulate Uruk dominance and influence for two reasons. First, because virtually nothing was known about the local polities of the neighboring subregions, they were assumed to be backward and easily amenable to Mesopotamian control. Second, the presence of Uruk colonies or material culture in north Syria, southeast Anatolia, and western Iran was automatically assumed to be evidence for either political or economic control by Mesopotamia. Neither of these blanket assumptions holds up under close scrutiny. By documenting the indigenous societies of southeast Anatolia both before and during the period of intensive contact with Mesopotamia, the Hacınebi data require us to rethink our models of how the Uruk interregional interaction network actually functioned.

Notes

The Hacınebi excavations were conducted with the permission of the Turkish Ministry of Culture, General Directorate of Monuments and Museums. Thanks are due to the staff of the Şanlıurfa Provincial Museum and its directors—the late Adnan Mısır and his successor, Eyüp Bucak—for their administrative assistance. The project was funded with support from the National Science Foundation (grant number SBR-9511329), the National Endowment for the Humanities (grant numbers RO-22448, RK-20133-94, and RZ-20120), the National Geographic Society (grant numbers 4853-92, 5057-93, 5295-94, and 5892-97), the Wenner-Gren Foundation for Anthropological Research (grant number 6309), the Kress Foundation, the American Research Institute in Turkey (ARIT), the de Groot Fund of the Metropolitan Museum of Art, Faculty Research Grants from Northwestern University, and the generosity of private donors.

I also wish to thank Mitchell Rothman for the opportunity to participate in this SAR seminar and the other seminar participants for their critical insights about my paper during our group discussions. In particular, I thank Guillermo Algaze for his careful reading and comments on the conference draft of the paper. Any remaining errors of interpretation or fact are my own.

9

Centralization Processes in Greater Mesopotamia
Uruk "Expansion" as the Climax of Systemic Interactions among Areas of the Greater Mesopotamian Region

Marcella Frangipane

Relations between Lower Mesopotamia and the northern regions of the Tigris and Euphrates Basins as far as the mountainous areas of eastern Anatolia have become a key topic in the debate over the formative phases of the state in this part of the world. They dominate the debate on whether relations were catalyzed by the south, primarily because of its requirements, or whether they can be interpreted as multidirectional, driven by several centers, in opposition to the southern Uruk–oriented perspective. Interest in the problem of intraregional relations has been aroused by the increase in archaeological activities in the northern areas (Palmieri 1985), which have revealed that centralized societies emerged very early on even in the north, while many southern cultural elements were very prominent in these contexts. From the traditional point of view, one that considers the Mesopotamian alluvium the formative center of urbanization and the state—traditionally considered to be mutually associated—the model that best explained the radical changes taking place in the northern societies was that of the "world system." This model accounts simultaneously for the cultural affinities with the south and the obvious aspects of regional autonomy, in which southern Mesopotamia operated as the politically and economically powerful "industrial center," leaving the regions between the Upper Euphrates and the Upper Tigris with a "peripheral" role as suppliers of raw materials (Algaze 1993a).

That interpretation of the Uruk period and phenomenon is, in my opinion, fairly questionable both historically, in terms of interpreting the archaeological evidence, and theoretically, in terms of the applicability of the world system model to early state and even pre-state societies. The creation of a system of interdependent economic relations between different and distant subregions in which some (the centers) played a decisive role in promoting those relations, dictating the rules to suit their own needs, while others (the peripheral regions) simply had to accept them, even though they organized their response to them autonomously, presupposes a number of factors:

1. There existed, at least in the center, institutions able to wield economic and political control over their own territory to the extent that they were able to manage the social needs and organize trading activities within the framework of a general economic system.

2. The central system was able to exploit the peripheral systems to the point of creating, on a wider scale, a single economic super-system comprising various regional subsystems (Champion 1989; Ekholm and Friedman 1993). Direct or indirect interference in the organization of subregions that were also quite distant, implicit in this model, could only have been exercised if mechanisms existed to regulate the flow of goods in such a way that they became standard and functional to the economic systems of both poles of interaction.[1] Mechanisms of this kind can vary widely, from coordination by the state institutions, which administer the work of the "merchant" organizations in highly centralized economies, to the modern capitalist systems of indirect economic coercion through the principles of the market.

I do not think that such institutions can be envisaged in the case of the first centralized societies in the Middle or Late Uruk (LC 3–5) periods. At this point the crucial issue to be analyzed, as far as this is feasible, is the character of the economies in Mesopotamian societies.

SOCIAL AND ECONOMIC RELATIONS IN SOUTHERN MESOPOTAMIA IN THE FOURTH MILLENNIUM

Whatever ability the Mesopotamian elites had to govern, or even only to guide intraregional relations, depended on their ability to intervene in the local economy and control the production and circulation of goods within their territory. The boundaries of the specific territory to which they belonged also depended on, and were at the same time dictated by, the capacity of these elites to establish their own, unchallenged right to exert political authority over that territory and to regularly extract surpluses from it.

There is no doubt that the leaders of the temple institutions and, more generally, the public institutions in Late Uruk period (LC 5) Mesopotamian centers centralized resources and controlled the management of certain productive activities. What becomes crucial at this point is to understand the way in which this control was exercised and also to reconstruct its scope. The concept of "centralization," like "redistribution," is far too generic to enable definition of specific types of economies without further qualification of their nature and the relations they underlay. The nature of centralization, and consequently the power underpinned by it, essentially depended on the degree of involvement of the urban and rural populations in the "central" economic system, and hence on the encroachment of the constraints imposed by the elites on the economy of the community. In other words, what needs to be known is what resources the paramount authorities were able to centralize, and to what extent; which segments of society provided those resources; and how goods and labor circulated—regularly or only occasionally, in the form of tribute or spontaneous offerings, services provided by the majority of the population under specific circumstances, or regular work by some employees. The answers to these questions in contexts for which we have almost no written sources—the pictographic tablets from Warka IVa–III can only give us general ideas of the ration system and the productive sectors involved in central activities—are obviously highly problematic, but they are nevertheless crucial.

One central aspect of the problem is the relationship between the "governing" elites and households. Certainly, there were large houses from the earliest phases in the occupation of the southern Mesopotamian

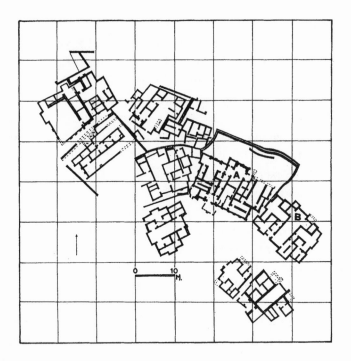

FIGURE 9.1

Plan of the Tell Abade Ubaid village, Iraq.

plain (see, e.g., the tripartite buildings of Tell es-Sawwan I–II and the houses at Tell Oueili). Coupled with the data from Early Dynastic and subsequent tablets, this evidence indicates that Mesopotamian society in the alluvial plain most probably comprised extended families, the basic social units for primary production (agriculture and livestock). It was probably from these families that the high-ranking groups emerged for the political management of the community (Frangipane 1996:87–125).[2] One or more households were likely to have wielded authority and held a high social status from the earliest formative phases in Mesopotamia. This differential status is suggested, for example, by the architecture in an Early Ubaid site like Tell Abade, which, despite the fact that it is north of the alluvial plain, is one of the very few sites from this period that have been extensively excavated. At Abade there are two houses with characteristic floor plans that are similar to all the others in terms of their basic layout, except that they are larger and more complex (fig. 9.1). One of the houses possesses very unusual features, such as the concentration of tokens and child burials under the floor (Jasim 1989). This suggests that the occupants of the house played a prominent role, both as an ideological benchmark for the community (the burial of children) and in terms of the economic and organizational tasks (the tokens) of the residents.

The probable relationship between the origin of the Mesopotamian elites and the social and kinship system that regulated the communities on the alluvial plain does not, however, in itself explain the functions that the elites actually performed in the society that they "governed" and from which they derived their power. One approach has viewed their role as a means of coordination to improve the functioning of the entire socioeconomic system (Adams 1966; Wright and Johnson 1975); another view considered them as one component competing against other social and production units to control the means of subsistence (Godelier 1978; Khazanov 1978; Liverani 1998). This dichotomy has triggered one of the most heated debates among different schools of anthropological thought regarding the birth of hierarchical systems.

The nature and legitimization of the authority of the emerging households were, in my opinion, largely dependent on the ways in which primary commodities were produced and consumed within the communities concerned. The existence of status hierarchies in the kinship or social systems, albeit in embryonic form, must have been significant in that they indicated a fragmented and potentially competitive organization of the basic economy. Alternatively, with the collective/community management of the means of production or the products themselves, it was necessary to maintain a highly egalitarian social structure that helped cooperation. The fact that there may have been wide-ranging and clearly distinct and visible household units within the Mesopotamian communities, coupled with the absence of any evidence of communal storage facilities,[3] seems to indicate that southern Mesopotamia adopted the first model, in which households were separate production units, competing rather than cooperating with each other. This social structuring is indicated by the marked separation of the houses in the residential areas, the presence of emerging nuclei represented as such in the oldest villages from the beginning of the fifth millennium, and the documented presence of domestic storage in such cases as the Tell es-Sawwan houses of level IV (Breniquet 1991).

The organization of societies into comparatively autonomous socioeconomic units is even more evident in the Late Uruk period (LC 5). At that time a wide range of different administrative instruments (clay sealings, bullae, and numerical tablets) and huge amounts of mass-produced bowls, even in private houses, are evidenced at Susa and Jebel Aruda (Le Brun 1978; Van Driel and van Driel-Murray 1983).[4] This evidence shows that some household production units were able to manage resources and labor on a large scale. The entire range of the Late Uruk (LC 5) administrative materials, including numerical tablets, has in fact been found in a house of level 17B at Susa (Le Brun 1978), as well as in the main buildings of the preeminent district at Jebel Aruda, where thousands of mass-produced bowls have also been found. It is unlikely that these materials were used within the domestic units in activities carried out by the families themselves. In this case, it would be difficult to explain both the function of the sealing practices and the huge number of bowls. It is possible that the management of the land and the fruits thereof might have been entrusted to individual household units, probably extended families, supporting evidence for which comes from third-millennium land conveyance documents (Diakonoff 1954).

An organization of this kind, in a highly productive but unstable environment of the kind that existed in the alluvium, by being a source of risk and competition, must have created inequalities, that is, impoverished people working for stronger groups. At the same time, elite groups had an ideological role that served to protect the whole community, as evidenced by the remarkable and early development of the temple areas. The economic and administrative activities documented in the ceremonial/religious complexes, in fact, appear to be the same as those attested in a few of the houses, but on a larger scale. The competitive strength of the elites, by virtue of their privileged status, must have developed because of their considerable capacity to hoard surpluses and labor, which was certainly ideologically filtered but may also have been viewed as a possible safety net for the weaker members of society. This dialectic between the public function and "private" interests seems to have run throughout the history of the oldest centralized Mesopotamian systems, preserving a potential for conflict between the elites and their clients. The possible clash of interests between the most powerful groups and the other members of the community was probably reflected in a "rural-urban dialectic" (Schwartz and Falconer 1994:3–4). This, in my opinion, is the way to interpret the arduous and slow process of establishing fully fledged state entities—in other words, institutions with which the population of a particular territory are able to identify—and hence the creation of stable political units.

The lack of any real integration in the Uruk period postulated by Adams (1981) for the territory of southern Mesopotamia, in contrast with Johnson's rather abstract model of a strong rationalization and integration of specialized functions between the various sites (Johnson 1975), takes us back once again to this fluidity in relations that I have suggested. The substantial productive autonomy of the smaller centers where a wide variety of craft activities were practiced, over which the local elites exerted autonomous administrative management, has been confirmed in several cases (Adams 1981:76–81; Pollock, Pope, and Coursey 1996:697; Wright, ed. 1981). The elites were probably not very successful in controlling the flow of goods produced in the villages, but they were certainly able to increase their resources by extracting labor, as has been amply shown by the type of transactions recorded on the Uruk pictographic tablets from Eanna (Nissen 1986b). In the Uruk period, public areas were characterized by intense administrative and redistribution operations (huge numbers of mass-produced bowls for what might have been the distribution of meals, and large concentrations of clay sealings for administration). At the same time they lacked large warehouses or other areas to store large quantities of goods. It is now evident that the concentration of clay sealings in public areas is an indication of control over outgoing goods—in other words, the distribution of goods to employees or individuals working on behalf of the central institutions—rather than revenues (offerings and tributes). This assumption is clearly demonstrated by the detailed study of the administrative system evidenced at Arslantepe, which, even though it is in another area, nevertheless reveals a wholly similar organization to that found in southern Mesopotamia (Ferioli and Fiandra 1983, 1994; Frangipane and Palmieri 1983b). The large numbers of seals (more than 120) impressed on thousands of sealings, together with other considerations regarding the notary functions of the seal as a receipt for a completed transaction (Fiandra 1981), indicate that the seals were not applied by the officials responsible for the stores. Rather they were placed by the individuals who withdrew the goods for themselves and for groups of employed workers. More than 30 seal designs impressed on 130 clay sealings found in situ in a small storeroom in the palatial complex at Arslantepe (Frangipane 1994a) confirm this hypothesis. This interpretation is also supported on the basis of the intrinsic requirements of the system. These include security against possible embezzlement by the persons who managed the goods as well as the certification of the accuracy of the account accomplished by the recipient's sealing. The enormous quantity of mass-produced bowls, which increased as centralization grew, and their association with the clay sealings confirm that they were used to distribute meals to large numbers of people. The size of the assemblage also supports the hypothesis of a concentration of workers employed on a full- or part-time basis by the public institutions.

Once again, at Arslantepe, which is one of the rare sites in which central stores have been identified in the Late Uruk period (LC 5), the stores were found in two rather small rooms, measuring about 3.5 by 2.5 and 6 by 2 meters, respectively. The smaller was clearly used for redistribution, as indicated by the presence of hundreds of sealings and bowls, both absent in the other storeroom (Frangipane and Palmieri 1989). The same general situation, an enormous amount of administrative material and bowls and a lack of any clearly defined storage areas, is also recorded in what is known as the "administrative quarter" of the colonial site at Jebel Aruda (Frangipane and Palmieri 1989; van Driel and van Driel-Murray 1983). Jebel Aruda is closely related to the Mesopotamian world—it is considered a colony of southerners in the Middle Euphrates. The number of seal designs is fairly large, although it is not comparable to the Arslantepe assemblage. The Jebel Aruda sealings in fact come from a "private" elite area, where a substantial quantity of sealings was discarded in two small rooms (36 and 37) in the main building (SI). The activities therefore seem to have been more closely related to centrifugal than centripetal movements of goods. The strongest sectors of the society seem to have exercised their control over the labor force, as the central institutions did, but probably neither had the ability to draw large amounts of products (large storage areas are lacking). Goods controlled by central institutions or privileged social sectors seem to have been reinvested mainly to reward workers.

The organization of the centralized Late Uruk structure therefore seems to be much closer to the model of a "segmentary state" based on the Alur polity in East Africa (Mair 1962; Southall 1988; also considered in Stein 1994c; Rothman 1988) rather than an integrated state organization that was capable of channeling regular tribute and taxes from the countryside. As in the case of the Alur, "tribute tends to be more frequently in the form of labor rather than goods," and "the centralized authorities exercise only limited control over peripheral foci of administration" (Stein 1994c:11–12). If this is true, the economic and political links must have been rather fluid, even in the immediate hinterland of the urban centers, and their territorial sovereignty must have been rather weak.[5] I argue here that the public sector of the economy, despite the fact that it was certainly expanding all the time, was not able to exercise any real and widespread control over the circulation of staple goods in its own hinterland. Therefore, it must have been even less capable of influencing the management of economic activities over large distances, and certainly of provoking the physical movement of large segments of the population into distant areas to meet its own operational requirements.

The new demands and needs of the elites certainly encouraged the development of handicrafts, creating an increased demand for luxury goods. The increased organizational capacity of the central authorities to control at least some of the activities and the easier internal movement of goods as a result of urbanization certainly facilitated these trends. Increased demand must have expanded the desirability of external trade, but we cannot assume that trade could be centrally regulated over long distances because this would have required full-fledged trading agencies, for which there is no evidence whatsoever.

Trade, moreover, could not have been an activity of vital importance for the survival of the elites and the system that was built around them (despite the fact that it must have taken on a much more significant role than in the past in reproducing power relations by guaranteeing selective access to certain hard-to-come-by goods). The goods produced using exotic raw materials were still used mainly by the elites (ornaments, prestige objects, and, to a lesser degree, weapons) and did not enter the distribution circles for daily use, even though the quantity and the variety of these products had increased considerably, and productive techniques such as metallurgy, which had previously not been particularly important, also developed. The heightened importance of imported raw materials, to my mind, should be linked to the expansion of urbanization and, consequently, the greater integration and dovetailing of different specialized sectors within the towns, rather than to centralization. There must have been an impetus to establish much closer contact with the areas that provided the raw materials, as evidenced in the north. However, there is no evidence to suggest that these relations were planned and deliberately organized by the southern centers. The layout of colonies with large populations, such as Habuba Kabira, and the variety of different contexts and forms of "contacts" found in the north make it unlikely that these population shifts were designed solely for trade. If they had been, there would have been a guaranteed and regular outlet in the centers of origin, which could have been achieved only with a high level of centralization of these activities. There is no clear evidence for this level of organization, nor is it likely that it could have developed in fourth-millennium Mesopotamia. Furthermore, if the emergence of colonial settlements in the north had been linked to what were primarily commercial needs, there should be far more archaeological remains connected with exchange activities or the crafts linked with them in these communities. Yet not even in the most typical of all the colonial sites in the Middle Euphrates, Habuba Kabira, which has been extensively excavated, have any clear traces of such activities been found.

THE ECONOMIC AND SOCIAL STRUCTURE OF THE NORTHERN COMMUNITIES: TRADITION, CONTACT, AND CHANGE

The soundest approach to solving the problem of north-south relations in the Uruk period is to view the phenomena also from the north, not in terms of the degree to which the northern and southern societies resembled each other or differed, but rather in terms of analyzing the features and processes that characterized the development of northern communities as well as the historical roots of their external relations. If we examine the evidence from this viewpoint, the variety and the complexity of the different ways in which the cultural components interacted in these subregions will reflect the different forms of penetration by southern groups. That same approach helps to explain the specific organizational features of the northern communities, while revealing the influence that the needs of these northern communities had in determining the kind of relations that were established with the outside world, as Rothman (this volume) also asserts.

The varying presence of alien groups and their influence in the sites that have been investigated seem to be closely related to the importance and the presumed role played by these sites in their respective subregions. Influence therefore largely seems to depend on the needs of the northern communities and the scope of their actions in response to external interference. The presence of "foreigners" can only be recognized with a substantial degree of clarity in the few wholly colonial settlements in the Middle Euphrates, such as Sheikh Hassan, Habuba Kabira, and Jebel Aruda. There, Uruk cultural traits are found exclusively throughout the settlements, which had not existed previously (Boese 1995; Strommenger 1980; van Driel and van Driel-Murray 1983). Alternatively we have evidence from small sites such as Hacınebi and Hassek Höyük, where small areas with typical Uruk materials apparently were isolated in already existing, but smaller and probably rural, settlements (Behm-Blancke et al. 1984; Stein, Bernbeck et al. 1996).

The gradual increase in Uruk culture elements in the large and important centers of the central and eastern parts of Upper Mesopotamia, such as Tell Brak and Nineveh (Oates and Oates 1993a, 1994; Gut 1995), is much more difficult to interpret. In these sites the excavations are not sufficient to reveal the spatial distribution of the complexes of materials found at different levels, and hence the nature of these seemingly foreign traits. However, at least as far as Brak is concerned, the sequences recognized in two far-apart soundings on the main mound (areas CH and TW) show that the site was already very large in the early/middle fourth millennium (LC 3 and 4). Recent excavations in the two trenches have discovered levels belonging to the Middle Uruk period (3600–3400 B.C.) (LC 3–4), when pottery and glyptics characterized as typical Uruk appear side by side with the traditional productions of the local fourth millennium culture, called

by J. Oates "Northern Early Uruk." The early phases of the fourth millennium consist exclusively of local materials characteristic of Upper
Mesopotamian and Syro-Anatolian subregions. The marked increase in
occurrence of Uruk elements in this site, first within a localized cultural
context and then, at the end of the period, clearly predominant or
completely replacing the local traits, might be due to a number of factors. One factor might be the presence at the site of small groups of
southern origin, taken into the centers and integrated into the productive structure of the communities that were already very strongly hierarchically organized and, at least in the case of Tell Brak, urbanized.
Another might be the adoption by the elites or local artisans of typically
southern models and technologies as a consequence of an intensification of relations. This latter possibility would indicate a new cultural
assimilation over the whole of the Mesopotamian area, probably implying yet again, as in previous periods, a widespread circulation of individuals but this time with new forms and partially new needs, of which
the colonies themselves were probably the most evident sign. The interaction between kin groups and cultures and the complex effects of this
interaction in the Uruk period can only be analyzed by reviewing the
roots of the phenomenon.

Crossing Pathways: The Foundation of Greater Mesopotamia

If we examine the developments that preceded the great changes
of the second half of the fourth millennium, we also discover the long
time frame over which intensive relations with the south were established. The so-called Uruk Expansion appears more than anything else
to have been a new manifestation of relations that were deeply rooted
and whose form, and in some cases whose nature, probably changed
under the influence of the overall changes taking place in the societies
concerned.

In reality, the area of Greater Mesopotamia became one single
region during the Ubaid period, even though it was by no means
homogeneous. This does not mean, however, that it was a territorial or
economic unit. The concept of territoriality in these phases is difficult
to define and raises highly complex problems. I think one can assume
that the cultural expansions taking place in the Halaf period, and to an
even greater extent in the Ubaid, are related to weaknesses in the link-

age between "political" unity and ethnic or territorial unity. This does not mean that the communities did not relate themselves to a particular territory. On the contrary, the appearance of agriculture, which transformed land into a new kind of means of production, is traditionally associated with a strengthening of bonds between the communities and their territories during the Neolithic. But this linkage must have been related mainly to rights of possession and use for economic purposes; the concept of territory was presumably not yet relevant to defining polities. I assume that whatever form authority took, rather than being exercised over a particular territory, it was exercised over a number of communities that were coordinated politically in order to make decisions in their joint interests.

In the sixth millennium B.C., northern and southern Mesopotamia were characterized by communities with very different forms of economic and social organization. However, they shared a common trait—the tendency to establish among themselves a geographically broad communication network, thus maintaining links even at extensive distances. This trend, which has also been found in other regions, was probably a structural feature of the societies born during what we now call the "second Neolithic revolution," whose cultures were progressively expanding over increasingly wide areas as a consequence of growing populations. These links were of two types. First were ties between population units that shared the same culture and probably had the same origin, evidenced by the diffusion of structural elements, such as settlement types, house planning, and types of subsistence economy (for example, the ties that gave rise to the Halaf cultural homogeneity over a very large and expanding territory). Second were ties with other groups as indicated by the diffusion of formal features in the material culture, such as ceramic vessels.

Shortly after its first appearance, pottery seems to have acquired an important social function for symbolic identification of groups of people—we do not how large—as both the manufacture of fine wares with varied and standardized painted designs and the ways in which they circulated suggest. The mechanisms of pottery circulation in these periods and the quantities involved indicate the nature of the relations, marking, on the one hand, the limits of areas where people with the same cultural identity settled and, on the other, the existence of intercultural relations. The beautiful, sophisticated pottery of the sixth millennium marks the boundaries of the Halaf, Samarran, and Eridu-Hajji Mohammad cultures, and at the same time few items from each of these style groups circulated widely in other subregions. Moreover, the circulating items were mainly open vessels, like dishes and bowls, and they moved in all directions, as chemical analyses carried out on Halaf pottery also suggest. We therefore hypothesize that ceramics were symbols of their producers and often accompanied their makers from one place to another.

The ways in which people circulated, however, seem to have been substantially different in the northern, Halaf environment and in the southern, Ubaid area. Whereas movements appear, in my opinion, to be a structural trait of the Halaf societies from their beginning, the southern communities were characterized by a completely different, sedentary organization. In the northern regions, with rainfall and possibly rotating agriculture as well as several ecological niches at varying altitudes, the Neolithic communities developed a mixed economy, with pastoral and agricultural activities possibly carried out by the same groups, integrated by hunting and perhaps other resource exploitation. This pattern is likely to have resulted in small settlements and a cooperative economic organization with communal storage and substantial integration among villages (Frangipane 1996:69–87). This trend is demonstrated by the small size of the Halaf sites and the economic specialization (for example, in hunting activities) of some of them. It is also marked by the architecture, which shows the functional integration of round structures of different dimensions without any definition of individual domestic spaces, and the appearance in the villages of large rectangular buildings (thus far usually one documented per village) that seem to have been places for communal activities (in some cases, as at Sabi Abyad, probably for storage; Akkermans 1993).[6]

The egalitarian basis of Halaf society probably pushed groups to split up under population pressure, and the social cohesion required by the economic ties created a system, possibly with exogamous marriage rules (Forest 1996), that encouraged people to circulate. On the contrary, the hierarchical structure of the societies of the alluvium, as hypothesized above, permitted the individual settlements to grow, increasing their organizational complexity yet remaining basically stable. However, southern people also moved, although in a different way and probably for different reasons. Not only is southern pottery found in the north from the Hassuna period, but also, starting with Ubaid phase 3 of the fifth millennium, the southern culture gradually expanded to the north, accompanied by its typical house plans and a change in the entire socioeconomic system. The superpositioning of the new cultural features and a new model of society on the Halaf substratum is clearly documented at, among other sites, Tepe Gawra, where the tripartite houses appear in level XV (Tobler 1950). These examples strongly recall the Ubaid houses in the Hamrin and introduce a new component, probably brought by foreign groups.[7] Tepe Gawra is also the only site that, having been excavated over wide horizontal areas covering a long sequence of levels from the end of Halaf to the end of the Ubaid period, shows the gradual transformation in its settlement pattern and pottery repertoire. In the earliest transitional levels (XIX–XVII), the first tripartite houses sit beside large buildings in the Neolithic tradition—large structures used for communal purposes—and round structures in the Halaf style, along with the apparently contemporary late Halaf and Ubaid painted pottery. The introduction of Ubaid ceramics in late Halaf contexts is confirmed by recent data from other sites, such as Khirbet Derak, sites in the Balikh Valley (Akkermans 1993), and Domuztepe in Anatolia (Campbell et al. 1999). Imitations of the Ubaid style are attested in pottery fragments that are Halafian in fabric at Khirbet Derak (Huot 1994:184). After the appearance of two tripartite buildings of the typical Hamrin type at Tepe Gawra XV, the site undergoes a substantial change. A completely different model is evident at the very end of the period, in level XII, which appears as an agglutinated village with several tripartite houses, one of which is clearly outstanding in terms of size and other unusual traits—white-plastered walls, concentration of infant and child burials.

The diffusion over vast areas of not only formal but also structural elements must in fact have entailed the physical movement of individuals and therefore necessitated a certain flexibility when defining the territories to which they belonged. This assumption is indispensable for understanding the far-reaching osmosis from south to north between the various areas around the Tigris and the Euphrates, founding a lengthy common history of parallel and uninterrupted processes of two-way relations for what would become Greater Mesopotamia.

Nevertheless, interaction in the north between the Ubaid component and the Halaf communities, which were completely different in character, as well as the distinct environmental features of the northern regions, created far-reaching differences between the southern and northern societies. This differentiation is revealed in their economic, social, and political organization.

The environmental conditions in the north, as discussed above, may have offered less scope for the expansion of agriculture, which was traditionally combined with the pastoral sector of the economy. At the same time, the hypothesized cooperation in the conduct of the primary economy and the egalitarian structure of the Halaf communities probably resulted in dialectic relations with the different structures and modes of production of the groups of southern origin. This gave rise to social and economic inequalities previously unknown in the north. One example is the fairly widespread appearance, in several private Ubaid houses of the northern regions (Tepe Gawra and Değirmentepe), of administrative practices (seals and sealings) (Rothman 1994b; Esin 1994; Esin and Harmankaya 1987). Though the use of sealing is attested from the Neolithic in northern regions, and the Halaf period is characterized by a wide diffusion of a variety of seals, in fact it is during the Ubaid period that both clay sealings and seals for the first time appear to have been widely used within individual domestic units. The social and economic function of these tools seems therefore to have changed from a means of administering the redistribution of goods within egalitarian societies to a means for administering the movement of goods controlled by individual families. The appearance of social and economic inequalities is also suggested by the development, at the end of the period, of the mass production of bowls, which must have already been related to the distribution of meals to persons not belonging to the family, and possibly working for it.

If this interpretation is correct, the inequalities that can be inferred from the data may have arisen from the interaction between different socioeconomic systems and, possibly, different cultural and ethnic groups (Halaf and Ubaid). They may therefore not have had the same well-grounded basis in the social structure of the local population as they probably had in the south. All this means that the north lacked a large estate system and that the social hierarchies were weaker than in the south. We also observe a lower degree of urbanization, which varies in each subregion according to its agricultural potential to maintain urban population, resulting in a lower capacity for centralization in the north.

The structural differences and the contemporaneous presence of a number of significant similarities, which are the sign of shared cultural traditions and indicate the common roots of the northern and southern cultures, are the basis upon which to study the Uruk phenomenon.

The Emergence of Territorial Ties in the Fourth Millennium

In this perspective, the probable colonial sites—I consider them to be far fewer in number than those identified by Algaze (1993a), and only along the Euphrates—seem to reflect repeated shifts of sections of the population throughout a territory that was traditionally known to and frequented by them, but which took on different forms from the past (the "colonies"). These shifts occurred over a very long period of time, judging from the probable chronological span of sites such as Sheikh Hassan and Habuba Kabira. This new way of occupying the land could, in my opinion, reflect an embryonic formation of political units with a more stable territorial base in the first half of the fourth millennium.

The growth of urban centers may have increased the need to establish well-defined limits to the rural landscape that the towns could exploit for their sustenance. This need must have been particularly pressing in the southern alluvium, where the enormous expansion of urbanization resulted in centers requiring growing quantities of resources. The more the urban population and the elite activities that took place in those centers expanded, the greater the requirements for regulation of the flows of goods became. This may have brought about gradually increasing political control over the hinterland, with a possible consequent expansion of sectors involved in the central administration. The archaeological evidence for such a process is not very strong, but we may interpret both the construction of town walls around Mesopotamian centers and the initial "regionalization" in the more varied environment of northern Mesopotamia during the fourth millennium as evidence of the improved definition of territories. This hypothesis is supported by the results of such processes recognizable at the beginning of the third millennium. This was a time when the still fluid and vaguely bounded cultural regions that appear in the Late Chalcolithic (Tigris and eastern Jazira, Euphrates Valley and western Jezirah, areas west of the Euphrates, Anatolian lands north of Taurus) become better defined cultural areas coinciding with the clearly distinct territories of the Ninevite V and western Early Bronze I cultures (the central-eastern Jazira and the middle/upper Euphrates Valley, respectively). At that time the Jazira towns also seem to have had stronger economic and perhaps political control over their rural landscapes, as suggested by a large-scale storage of cereals in rural villages (such as Tell al-Raqa'i and Telul eth-Thalathat, discussed below).

Clearer political definition of the territories must have brought with it a stronger identification by the groups with their place of origin, and hence greater distinction and separation of them, even concentrating in a defined "urban" space, when they came into contact with other populations. This tendency to define the territory over which political control is exercised is a sign of increased authority and power by the institutions responsible for exercising it, and it involves a growing variety of functions and duties within the territory, which consequently gives a distinct role to the sites. This situation, together with the fact that the process was in its initial stage and therefore outsiders would not yet have had to deal with politically integrated territorial units, could account for the variety of forms, degrees, and modes of penetration recognized for the "alien" presence in the north, and the different responses by the individual local communities to their stimuli and/or pressure (fig. 9.2).

For example, the relations that might be established with the population and the authorities in a dominant center, such as Tell Brak and perhaps Nineveh, would differ from those established with the population and authorities of a site with less political weight (such as Hacınebi). There may also be a different degree of interest in establishing these relations, to the point of completely ignoring certain sites altogether (for example, Tell Leilan, Hayaz, Tepe Gawra). Perhaps, however, the new chronology indicates that these centers were not occupied in the periods with the most intensive interactions.

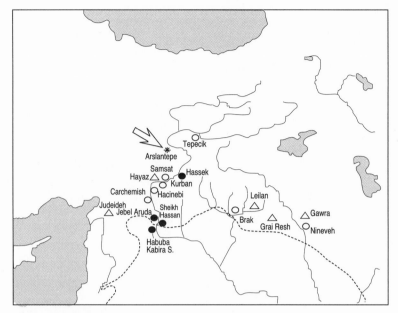

● = Uruk settlements (colonies?)
○ = Local LC settlements in which Uruk (probably alien) groups interacted with the
     indigenous population or interfered in the site occupants' lives.
△ = Local LC sites with no substantial Uruk presence
✳ = Local Uruk-influenced center

FIGURE 9.2

Northern Late Chalcolithic sites mentioned in the text.

ARSLANTEPE: ORIGINALITY AND SHARED FEATURES IN A POWERFUL CENTER NORTH OF THE TAURUS RANGE

Arslantepe is one of the nodes on this network of complex relations with differentiated points. It is also emblematic of the formation
of a centralized structure in the most "peripheral"context within the
regional framework defined as Greater Mesopotamia in geographical,
as well as ecological and cultural, terms.

The environment, on the northern slope of the Anti-Taurus, is
mountainous, with a much higher annual rainfall than in the regions
south of the Taurus but with fewer open plains. Particularly important
is its position on the Malatya Plain, which was fertile and abundantly
irrigated by the tributaries of the Euphrates, and by the myriad streams
created by runoff from the mountains. The settlement pattern in this
region also seems to have been very different in character not only

325

from the Mesopotamian alluvium, but also from the Jezirah steppe. It is characterized by tiny sites dominated by one single center, Arslantepe. Despite its small size by Mesopotamian standards, Arslantepe remained the preeminent site in terms of size, continuity of occupation, and political centrality for millennia.

This feature, together with the fact that it has been excavated over a very long period of time, has made it a key site for the study of the history of the region. A detailed sequence of periods of occupation has been brought to light over large areas. The sequence relating to the Late Chalcolithic reveals a very long and continuous occupation, with numerous rebuilding phases by a local culture (period VII in the internal sequence of the site). This period must have covered much of the fourth millennium, even though ^{14}C dating attained thus far covers a smaller period between 3700 and 3500 B.C.[8] The lengthy duration proposed for this cultural phase not only reflects the number of superimposed levels (about seven), reaching in some places to a depth of almost 3 meters, it also takes into account the chronological attribution of the preceding and following levels. The oldest is period VIII, which is thought to correspond to a Post-Ubaid/Early Gawra horizon (LC 1–2). We have obtained three ^{14}C dates for the final level of period VIII, all between 4300 and 4000 B.C. Period VIA, following period VII and corresponding to Late Uruk (LC 5), yielded numerous dates that on average indicate the last three centuries of the fourth millennium, between 3350 and 3000 B.C. (Alessio et al. 1983; Calderoni et al. 1994; Wright, this volume).

Determining the precise time frame of period VII, based on clear comparisons with archaeological material from other sites, is made difficult by the distinctive characteristics of the material produced at Arslantepe in that period—in particular, the pottery. Although it exhibits the general features of the pottery manufactured by the northern Mesopotamian cultures in the first half of the fourth millennium, it nevertheless has a number of essentially local traits. The best comparisons can be found with phase F of the Amuq sequence (Braidwood and Braidwood 1960), suggesting that this cultural corpus was mainly distributed in the area west of the Euphrates. This geographical range seems to be recognizable fairly early in the Late Chalcolithic period, when elements of "southern" Middle Uruk (LC 3) culture (Hacınebi,

Tell Brak TW 16–13) began to emerge in the areas to the south of the Taurus in sharp contrast with ceramics in Arslantepe VII contexts. However, the situation is not as clear at the beginning of the fourth millennium. In this period, both south of Arslantepe at Tepe Gawra and north of it at Norşuntepe (Hauptmann 1976), the so-called Gawra XI–IX (LC 2) corpus has been recorded. The lack of connection with Arslantepe VII may be due to the fact that the period VII occupation at the latter site may have postdated LC 2. Still, we cannot exclude the possibility that there were geographical differences, at least not until we carry out a thorough analysis of period VIII remains (Frangipane 1994b).[9]

What is of interest to us here, however, is the fact that towards the mid-fourth millennium Arslantepe manifested a local culture, which was distinctive and well established. Its distinctiveness as a society with recognizable internal hierarchy was expressed both in the architecture and in the development of particular products that reveal new social needs. Imposing period VII buildings with mud brick columns on the higher part of the mound must have been reserved for the elites, even though the mound itself seems not to have had "public" functions as indicated by a lack of religious or administrative features (Frangipane 1993). The emphasis on mass production of bowls, both flint-scraped and conical with flat bases, suggests a parallel development of requirements that may not have been new—reminiscent of the Coba bowls at the end of the Ubaid period—but that required a more structured response and greater organization to meet them. The continuity that one finds in the Arslantepe sequence from period VII to period VIA in the developmental steps of mass-produced bowls, from the flint-scraped to the wheel-made string-cut bowls, is a sign of the internal growth of this society. It demonstrates the development and then perfection of original technical and organizational solutions to meet the needs of a society that was becoming increasingly hierarchical in socioeconomic terms. It is no coincidence that only a very few fragments of beveled-rim bowls have been found on the site, which has been widely excavated at these particular levels, indicating that they were not mass-produced at the site.

The existence of well-structured hierarchies, which had hitherto only been suggested by the data, was proven irrefutably in the 1998

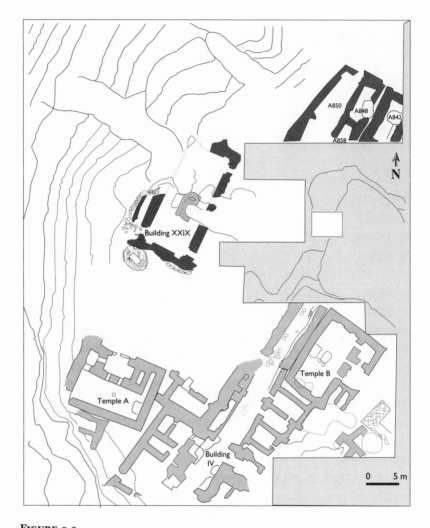

FIGURE 9.3

Arslantepe, Malatya (Turkey): plan of monumental buildings, both public and "residential,"
periods VIA and VII.

campaign with the finding of an imposing ceremonial building from
period VII on the northwestern border of what became the public area
in the subsequent VIA period (LC 5) (fig. 9.3). The public function of
this building is indicated by its extraordinary size—the main room is 18
meters long, the walls are 1.60 meters thick; its prominent position—it
rose in full relief on a raised basement made of huge stone slabs and

two layers of mud bricks; and the materials found in the rooms. These materials consisted almost exclusively of mass-produced bowls spread everywhere over the floors and a collection of clay sealings—the first to be found in levels from this period—discarded in an adjoining room. The ground plan is very similar to that of the subsequent period VIA temples, but in addition to being larger it is also distinguished by the numerous entrances to the main hall and its isolated raised position on the mound. These features, along with the wall paintings preserved in a niched corner of the large room (an eastern Anatolian trait), suggest that redistribution was the main activity performed there, and it probably took the form of the ceremonial or ritualized distribution of meals.

It therefore appears that a centralized system based on corvée labor and expressed through redistribution was already operating in the first half of the fourth millennium. This was a completely local society, apart from the Mesopotamian cultural roots it had probably shared, at least since the Ubaid period, with all the other regions of Greater Mesopotamia. Centralization already seems to resemble the more clearly documented features of the subsequent VIA period, although at present it appears to have been performed through a more markedly ideological mediation.[10]

The gradual nature of the transformation process has also been shown by the discovery of a level with massive constructions, revealing an interesting transition between the end of period VII and the beginning of VIA (fig. 9.3: A850, A848–58, A842). These buildings, whose function is not yet clear, but which could not have been houses or full public buildings, were perhaps originally stores or places where activities directly or indirectly connected with handicraft production were performed. This may be inferred from the presence on the floors of a quantity of ochre, a number of fragments of semiprecious stones and minerals, and assemblages of numerous obsidian arrowheads, the majority of which had not been used. The floor levels had been rebuilt after a partial burying of the ruins, but their use does not seem to have changed substantially through time, except for the presence, in one of the rooms, of about 70 clay sealings, which were again associated with a large number of mass-produced bowls. Interestingly, whereas on the lower floors the pottery consisted of the typical wares and forms of period VII, on the upper, rebuilt floors some wheel-made reserved-slip ware and a few examples of typical VIA shapes of red-black pottery were found for the very first time, along with period VII ceramic types. The mass-produced bowls here, as in the ceremonial building, show late traits with traditional period VII shapes and new manufacturing techniques indicated by the string-cut bases.

The presence of this level, which immediately underlies a complex of monumental, but not public, buildings belonging wholly to period VIA, reveals a continuity of development from the so-called local aspects to the Late Uruk–influenced aspect. This continuity is also emphasized by the use of the same areas in the settlement for similar purposes: the central and higher part of the mound used for residential buildings, probably for high-ranking people, and the southwestern zone designed for public functions.

Arslantepe VIA society shows the centralized system in its full flowering, which brought about significant changes in terms of organization and production. These changes are recognizable in the primary economy, where a remarkable increase in sheep to the detriment of other domestic species more suitable for rural family management, such as pigs, may be interpreted as the result of more marked intervention by the central institutions in the management of animal breeding. Either those institutions developed their own flocks or influenced community pastoral activities as a result of their demands, or they strengthened their economic relations with nomadic groups moving around the area (fig. 9.4). Sheep are ideal for centralized management, because they are small and offer potential for secondary products (Zeder 1988).

One probable influence of central demand can also be seen in the area of craft production. The radical transformation of the pottery repertoire with the disappearance of coarse chaff-faced wares, the standardization of vessel shapes and sizes, and the widespread use of the potter's wheel is an indication of a change in the organization of manufacture, probably resulting from pressure by the central institutions. A similar pattern is represented by metallurgy that is documented for this period.

The structural changes were associated with the introduction of formal features related to the Mesopotamian world, especially with regard to pottery. The introduction of new elements, however, was not due to the penetration into the local context of alien components,

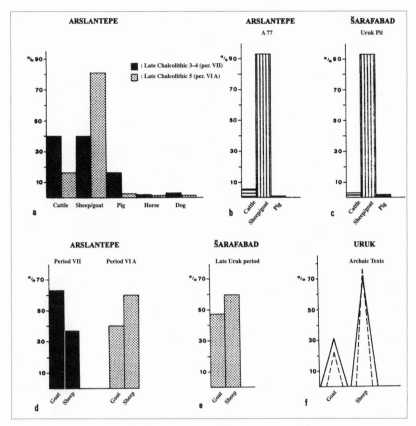

FIGURE 9.4

Comparison of animal breeding patterns at Arslantepe VII and VIA, Šarafabad, and Uruk-Warka.

along the lines of what happened at Hacınebi. The fine wares and the reserved-slip decoration, for example, are not related to any typical Uruk inventory as one would otherwise expect if these items had been introduced from a southern repertoire. They are more a product of a local elaboration of what are generically Mesopotamian models, which was clearly manifested at the height of period VIA. Furthermore, the development of mass-production of bowls did not introduce any external elements such as beveled-rim bowls; on the contrary, a gradual growth is apparent from a tradition that was deeply rooted throughout the whole of the north. A third element is the emergence of red-black ware. This ceramic type, which was completely alien to the

Mesopotamian cultural environment, is evidence of a general enlargement of the sphere of interaction of the Arslantepe community, which had broader contacts also with Anatolian and Transcaucasian groups. The discovery of a fragment of a small black jar on the lower floor of one of the rooms of the "transitional" building (A858), together with pottery that was exclusive to period VII, suggests that these contacts may have already begun before the evidence of Uruk influence on Arslantepe pottery.

All these elements are fully established in period VIA, when they are contemporary with what was virtually the total disappearance of products belonging to the cultural horizon of period VII. The far-reaching changes in the pottery repertoire at the end of the fourth millennium, with the development of fine wares and the sharp distinction between three types of production—wheel-made in the Mesopotamian environment, the Anatolian type handmade black burnished ware, and kitchen ware—suggest that the organization of production is now differentiated into specialized sectors, both centralized and otherwise (for the first two classes), and sectors of "domestic production"(for the kitchen ware).

This change took place together with many others, marking the emergence of a highly centralized society with a strong ruling class that controlled considerable resources and power. We are now familiar with the extension and the imposing nature of the public area at Arslantepe in this period, and the way in which central functions and activities such as storage and redistribution were concentrated in it, the movement of goods was administered, and religious activities were performed (Frangipane 1997b). This is revealed through the complexity of the buildings themselves (fig. 9.5). The public area housed different functions (temples, stores, courtyards, special areas for discarding administrative material), all linked by a single architectural plan. It combined features of many traditions. From the "Mesopotamian" tradition, the temples had a main room equipped with altars, niches in the walls, podiums, rectangular hearths, and plastic decoration on the walls. From the Anatolian culture came the adjoining position of buildings, their terraced arrangement, and probable overhead passages between one building or sector and another. The public area also exhibited elements unique to this site and cultural area, such as the

FIGURE 9.5

View of the period VIA temple-palace complex at Arslantepe.

bipartite (rather than tripartite) layout of the temples and the pictorial decorations on the walls.[11]

This combination of local features and elements shared with the Mesopotamian traditions is visible in virtually every aspect of the organization and culture at Arslantepe from this period. The forms of economic centralization are characterized, as they were at Uruk-Warka, by widespread administrative control, which seemed to emphasize the management of activities and labor rather than goods collected in the forms of taxes or tribute. This is indicated by the small size of the storerooms compared with the huge quantity of clay sealings and mass-produced bowls—now being made on the fast wheel—indicating a constant movement of goods, particularly withdrawals (figs. 9.6 and 9.7).The sealings were found in large assemblages in specific places within the palatial complex, and they were all in situ. They were recovered from two types of locations. Sealings were either found along with

FIGURE 9.6

Mass-produced bowls and clay sealings from Arslantepe, period VIA.

FIGURE 9.7

Example of Arslantepe VIA sealing.

334

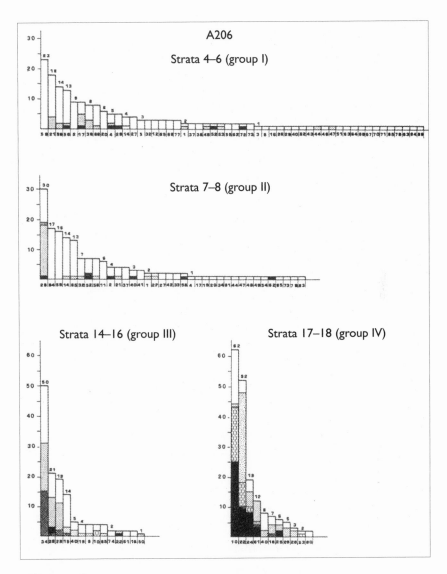

FIGURE 9.8

Histograms showing the stratigraphic distribution of the sealings from the main dumping place in the Arslantepe public area. The x-axis refers to the seals impressed on the clay, the y-axis to the sealed objects (pots, sacks, locks, door pegs) (Frangipane and Palmieri 1988–89:fig. 5).

vessels in one of the storerooms, both close to the vessels and put aside in one corner of the room (Frangipane 1994a), or they were heaped in special dumping places in the buildings themselves, having been discarded after their removal, and probably their auditing or recording. In the latter case sealings were grouped together in the dump layers by seals and types of sealed containers (fig. 9.8) (Ferioli and Fiandra 1983, 1994; Frangipane and Palmieri 1983b). Each location had particular seal designs impressed on the sealings, suggesting that each administrative sector within the palace had its own officials. The number of officials indicated by the seals, reconstituted by the impressions (approximately 190 on almost 2,000 clay sealings), is also very high and suggests that there was probably an internal organization of delegated powers and functions, somewhat like that reflected in the Uruk-Warka Professions List (see Nissen, this volume). Some seals had been mainly put on door closings, indicating individuals responsible for the storerooms; others were primarily on mobile containers (pots and sacks with different closing systems). The latter are the majority and, together with the very large amount of seals employed and the numerous cases of sealings taken away when they were still wet (i.e., no more than 24 hours after having been put on the container), suggest intensive administrative activity involving an extraordinarily large number of persons who worked under the control of the central institutions and were probably responsible for withdrawing the goods for themselves or other people under their charge. This activity entirely or almost entirely concerned internal circulation of goods, probably foodstuffs, as is indicated by the homogeneity of the operations, containers, and clay.[12] The actual storerooms, however, were very small (only two rooms found so far), and the sealing activity was concentrated in the smallest of the two storerooms, where they were associated with a few large containers and more than one hundred mass-produced bowls (Frangipane 1994a).

Although we do not have tablets of any kind, the study of the extraordinary assemblages of sealings found at Arslantepe has enabled us to demonstrate that the administrative system evidenced in this northern Anatolian site is comparable to that proposed for Uruk-Warka itself, though on a smaller scale. However, the glyptic is very different from typical Late Uruk production, as a result of a highly developed handicraft activity deeply rooted in the region. In the sophistication of the

designs, the carefully elaborated use of space-fillers, the symbolic elements, and the precise definition of different styles, it reveals the existence of workshops with a long local tradition. These traditions were
established at least as far back as the Ubaid period throughout the
north from Tepe Gawra to Değirmentepe (see Pittman, this volume).
Only on the cylinder seals, which constitute a very small minority, does
one find southern elements that were widespread in the Late Uruk
environment. Their designs include such elements as animals rampant
with intertwined tails, intertwined serpents, rows of vessels in carrying
devices, and the well-known scene of the transport of a preeminent person on a sledge vehicle.

Another structural feature that resembles those of other Mesopotamian traditions is the use of a powerful ideological apparatus that
functions as a means of reproducing the system. However, the expres-
sive forms and the specific ideologies also appear to be extremely original. The most outstanding examples are the wall paintings in the
passages of the palace (doors, corridors), designed to impress the people entering the building. In addition to the well-known anthropomorphic figures painted in a hieratic position on both sides of a door in the
central room of the stores complex, what is particularly interesting in
this regard is the painting (still being restored) of a complex narrative
scene in the corridor of the palace. It depicts two bulls facing one
another, perhaps both pulling a cart, one driven by a coachman and
probably coming out of a building represented geometrically, and the
other entering from the direction of the palace access gate (fig. 9.9).
They probably refer to mythical figures and events with which everyone
would have been familiar. They are full of references to an ideology of
power. Both the form of expression (the stylized paintings) and the
symbolic elements, as well as the narration itself, are dissimilar to any
other representations in the Mesopotamian environment. The only
common element is the symbol of the cart drawn by a cow or bull and
driven by a coachman, which is also present in the glyptic iconography
of both Arslantepe and Uruk-Warka.

The overall organization of this society also has a number of substantial characteristics, perhaps shared with other communities in
Upper Mesopotamia but quite distinct from the "early state" structures
further south. At Arslantepe, the marked development of a powerful

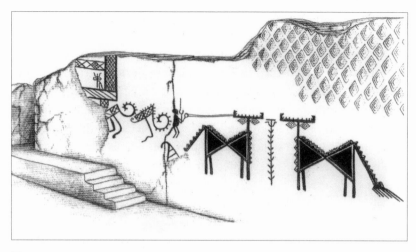

FIGURE 9.9

Wall painting from the corridor in the period VIA "palace" at Arslantepe.

political/administrative apparatus was not accompanied by a parallel process of urban growth, evidenced not only by the small size of the site but also by a further loss, during this period, of residential areas. Its development was based on social and economic conditions quite different from that which occurred on the southern alluvium plain, and also in the Syro–northern Iraqi plains. Arslantepe's ecological situation must have permitted a flourishing agricultural regime, but production capacity was limited by the mountains and may have been insufficient to support a large urban population. In fact, no real cities ever developed in this region in the early historical periods. It is therefore quite likely that the land ownership or usufruct system and the social base for managing the land differed from the situation in the alluvial plains. There were probably no large landowning families, and the lessened role of family groups in this subregion is suggested by the lack of isolated large houses otherwise typically found in Mesopotamia. The elites in this case probably did not have as strong a social and economic base underpinning their power as existed in the south, and they probably had a smaller capacity for expansion in the area of the primary economy. The lack of a hierarchically stratified society in terms of large family units may have made the power of the leaders much more vertical, in the sense that the society appears to have been divided into two basic social strata—the ruling class and the community—instead of showing the plurality of relations of inequality assumed for the later Mesopotamian world. In this way, if our reconstruction is correct, the Arslantepe system as a whole was less broadly based and less firmly rooted, and it was therefore weaker.

Yet the public institutions at Arslantepe at the end of the fourth millennium seem to have acquired an enormous amount of power. What was this power based on? I cannot accept the hypothesis that Arslantepe was a secondary state, the result of a powerful outside impetus from the south, for all the reasons I have already mentioned. In combination, the elements of different cultural origins that one finds at Arslantepe VIA are only superficially similar to southern Mesopotamia. In reality, it is the expression of a culture from the periphery of Greater Mesopotamia that, for millennia, had shared cultural patterns and routes of development with the other areas in this composite cultural region, actively contributing to the formation of Greater Mesopotamia and the network of interactions that created it. The architectural and administrative traditions and the external relations that linked the society of the Malatya Plain at the end of the fourth millennium to the "core" Mesopotamian areas are the result of a long history of very close relations and parallel developments.

This is certainly not to deny the magnitude of the influence of the southern groups on the north in the latter half of the fourth millennium. That influence must have been felt at Arslantepe, as shown by the few elements of undisputed southern culture found in its large public area. For example, while the pottery is similar but clearly distinguishable from the classic Late Uruk production patterns in terms of both the variety and number of shapes making up the repertoire and the specific profiles, a number of vessels mirror the shape and sometimes even the technique of manufacture of typical southern Mesopotamian items. Where these few objects have been found in situ, they were concentrated in particular places within the monumental complex: three vessels in the main room of Temple B, a spouted bottle in Temple A, and another in one of the storerooms in the "palatial" building, where it was found in association with four other spouted bottles of local production. Moreover the latter examples were unusual within the Arslantepe repertoire. The rarity and particular location of these findings clearly indicate that they were either imported materials or made locally on the basis of foreign typological models. This is suggested by the fact that they were not made using a homogeneous manufacturing technique: only very few of them show an unusual gritty paste, whereas others have fabrics more similar to the rest of the Arslantepe pottery. The ongoing chemical and mineralogical analyses have thus far provided equivocal answers to these questions. In addition to these indications of direct or indirect contacts with foreign groups, there are a number of references to southern images and symbols. These include certain representations on the glyptic and the decorative motifs impressed in the form of concentric lozenges on the walls of the temples and the corridor leading to the building complex, which may well have been elements that circulated at the level of the elites.

NORTH-SOUTH RELATIONS IN THE LATE URUK (LC 5) PERIOD: THE BEGINNING OF TERRITORIAL DOMINANCE

All of these clues indicate that southern groups were present in the north, where they probably migrated to what they might have considered "neighboring" regions, even areas very far from their native lands.[13] I think that the traditional cultural neighborhood was still recognized as such, and this may also have made Uruk people ideal partners for the northern elites without having to resort to hypothetical pressures from centers in their "motherland."

The far-reaching and well-entrenched interaction of the communities of Greater Mesopotamia, whose unity was also based, according to our initial hypothesis, on continuous movements of segments of the population and in turn encouraged these movements, showed an intensification in the second half of the fourth millennium. At the same time, a change in the way these movements occurred made them more visible. We do not know why substantial sections of the population moved and settled elsewhere, nor do we know whether the mechanisms that produced these population shifts were of the same nature, or the same magnitude, as those that had led to the fissioning and wide-ranging movement of groups in previous ages. Certainly, the geographic spread of the population shifts does not seem to be very different from earlier periods, and there is no significant evidence that their purpose was primarily commercial. As I have already pointed out, no archaeological remains suggest the existence of significant trade activities either in the colonies or in other sites where the presence of southern groups is attested. Even the soaring development of metallurgy at Arslantepe, while probably linked to trade with the southern Mesopotamian areas, was mainly in response to the strong demand from the internal elites, as shown from the type of objects produced there (weapons, ornaments, luxury household items) and their plentiful remains in the public buildings. Their limited circulation in the Malatya and neighboring regions suggests that the main object of trade, if metals were traded, was probably raw materials or ingots, whereas the development of metallurgical technology may have been stimulated by local demand. The mainly local destination of metal products is also indirectly supported by the continuity of the types of objects and the use of metal in the period immediately following the collapse of the centralized Mesopotamian-type structures. In an imposing "royal" tomb from the beginning of Early Bronze 1 was found an extraordinary concentration of objects that reveal a clear continuity with the tradition of period VIA in terms of both the shapes and in the smelting and casting technologies used (Frangipane 1998).

In the Late Uruk period (LC 5), the form taken by population shifts and the physical definition of the places in which people settled, including the founding in some cases of new towns surrounded by walls, indicate that the northern territories were less penetrable, and the groups coming into contact with each other had a much stronger political identification. They probably tried to maintain their own identity more than before, as is clearly evidenced in the archaeological material. As a result of strengthening the central institutions, there was a new way of bringing different cultures together. They met as distinct and separate political entities and probably sometimes clashed.

The economic interrelation between central institutions and the rural environment that provided the resources was legitimized by an ideology linking people, the land, and the developing urban centers together. Increased economic dominance and power mechanisms gradually reinforced the political importance of territorial units. The appearance of town walls in the alluvium and northern steppes in the

Late Uruk period was not only a possible response to heightened conflict, but was probably the symptom of a dawning conception of urban spaces as well-defined political entities with which the surrounding rural communities may also have identified. Another crucial factor in the formation of stable links between centers and their hinterland must have been the need to regulate relations with the nomads, over whom economic and political control was probably very important (Adams 1981). The significant development in sheep rearing in all the Late Uruk centers (Green 1980; Wright, Miller, and Redding 1980) seems to indicate the importance of these animals in the central economy. The effectiveness of this control must also have depended on the nomads identifying the towns as their reference points when they came into contact with the rural communities of a given territory.

This process must still have been in an initial phase at that time, because it did not entirely wipe out the capacity of the sociocultural entities that made up the Mesopotamian mosaic to "host" and absorb each other, even though the political relations began to be regulated in a new and different way. The societies perhaps fully exploited their traditional capacity to relate to one another on a vast geographical scale at that time, but a mechanism of centralized governance was introduced that gradually changed these relations.

THE COLLAPSE OF THE LATE URUK SYSTEM AND THE RISE OF POLITICALLY BASED STATES

The system of Late Uruk relations was probably the most widespread and intensive of any society in Mesopotamia prior to the founding of territorial states or empires, and it must have marked the peak of development of the "nonterritorial" centralized systems. It is precisely at that moment that Arslantepe seems to have projected its external relations in every direction, probably incorporating into the economic structure of the state the nomadic pastoral communities of Transcaucasian origin, who must have already been frequenting that area at the end of the fourth millennium. Indications of this involvement can be found in the adoption of new forms of pottery of northeastern origin and in the metallurgy, which showed such strong similarities to the Transcaucasus in the technology and composition of the metals that the Arslantepe smiths might well have used the same

(Transcaucasian) raw materials. This involvement of societies from northeastern Anatolia with the mediation of such centers as Arslantepe further extended the network of traditional relations of Mesopotamian societies.[14]

The nascent early state structures, with their increasing control over more compact and well defined territories and with the formation of political entities of varying strengths, introduced an element of contradiction and conflict into this permeable system and was probably the root cause of its crisis. The so-called collapse of the Uruk system was probably the dramatic moment of transition from the traditional system of relations to one based on more clearly defined political structures, and not the result of the withdrawal of the southern communities. On the contrary, the formation of Early Dynastic territorial states in the south is the sign of a reorganization that represents continuous development.

In the north, less economically strong centralized structures, which had less co-penetration with "civil" society, showed clear signs of crisis in this transitional phase. Each varied widely in outcome from one region to another. Where the crisis was overcome, the result was once again the emergence of smaller and more clearly defined political and territorial arrangements. Ninevite V territorial organization in central and eastern Jazira shows clear signs of this transformation (fig. 9.10; see also Rothman, this volume). There is evidence, on the one hand, of a significant growth of the main urban centers, such as Tell Brak, Halawa, Tell al-Hawa, and probably Leilan. On the other, small rural sites such as Tell al-Raqa'i and Telul eth-Thalathat have large central storage buildings, which may have been intended for the accumulation of the village's agricultural surplus (fig. 9.11) (Fukai, Horiuchi and Matsutani 1974: pl. XL, XLI; Schwartz and Curvers 1992). Since the socioeconomic organization of third-millennium societies does not seem to have been either egalitarian or communal, such buildings, which might also have been present in other villages, may be interpreted as places where the community surplus was collected to be sent to the towns (Schwartz 1994b). If this interpretation is correct, it implies central regulation of flows of staple products from the countryside to the towns, which in turn entails a strong stable relation between urban centers and *their* hinterland. The organizational experience in the

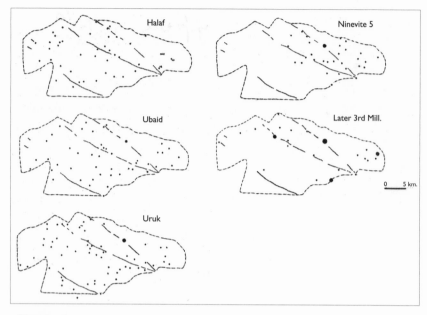

FIGURE 9.10

Changes in territorial organization in the northern Jazira (from Wilkinson 1990c:figs. 6–7).
The location of villages around the main center in the Ninevite V period, which results in an
empty space at the margin of this area that anticipates the more evident change in the later
third millennium, suggests that the process of the formation of separate political entities had
already started.

running of collective economies acquired by the Jazira communities in
previous millennia[15] probably helped the management of the new
forms of control. The socioeconomic and political relationships
involved in the new system, however, were completely different. By
increasingly extending its territorial capillary organization, this system
may have created the first real, though small, state entities.

North of the Taurus, the crisis was more radical and more final, perhaps partly owing to the newly acquired strength of the Transcaucasian
pastoral societies that placed their mark on the cultures of the Upper
Euphrates throughout the rest of the third millennium. Intensive contacts with the Syro-Mesopotamian areas were broken off forever. In any
event, both in the south and in the north, the end of the Late Uruk
period also brought to an end the long history of Greater Mesopotamia,
which is also the history of societies without "nations."

344

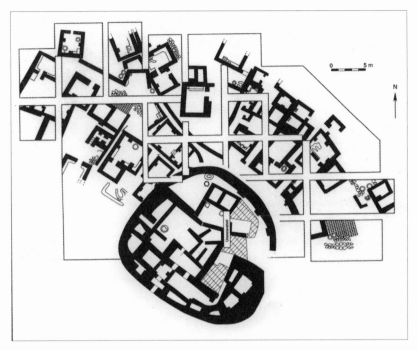

FIGURE 9.11

Plan of the Ninevite V village of Tell al-Raqa'i, Syria (Schwartz 1994b:fig. 9).

Notes

1. Otherwise there would have been a heterogeneous and discontinuous relationship between groups of individuals, interacting at irregular intervals, which is probably what occurred throughout the majority of prehistoric ages.

2. In the Early Dynastic, the palace was still the "great household" (in Sumerian, *é.gal*).

3. It is still difficult to interpret the storage buildings at Tell Oueili, whose dimensions vary in the different Ubaid phases (Huot 1994:117–30, 167–72). Not knowing the number of these buildings and their relationships to the houses and the rest of the settlement, it is impossible to know for which social units and products (the whole of the harvest or part of the surplus harvest) they were used.

4. These are obviously elite, not public, buildings.

5. The very term "early state," which I myself have used, is still perhaps inappropriate for the Late Uruk centralized system, even though I think that it is

345

equally inappropriate to use the concept of "chiefdom," which is awkward when applied to highly bureaucratized systems probably based on an established dominant class with internal hierarchies and an organization based upon delegated powers. I also dislike the terminology of "simple" versus "complex" chiefdoms, because they neither explain nor describe anything. Despite this classificatory difficulty, I would like to emphasize that societies of this kind cannot be written off by defining them as "transitional." They were full forms of society per se, which took in and integrated new relations and traditional relational systems that, taken together, made up a new structure.

6. The roots for this system can be found in the pre-Halaf communities of the Jezirah, with small specialized villages and large communal storage buildings. The finding of an extraordinary assemblage of clay sealings in the Neolithic pre-Halaf village of Sabi Abyad is well in keeping with our reconstruction (Akkermans and Duistermaat 1996; Frangipane 2000).

7. It is not plausible, in my opinion, that the form of the house was imitated, especially since it is so different from the local examples in terms of the use of domestic space and the concomitant structure of the families.

8. These dates, like the others mentioned in this chapter, are calibrated.

9. Unfortunately, the gap in the sequence at Norşuntepe and the uncertainty about the stratigraphic continuity of Gawra do not help to clarify the relationship between cultural and chronological factors.

10. No separate area for storage or other economic-administrative activities has been found as of yet.

11. These represent a typical Upper Euphrates cultural tradition, as evidenced by the older examples at Değirmentepe, Norşuntepe, and Arslantepe.

12. Neutron activation analyses have been carried out by James Blackman at the Conservation Analytical Laboratory of the Smithsonian Institution and are not yet published. I would like to take this opportunity to thank Mitchell Rothman for his help in arranging the contacts with Dr. Blackman and drilling the samples in Malatya. One of the most interesting initial findings is that the administrators of Arslantepe did not use the pure clay mix of most other sites, but a clay-stone conglomerate.

13. This phenomenon may be compared with the model of Greek colonies in southern Italy, to which Greeks traveled following routes known since the Mycenean period (Schwartz 1988b).

14. It is interesting here to note the presence at Uruk-Warka, in the

Riemchengebäude, of a javelin point made of a very unusual copper-silver alloy of which a great quantity was found in the Arslantepe Royal Tomb.

15. I refer to the above-mentioned evidence of collective storage in Neolithic and probably Halaf communities.

10

The Tigris Piedmont, Eastern Jazira, and Highland Western Iran in the Fourth Millennium B.C.

Mitchell S. Rothman

What one sees in the local community, then, is the outcome of two sets of forces, ecological on the one hand, economic, political and ideological in the other. The resulting interplay at the local level influences not only what goes on "on the ground"; it also influences the nature and capacity of the larger system in the "outside" world. The characteristics and capabilities of such a system depend directly upon the successful or unsuccessful outcomes of these local interplays. In this view, neither the local system or the larger world can be understood as if it constituted a closed system.... They are products of the shifting relations obtaining between them

—J. Cole and E. Wolf, *The Hidden Frontier*

One contrast between colonial and independent countries is that independent countries can base infrastructural development on even a single export while colonies lack the political means to do so.

—E. P. Durrenberger, *A Local Elite and Underdevelopment in a Peripheral Economy: Iceland in the Eighteenth–Twentieth Centuries*

The other contributions to this volume have illustrated that the phenomenon called the Uruk Expansion is quite variable across time and space. Also, rather than being some unitary movement of population, political and economic domination, or increased interaction over a short period of time, the phenomenon began much earlier than was once thought. As it continued over a period of approximately 500 years, many aspects of the relations among players, local and regional, changed considerably.

The focus of attention in understanding this phenomenon has been on the basins of the Euphrates River and its tributaries, the Khabur and Balikh Rivers. Some of the most dramatic changes occurred there, such as the founding of early outposts at Hacınebi, perhaps Hassek Höyük, and Sheikh Hassan; the occupation by Southerners at sites along the Euphrates like Habuba Kabira South and Jebel Aruda; and the emergence of major local centers on the upper Euphrates at Samsat and Arslantepe. It is also logical to focus on this area because those who propose that trade was the major impetus for the so-called expansion can rightly point to the Euphrates River as a transportation route that could speed the shipping of goods, at least in a southerly direction. Although a Tigris route up toward modern Mosul and then across the Jazira toward Tell Brak and the Euphrates Basin is well attested, timber for building (see Wright, chap. 4, and Algaze, chap. 2, this volume) would be most practically and cheaply transported by river barges down the Euphrates. Metal, another critical resource desired by Southerners, was already being mined at Ergani and refined and molded into tools at sites in close proximity to the Euphrates River.

Polities along the Tigris River and its tributaries, the upper and lower Zab Rivers,[1] are of particular interest for this discussion because of the difference in their evolution from that of sites in the Euphrates Basin. From the point of view of resource extraction, the Tigris sites are, in fact, closer than those on the Euphrates to sources of obsidian, gold, lapis lazuli, carnelian, and many metal ores.[2] Historical trade routes from the south along the Tigris and from the Zagros front of western Iran (see Algaze 1993a: fig. 20; also see fig. 1.1, this volume) ran through this area. However, in the Tigris Basin there are no comparable sites to Habuba Kabira South/Qannas or Jebel Aruda.[3] As Algaze (this volume) notes, all of the major sites were occupied before the Middle Uruk (our LC 3–4), and none seems to have the whole set of classic southern artifacts and artifact styles, as was the case with Habuba Kabira South/Qannas and Jebel Aruda. The possible exception is Nineveh, which Algaze (this volume) argues came close to being a northern emplacement. Based on a tiny sample of a large site it is possible to argue that Southerners dwelled in Nineveh, but whether it was a southern town like Habuba Kabira is far less clear (see below). Some of the major centers in this zone with an admixture of northern and southern artifacts—for example, Tell al-Hawa—grew to a considerable size, 35–50 hectares (Wilkinson and Tucker 1995), rivaling all but the largest centers of Tell Brak, Hamoukar, Uruk-Warka, and perhaps a few other places. How then do we come to understand developments in this zone?

In this chapter, I will

1. discuss the approach that has been taken toward understanding the so-called Uruk Expansion, arguing that it has placed too much emphasis on the power and role of the south and also makes a number of questionable assumptions about the behavior of northern "precontact" societies;

2. review the data from the Tigris piedmont and eastern Jazira in terms of the changing conditions over the whole of the fourth millennium; and

3. discuss the best documented site in this zone, Tepe Gawra, and its implications for our understanding of the evolution of northern societies, especially in the LC 1, LC 2, and beginning of the LC 3 (Terminal Ubaid, Early Uruk, and early Middle Uruk) periods.

THEORETICAL CONSIDERATIONS

The history of research in any field inevitably has an effect on the possible interpretations of patterns of artifact distribution. Every researcher carries with them the assumptions of their teachers and earlier literature in creating the mental map that they use to interpret new data. Studies of the ancient Near East are no exception.[4] As some argue (Nissen, this volume; Stein 1994c), the study of early complex societies in this region has two intellectual forebears: an early textual tradition and a focus by earlier archaeologists on excavating the monumental districts of the largest settlements. Cuneiform tablets, as Nissen argues in chapter 5, were created by and for the rulers and other leaders of the society in order to meet the administrative need for information on mundane matters. In this tradition, the world, of course, should be looked at from the top down. This approach should therefore be applicable in any locality where rulers controlled large populations and technologies such as writing, and it should work on a regional scale if the "core" south dominated the "peripheral" north and east.

Every author in this volume has avoided the most obvious and unsubtle version of this top-down, "alluvio-centric" viewpoint. Nevertheless, a certain willingness to overemphasize the roles of the states of the southern alluvium in the north persists. I am mostly referring to ideas that relate to Algaze's theory of the Uruk expansion. As Wright (1995) notes, Algaze's thesis is especially powerful because it brings together a series of economic and cultural factors in one unified theory. The rise of the state and the city in the south plus the Southerners' need for raw materials yielded the very colonial system that Algaze sees represented in a dendritic arrangement of sites with southern artifacts in the north.

The question that must be asked again is whether these three factors actually correlate in the way that Algaze's construct predicts, and if not, then how else can their correlation be understood to yield the same basic patterns of artifact distribution. In my opinion, Algaze's thesis brings together three elements in trying to explain the spread of clearly southern Mesopotamian (Uruk) artifact styles and the physical presence of Southerners in the north and east, the steppes and hilly country of Greater Mesopotamia. The first (Algaze, this volume) is that once a state-level society evolved in the southern alluvium, a number of processes inevitably began. One was geographical expansion, in this case to garner the natural resources its leaders and citizens valued. According to Algaze, this expansion is in the very nature of all states. Because of this expansion, a series of networks based largely on trade developed. In generating these new networks the more administratively elaborated societies of the south generated what has been called a World System (Peregrine 1996:3). Algaze asserts that the Southerners received raw materials, processed them, and manufactured goods that were distributed through southern economic systems, and also presumably traded back to northern and eastern polities in some as-yet-undetermined amounts. Therefore, members of northern and eastern societies were classic colonists in an economic sense. By sending non-value-added raw materials to the south and receiving value-added goods manufactured in the south, development was catalyzed primarily in the south, not in the north. This is the essential concept of Wallerstein's World Systems (Peregrine 1996:3). In the creation of the trading networks that impelled southern dominance, no military force was used, although the trading diaspora sites like Habuba Kabira South were controlled by southern leaders from one of a number of city-states. When these southern emplacements were abandoned at about 3000 B.C., the economic, political, and social structures of northern societies collapsed. Lastly, Algaze proposes that prestige or luxury trade in semiprecious stones, gold, silver, obsidian, metals, and slaves (Algaze 1993a:74–84), rather than bulk trade in crops and domestic animals, was at the heart of these exchange networks. Possible exceptions to this may be wool and timber.

Development of State and Pre-State Polities

In trying to explain the pattern on the ground, I will address each of the issues raised by the Uruk expansion theory. First, the issue of the state: one should, it seems to me, ask why states came into being. As Nissen (this volume) asks, what was the need? If, as Algaze proposes, the growth of the city-states of the south, especially Uruk-Warka, is to a significant extent based on their external, cross-cultural relations, those issues should play a major part in initial state development. To the contrary, although any number of theories have been offered to explain state origins (for example, for the Susiana Plains: Rothman 1987; Wright 1977b, 1994; Wright and Johnson 1975), they all seem compelled by local conditions. Algaze cites the far more agglomerated population of the southern city-state as an economic advantage in manufacturing and trade, but it is equally a political and administrative disadvantage. As I read Adams (1981) concerning the city—and extend it to political organizations like the state—the major concern of the centralized institutions of palace and temple alike was local and economic. That is, they seemed to care about land, water, crops, animals, and the labor of people to turn the resources of the south into products for storage, consumption, and *local* exchange. "In the largest sense, Mesopotamian cities can be viewed as an adaptation to this perennial problem of periodic, unpredictable shortages. They provided concentration points for the storage of surpluses, necessarily soon walled to assure defensibility. The initial distribution of smaller communities around them suggests primarily localized exploitation of land with much of the producing population being persuaded or compelled to take up residence within individual walled centers rather than remaining in villages closer to their fields" (Adams 1981:244). This emphasis on local workers appeared more and more in administrative seal designs of the LC 4 and 5 south. As Pittman writes (1993:243), "the images [in the sealings of the Late Uruk] when read closely show us the monitoring of the production and the feeding of a labor pool who produced commodities…. We also see the counting of capital investments such as animals on the hoof and the deposition of grain in the granary."

Politically, we see rulers engaged in competition for water and land with other city-states. Late Uruk prisoner scenes (Nissen, Damerow, and Englund 1993: fig. 15) emphasize armed competition, and because they seem to represent the defeat of a leader (man with a beard; see this volume, figs. 11.17 and 11.23) these images likely refer to local conflicts, not long-distance ones. Military incursions into "foreign"[5] lands are not depicted until the Akkadian period of the late third millennium B.C. when militarily subjugated colonies are historically attested. Certainly, the early and continuing conflicts between the city-states of Umma and Lagash (Cooper 1983) and Isin and Larsa (Edzard 1967:161–63, 189–94) from the mid-third into the early second millennium B.C. were about water for irrigation and arable land. Similarly, the earliest writing systems emphasized the receipt and dispersal of grains and animal products and the payment of temporary workers, male and female, often engaged in agricultural activities like grain processing (Nissen, Damerow, and Englund 1993). The nonwriting administrative system at Arslantepe seems to have been geared to staples as well (Frangipane 1994a, 1997b:66–68).

Within the local polity, the scope of activities that the administrative systems, which emerged in the late fourth millennium B.C. south, could control seem limited. Even a millennium and a half later in the Old Babylonian period of the early second millennium B.C., for which we have good documentary evidence, the grip of kings was limited to a core set of activities, and they cannot be said to have dominated most aspects of their societies (Stone 1987). Kings spent much effort at controlling their own agricultural land (Rothman 1994c). Competing organizations like the "city" (a council of some kind)[6] and guilds of merchants and other occupations coexisted (Oppenheim 1977:95–125). As Stein (1998) points out, increasing distance from the capital leads to the degradation of control. The point here is that the administration of states in the southern alluvium appears to have been built on local control and also to be quite limited in terms of the activities and the area over which they hold sway. Therefore, issues of exchange, though important, may be overemphasized in our understanding of the development of southern states, and, as I will argue, northern polities.

This assumption that development of the southern city-states was significantly determined by their "foreign" trade is also largely contradicted by the fate of its largest settlement, Uruk-Warka, after the withdrawal of the northern settlements. One would expect to see something of a collapse at Uruk-Warka as well, if this long-distance trade were such a key to its economic and political development. This is certainly what happened to England in a very few decades after portions of its empire, especially India, broke away. However, no such thing seems to have happened in Mesopotamia. Uruk-Warka and other cities and city-states continued to grow during the succeeding Sumerian period, and resources of metals and other goods continued to arrive in significant numbers, perhaps even in increasing numbers (Nissen, this volume).[7] The Sumerians hardly suffered an embargo of metals or other exotic goods.

I take it as axiomatic, as Cole and Wolf (1974:21, quoted above) contend, that regional dynamics always begin at the local level. Unless one culture is able by force of arms, technology, and numbers to overwhelm another culture—examples include the Native American tribes, British colonial India, or Dutch Java—cross-cultural interaction always involves some level of give-and-take. Even in the example of the Native American populations, which were moved out of their original ecological niches and decimated in terms of numbers, political and economic interaction continues, albeit in a new guise. Nissen (this volume) illustrates this point in explaining the development by southern scribes of the cuneiform writing system of the third millennium B.C., in which spoken languages initially foreign to the cuneiform scribes had to be accommodated as the cuneiform signs were modified. All players must be willing to play, or the game simply never happens, no matter how unequally the sides are matched during the eventual contest. Therefore, I think we would best be able to understand the Uruk expansion by looking carefully at a number of local systems and determining their developmental trajectories before the LC 3, and then through the first "contact" to the beginning of the third millennium B.C. This strikes me as the only way to sort out whether we are seeing direct influence, migration largely for trade (a diaspora) (Stein, this volume), migration to escape the south (Johnson 1988–89; Schwartz 1988b), colonial occupation (Algaze 1993a, this volume), or simple emulation of southern, "foreign" styles by leaders (Stein 1998) to achieve various ends.

I therefore reject the World Systems perspective that "the fundamental unit of social change is the world-system and not the society" (Hall and Chase-Dunn 1996:11–12). Ironically, I think Algaze might agree with me on this point. As an alternative, we must not let the seemingly grand scheme of regional trade networks overwhelm the perspective gained by looking inside the societies in question. As D'Altroy (chap. 12, this volume) writes, there is a tendency not to weight the non-state, noncentralized segments within each society appropriately, or to assume that they do not matter in larger-scale cultural dynamics. There is not enough emphasis on other modes of organization and action: kinship, "ethnic" (subregional self-defined and recognized by others) groups,[8] occupational groups, or political factions. An equally common problem of those writing about complex societies is the use of the term "elites" as a general code for a multiplicity of phenomena. Are all elites at the center of political *and* military decision-making? Are they all economic leaders? Do all leaders necessarily coordinate their efforts? History would say otherwise. For example, relations between the long-distance traders, the *tamkarû* (or *dám.gar*), and the governing elites documented in early third millennium B.C. texts and in the more detailed second millennium documents appear quite informal. Guilds of some kind seem to have regulated traders, maintaining investment funds independent of the crown (Rothman 2000). For example, the traders at the *karum* of Kanesh do not seem to be working for the king, but for their own personal advantage (Larsen 1967). *Tamkarû* at times seem to have had the patronage of the king, as troops were sometimes sent along as bodyguards, but again they seem less directed by the governing elites than having a temporary alliance with them for mutual benefit (Leemans 1950; Rothman 2000).

At the same time the opportunities for traders in the "periphery" may well have had to do with economic demand for goods generated by a state level of complexity at home. A greater division of labor, which is necessary for the rise of marketplaces with specialized goods,[9] also tends to correlate with city dwelling. In short, Algaze is right in seeing the rise of societal complexity typical of the state as critical for explaining the increasing trade and probable movement of people on a regional scale. He is perhaps wrong in focusing on the role of the state's leaders in setting up and operationalizing the exchange networks that ensued.

Much of the discussion of the Uruk phenomenon appears to assume that the leadership of states is based on economic issues, especially external trade. However, there are multiple sources of authority and influence. An emphasis on exchange has driven most theories but perhaps has given us a one-dimensional image. Blanton, Feinman, Kowalewski, and Peregrine (1996) divide sources of authority and influence into two general types: *(a)* objective and *(b)* ritual, knowledge-based, or ideological. Objective sources include wealth and control of production. Ideological sources involve the propitiation of the gods, and also manipulation of cultural perceptions and cultural knowledge. Those "who command attractive explanatory systems gather followers, or...exchange partners who become indebted in a commerce of ideas [and goods]" (Blanton, Feinman, Kowalewski, and Peregrine 1996:3). As Southall (1956:261) writes of Alur segmentary states, which probably are better classified as pre-states: "ritual supremacy is often accepted where political controls are not, and segmentary states may characteristically be more highly centralized ritually than politically."

Ritual and Complexity

One of the more interesting aspects of the Mesopotamian scene, and perhaps of early social complexity in general, is the relation of religious ritual and ideology to economics and politics. The ethnographic literature documents many cases of the use of religious ideas and ritual both in the regulation of practical economic activities and in the game

357

of politics. According to the global explanatory models or worldviews discussed by Blanton et al. (1996), societies evolve a perspective or cognitive map that explains not only the ways of the divine but also the reflection of the divine in the secular world.

An example of the practical use of ritual and religious ideas comes from Bali, where irrigated terraces are used for growing rice (Lansing 1995). One of the major problems of this agricultural regime is regulating the timing and the amount of water distributed to each of the terraces owned or cultivated by farmers. The Balinese have developed a system in which their fealty to one of the two chief gods of the island, the Goddess of the Lake, forms the basis for water management. This role of religious observance and water use is quite explicit. One manuscript intones, "because the Goddess makes the waters flow, those who do not follow her laws may not possess her rice terraces" (Lansing 1995:77). A possibly common theme in Mesopotamia involves the images of gods and leaders with the flowing waters of life. The investiture mural in Zimri-Lim's palace at second millennium B.C. Mari has one panel in which the god is handing the staff of rule to the king. In the panel below, water is flowing from pots. This "sacred" water nourishes the stalk of a plant and spawns fish (Weiss 1985: fig. 42).

The Mari wall painting emphasizes another aspect of religion and rule. Rulers, especially in times of trouble or transition, often invoke the power of the divine. This process is called sanctification (Drennan 1976). Moorey (1977) has proposed that the death pits from among the Royal Tombs at Ur represent part of this process. He argues that those who enacted the annual mating of the god Dumuzi and goddess Inanna as guarantors of the fertility of the land were given godlike status in death. Contemporary records indicate that the players in this ritual were often members of the king's immediate family. Similarly, in the prologue to the so-called Hammurabi stele, under an image of Hammurabi receiving the symbol of rule, Hammurabi makes it clear to all who can read that his rule is by divine right. Specifically, he records the judgments on various matters and invokes the old idea that to be a good ruler he must establish justice (Saggs 1962:197f.) As Drennan (1976:346) writes, "It seems highly unlikely that the natives of Mesoamerica [or Mesopotamia] accepted the social conventions granting higher status to a restricted set of individuals because they realized that it was necessary in order to maintain a system of economic symbiosis, which in turn enabled them to enjoy various economic advantages of specialization."

This confluence of religion and secular rule was originally interpreted as a theocratic state (Falkenstein 1974). Based on records from the city of Lagash in the southern alluvium, Falkenstein interpreted records of extremely large temple estates mentioned in conjunction with city rulers as evidence of priest-kings. Additional land exchange and other documents led to a major revision of Falkenstein's model (Yoffee 1995:289–90). The nature of the relations between the temples and the palace, the house of the god and the great household, varied through time. Each was a distinct institution, and they were not the only landowning institutions.

A less often mentioned but crucial aspect of religious ritual is its integrative function. The Kede of modern Nigeria comprise a segmentary state that exists within a multiethnic region (Nadel 1940). Kede traders and colonists often live in areas where they are at least temporary minorities. They maintain their societal integration and also bring other ethnic groups into their sphere of control through religious ritual. One such ritual has to do with the river, used for both transport and agriculture. This ritual is supposed to be for the whole riverine community, Kede and others. "The priest climbs a rock in midstream and throws a stone toward the bank; the spot where the stone falls is believed to mark the line to which the river will rise that year" (Nadel 1940:191). It promotes fertility. The chief often provides the goods needed for rituals, even ones he cannot attend. Therefore, "a single belief and a common cult comprise both rulers and ruled, notwithstanding the religious barriers which otherwise separate the two, and add to the political dependence...another, spiritual, dependence" (Nadel 1940:191).

Certainly, throughout the extended period from the fifth through the third millennia, we know that people moved around Greater Mesopotamia—not only nomadic groups, but cultivators and craft workers as well. As I have written about Gawra (Rothman 1988; Rothman and Peasnall 1999), I find the increasing importance of the temple and its cult an integral part of forming and maintaining polities and exchange networks. The symbolic transition of the tripartite

(Mittelsaal) house from an extended family residence to a specialized temple makes sense in this context.

The nature of ritual and the ritual buildings may provide an indication of ritual's role, certainly in the sanctification (Drennan 1976) of leaders and in their increasing authority to the exclusion of other segments of society. In chapter 9, Frangipane points out that in the period VII temple complex at Arslantepe, multiple doors lead into the main sanctuary. That sanctuary is quite large, even compared with the later VIA temple. The progression Frangipane notes in political organization is an increasingly exclusionary one. One could certainly speculate that as the political organization became more exclusionary, access to the holy sanctum within the temple of the formal "state" religion would become more exclusionary as well. These issues are discussed in greater detail by Heinrich (1982).

It is likely that religion played roles of sanctification of rule, social integration, and cultural identity in fourth millennium B.C. Mesopotamia.

The Nature of Regional Networks and Their Reflection of Cross-Cultural Interactions

How then should we view intraregional, cross-cultural exchange? Even if we accept a major role for leaders in the Uruk expansion as well as external exchange as keys to understanding larger trends in Greater Mesopotamia during the fourth millennium B.C., we must also look at differing goals and options for them in their relation to various segments of society. We again must see a possible multiplicity of leadership groups or "elites." Even if the strong leaders are at the top of clear political and social hierarchies, the power and role of leaders may be restrained or heterarchical. In what Blanton, Feinman, Kowalewski, and Peregrine (1996:2) call an "exclusionary power strategy," political actors seek to amass for themselves wealth, status, or political authority. An alternate but equally common "corporate strategy" shares authority, decision-making, and rewards across "groups and sectors of society in such a way as to inhibit exclusionary power" (1996:2). According to Blanton and colleagues, the exclusionary strategy in economic terms can be seen as a "network strategy" in which those who wish to garner wealth, status, and political authority must establish ties outside their local polity. These ties are represented in exchange relationships in a wider network outside their own local exchange sphere. This strategy is especially clear when leaders attempt to control the distribution of rare and highly valued goods, or their manufacture for export. This strategy may have been common in the northern and eastern sites that exhibit extensive emulation of southern Uruk artifacts.

Arslantepe appears to be a classic case of network strategy, as that determinedly local site clearly based its amazingly centralized palace system on its role as a production center, especially for metals, and as a trading intermediary (Frangipane and Palmieri 1983; Frangipane 1993). It was not a case of imperialism or of colonialism. As the quotation by Durrenberger at the beginning of this chapter implies, Arslantepe was part of an independent polity ("country," in his terms) and by the end of the fourth millennium probably at the sociopolitical level of a city-state. The site was never "taken over" by Southerners, but its leaders' attempts at a network strategy brought both southern artifact styles and administrative technology—as well as Transcaucasian manufacturing technology and wares—into the site.

Networks of various kinds may be at work, and not all of the networks created involved primarily economic exchange. The boundaries of networks of exchange, as well as those of politics, military might, information, and style, may not be identical. As Hall and Chase-Dunn (1996:14) write, "all regularized material exchanges should be included as criteria of system boundedness. Thus, it is necessary to consider how relatively localized systems of bulk-goods exchange are nested within much larger networks of prestige-goods exchange in any system." Hall and Chase-Dunn (1996:14) also point out that military involvement may well describe a larger area than local bulk exchange, probably much like the inter–city-state conflicts I cited above. One must add to these bases for network building other "information sharing" networks: "networks of information in a variety of forms, including, but not limited to, ideology, religion, technical information and culture must also be included as bounding mechanisms. We do not expect that the information network will necessarily coincide with any of the other networks, [although] the information net will be of the same order of size as the prestige-goods net: sometimes larger, sometimes smaller" (Hall and Chase-Dunn 1996:14). The Ubaid regional system is probably best described as an information network. In the Ubaid system a new technology of slow-wheel pottery manufacturing spread rapidly across Greater Mesopotamia, causing seemingly identical styles of pottery decoration(Nissen, this volume) that should not be taken to imply cultural assimilation. As Nissen states in chapter 5, a number of different technologies seem to accompany the slow wheel: stamp seals, Mittelsaal house plans, and one could add canal irrigation. To be adopted these technologies must fill some local need. For example, the Mittelsaal house plan may have provided developing local chiefly systems with an appropriate residence for extended families (Forest 1983; Rothman 1988; Rothman and Peasnall 1999). As pointed out above, the development of the Mittelsaal plan as the model for fourth millennium temples is probably not coincidental, either. Similarly, irrigation agriculture with its potential for increasing yields would fit the goals of a newly developing tributary economic system (Wolf 1982).[10] The point is that some southern cultural items may represent answers to existing needs in the north rather than a geographical expansion of southern population and control. The "Uruk Expansion" may have been less a matter of significant trade or influence and more a result of information exchange.

Assuming that a regional network of information and goods exchange did exist, how do the various polities fit in it? Was there southern dominance? Algaze's idea of an informal, *peaceful* empire in which only the Southerners got a significant return has long troubled me (Rothman 1993). As Chase-Dunn (1989:23) writes, "In the periphery extra-economic coercion plays a much greater part in production relations." The following could easily be a summary of Algaze's thesis: "Under circumstances such as these, it was unnecessary (indeed for geographical reasons it was impractical) to build an empire in the *political* sense of the word, overturning the ethnic, institutional, or administrative structure of the conquered nations. It was enough that the conqueror's presence be everywhere visible, and everywhere strong enough to prevent the subject peoples from refusing what was required of them: heavy contributions in the native products, and free access by the conqueror's agents to the native natural resources, which must at their direction flow freely toward the capital" (Bottéro 1967:111). This is a description of the Akkadian Empire 1,000 years after the so-called

Uruk Expansion. Bottéro continues, "It was enough, that is, in an *economic* empire of this kind, to add to the native and political and administrative machinery a military occupation force, intended to hold it to obedience" (1967:111). Uruk-Warka is much farther south than the Akkadian capital, which would make it even harder to exert control, military or otherwise, as Stein (1999) has suggested.

As Kohl (1987:20) argues for societies of third millennium B.C. Mesopotamia, "peripheries...were far from helpless in dictating the terms of exchange; they could develop or terminate relations depending upon whether or not these relations were perceived to be in their best interest." In practical terms, this means that individuals or groups within northern societies must have seen advantages to an exchange relation with Southerners, or they certainly could have denied Southerners access to resources or simply killed them. Whether or not there was a wall, the small communities of Southerners that we see at Hacınebi and perhaps Hassek Höyük and even the larger ones at Habuba Kabira South/Qannas and Jebel Aruda could not have sustained themselves that far from home without the cooperation or at least tolerance of local northern and eastern communities, as Algaze (this volume) now agrees.

Algaze's construct also seems to raise questions even in its own terms. Evidence for one of the most important and prolific economic exchanges, metals, indicates a tradition of metallurgy from extraction through smelting and refining to final product in the north. Metallurgical material at Hacınebi begins in the Hacınebi A, precontact, late LC 2 period (Stein et al. 1998), and even earlier at Değirmentepe (Esin 1982:109). Certainly lapis lazuli, carnelian, gold, silver, bitumen, obsidian, chlorite, and other minerals were processed and manufactured into very technically fine products before the so-called contact period (see below for Gawra). Textiles were being manufactured as cottage industries, but also on a larger scale at Gawra early in the fourth millennium B.C. Ceramics were mass-produced at an early date, if one accepts Akkermans's (1988:127–28) assertion that chaff-faced wares were adopted because of their speed of production. In short, what was the advantage of exchange for the northerners and easterners, who do not seem to *need* any of the suggested southern exports? Unlike Britain's American or Indian colonies, no one claims that Southerners had the military or political power to tax or to force their neighbors *not* to manufacture needed goods, such as tea or cloth. In classic colonial systems most colonists were immigrants, such as Stein (this volume) describes, or were local populations who were utterly dominated by a contingent from the colonizing society. We should perhaps be looking at the residents of Habuba Kabira and Jebel Aruda as the colonists, and not focusing so much on the surrounding precontact polities as being colonized. Algaze's thesis might best explain the collapse of the Uruk colonies at Habuba Kabira South and Jebel Aruda. The latter site was already in decline before its abandonment near the end of the fourth millennium B.C. (van Driel 1998). Ironically, it may be changes in southern city-states that created new economic demand and the formation of entrepreneurial groups of individuals like those at Hacınebi rather than formal, government-administered colonies.

The Kede of northern Nigeria may once again provide a modern example. The Kede were an independent segment of the Nupe state (Nadel 1940). Their homeland is at the confluence of the Niger and Kaduna Rivers The Kede are well-organized traders who traditionally controlled the river route and became transport specialists carrying goods between their homeland and non-Kede farming and fishing groups. In search of new trading opportunities, groups of Kede emigrated upriver. As Nadel (1940:173) writes, "the Kede territorial expansion did not proceed step by step, in continuous stages, but rather in a series of leaps, which may leave gaps between outpost and outpost." These new colonies were not set up by the primate chief, but by small groups of independent entrepreneurs. Only after a considerable time did these trading colonies come under the control of leaders in the capital. "From the history of modern Kede settlement we learn that there is a certain time lag between the first occupation of a new place by Kede immigrants and its eventual rise to the status of a political outpost" (Nadel 1940:173). Perhaps as it did to the residents of Habuba Kabira South, "the new economic development of the country ...attracted Kede emigration to places far outside the orbit of their political organization; thus at the busy trading-place on the confluence of the Niger and Benue [Rivers], Lokoja, a large and prosperous Kede colony has grown, which combines all the stages of Kede settlement, permanent and semi-permanent houses in which Kede families have made their home" (Nadel 1940:173–74). The Kede regard the local population, however well organized, as "aboriginals."

Our task is to understand local developments and their implications for development and change in each subregion. In trying to determine the implications of an exchange network's impact on local political and economic development, we must also establish, and not assume, what was obtained through this network and what their social meanings were in each node of the network. Not all goods have the same meanings and the same social or political uses in every society. As Schortman and Urban (1996:99) write, "A prestige good, like any other item, derives its behavioral significance in part from the manner in which it is used by people attempting to accomplish specific objectives. One of those goals is the acquisition of power, and social valuables can have a role in such machinations. That is not to say that prestige goods structure economies or political systems. Such structures are created by people who may well use social valuables." Is a leader who wishes to confirm his or her authority more likely to go to a ceremony with a new lapis lazuli pin or distribute metal plowshares to clients? As D'Altroy writes (this volume), "ceremonial hospitality and redistributional relations mediate group re-affiliations and provide the context within which political activities are carried out." Are the aforesaid leaders better off distributing grain rations or a few fancy pots?

Schortman and Urban (1996) use the examples of obsidian blades and marine shell in Mesoamerica. Both are made of imported raw materials by skilled artisans but were used in two very different ways to maintain hierarchies or social status. In the case of the blades, giving them to individuals lower on the hierarchical ladder established a client relationship. The marine shell ornaments were used for competition among would-be leaders within a polity. Those able to obtain and display prestige goods were accorded respect. Shells were also used as an exchange good between elites, much as the gift of the *mwali* shells is used to establish a partner relationship at a more egalitarian level in the New Guinea Kula Ring (Malinowski 1961). In the Kula Ring the goal of the trading system is to obtain more practical bulk goods. The shells are symbolic gifts used to open exchange networks. In short, simply establishing that trade in rare goods or even bulk goods existed does not tell us all we need to know in order to understand how people use socially valuable items for political ends, or what effect exchange had on economic and political action and organization. It is not, as Algaze asserts, necessarily a case of administratively superior polities imposing themselves and their ideas on peripheral, underdeveloped societies.

We must discover the patterns of distribution and consumption of goods. Knowing which products went to which members of the receiving society and what use was made of them is a key to their interpretation as economic and political tools. As D'Altroy notes in chapter 12, Algaze and others seem to assume that only elites receive goods imported from a distance, and they use them in the same way. Evidence from Hacınebi indicates that large amounts of bitumen were traded (M. Schwartz, Hollander, and Stein 1999). Were only elites getting bitumen and giving it out? Were they using all the bitumen themselves? It strikes me as implausible that leaders of the fourth millennium could control the movement of all valuable goods, or even tried.

Other factors need to be considered. Was the trade in bulk products or easily transported luxury items? The mechanisms of exchange (down-the-line, direct, administered) must also be considered, especially since we cannot assume that all goods were distributed in the same way, locally or regionally. Each good and type of good must be understood on its own.

In trying to investigate a large region over a long period of time at a critical point in human social evolution, we researchers have made, perhaps of necessity, certain assumptions about the region's networks and their impact on northern and southern societies in Mesopotamia. In order to take the next steps in understanding the evolutionary processes involved, we must dig more deeply into individual polities and examine what happened in each one. The grander regional patterns will emerge only after we understand local contexts and their relation to the buildup of regional networks. This is not to advocate a return to particularism in which the data somehow are important in and of themselves, but rather a plea to document particular cases better in order to understand general trends in their real world messiness.

Emulation, Adoption, and Colonization

Algaze's theory has gained currency, as I have already said, in part because it explains a regionwide pattern of artifact distribution. The explanation of that pattern has been questioned (Pollock 1992; Rothman 1993; Stein 1998; Stein et al. 1996; Wattenmaker 1990). One of the key issues has been whether the presence of clearly southern style artifacts in the north and east indicates emulation, adoption, or the physical presence of Southerners. Stein (this volume) presents a set of criteria for determining whether sites with this material actually housed Southerners. We still need to find a way to understand southern material at sites where Stein's criteria would suggest that Southerners did not live in any significant numbers. What does the presence of this material mean? To some degree I have already discussed this in questioning how "elites" may use foreign, valued items in a political realm. Stein (1998), Frangipane (1997), and others have proposed that these foreign goods in the "periphery" resulted from elite emulation. Hellwing (1999) asserts that many of the southern-style vessels at Hassek Höyük were copies of that style using local techniques. Because processes that probably happened in decades are hidden behind our more than 200-year-long periods, these questions may be difficult to answer at this time.

One way to understand the process of elite emulation and then more general adoption may be language. Pottery style is associated with specific groups or "cultures" at certain times and places, based on the assumption that potters symbolically express common traditions or inclusion in the same political or economic entities. In others words, pottery style zones, if they are anthropologically meaningful, are expressions of a definable group's physical propinquity and common identity. In many ways language covers the same social and cultural ground. For example, Sumerian and Latin as spoken languages died long before their use as literary or legal languages ceased. In terms of emulation, the spread of dialectic differences in languages, which can begin as elite affectations and then are adopted more broadly by the general population and become markers of regions or ethnicity, may be a useful way to view these issues. The so-called Brooklyn accent of New York is just such a case. Individuals from New York's upper classes emulated an upper-class speech pattern from London in the mid-nineteenth century, as did elites in places stretching in a band from Virginia to New Orleans. This same dialect was later adopted by middle- and lower-class residents of Brooklyn and overlaid on a generalized New York accent. In the southeastern United States, southern "drawls" were overlaid on the old elite dialect (Labov 1972:143–45, 171–78). Some typical phonemes of the "Brooklyn" accent can still be heard among older persons from the southeast United States. Like pottery in the Ubaid period, combinations of recognizable local and "foreign" elements existed side by side. The process of emulation by a limited segment of society, followed by a general adoption, seems to be a similar pattern to the distributions of southern Uruk pottery in the north. First, there are pockets of original southern types at sites like Hacınebi and then a much broader use—at Hassek, copying—in the LC 5 at places like Tell al-Hawa, Brak, or Nineveh.

Part of the problem may be the way we have come to see the nature of cross-cultural contacts over the late fifth through fourth millennia. Many of the recent articles and books written about this period refer to LC 1, LC 2, and early LC 3 as "precontact." I, too, use this nomenclature. However, this term to some degree distorts the ancient reality, as Nissen (this volume) states. Contacts across the whole of Mesopotamia had been numerous for more than a millennium and a half before this so-called contact began. Ironically, the Mittelsaal or tripartite house is listed as one of the markers of southern Uruk presence in the north (Sürenhagen 1986a). Yet, virtually every house type from Habuba Kabira South (Kohlmeyer 1996) can be found at Tepe Gawra from levels XII to IX, all before "contact." Similarly, hammerhead bowls, markers of the LC 3 (see Schwartz, this volume) that were gradually adopted in the north, appeared in Susiana quite suddenly (Wright, comment in Rothman 1989:283). A very similar style of administrative tool, the stamp seal, existed in both the north and south for many hundreds of years before contact. Put simply, contact started millennia before the Uruk period and never stopped. Goods and ideas clearly moved in both directions in the precontact period and after the Uruk period. What seems to have happened in the last 600 years of the fourth millennium is not a sudden contact, but an intensification of already existing interaction or, perhaps, a new kind of interaction. This contact did not cease at the end of the fourth millennium B.C., but it did change insofar as it can be monitored in different subregions.

The Uruk Collapse

The idea of an Uruk expansion has traditionally presupposed an end of that growth. An integral part of the explanations of this phenomenon offered to date has been that the withdrawal from the Uruk colonies at Habuba Kabira South, Jebel Aruda, and other sites marked the end of the expansion. This withdrawal, seen as a collapse, presumably exposed the underdeveloped nature of northern polities because they retreated into village life, not to return to a florescence of urbanism until 500 or so years later. The prime example of this trend is in the Euphrates Basin, the Syrian Tabqa and Tishrin, and the Turkish Euphrates south of Birecik.

Even if settlement in the Upper Euphrates changed at the end of the Late Uruk period, was there a general collapse? Arslantepe VIA continued in full glory after Habuba Kabira LC 5 levels ended according to radiocarbon dating (Wright and Rupley, this volume). Its demise probably had more to do with the movement of Transcaucasians than with events in the southern alluvium (Rothman et al. 1998). Habuba (north, not the famous southern one) had post–LC 5 material, although it is largely unpublished (Lupton 1996:79). As I will argue below, societies in the Iraqi Jazira and Tigris piedmont do not seem to have "collapsed" at all. Lupton argues that the Karababa center of Samsat also did not decline. Other sites in the Karababa (Algaze et al. 1990; Behm-Blanke 1985; Behm-Blanke et al. 1981), the Tabqa (Dornemann 1988), and near Birecik (Rothman et al. 1998) do not seem to have been abandoned at the beginning of the Early Bronze Age.

Related to this, I argue below that many of the sites that Algaze sees as controlled by the south, even sites with southern artifacts in profusion, may have been within "independent countries," as the Durrenberger quotation at the beginning of this chapter calls them. Perhaps internal changes in these polities led to dramatic alterations in the north, not the withdrawal of southern cities in the Euphrates Basin of Syria and southeastern Turkey. Even if so-called colonies in the Euphrates Basin of Syria and southeastern Turkey collapsed, the large Ninevite V occupations of Nineveh, Tell al-Hawa, and other sites in the Tigris Basin do not represent collapses at all. Perhaps the areas that did retrench had overextended their administrative and economic capabilities. As one could write about the Euphrates Basin in the last 400 years of the fourth millennium B.C., "Even in an independent, peripheral state, local elites making a living from the export trade and enjoying well-established connections with core economies had every incentive to maintain export economies even in times of trouble" (Durrenberger 1996:72).

Given the issues raised above, what can the Tigris piedmont and the eastern Jazira tell us about the nature of societies and their interactions during the fourth millennium B.C.?

THE TIGRIS PIEDMONT AND THE EASTERN JAZIRA

Chronological Issues

The chronology of the Tigris piedmont and eastern Jazira has benefited from comprehensive new analyses by Gut (1995), Rova (n.d.), and Truffelli (1998), among others. In outline it is becoming fairly clear. Some of the older excavations—for example, Tepe Gawra, Grai Resh, and Nineveh—lack radiocarbon or other absolute dates and were at times not excavated according to modern stratigraphic standards. More recent excavations in the eastern Jazira and Saddam Dam catchment are providing a new stratigraphic framework for levels in older excavations. Levels associated with each of the LC 1–5 periods proposed in this volume were occupied at various sites in this subregion, although surprisingly few sites, even Nineveh, seem to have had settlements that spanned all of these periods. A more complete analysis of the relative chronology of this part of Mesopotamia in relation to Tepe Gawra will appear elsewhere in the near future (Rothman n.d.), so only a general outline of the chronological issues will be presented here.

A good way to begin a chronological analysis for this time and place is to understand that there seem to be clusters of design elements, certainly in pottery and at times also in seal design, architecture, and various small finds. These clusters tend to define geographical zones, often ones with ecological similarities (Lupton 1996: figs. 2.4, 3.19, 4.18, and 9.1). In the LC 1 and 2 periods, the north can be divided into (1) the whole of the Tigris drainage north of the lower Zab to the Murat River east of Elâzig and the eastern part of the Khabur River basin (the area covered by this chapter), (2) an area west of the Euphrates to the Levantine Coast (see Schwartz, this volume), and (3) an area east of the Euphrates into the Balikh and Khabur Basins (see Schwartz, this volume). Within these zones, stylistic repertoires include material from two adjoining areas. Tell Brak falls into a zone of overlap during the LC 1 to early 3 phases. After the beginning of LC 3, the zones change. One zone—the one into which Southerners moved to live at Habuba Kabira South, Jebel Aruda, and so on—consisted of the middle Euphrates River and lower parts of the Balikh and Khabur. A second zone swept across the whole of the Assyrian (eastern) and north Syrian (western) plains from the Tigris piedmont to the Euphrates. The final zone is restricted to what for the early third millennium Buccellati (1979) called the Outer Fertile Crescent—places at a higher elevation along the most northerly sections of the Tigris and Euphrates Rivers and the area where the Murat River crosses the Malatya and Altınova Plains. This area, especially the key site of Arslantepe, has been called the gateway to the highlands (Burney 1993). In the Early Bronze 1 period, beginning in Mesopotamia at 3000 B.C., the style zones changed again, this time in many ways coming closer to the pre-contact pattern, with the exception of a band of Early Transcaucasian red-black wares in the northern, Eastern Turkish zone.

The shifting of areas dominated by certain styles indicates to some degree shifting patterns of interaction. Although that interaction could be only a sphere of information exchange, given the preponderance of evidence a more likely explanation is that as southern traders and set-tlers came north, exchange relations, marked in part by the emulation and adoption of "southern" styles, increased. As the Euphrates zone (style zone 3) began to decline, older, more informal boundaries returned. Those boundaries were not identical to the precontact ones because new players from the Transcaucasian region entered the Outer Fertile Crescent, but zones 1 and 2 retrenched in their east-west and north-south exchanges, respectively. Again, they did not collapse; they changed.

A few of the chronological markers of the LC 1–5 periods in the Tigris piedmont and the eastern Jazira are illustrated in figures 10.1 and 10.2. The LC 1, also called the Terminal Ubaid, is a transitional phase from the Ubaid 4 to the Early Uruk period in the older nomen-clature. Its distinctive markers, again for the Iraqi Jazira and hills only, includes Sprig Ware jars and bowls, Wide Flower Pots with extended

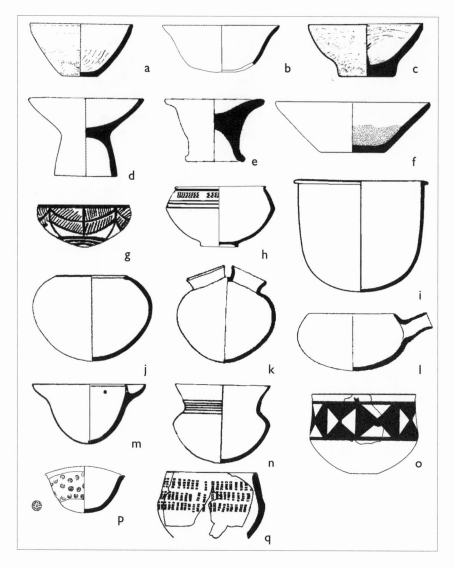

FIGURE 10.1

Pottery of the northern LC 1 to early LC2.

KEY

a. Değirmentepe (Esin 1983:fig. 5, 1), pinkish, chaff temper, flint-scraped. D = 19 cm.

b. Hammam et-Turkman IVD (Akkermans 1988:fig. 7, 110), plant and lime temper, scraped surface, orange, dark core. D = 35 cm.

c. Norşuntepe, J/K 17 (Hauptmann 1982:pl. 36, 1), bright red-brown, lightly speckled [chaff faced]. D = 16.5 cm.

d. Norşuntepe, J/K 17 (Hauptmann 1982:pl. 38, 8), red ocher–colored, coarse ware, black core; chaff, limestone, and coarse sand temper. D = 13.5 cm.

e. Tepe Gawra XII (Rothman n.d.:pl. 11, 226), red-brown ware, burnished, quartz and chaff temper. D = 9.7 cm.

f. Tepe Gawra XII (Rothman n.d.:pl. 11, 239), brown ware, chaff temper, bitumen inside. D = 21.5 cm.

g. Tepe Gawra XII (Rothman n.d.:pl. 13, 321), gritty brown ware, red slip, black paint. D = 8.4 cm.

h. Tepe Gawra XIB (Rothman n.d.:pl. 14, 803), no detail. D = 19.6 cm.

i. Tepe Gawra, grave below XII (Tobler 1950:pl. CXXVI: 274), coarse gray ware. D = 60 cm.

j. Tepe Gawra XIAB (Rothman n.d.:pl. 14, 775), brown ware, burnished. D = 22 cm.

k. Tepe Gawra XI (Rothman n.d.:pl. 19, 1444), gray brown ware, dark red slip. D = 20 cm (body), 8.8 cm (spout).

l. Tepe Gawra XIAB (Rothman n.d.:pl. 15, 767), green gray ware, quartz grit and chaff temper. D = 17.0 cm.

m. Tepe Gawra XIA (Rothman n.d.:pl. 15, 795), coarse buff ware, wet-smoothed. D = 48 cm.

n. Tepe Gawra XI (Rothman n.d.:pl. 18, 1396), greenish buff ware. D = 6 cm.

o. Norşuntepe J/K 18-19, Late Chalcolithic (Hauptmann 1976:pl. 50, 9), chalky white, slightly burnished, with black paint; grit and lime temper. D = 13.5 cm.

p. Tepe Gawra XI (Rothman n.d.:pl. 18, 1415), buff ware, lime temper. D = 9 cm.

q. Norşuntepe J/K 18-19 (Hauptmann 1976:pl. 42, 8), reddish gray; chaff, lime, and grit tempering. D = 10 cm.

bases,[11] U-shaped urns, and small, footed bowls (like braziers) (fig. 10.1). LC 2 or early Uruk markers (Gut's Gawra A) include stamped and appliqué wares; early Wide Flower Pots (western Cobas); carinated tumblers (often with incised lines); double- or channel-rim bowls; double-spouted jars; gray, lightly burnished, hole-mouth jars (often with an interior beveled edge); and bowls with cannon spouts. Gut's Gawra B assemblage type includes bowls and jars with triple paint blobs on the interior edge; globular jars with short, out-flaring rims; early red-slipped, burnished wares; and jars with descending crosshatch triangles

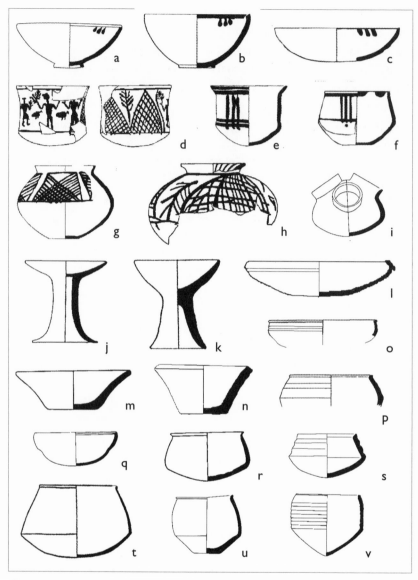

FIGURE 10.2

Pottery of the northern late LC 2 to LC 3.

KEY

a. Tepe Gawra XA (Rothman n.d.:pl. 21, 1819), brown ware, dark brown paint. D = 35.5 cm.

b. Musharifa Late Chalcolithic (Oguchi 1987:fig. 14, 11), reddish brown with vegetable and white grit temper, cream slip, red-brown paint. D = 18 cm.

c. Norşuntepe J/K 18-19, Late Chalcolithic (Hauptmann 1972:pl. 71, 6), reddish brown ware with flat dark red paint, dark gray core, a bit of grit and micaceous sand temper. Diameter not recorded.

d. Tepe Gawra X (Rothman n.d.:pl. 24, 1949), fine light brown ware. D = 20.5 cm.

e. Tepe Gawra X (Rothman n.d.:pl. 24, 1924), buff ware, cream slip, black paint, wheel-made. D = 12 cm.

f. Norşuntepe J/K 18-19, Late Chalcolithic (Hauptmann 1972:pl. 71, 2), matte reddish brown on yellowy buff clay. Diameter not recorded.

g. Norşuntepe J/K 18-19, Late Chalcolithic (Hauptmann 1972:pl. 71, 1), buff ware with dark reddish brown paint. Diameter not recorded.

h. Tepe Gawra X (Rothman n.d.:pl. 23, 1942), red ware, cream slip. D = 14 cm.

i. Tepe Gawra VIIIA/B (Rothman n.d.:pl. 29, 2789), buff ware, basalt grit and chaff. D = 9.9 cm.

j. Grai Resh, Lloyd 1940:fig. 7, 6), no detail. D = 11 cm.

k. Tepe Gawra IX (Rothman n.d.:pl. 26, 2250), orange red ware, buff slip, quartz grit and chaff temper. D = 19 cm.

l. hammerhead bowl.

m. Tepe Gawra IX (Rothman n.d.:pl. 25, 2243), buff ware. D = 25 cm.

n. beveled-rim bowl.

o. Hammam et-Turkman VB (Akkermans 1988:fig. 9, 139), plant and lime temper, burnished surface, dark core. D = 31 cm.

p. Umm Qseir (Tsuneki and Miyake 1998:fig. 63, 6), fine ware, slight chaff inclusions, reddish brown, light orange surface, lower exterior scraped. D = 11 cm.

q. Tepe Gawra VIIIC (Rothman and Peasnall 1999:pl. 28, 2826), buff ware, wheel-made, wet-smoothed. D = 12 cm.

r. Tepe Gawra VIIIA (Rothman and Peasnall 1999:pl. 29, 2830), buff ware, wheel-made. D = 11.8 cm.

s. Tepe Gawra VIII (Rothman n.d.:pl. 29, 2774), brown ware, wheel-made, wet-smoothed. D = 10.5 cm.

t. Mohammad Arab period 1 (Roaf 1998:fig. 3, 32), buff fabric, grit temper, cream slip.

u. Tepe Gawra VIII/VI (Rothman n.d.:pl. 29, 2794), green gray ware, wet-smoothed, wheel-made, sand temper. D = 9 cm.

v. Tepe Gawra VIII (Rothman and Peasnall 1999:pl. 29, 2811), gray greenware. D = 9.8 cm.

and occasionally plant sprig painted designs (fig. 10.2). LC 3 markers consist of the earliest pottery made using fast-wheel technology; beveled-rim and nose-lug bowls; "Uruk" gray ware; carinated and interior-ledge-rim bowls; and chaff-faced wares including the earliest hammerhead bowls, casseroles, and internally corrugated rim jars, the latter three more numerous in LC 4. In other words, LC 3–5 in the Tigris Basin is very much like the Syrian sequence described by Schwartz (this volume). Post–LC 5 northern wares, the so-called early Ninevite V pottery, were painted, incised, or ribbed fast-wheel-thrown pots, including new forms of goblets with pedestal bases, pointed-base cups, and bowls.

Although I generally agree with our mutual chronological chart (table 1.1), I do think that there are problems with placing Hammam et-Turkman. The painted pottery illustrated by Akkermans (1988) appears to be identical to Gawra XIIA/XIII, which would place them before LC 1. Perhaps there was a hiatus or mixing of layers.

Ecology of the Tigris Zone

The ecology of the Tigris piedmont and eastern Jazira includes rolling steppe and some hill country to the east. The area is generally well watered, more so in the piedmont area than the central Jazira Plain. Precipitation would have been more than adequate for rainfall agriculture. If anything the climate during the fourth millennium B.C. may have been a bit moister and cooler than it is today (Wilkinson and Tucker 1995:85–86).

Historically and in modern times this area has been a rich source of grain and pastureland. The Erbil Plain, where Qalinj Agha is located, is among the prime rainfall agricultural zones in modern Iraq. "The whole plain is cultivated and presents a green rolling landscape in spring. Many of the streams are perennial. The principal crops are wheat and barley, and the district is probably the best wheat-producing region of Iraq" (British Admiralty 1944:93). The same applies to the area north of the greater Zab River, where Nineveh and Tepe Gawra are located. As described by the same intelligence report (British Admiralty 1944:95), "The whole plain between the Tigris and the lower Khazir Su and the Great Zab has rich, heavy soil and is well cultivated, though now entirely dependent on rainfall. It was the granary of the ancient Assyrians." In other words, although the yields per hectare may be higher under irrigation in the south, the total yields under rainfall agriculture in the north may be greater (Weiss 1986:40). As one heads further north into the hilly country near Dohuk, the land is hardly less fertile, although other crops are added to the grains: "the Rubal Dohuk waters a fertile valley between the Tang-i-Daria and the outer hills. Much fruit is grown in this upland valley and there are extensive vineyards....the chief crops are wheat and rice, but much of the ground becomes very dry in summer" (British Admiralty 1944:96). The northern Jazira, where Tell al-Hawa is located, is less agriculturally rich than the piedmont, but it can sustain a significant population through rainfall cultivation. With proper fallowing, even the steppes of the northern Jazira can produce reliable grain yields (Wilkinson and Tucker 1995:7–9).

Animal resources must also be factored into our understanding of trends in this area. Pastureland is plentiful throughout the area, and caravan traffic historically favored a route across the northern Jazira in part because of widely available pasture for camels and horses (British Admiralty 1944:80). Wild animals have long been plentiful. As late as the beginning of the twentieth century, the following large mammals roamed the entire area: onager, oryx, ibex, gazelle, wolf, Asiatic lion, and wild boar (Wilkinson and Tucker 1995:10). Hunting, especially east of the Tigris River where the steppe and the hills meet, would have been a rich source of protein. Unfortunately, at sites like Gawra, excavated earlier in this century, animal bone was rarely saved, so we do not know for certain the percentages of wild versus domesticated animal consumption. There is evidence of sheep/goat, possibly raised for meat and definitely used for wool, milk, and (the bone) tools. Stands of wild flax in the nearby hills provided an alternative to wool (Watson 1979:108).

Mineral resources are close at hand. Various flints used for tools are found in the limestone formations of the eastern hills and in the Jazira Plain. Basalt and marble are locally available (Tobler 1950:176), as is chlorite (Solecki and Solecki 1970). Oil seepage and bitumen sources occur in the same area (see Forbes 1964[I]:2). Sources of obsidian, metal ores, gold, and other resources are not very far away in modern eastern Turkey.

The topography in this area limited and directed travel (and

trade), and it circumscribed the areas in which cohesive human organizations were likely to develop. For example, the Greater Zab River,
which separates Tepe Gawra from Qalinj Agha, is passable only during
the dry months. Once the rainy season begins, it serves as a natural
boundary for foot or caravan traffic. Travel into the Iranian highlands
and further east to lapis lazuli sources usually passes through the Jebel
Maqlub. The Jebel Maqlub limited incursions from Parthians and
Sassanians. The Jebel Sinjar also forms a natural barrier that made the
northern Jazira a defensible area. A Roman *limes* or border post there
was used for military operations in World War I (British Admiralty
1944:80).

Settlement and Development in the Eastern Jazira and Tigris Piedmont

Developments in the eastern Jazira and Tigris piedmont over the
period from about 4300 to 3000 B.C., as implied by the quotation at the
beginning of this chapter, were based on the local ecology as well as a
number of political, economic, and ideological factors. This section
will discuss the settlement pattern data in the subregion at large.
Modern survey has been conducted in the northern Jazira and to a
lesser extent in the catchment of the Saddam Dam north of Eski Mosul
(Ball, Tucker, and Wilkinson 1989; Wilkinson and Tucker 1995). The
remainder of the sites were drawn from the *Archaeological Map of Iraq*
(1968), summaries of that map by Abu al-Soof (1968), and references
to unpublished material by Rova (n.d.).

Assigning LC dates to the sites in this region is difficult at best,
given the spotty publication of finds, the necessarily quick and dirty
excavations by salvage teams, and the abundance of material from
older excavations, most without radiocarbon dating. These maps
should therefore be taken as general guides.

Our baseline in the LC 1 shows a fairly sparsely occupied zone with
significant sites in each area within the larger zone (fig. 10.3). Lacking
information comparable to that provided for the "Uruk" by Abu al-
Soof, this first map is the least comprehensive. Nonetheless, we can
make a few general statements about this zone: sites were small, were
placed in the most optimum place for agricultural exploitation, and
were already connected in a loose network of exchange. Lapis lazuli

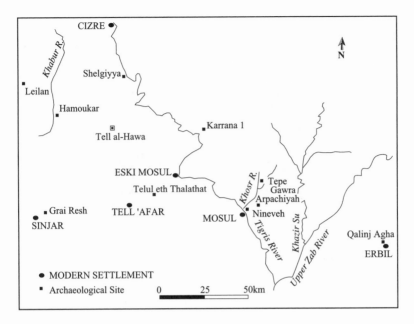

FIGURE 10.3

Distribution of LC 1 sites in the northern piedmont.

had appeared at Tepe Gawra, for example, in the Late Ubaid period level XIII. Worked copper is found for the first time in level XIII: a single copper awl or pin, most likely hammered (Tobler 1950:212). Four crudely smelted copper objects appeared in Gawra XII (Vince Pigott, MASCA, personal communication 1990). Obsidian also began to appear in Gawra XIII and increased through level XI, decreased in levels X and IX (Tobler 1950:200–201), and increased dramatically in level VIII when the numbers of both blades and cores of obsidian increased exponentially (Rothman 1988, n.d.). It is interesting to note that Pollock (chap. 6, this volume) finds the greatest quantity of obsidian blades in the southern surveys from LC 2–4. These items, or at least their raw materials, must have been imported over considerable distances. The probable sources of this material are fairly widespread, stretching from Afghanistan to central Anatolia (for lapis lazuli, see Hermann 1968; for obsidian, G. Wright 1969). Salvage excavations at Shelgiyya on the upper Tigris indicate that specialized production of fine pottery, specifically, Sprig Ware, may have already begun in the LC

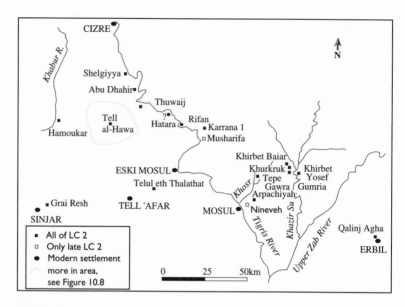

FIGURE 10.4

Distribution of LC 2 sites in the northern piedmont.

1 (Ball 1997). A concentration of Sprig Ware was also recovered from early Tell al-Hawa. Taken together, this material shows that a far-flung network of exchange relations had already begun in the fifth millennium B.C., but especially in LC 1. Nineveh seems unoccupied by the end of this period.

LC 2 is the period when most of the levels of Tepe Gawra relevant to our discussion were occupied. In figure 10.4, an apparent increase in sites is notable. These sites seem to fill in the areas little occupied in LC 1. For the so-called precontact period, this was a time of tremendous economic and political development. Tell al-Hawa grew to an extraordinary size at this time. "Concerning the possible introduction of urban concepts into the north by such southern implants, the investigations at Tell al-Hawa…suggest that the period of greater urban expansion was in the Earlier part of the Uruk period, while southern Mesopotamian colonies are from the Later part" (Ball 1997:6). Quite a number of apparently important sites were located away from the major river channels. In fact, Nineveh has yielded none of the wares typical of the early LC 2 (Gawra XIA/B-XI, Gut's Gawra A). As Gut (1995:238) points out, this may be because of the small sample taken in Mallowan's deep sounding; however, earlier pottery was recovered from the sounding. This potential hiatus may also exist at Tell Leilan where these same wares are missing between Leilan VIB and V. As Schwartz (1988a:74) notes, "Although Periods V and IV must correspond temporally to Gawra XIA-VIIIB, no clear parallels between the assemblages are obvious." Again, the exact chronological position of early chaff-faced ware casseroles and hammerhead bowls may indicate a shorter hiatus at Leilan, but Nineveh falls well within the eastern Jazira and Tigris piedmont zone and should have yielded some of these pottery types. New sites came into existence east of Gawra along the Khazir Su. The settlement pattern data seem to indicate growth and the likelihood of evolving societal complexity, involving exploitation of the area's agricultural potential and increasing trade. This trend is not limited to the Jazira, however. "Although larger in size (possibly owing to the greater availability of good quality agricultural land) and probably somewhat more integrated, the north Jazira [sub-] regional system exhibits the same highly centralized nature as that seen in the Karababa area. As with Samsat, the disproportionate size of Tell al-Hawa vis-à-vis surrounding settlements may be the result of its preeminent functional role and its participation in inter- [and intra-] regional exchange networks. Like Samsat in the Karababa area, Tell al-Hawa acted as the regional conduit between the north Jazira settlement system and the wider supra-local precontact period world that was characterized by wide-reaching interaction spheres" (Lupton 1996:26). All of this is in the apparent absence of a significant southern presence, although this is not to say that trade was not going to the south. The pattern indicates a local development, one in which it is not difficult to see a role for sites like Tepe Gawra. Gawra and other sites occupied contemporaneously, like Qalinj Agha near Erbil and Nuzi near Kirkuk, would have had more direct access to a number of raw materials and goods that might be important for larger networks of exchange. Also as I noted above, transport between these areas may have been blocked in some seasons. Each would have constituted its own world.

LC 3 (fig. 10.5) was marked by the abandonment of Tepe Gawra and Grai Resh, Qalinj Agha, Musharifa, Rifan, Arpachiyah, Khirbet Yosef, and so on, somewhere early in the period. Tell al-Hawa

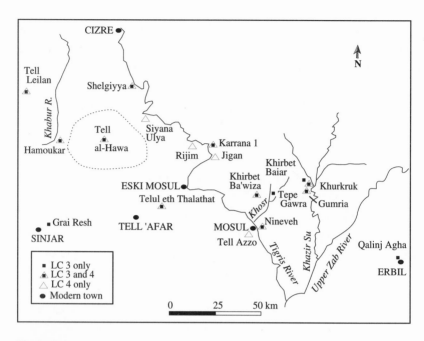

FIGURE 10.5

Distribution of LC 3–4 sites in the northern piedmont.

decreased in size although its central place in the north Jazira does not seem to have changed drastically (Lupton 1996:57–59). Nineveh was reoccupied and continued to grow. The Gawra mound was so narrow by the end of level VIII that only fortresses and a few special-function buildings would be built on it afterwards. It is even possible that Gawran leaders moved their base of operation west, possibly to Nineveh itself, although there is no way to verify this. For LC 3 and 4— the lack of differences prevents us from separating these two phases chronologically or otherwise—change seems minor. The settlement pattern already established in the LC 2 continued, despite the early influx of Southerners at sites like Hacınebi and Sheikh Hassan. As Lupton (1996:57) writes, "Contact with the Late Uruk world seems to have had little effect on the organization of [sub-] regional settlement in the north Jazira area. The continuing primacy of the north Jazira system suggests that inter [and intra-] regional exchange was probably still channeled through the area's dominant site, Tell al-Hawa. I would argue that the elites resident at Hawa used their advantageous position

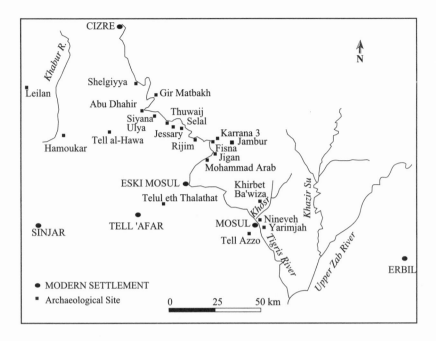

FIGURE 10.6

Distribution of LC 5 sites in the northern piedmont.

to minimize politically the economic and/or political expansion of the surrounding lower order centers."

The LC 5 (fig. 10.6) in this region saw a growth in the number of sites in Saddam Dam area. All were typified by what we have come to call the classic Uruk wares: droopy spouted and lugged jars, reserve slip and incised designs, tall flowerpots, strap handle jars, and so forth (see fig. 5.7, this volume). The lack of current publications precludes our ability to determine whether local wares comprise a large percentage of these sites' LC 5 repertoires. Algaze (this volume) argues that since the full repertoire of Uruk pottery types and Uruk administrative techniques (numerical tablets, glyptic style, cylinder seals) is found at LC 4/5 Nineveh, it was a southern emplacement. The clay sickles from stratum 35 (Mallowan 1933: pl. LXXI) support his argument. Stratum 35 is contemporaneous with the Hacınebi B2 southern community. What argues against an LC 5 takeover by Southerners is that, as at Brak, which certainly held a similarly key role in exchange networks, most large emplacements were at newly founded sites rather than deeply

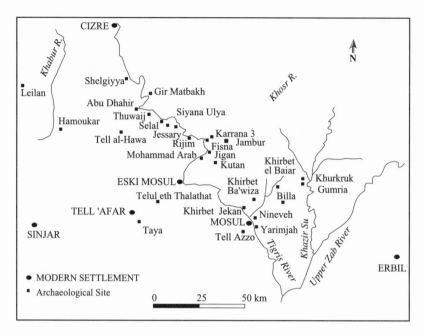

FIGURE 10.7

Distribution of Early Ninevite V sites in the northern piedmont.

occupied sites of the preceding LC 1–3 periods and before. Also, during the 150 or more years since some of these ceramics first appeared in the north in LC 3 and 4, one would expect that there was time for the adoption of previously elite-only styles by the general population. Samples come from very small exposures at sites with these periods, and earlier excavators' dislike of plain pottery has left unrepresentative samples of potsherds (Gut, personal communication 1997).

Following the end of the fourth millennium B.C. the Tigris piedmont and eastern Jazira settlement systems did not collapse. "Though Tell al-Hawa continued to be the dominant site in the north Jazira, substantial changes occurred resulting in a more nucleated post-contact period settlement pattern. In spite of a 26% increase in population, much of the west and south-western parts of the plain were abandoned as the area's inhabitants concentrated in a series of emerging population centers" (Lupton 1996:90; see figs. 10.7 and 10.8). If this subregion were analyzed without taking into account trends in the Syrian Euphrates Basin, no one would be writing about a collapse. In the

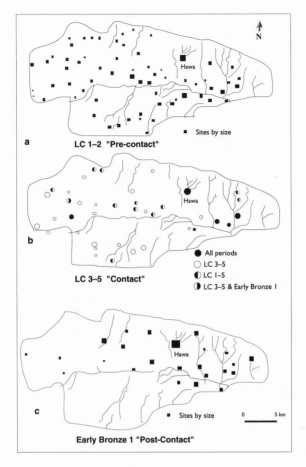

FIGURE 10.8

Changes in settlement around Tell al-Hawa, LC 1–Ninevite V (after Lupton 1996:figs. 2.11, 3.15, and 4.15).

Tigris piedmont zone, new sites were founded, and older ones, which appear to have been abandoned in the LC 5, were reoccupied. The same can be said about the Karababa (Lupton 1996:90). The survey around Tell al-Hawa discovered detectable routes or "hollow ways" in the LC 5, emanating from the central sites (Wilkinson and Tucker 1995:86). Wilkinson interprets them as transportation routes. He and Tucker note, "there was eventually a significant increase in the percentage of sites on major routes during the Ninevite 5 period" (1995:86). They continue, "Late Uruk sites were apparently significantly related to routeways. The correspondence between the development of urban centres and routes suggests that communications were stronger and settlement growth may have been stimulated by these links and perhaps trade along them" (Wilkinson and Tucker 1995:86).

Those areas most directly in contact with southern Mesopotamian colonies do seem to have had declining populations. Like Arslantepe these areas have smaller central sites. Interestingly, in redefining themselves in the post-Uruk period, residents in the Ninevite V occupied areas returned to styles that must have been copied from older Ubaid and LC 1 painted samples (for examples see Gut 1995: tafel 71–77).

The picture from the Tigris piedmont presents a very different view than the one proposed in the Uruk expansion theory. A similar pattern of local development and some contact is evident in the Zagros of western Iran (Henrickson 1994). The period VI stylistic group, which marks the Zagros for much of the Late Chalcolithic, should be contemporaneous with the changes during LC 2–5. The area encompasses a series of narrow intermontane valleys north of the lowland Khuzistan Plain. According to Henrickson, the sites tend to be small and isolated, although high-intensity survey is limited to the MahiDasht, Kangavar and the Hulailan valleys. In the LC 4–5 this region saw some increased interaction, presumably with Susa. Seals of types typical of Gawra and Susa were found at Giyan, mostly out of context (Caldwell 1976:234). Giyan sat on the best north-south route through the Zagros for carrying lapis lazuli and other goods from the north to the Susiana Plains, which may explain these similarities. Except for one notable exception, the Oval at Godin, most signs of Uruk penetration are simply beveled-rim bowls (Henrickson 1994: table 2).

I will now look at trends in the precontact, LC 1–3 period at a small local center in the Tigris piedmont.

THE CASE OF TEPE GAWRA

Tepe Gawra was clearly a small center in the LC 1–3 periods (see Blanton 1976 for a definition of "center"). For much of the time between level XII and VIII there were more productive, religious, and administrative activities than were needed for the subsistence of the residents and management of the town. These activities clustered in certain areas and were unlikely to be found in other parts of the immediate area. The site's importance for our discussion derives from the wide horizontal exposure of the relevant levels, which provides a view of most of the buildings and the remains of activities for much of the town.[12] By mapping the clusters of activities into the buildings and open spaces on the mound, we can see patterns of site function and also of obvious specialization. If a large building or area of the mound has a concentration of one activity or related activities to the exclusion of others, a specialized function is likely. Certainly, at a site as small as Gawra, with a population probably not exceeding about 200 people during the periods in question, the craft and food processing needs of its residents would have been equally small, so production for subsistence would require little specialization. Claims for a lower town off the main mound, which would contradict this view, are based on one person who visited the site many years after archaeological excavation ended. Other eyewitnesses did not corroborate what that one visitor saw, and there are other reasons to doubt a fourth millennium B.C. lower town (Rothman 1988, n.d.).

To summarize what we know of Gawra (see Rothman n.d., Rothman and Peasnall 1999 for detail), the earliest Terminal Ubaid (LC 1) level following the end of Ubaid 4 (level XIIA) is XII. From XII to VIII, a trend from extended family, multifunction buildings to almost exclusively specialized buildings is evident. The large, probably two-story, tripartite (Mittelsaal) buildings of level XII each contained domestic, craft production, and ritual areas. Other than these buildings a central storage silo, presumably for grain, and a storage and sorting area for goods, likely for exchange, marked the site as a possible center, serving as a collection and presumably distribution site for goods. In succeeding level XIA/B, smaller two- or three-room houses were built alongside multifamily residences like the ones in XII. A specialized craft building was also uncovered, much like in level XII. The Round House, a thick-walled round structure apparently used for grain storage and defense, was built at the end of XIA/B. By level XI/XA few large residences existed, and crafts such as weaving, woodworking, and bead carving were centralized in special-function buildings. A temple with its doors facing out onto the countryside was also built, as was a building in the form of the old extended family residences, but housing administrative rather than residential activities.

Levels X and IX retained and expanded XI/XA's religious and administrative functions, while a warren of small residences with evidence of cottage crafts occupied much of the mound. By VIII the temple and administrative functions remained, but residences were few. A host of new, specialized craft buildings appeared.

The evidence of clusters of activities and their distribution among the buildings and open spaces from XII to VIII indicate that the strategies of various political actors had changed over the span of perhaps 700 years. The site retained functions in each level that were aimed at an audience greater than the occupants of the mound itself, although the physical space on the mound continued to decrease. Leadership organization of some kind developed.

The remains of administrative technology (seals and sealings) give a clear indication of how such leadership may have been structured and perceived (Rothman 1994a, 1994b; Rothman and Blackman 1990). Seals exist as markers of identity, either as individuals or as members of an institution, whether one of extended family, a descent group, or an administrative/leadership institution (Rothman 1994a, 1994b). By using clay locks on doors, boxes, sacks, jars, or other containers sealed with one's official or personal seal, individuals controlled access to craft products, raw materials, and foodstuffs.

Evidence of seals and sealings in coordination with the distribution of activities described above can give us better evidence for the nature of leaders' strategies as they represent control mechanisms. In level XII the distribution of seals and sealings clearly indicates a less centralized strategy (Rothman and Peasnall 1999). That is, the items sealed represent a wide range of goods that individual actors might want to control. In terms of design and find spot, almost no pattern is discernible. All but one building have remains of sealings and/or seals. This indicates an organization in which many different players have a similar role. I would propose that if sites in the orbit of Gawra were excavated, one would see a different pattern from Gawra itself, as Gawra had taken on the role of a center. Within Gawra, despite the presence of central grain warehouses and goods sorting areas, no separate leadership had emerged overall. The possibility of a strategy to create positions of rank through exchange existed but does not seem to have developed. A corporate strategy, most likely coordinated by heads of extended family units, apparently existed at this center.

In level XIA/B, the pattern of XII is changed somewhat. There is still a fairly wide dispersal of control devices in private houses as well as more public institutions. However, there are two real concentrations of seals and sealings in the Round House fortress and the special-function tripartite craft building in the northern part of the site. Those in the Round House were from large jars, presumably rations for site defenders. A generalized leadership probably existed within the site, although the leaders of Gawra may have begun developing centralized institutions in relation to neighboring groups.

In XI and XA, yet another new pattern is evident, although the problems in the excavation of XA make inferences from that phase tricky. In those strata, seals and sealings in good context are virtually absent from private homes. They do exist in considerable numbers, but all in specialized craft, temple, or administrative buildings. In addition, two design subjects from seals, herds of caprids and predation scenes, were recovered from the temple, on the one hand, and from workshops and the administrative building, on the other hand (Rothman 1994a). However a large number of seal designs from the site do not fit in either category. In other words, control functions are now focused on specialized activity areas. At the same time, a fairly wide distribution of control still seems evident despite increasing specialization and spatial differentiation of activities.

Levels X to VIII indicate a real change in the strategy of political actors, reaching its height in VIIIA. That strategy seems to indicate the development of hierarchically ranked administrative positions. This change is also evident in the burials (see below). To reiterate, the temple in Gawra X became *the* central institution, and craft activities were scattered throughout a series of private houses. The majority of sealings were found in association with the temple. A series of sealings stamped with the same seal or with very similar seal designs of a caprid facing a building came from that context and from a building at the edge of the mound, which seems to have been a receiving station for sealed containers. It is rare to have multiple sealings with the same stamp at Gawra, and their find spots near the temple and a receiving station would indicate control by this centralized institution of imported goods. Elsewhere among the residences a variety of designs appeared.

The most drastic change occurs in level VIII in which few residences existed. In the middle stratum, VIIIB, both seals and sealings are found in every building. However, in the tripartite building nearest the warehouse were found a series of sealings depicting a bull, dog, and snake. This same design appears in each of the other buildings. In the temple excavators recovered a piece of the same sealing with a perfect fit to one near the warehouse. Whatever actors were controlling the warehouse appear to have controlled the flow of goods to all the other institutions, each of which has different sets of stamp seal designs. The political actors controlling the warehouse appear to have evolved a strategy largely based on centralized control, presumably for their own benefit. This strategy appears to have developed at the same time as early trading posts of Southerners appeared in the north. The increased demand for goods, both prestige/luxury (gold, lapis lazuli, carnelian, etc.) and practical (metals and obsidian for tools), drew Southerners to the north and also gave the leaders of northern centers greater opportunities to pursue an exclusionary power strategy by controlling exchange networks.

The mortuary practices indicate a pattern of increasing social differentiation similar to the correlation of activity clusters, building types, and seals/sealings. This can be measured on a number of dimensions. The graves sunk from level XII were usually those of children (Tobler 1950:118–19). In fact, most of the burials before level X appear to be of children or infants. However, burial types range from simple pit burial to pot burial to "sidewall" burials to cist grave to constructed *libn* (mud brick) tombs. Through time, fewer types were used, until libn tombs or common interments marked the graves of both children and adults (see Peasnall n.d. or Rothman and Peasnall 1999: fig. 2). The graves of levels XI and XIA/B have few grave goods (table 10.1). By level X the goods in the best-endowed children's and adult's graves are rich by any standard. In short, as more specialized and centralized institutions with their attendant ranking evolved, social differentiation is evidenced by mortuary practice.

That practice gives us an unusual look at two issues raised above in the theoretical section: how trade goods were consumed and whether leaders controlled exotic goods exchange as a major part of their strategy. I follow Pollock (1983) in asserting that goods placed in graves, especially those of high status, represent markers of prestige, in the sense that those able to obtain and display prestige goods were accorded more respect. Table 10.1 gives an impression of some of the adult and child graves from VIII to XIA/B. Table 10.2 lists goods from what Peasnall found to be clusters of graves in levels XIA/B–VIII (note that in this table child and adult burials are mixed). From these I will determine what sorts of materials and/or goods from graves were marked symbolically as prestigious. I will then map the distribution of these same materials and/or goods in the settlement of the living. In this way, it should be possible to get a general idea of how imported, symbolically powerful goods were distributed by residents.

Objects that might be related to status were found in some adult burials: an eye idol and animal bones with a green powdered substance in tomb 31 and maceheads in tombs 34 and 114. A wolf's head made of electrum was recovered from tomb 114, which may be in the same symbolic category as the predation designs in seals (recall that predation designs were associated in level XI/XA with administrative and specialized craft activities). Many of the skeletons found in prestigious burials are coated with the same powdered substance. Eye idols appear to have some religious meaning (Rothman 1988:226–27, n.d.). It is therefore possible, though tentative, to conclude that individuals with the greenish powder and eye idols had some religious role or symbolic connection, while the holder of the maceheads, a military weapon, was associated with secular administration.

Among the exotic, apparently prestigious materials at Gawra were ornaments with gold, carnelian, lapis lazuli (more the quantity of the material than what is made from it), electrum, copper, turquoise, dentalium shells, and diorite or chlorite, the last carved into bowls or seals. Surprisingly, with the exception of tomb 114 with its obsidian bowls and beads, obsidian does not seem to serve as a symbol of prestige. The same appears to apply to metal tools. Table 10.3 lists these materials by level.

Clearly, exchange relations of some distance are bringing exotic goods into the Tigris piedmont. Unfortunately, not all of these objects can be mapped onto precise find spots. Figures 10.9 through 10.11 illustrate the distribution of those items that can be reliably placed in their original provenience. Although the small numbers of artifacts

TABLE 10.1

Well-Endowed Burials from Tepe Gawra

Burial	Stratum	Type	Age	Contents
031	VIII/IX	Libn tomb	Adult	32 white shell beads, 57 carnelian beads, 1 pink carnelian pendant, 29 lapis beads, 120 turquoise beads, 2 crystal beads, 16 gold spherical beads, 1 alabaster ointment vase, 1 bone zigzag hair ornament, 1 serpentine ointment dish, 1 gold foil rosette ornament, 11 gold over bitumen core hemisphere studs, 1 oolite ointment vessel, 1 ivory or bone plaque seal, 256 beads, 1 Mosul marble dish, 1 Mosul marble hut idol, 1 bone comb, green pigment on chest, reed matting, animal bones with green pigment
013	VIII/IX	Loose burial	Infant	15 turquoise ring beads, white stone ring, 12 variegated stone ring beads, 29 white spherical beads, 81 black stone ring beads, 1 amethyst irregular bead, 1 cowrie shell, 1 gold ornament, shell ring beads, 186 white ring beads, 5 white shell barrel beads, 175 black stone ring beads, 1 turquoise ring bead, 3 "bronze" flat, band ring, white shell ring beads, 89 white ring beads, 85 black stone ring beads, 3 carnelian ring beads, white shell, spherical beads, black stone ring beads, 2 gray stone ring beads, green stone ring beads
012	VIII/IX	Libn tomb	Infant /Child	1 gold over bitumen core ornament, 2 lapis bird figurines, 1 ivory irregular pendant, 4 gold beads, white paste beads, 28 carnelian beads, 1 carnelian pendant, 1 lump of iron, 1 black stone bead, 1 gold over bitumen core ornament, 242 small white beads, 37 turquoise ring beads, 1 turquoise pendant, 10 lapis beads.
109	X	Libn tomb	Adult	1 marble jar, 1 oolite bowl , 1 alabaster bowl, 1 gold rosette ornament, 447 turquoise beads, 1 gold ribbon-rosette, 3 gold rosette ornaments, 6 gold ornaments, 50 gold studs, 20 gold crescent ornaments, 1 gold ferrule, 3 gold and lapis eye shaped ornaments, 90 gold bangles, 125 gold beads, 37 large electrum beads, 76 small electrum beads, 472 lapis beads, 1 lapis stamp seal, 16 large lapis beads, 451 turquoise beads, 461 carnelian beads, 1 unidentified ceramic object, 1

No.	Period	Burial type	Age	Contents
114	X	Libn tomb	Adult	gold and lapis fly figurine, 1 bone comb, 145 shell beads, 1 ceramic sphere, 1 bone, gold, lapis, and turquoise hair ornament, traces of blue pigment on head, chest and forearms, 9 electrum beads, 2 obsidian blades; 1 electrum wolf head, 8 lapis beads, 1 turquoise bead, 1 honing stone with gold, 1 hematite macehead, 1 alabaster macehead, 6 red jasper stones, 1 bone with gold hair ornament, 3 bone ornaments, 40 lapis beads, 24 turquoise beads, 33 gold beads, 55 carnelian beads, 234 lapis beads, 374 turquoise beads, 29 gold beads, 1 gold rosette with lapis, 1 lapis stamp seal, 45 shell - beads, 33 carnelian beads, 2 gold beads
102	X	Libn tomb	Youth	2 marble discs, 3 marble stones, 1 obsidian spouted pot, 1 obsidian spouted bowl, 1 marble macehead, 7 marble spheres, 204 shell ring beads, 56 carnelian carinated and ring beads, 24,067 white ring beads, 1,125 obsidian ring beads, 1 red ware bowl
36-134	XI/XA	Libn tomb	Adult	1 copper spiral pendant, 1 obsidian pendant, 1 gray ware vessel
36-110	XI/XA	Libn tomb	Adult	1 black steatite seal, 1 small buff jar
142	XI/XA	Loose burial	Child /Youth	1,348 tiny white ring beads, 129 white carinated beads, 733 small black stone beads, 1 carnelian ring bead, 1 lapis grooved bead, 1 gold rosette ornament, 1 slate ax head
180	XI/XA	Libn tomb	Child	1 lapis pendant, 320 small white ring beads, 378 small white beads, 1 white, stone irregular bead, 29 carnelian ring beads, 10 carnelian carinated beads, 1 lapis cylinder bead, 20 dentalia shells, various types of beads
36-060	XIAB	Libn & stone tomb	Child	1 small brown ware jar, 3,075 unidentified beads, 3,300 ring beads, 1 yellow paste rosette pendant, 1 ivory rosette ornament, reed matting

Source: After Peasnall n.d.

TABLE 10.2

Clusters of Artifacts in Graves at Tepe Gawra

Class	Level XIA/XIB	Level XI/XA	Level X	Level VIII/IX
1	White and black beads (6)	Turquoise and carved beads (4)	White beads (4)	Gold and copper ornments, exotic beads other than lapis (10)
2	Ceramic vessels (6)	White beads plus lapis, carnelian, turquoise, quartzite, shell beads, gold rosettes and ornaments. One with macehead (10)	White, black, carnelian beads (8)	Similar to 1, but lapis beads and no gold or electrum ornaments (7)
3	Stamp seals (2)	White beads (8)	Gold rosettes, ornaments, macehead, blades, combs, ointment vessels, hair ornaments, stamp seals (4)	Similar to 2, but lacks more elaborate ornaments, combs, and hairpieces (2)
4	Macehead, bone bead (1) ,	Ceramic vessels, two with stamp seals (6)	Ceramic vessels (4)	Elaborate gold rosettes and ornaments, stamp seals; like level X group 3 (3)
5		Gold beads, rosettes (1)		White beads, one with copper bead (3)

Note: Numbers in parentheses indicate the number of graves in the cluster.

make a conclusive answer improbable, such patterns that are discernible fit the other data. In level XII cores of obsidian are in evidence. Given that only 16 blades and four cores were recovered, it is likely that obsidian was imported as cores, which were knapped locally. The four cores were found near blades associated with three tripartite

TABLE 10.3

Occurrence of Imported Raw Materials and Goods by Occupation Level at Tepe Gawra

Level	Lapis Lazuli	Gold	Carnelian, Serpentine, Turquoise	Shell	Obsidian Tools	Flint Tools	Obsidian Cores	Metal Tools	Copper Ornaments
XII	1	2	3	2	16	4	4	4	0
XIA/B	0	0	1	0	10	4	2	5	1
XI	0	1	2	2	18	4	3	13	3
XA	1	2	0	0	4	2	0	2	0
X	0	0	0	1	4	1	0	2	0
IX 1	1	1	1	0	56	12	0	3	0
VIII	1	2	4	6	118	52	3	31/7[a]	3

[a] The seven are probably in terrace from VI.

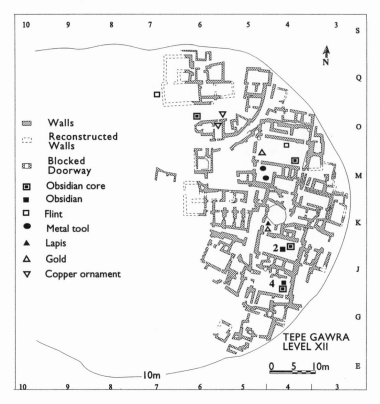

FIGURE 10.9

Distribution of imported materials, Tepe Gawra level XII, LC 1.

houses, and the area of goods sorting behind the entrance road to the site. A single gold and lapis pin was found in a side room of one of the extended-family houses. The other gold and copper beads were found in association with the largest house, the one with the White Room, and in the storage and sorting area. Metal tools were recovered from the area of the White Room. In other words, no real indication of central-ized control or marked social stratification within the site is visible.

Increased specialization has been noted in activities in phase XI of level XI/XA, and more hierarchical control is evident in administration. Metal tools were found near the temple, a shrine, the administrative/craft building, and a large kiln area, just the places where increasingly powerful groups would work or live. A metal tool was also found in a house in the western part of the excavated area. A concentration of tools

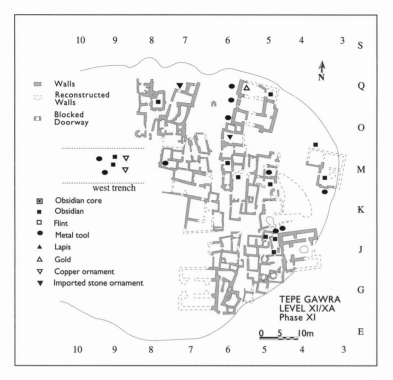

FIGURE 10.10

Distribution of imported materials, Tepe Gawra level XI/XA, phase XI, early LC 2.

and other imported goods was found in the quickly excavated West Trench. Tobler claims that this part of the mound was empty, but field notes indicate that buildings and associated fill were most likely thrown over the edge of the mound (calling into question Tobler's conclusion). Obsidian blades show a distribution similar to that of the metal tools. A single gold bead and a serpentine bead were found in the administrative building. The other serpentine bead was found near a private house, and a carnelian bead was found in the West Trench.

Level VIII was occupied in the early period of southern trade communities in the north. Table 10.3 indicates a huge increase in blades, many of them unused. The largest collection, more than 66 (although a precise count is difficult because of poor recording methods under Speiser and his conflation of most artifacts in the three phases of VIII), was recovered from the central warehouse, which sealings of VIIIB

397

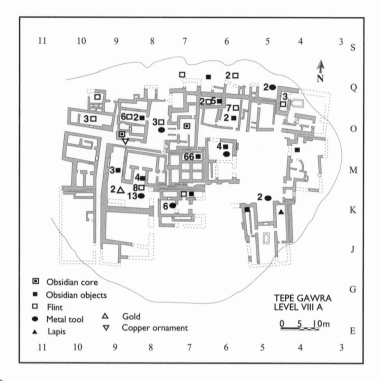

FIGURE 10.11

Distribution of imported materials, Tepe Gawra level VIIIA, early LC 3.

indicate was a central control node (Rothman and Blackman 1990). Excavators recovered many metal items from the adjoining tripartite building and the one to its west. This last building proved an interesting though functionally hard-to-interpret structure with a room with an arched ceiling, somewhat like the building uncovered by Campbell-Thompson and Mallowan (1933) in Late Uruk, LC 5 Nineveh. The two gold beads in this level came from this same building. The one lapis bead in this level came from the temple. In the residential or craft-producing (maybe even exchange) area of the northwestern quadrant of the mound, locally available flint blades were more common than obsidian ones.

The grave goods and find spots of Gawra XII–VIII indicate that exotic or imported goods served as symbols of status for a long period of time. This was true more of ornamental uses of these goods than practical, tool-making applications. A fairly egalitarian distribution characterized the earliest (LC 1 period) distributions of exotic materials in graves and in the living spaces of the mound. Again, if other contemporary sites within Gawra's sphere were excavated, I predict that fewer of these goods would be found. As the site developed its economic role and internal organization, a less and less egalitarian distribution marked both the living and the dead. By level VIII in the so-called contact period a significant increase in trade is evident. The graves are not much richer than in level X, which should have been before contact, in a less trade-oriented time. What is perhaps most interesting is that we cannot conclude from this that long-distance trade structured the economy or politics of the small Gawran center. The place of religion and local production and exchange lies beneath the most spectacular exotic items. After all, if one took all the gold, lapis, carnelian, copper, and so on from Gawra XII to VIII and put it in a skull box, it would still rattle around in the empty spaces.

CONCLUSION

The Tigris piedmont and eastern Jazira Plain subregion of Mesopotamia present a very complex picture of development over a longer period of time than that of the Euphrates Basin. Certainly, the idea that this area was taken over by an outside force in a formal or informal, coercive or peaceful economic empire simply does not fit the data. As I said above, Algaze is probably right in seeing the development of the north as being catalyzed by events in the south. Many of these areas comprised, in effect, independent "countries" in Durrenberger's terms, which had undergone a long period of economic and political development. This area did not "roll over" in response to Southerners and it did not witness a collapse. Rather than the Uruk expansion being an administratively controlled, consciously imperial plan by elite leaders of southern states, a much less controlled, more incremental parry and response by northern leaders in the face of new economic opportunities presented by the south seems more plausible. The same can probably be said of the sites of the Karababa and the Arslantepe area. The story in the Euphrates Basin may be different as a significant migration represented by new southern cities occurred there. Local leaders may have become more dependent on exchange with larger numbers of entrepreneurs. If the Kede example offered above is a valid analogy, a more likely scenario would be a group of Southerners moving northward first as traders within local communities and then in newly founded cities. Only after some time did their connection with the south, especially southern leaders, become formalized. An alternative way to view the "collapse" might be the impact of interference by those southern leaders. What *did* collapse was the southern colonies themselves, Habuba Kabira South/Qannas and Jebel Aruda. That collapse did have an effect on their nearest neighbors in the Euphrates and Khabur subregions, but probably not because Southerners colonized those neighbors in any sense.

We are making considerable progress in interpreting this critical period, but our work is not done. New analyses of already excavated material are necessary, as is further, focused field research.

Notes

1. This area encompasses the eastern Jazira immediately to the west of the Tigris River and the Tigris piedmont to its east.

2. The Ergani mines were undoubtedly used from pre-expansion times through the fourth and into the third millennium and beyond. How much of the material exported to the south came from this source is less certain.

3. Admittedly, this part of Mesopotamia has not had the modern survey coverage that the Euphrates Basin has had, but the building of dams has brought a few modern surveyors to the Jazira, the upper piedmont zone, and just south of this area, the Hamrin. This area had also been explored by a few generations of biblical archaeologists, who were captivated by the Neo-Assyrian heartland.

4. In writing about the theories proposed for explaining the so-called Uruk Expansion, I stand with others on three large pairs of shoulders, two of whom have participated in this advanced seminar. The shoulders in question belong first to Robert McCormick Adams, whose pioneering work using archaeological survey to investigate a series of complex cultural phenomena, primarily the origin of cities in Mesopotamia, set the agenda for following generations. The second is Henry Wright, who refocused our research on the causes and measurement of the sorts of cultural or societal organizational change that spawned cities, primarily state origins. For my generation, the explanation proposed by another Adams student, Guillermo Algaze, has set in motion more than a decade of research, including many of the projects and ideas discussed in

these pages. I also want to acknowledge Hans Nissen, whose European approach of combining information on early historical texts, survey, and excavation in the Mesopotamian south has been an inspiration to many. Whether or not in the end there is consensus on the propositions offered by these four scholars, we are all indebted to them.

5. The Naram Sin stele uses the convention of an oversized king climbing a mountain, followed by troops (Frankfort 1970: fig. 91).

6. Probably similarities between the "city" and the modern legislature are fairly few, but we know little about it.

7. Chemical sourcing of metal ores and studies of manufacturing processes will be useful in this regard.

8. The definition of an ethnic group as those who think they are members (and symbolize that membership) and those outside the group who think others belong to that group (self-ascription and ascription by others) remains useful here.

9. It is necessary to distinguish between physical bartering (market) places and trade and modern market principles (Rothman 2000).

10. Wolf (following Marx) defines three modes of production: kinship, tributary, and capitalist. Each is correlated with a type of social organization. The tributary mode of production is most common in complex chiefly, primary, and Asiatic states.

11. The term "Coba bowls" may be more confusing than helpful chronologically. There seem to be three varieties (and a fourth that is really not a Coba bowl by anyone's definition), often subsumed under the same term, each of which is distinct and chronologically sensitive. All are fairly crudely made—the three traditional ones by hand, as fingerprints can be seen on the bottoms where they were held. All have marks of flint scraping near their base. The first is a rounded bowl with concave sides. Trufelli (1997:8–9, fig. 2) calls these "western Cobas." The other is a flat-bottomed, flaring-sided bowl, which Trufelli calls "eastern Cobas." Early in Gawra XII and at Norşuntepe these have extended bases. Later they are flat, and are usually called Wide Flower Pots. By LC 2, these flaring-rim versions are either wet-smoothed or slow-wheel-turned and are universally called Wide Flower Pots.

12. Levels VIII, IX, and X were completely excavated. About two-thirds of the levels XI/XA and XIA/B town was excavated. About half of level XII was uncovered. The same approximate area was excavated for each, because the outward curve of the mound made each level larger than the preceding one.

11

Mesopotamian Intraregional Relations Reflected through Glyptic Evidence in the Late Chalcolithic 1–5 Periods

Holly Pittman

The era of state formation in Mesopotamia is known through myriad archaeological details. Scholars apply interpretative strategies or models to those archaeological data in order to interpret them and assign coherent meanings. Among the data long available for interpretation is abundant evidence for a remarkable increase in the use and variety of products of symbolic behavior within the domain of what can be broadly construed as administration. This increase apparently reflects a desire on the part of the ancients to record details of human relations within their communities in ways that would allow for their reconstruction without relying solely on human memory. We have large and well-organized samples of the material residues of this ancient symbolic behavior. With it, some six thousand years later, we can attempt to reconstruct the outlines of those ancient relations. With the benefit of hindsight, our analyses can extend over long periods, encompassing the millennium between approximately 4200 and 3000 B.C. during which states formed for the first time in southern Mesopotamia. The administrative evidence consists of both the symbolic messages and the media on which they were carried, including glyptic art, series of intentional marks, and various document types. This discussion will focus on glyptic art found on seals and sealings. Examples of glyptic art will be examined as a measure of the changing regional character as well as of the extent and intensity of contact between regions during the millennium of Mesopotamian state formation. Such an analysis must be integrated with others focused on other data categories and combined with theoretical reconstruction in order to acquire any explanatory power.

Glyptic art is a hallmark of ancient Near Eastern cultures. It first appears in the seventh millennium B.C. and continues in essentially uninterrupted use until Hellenistic times. Whenever we find seal-impressed clay masses—either as freestanding documents or as locking devices—we identify them as residue of administrative activity broadly construed. Although there is no agreement on the specific cultural value of imagery carried by glyptic art, from its origin, glyptic was used to make repeating impressions of images on malleable material, most commonly clay. It is, indeed, the infinitely reproducible nature of this impressed mark that gives glyptic its unique administrative value. The capacity of imagery carried on clay to store and transmit information is the trait that enables these actions to be understood as administrative. The seals also served other symbolic purposes, acting as amulets as well as votive objects and objects appropriate as burial goods.

State formation in Mesopotamia is closely associated with the Uruk horizon, which is defined on the basis of a ceramic sequence constructed from sites in southern Mesopotamia, most notably Nippur and Uruk-Warka. The Uruk horizon has been dated to the late fifth and fourth millennia B.C. through radiocarbon analysis (see Wright and Rupley, this volume). The presence of diagnostic ceramic types in regions beyond the southern Mesopotamian heartland suggests that the process of state formation in the south was not solely a local development. Indeed, the distribution of ceramics together with architectural and other artifactual evidence indicates that long-distance relations played an important, and perhaps seminal, role in the evolution of social complexity and underlies the formation of Mesopotamian states. The goal of this discussion is to enrich the texture of our description of these interregional relations. Sustained attention to glyptic art, which was one of the essential symbolic technologies used to mediate human interactions during this process of radical social change, provides an essential tool.

Glyptic art, together with the evidence of its use, is widespread during the Uruk period (Late Chalcolithic [LC] 1–5) and has served as a marker for the state formation process. In that respect, it is like the ubiquitous beveled-rim bowl of the Uruk period. At the simplest level of analysis, presence (or absence) of seals and sealings tells us about information-processing behavior. When treated comprehensively, glyptic artifacts, like ceramic evidence, allow us to measure degrees of similarity and difference among human communities along both temporal and spatial dimensions. These comparisons can be made at various levels, from single assemblages of two or more exemplars to diverse assemblages documented across vast distances during the same or different time horizons.

As a general practice, we can compare glyptic across cultural horizons when we are confident that the same general functional parameters obtained cross-culturally. By "function" I mean that glyptic art was used for administrative purposes as well as for others. Comparisons are made by measuring the degrees to which seal morphology, imagery, style, and other factors are shared or unique within and between regions. These comparisons allow us to confirm or refine relative chronology of archaeological deposits defined through ceramic analysis and establish the presence and extent of shared ideology, technology, and administrative praxis.

For the purposes of defining changing regional character and describing intraregional relations, I will employ three discrete measures of similarity in seal imagery. The closest degree of similarity reflects systemic or "cultural" identity. In this category, literal identity is not the point. Rather this highest degree of similarity exists when features of seal designs are judged to belong to the same semiotic system employed by a single cultural tradition. In this category of systemic or cultural identity, there must be technological, morphological, iconographic, and stylistic isomorphism among seal assemblages.

A second degree of relation is one that corresponds generally to the notion of "cultural emulation," which is frequently invoked in discussions of state formation in Mesopotamia. Cultural emulation suggests that fundamental features of a particular style and/or iconography are borrowed from one cultural group by another and used in the local production and use of glyptic artifacts. These features can include any combination of stylistic, iconographic, or morphological traits. A few clear examples of cultural emulation within glyptic art are discussed below.

Finally, we can recognize a degree of similarity that corresponds to the shared symbolic domain elaborated upon by Gil Stein (chap. 8). He invokes a "shared ideological system" to infer the existence of communication between independent chiefdom elites. Before Mesopotamian state formation, this shared symbolic system describes the relations between distant regions as reflected in the glyptic art. This rather generic degree of similarity tells us that groups shared basic life ways and perhaps basic beliefs, a mutual awareness of each other, and similar levels of hierarchical or information-processing complexity. Within regional style groups we see a greater or lesser degree of identity among individual seals. Between regions there will be far less sharing.

A final consideration is the assumption concerning the point of origin of any specific item of administrative residue. Only in the case of door sealings, which are rarely encountered in proveniences dating to the fourth millennium B.C., can we be sure that clay administrative documents originated at the site where they were found. In the case of inscribed documents, we assume that they originate where they tell us they were written. In the case of preliterate administrations, however, only physical analyses such as neutron activation will provide independent proof for this important issue of origin (Rothman and Blackman 1990). Particularly when considering instances of shared cultural or systemic identity, we need to know if the artifact has traveled from place of origin to place of deposition. With sealings used to close portable containers, the situation is fraught with even more interpretive problems. One intuitively assumes that a commodity was packaged before it was sealed and was sealed in order to keep it secure while moving. Is that an accurate assumption? How far did the sealings travel? Did they come long distances or from the immediate hinterland of the site where they were found? Indeed, perhaps sealings do not represent any movement at all but were a purely administrative step used to control the internal distribution of goods. Until reliable data from neutron activation analysis are forthcoming, for the purposes of this discussion I assume that clay sealings were meaningful within the community where they were found and that therefore they can, as a general rule, be used to describe regional character.[1] This guideline is obviated when specific evidence is unique within a given glyptic assemblage. Then one should try to determine possible origin of the clay mass or of the seal with which it is impressed through comparisons to material from other regions.

OVERVIEW OF THE SUBREGIONS

Seven contiguous subregions have been recognized for the era of state formation in Mesopotamia: southern Mesopotamia, Khuzistan, the Western Zagros, Upper Tigris, Iraqi and Syrian Jazira, middle Upper Euphrates, and Upper Euphrates (see fig. 1.1). While ecologically distinct, all of them are interconnected either overland or along the Tigris River or rivers of the Khabur drainage basin. Direct communication along the Euphrates River was not extensive until the early third millennium B.C.

Based on site size and density, the southern Mesopotamian alluvium is the location of greatest social complexity during the era of state formation. From the perspective of seal use and information processing technologies, this is certainly true by the end of the period; it is less evident from the accumulating evidence for the beginning of the era. Notwithstanding recent survey and excavation data on changing settlement size, and the refinement and extension of the ceramic sequence from Nippur, Uruk-Warka is still the only site that has produced a coherent body of glyptic art in anything approaching a stratified context. Even at Uruk-Warka, the tertiary nature of the deposits limits us to *terminus ante quem* relative dates for most of the glyptic evidence (Nissen 1986a, this volume). Telloh, ancient Girsu (Genouillac 1934–36), also produced a significant body of glyptic art. Its archaeological context is also problematic, not because of the deposition but because of the methods of retrieval.

Sites in the eastern extension of the southern alluvium, the archaeologically productive region of Khuzistan, never attained the size of those in southern Mesopotamia during the fourth millennium (Johnson 1987a). In fact, there is evidence for a radical decrease in sedentary occupation of the plain at the end of the Uruk period

(Johnson 1973). This change in settlement patterns appears to coincide with a profound change in the nature of the glyptic art. However, measured solely in terms of administrative evidence, the complexity of these communities during the Early and Middle Uruk periods (LC 2–4) would seem to be closely comparable to that known at Uruk-Warka. Only in the Late Uruk period (LC 5) do they diverge. Mesopotamian administrative practices become far more complex with the appearance of proto-writing. In Khuzistan, the important sites for our knowledge of glyptic art and administration include Sharafabad (Wright, Miller, and Redding 1980), Susa (Amiet 1972, 1980; Le Brun 1971; Le Brun and Vallat 1978), and Chogha Mish (Delougaz and Kantor 1996). All chronological phases considered in this review of glyptic evidence are documented in Khuzistan, but not at all sites. The radical reorganization that marks the beginning of the Late Uruk (LC 5) phase in Khuzistan may reflect competition between Susa and Chogha Mish. Whatever its cause, the latter site was abandoned at the beginning of the Late Uruk phase. Susa suffers some kind of retrenchment by the end of the phase.

Although incompletely known, the Western Zagros region seems to have had a thriving tradition of glyptic art during the Late Ubaid/Early Uruk (Ubaid, LC 1, LC 2) phases and continuing into the early third millennium (Amiet 1980; Rashad 1990). Unlike other subregions drawn into the process of state formation, the Western Zagros, for the most part, continued to use stamp seals throughout the entire millennium, only rarely adopting the cylinder seal for administration until the middle of the third millennium. This makes establishing chronological relations through glyptic comparisons difficult because iconographic and stylistic features continue in use much longer in the Western Zagros than in other regions. An important exception to this tendency is Godin Tepe, where an "implantation" of a community of people from Khuzistan or the Diyala occurs at the beginning of the Late Uruk period. Among the strongly southern artifact assemblage are cylinder seals and numerical tablets closely comparable to those from Susa (Weiss and Young 1975).

The fourth zone is the Upper Tigris piedmont. The glyptic traditions for various stages of the era of state formation are well documented at Gawra (Rothman n.d.), Nineveh, and Arpachiyah (von

Wickede 1990). This subregion has produced abundant evidence for the early and extensive use of stamp seals, which developed early in the Ubaid period and continued through the Early Uruk phase (LC 2). However, apart from the important evidence from Nineveh for administrative identity with southern administrative systems, the glyptic art from the Upper Tigris subregion has a distinct regional character. Until recently, our understanding of the distinct character of the region has been affected by our incorrect interpretation of relative chronology, which placed Gawra VIII in the Late Uruk phase. The ceramic chronology proposed in this volume now places the occupation of level VIII of Gawra at the beginning of the expansion of the southern presence into the north in the early Middle Uruk/LC 3 phase. In the Upper Tigris, only at Nineveh do we have evidence thus far for administrative and glyptic materials identical to those used in the late Middle and Late Uruk (LC 4–5) contexts in the south (Collon and Reade 1983).

The fifth zone is the Syrian and Iraqi Jazira, the steppelike land that supports rainfall agriculture and lies between the Euphrates and the Tigris. This subregion is watered and drained by the Khabur and Balikh river systems. From an early period, Tell Brak, strategically located halfway across the plain on the Jaghjagh River, was a prominent settlement in the region. Recent excavations at Brak are enabling us to make greater sense of the role played by the site in this period. It has become increasingly clear that Brak is crucial to an understanding of the relations between the east and west as well as north and south during the era of state formation. Although evidence has been available since Mallowan's excavations in the 1930s, only now are we beginning to grasp the importance of this site as a vibrant point of intraregional mediation during the Middle Uruk period (LC 3–4). Other sites in the Jazira will undoubtedly show similar features. Most recently Hamoukar to the east of Brak has produced abundant finds of the period (*New York Times,* May 23, 2000).

Along the Euphrates, three points of interaction in the state formation process have been identified. As Gil Stein has observed for the ceramics, the glyptic evidence found along the Euphrates seems to reflect a direct correlation between distance and the level of interaction between north and south (Stein 1998). Qraya (Simpson 1988), at the confluence of the Khabur and the Euphrates, is the southernmost site that has yielded Middle Uruk seal-impressed administrative materials (LC 3–4).[2] The glyptic from the important cluster of sites some 250 kilometers to the north and also on the Euphrates River—Sheikh Hassan, Habuba Kabira, and Jebel Aruda—also provides the evidence for close, direct, and sustained contact with sites in the south. This begins in the early Middle Uruk period (LC 3) and continues through the Late Uruk (LC 5). Administrative materials and glyptic art from these sites are either identical to material known from the south or emulate it in form, iconography, and style. Further upriver at Hacınebi, the contact between the southern sites is limited to the early Middle Uruk period (LC 3) in ceramic terms. In addition, all three categories of glyptic evidence were found at Hacınebi: administrative material identical to that found in the south; glyptic art made locally and emulating morphological, stylistic, and iconographic features of southern glyptic; and material unrelated to the southern traditions and closely related to regional styles found in the Jazira and in eastern Anatolia. Even further upriver, at Hassek Höyük, it is difficult to judge if any of the glyptic evidence is identical to that from the south or whether it is all emulative. Finally, at Arslantepe, west of the Euphrates, no evidence that is culturally identical to southern glyptic has been found, although there is abundant evidence for emulation together with masses of Anatolian regional glyptic material that bears no relationship whatsoever to southern practice.

A REGIONAL SURVEY OF THE GLYPTIC EVIDENCE

In the absence of datable inscriptions, ceramics have long served as the backbone of Greater Mesopotamian relative chronology, while radiocarbon sequences give the range of absolute dates. In this analysis, glyptic art and administrative materials are fit into ceramically defined sequences as reflected in table 1.1. Dates are therefore assigned independently of changes (or continuities) in glyptic art. Our understanding of the sequence of development and interregional relations reflected in the glyptic and administrative materials is thus based on temporal relations established through external criteria.

The present survey covers a much longer period of time than the one on which this volume focuses. As Nissen argues in this volume, the

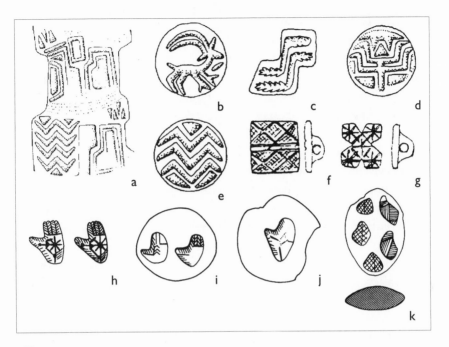

FIGURE 11.1

Seal designs of the Halaf period. (a–e) Impressions on ancient clay sealings from Sabi Abyad, level 6, Early Halaf period. Both geometric and figural imagery is recorded from the site. Shapes include both circular and right-angled straight-sided geometric forms. (f–g) Stamp seal impressions on clay sealings from Domuztepe, eastern Anatolia, Late Halaf period. (h–k) Impression on clay sealings in the shape of a right hand; disk-shaped clay sealings from Arpachiyah impressed by a stamp seal in the shape of a right hand; multiple impressions of a crescent-shaped stamp, and a triangular stamp, Late Halaf period. Not to scale. Sources: a–e, Duistermaat 1996:figs. 5.3–5.5; f–g, Campbell et al. 1999:fig. 14; h–k, von Wickede 1990:57, 58, 60b, 59.

processes of development, interaction, and change began much earlier than the fourth millennium. To see the full picture a brief discussion of the earliest material is necessary.

Halaf and Ubaid

By the beginning of the era of state formation, glyptic art had been in use for millennia in Greater Mesopotamia (Porada et al. 1992; Rashad 1990; von Wickede 1990). The typical seal form was the stamp, whose shape as well as engraved imagery carried meaning. By the middle Halaf levels at Sabi Abyad on the Euphrates in Syria (Akkermanns and Duistermatt 1996) we know that some of the administrative practices used later were fully developed. Seal imagery included geometric and figural representations. Sealing practice included multiple impressions and counter sealing both on locks for portable containers and on freestanding clay documents (fig. 11.1a–e).

From Domuztepe (Campbell et al. 1999) in eastern Anatolia to Arpachiyah in the Upper Tigris piedmont we have evidence that these practices continued across the extensive regional embrace of the late Halaf horizon. Although limited figural imagery continued to be used, geometric patterns (especially quadrilles) dominate the iconography. Differentiation among seals is now far more clearly expressed through seal shape than through design (fig. 11.1f–k).

The glyptic art of the Late Ubaid phase is best known from Tepe Gawra levels XVI–XIII. Stamp seal imagery there gradually came to include representations of not only geometric patterns and horned animals but also snakes, vultures, and humans. A humanoid figure with the head of an animal appears (fig. 11.2). Although the precise identity of this figure is unknown, its depicted demeanor suggests a shaman.[3] To the west, this subject matter is well known at Değirmentepe, in a distinctive regional style (fig. 11.3a–c). This individual continues to figure prominently in the early phase of the Late Chalcolithic period. To date there is only slim evidence for this personage in the glyptic art of this period from the southern alluvium of the Tigris and Euphrates; we have one example from southern Mesopotamia (Oueili) (fig. 11.3d). From Susa, however, this figure may be documented as early as level 27 in the Acropole sounding (fig. 11.3e).

Terminal Ubaid/LC 1

The relative chronology based on ceramic sequences equates Eanna XVI–XIV, Susa Acropole levels 27–23, and Gawra XII and XIA/B and the Gawra A phase at Nineveh.

In the meager material that we have from the site of Uruk-Warka there is no suggestion of a flourishing glyptic tradition in southern Mesopotamia, although further excavation is needed to confirm this impression. This stands in stark contrast to the vigorous glyptic traditions known from Susiana, Giyan in the Zagros, Gawra, Nineveh, and

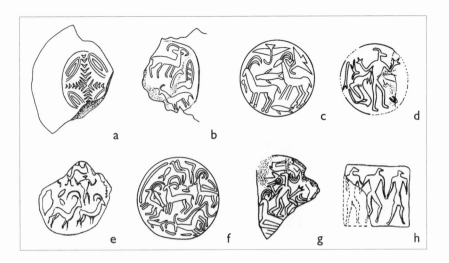

FIGURE 11.2

Stamp-seal-impressed clay sealings from Tepe Gawra, Late Ubaid levels XIV–XIII. Both circular and rectangular stamps occur. While geometric imagery continues, there is an increase in use of figural representation. The figural scenes are complex and are composed along a horizontal axis or a circular rotation. Not to scale. Sources: a–d, f–g, von Wickede 1990:244, 249, 245b, 250b, 248, 252a; e, h, Amiet 1980:36, 49.

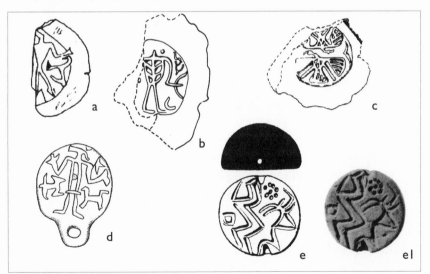

FIGURE 11.3

Late Ubaid stamp seal designs impressed on clay sealings: human, vultures, "shaman" figures. (a–c) Eastern Anatolia (Değirmentepe, Late Ubaid). (d) Stone pendant with incised image of horned "shaman" from southern Mesopotamia (Oueili, Late Ubaid). (e) Drawing and photo of seal from Susa, Acropole level 27. Not to scale. Sources: a, drawing after von Wickede 1990:358; b–d, von Wickede 1990:363, 348, 227; e–e1, Le Brun 1971:fig. 35, pl. 22.

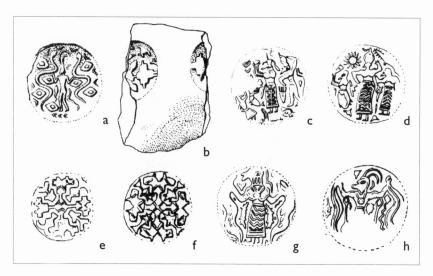

FIGURE 11.4

Stamp seal impressions on clay sealings from Susa. (a–b) Acropole level 25. (c–h)
Unstratified material. Dominant themes in the stamp seals from Susa at this period are the
"shaman" figure, now wearing a long skirt with distinct patterning as well as an animal
headdress, engaged in a significant (i.e., "ritual") activity. Another common theme is the
abstracted representation of animal head standards (e–f). Not to scale. Sources: a–b, Le
Brun 1971:fig. 35; c–h, Rashad 1990:821, 822, 804, 805, 810, 811.

Arpachiyah in the Upper Tigris region, and Değirmentepe in eastern
Anatolia, to name only the most obvious. Unlike ceramics, which begin
to show profound change, the glyptic form and administrative practice
continues essentially unchanged from the preceding period. Familiar
among the unstratified material from Susa are seal impressions found
in well-controlled contexts in Acropole level 25 (fig. 11.4a–b). This type
is abundantly represented among the unstratified material at Susa (fig.
11.4c–h). It is also found in the western Zagros Mountains at the site of
Tepe Giyan (fig. 11.5a–c). Unfortunately the Giyan sample is poorly
provenienced, but it seems likely that the local tradition continued into
a period equivalent to the Early Uruk (LC 2) and beyond. Regardless of
its end date (which could be as late as the beginning of the third millennium), the Western Zagros material represents the unbroken continuation of the Late Ubaid figural tradition. Gawra provides the
best-controlled sample of this glyptic type. Appearing first in Gawra

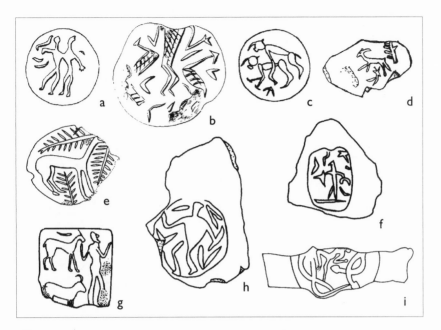

FIGURE 11.5

Stamp seal imagery from the Early Uruk/LC 2 phase. Dominant imagery includes humans and animals, shamans, and horned animals. (a–c) Western Zagros (Giyan). (d–i) Upper Tigris (Gawra XII). Not to scale. Sources: a–b, Amiet 1980:88, 84; c, Rashad 1990:fig. 3, 77; d, f, h, Rothman n.d.: pl. 25, 465, pl. 24, 433, pl. 28, 472; e, g, i, von Wickede 1990:259, 268, 261.

XIV and represented most clearly in Gawra XIII, the type is abundant in XII (fig. 11.5d–i). Its imagery is somewhat expanded from the Late Ubaid but is essentially unchanged. Common images include the shaman figure, copulating humans, humans and animals, and caprids.

Early Uruk/LC 2

The relative chronology based on the ceramic sequence equates Eanna XII, Tell Brak TW 19–18, Gawra XI/XA, and Hacınebi A.

We have extremely poor knowledge of this phase from the south, but evidence from the Upper Tigris and Upper Euphrates indicates that the stamp seal traditions begun in the earlier Ubaid phase continued to develop. The most noticeable trend is the introduction of a number of new scenes, especially apparent at Gawra.

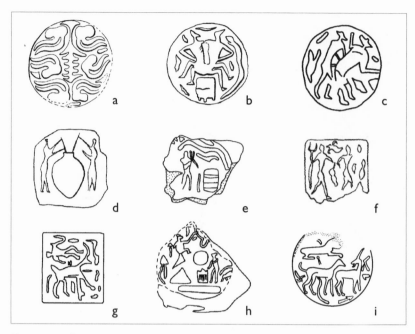

FIGURE 11.6

Stamp seal imagery from the Early Uruk/LC 2 phase, Upper Tigris. Dominant imagery includes groups of humans engaged in complex activities of drinking, farming, and ritual. Also seen are caprid heads, intertwined snakes, and a horned animal with a vulture. Not to scale. (a) Uruk-Warka Eanna deep sounding, level XII. (b–d) Gawra XII–XIA. (e–i) Gawra XI/XA. Sources: a, g, i, von Wickede 1990:482, 284, 278; b, d, f, Amiet 1980:41, 43, 45; c, e, h, Rothman n.d.:pl. 37, 1077, pl. 40, 1005, pl.36,1061.

The earliest stratified glyptic from Uruk, from the deep sounding in Eanna level XII (fig. 11.6a), is a single stamp seal impression with six heads of horned caprids arrayed on either side of a central vertical form. This composition of animal heads is comparable to seals from Susa (fig. 11.4b, e, f). This seal imagery may have been created by a drill rather than by a gouging tool. The use of the drill, as we will see below, marks the transition from the late Ubaid tradition to the Uruk tradition in seal production in the south.

The absence of stratified material among the finds from Susa makes it difficult to identify trends. The ceramic evidence suggests the possibility of a hiatus in the occupation of the site.

In the Upper Tigris, abundant glyptic evidence from Gawra level

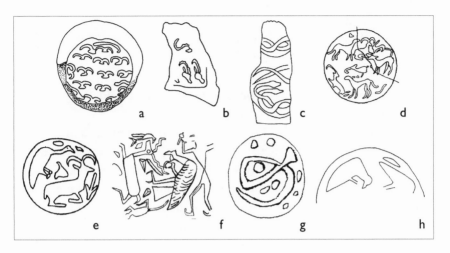

FIGURE 11.7

Stamp seal imagery. (a–e) Early Uruk/LC 2 phase from Upper Tigris, Gawra XI/XA. (f–h) Early Uruk/LC 2 phase from the Upper Euphrates, Hacınebi phase A. The imagery of both regions presents the "shaman" figure, the vulture, the caprid, and twisted snakes. Not to scale. Sources: a–b, d–e, von Wickede 1990:279, 291, 286, 296; c, Rothman n.d.:pl. 49, 1844; f–h, author.

XIA/B documents certain trends. Most important, the repertoire of human figures expands from the single shamanic figure to extended groups of figures engaged in a variety of activities (fig. 11.6b–h). These activities include mating, communal drinking (suggested by groups in association with a large vessel and straws), and subsistence (groups with or without tools in association with animals). The stamp seals with animal representations have a horizontal orientation (figs. 11.6i and 11.7a–b, d–e), unlike those of earlier levels, which were arrayed around the seal surface. Free-floating heads of horned animals are represented for the first time (fig. 11.7a–b). Copulating snakes continue to be depicted (fig. 11.6c). In addition, in a composition almost identical to one from Hacınebi A, a vulture hovers over the back of a caprid (fig. 11.7f). To date no stratified examples have been reported from Tell Brak; however, examples have been found on the surface.

At the crossing of the Upper Euphrates into Anatolia, in contexts dated to this phase on the basis of ceramics, Hacınebi A levels have produced a comparatively large number of actual seal stones in addition to a small number of sealings (fig. 11.7f–h). One of the seal stones (fig. 11.7f) is closely comparable to similar compositions seen in Gawra XI A/B and Gawra XI/XA (fig. 11.7e).

Commentary on the Glyptic Art of Terminal Ubaid–Early Uruk/ LC 1 and 2

Seals of the Late Ubaid through Early Uruk belong to a single tradition. Seals found in these levels are all stamp seals; they are all engraved rather than drilled (with the possible exception of the Eanna XII example); and their iconography frequently includes a humanoid figure with animal attributes, who is associated with caprids, vultures, or snakes. They are notably absent in the south, but otherwise their distribution extends through all of the subregions that are later drawn into the process of state formation in the south (including Khuzistan), the Upper Tigris, and the Upper Euphrates. Although there is a high degree of similarity in the iconography of these subregions, regional styles of carving are evident. There is no strong evidence for either exchange of actual seals or close contact between the seal carvers. This is to say that neither cultural identity nor conscious emulation underlies the features shared across the region. Rather, as displayed in the pottery of the late Ubaid phase, we continue to see in the glyptic traditions the use of a "shared symbolic ideology." Their common technology, morphology, and general iconography indicate that they belong within the same cultural horizon. There are, however, obvious differences that distinguish subregions in details of form, carving, and imagery. Thus, while they reflect general cultural familiarity, their differences do not allow us to see them as closely chronologically synchronous or as evidence of direct contact between distant places. What they tell us is that communities shared general administrative as well as production technology and that they shared social institutions that were symbolized in similar ways. They do not tell us that these sites were in direct and continuous administrative contact with each other. Certainly, this general level of similarity is not evidence for political or economic hegemony of any subregion over any other.

Early Middle Uruk/LC 3

The relative chronology based on the ceramic sequence equates

Eanna IX–VIII, Nippur XX–XIX, Susa 22–19, Gawra VIII, Tell Brak TW 17–14, Hacınebi Tepe B1, Sheikh Hassan 13/10–8, and Qraya.

Although the change from the Ubaid to the Uruk horizon is slower for glyptic than for the ceramics, both glyptic art and administrative practice change as radically. One essentially stylistic feature that must be discussed is the introduction of the drill as the primary tool for carving seal imagery. From available evidence, this change in the technology of production appears simultaneously at sites in the north and south. However, it tends to dominate in the south. We cannot yet know if the drill-based technology was introduced and then developed in the south or if it was introduced in the north and then adopted and developed in the south. It is likely that the former will prove to be the case because in the north drilling technology is not typical of regional styles whereas in the south the use of the drill is increasingly well developed. Together with the increased use of the drill for carving, a new form of seal, the cylinder, is introduced. Once introduced, the cylinder seal becomes the glyptic form of choice in southern Mesopotamia, whereas it has a relatively short and highly derivative use in the surrounding regions. From the moment of its introduction the drill is used to cut both stamp seals and cylinder seals.

The simultaneous introduction of drilling technology and the cylinder seal is probably not coincidental because wheel-based technology underlies both. Behind the radical change in ceramics lies the gradual use of slow- and then faster-wheel modes of production. The wheel-based technology of ceramic production may have served as the direct source or at least the primary inspiration for basic changes in lapidary technology. Regardless, there is no question that rotary technology underlies the tools of choice in the cutting of seal stones. A further speculation about causal relations linking these various artifacts is that hollow drill technology was used to produce stone vessels. This technique produced cylindrical stone cores that would have served very effectively as blanks for cylinder seals. Thus, the cylinder seal as object may have originated as the residue produced from coring stone blocks with a hollow drill to produce stone vessels.

Although the data are meager and poorly controlled, a fragmentary chain of evidence suggests that we should seek the origins of this change—a change that undoubtedly reflected profound reorganization

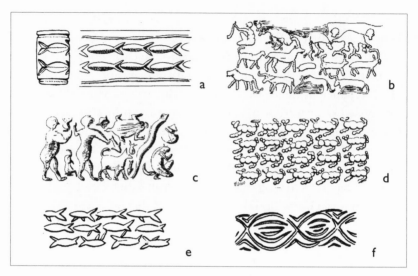

FIGURE 11.8

Imagery on cylinder seals from southern Mesopotamia and Khuzistan, early Middle Uruk/LC 3 phase. Both the cutting disk and the rotary drill are used. (a) Drawing of a cylinder seal found in the Susa Acropole sounding in level 21. (b) Drawing of cylinder seal found out of context in the Uruk-Warka Eanna sounding, level III. (c) Drawing of cylinder seal found on the Anu Ziggurat at Uruk-Warka between levels C and D. (d–f) Telloh. Not to scale. Sources: a, Le Brun 1971:fig. 43; b–f, Amiet 1980:1598, 219 (pl. 12), 297, 352, 357.

in the society—in southern Mesopotamia and Khuzistan. While Uruk-Warka and Telloh provide some evidence, as we shall see below, the change can be charted most clearly in the unstratified materials from the early excavations at Susa. These materials are from levels equivalent to Susa Acropole sounding levels 22–19.

One of the very few items from those levels at Susa that have been published is the wheel-cut seal reported from level 21 in the Acropole sounding (fig. 11.8a). This seal, of a type that is well known in southern Mesopotamia and has been found as far afield as Upper Egypt, is a fine example of the earliest use of rotary technology in the form of a cutting disk. Until now this seal has been treated as if it were out of context. However, given a consideration of the wider field of evidence, we can see that this seal indeed belongs to the level in which it was found and is certainly one of the earliest stratified cylinder seals known to date.

The other style of seal associated with the early Middle Uruk (LC

3) period has been labeled the "baggy style." This term, introduced by Amiet, graphically describes the visual quality of the figures. The imagery is cut with a ball drill in a manner that leaves the drill marks manifestly obvious. No baggy-style seals have been found at Uruk-Warka in the Eanna precinct in a Middle Uruk context. However, a large cylinder seal found out of context in Eanna level III (fig. 11.8b) is cut in the baggy style and certainly belongs to an earlier level. Middle Uruk levels on the Anu Ziggurat (between levels C and D) yielded one seal of this type (fig. 11.8c).

The other site in southern Mesopotamia that has produced examples of the "baggy style" is Telloh (fig. 11.8d). Significantly, this seal was found together with the wheel-cut style comparable to those from Susa Acropole 21 (fig. 11.8e, f). Although no well-controlled stratigraphic context is preserved for those finds, the ceramic material associated with the baggy-style seal also belongs to the (early?) Middle Uruk horizon.

At the same time as the cylinder was introduced in the south, a new stamp seal type was also developed. This new type is either geometric (hemispheric, square, or rectangular) or theriomorphic, appearing as protomes, worker figures, horned animals, rabbits, etc. These seals carry images that are drilled rather than engraved. This technique links them directly to the images on the earliest cylinders. Until now, these highly distinctive stamps have been dated to the Jemdet Nasr phase. While many are found in later contexts, a significant number have been found in contexts with ceramics that are now understood to be early Middle Uruk. Telloh, Susa, Tell Brak, Sheikh Hassan, and Tell Qraya all provide compelling evidence for the early Middle Uruk (LC 3) date for the appearance of this stamp seal type. This early date also coincides with the stylistic development (the use of the drill) that begins in the early Middle Uruk phase (LC 3). Accompanying this new technology is a new repertoire of images. The image of the worker as the centerpiece of this new iconography is, I believe, significant in this context of state formation. This drill style and its new iconography is, as I argue elsewhere, the basis for the idealized naturalism that emerges during the later phase of the Middle Uruk and continues into the Late Uruk period, particularly in southern Mesopotamia. Through its iconography, as I will develop in a separate study, we can begin to describe a social, economic, and political history of this crucial phase in human social evolution.

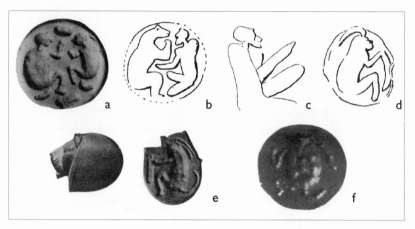

FIGURE 11.9

Imagery on stamp seals from Susa, early Middle Uruk/LC 3 phase. The imagery engraved on the bezel of this type of stamp seal frequently shows seated worker figures, either male or female. The drill is used exclusively to execute the imagery in the "baggy" style. Not to scale. Source: Rashad 1990:1047, 1051, 1046, 1045, 1100, 1043.

At Susa, it is significant that the baggy style was not found in level 18 or 17 of the Acropole sounding, as represented by the materials published to date. The baggy style is, however, abundantly documented among the unstratified material from Susa, where it is found most clearly among the stamp seals (fig. 11.9). In addition, some hollow clay balls from unstratified contexts are impressed by seals of the baggy style (fig. 11.10) that are comparable to the cylinder known from Anu between C and D. Many are counter-impressed with stamp seals. No examples of the baggy style are found on numerical tablets or tags. Although it is difficult to be certain from the drawings, Chogha Mish does seem to have examples of the baggy style seals impressed on hollow clay balls that are counter-impressed by stamp seals.

In the Upper Tigris, there is precious little evidence for this early Middle Uruk (LC 3) phase. Yorgan Tepe (the local name of the Nuzi mound) has produced a series of drilled stamp seals in a pit context that apparently produced no ceramics (fig. 11.11). Gawra VIII is dated to the early Middle Uruk period on the basis of ceramics. If this temporal assignment is indeed correct, a new composition was introduced in this period that becomes important in later southern traditions. This

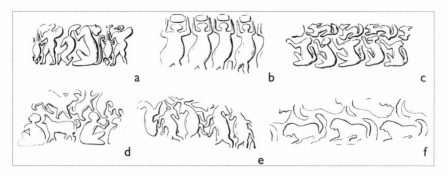

FIGURE 11.10

Imagery of impressions of cylinder seals from Susa on hollow clay balls, sealings, and tags, early Middle Uruk/LC 3 phase. The imagery on this type of cylinder seal shows workers, animals, and felines. The drill is used exclusively to execute the imagery in the "baggy" style. Not to scale. Source: Amiet 1972:567, 678, 565, 570, 465, 553.

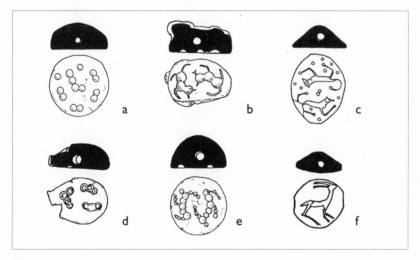

FIGURE 11.11

Imagery engraved on limestone stamp seals found at Yorgan Tepe (the mound of Nuzi) in the Upper Tigris subregion, early Middle Uruk/LC 3 phase. Most of the seals are carved with the drill; c and f are cut, partially, by means of a graver. Not to scale. Source: Starr 1937–39:A1-2, C1-2, G1-2, J1-2, L1-2, F1-2.

composition is crossed-necked animals (fig. 11.12a–c). The crossing of animal necks is common on seals from Uruk-Warka and Susa in the Late Uruk period. It is likely that this composition was developed in the

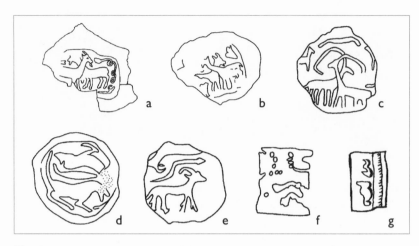

FIGURE 11.12

Early Middle Uruk/LC 3 phase, Gawra VIII. (a–e) Drawings of stamp seal imagery impressed on clay masses from the Upper Tigris subregion. (f–g) Bone cylinder seals carved with illegible imagery by means of a drill. Not to scale. Source: Rothman n.d.:pl. 59, 2923, pl. 57, 2952, pl. 58, 2930, pl. 61, 2967, pl. 60, 2966, pl. 63, 2938, pl. 57, 2959.

last stages of this Ubaid type stamp seal tradition seen at Gawra VIII and then borrowed by southern seal makers for use in their cylinder compositions. Another composition that appears here for the first time is the *tête beche* organization of animals in which one is placed above and mirrors the other (fig. 11.12d–e). This compositional formula is also used extensively in Uruk cylinders and it continues to be used in later stamps. Finally, in Gawra VIII two fragments of what may be bone cylinders drilled with random patterns may be the northern experiments of cylinder seals carved in the baggy style (fig. 11.12f–g).

Although we have little to date from levels TW 17–14 at Tell Brak in the Jazira, more will be forthcoming. In TW 16 two impressions of what has been called a cylinder seal but is more likely a stamp seal are recorded (fig. 11.13a) along with a stamp seal impression (fig. 11.13b). Hacınebi Tepe level B1 produced a small but interesting collection of glyptic art that displays connections to Gawra VIII, to Brak, and to northern Anatolian glyptic styles (fig. 11.13c, d, e, respectively). It is significant that no baggy style seals have been found in phase B1 of Hacınebi.

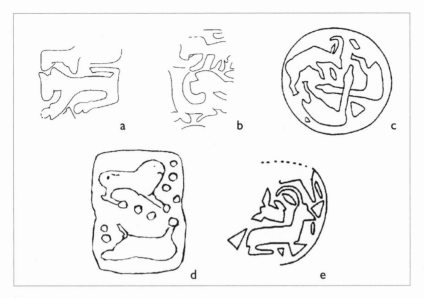

FIGURE 11.13

(a–b) *Drawings of stamp seal impressions from the Jezira, Tell Brak area TW, level 16 and early level 14, Middle Uruk/LC 3–4 phase.* (c–e) *Drawings of impressions and actual stamp seals from the Upper Euphrates, Hacınebi phase B1, Middle Uruk/LC 3–4 phase. Not to scale. Sources: a–b, Oates and Oates 1993a:fig. 32; c–e, author.*

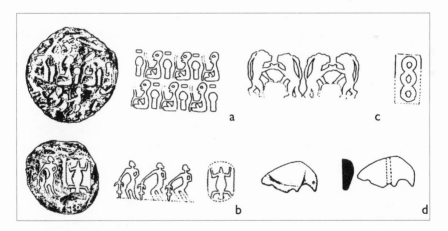

FIGURE 11.14

(a–c) *Drawings of impressions of cylinder and stamp seals on hollow clay balls from the Euphrates.* (d) *Drawing of a vulture pendant seal carved from white limestone, Sheikh Hassan level 10, early Middle Uruk/LC phase 3. Not to scale. Source: Boese 1995:figs. 37, 38, 39, 40.*

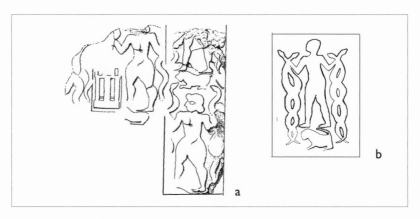

FIGURE 11.15

Drawings of seal impressions on hollow clay balls from southern Mesopotamia and Khuzistan. Subject of naked hero mastering snake is one of many themes shared between the two regions. Not to scale. (a) Eanna level V–IV. (b) Chogha Mish Uruk levels, late Middle–Late Uruk/LC 4–5. Sources: a, Amiet 1980:1599; b, Delougaz and Kantor 1996:pl. 156.

Ceramics from Sheikh Hassan level 10 are assigned to the early Middle Uruk phase. The poor-quality illustrations of the three hollow clay balls from that level make them difficult to evaluate. The balls are impressed by cylinders and counter-impressed by stamp seals. This practice is typical of the unstratified hollow clay balls from Susa and Chogha Mish. Further indication of the early Middle Uruk (LC 3) date of these levels at Sheikh Hassan is a pendant in the form of a vulture, a common shape for the stamp seals (fig. 11.14d).

Finally, at Tell Qraya at the confluence of the Khabur and the Euphrates were apparently found hollow clay balls and clay sealings impressed with such early-style cylinder seals and counter-impressed by a stamp seal (see note 2).

Late Middle Uruk/LC 4

The relative chronology determined through ceramic comparison equates Eanna VII, Nippur XVIII, Sharafabad, Susa early level 18, Brak TW13, and Hacınebi Tepe level B2.

No securely stratified glyptic or administrative material of the late Middle Uruk phase has yet been reported from sites in southern

Mesopotamia. The closest example comes from Eanna level V. This massive hollow clay ball was impressed by a very large cylinder carrying the image of a nude male master of snakes who stands on top of an architectural structure (fig. 11.15a). Stylistically the image is very similar to ones impressed on hollow clay balls from Susa and Chogha Mish (fig. 11.15b) that represent further development from the "baggy style." Characteristic of this early modeled style is smoothing of the drilled forms of the true "baggy" style with a graver. No longer are human figures made of contiguous series of drillings. Rather they are highly modeled and fully sculptural with increasing anatomical detail.

Both the seal from Anu (see fig. 11.8c) and the impression from Eanna V (fig. 11.15a) show subject matter that is characteristic of Uruk period glyptic and that distinguishes it from that of the earlier Ubaid period. Now anonymous workers and domesticated or herded animals are the dominant subject matter. The horned shaman was transformed into a nude human hero who masters the forces of nature. Soon, this figure is replaced by the "priest king" of the Late Uruk phase.

With little comparable evidence from Uruk-Warka, it is difficult to characterize the relationship between southern Mesopotamia and Khuzistan. What little data we have suggest that the two subregions underwent a common development. There is no suggestion of political or economic hegemony of one subregion over the other. Also, there is no suggestion that one subregion was emulating the other. The apparently continuous contact between the two subregions explains the commonality that we will probably see when further exploration of southern Mesopotamia is possible.

The sounding in the Acropole at Susa provides us with a skeletal sequence through which we can order the mass of unstratified administrative material. This sequence also helps us to understand the material from Chogha Mish. Through these various bodies of evidence we can define a late Middle Uruk glyptic phase that can be distinguished both from the early middle phase of the baggy style and from the "classic" style seals of the Late Uruk phase, which are associated with the earliest written documents.

The glyptic of Susa Acropole level 18 (fig. 11.16) depicts heroes mastering animals, humans producing goods, animal files (lines of animals) as well as humans engaged with animals, animal combat, humans

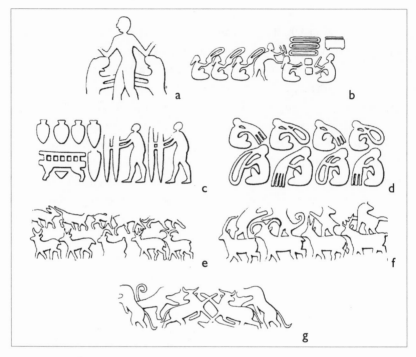

FIGURE 11.16

Drawings of impressions of cylinder seals on clay administrative documents (hollow clay balls, sealings, numerical tablets), Khuzistan, Susa Acropole level 18. Subject matter includes heroic master of animals, worker scenes, animal files, and animal combat scenes. Late Middle Uruk/LC phase 4. Not to scale. Sources: Le Brun and Vallat 1978:figs. 6–7.

and animals associated with a niched structure, and lists of commodities arranged in double registers. Characteristic of all of these compositions is the tendency to divide the image field into registers (fig. 11.16d), sometimes of changing and unequal heights (fig. 11.16a–c), thereby filling the entire surface with images of varying scales. Another feature typical of this phase is seen in the bodies of animals, which tend to be bulky yet dovetail into each other in a distinctive manner (fig. 11.16e–f).

During this late Middle Uruk (LC 4) period, the figures continue to be made with a drill, but the marks are now smoothed out through the secondary use of a graver. Further, conventions of representation seem to have been resolved for the most important subjects. For exam-

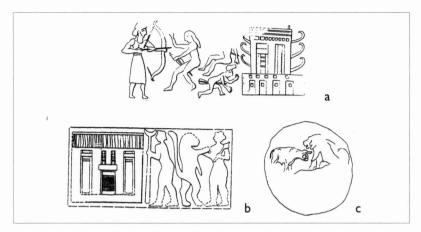

FIGURE 11.17

Drawings of impressions of cylinder seals on clay administrative documents. Late Uruk/LC phase 5. (a–b) Khuzistan (Susa old excavations; Chogha Mish, Uruk phase). (c) Upper Tigris (Nineveh deep sounding). Not to scale. Sources: a, c, Amiet 1980:659, 1679; b, Delougaz and Kantor 1996:pl. 154.

ple, the worker figure's posture is now fixed with one leg up and one under the body (fig. 11.16, d). At this stage in the Uruk period the widest iconographic range is seen in the glyptic art.

At Susa and Chogha Mish, where the types are most extensively represented, the human figures, nude and bald or dressed and wearing a long pigtail, are distinguished by their actions and their attributes. One recognizable headgear, the hair roll and heavy band associated with the paramount ruler of Uruk, is seen, but rarely, on seals found in Khuzistan (fig. 11.17a–b). While internal evidence cannot identify this figure, the consensus interpretation is that he represents a generic leader rather than a single centralized institution of power.

Although there are differences in the seal repertoire at Chogha Mish and Susa, the similarity of the glyptic imagery and the entire administrative assemblage from the two sites is remarkably close. What such similarity implies for the political or economic relationship between Susa and Chogha Mish is still a matter for speculation; there is no question that they shared details of the symbolic technology used in the administrative toolkit. It is important to emphasize the closeness of the two samples because it is extended when we compare the symbolic

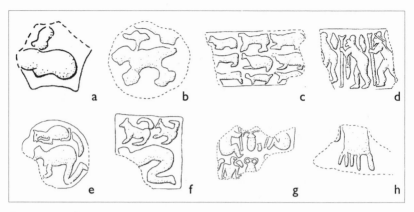

FIGURE 11.18

Imagery of impressions of cylinder and stamp seals found in a seasonal pit at Sharafabad, Khuzistan, early Middle Uruk/LC 3 phase. All imagery is rendered in the "baggy"style by use of the drill. Not to scale. Source: Wright, Miller, and Redding 1980:fig. 6.

technologies of the sites on the Euphrates with Tell Brak, and especially Hacınebi level B2.

To the degree that we have comparable material from the late Middle Uruk (LC 4) phase from Uruk-Warka, we find the same themes. What we cannot do is compare the imagery from Susa 18 and Chogha Mish with images found in Uruk-Warka Eanna levels IVa and III (Late Uruk/LC 5 and later). The subject matter of the two groups is strikingly different. But until we have more glyptic evidence from Uruk that is securely dated to the late Middle Uruk (LC 4) phase we cannot confidently conclude that the two regions did not share iconographic as well as stylistic and morphological features during this phase. It is during the Late Uruk phase that they diverge.

The site of Sharafabad in Khuzistan provides the well-controlled examples of the material culture of the late Middle Uruk (LC 4) phase. In a seasonal pit we see the continued use of the baggy style, which is not present in the contemporary levels at Susa or Chogha Mish (fig. 11.18). If the ceramics from this provenience can really be assigned to that date, then the true baggy style seals continue in use throughout the Middle Uruk period and cannot be limited to the early part of the period. We see the same situation in Tell Brak level 13. At Sharafabad, impressions of both stamps and cylinders carrying baggy-

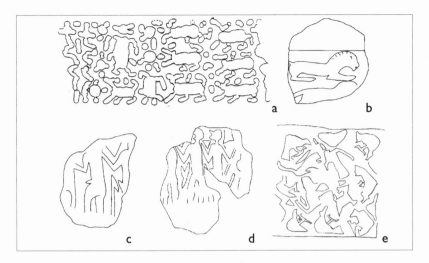

FIGURE 11.19

Drawings of (a) a cylinder seal image from Brak TW 13, (b–d) impressions of cylinder seals on clay administrative documents, and (e) imagery engraved on a stamp seal from Brak HS1, late Middle Uruk/LC phase 4. Not to scale. Sources: a, Oates and Oates 1993a:fig. 31; b–d, Matthews 1994:fig. 4; e, drawing after Matthews 1994:fig. 7.

style images of workers and animals were found on clay sealing devices. No hollow clay balls or numerical tablets were found among these administrative devices. However, semicircular clay cups with seal impressions found in the Sharafabad pit are probably a local adaptation of the hollow clay ball technology in what is a small rural enclave whose administrative praxis lags behind that of the larger centers of Susa and Chogha Mish.

During the late Middle Uruk phase in the western Zagros Moun-tains and in the Upper Tigris, stamp seals of the Late Ubaid/Early Uruk type continue to be used. If our ceramic chronology is correct, Gawra was abandoned by this time. A seal-impressed jar sealing from Nineveh (fig. 11.17c) can be dated to this phase on the basis of comparison with examples from Susa.

In the Khabur, the late Middle Uruk (LC 4) phase is documented in area TW 13 at Tell Brak. From that level comes a fine example of a baggy-style seal (fig. 11.19a). Apart from the bone cylinders from early Middle Uruk Gawra VIII, this is the first evidence for this stylistic type in the Jezirah. It is closely comparable to examples found at Telloh and at Uruk-Warka in Eanna III and ones preserved as impressions from Susa, Chogha Mish, and Sharafabad.

The glyptic and administrative finds from Tell Brak suggest that during the Middle Uruk (LC 3–4) period Brak was a pivotal point in the relations between north/south and east/west. Combined with the evidence from Hacınebi, evidence from Brak confirms the general contemporaneity of three distinct glyptic traditions. In area HS1, Middle Uruk pottery was associated with cylinder seal impressions (fig. 11.19b–d) closely comparable to images from Sharafabad, Susa, Chogha Mish, and Sheikh Hassan. Found in the same context with these Middle Uruk cylinder sealings are impressions of the Jazira regional style stamp seal (fig. 11.19e). Mallowan found a number of similar stamp seals (see fig. 11.21d–f) in his excavations of the earliest levels of the Eye Temple together with many theriomorphic stamps. This type was manifest in the early Middle Uruk contexts at Sheikh Hassan (fig. 11.14d). Clearly it continues in use through the Middle Uruk period. By the Late Uruk (LC 5) period, I think that this type was no longer administratively functional and thus fell out of production. If that is the case, then the examples found in later contexts must be considered heirlooms, a likely possibility given their intrinsic charm as objects. They were collected into groups and deposited in later contexts, perhaps as a votive or other meaningful act.

In addition to the types already described, a small number of theriomorphic stamp seals engraved by a drill (fig. 11.20c) were found at Tell Brak, together with numerous theriomorphic stamps that are engraved with a gouging tool (fig. 11.20a, b, d–f). Among these are a number of examples carved in bone, including a recumbent lion, a caprid, and a squatting worker. This version of the theriomorphic stamp seal with engraved rather than drilled imagery rarely occurs in the south. It may represent a northern variation on the drilled theriomorphic or geometric stamp seal type. Perhaps with more evidence we will be able to use these two types as indicators of direct contact between the two regions. This seal type is found in great abundance at Hacınebi Tepe in phase B2 contexts that are spatially distinct but contemporary with late Middle Uruk (LC 4) finds.

There are few late Middle Uruk (LC 4) period contexts from the Upper Euphrates, as determined by the ceramic sequence. However,

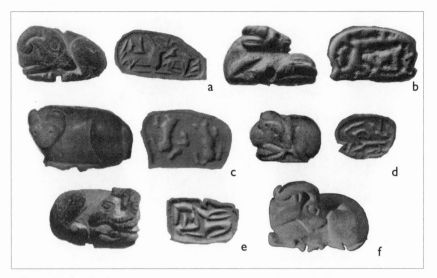

FIGURE 11.20

Theriomorphic stamp seals carved from limestone and from bone from the north, found in the Eye Temple, the lowest level of the gray brick stratum at Tell Brak. All but one (c) is carved by means of a graver. It is possible that the one drilled rather than engraved belongs to the southern rather that the upper Tigridian type of theriomorphic stamp seal. Not to scale. Source: Mallowan 1947:pl. 11–13.

both the ceramics and the glyptic art from B2 contexts at Hacınebi Tepe belong to this phase. The seals find close parallels to examples from Susa level 18. Of the ten images of Middle Uruk type (a selection of which is shown in fig. 11.22a–g), five depict human beings, four show animals, and one carries ear-shaped forms arranged in rows. Nine are "identical" to seal images from Susa level 18 and/or Chogha Mish. Only one seal, showing a double register of felines walking in opposite directions, emulates a Middle Uruk type (fig. 11.22e).

In addition to the cylinder seals closely paralleled in the south, Hacınebi level B2 produced three kinds of regional glyptic evidence. One seal in the shape of a kidney (fig. 11.22h) is identical to stamp seals known in abundance from Tell Brak (fig. 11.21a–c) and found most recently at Hamoukar. The second parallel is a theriomorphic stamp in the shape of a recumbent lion engraved on the bezel with gouged animal figures (fig. 11.22i). The third type of stamp seal found at Hacınebi is either local to the immediate region or exhibits stylistic

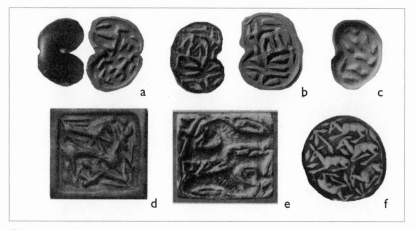

FIGURE 11.21

Stamp seals carved in stone with kidney-shaped, square, and circular forms. Late Middle Uruk/LC phase in the Jezira, found in the Eye Temple, the lowest level of the gray brick stratum at Tell Brak. Not to scale. Source: Mallowan 1947:pl. 17–19.

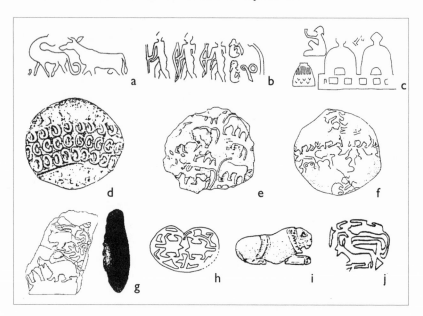

FIGURE 11.22

Drawings of seal impressions on administrative documents from the northern Euphrates, early Middle Uruk/LC 3 phase. (a–g) Hacınebi phase B2, from contexts with southern Uruk–type pottery. (h–j) Hacınebi phase B2, from contexts with only Late Chalcolithic pottery. Not to scale. Source: author.

434

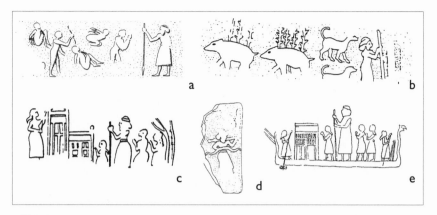

FIGURE 11.23

Drawings of cylinder seal imagery impressed on administrative documents from southern Mesopotamia, Uruk, Eanna precinct level IV. A prominent image in this phase is the male figure wearing a long skirt and a headband engaged in activities of combat, hunting, and procession toward a monumental structure. Late Uruk/LC 5 phase. Not to scale. Sources: a, *Brandes 1979:tafel 1, top;* b–d, *Amiet 1980:187–88, pl. 13bis (A), 665;* e, *Lenzen 1961:pl.26A.*

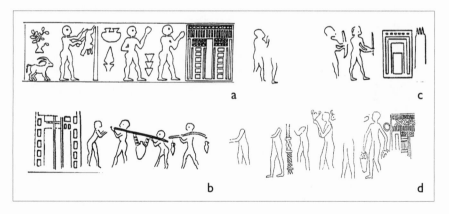

FIGURE 11.24

Drawing of cylinder seal imagery impressed on administrative documents from southern Mesopotamia, Uruk, Eanna precinct level IV. A prominent image in this phase is the procession of laden male figures toward an architectural structure. Late Uruk/LC 5 phase. Not to scale. Sources: a, *Brandes 1979:pl. 30;* b–d, *Amiet 1980:pl. 13bis (D), 203A, 1607.*

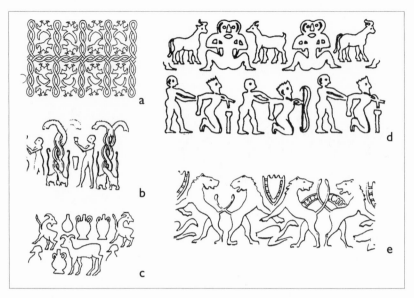

FIGURE 11.25

Drawing of cylinder seal imagery impressed on administrative documents from southern Mesopotamia, Uruk, Eanna precinct level IV. Prominent images in this phase include various subject matter arranged in repeating or heraldic composition. Late Uruk/LC 5 phase. Not to scale. Sources: a, c–d, Brandes 1979:pl. 29, 15, 13; b, Amiet 1980:pl. 13 bis; e, Amiet 1980:199.

similarities with material from the eastern Anatolian highland (fig. 11.22j).

Late Uruk Phase/LC 5

The relative chronology established through ceramic analysis equates the Uruk IV, Susa 17, Habuba Kabira, Jebel Aruda, Hassek Höyük, and Tell Brak TW 12.

LC 5 is the phase we associate with "classic" style Late Uruk glyptic art known through famous sculptural masterpieces. Retrieved in large numbers from the various phases of level IV in the Eanna precinct at Uruk-Warka, the glyptic art from that site is distinctive both stylistically and iconographically (figs. 11.23–11.25). In southern Mesopotamia seals of this style have been found not only at Uruk-Warka but also at Tell 'Uqair and Jemdet Nasr. The imagery sometimes depicts either cult activity or social conflict. In these scenes, the so-called priest/king is

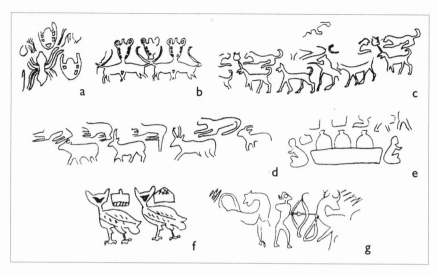

FIGURE 11.26

Drawings of cylinder seal imagery impressed on administrative documents from Khuzistan, Susa Acropole sounding level 17. Prominent imagery includes repeating elements, heraldic compositions, animal files, worker scenes, and hunt scenes. Late Uruk/LC 5 phase. Not to scale. Source: a–b, f–g, Le Brun 1971:fig. 44; c–e, Le Brun 1978:figs. 9, 10.

shown or implied. The defeated are shown bound and captive (figs. 11.23a, 11.25e). Other themes on Late Uruk (LC 5) seals from Uruk-Warka are human processions toward a structure (fig. 11.24) and animal files in one or several registers (fig. 11.25c) or arranged in heraldic scenes (fig. 11.25a–b, e). At the very end of this phase, the symbolic technology of writing appears for the first time. This technology was not transferred to other subregions engaged in the processes of state formation, with the important exception of Susa where a short-lived script (Proto-Elamite) recorded what might have been an Elamite language.

The Acropole sounding level 17 at Susa produced a small number of seals and administrative objects (fig. 11.26). Although we can see clear continuity from level 18, new features were introduced. Stylistically, the figures are more finely rendered, and they tend to be smaller. Compositions are denser with greater numbers of elements. In addition, they are more legible because there is less dovetailing of the individual design elements. The register principle is more common. A new theme

437

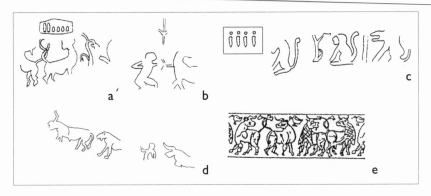

FIGURE 11.27

Drawings of cylinder seal imagery impressed on administrative documents and imagery of a cylinder seal. Western Zagros, Godin Tepe level V, Late Uruk/LC 5 phase. (a–d) Heraldic composition, animal files, and hunt scenes are found impressed on numerical tablets and jar stoppers. (e) The imagery of this seal belongs to the early Proto-Elamite phase in terms of both its iconography and its style of carving. Not to scale. Sources: a, d–e, Weiss and Young 1975:fig. 5; b–c, Amiet 1980:1675, 1676.

of an archer actively engaged in hunting game (fig. 11.26g) is shared along the Tigris piedmont, both at Godin Tepe level V and at Nineveh.

Design elements that strongly prefigure the Proto-Elamite style can be seen in the glyptic recovered from level 17 of the Acropole sounding at Susa (fig. 11.26f). While not of primary interest to us here, these new elements suggest that a new regional character was evolving in Khuzistan that was different from the previous traditions, which were closely shared across the entire alluvium in the Middle Uruk (LC 3–4) period. Among the unstratified materials from Susa that can be associated with level 17 on the basis of their seal impressions is a group of about twenty tablets that carry one or at the most two signs. These are the regional response to the invention of writing that was occurring in southern Mesopotamia and that was the basis for the subsequent development of the Proto-Elamite script.

Until now we have not seen the Middle Uruk seal style in the Zagros Mountains, where the Late Ubaid/Early Uruk seal tradition continued unaffected by developments to the west. However, at Godin Tepe we have a situation similar to that seen at Hacınebi. Southern administrative materials, this time closely comparable to those from

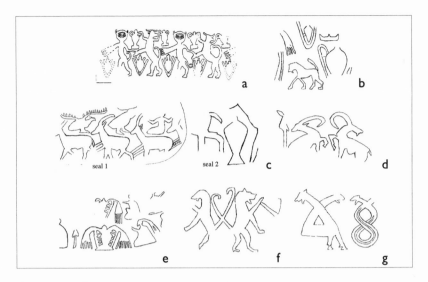

FIGURE 11.28

Drawings of cylinder seal imagery impressed on administrative documents from the Jezirah, Tell Brak TW level 12 pit. Found with southern-type ceramics. Repeating elements, heraldic composition, animal files, and twisted snakes appear in the imagery. Late Uruk/LC phase 5. Not to scale. Source: Oates and Oates 1997:fig. 14.

Susa 17, including strong precursors to the Proto-Elamite administrative tools, appear in Godin V (fig. 11.27a–e).

At Tell Brak, the Late Uruk phase is well documented in the most recent excavations in TW level 12. There are a large number of sealings (fig. 11.28) impressed with seals identical to ones from Susa and from Uruk-Warka. This commonality confirms the continued strong connection of Brak with the south (see fig. 11.25a–e).

When it was excavated in the 1960s, Habuba Kabira was the first site to give us clear evidence for people from the south living in the upper reaches of the Euphrates River basin. Shortly after the first results from Habuba Kabira were reported, this impression was confirmed by finds at Jebel Aruda. From more recent work at Sheikh Hassan and Tell Qraya, we now know that Habuba was late in the long period of southern presence at sites along the Euphrates. While Sheikh Hassan continued to be occupied, Habuba Kabira and the surrounding sites were established in the Late Uruk phase as a major southern presence. The administrative materials do not include writing. Rather the hollow clay balls, tags, and

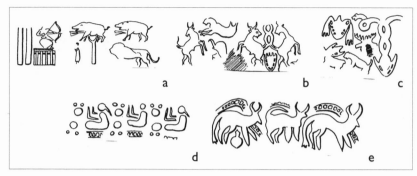

FIGURE 11.29

(a–d) *Drawings of cylinder seal imagery on administrative documents from Habuba Kabira.*
(e) *Drawing of cylinder seal imagery from Habuba Kabira. Not to scale. Source: Amiet 1980:*
1632, 1630, 1631, 1634, 1633.

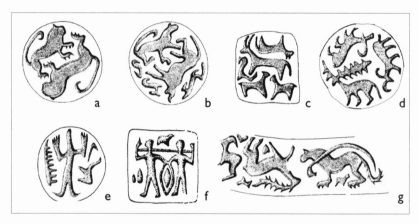

FIGURE 11.30

Drawings of stamp and cylinder seal imagery impressed on administrative documents from
eastern Anatolia, Arslantepe level 6. Not to scale. Source: Frangipane and Palmieri
1983a:figs. 68–71.

numerical tablets are identical to ones known from Susa level 18. The
glyptic style preserved on the administrative documents is identical to
that from Susa 17 and to Eanna IV (fig. 11.29a–d). In addition, a seal
from Habuba (fig. 11.29e) is cut locally in a style that emulates southern seal morphology (the cylinder) and iconography (a file of animals
with a ladder pattern) but clearly belongs within the Anatolian regional
style as we know it from Arslantepe (fig. 11.30).

Contrary to the many connections I have drawn between some sites in the north and Susa or Uruk-Warka, none of the incredibly abundant administrative materials from Arslantepe can be categorized as identical to ones from southern Mesopotamia or from Khuzistan (fig. 11.30). It seems that Arslantepe belongs entirely to another sphere, one that has knowledge of the developments toward state formation in the south but does not have any sustained, direct contact with those distant communities. At Arslantepe a small number of cylinder seal impressions is carved with subject matter that emulates the southern styles (fig. 11.30g). Scenes with human figures and with animal files are both preserved. Both the style of carving and the details of subject matter (the *tête bêche* composition of caprids, for example, and the use of gouging tools) can be identified as features of an Anatolian regional style. Among the numerous impressions of stamp seals, Arslantepe has a wide range of what might be called the "Anatolian regional style." Like the Jazira style, this style is made up exclusively of stamp seals. However, unlike those of the Jazira, which have densely packed image fields, the Anatolian style most often depicts single animals or pairs of animals composed to fill the image field. The style of carving seen on these seals, with the pointed digits and generally gouging carving, may also be typical of the type (fig. 11.30a–e).

CONCLUSION

A few overarching conclusions about intraregional relations during the era of state formation in southern Mesopotamia can be drawn from the glyptic evidence. It is clear that at the beginning of the process no one area was more highly advanced than another. Traditions of administrative tools were well established in all of the areas that are reviewed here. Further, the subregional traditions were never eradicated. During the Middle Uruk (LC 3–4) period, the traditions either continued to evolve internally, borrowed features in emulation of other subregional styles, or used administrative tools that for all intents and purposes belong to other traditions (the condition of "identity").

Although there is evidence for emulation of southern styles in the north at Tell Brak, Hacınebi, Habuba Kabira, and Arslantepe, there is no clearly identifiable emulation of northern regional style in the south. However, the rare examples of northern types of seals found in the south suggest that contact and influence was not unidirectional.

The radical changes in the administrative toolkit and the symbolic technology that occur in the south do not occur in the north except in contexts where there is clear evidence for the presence of southern influence. It is at this point that the south becomes more administratively and symbolically complex than the north. However, at sites of comparable size in the north (e.g., Tell Brak) there is a parallel development in the administrative and symbolic technology that is independent of changes in the south. This strongly suggests that the north has an independent tradition that, while perhaps not as complex, is integrated with the southern administrative system during the Middle Uruk (LC 3–4) phase.

Probably the most important contribution that the glyptic evidence makes to a more refined understanding of the era of state formation in Greater Mesopotamia is establishing the existence of nodes where both traditions were equally strong. This is what the materials now known from Brak suggest. Further excavations will soon clarify these relations. The existence of these nodes does raise an essential question. The residents of Hacınebi had clear physical interactions with a group of Southerners. Contemporaneous Tell Brak did as well. Why then is there virtually no evidence at Hacınebi for the interaction of the two traditions?

The time depth that can be traced through the glyptic suggests that the contact between north and south lasted for a long period of time. That contact was not isolated but needs to be considered as one of a series of long-distance relations that perhaps went up the Euphrates but even more consistently went up the Tigris corridor, across the Jazira, and into the Anatolian highlands. At each point along the various routes there were connections to other centers, both more distant and nearby.

Perhaps Tell Brak was a central node in intraregional relations from the beginning of the era of state formation. Like Susa, Brak had active relations with centers in the south from the very beginning of the era. Unlike Susa, however, Brak was at a crossroad joining three distinct regions—the south, the east, and the west. As Lupton (1996) points out, ceramic style zones of the Euphrates and the Tigris Basins overlap at Brak in the LC 2–4. At some point a bit later, equivalent to the late

Middle Uruk (LC 4) phase, groups working through Brak extended their reach, perhaps from Brak to the Euphrates, at sites like Hacınebi. At the same time southern presence was also established at such sites as Sheikh Hassan, but without the mediation of Brak. In the LC 5, the southern presence may have increased further, as evidenced by settlements at Habuba Kabira and Jebel Aruda. With such a substantial presence there, Hacınebi fell out of use, perhaps with the route from Tell Brak diminishing in importance for some reason (although Brak itself remained pivotal to the movement in the Jazira). The influence of the southern system was felt as deep into the Anatolian highland as Arslantepe. At the same time as the Euphrates route became primary over the Jazira route, a similar change in the patterns of interaction from Susa occurs. At the site of Godin, administrative materials derived from Susa appear. Further to the north, the southern-type materials from Nineveh suggest the same source.

Notes

1. A recent neutron activation analysis of 150 sealings from fourth millennium B.C. Arslantepe reveals that those sealings were not clay, but a soft stone conglomerate thus far found to have been used for this purpose only at Arslantepe.

2. Simpson reports that no seals or administrative materials were found at Qraya. However, in the Dier Ezor Museum three sealings and a hollow clay ball are clearly labeled as coming from Qraya (personal observation, April 2000).

3. The "shaman" in early Mesopotamian art is the subject of a paper that I presented at the American Oriental Society's annual meeting in Toronto on March 30, 2001.

12

A View of the Plains from the Mountains

Comments on Uruk by an Andeanist

Terence N. D'Altroy

Uruk Mesopotamia occupies a paradoxical position for archaeologists and historians who are interested in the emergence of early complex societies but work elsewhere. Because of the precocious sociopolitical and economic formations of Greater Mesopotamia and the ingenuity of the scholars who have worked to explain them, Uruk has stood as *the* model for the study of the rise of state society for several decades. It provides both the conceptual and organizational standards against which we most often compare the developments in the other regions where we work. That very reliance on Uruk research, and especially on the importance of urbanization and the administrative paraphernalia of the state, has often led us to formulate our explanations of state formation in opposition or conformity to Uruk, as if precedence conferred the status of a standard.

As Mesopotamian scholars are well aware, however, there is no necessity that the world's first state societies developed under conditions or along courses that were precisely analogous to those seen elsewhere and at a later time. One of the compelling questions that faces us therefore concerns the ways in which the features and trajectories of

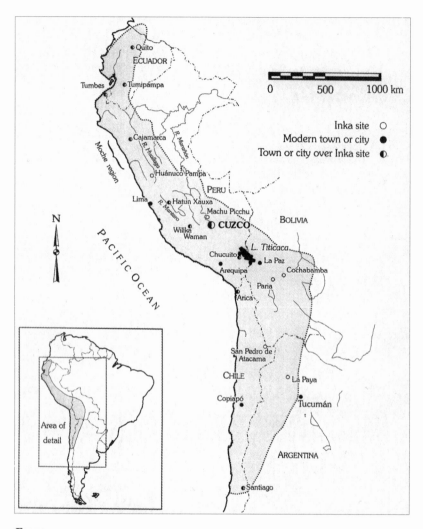

FIGURE 12.1

The Inka Empire, showing the principal road network and provincial centers (modified from Hyslop 1984:frontispiece).

Uruk are representative of early states, variations on a limited number of themes, or historically contingent. Thus, it is striking how infrequently the literature on Uruk seems to make explicit comparative reference to state development in other parts of the world. The exceptions, such as work by Adams (e.g., 1966), Wright (e.g., 1984), Knapp (1988), and Stone (e.g., 1997), and Algaze's chapter in this vol-

446

ume, stand out precisely for their uncommon character. A corollary issue centers on the ways that our images of the formation and nature of pristine states—not just Uruk—have been defined by the vagaries of archaeological preservation in Mesopotamia, and by the selection of research locations, especially for excavation.

Because of the long history of research and the exceptional intellects that have been applied to Mesopotamian archaeology, many aspects of Uruk have appeared to be relatively well defined to many of us looking in from outside, even granted the substantive debates among investigators. Yet clearly, this conference would not have been organized if the region's researchers were equally sanguine about the cultural sequences and processes involved. The fact that each participant was asked to discuss both the chronology and character of the archaeological complexes in his or her geographical area of interest underlines the serious concerns about the adequacy of the baseline data from which interpretations are drawn. Mitchell Rothman is to be congratulated for recognizing the opportunities that a comparative symposium could offer, for organizing the meeting, and for shepherding the resultant volume through to the end. I would also like to compliment the authors for their insightful contributions. Although there still are significant differences of interpretation among them, their free sharing of information serves the collective enterprise of advancing our knowledge in the best tradition of scholarly research.

In this chapter I comment on the advances made by the volume's contributors and make some observations on issues that appear, to an outsider, to be unresolved. In raising these issues, the discussion will bring in material from the Andes to provide some comparative perspective and help illustrate the issues at hand. I am especially interested in the inner workings of Uruk society and in the social transformations that occurred in the transition from the Ubaid, although perhaps these are issues that may currently be beyond the available evidence on the Early Uruk. Consequently, this chapter may not resolve any substantive disputes, but it is my hope that it will help focus research in useful ways.

Before examining more specific topics, I would like to make a few general points. One concerns what scholars elsewhere draw most frequently from research on Uruk. At a theoretical level, one cannot overemphasize the impact of arguments that have their roots in explanations of the history of Greater Mesopotamia. The logical starting point is Childe's (e.g., 1941) early and astute emphasis on explaining the emergence of civilization as a process in which social, political, economic, and environmental features were interdependent. Many of the themes that he emphasized—among them urbanism, class formation, the social control of labor, and technological inventiveness, especially in writing and the exact sciences—required both framing a big picture and paying attention to detail in a vision that still seems current, even if many of his specific arguments have been superseded. Similarly, it is difficult to overestimate the impact of Adams's and Nissen's work on the development of archaeology as a regional, ecological, historical, and social discipline (see also Redman 1978).[1]

Perhaps the most influential elements with roots in Mesopotamian research, however, have been the notion of a precocious theocratic state (see Foster 1981), the application of economic geography to settlement and exchange systems (see also Smith 1976), and the analysis of political complexity in terms of decision-making hierarchies (with acknowledgments to Flannery 1972). Regrettably, applications of those ideas have not always been as judicious as they might have been. New World archaeologists have long contributed independently to theories of state formation, of course, and in recent years have become more discriminating in the ways that they have approached these issues. Still, we do not have to look far in past Americanist publications to see priesthood as the default choice for the core power of all emergent states, hexagons draped over mountains and lakes, and site hierarchies translated directly into state administrations. We (including myself) have all too often taken the theoretical premises, the evidentiary basis for process, and the historical developments of Uruk as a linked package. One trend to the contrary arises in the comparisons among early states in Uruk, the Maya, and early China (see Feinman 1994:227; Nichols and Charlton 1997; Yoffee 1991:290), but those explicit comparisons still form only a minor element in the debates. Part of my discussion here, therefore, will be to suggest how some of the changing views on the natures and trajectories of some New World states may help us look at Uruk from a slightly different viewpoint.

A related point concerns the emphasis on explaining innovation or transformation at the expense of accounting for continuity or stability. It seems to me that an adequate explanation of the course of Uruk societies must take into account both that which was transformed and that which remained stable from Ubaid and other predecessor cultures. Here, I am thinking most particularly of activities and relationships that took place outside the purview of elite, state, and religious institutional control. It seems unlikely that all important aspects of life were radically reconstructed with the advent of the state, no matter how transformational it was; neither did the state control all aspects of life. How we recognize and explain elements that remained stable, not simply through tradition or inertia, ought to be part of a full discussion of the emergence of state society. A number of scholars have made that point for Uruk, of course (e.g., Nissen, this volume), but enduring features seem to be underplayed in the literature. That is surprising in a way, considering, for example, the remarkable persistence of the structure of socioeconomic relations presented in the Standard Professions List (Nissen 1986b).

That point leads to a final general concern: the common, almost overwhelming research interest in elite organization and activities at the expense of the daily life of the vast bulk of the population. Even though many of the most radical changes revolved around elite-driven activities, if one of our goals is to explain the nature of early states in their entirety, studies of the elite, the powerful, and the exotic, on the one hand, must be balanced with studies of the common, the quotidian, and the drab, on the other. Thankfully, that imbalance is being redressed by interest in household archaeology and by textual analyses of the more mundane aspects of life (e.g., in Wright, ed. 1981; Van De Mieroop 1993), but there is still a long way to go. Overall, a great deal of explanatory weight still seems to be accorded to what appears to be a limited set of exotic materials. Without discounting the importance of control of long-distance materials in the manipulation of political relations, I tend to cast my lot with those who place the greatest analytical emphasis on local relationships in searching for the processes leading to greater social complexity.

There are good reasons for those emphases, of course. One of them arises from the vagaries of preservation and the difficulties of finding an intact deposit associated with architecture. Another stems from the time-honored predilection among field investigators to excavate in the grand, elite, mortuary, and ceremonial contexts in the largest sites. In this regard, the enforced hiatus in fieldwork in the core part of Mesopotamia has had several positive repercussions, much like the situation in Peru in the 1980s, apart from the regrettable loss of opportunity to undertake new research in the rapidly diminishing and damaged material record. One benefit has been the opportunity to reanalyze recorded data in more detail than would otherwise be possible, and thus to catch up on publications that have been languishing in various states of completion. A second dividend has been the theoretical and methodological ingenuity that has been inspired by a need to squeeze more information out of an essentially static database in important regions. Johnson's (e.g., 1987a, 1988–89), Wright's (1987, 1995), and Algaze's (1989b, 1993a) writings stand as important cases in point, as do many chapters in this volume. Third is the increased emphasis on fieldwork in regions that border the heartland, exemplified by Frangipane, Rothman, Schwartz, and Stein especially in this conference. As a result, a much more nuanced macro-regional picture has been sketched out for the emergence of complex society than had existed a couple of decades ago. Regrettably, however, these theoretical and methodological advances exist in a climate in which the opportunity to test new ideas anytime soon remains a faint hope for much of the heartland.

CHRONOLOGY

The conferees' concern with sorting out the chronology of Uruk and its related cultures underscores the need to establish the sequence of events as an antecedent to explaining them. Wright and Rupley's invaluable synthesis of the radiocarbon dates along with the information provided by the other seminar participants bring two points to the fore. One is that the tools needed to establish the linkages among the various components of the Uruk phenomenon are only now becoming adequately refined. As the participants repeatedly noted, explanations of the Uruk expansion must establish the local sequences with a fair degree of specificity before any models can be rigorously tested with field data. It now seems secure that the transition from Ubaid and other regional cultures to Uruk was not simultaneous in all regions (Hole 1994; contributors herein), calling into question explanations that presume a unitary or integrated process. Moreover, Nissen's reiterated concern about the poorly reported contexts of Middle to Late Uruk ceramics from Warka has given all Uruk scholars pause to consider how reliable any settlement pattern sequence or grand-scale explanations based on ceramic affiliations may actually be.

The new temporal framework doubles the length of the Uruk era from a half to a full millennium. That remarkable change opens the door to a new appreciation of the dynamics of state formation. As all of the authors here stress, it also provides abundant room for spatial and temporal variations in the relations among southern alluvial societies and those of Greater Mesopotamia. Most particularly, the chronology now identifies two waves of Uruk expansion, each of a different character, and refines the links among occupations in different subregions. Archaeologists seldom need to be reminded of the importance of temporal control, but this reconception emphasizes the point dramatically.

The second point, accentuated by Frangipane, Rothman, Schwartz, and Stein, is that reliance upon Uruk artifacts and architecture as chronological markers sidesteps the problems of (a) how to investigate settlement dynamics across long periods of time, when the database draws heavily from surface collections, and (b) how to deal with potentially coeval occupations, whether sites or architectural sectors, that lack those markers. With respect to the former, Pollock's and Wright's chapters both represent efforts to apportion occupations to different phases and, by extension, to reconsider demographic processes in the heartland. Although there may be questions about some of the assumptions underlying the estimates, the authors argue effectively that the reduction in estimated population sizes for settlements and changes in regional site hierarchies point to new ways of thinking about demographic pressure on resources, urban scale, and urban-rural relations.

How best to use chronological markers is a nettlesome problem for those of us who work on the Inkas or any other expansionist state. Because it is difficult to recognize contemporaneous occupations in the absence of materials diagnostic of Inka culture, archaeologists tend to concentrate on the features that are related directly to the empire. That approach differs notably from that of documentary studies, in which the nature of local societies is an important independent subject for investigation. Studies of Uruk on the grand scale may exhibit an analogous problem: how to deal with coeval occupations that lack readily identifiable temporal markers. For explanations of colonial and peripheral relations, that issue must be addressed squarely, or the suspicion will linger that patterns look overwhelmingly Uruk-related because that is the predominant evidence admitted into consideration. Nissen's discussion of the transition from Ubaid to Uruk in Greater Mesopotamia frames the question well and provides some avenues for future research when the opportunity arises. Similarly, the chapters on the colonized subregions present information on complex pre-Uruk societies that have stimulated the participants to rethink the relationships between the south and the adjoining lands (see below on "Colonies and External Relationships").

THE NATURE OF POWER

One of the most striking features of the emergent city-states of Uruk was the development of highly centralized, powerful, decision-making hierarchies that were concerned with close control of labor and its product (e.g., Nissen 1988; Wright 1977b; Wright and Johnson 1975). The evidence adduced to support this position has been extensively described and will not be recapitulated at length here (see Algaze, Wright, Nissen, and Pittman, this volume). Among the most important features are settlement hierarchies that became increasingly well integrated in Late Uruk, the construction of monumental architecture, and the remarkable evidence for standardized record-keeping, tribute, storage, control over some aspects of craft production, and provisioning of rations. My reading of this perspective is that life in Late Uruk societies was run from the top down, in a way that does not seem to have been matched in any other pristine state with which I am familiar.

An alternative viewpoint of early Mesopotamian states emphasizes the multiplicity of interest groups and the existence of an ideology of nominally consensual leadership, at least in the Early Dynastic (Jacobsen 1970; Stone 1997; see also Small 1997). Using the models of the Yoruba and late medieval Islamic states, Stone (see also Gelb 1979) argues that the powers at the core of such societies were structured more along kinship than class lines. She suggests that power was kin-based and vertically oriented, characterized by factionalism, and unstable across generations. Maintaining power required high levels of generosity, much as has been argued elsewhere for complex chiefdoms (e.g., Wright 1984; Earle 1997) and for Eisenstadt, Abitbol, and Chazan's (1988) *congruent* states. In such a situation, the paramount leadership was restricted in scope and potency, largely because of its inability to monopolize the means of production. Some paramounts may therefore have played a more highly symbolic role than the central managerial position often attributed to them.

A central point of this second view is that multiple hierarchies of power were at work at the same time. This model recalls the paradigm of heterarchy put forward most forcefully by Crumley (1990). In essence, her position is that complex social systems exhibit multiple hierarchies of power, each of which is contextual. Some are only temporarily invoked to resolve particular problems. Heterarchical organization lends flexibility to the negotiation of power relations and "the individuals who interpret, explain, and integrate values...play a pivotal role in maintaining order" (Crumley 1990:5, cited in Small 1997:117). I am uncomfortable with the ways in which the model has sometimes been applied (see examples in Ehrenreich 1995), in that I find it hard to accept the idea that there was even a rough democracy of hierarchies in pristine states. Nonetheless, it does seem likely that individuals' and groups' roles were partially contextual and that there were multiple competing sources of power within the society.

Each position—the powerful state and the multiple interest group model—has much to commend itself, but I find reconciling them to be a challenge. As is Pollock (1992), I am uneasy with the degree of regulation that the first model concludes was practiced in (Late) Uruk. I wonder if, in the face of extensive evidence for institutional control, we assign it a power that was more contextual and restricted than it appears (see Adams 1966, 1981) precisely because of our analytical focus on the evidence for regulation. That is, control was high in some contexts, but restricted in scope. In a number of works that present detailed analyses, Wright and his colleagues (e.g., Wright ed. 1969, 1981) discuss evidence for apparently nonregulated activities at sites that also exhibit some evidence for regulation. What intrigues me is the balance between the two. Were certain limited domains of life regulated, or some aspects of almost every domain? My perception is that

Uruk scholars are aware of the analytical emphasis on control but consider the transformations toward complexity to be of greatest interest. This issue will come up again with respect to colonies and craft production (see below).

There is also a strong implication that, since production, movement, and consumption of certain classes of goods in key contexts were regulated, institutional control was the dominant means of maintaining social order and channeling social relations. However, I still do not have a good sense of how different forms of power worked on a day-by-day basis as the states were forming. There seems to be a working assumption that increases in the specificity of recording were paralleled by increases in regulation of the social order. That may well be true by Late Uruk, but it is also possible to envision part-time or contextual administrators in much the same way as we envision part-time artisans. Wright and Johnson (1975) have provided an ingenious and enormously influential model of administrative complexity through which to recognize emergent decision-making hierarchies in the transition to state society. That process surely signified major changes in the disposition of power and access to resources. But it is also true that understanding the hierarchy's structure does not necessarily inform us well about the proportional allocation of labor and resources to different elements of the society during the developmental stages (see below, "Labor Mobilization and Craft Production").

That point brings me to an intriguing feature of Uruk leadership—how was the membership of the leadership institutions formed? Most of the major theoretical arguments recently put forth concern the interaction among power groups and institutions. Despite repeated calls for integrated analyses by a number of the scholars noted above, it appears that the analysis of different institutions in early Mesopotamia is still largely focused on identifying separate spheres of organization, power, and resource use. Getting a grasp on those elements is certainly crucial to understanding the nature of the emergent state, but so too is understanding the contexts and nature of interaction. Did families or larger kin groups place members in multiple institutions? Did important individuals play roles in multiple institutions, changing hats as the circumstances dictated? How were they bound together? Were they competitive during the era of state formation? How were the local and regional elites tied into the regional system on a practical basis? Was it through marital ties, patron-client relationships, or extended kin groups, as have been variously proposed? How do the material correlates of such relationships differ from one another? Here, I find Adams's social characterizations most persuasive, but obtaining the archaeological evidence to test for different kinds of linkages remains a challenge. Nissen (1986b:329) aptly cautions us about the uncertainty of the status of important positions *(Lu.gal* and *En)* even in Late Uruk (LC 5) texts, illustrating the difficulties that face anyone addressing the problem.

The best comparative material that I can draw from the Andes takes us to the Moche states of Peru's north coast (A.D. 100–600). There is a long history to the view that a priesthood sustained by an elaborate elite ideology formed the power at the core of the Moche. New finds from the extraordinarily rich tombs at Sipán and San José de Moro, however, are providing clues as to how different sources of power were linked in Moche leadership (Alva and Donnan 1994; Castillo and Donnan 1994; Uceda and Mujica 1994). The individuals in several tombs (spanning over 300 years) were dressed as figures in a frequently repeated scene in Moche iconography, now called the Sacrifice Ceremony. In that scene, prisoners were sacrificed and their blood (maintained chemically in a liquid state) was presented by elaborately dressed priests to a paramount figure who was even more elegantly dressed, in one case in a full suit of gold plate, with assorted pectorals, necklaces, feathers, and the like. Those remains provide evidence for a widespread melding of ideological and social leadership in a set of elite individuals of both sexes, apparently linked to militarism and human sacrifice. At the same time, there is varied evidence (e.g., brickmakers' marks and segmentary construction) for large-scale mobilization of labor, as either corvée or sponsored groups, to build monumental architecture. The Temple of the Sun in the Moche Valley, Peru, is estimated to have required about 140,000,000 mud bricks—truly a state-level enterprise. Conversely, there is no direct accounting or architectural evidence for bureaucratic institutions or for segregation of political and religious leadership roles in the first Andean state societies comparable to that cited for Uruk.

My question is this: given the lamentable lack of mortuary remains for Uruk, is it still possible to recognize analogous intersections of different forms of power among early Mesopotamian elites? The epigraphic evidence associating kings with deities seems to provide some evidence to that effect (see chapters by Algaze and Pittman, this volume). Without drawing the parallels too exactingly, another possible avenue arises from the Greek city-state evidence analyzed by Humphreys (1978, cited in Small 1997), Morris (1997), and Small (1997). Humphreys identifies a variety of public contexts in which distinct kinds of social interactions took place: for example, "the council, the assembly, the law court, the military, the theater, the symposium, the gymnasium, and the funeral celebration" (Small 1997:113). The point is that overlapping sets of elites participated differentially in leadership roles in distinct contexts. I wonder if the institutional identities of public entities that were clearly differentiated by the third millennium—and are often cited as organizational referents for the pristine state—still intersected considerably in Uruk society.

An additional aspect of political interaction that has received attention in the Americas in recent years is factional competition among elites in emergent complex societies (Brumfiel and Fox 1994; see also Earle 1997). It seems plausible that in the climate that prevailed during the transition from Ubaid to Uruk, political restructuring entailed a mix of inducement and coercion in factional competition, in conjunction with the formation of more elaborate hierarchies (see Adams 1981; Wright 1977b). The long-standing recognition that even elite institutions were cast as households (Gelb 1979) underscores the key role of kinship ideology in the power structures of early Mesopotamia (G. Emberling, University of Michigan, personal communication 1999). A key issue may have been not simply the mobilization of labor for elite or institutional goals, but the attraction of adherents whose productivity could usefully be applied to multiple, potentially reinforcing, interests. As Price (1984; see also Wright 1984) observes, in societies in which labor is a key to power (rather than wealth, for example), the political economy is often structured around maintaining elites and retainers, and attracting new constituents. In such a situation, ceremonial hospitality and redistributional relations mediate group re-affiliations and provide the context within which political activities are carried out. How that kind of arrangement may have played out in Uruk's political life strikes me as an intriguing question.

From this perspective, the purpose of acquiring or producing and then distributing preciosities is not solely to display status or to reward associates, though those are certainly important goals (see Algaze 1993a, and this volume). Instead, the ceremonial hospitality can serve an overtly political purpose by announcing group labor capacities, thus allowing kin groups to assess the advantages of re-affiliation. The relationship between demographic and political restructuring, mediated by ceremonialism, is at least partially explicable in terms of intrapolity competition. Whether that competition is between powerful kin groups ("great families"), institutions (state vs. temple), city-states, or between kin groups and institutions is likely a historically contingent issue. Considering the remarkable degree to which populations were concentrated in southern urban centers in Late Uruk, and the fluctuating pattern of establishment and abandonment of rural settlements described by Pollock (this volume), I wonder exactly how political affiliations were constructed.

In order to address such problems archaeologically, a broad spectrum of contexts must be examined, of which I will touch on only one here. A key point is that the remains of comestibles and food processing, serving, and storage tools in elite households may be evidence of access to resources, but not necessarily of their consumption. Johnson (1989:374–5; see Wright, ed. 1981) points out that the distribution of faunal remains at Farukhabad suggests that elites were enjoying gazelle meat a millennium before the advent of the state, while the rest of the populace made do with other ungulates. It may be useful, however, to think of that situation more as evidence of unequal sociopolitical relationships than as an indication of the resources consumed directly by household members (see Hastorf 1990). Only through direct skeletal analyses might it be possible to ascertain with any surety when the elites (males?) consumed a diet that was superior to that of the populace as a whole. There is a marked difference between having the privileged obligation of hosting events and skimming the cream off the productivity of the society. The two are often interlinked in practice, but determining how the balance shifted toward extraction is one of the most important challenges in explaining the permanent investiture of elites. It would therefore be very interesting to be able to compare the household and institutional evidence for feasting activities (assuming such evidence is available) to see if and when household ceremonial activities were supplanted by institutionally sponsored events.

COLONIES AND EXTERNAL RELATIONSHIPS

The interaction between the peoples of the Uruk heartland and the rest of Greater Mesopotamia provides one of the most interesting dynamics of the fourth millennium. Algaze's (1989b, 1993a, this volume) publications in particular have placed colonization at the forefront of the debate over the nature of the Uruk period. Many scholars have expressed regard for the integrative nature of his work, which drew on Wallerstein's (1974) world systems model, while still expressing reservations about aspects of that argument. Wright (1995), for example, pointed out that it has the merit of linking disparate data sets within a coherent, testable model. Algaze also observes correctly that Wallerstein's view of preindustrial empires as fundamentally political in character and internally homogeneous are off the mark. To the contrary, some early empires were extractive economic systems underwritten by force (e.g., the Aztecs: see Hassig 1985, 1988; Smith 1996), and the overwhelming political characteristic of the early empires was their heterogeneity (Sinopoli 1994). Moreover, there seems little doubt that the ranges of economic and political control were seldom congruent in early empires, as Wallerstein's original discussion envisioned. Finally, Wallerstein's view that preciosities were of negligible importance in early states has also been amply refuted (e.g., Schneider 1977), although their significance may well have been overstated in some cases. For this volume, Algaze has modified his viewpoint to some degree and effectively integrated new information into his model. Two essentials of the argument remain the same, however. That is, the Uruk expansion was driven by economic concerns related to consumption by Uruk city-states, and the interaction was dominated by the city-states.

Despite the focus that Algaze brought to the issue, like several of the participants in this volume I have not been convinced that those arguments fully cover the complexities of the situation. Several chapters provide evidence for distinct kinds of relationships between the societies of northern Mesopotamia and the southern heartland. Most importantly, they have collectively identified two phases of relationships, one interactive and one more clearly colonial. Wright (with Johnson) and Nissen point out that the Uruk materials in the Susiana subregion exhibit a distinctly local style, indicative more of imitation than of colonization by people from the heartland. As Frangipane, Schwartz, and Stein observe for Syria and Turkey, substantial Chalcolithic settlements were already thriving when the southern enclaves first appeared. Arslantepe and Tell Brak, for example, were urban centers at the core of complex societies with long histories. These authors emphasize that the northern and western societies had established long-distance exchange relationships well before the advent of colonies from the south. Even for some areas in which Uruk stations or intrusive colonies were present (e.g., Hacınebi; see Stein, this volume), the evidence discussed does not seem to register a significant *imposed* impact of Uruk culture on the local societies. Instead, mutuality or emulation appears to explain the situation better. In these cases, the evidence often seems to point in the direction of continued local autonomy, not annexation or domination.

The clearest evidence for colonization lies in newly founded sites, such as Habuba Kabira, Jebel Aruda, and Sheikh Hassan in the Syrian Upper Euphrates. Their creation raises an interesting question: what is the relationship, with respect to the activities conducted, between the Uruk assemblages of the colonies and those of the heartland? Even if a full array of such Uruk artifacts as seals, sealings, and vessel forms is present, are goods of daily life and state rule present in proportions substantially similar to or different from those of the alluvium? The point is to assess if the colonies resulted from marginalized populations transplanted wholesale from the south (e.g., Johnson 1988–89) or if they were settlers disproportionately pursuing a limited array of state-related activities, as Algaze's model suggests. In this regard, Pollock's suggestion that the demographic and political dynamics of the Nippur-Adab subregion were substantially different from those in the far south, and that the colonization in Syria was potentially a northern effort, is very intriguing. If that assessment is correct (determination of which I leave to the regional scholars), then the model of colony-heartland relationships may have to be reconsidered even further.

If we return to the Andean material for comparison, there is ample evidence for community and state-sponsored colonies in prehistory.

Intriguingly, there are sites that indicate colonization both within and
outside territories politically dominated by a powerful state. The Wari
and Tiwanaku states of the Andean highlands established colonies on
the Pacific coast in what is now southern Peru and northern Chile during the latter half of the first millennium A.D. Tiwanaku also seems to
have colonized the Cochabamba region of the eastern Bolivian lowlands. They appear to have been seeking warm-weather crops, such as
maize and coca, and localized natural resources, such as guano and
minerals, in establishing their colonies.

Under Inka rule, both the state and local lords founded colonies
to produce goods or procure special resources. In fact, no Inka policy
affected the social landscape more than resettlement, as perhaps three
to five million people out of a total population of about twelve million
moved to new locales. Cobo (1979 [1653]: book 2, chap. 23, p. 189)
wrote that, in principle, the Inkas selected six or seven thousand families from each province (of 20,000–30,000) to be resettled as part of
their standard approach in new territories. Rowe (1982:107) has estimated that 10–80% of the population of individual provinces was resettled. The most renowned program moved entire communities
hundreds of kilometers to create enclaves of internal colonists called
mitmaqkuna. Espinoza Soriano (1970, 1973) has published numerous
early sources that detail how particular groups of people were used to
meet military, political, and economic ends. Among the economic
colonists were artisans, such as weavers, potters, and metalsmiths; farmers, especially for maize, coca, and peppers; and herders, masons, and
miners. Another motive for resettling colonies arose from the Inkas'
interests in claiming a divine mandate over the peoples of the Andes.
That vision was given its most conspicuous form in the ethnic micro-
cosm created around Cuzco, but the sanctuary that housed members of
42 ethnic groups at Copacabana, on Lake Titicaca, may have been
designed for the same purpose (see Julien 1993).

The Inka colonists were administratively subject to the state officials of their new provinces, but they were maintained on the census
rolls of their homelands. They were supported from state resources for
only a year or two, after which they had to fend for themselves. The
Inkas went to some lengths to make sure that the *mitmaqkuna* owed
their allegiance to the state. They had to wear their traditional clothing

and to speak their own languages, and their interaction with the local societies was restricted in some ways (see Rowe 1982). The colonists were resented since they were often given fine lands and other resources at the expense of the local communities. Even so, the *mit-maqkuna* occasionally forged working relationships with their neighbors to obtain a variety of goods that they might otherwise be unable to obtain.

One might think that such a vast resettlement program would have produced a melange of ceramic types, house forms, mortuary practices, and the like, as ethnic groups were intermixed. Surprisingly, however, *mitmaqkuna* communities are notoriously hard to find archaeologically. Inka state remains, in contrast, are unmistakable. In recent years, stylistic and chemical sourcing analyses of pottery have helped to identify resettled groups in various locations (e.g., D'Altroy and Williams 1998; Williams and Lorandi 1986), but the lack of a clear archaeological signature for colonists suggests that perishable textiles most clearly distinguished one group from another. Overall, if it were not for the hundreds of documents testifying to the program, we might well underestimate the scale of resettlement by a couple of orders of magnitude.

Without translating the Inka case directly onto the Mesopotamian situation, three aspects of Andean colonization seem pertinent here. One is that the colonies often served explicitly elite or state ends, but that the umbrella of state activity offered the broader populace chances to exploit more diverse and distant ecological zones than otherwise might have been available. The suggestion that entrepreneurial traders were involved in early Mesopotamian interactions may be broadly analogous (e.g., Adams 1974a). Second is that some, but not all, colonies may have been designed to meet the economic goals of the core state institutions. McCorriston's (1997) argument for an expansion into the Upper Euphrates to meet the southern demands for wool fits nicely into this scenario. The third is that the material signatures of Inka colonies are far more difficult to recognize than we might have expected. As various scholars have observed (e.g., Rothschild 1990; Deagan 2001; Stein, this volume), the degree to which colonists become fully assimilated or maintained a discrete identity is partially a historically continent issue.

As a result, I am a little uneasy about arguments that associate the first colonial relationships with components that contain the material markers of Uruk administrative culture. Traders may well have been present without leaving a clear set of cultural markers, so that the appearance of Uruk materials may indicate more a change in the terms of the interaction than the initial physical presence of Southerners. Conversely, the presence of some Uruk markers does not necessarily imply domination by southern states nor even the presence of colonies. Stein's complex Uruk assemblage at Hacınebi provides a convincing case for a state interest, as do the occupations at Habuba Kabira and Sheikh Hassan (see Schwartz, this volume). Nonetheless, the authors here have made the point clearly that the Uruk expansion(s) most likely encompassed a wide range of interactions, of which direct colonization was only one type.

RELIGION, CEREMONY, AND CORPORATE ARCHITECTURE

In reviewing the contributions to this volume and other recent literature on Uruk, I am struck by the marked differences in the ways in which hierarchically organized religion and ceremony are treated in Uruk and in the early states of the Americas. In the Andes and Mesoamerica, ideology is often treated as a vigorous, active aspect of early complex society—perhaps morbidly so, given the frequent evidence for human sacrifice, bloodletting, and use of hallucinogens. Economic activities are only of peripheral interest, if any, in current studies of institutionalized religion. In contrast, with the partial retreat of the theocratic model of early Mesopotamian societies, Uruk temples seem to be analyzed predominantly for their roles as economic enterprises. Recent treatments of the actual activities pursued in Uruk temples from an architectural and artifactual perspective (Forest 1999; Heinrich 1982) should be integrated into the analysis. Discussions of religion(s) seem to exemplify the ongoing split between archaeological and epigraphic approaches to the field (nicely paralleled by archaeological and historical disciplines in the Americas). With some exaggeration, archaeological approaches strike me as coming close to treating the early temple and its priesthood as a despotic Vatican treasury: that is, an economic enterprise in church's clothing enriching itself by using the labor of the populace on appropriated resources, while working nominally for the public good on earth and in the hereafter. Studies of seals and representational art, in contrast, seem to focus heavily on the identity of the imagery often retrodicted from better understood images made a millennium later. Some of those analyses are truly ingenious, but I am always concerned about interpretations that assume an unchanging correspondence between image and meaning over many centuries, especially in such a dynamic sociopolitical climate.

In keeping with my interests in the inner workings of society, I would very much like to know what people were actually *doing* inside restricted precincts and temples and if civic and religious ceremonies became increasingly exclusionary as well as majestic over time. Did the temple elites provide a forum for resolution of disputes? Were the ceremonies massed ensemble performances? processional? ecstatic? In Ubaid times, were they more broadly participatory? Surely, sacrifices and prayers formed a significant part of the activities, but many scholars have underscored that Mesopotamian religious institutions also concerned themselves with the manipulation of power. I assume that scholars are working on these questions and that I am simply unaware of their work. Noting that Pollock's (1992) recent review of the Uruk period was silent on the archaeological assessment of ideological leadership, particularly through architectural analysis, however, I will take the opportunity to follow the lead out a little further.

My image of Uruk institutional ceremonial activity is that it was spatially and socially exclusionary, directed toward enclosed areas and building interiors, and performance-oriented rather than participatory, at least with respect to the general populace. If that impression is close to being correct, then who exactly were the audiences for ritual performances—representatives of elite families and kin groups? What were the relationships between the participating and observing groups? How did the leadership propose to serve as intermediaries between the populace and the cosmological, natural, or ancestral forces? In what ways were they participatory events, with consensually recognized leaders? Were there competitive cult groups within cities, vying for the support of kin or political factions? By extension, how did the temple institutions attain such concentrated power, and what messages were they attempting to transmit to their audiences? Did priests who were integrated across cities stage religious ceremonies? Did the religious institutions play an independent organizational or mediating role among kin/political groups within society?

Mesopotamian scholars have often sought answers to such questions by drawing on later, written sources. Along with other scholars (e.g., Wright in Adams and Wright 1989:448), however, I am chary of retrodicting the cultural or organizational features of mid-third millennium societies back into Uruk. Carefully considered direct historical analysis can be rewarding, especially if independent corroborative evidence is sought (e.g., Marcus and Flannery 1992; Nissen, Damerow, and Englund 1993), but I feel some discomfiture with what seems to be a recurrent interpretive practice for societies in which crucial organizational shifts antedated the written evidence by centuries or more.

Moore's (1996) recent book on developmental trends in Andean monumental architecture provides some directions as to how we might approach such questions archaeologically. He suggests, for example, that analysis of sight lines, areas for potential aggregation, the acoustics, and the accessibility of visual detail for both participants and observers can provide means of ascertaining the nature of ceremonial activities. The layout of ceremonial or other public architecture should provide indications as to whether the activities were intended as performance for an audience (whether large or select) or as participatory events, or whether they were static or mobile. His work suggests that by understanding whether the audiences were collaborative or passive, how detailed a message they could see and assimilate, and how large a gathering was present (in absolute terms or as a proportion of the population), we may gain a more nuanced understanding of the changing relationships between the ideological institutions and the society at large.

To cite the evidence from the Andes for comparative purposes, the broad trends during the period when political complexity moved from a ranked to a state-level society seems to have passed from secretive, small-scale, enclosed ceremonies to group processions to large-scale performances in front of massed audiences. Those trends are paralleled by an increase in social differentiation recognizable through the mortuary record (a sad point, from the Uruk perspective). In addition, the evidence from the Moche state(s) cited above shows that particular priestly roles may have been codified and practiced in more than one state polity within the same culture region.

Moving back in time 2,000 years, we can cite some examples of Initial period monumental constructions in the Andes that are comparable to those of Uruk and yet are usually considered by Andean scholars to have substantially antedated state society. From the Late Preceramic (ca. 2500–1800 B.C.) through the Initial period (ca. 1800–800 B.C.), societies inhabiting the central and north coasts of Peru erected at least 45 monumental sites that shared essentially the same U-shaped layout. The open end lay upstream, toward the east, with pyramids at the base and long mounded arms that enclosed open plazas and, often, large, open pits. A number of the pyramids retain grand-scale art on their facades, executed sometimes in brilliantly colored clays and others in carved stone. An especially large construction lay at La Florida (ca. 2150–1750 B.C., uncalibrated), just south of Lima, Peru. Patterson (1991) estimates that the main pyramid has a volume of 1,010,500 cubic meters and that its construction would have required the labor of about 500 to 1,000 people for two centuries. Similarly, the site of San Jacinto, built around an open space of about 30 hectares, would have required the movement of about two million cubic meters of earth just to create the flat surface on which the architecture was arrayed (Williams 1991). In the Casma Valley alone, there are five to eight such grand complexes. The largest, at Sechín Alto, covers about 56 hectares, with four plazas and associated architecture all laid out according to an axial arrangement that extends 1.5 kilometers from the main mound (Burger 1992). The immense main pyramid was the largest construction in the Americas during the second millennium B.C.; covering an area of 250 by 300 meters at the base, it rose to a height of 44 meters. The facade of the main pyramid at nearby Cerro Sechín exhibits about 400 granite sculptures, arranged as a single scene, consisting of two sets of warriors advancing along lateral walls through the carnage of their adversaries, with banners displayed at the heads of columns (Burger 1992).

Despite the organizational and energetic requirements of erecting those monuments and the graphic evidence for the exertion of coercive force, there is prolonged and profound disagreement over the character of the iconography and the nature of the society responsible for the constructions. Burger (1992:78), for example, argues for a relatively simple organization in many locales. He suggests that the imagery is indicative of ritual warfare and small-scale raiding and that many of the monuments were actually built over centuries, by accretion of layers each a meter or so thick. Conversely, Moseley (1975) and the Pozorskis (1987, 1993), who have also worked on such sites over a long period, argue that the iconography is indicative of conquest and that the monumental constructions would have required potent leadership, perhaps even a state. They also observe that there are associated architectural complexes (e.g., at Pampa de Las Llamas-Moxeke) that were apparently storage facilities to which access was restricted (see also Wilson 1997:239–41).

Why there is such a disjuncture between many Andeanist and Mesopotamian interpretations of the relationship between *(a)* the scale and complexity of early monumental complexes and *(b)* the organization required to plan the constructions, recruit the labor, and maintain social cohesion merits some attention. Part of the difference may arise from a reticence on the part of many Andean scholars to give comparable weight to the organizational accomplishments of religiously based institutions and to those of more secular political institutions. That is, the managerial skills, corvée mobilization, and decision-making hierarchies needed to erect enormous monumental constructions are not considered to be of a significance equal to those required for other centrally driven tasks. Alternatively, we may be stuck in our own versions of early theocratic leadership, associating the monumental and the visual with the powerful, but not political.

The differences may also revolve around three features that are characteristically taken to imply state organization in Uruk, but are conspicuously missing in the Andes at the time of the early monumental constructions. They are hierarchical urban formations, administrative architecture, and evidence for the regulation of activities or movement of goods through accounting devices. The first urban settlements date to the last two or three centuries B.C., for example in the Gallinazo Group of the Virú Valley (Willey 1953). Previously, the population appears to have been largely dispersed throughout or adjacent to irrigated agricultural lands. Not until the Early Intermediate period (ca. A.D. 100–700) is there solid evidence for systematic accounting of labor input in the form of makers' marks on adobes, and not until the mid-first millennium A.D. do the first standardized administrative buildings and indisputable accounting devices appear (Middle Horizon *khipu*, or knotted strings). In essence, several of the features that appear to be organizationally linked in the early states of Greater Mesopotamia do not appear to have been comparably associated in Andean societies. Only with the advent of differentiated social classes comparable to those of the Early Dynastic, valley-wide and even multi-valley irrigation systems, and the urban society of the Early Intermediate, are scholars willing to agree that state society had emerged in the Andes.

These issues collectively point our attention to a consideration of the ideological foundations, religious institutions, and practices of Uruk and its immediate antecedents. Stein (1994b), working with a model of locally organized staple finance, has suggested that Ubaid temples in the larger settlements may have been mobilizing surplus grain production from outlying villages. He further suggests that they were organized as collaborative community enterprises—not independent institutions—directed by elite families whose positions arose from their ability to command labor through kin ties. That model is supported in part by the nature of temple and storage architecture and the distribution of agricultural tools, although some finer chronological resolution would help in assessing the amount of surplus potentially mobilized. Stein's argument has the additional asset of focusing on local relations as the key to the emergence of both elites and temple institutions. One question of interest here is the degree to which such centralized accumulations had supplanted household storage as a source of day-to-day supplies or as a buffer against interannual variations in productivity.

That question leads to a model of religious organization that does not seem much elaborated for Ubaid and Uruk (at least in what I have read): collaborative or competitive sponsorship. Uruk temple institutions apparently developed as well-integrated and unified bodies with the capacity to own resources and mobilize the labor to work them as well as to erect corporate architecture. For the Moche state, Shimada (1994, n.d.), conversely, has argued that the construction of monumental architecture is as readily explicable by elite or group sponsorship as it is by labor taxation. Makers' marks on bricks thus would have implied nominally voluntary contributions, not expropriation of labor. His example is that of Gothic cathedrals, for which individual elite sponsors sometimes put up their resources for the construction of particular elements, such as naves and sacristies. It would thus be interesting to know if there is any evidence in Uruk architecture for segmentary construction practices or for architectural signatures that might be labels of group contributions. By extension, I wonder if it would be possible to distinguish Uruk sealings that were related to collaborative ventures or contributions, rather than extractions.

This leads to a final point concerning the nature and legitimization of leadership. It is often observed these days (e.g., Demarest and Conrad 1992) that the presence of centralized ideologies does not imply that all members of society bought into the package or that there was a single, dominant, unified ideology. It would therefore be intriguing to explore the divergences between the representation and the actuality of relationships of power. Morrison and Lycett (1994), for example, have noted that local elites and paramount elites in Vijayanagara, India, exhibited their statuses in different contexts. They make the point that the representation of status may have been as much a claim to power as an expression of reality. I wonder, similarly, if it would be possible to recognize whether individuals or groups in Mesopotamian societies were attempting to assert legitimacy or status through manipulation of symbols of rank or power. That is, is it possible to disentangle the relationships between the depiction of status and the exercise of power? One way of addressing such issues might be by relating the contextual patterning of the symbols associated with the exercise of power (e.g., seals and sealings) to the patterning of architecture and artifacts. Rothman (1994b, this volume) has used the evidence for Tepe Gawra to make a very useful foray into this territory, albeit to a different end, and it would be intriguing to see this line of inquiry followed up elsewhere.

LABOR MOBILIZATION AND CRAFT PRODUCTION

One of the most fruitful lines of inquiry for scholars working on social complexity in the fourth millennium B.C. has been a consideration of the changes in forms of labor that accompanied state formation. Here, I would like to raise just a few points. The first concerns an issue that has been of interest to scholars working on early Mesopotamian states for some time. That is, how did multiple kinds of labor mobilization (e.g., family/household, extended kin group, elite retinues or retainers, the community, the state, and the religious institutions) operate at the same time? Each kind of labor organization implies a distinct scale, different obligations or inducements, perhaps distinct tasks, and partially overlapping schedules—probably drawing in large part from the same labor pool.

The increasingly creative discussions of the changing nature of labor and resource-holding institutions (esp. Zagarell 1986 and comments) take us beyond the standard divisions of temple, state, and kin, and private estate, public/communal, and kin. Even so, there is still a tendency to treat social groups or statuses as though they were internally homogeneous. It is a welcome development that the roles of men and women are starting to be treated with greater refinement, but there is much room for exploration here. As Stone (1986:425) observes, Zagarell's analytical model (mode of production) treats women as a unitary, exploited group, an approach that likely masks crucial differences that existed in women's varied statuses, roles, and perquisites of power. What often seems to be missing from the published discussion is a nuanced treatment of the archaeological evidence needed to test those divisions and their interaction with one another (see McCorriston 1997 and comments). Perhaps that is largely a product of the quotidian activities of the bulk of the population being a relatively recent research interest (although see publications by Wright and colleagues cited above), and of the difficulties of recovering the kinds of material remains to address such questions.

Cross-culturally, Netting, Kramer, Wilk, and G. Stone have considered ethnoarchaeologically how the differing labor demands of distinct institutional settings, phases of household cycles, and stages of agricultural intensification (e.g., frontier development, construction of irrigation systems, intensification of garden plots) could have affected household composition and labor scheduling. Stone (1996), for example, finds that among the Kofyar of Nigeria's Jos Plateau, households moving into virgin lands could consist of more than a dozen adult males, with few women or children present. In contrast, households in well-developed areas would exhibit more conventional age-sex profiles. Bernbeck's (1995) provocative analysis of Hassunan and Samarran household composition and labor investment is a step in a similar direction, as is McCorriston's (1997) argument for the transformation of labor organization with the shift from linen to woolen clothing during the Uruk period.

My question is whether it would be possible, with present evidence, to examine the architectural and artifactual materials throughout Uruk to determine if there were recognizable differences in household composition *(a)* across time, *(b)* from urban to rural contexts, or *(c)* from marginal to intensively cultivated locations at the local level. Such an approach might provide a more dynamic sense of the social variations present among the general populace. Similarly, it would be intriguing to follow out some of the artifactual evidence to see if the proposed shift toward woolen textiles is reflected in the tools of the trade in household contexts (McCorriston 1997). In comparison, Costin's (1993) analysis of spindle whorls and weaving tools in Xauxa peasant households demonstrates a doubling in the intensity of household weaving under Inka rule. She interprets that evidence, quite reasonably, to imply that the state appropriated the labor of women in the household to meet state ends, outside the specialized weaving enclaves that were also established.

With some reservations, arising from comparing a pristine state to a late empire, I would like to examine the Inka case for insights into how to reconcile documentary and archaeological sources on labor organization.[2] There were manifold differences between the Inkas and Mesopotamia, of course, among them scale of organization, duration, ethnic and cultural variety, and degree of urbanization, but there are also some intriguing parallels that invite comparison at a general level. One is that there were several intersecting institutions within the Inka state: the state, the state church, and the royal and aristocratic families, each of which was supported primarily by corvée and encumbered labor groups. Second is that the state cast itself in terms of traditional relationships based on local hierarchies and kin structures (Murra 1980). Third is that the recording system was largely dedicated to keeping track of activities in service of economics. Finally, there were hierarchically ranked lists of labor services, remarkably similar in principle to the Mesopotamian Standard Professions List (Nissen 1986b:328-9).

The Inka labor tax was levied on the heads of household, that is, married men who belonged to an age category that corresponded to about 25–50 years of age, or about 15–20% of the empire's population. Generally speaking, a householder's assignment required two or three months of work per annum, but the Inkas did not require that the laborer work for a specified period or even undertake the duty by himself. Instead, what mattered was that the duty was accomplished. As a result, whole families could take on the job, and the larger the family, the quicker the task was done. Thus, a man with a large family was thought to be well off. Over time, the Inkas modified the ways in which they extracted labor service from their subjects. In the later decades of their rule, they increasingly replaced rotating corvée workers with permanent specialists (Murra 1980). They created several specialized labor statuses, the most important of which were *(a)* forcibly resettled colonists installed to meet military and economic needs *(mitmaqkuna)*, *(b)* individuals detached from their kin group and assigned permanent duties *(yanakuna)*, and *(c)* young women *(aqllakuna)* assigned to live in segregated precincts within state installations, where they wove cloth and brewed beer.

Some early sources wrote that there were standard categories of duties, which were reported in an order that reflected cultural importance rather than the numbers of personnel involved. The chroniclers Falcón (1946 [1567]:137–40), Murúa (1986 [ca. 1605]: book 2, chap. 21, pp. 402–4), and Guaman Poma (1980 [1614]: / 191[193], p. 183) itemized lists of labor service due the state. Falcón specified 32 categories for coastal societies and 37 for highland populations, not counting the two kinds of taxes that likely demanded the greatest input: general agricultural labor and military service (see D'Altroy 1994b). Both Murúa's and Falcón's lists, which correspond well, regularly distinguished between artisans who produced fine quality objects and those who made more ordinary goods. From our present perspective, it is hard to be sure that the order precisely reflected Andean categories of importance, since the lists do not conform exactly to the local labor assessments that are available (see below). It is also important to emphasize that those lists did not cover the full range of social ranks or labor services within Inka society, as the highest social ranks were not recorded. There was some flexibility in the way policies were enacted locally, even if administrators were supposed to assign duties equitably (Julien 1988). Moore (1958) has pointed out that the administrators could use their discretion in assigning service as leverage in local relations. And in some cases, the assignment of duties was left up to the local lords (Santillán 1927 [1563]:44; Polo 1916 [1571]:102). In such a system, notions of equal service could be construed many ways in practice, so that political favor and kin ties carried a great deal of weight in the assignment of tasks.

Although each household was supposed to render labor duty, many were exempt from the standard corvée service. Officials with responsibilities over 100 or more households seem to have been excused from labor service entirely. Certain ethnic groups were favored for particular duties because they were thought to have special talents, while others were thought to be virtually useless for state purposes but were put to work anyway.[3] Other groups were required to render natural products, such as spears and gold dust. In one of the more eccentric duties, one scorned people had to turn in a basket of live lice three times a year, just so they would learn the obligation of service (Cieza 1967 [1553]: chap. 18, p. 56).

Our best evidence on how labor was assigned locally comes from Spanish inspections, called *visitas,* recorded in the first few decades of the colonial era (Helmer 1955–56 [1549]; Ortiz de Zúñiga 1967 [1562], 1972 [1562]; Diez de San Miguel 1964 [1567]). The 1549 Huánuco inspection provides specific figures for the application of labor taxes to 4,108 Chupaychu and Yacha households. Julien's (1982, 1988) and LeVine's (1987) analyses show that levies were tailored to microenvironmental variations. The lists provide a breakdown of the households dedicated to cultivating state fields; to building or maintaining the roads, bridges, and state installations; to artisanry; to extracting natural materials; and to providing other services. Many individuals in the last group were either military guards or security personnel for elite individuals. In interpreting the numbers, we need to keep in mind that some duties, like farming, lasted only a couple of months a year, whereas others, such as construction at Cuzco, required continuous duty (Julien 1993). The laborers can be summarized as follows: 11.0% (440–460) to extract natural materials, 13.6% (560) to make material goods, 24.3% (1,000) to farm state lands, 9.7% (400) to work on the physical infrastructure, and 41.3% (1,698) to provide services that did not yield an obvious material product (e.g., portage, household service, guard duty).

From the perspective of reconciling documentary and archaeological data, the Huánuco figures are sobering. Only one of every nine individuals performed work that yielded constructions and pottery, the two principal kinds of remains that archaeologists use to study the Inkas. There were ten times as many weavers as potters, a ratio that is seen elsewhere in the empire (Spurling 1992) but would be hard to pick up from the material record. More than 40% of the workers rendered personal and guard services that would not be likely to yield much in the way of archaeological remains. In addition, all 400 construction workers were sent to Cuzco, the imperial capital. None worked on local installations, even though they served the most elaborate provincial center in the empire, Huánuco Pampa.

The disparities between the lists of labor duties and the material record remind us that the most visible archaeological remains are only indirectly related to the activities that people were performing on a regular basis. Conversely, hierarchical lists of labor obligations provide great insight into organization and cultural values but do not always inform us directly about the proportional allocation of resources. It is also worth emphasizing that the majority of the labors of the subject populace and the bulk of the material record of the Inka era were *not* the products of state activities. Instead they arose from the daily life of the great majority of the populace, the peasantry. My purpose in directing attention to these aspects of the Inka economy is not to draw a close parallel between the Inka and Uruk cases. Instead, it is primarily to highlight the point that a closer consideration of the proportions of labor dedicated to the central institutions and to other social formations in Uruk society might provide some insights into the nature and depth of state organization.

CONCLUDING COMMENT

In concluding this chapter, I would like to reiterate my regard for the scholars, both the authors in this volume and their intellectual ancestors, who have worked so effectively to explain the rise and nature of the world's first state societies. It is not just the chronological precedence of Uruk that has stimulated those of us who work elsewhere to turn to Mesopotamia for insight into early civilizations, but the theoretical arguments and methodological ingenuity that have been put into action. The chapters here will move discussion forward on several fronts. For regional scholars, the chronological refinements will change the perception of the duration of the Uruk era at the same time that they provide a framework for explaining interactions on the grand scale. The comparative evidence for the timing and nature of southern Uruk society's relations with those of Greater Mesopotamia should also improve our understanding of the balance of complexity and power in the region, which had previously been within the grasp of only one or two conference participants. What is especially interesting to me is the range of forms that those interactions have been shown to encompass. As a result of this conference, explanations of the Uruk expansion are now better grounded, deeper, and subtler than before. From a comparative standpoint, the chapters in this book help to focus attention on the variegated sociopolitical context within which the first states arose. It has been pointed out before that pristine states developed in complex circumstances, not cultural vacuums. This volume has described those conditions in Greater Mesopotamia and, in the process, should help to provide richer comparative models, even if the participants did not achieve unanimity concerning the processes involved.

- This chapter was not intended to resolve problems concerning Uruk, but rather to float some ideas that might be of interest in exploring life in the era further. My inclination has been to address some of the main themes to which the conferees have applied themselves and to raise issues about Uruk Mesopotamia that have piqued my interest over the years. I realize that some of these interests may be tangential to what can be addressed, given the nature of the present data, but such an exchange may prove to be useful down the line. In closing, I can only express the hope that the ideas that have been presented throughout the volume will have the chance to be put to the test in the near future.

Notes

I would like to express my appreciation to Mitchell Rothman for granting me the privilege of participating in this conference as the appointed outsider. Those of us who study complex societies in the Andes rarely get the opportunity to comment comparatively on the emergence of social complexity in Mesopotamia, but I think that the effort is well worthwhile, especially since scholars historically have often drawn on Mesoamerican societies for comparisons between Old and New World societies (e.g., Adams 1966; Feinman 1994). To provide some perspective on my comments, I should note that I am an archaeological anthropologist and that Adams, Wright, and Johnson have been influential in forming my views of the emergence and transformation of complex societies. In fact, Wright taught the first archaeology course I ever took. My point of view is predominantly archaeological, even though my own research draws equally from documentary and archaeological sources. In addition, because I have read only a little of the Assyriological literature and do not have a command of German, readers with an intimate knowledge of the region may find that I am raising concerns that have already been addressed elsewhere. For those deficiencies, I apologize and ask indulgence. I would also like to thank Mitchell Rothman, Gil Stein, David Small, and Geoffrey Emberling for reading drafts of this chapter and saving me from some egregious gaffes. Any errors and needlessly complex language that remain are my responsibility.

1. Paralleled by the work of Willey, Sanders, Flannery, and their colleagues in the Americas.

2. This section summarizes material that I have presented elsewhere (D'Altroy 1994a, 1994b, 2001). I repeat the information here because scholars interested in Uruk may not readily come across publications on the Inkas.

3. The Rucanas were employed as litter bearers, the Qolla as masons, the Chumbivilcas as dancers, and the Chachapoyas, Kañares, Chuyes, and Charkas as warriors (Rowe 1946; Espinoza 1980).

References

Abu al-Soof, B.

1968   Distribution of Uruk, Jamdat Nasr and Ninevite V Pottery as Revealed by Field Survey in Iraq. *Iraq* 30:74–86.

1985   *Uruk Pottery.* Baghdad: State Organization of Antiquities and Heritage.

Adams, R. McC.

1962   Agriculture and Urban Life in Early Southwestern Iran. *Science* 136:109–22.

1965   *Land behind Baghdad.* Chicago: University of Chicago Press.

1966   *The Evolution of Urban Society.* Chicago: Aldine.

1974a   Anthropological Perspectives on Ancient Trade. *Current Anthropology* 15:239–58.

1974b   The Mesopotamian Social Landscape: A View from the Frontier. In *Reconstructing Complex Societies,* edited by C. Moore, pp. 1–12. Boston: Supplement to the Bulletin of the American Schools of Oriental Research 20.

1978   Strategies of Maximization, Stability, and Resilience in Mesopotamian Society, Settlement, and Agriculture. *Proceedings of the American Philosophical Society* 122:329–35.

1981   *The Heartland of Cities.* Chicago: University of Chicago Press.

1992   Ideologies: Unity and Diversity. In *Ideology and Pre-Columbian Civilizations,* edited by A. A. Demarest and G. W. Conrad, pp. 205–22. Santa Fe: SAR Press.

1996   *Paths of Fire: An Anthropologist's Inquiry into Western Technology.* Princeton: Princeton University Press.

Adams, R. McC., and H. L. Nissen

1972   *The Uruk Countryside.* Chicago: University of Chicago Press.

Adams, R. McC., and H. T. Wright

1989   Concluding Remarks. In *Upon This Foundation: Ubaid Reconsidered,* edited
         by E. F. Henrickson and I. Thuesen, pp. 441–56. University of
         Copenhagen Museum. Copenhagen: Tusculanum Press.

Adams, W.

1984   The First Colonial Empire: Egypt in Nubia, 3200–1200 B.C. *Comparative
         Studies in Society and History* 26:36–71.

Aitchison, T., B. Ottaway, and A. S. Al-Ruzaiza

1991   Summarizing a Group of 14C Dates on the Historical Time Scale, with a
         Worked Example from the Late Neolithic of Bavaria. *Antiquity* 65:108–16.

Akkermans, P. M. M. G.

1988   The Period V Pottery. In *Hammam et-Turkman I,* edited by M. van Loon,
         pp. 287–350. Leiden: Nederlands Historisch-Archeologisch Instituut te
         Istanbul.

1993   *Villages in the Steppe.* Ann Arbor, Michigan: International Monographs in
         Prehistory.

Akkermans, P. M. M. G., and K. Duistermaat

1996   Of Storage and Nomads: The Sealings from Late Neolithic Sabi Abyad,
         Syria. *Paléorient* 22(2):17–32.

Alden, J.

1982   Trade and Politics in Proto-Elamite Iran. *Current Anthropology* 23:613–28.

**Alessio, M., L. Allergri, C. Azzi, F. Bella, G. Calderoni, C. Cortesi, S. Improta,
and V. Petrone**

1983   C14 dating of Arslantepe. In Perspectives on Protourbanization in Eastern
[1988]   Anatolia: Arslantepe, Malatya. *Origini* 12:575–80.

**Alessio, M., F. Bella, S. Improta, G. Belluomini, G. Calderoni, C. Cortesi,
and B. G. Turi**

1976   University of Rome Carbon-14 Dates XIV. *Radiocarbon* 18:321–49.

Algaze, G.

1986a   *Mesopotamian Expansion and Its Consequences: Informal Empire in the Late
         Fourth Millennium B.C.* Doctoral dissertation, University of Chicago.

1986b   Habuba on the Tigris: Archaic Nineveh Reconsidered. *Journal of Near East
         Studies* 45(2):125–37.

1986c   *Kurban Höyük and the Late Chalcolithic Period in the Northwest Mesopotamian
         Periphery. In Ğamdat Naşr: Period or Regional Style?* edited by U. Finkbeiner
         and W. Röllig, pp. 274–315. Beihefte zum Tübinger Atlas des Vorderen
         Orients, Reihe B, Nr. 62. Wiesbaden: Ludwig Reichert.

1989a   A New Frontier: First Results of the Tigris-Euphrates Archaeological
         Reconnaissance Project, 1989. *Journal of Near Eastern Studies* 48(4):241–81.

1989b   The Uruk Expansion: Cross-cultural Exchange in the Early Mesopotamian Civilization. *Current Anthropology* 30:571–608.

1993a   *The Uruk World System.* Chicago: University of Chicago Press.

1993b   Expansionary Dynamics of Some Early Pristine States. *American Anthropologist* 95:304–33.

1995   Fourth Millennium Trade in Greater Mesopotamia and the Question of Wine. In *The Origins and Ancient History of Wine,* edited by S. Fleming, P. McGovern, and S. Katz, pp. 89–96. New York: Gordon and Breach.

2001   Initial Social Complexity in Southwestern Asia: The Mesopotamian Advantage. *Current Anthropology* 42:199–233.

Algaze, G., R. Breuninger, and J. Knudstad
1994   The Tigris-Euphrates Archaeological Reconnaissance Project: Final Report of the Birecik and Carchemish Dam Survey Areas. *Anatolica* 20:1–96.

Algaze, G., R. Breuninger, C. Lightfoot, and M. Rosenberg
1991   The Tigris-Euphrates Archaeological Reconnaissance Project: A Preliminary Report of the 1989–1990 Seasons. *Anatolica* 17:175–240.

Algaze, G., M. E. Evans, M. L. Ingraham, L. Marjoe, and K. A. Yenu
1990   *Town and Country in Southeastern Anatolia,* vol. 2: The Stratigraphic Sequence at Kurban Höyük. Oriental Institute Publications 110. Chicago.

Algaze, G., A. Mısır, and T. Wilkinson
1992   Sanlıurfa Museum/University of California Excavations at Titris Höyük, 1991: A Preliminary Report. *Anatolica* 17:33–60.

al-Moslimany, A. Paxton
1994   Evidence of Early Holocene Summer Precipitation in the Continental Middle East. In *Late Quaternary Chronology and Paleoclimates of the Eastern Mediterranean,* edited by Ofer Bar-Yosef and R. S. Kra, pp. 121–30. Tucson: Radiocarbon.

Alva, W., and C. B. Donnan
1994   *Royal Tombs of Sipán,* second ed. Fowler Museum of Cultural History, University of California at Los Angeles.

Amiet, P.
1972   *La glyptique susienne.* Mémoires de la Délégation Archéologique en Iran 43. Paris: Paul Geuthner.

1980   *La glyptique Mésopotamienne archaïque.* Paris: Centre National de la Récherche Scientifique.

1985   La periode IV de Tepe Sialk reconsiderée. In *De l'Indus aux Balkans: Recueil à la mémoire de Jean Deshayes,* edited by J.-L. Huot, M. Yon, and Y. Calvet, pp. 293–312. Paris: Éditions Récherche sur les Civilisations.

Amiet, P., and M. Tosi
1978   Phase 10 at Shahr-i Sokhta Excavations in Square XDV and the Late Fourth Millennium Assemblage at Sistan. *East and West* 28:9–21.

Anderson, P.

1983 L'utilisation de certains objets en céramique de Tell el-'Oueili (Obeid 4): Rapport préliminaire sur les microtraces. In *Larsa et 'Oueili: Rapport préliminaire,* edited by Jean-Louis Huot, pp. 177–91. Paris: Éditions Récherche sur les Civilisations.

Anderson-Gerfaud, P., and F. Formenti

1996 Fonctionnement de "faucilles" en céramique de Tell el Oueili: Rapport sur de nouvelles expériences et tentatives d'analyse de traces d'utilisation. In *Oueili: Travaux 1987 et 1989,* edited by Jean-Louis Huot, pp. 373–79. Paris: Éditions Récherche sur les Civilisations.

Andrae, W.

1922 *Die Archaischen Ischtar-Tempel in Assur.* Wissenschaftliche Veröfeentlichung der Deutschen Orient-Gesellschaft 39. Leipzig: J.C. Hinrichs.

Bachmann, F.

1998 Ein "Habuba Kabira Süd Horizont" am Tell Sheikh Hassan? *Mitteilungen der Deutschen Orient Gesellschaft zu Berlin* 130:51–67.

Badler, V.

1998 Gender and the Archaeology of the Ancient Near East. Paper presented at the XLV Rencontre Assyriologique Internationale, July 7, Boston.

Badler, V. R., P. E. McGovern, and D. L. Glusker

1996 Chemical Evidence for a Wine Residue from Warka (Uruk) inside a Late Uruk Period Spouted Jar. *Baghdader Mitteilungen* 27:39–43.

Baines, J., and N. Yoffee

1998 Order, Legitimacy, and Wealth in Ancient Egypt and Mesopotamia. In *Archaic States,* edited by Gary Feinman and Joyce Marcus, pp. 199–260. Santa Fe: School of American Research Press.

Bairoch, P.

1988 *Cities and Economic Development.* Chicago: University of Chicago Press.

Bakker, J. A., J. Kruk, A. E. Lanting, and S. Milisauskas

1999 The Earliest Evidence of Wheeled Vehicles in Europe and the Near East. *Antiquity* 73:778–90.

Ball, W.

1997 Tell Shelgiyya: An Early Uruk Sprig Ware Manufacturing and Exporting Centre on the Tigris. *Al Rafidan* 18:93–101.

Ball, W., D. Tucker, and T. J. Wilkinson

1989 The Tell al-Hawa Project: Archaeological Investigations in the North Jazira, 1987–88. *Iraq* 51:1–66.

Bartel, B.

1989 Acculturation and Ethnicity in Roman Moesia Superior. In *Centre and Periphery,* edited by T. Champion, pp. 173–85. London: Unwin Hyman.

Becker, A.

1993   *Uruk, Kleinfunde I: Stein*. Mainz: von Zabern.

Behm-Blancke, M.

1986   Die Ausgrabungen auf dem Hassek Höyük im Jahre 1985. *Kazı Sonuçları Toplantısı* 8:139–48. Ankara: Eski Eserler ve Müzeler Genel Müdürlügü.

1989   Mosaikstifte aus der Uruk-Zeit am Oberen Euphrat. *Istanbuler Mitteilungen* 39:73–83.

1992a   *Hassek Höyük: Naturwissenschaftliche Untersuchungen und Lithische Industrie.* Tübingen: Ernst Wasmuth.

1992b   Hassek Höyük: Eine Uruk Station im Grenzland zu Anatolien. *Nürnberger Blätter zur Archäologie* 8:82–94.

Behm-Blancke, M. R., H. Becker, J. Boessneck, A. Von Den Driesch, M. R. Hoh, and G. Wiegand

1981   Hassek Höyük: Vorläufiger Bericht über die Ausgrabungen in den Jahren 1978–80. *Istanbuler Mitteilungen* 31:11–94.

Behm-Blancke, M. R., M. R. Hoh, N. Karg, L. Masch, F. Parsche, K. L. Weiner, A. von Wickede, and G. Wiedermeyer

1984   Hassek Höyük: Vorl. Bericht über die Grabungen in den Jahren 1981–83. *Istanbuler Mitteilungen* 34:31–150.

Benco, N. L.

1992   Manufacture and Use of Clay Sickles from the Uruk Mound, Abu Salabikh, Iraq. *Paléorient* 18(1):119–33.

Bernbeck, R.

1993   *Steppe als Kulturlandschaft*. Berlin: Dietrich Reimer.

1995   Lasting Alliances and Emerging Competition; Economic Developments in Early Mesopotamia. *Journal of Anthropological Archaeology* 14:1–25.

1997–98   Rezension zu Tony Wilkinson and David Tucker. Settlement Development in the North Jazira, Iraq. *Archiv für Orientforschung* 44–45:457–67.

1999a   An Empire and Its Sherds. In *Iron Age Pottery in Northern Mesopotamia, Northern Syria and Southeastern Anatolia,* edited by Arnulf Hausleiter and Andrzej Reiche, pp. 151–72. Münster: Ugarit-Verlag.

1999b   Landflucht und Ethnizität im Alten Mesopotamien. In *Fluchtpunkt Uruk: Archäogolische Einheit aus Methodischer Vielfalt,* edited by Hartmut Kühne, Reinhard Bernbeck, and Karin Bartl, pp. 296–310. Rahden/Westf.: Marie Leidorf.

Beyer, D.

1991–92   Le campagne 1991 de Tell Ramadi (Syrie). *Orient-Express* 1991–92:16.

1998a   Évolution de l'éspace bâti sur un site de la vallée du Khabur au IVᵉ millénaire: les fouilles françaises de Mashnaqa. In *Éspace naturel: éspace habité en Syrie du Nord (10ᵉ–2ᵉ millénaires av. J-C.),* edited by M. Fortin and O. Aurenche Lyon, pp. 139–48. Maison de l'Orient. Bulletin of the Canadian Society for Mesopotamian Studies 33.

1998b   Mashnaqa 1997: travaux de la mission archéologique française. *Orient-Express* 1998(1):8–11.

Bigelow, L.

1998   Faunal Perspectives on Socio-Economic Organization and Ethnicity at Hacınebi. Paper presented at the Annual Meeting of the Society for American Archaeology, Seattle.

1999   Zooarchaeological Investigations of Economic Organization and Ethnicity at Late Chalcolithic Hacınebi: A Preliminary Report. *Paléorient* 25:83–9.

Bittel, K.

1939–41   Bemerkungen über einige in Kleinasien gefundene Siegel. *Archiv für Orientforschung* 13:299–307.

Blackman, M. J.

1999   Chemical Characterization of Local Anatolian and Uruk Sealings from Hacınebi. *Paléorient* 25(1):51–56.

Blanton, R.

1976   Anthropological Studies of Cities. *Annual Review of Anthropology* 5:249–64.

Blanton, R., G. Feinman, S. Kowalewski, and P. Peregrine

1996   A Dual-Processual Theory for the Evolution of Mesoamerican Civilization. *Current Anthropology* 37:1–14.

Blanton, R., and P. Peregrine

1997   Main Assumptions and Variables for Economic Analysis beyond the Local System. In *Economic Analysis beyond the Local System*, edited by R. Blanton, P. Peregrine, D. Winslow, and T. Hall, pp. 3–11. SEA Monograph 13. Lanham: University Press of America.

Boardman, J.

1980   *The Greeks Overseas: Their Early Colonies and Trade*. New York: Thames and Hudson.

Boehmer, R. M.

1974   Das Rollsiegel im prädynastischen Ägypten. *Archäologischer Anzeiger* 1974:495–514.

1991   Uruk 1980–90—A Progress Report. *Antiquity* 65:465–78.

1999   *Uruk Früheste Siegelabrollungen*. Mainz: von Zabern.

Boehmer, R. M., G. Dreyer, and B. Kromer

1993   Einige frühzeitliche 14C-Datierungen aus Abydos und Uruk. *Mitteilungen des Deutsches Archäologische Instituts Abteilung Kairo* 49:63–68.

Boese, J.

1986–87   Excavations at Tell Sheikh Hassan: Preliminary Report on the Year 1987 Campaign in the Euphrates Valley. *Annales Archéologiques Arabes Syriennes* 36–37:67–100.

1995   *Ausgrabungen in Tell Sheikh Hassan I*. Vorläufige Berichte über die Ausgrabungskampagnen 1984–90 und 1992–94. Saarbrücken: Saarbrücker Druckerei und Verlag.

1995–96 Tell Sheikh Hassan in Nordsyrien. Eine Stadt des 4 Jahrtausends v. Chr. am Euphrat. *Nürnberger Blätter zur Archäologie* 12:157–72.

Boserup, E.
1965 *The Conditions of Agricultural Growth.* Chicago: Aldine.

Bottéro, J.
1967 The First Semitic Empires. In *The Near East: The Early Civilizations,* edited by J. Bottéro, E. Cassin, and J. Vercoutter, pp. 91–132. New York: Delacourte Press.

Braidwood, R., and L. Braidwood
1960 *Excavations in the Plain of Antioch: The Early Assemblages.* Oriental Institute Publications 61. Chicago: University of Chicago Press.

Brandes, M.
1979 *Siegelabrollungen aus den archaischen Bauschichten in Uruk-Warka.* Freiburger Altorientalische Studien 3. Wiesbaden: Franz Steiner.

Brandt, R.
1978 The Other Chalcolithic Finds. In *Korucutepe,* vol. 2, edited by M. van Loon, pp. 61–63. Amsterdam: North Holland.

Breniquet, C.
1991 Tell es-Sawwan. Réalités et problems. *Iraq* 53:75–90.

British Admiralty, Naval Intelligence Division
1917 *A Handbook of Mesopotamia,* vol. 1. Oxford.

British Naval
1944 *Iraq and the Persian Gulf.* Geographical Handbook Series BR 524. London: Naval Intelligence Division.

Bronk Ramsey, C.
1995 Radiocarbon Calibration and the Analysis of Stratigraphy: The OxCal Program. *Radiocarbon* 37:425–30.
1998 OxCal v3.0beta. Oxford Radiocarbon Accelerator Unit <http://www.rlaha.ox.ac.uk>.

Brumfiel, E. M., and J. W. Fox (editors)
1994 *Factional Competition and Political Development in the New World.* Cambridge: Cambridge University Press.

Buccellati, G.
1990 Salt at the Dawn of History: The Case of the Bevelled Rim Bowls. In *Resurrecting the Past: A Joint Tribute to Adnan Bounni,* edited by P. Matthiae, M. van Loon, and H. Weiss, pp. 17–40. Leiden: Nederlands Archeologisch-Historisch Instituut te Istanbul.

Buccellati, G., D. Buia, and S. Reimer
1991 Tell Ziyada: The First Three Seasons of Excavation (1988–90). *Bulletin of the Canadian Society for Mesopotamian Studies* 21:31–61.

Buccellati, M. K.

1979   The Outer Fertile Crescent Culture: Northeast Connections of Syria and Palestine in the Third Millennium B.C. *Ugarit Forschungen* 11:413–30.

Buck, C. E.

1996   *Bayesian Approach to Interpreting Archaeological Data.* Chichester, England: Wiley.

Burger, R. L.

1992   *Chavín and the Origins of Andean Civilization.* London: Thames and Hudson.

Burghardt, A. F.

1971   A Hypothesis about Gateway Cities. *Annals of the Association of American Geographers* 61:269–87.

Burney, C.

1993   Arslantepe as a Gateway to the Highlands. In *Between the Rivers and over the Mountains,* edited by M. Frangipane, H. Hauptmann, M. Liverani, M. Matthiae, and M. Mellinck, pp. 311–18. Università di Roma "La Sapienza."

Byock, J.

1988   *Medieval Iceland.* Berkeley: University of California Press.

Calderone, L., and H. Weiss

1988   The End of the Ninevite 5 Sequence at Tell Leilan. Paper presented at a conference on the Origins of North Mesopotamian Civilization, December 15–19, Yale University.

Calderoni, G., I. Caneva, A. Cazzela, M. Frangipane, and V. Petrone

1994   Department of Earth Sciences at the University of Rome Radiocarbon Dates 3. *Radiocarbon* 36:143–52.

Caldwell, D. H.

1967   *Investigations at Tal-i-Iblis.* Springfield: Illinois State Museum.

1976   The Early Glyptic of Gawra, Giyan, and Susa and the Development of Long Distance Trade. *Orientalia* 45:227–50.

Caldwell, J. R.

1968   Tell i-Ghazir. *Reallexikon der Assyriologie* 3:348–54. Berlin: de Gruyter.

Campbell, S., E. Carter, E. Healey, S. Anderson, A. Kennedy, and S. Whitcher

1999   Emerging Complexity on the Kahramanmarash Plain, Turkey: The Domuztepe Project, 1995–97. *American Journal of Archaeology* 103:395–418.

Campbell-Thompson, R., and M. Mallowan

1933   The British Museum Excavations at Nineveh. *Liverpool Annals of Archaeology and Anthropology* 20:71–186.

Cancian, F.

1980   Risk and Uncertainty in Agricultural Decision Making. In *Agricultural Decision Making: Anthropological Contributions to Rural Development,* edited by Peggy Barlett, pp. 161–76. Orlando: Academic.

Carter, E.

1971   *Elam in the Second Millennium B.C.: The Archaeological Evidence.* Doctoral dissertation, Department of Near Eastern Languages and Civilizations, University of Chicago.

Carter, E., and M. W. Stolper

1984   *Elam: Surveys of Political History and Archaeology.* Berkeley: University of California Press.

Castillo B., L. Jaime, and C. B. Donnan

1994   La ocupación moche de San José Moro, Jequetepeque. In *Moche: Propuestas y Perspectivas,* edited by Santiago Uceda and Elías Mujica. Travaux de l'Institut Français d'Etudes Andines 79:93–146. Lima.

Cauvin, J., and D. Stordeur

1985   Une occupation d'époque Uruk en Palmyrène: le niveau supérieur d'El Kowm 2-Caracol. *Cahiers de l'Euphrate* 4:191–206.

Cecchini, S., and S. Mazzoni (eds.)

1998   *Tell Afis (Siria): Scavi sull'acropoli 1988–1992* (The 1988–92 Excavations on the Acropolis). Pisa: Edizioni ETS.

Champion, T.

1989   Introduction. In *Centre and Periphery,* edited by T. Champion, pp. 1–21. London: Unwin Hyman.

Charvát, P.

1997   *On People, Signs and States: Spotlights on Sumerian Society, c. 3500–2500 B.C.* Prague: Oriental Institute of the Academy of Sciences of the Czech Republic.

Chase-Dunn, C.

1989   *Global Formation: Structures of a World Economy.* Cambridge: Basil Blackwell.

Childe, V. G.

1941   *Man Makes Himself.* London: Watts.

Christen, J. A.

1994   Summarizing a Set of Radiocarbon Determinations: A Robust Approach. *Applied Statistics* 43:489–503.

Cieza de León, P. de

1967   *El señorio de los Incas. Segunda parte de la crónica del Perú.* Lima:
[1553] Instituto de Estudios Peruanos.

Cioffi-Revilla, C.

2000   The First International System: Preliminary Polity Data Set of the West Asian Macro Social System in Southern Mesopotamia, 6000–1500 B.C. Paper presented at the Meeting of the International Studies Association, Los Angeles.

Clark, J. E., and M. Blake

1994   The Power of Prestige: Competitive Generosity and the Emergence of
Rank Societies in Lowland Mesoamerica. In *Factional Competition and
Political Development in the New World,* edited by E. M. Brumfiel and J. W.
Fox, pp. 17–30. Cambridge: Cambridge University Press.

Clark, R. M.

1975   A Calibration Curve for Radiocarbon Dates. *Antiquity* 49:251–266.

Cobo, B.

1979   *History of the Inca Empire.* Austin: University of Texas Press.
[1653]

Cohen, A.

1971   Cultural Strategies in the Organization of Trading Diasporas. In *The
Development of Indigenous Trade and Markets in West Africa,* edited by C.
Meillassoux, pp. 266–81. London: Oxford University Press.

Cole, J., and E. Wolf

1974   *The Hidden Frontier.* New York: Academic Press.

Collon, D., and J. Reade

1983   Archaic Nineveh. *Baghdader Mitteilungen* 14:33–43.

Connan, J., and O. Deschesne

1991   Le Bitume dans l'Antiquité. *La Récherche* 22(229):152–59.

1996   *Le Bitume à Suse: Collections du Musée de Louvre.* Paris: Reunion des Musées
Nationaux.

Cooper, J. S.

1983   *Reconstructing History from Ancient Inscriptions: The Lagash-Umma Border
Conflict.* Sources from the Ancient Near East, vol. 2(1). Malibu, California:
Undena Press.

Costin, C. L.

1993   Textiles, Women, and Political Economy in Late Prehispanic Peru. In
Research in Economic Anthropology, edited by Barry Isaac, pp. 29–59.
Greenwich: JAI Press.

Costin, C. L., T. K. Earle, B. Owen, and G. S. Russell

1989   Impact of Inka Conquest on Local Technology in the Upper Mantaro
Valley, Peru. In *What's New? A Close Look at the Process of Innovation,* edited
by Sander E. van der Leeuw and Robin Torrance, pp. 107–39. One World
Archaeology Series, vol. 14. London: Unwin and Allen.

Coursey, C.

1997   *Shaping, Stewing, Serving, and Brewing: Uruk Period Pottery Production and
Consumption in Alluvial Mesopotamia.* Doctoral Dissertation. Ann Arbor:
University Microfilms.

Crabtree, P. J.

1990   Zooarchaeology and Complex Societies: Some Uses of Faunal Analysis for the Study of Trade, Social Status, and Ethnicity. *Archaeological Method and Theory* 2:155–205.

Crawford, H. E. W.

1973   Mesopotamia's Invisible Exports in the Third Millennium. *World Archaeology* 5:232–41.

Creamer, W., and J. Haas

1985   Tribe vs. Chiefdom in Lower Central America. *American Antiquity* 50:738–54.

Crumley, C. L.

1990   A Critique of Cultural Evolutionist Approaches to Ranked Society, with Particular Reference to Celtic Politics. Paper presented at the Fifty-fifth Annual Meeting of the Society for American Archaeology, Las Vegas.

Curtin, P. D.

1975   *Economic Change in Precolonial Africa.* Madison: University of Wisconsin Press.

1984   *Cross-Cultural Trade in World History.* Cambridge: Cambridge University Press.

Curvers, H.

1989   The Beginning of the Third Millennium in Syria. In *To the Euphrates and Beyond: Studies in Honour of Maurits N. van Loon,* edited by O. Haex, et al., pp. 173–93. Rotterdam: Balkema.

1991   *Bronze Age Society in the Balikh Drainage (Syria).* Doctoral dissertation, University of Amsterdam.

Curvers, H. H., and G. M. Schwartz

1990   Excavations at Tell al-Raqa'i: A Small Rural Site of Early Urban Mesopotamia. *American Journal of Archaeology* 94:3–23.

D'Altroy, T. N.

1992   *Provincial Power in the Inka Empire.* Washington, D.C.: Smithsonian Institution Press.

1994a   Comments: Re-thinking Complex Prehistoric Societies in Asia. In *Landscapes of Power,* edited by K. Morrison, pp. 354–83. Asian Perspectives (special issue). Honolulu: University of Hawaii.

1994b   Public and Private Economy in the Inka Empire. In *The Economic Anthropology of the State,* edited by E. M. Brumfiel, pp. 171–222. Society for Economic Anthropology Monograph 11. Lanham, Maryland: University Press of America.

2001   *The Incas.* Oxford: Blackwell.

D'Altroy, T. N., and V. I. Williams

1998   Provisioning the Inka Economy in Kollasuyu. Final report to the National Science Foundation (SBR-97-07962). Department of Anthropology, Columbia University.

Damerow, P., and R. K. Englund

1989   *The Proto-Elamite Texts from Tepe Yahya.* American School of Prehistoric Research, Bulletin 39. Peabody Museum of Archaeology and Ethnology, Harvard University.

Deagan, K.

2001   Dynamics of Imperial Adjustment in Spanish America: Ideology and Social Integration. In *Empires: Perspectives from Archaeology and History,* edited by S. Alcock, T. D'Altroy, K. Morrison, and C. M. Sinopoli, pp. 179–94. Cambridge: Cambridge University Press.

de Contenson, H.

1985   Le matériel archéologique des tells. In *Holocene Settlement in North Syria: Résultats de deux prospections archéologiques effectuées dans la région du nahr Sajour et sur le haut Euphrate syrien,* edited by P. Sanlaville, pp. 99–162. Oxford: BAR International Series 238.

de Jesus, P. S.

1980   *The Development of Prehistoric Mining and Metallurgy in Anatolia.* BAR International Series 74. Oxford.

Delougaz, P., and H. J. Kantor

1996   *Chogha Mish I: The First Five Seasons of Excavations, 1961–71,* edited by A. Alizadeh. Oriental Institute Publications 101. Chicago: Oriental Institute.

Delougaz, P., and S. Lloyd

1942   *Pre-Sargonid Temples in the Diyala Region.* Oriental Institute Publications 58. Chicago: University of Chicago Press.

Delougaz, P., H. Hill, and S. Lloyd

1967   *Private Houses and Graves in the Diyala Region.* Oriental Institute Publications 88. Chicago: University of Chicago Press.

Demarest, A., and G. Conrad (editors)

1992   *Ideology and Precolumbian Civilizations.* Santa Fe: School of American Research Press.

DeMarrais, E., L. J. Castillo, and T. Earle

1996   Ideology, Materialization, and Power Strategies. *Current Anthropology* 37:15–31.

de Noblet, N., P. Braconnot, S. Joussaume, and V. Masson

1996   Sensitivity of Simulated Asian and African Summer Monsoons to Orbitally Induced Variations in Insolation, 126, 115, and 6 kBP. *Climate Dynamics* 12:589–603.

Dercksen, J. G.

1996   *The Old Assyrian Copper Trade in Anatolia.* Istanbul: Nederlands Historisch-Archaeologisch Instituut te Istanbul.

Descoeudres, J. P. (editor)

1990   *Greek Colonists and Native Populations.* Oxford: Clarendon.

Dewar, R.

1991   Incorporating Variation in Occupational Span into Settlement Pattern
Analysis. *American Antiquity* 56:604–20.

Dewar, R., and H. T. Wright

1994   Changing Population Patterns during the Early Phases of Occupation on
the Deh Luran Plain. In *Early Settlement and Irrigation on the Deh Luran
Plain: Village and Early State Societies in Southwestern Iran,* by J. A. Neely and
H. T. Wright, pp. 200–11. Technical Report of the Museum of
Anthropology 26. Ann Arbor: University of Michigan.

Diakanoff, I. M.

1954   *Sale of Land in Pre-Sargonic Sumer.* Moscow: International Congress of
Orientalists, Assyriology Section.

Diamond, S.

1974   *In Search of the Primitive: A Critique of Civilization.* New Brunswick:
Transaction Books.

Diez de San Miguel, G.

1964   *Visita hecha a la Provincia de Chucuito por Garci Diez de San Miguel en*
[1567]   *al año 1567.* Lima, Peru: Casa de Cultura.

Dillemann, L.

1962   *Haute Méstopotamie orientale et pays adjacents.* Paris: Guethner.

Di Nocera, G. M.

1998   C-14 Datings at Arslantepe and Bronze Age Chronology in the Upper and
Middle Euphrates. Paper presented at the 1st International Congress on
the Archaeology of the Ancient Near East, Rome.

Dittmann, R.

1986a   Seals, Sealings, and Tablets. Remarks on the Changing Pattern of
Administrative Control from the Late Uruk to the Proto-Elamite Period at
Susa. In *Ǧamdat Naṣr: Period or Regional Style?* edited by U. Finkbeiner and
W. Röllig, pp. 332–66. Wiesbaden: Ludwig Reichert.

1986b   *Betrachtungen zur Frühzeit des Südwest-Iran.* Berliner Beiträge zum Vorderen
Orient 4. Berlin: Reimer.

1986c   Susa in the Proto-Elamite period and Annotations on the Painted Pottery
of Proto-Elamite Khuzestan. In *Ǧamdat Naṣr: Period or Regional Style?* edited
by U. Finkbeiner and W. Röllig, pp. 171–96. Wiesbaden: Ludwig Reichert.

1987   Bemerkungen zum proto-elamischen Horizont. *Archäologische Mitteilungen
aus Iran* 20:31–63.

Dornemann, R.

1988   Tell Hadidi: One Bronze Age Site among Many in the Tabqa Dam Salvage
Area. *Bulletin of the American Schools of Oriental Research* 270:13–42.

1997   Qarqur. In *The Oxford Encyclopedia of Archaeology in the Near East,* edited by
E. Meyers, pp. 370–71. New York: Oxford University Press.

Doyle, W. M.

1986   *Empires.* Ithaca: Cornell University Press.

Drennan, R.

1976   Religion and Social Evolution in Formative Mesoamerica. In *The Early Mesoamerican Village,* edited by Kent V. Flannery, pp. 345–68. New York: Academic Press.

Duistermaat, K.

1996   The Seals and Sealings. In *Tell Sabi Abyad: The Late Neolithic Settlement,* vol. 2, edited by Peter M. M. G. Akkermanns, pp. 339–403. Istanbul: Nederlands Historisch-Archaeologisch Instituut.

Durrenberger, E. P.

1997   A Local Elite and Underdevelopment in a Peripheral Economy: Iceland in the 18th–20th Centuries. In *Economic Analysis beyond the Local System,* edited by R. Blanton, P. Peregrine, D. Winslow, and T. Hall, pp. 71–86. SEA Monograph 13. Lanham, Maryland: University Press of America.

Dyson, R. H.

1987   The Relative and Absolute Chronology of Hissar II and the Proto-Elamite Horizon of Northern Iran. In *Chronologies du Proche Orient* (Chronologies in the Near East), edited by O. Aurenche, J. Evin, and F. Hours, pp. 647–78. British Archaeological Reports 379. Oxford.

Dyson, S. (editor)

1985   *Comparative Studies in the Archaeology of Colonialism.* BAR International Series 233. Oxford.

Earle, T.

1982   The Ecology and Politics of Primitive Valuables. In *Culture and Ecology: Eclectic Perspectives,* edited by J. Kennedy and R. Edgerton, pp. 65–83. American Anthropological Association Special Publication 15.

1991   The Evolution of Chiefdoms. In *Chiefdoms: Power, Economy, and Ideology,* edited by T. Earle, pp. 1–15. Cambridge: Cambridge University Press.

1997   *How Chiefs Come to Power.* Stanford: Stanford University Press.

Edens, C.

1996   Hacınebi Chipped Stone, 1995. In Hacınebi, Turkey: Preliminary Report on the 1995 Excavations, by Gil J. Stein, Christopher Edens, Hadi Özbal, Julie Pearce, and Holly Pittman. *Anatolica* 22:100–104.

1997   Hacınebi Chipped Stone. In Excavations at Hacınebi, Turkey, 1996: Preliminary Report, by G. Stein, K. Boden, C. Edens, J. P. Edens, K. Keith, A. McMahon, and H. Özbal. *Anatolica* 23:124–27.

1998a   Hacınebi Chipped Stone, 1997. In Southeast Anatolia before the Uruk Expansion: Preliminary Report on the 1997 Excavations at Hacınebi, Turkey. *Anatolica* 24:155–60.

1998b   The Chipped Stone Industry at Hacınebi: Technological Styles and Social Identity. Paper presented at the Annual Meeting of the Society for American Archaeology, Seattle.

Edens, J. P.

1997   Hacınebi Ceramic Analysis, 1996. In Excavations at Hacınebi, Turkey, 1996: Preliminary Report, by G. Stein, K. Boden, C. Edens, J. Edens, K. Keith, A. McMahon, and H. Özbal. *Anatolica* 23:127–32.

Edzard, D. O.

1967   The Early Dynastic Period. In *The Near East: The Early Civilizations,* edited by J. Bottéro, E. Cassin, and J. Vercoutter, pp. 52–90. New York: Delacourte Press.

Ehrenreich, R. M. (editor)

1995   *Heterarchy and the Analysis of Complex Societies.* Archaeological Papers of the American Anthropological Association 6.

Ehrich, R. W. (editor)

1992   *Chronologies in Old World Archaeology.* 2$^\text{d}$ ed. Chicago: University of Chicago Press.

Eichmann, R.

1989   *Uruk, Die Stratigraphie.* Mainz: von Zabern.

Eidem, J., and D. Warburton

1996   In the Land of Nagar: A Survey around Tell Brak. *Iraq* 58:51–64.

Einwag, B.

1993   Vorbericht über die archäologische Geländebegehung in der West-Gazira. *Damaszener Mitteilungen* 7:23–43.

Eisenstadt, S., M. Abitbol, and N. Chazan

1988   *Early State in African Perspective.* Leiden: E. J. Brill.

Ekholm, K.

1977   External Exchange and the Transformation of Central African Social Systems. In *The Evolution of Social Systems,* edited by J. Friedman and M. J. Rowlands, pp. 115–36. London: Duckworth.

1981   On the Structure and Dynamics of Global Systems. In *The Anthropology of Pre-capitalist Societies,* edited by J. S. Kahn and J. P. Llobera, pp. 241–62. London: Macmillan.

Ekholm, K., and J. Friedman

1979   "Capital" Imperialism and Exploitation in Ancient World Systems. In *Power and Propaganda,* edited by M. T. Larsen, pp. 41–58. Copenhagen: Akademisk Forlag.

1993   "Capital" Imperialism and Exploitation in Ancient World Systems. In *The World System,* edited by A. Gunder Frank and B. K. Gills, pp. 59–80. London: Routledge.

Emberling, G.

1997   Ethnicity in Complex Societies: Archaeological Perspectives. *Journal of Archaeological Research* 5:295–344.

Emberling, G., J. Cheng, T. Larsen, H. Pittman, T. Skuldboel, J. Weber, and H. T. Wright

1999   Excavations at Tell Brak 1998: Preliminary Report. *Iraq* 61:1–41.

Englund, R.

1983   Dilmun in the Archaic Uruk Corpus. In *Dilmun: New Studies in the Archaeology and Early History of Bahrain,* edited by D. T. Potts, pp. 35–38. Berliner Beiträge zum Vorderen Orient 2. Berlin: Dietrich Reimer.

1994   *Archaic Administrative Texts from Uruk: The Early Campaigns.* Archaische Texte aus Uruk 5. Berlin: Mann.

1996   The Proto-Elamite Script. In *The World's Writing Systems,* edited by P. T. Daniels and W. Bright, pp. 160–64. Oxford: Oxford University Press.

1998   Texts from the Late Uruk Period. In *Mesopotamien: Späturuk-Zeit und Frühdynastische Zeit,* edited by P. Attinger and M. Wäfler, pp. 15–236. Freiburg, Switzerland: Universitätsverlag, and Göttingen, Germany: Vandenhoeck and Ruprecht.

Englund, R. K., and H. J. Nissen

1993   *Die Lexikalischen Listen der Archaischen Texte aus Uruk.* Archaische Texte aus Uruk 3. Berlin: Gebr. Mann.

Esin, U.

1975   Tepecik 1974. *Anatolian Studies* 25:46–49.

1982   Tepecik Excavations, 1974. In *Keban Project 1974–75 Activities.* Middle East Technical University, Series I, no. 7, pp. 95–118. Ankara: METU (Middle East Technical University).

1983   Zur Datierung der vorgeschichtlichen Schichten von Değirmentepe bei Malatya in der östlichen Türkei. In *Beiträge zur Altertumskunde Kleinasiens,* edited by R. m. Boehmer and H. Hauptmann, pp. 175–90. Mainz: von Zabern.

1987   Die kulturellen Beziehungen zwischen Ostanatolien und Mesopotamien sowie Syrien anhand einiger Grabungs und Oberflächenfunde aus dem oberen Euphrattal im 4 Jt. v. Chr. In *Mesopotamien und seine Nachbarn,* edited by H. J. Nissen, J. Renger, pp. 13–22. Berlin: Reimer.

1990   Değirmentepe (Malatya) Kalkolitik Obeyd Evresi Damga Mühür ve Mühür Baskıları. In *X Türk Tarih Kongresi,* pp. 47–56, pl. 33–41. Ankara: Türk Tarih Kurumu Basimevi.

1994   The Functional Evidence of Seals and Sealings of Değirmentepe. In *Archives before Writing,* edited by P. Ferioli, E. Fiandra, G. G. Fissore, and M. Frangipane, pp. 59–81. Roma: Centro Internazionale di Recerche Archaeologiche, Anthropologiche e Storiche.

Esin, U., and S. Harmankaya

1987   Değirmen Tepe Kurtama Kazısı 1986. *IX Kazı Sonuçları Toplantısı,* I:79–125. Ankara: Kultur Müdürlüğü.

Espinoza S., W.

1970   Los mitmas yungas de Collique en Cajamarca, siglos XV, XVI, y XVII. *Revista del Museo Nacional* 36:9–57. Lima.

1973   Las colonias de mitmas múltiples en Abancay, siglos XV y XVI. *Revista del Museo Nacional* 39:225–99. Lima.

1980   Acerca de la historia militar inca. *Allpanvchis Phuturinqa* 14(16):171–86.

Evin, J.

1995   Possibilité et nécessité de la calibration des datations c-14 de l'archéologie du Proche-Orient. *Paléorient* 21(1):5–16.

Falcón, F. de

1946   Representación hecha por el Licenciado Falcón en concilio provincial
[1567]   sobre los daños y molestias que se hacen a los indios. In *Los Pequeños Grandes Libros de Historia Americana,* edited by Francisco A. Loayza, Series 1, T. 10, pp. 121–64. Lima: D. Miranda.

Falkenstein, A.

1974   *The Sumerian Temple City,* translated by M. Ellis. Malibu, California: Undena Press.

Falsoni, G.

1999   Tell Shiyukh Tahtani on the Euphrates. The University of Palermo Salvage Excavations in North Syria (1993–94). *Akkadica* 109–10:22–64.

Feinman, G. M.

1994   Social Boundaries and Political Change: A Comparative Perspective. In *Chiefdoms and Early States in the Near East,* edited by G. Stein and M. S. Rothman, pp. 225–36. Madison, Wisconsin: Prehistory Press.

Ferioli, P., and E. Fiandra

1983   Clay Sealings from Arslantepe VIA: Administration and Bureaucracy.
[1988]   *Origini* 12:455–509.

1994   Archival Techniques and Methods at Arslantepe. In *Archives before Writing,* edited by P. Ferioli, E. Fiandra, G. G. Fissore, and M. Frangipane, pp. 149–61. Rome: Centro Internazionale di Recerche Archaeologiche Anthropologiche e Storiche.

Fernea, R.

1970   *Shaykh and Effendi: Changing Patterns of Authority among the El Shabana of Southern Iraq.* Cambridge: Harvard University Press.

Fiandra, E.

1981   The Connection between Clay Sealings and Tablets in Administration. In *South Asian Archaeology 1979,* edited by H. Härtel, pp. 29–43. Berlin: Dietrich Reimer.

1994   Discussion. In *Archives before Writing,* edited by P. Ferioli, E. Fiandra, G. G. Fissore, and M. Frangipane, p. 168. Rome: Centro Internazionale di Recerche Archaeologiche Anthropologiche e Storiche.

Fielden, K.

1981   A Late Uruk Pottery Group from Tell Brak, 1978. *Iraq* 43:157–66.

Finet, A.

1977   L'Apport du Tell Kannâs a l'histoire Proche-Orientale de la fin du 4ᵉ millénaire à la moitié du 2ᵉ. In *Le Moyen Euphrate, Zone de Contact et d'Échanges,* edited by J. C. Margueron, pp. 107–15. Leiden: E.J. Brill.

Finkbeiner, U.

1995   Tell Bleibis, Eine Burg der Urukzeit am mittleren Euphrat. In *Beiträge zur Kulturgeschichte Vorderasiens: Festschrift für Rainer Michael Boehmer,* edited by U. Finkbeiner, R. Dittmann, and H. Hauptmann, pp. 139–44. Mainz: von Zabern.

Finkbeiner, U. (editor)

1991   *Uruk Kampagne 35–37, 1982–84: Die archäologische Oberflächenuntersuchung (Survey).* Ausgrabungen in Uruk-Warka Endberichte 4. Mainz: von Zabern.

Finkelstein, J. J.

1963   Mesopotamian Historiography. *Proceedings of the American Philosophical Society* 107:461–73.

Flannery, K. V.

1968   The Olmec and the Valley of Oaxaca: A Model for Inter-Regional Interaction in Formative Times. In *Dumbarton Oaks Conference on the Olmec,* edited by E. Benson, pp. 79–110. Washington, D.C.

1972   The Cultural Evolution of Civilizations. *Annual Review of Ecology and Systematics* 3:399–426.

1976   Empirical Determinants of Site Catchments in Oaxaca and Tehuacán. In *The Early Mesoamerican Village,* edited by Kent Flannery, pp. 103–17. New York: Academic Press.

1995   Prehistoric Social Evolution. In *Research Frontiers in Anthropology,* edited by C. R. Ember and M. Ember, pp. 3–26. Needham Heights, Massachusetts: Simon and Schuster.

Forbes, R. J.

1955   *Studies in Ancient Technology,* vol. 1. Leiden: E.J. Brill.

1964   *Studies in Ancient Technology,* Vols. I–XI. Leiden: Brill.

Forest, J.-D.

1983   *Les pratiques funéraires en Mésopotamie du 5ᵉ millenaire au debut du 3ᵉ.* Étude de CAS, Memoire 19. Paris: Éditions Récherche sur les Civilisations.

1996   *Mésopotamie. L'apparition de l'État VIIe–IIIe Millénaires.* Paris: Méditerranée.

1999   *Les premiers temples de Mésopotamie.* BAR International Series 765. Oxford.

Fortin, M.

1995   Rapport préliminaire sur la cinquième campagne à Tell 'Atij et la quatrième à Tell Gudea (printemps 1993). *Syria* 72:23–54.

Foster, B.

1977   Commercial Activity in Sargonic Mesopotamia. *Iraq* 39:31–44.

1981   A New Look at the Sumerian Temple State. *Journal of the Economic and Social History of the Orient* 24:225–41.

1993   International Trade at Sargonic Susa. *Altorientalische Forshungen* 20:59–68.

1997   A Sumerian Merchant's Account of the Dilmun Trade. *Acta Sumerologica* 19:53–62.

Frangipane, M.

1993   Local Components in the Development of Centralized Societies in Syro-Anatolian Regions. In *Between the Rivers and over the Mountains,* edited by M. Frangipane, H. Hauptmann, M. Liverani, P. Matthiae, and M. Mellink, pp. 133–61. Università di Roma "La Sapienza."

1994a   The Record Function of Clay Sealings in Early Administrative Systems as seen from Arslantepe-Malatya. In *Archives before Writing,* edited by P. Ferioli, E. Fiandra, G. Fissore, and M. Frangipane, pp. 125–37. Rome: Scriptorium.

1994b   Excavations at Arslantepe-Malatya, 1992. *Kazı Sonuçları Toplantısı* XV:211–18. Ankara: Kultur Müdürlügü.

1996   *La nascita dello Stato nel Vicino Orientale.* Roma-Bari: Laterza.

1997a   Arslantepe-Malatya: External Factors and Local Components in the Development of an Early State Society. In *Emergence and Change in Early Urban Societies,* edited by L. Manzanilla, pp. 43–58. New York: Plenum Press.

1997b   A Fourth Millennium Temple/Palace Complex at Arslantepe-Malatya. North-South Relations and the Formation of Early State Societies in the Northern Regions of Southern Mesopotamia. *Paléorient* 23:45–73.

1998   Arslantepe 1996: The Finding of an E.B.I "Royal Tomb." *Kazı Sonuçları Toplantısı* 19:291–309. Ankara.

2000   The Development of Administration from Collective to Centralized Economies in the Mesopotamian World: The Transformation of an Institution from System-Serving to Self-Serving. In *The Study of Cultural Change: Essays in Honor of Kent V. Flannery,* edited by G. M. Feinman and L. Manzanilla. Fundamental Issues in Archaeology, New York.

Frangipane, M., and A. Palmieri

1983a   (editors) Perspectives on Proto-urbanization in Eastern Anatolia:
[1988]   Arslantepe (Malatya). *Origini* 12:455–522.

1983b   A Protourban Centre of the Late Uruk Period. *Origini* 12:287–454.
[1988]

1983c   Cultural Beginnings at Arslantepe at the Beginning of the Third
[1988]   Millennium. *Origini* 12:523–74.

1987   Urbanization in Peri-Mesopotamian Areas: The Case of Eastern Anatolia. In *Studies in the Neolithic and Urban Revolutions, edited by L. Manzanilla,* pp. 295–318. BAR International Series 349. Oxford.

1989   Aspects of Centralization in the Late Uruk Period in the Mesopotamian Periphery. *Origini* 14:539–60.

Frank, A. G.

1998   *ReOrient: Global Economy in the Asian Age.* Berkeley: University of California Press.

Frankfort, H.
1970   *The Art and Architecture of the Ancient Orient.* Hamondsworth, England: Penguin Books.

Frenzel, B.
1966   Climate Change in the Atlantic/Sub-boreal Sphere: Botanical Evidence. In *International Conference on Climate from 8000–0 B.C.,* pp. 99–123. New York: St. Martin's Press.

Fukai, S., K. Horiuchi, and T. Matsutani
1974   *Telul eth Thalathat. The Excavation of Tell V.* Institute of Oriental Culture, University of Tokyo.

Gallagher, J., and R. Robinson
1953   The Imperialism of Free Trade. *Economic History Review* (second series) 6:1–15.

Galtung, J.
1971   A Structural Theory of Imperialism. *Journal of Peace Research* 2:81–117.

Garstang, J.
1953   *Prehistoric Mersin.* Oxford: Clarendon.

Gelb, I.
1979   Household and Family in Early Mesopotamia. In *State and Temple Economy in the Ancient Near East,* edited by E. Lipiski, pp. 1–97. Leuven, Belgium: Departement Oriëntalistiek.

Gelb, I. J., P. Steinkeller, and R. M. Whiting Jr.
1991   *Earliest Land Tenure Systems in the Ancient Near East: Ancient Kudurrus.* Publication 104. Chicago: Oriental Institute.

Genouillac, H. de
1934–36 *Fouilles de Telloh.* Paris: P. Geuthner.

George, A.
1999   *The Epic of Gilgamesh.* New York: Barnes and Noble.

Geyer, B., and J.-Y. Monchambert
1987   Prospection dans la moyenne vallée de l'Euphrate. *MARI* 5:293–344.

Giannessi, D.
1998   Late Chalcolithic and Early Bronze Age at Tell Afis. Poster presented at the 1st International Congress on the Archaeology of the Ancient Near East, Rome.

Gibson, M.
1972   *The City and Area of Kish.* Miami: Field Research Projects.

Godelier, M.
1978   Infrastructures, Societies, and History. *Current Anthropology* 19:763–71.

Goldstein, P.
1993   Tiwanaku Temples and State Expansion: A Tiwanaku Sunken Court Temple in Moquegua, Peru. *Latin American Antiquity* 4:22–47.

Goody, J.

2000   *The Power of the Written Tradition*. Washington, D.C.: Smithsonian Institution Press.

Green, M. V.

1980   Animal Husbandry at Uruk in the Archaic Period. *Journal of Near Eastern Studies* 39:1–35.

Green, M. W., and H. J. Nissen

1987   *Zeichenliste der Archaischen Texte aus Uruk*. Archaische Texte aus Uruk 2. Berlin: Gebr. Mann.

Guaman Poma de Ayala, F.

1980   *El primer nueva corónica y buen gobierno*, edited by John V. Murra and
[1614]   Rolena Adorno, translated by Jorge I. Urioste, 3 vols. Mexico, D.F.: Siglo Veintiuno.

Gut, R.

1995   *Das prähistorische Ninive: zur relativen Chronologie der frühen Perioden Nordmesopotamiens*. Mainz: von Zabern.

Hall, T., and C. Chase-Dunn

1996   Comparing World Systems: Concepts and Hypotheses. In *Pre-Columbian World Systems,* edited by P. Peregrine and G. Feinman, pp. 11–25. Madison, Wisconsin: Prehistory Press.

Haller, A. von

1931   Die keramik der archaischen Schichten von Uruk. In *4 vorl. Bericht über die in Uruk-Warka unternomenenen Grabungen,* by A. Nöldeke, E. Heinrich, H. Lenzen, and A. von Haller, p. 31–47. Berlin: de Gruyter.

Hammade, H., and Y. Yamazaki

1993   Some Remarks on the Uruk Levels at Tell al-'Abr on the Euphrates. *Akkadica* 84–85:53–62.

Hanbury Tenison, J.

1983   The 1982 Flaked Stone Assemblages at Jebel Aruda, Syria. *Akkadica* 33:27–33.

Hansen, D.

1965   The Relative Chronology of Mesopotamia, part 2: The Pottery Sequence at Nippur from the Middle Uruk to the End of the Old Babylonian Period (3400–1600 B.C.). In *Chronologies in Old World Archaeology,* edited by Robert Ehrich, pp. 201–13. Chicago: University of Chicago Press.

Harrison, S. P., D. Jolly, F. Laarif, A. Abe-Ouchi, B. Dong, K. Herterich, C. Hewitt, S. Joussaume, J. E. Kutzbach, J. Mitchell, N. de Noblet, and P. Valdes

1998   Intercomparison of Simulated Global Vegetation Distributions in Response to 6 kyr BP Orbital Forcing. *Journal of Climate* 11:2721–41.

Haselgrove, C.

1987   Culture Process on the Periphery: Belgic Gaul and Rome during the Late Republic and Early Empire. In *Centre and Periphery in the Ancient World*, edited by M. Rowlands, M. Larsen, and K. Kristiansen, pp. 104–24. Cambridge: Cambridge University Press.

Hassig, R.

1985   *Trade, Tribute, and Transportation: The Sixteenth-Century Political Economy of the Valley of Mexico.* Norman: University of Oklahoma Press.

1988   *Aztec Warfare.* Norman: University of Oklahoma Press.

Hastorf, C. A.

1990   The Effect of the Inka State on Sausa Agricultural Production and Crop Consumption. *American Antiquity* 55:262–90.

Hauptmann, H.

1976   Die Grabungen auf dem Norşun-Tepe, 1973. In *Keban Project 1973 Activities.* Middle East Technical University Series I, no. 6, pp. 61–78. Ankara: METU (Middle East Technical University).

1982   Die Grabungen auf dem Norşun-Tepe, 1974. In *Keban Project 1974–75 Activities.* Middle East Technical University Series I, no. 7, pp. 41–70. Ankara: METU (Middle East Technical University).

Hauptmann, A., K. Hess, H. Wright, and R. Whallon

1998   Evidence of Fourth Millennium B.C. Silver Production at Fatmall Kalecik, East Anatolia. *Metallurgica Antiqua* (Der Anschnitt), Beiheft 8:57–67.

Heinrich, E.

1934   Grabung in O XI–XII. In *5 Vorl. Bericht über die in Uruk-Warka unternommenen Grabungen,* by A. Nöldeke, E. Heinrich, and E. Schott. Berlin: de Gruyter.

1936   *Kleinfunde aus den archaischen Tempelschichten in Uruk.* Leipzig: Otto Harrassowitz.

1938   Grabungen im Gebiet des Anu-Antum-Tempels. In *Vorläufiger Bericht über die von der Deutschen Forschungsgemeinschaft im Uruk-Warka unternommenen Ausgrabungen* 9:19–30.

1982   *Die Tempel und Heiligtümer im Alten Mesopotamien.* Berlin: Walter de Gruyter.

Helmer, M.

1955–56   *La visitación de los Yndios Chupachos Inka et encomendero.* Lima and
[1549]   Paris: L'Institut Français d'Etudes Andines 5:3–50.

Helms, M. W.

1988   *Ulysses' Sail: An Ethnographic Odyssey of Power, Knowledge, and Geographical Distance.* Princeton: Princeton University Press.

1993   *Craft and the Kingly Ideal.* Austin: University of Texas Press.

Helwing, B.

1998   Cultural Interaction at Hassek Höyük, Turkey: New Evidence from Pottery Analysis. Paper presented at the Annual Meeting of the Society for American Archaeology, March 26, Seattle.

1999   Cultural Interaction at Hassek Höyük, Turkey: New Evidence from Pottery
            Analysis. *Paléorient* 25:91–99.

Henrickson, E.

1983   *Ceramic Styles and Cultural Interaction in the Early and Middle Chalcolithic of the
            Central Zagros, Iran.* Doctoral dissertation, University of Toronto.

1994   The Outer Limits: Settlement and Economic Strategies in the Central
            Zagros during the Uruk Era. In *Chiefdoms and Early States in the Near East:
            The Organizational Dynamics of Complexity,* edited by G. Stein and M.
            Rothman, pp. 85–102. Monographs in World Prehistory 18. Madison,
            Wisconsin: Prehistory Press.

Henrickson, E. F., and I. Thuesen (editors)

1989   *Upon This Foundation: The Ubaid Reconsidered.* Copenhagen: Museum
            Tusculanum Press.

Hermann, G.

1968   Lapis Lazuli: Early Phases of Its Trade. *Iraq* 30:21–57.

Hijara, I.

1980   Excavations at Tell Arpachiyah. *Iraq* 42:131–54.

Hole, F.

1985   The Organization of Susiana Society. *Paléorient* 11:21–24.

1994   Environmental Instabilities and Urban Origins. In *Chiefdoms and Early
            States in the Near East,* edited by G. Stein and M. S. Rothman, pp. 121–52.
            Madison, Wisconsin: Prehistory Press.

1997   Paleoenvironment and Human Society in the Jezireh of Northern
            Mesopotamia, 20,000–6,000 B.P.. *Paléorient* 23(2):39–50.

Hole, F., and G. A. Johnson

1986–87   Umm Qseir on the Khabur: Preliminary Report on the 1986 Excavation.
            Annales Archéologiques Arabes Syriennes 36–37:172–220.

Hole, F., K. V. Flannery, and J. A. Neely

1969   *Prehistory and Human Ecology of the Deh Luran Plain.* Museum of
            Anthropology Memoir 1. Ann Arbor: University of Michigan.

**Hole, F., with the collaboration of G. Johnson, N. Kouchoukos, J. McCorriston,
M. Zeder, S. Arter, and J. Blackman**

1991   Preliminary Report on the Joint American-Danish Archaeobiological
            Sampling of Sites in the Khabur Basin (1990). Submitted to Annales
            Archéologiques Arabes Syriennes.

Hole, F., G. Johnson, J. Arzt, and B. Diebold

1998   Tell Ziyadeh 1996. *Chronique Archéologique en Syrie* 2:59–67.

Hood, S.

1951   Excavations at Tabara el-Akrad, 1948–49. *Anatolian Studies* 1:149–83.

Hopkins, C.

1979   *The Discovery of Dura Europos.* New Haven: Yale University Press.

Humphreys, S. C.

1978   *Anthropology and the Greeks.* London: Routledge and Kegan Paul.

Huot, J. L.

1994   *Les premiers villageois de Mésopotamie, du village á la ville.* Paris: Armend Colin.

Hyslop, J.

1984   *The Inca Road System.* New York: Academic Press.

Jacobs, J.

1969   *The Economy of Cities.* New York: Vintage.

Jacobsen, T.

1939   *The Sumerian King List.* Chicago: The Oriental Institute.

1970   *Toward the Image of Tammuz.* Cambridge: Harvard University Press.

Jamieson, A. S.

1993   The Euphrates Valley and Early Bronze Age Ceramic Traditions. *Abr-Nahrain* 31:36–92.

Jasim, S.

1989   Structure and Function in an 'Ubaid Village. In *Upon This Foundation,* edited by E. F. Henrickson and I. Thuesen, pp. 79–90. CNI Publications 10. Copenhagen.

Joffe, A.

2000   Egypt and Syro-Mesopotamia in the 4th Millennium: Implications of the New Chronology. *Current Anthropology* 41:113–23.

Johnson, G. A.

1973   *Local Exchange and Early State Development in Southwestern Iran.* Museum of Anthropology Anthropological Papers, no. 51. Ann Arbor: University of Michigan.

1975   Locational Analysis and the Investigation of Uruk Local Exchange Systems. In *Ancient Civilization and Trade,* edited by Jeremy Sabloff and C. C. Lamberg-Karlovsky, pp. 285–339. Albuquerque: University of New Mexico Press.

1980a   Spatial Organization of Early Uruk Settlement Systems. In *L'Archéologie de l'Iraq du début de l'époque Néolithique à 333 avant notre ère,* edited by Marie-Thérèse Barrelet, pp. 233–63. Paris: Éditions du Centre National de la Récherche Scientifique.

1980b   Rank-size Convexity and System Integration: A View from Archaeology. *Economic Geography* 5:234–47.

1987a   The Changing Organization of Uruk Administration on the Susiana Plain. In *The Archeology of Western Iran,* edited by Frank Hole, pp. 107–39. Washington, D.C.: Smithsonian Institution.

1987b   The Ancient Economy, Transferable Technologies and the Bronze Age World-System: A View from the Northeastern Frontier of the Ancient Near East. In *Centre and Periphery in the Ancient World,* edited by M. Rowlands, M. T. Larsen, and K. Kristiansen, pp. 13–24. Cambridge: Cambridge University Press.

1988–89   Late Uruk in Greater Mesopotamia: Expansion or Collapse? *Origini* 14:595–611.

1989   Dynamics of Southwestern Prehistory: Far Outside, Looking In. In *Dynamics of Southwest Prehistory,* edited by L. S. Cordell and G. J. Gumerman, pp. 372–89. Washington, D.C.: Smithsonian Institution Press.

Johnson, G. A., and H. T. Wright

1986   Regional Perspectives on Southwest Iranian State Development. *Paléorient* 11(2):25–36.

Joyce, A.

1993   Interregional Interaction and Social Development on the Oaxaca Coast. *Ancient Mesoamerica* 4:67–84.

Julien, C.

1982   Inca Decimal Administration in the Lake Titicaca Region. In *The Inca and Aztec States, 1400–1800: Anthropology and History,* edited by G. A. Collier, R. I. Rosaldo, and J. D. Wirth, pp. 119–51. New York: Academic Press.

1988   How Inca Decimal Administration Worked. *Ethnohistory* 35:257–79.

1993   Finding a Fit: Archaeology and Ethnohistory of the Incas. In *Provincial Inca: Archaeological and Ethnohistorical Assessment of the Impact of the Inca State,* edited by M. Malpass, pp. 177–233. Iowa City: University of Iowa Press.

Kantor, H. J.

1984   The Ancestry of the Divine Boat (Sirsir?) of Early Dynastic and Akkadian Glyptic. *Journal of Near Eastern Studies* 43:277–80.

Karlsbeek, J.

1980   La Céramique de Serie du Djebel Aruda (à l'époque d'Uruk). *Akkadica* 20:1–11.

Keith, K.

1997   Spindle Whorls and Textile Production at Late Chalcolithic Hacınebi. In *Excavations at Hacınebi Turkey, 1996: Preliminary Report,* by G. Stein, K. Boden, C. Edens, J. P. Edens, K. Keith, A. McMahon, and H. Özbal. *Anatolica* 23:136–39.

Kelly-Buccellati, M.

1990   Trade in Metals in the Third Millennium: Northeastern Syria and Eastern Anatolia. In *Resurrecting the Past,* edited by P. Matthiae, M. van Loon, and H. Weiss, pp. 117–32. Leiden: Nederlands Historisch-Archeologisch Instituut te Istanbul.

Khazanov, A. M.

1978   Some Theoretical Problems of the Study of the Early State. In *The Early State,* edited by H. J. M. Claessen and P. Skalnik, pp. 77–92. The Hague: Mouton.

Killick, R. (editor)

1988   *Tell Rubeidheh: An Uruk Village in the Jebel Hamrin.* Hamrin Salvage Project Report 7. Baghdad: Directorate of Antiquities and British School of Archaeology in Iraq.

Klengel-Brandt, E., et al.

1997   Vorläufiger Bericht über die Ausgrabungen des Vorderasiatischen Museums auf Tall Knedig/NO Syrien, Ergebnisse der Kampagnen 1995 und 1996. *Mitteilungen der Deutschen Orient-Gesellschaft* 129:39–87.

Knapp, A. B.

1988   *The History and Culture of Ancient Western Asia and Egypt.* Chicago: Dorsey.

Knoke, D., and J. Kuklinski

1982   *Network Analysis.* Beverly Hills: Sage.

Kohl, P. L.

1987a   The Use and Abuse of World Systems Theory: The Case of the Pristine West Asian State. In *Advances in Archaeological Method and Theory,* vol. 11, edited by M. B. Schiffer, pp. 1–36. San Diego: Academic Press.

1987b   The Ancient Economy, Transferable Technologies and the Bronze Age World-System: A View from the Northeastern Frontier of the Ancient Near East. In *Centre and Periphery in the Ancient World,* edited by M. Rowlands, M. Larsen, and K. Kristiansen, pp. 13–24. Cambridge: Cambridge University Press.

Kohlmeyer, K.

1984   Euphrat-Survey. *Mitteilungen der deutschen Orient-Gesellschaft* 116:95–118.

1993   Zur frühen Geschichte von Blei und Silber. In *Handwerk und Technologie im Alten Orient,* edited by R. B. Wartke, pp. 41–48. Mainz: von Zabern.

1996   Houses in Habuba Kabira-South: Spatial Organisation and Planning of Late Uruk Residential Architecture. In *Houses and Households in Ancient Mesopotamia,* edited by K. Veenhof, pp. 89–103. Leiden: Nederlands Historisch-Archaeologisch Instituut te Istanbul.

1997   Habuba Kabira. In *The Oxford Encyclopedia of Archaeology in the Near East,* edited by E. Meyers, pp. 446–48. New York: Oxford University Press.

Koizumi, T.

1993   Ubaid Pottery from Kashkashok II: Typology and Chronology. *Al-Rafidan* XIV:19–67.

Kouchoukos, N.

1998   *Landscape and Social Change in Late Prehistoric Mesopotamia.* Doctoral dissertation, Yale University, New Haven.

Kramer, C.

1977   Pots and Peoples. In *Mountains and Lowlands,* edited by T. C. Young and L. Levine, pp. 91–112. Malibu, California: Undena Press.

1980   Estimating Prehistoric Populations: An Ethnoarchaeological Approach. In *L'Archéologie de l'Iraq du début de l'époque Néolithique à 333 avant notre ère,* edited by Marie-Therese Barrelet, pp. 315–34. Colloques Internationaux du CNRS 580. Paris.

Kramer, S. N.

1963   *The Sumerians.* Chicago: University of Chicago Press.

Kristiansen, K.

1991   Chiefdoms, States and Systems of Social Evolution. In *Chiefdoms: Power, Economy and Ideology,* edited by T. Earle, pp. 16–43. Cambridge: Cambridge University Press.

Kubba, S.

1990   The Ubaid Period: Evidence of Architectural Planning and the Use of a Standard Unit of Measurement (the Ubaid Cubit) in Mesopotamia. *Paléorient* 16(1):45–55.

Kuniholm, P. I.

1996   The Prehistoric Aegean: Dendrochonological Progress as of 1995. *Acta Archaeologica* 67:327–35.

Kurtz, D. V.

1987   The Economics of Urbanization and State Formation at Teotihuacan. *Current Anthropology* 28:329–40.

Kuzucuoglu, C., and N. Roberts

1997   Évolution de l'environnement en Anatolie de 20,000 à 6000 B.P. *Paléorient* 23(1):7–24.

Labov, W.

1972   *Socio-linguistic Patterns.* Philadelphia: University of Pennsylvania Press.

Lamberg-Karlovsky, C. C.

1995   Review of G. Algaze's "The Uruk World System: The Dynamics of Expansion of Early Mesopotamian Civilization." *International History Review* 17:767–68.

1996   *Beyond the Tigris and Euphrates: Bronze Age Civilizations.* Jerusalem: Ben Gurion University of the Negev Press.

Landes, D. S.

1961   Some Thoughts on the Nature of Economic Imperialism. *Journal of Economic History* 21:496–512.

1998   *The Wealth and Poverty of Nations.* New York: W.W. Norton.

Lane, F.

1966   *Venice and History: The Collected Papers of Frederic Lane.* Baltimore: Johns Hopkins University Press.

Langdon, S.

1924   *Excavations at Kish I.* Paris: Geuthner.

Lansing, J. S.

1995   *The Balinese.* Fort Worth: Harcourt Brace College.

Larsen, C. E.

1983   *Life and Land Use on the Bahrain Islands: The Geoarchaeology of an Ancient Society.* Chicago: University of Chicago Press.

Larsen, M. T.

1967   *Old Assyrian Caravan Procedures.* Uitg. v.h. Historisch-Archaeologische Institut te Istanbul 22.

1976   *The Old Assyrian City State and Its Colonies.* Copenhagen: Akademisk Forlag.

1979   The Tradition of Empire in Mesopotamia. In *Power and Propaganda,* edited by M. T. Larsen, pp. 75–106. Copenhagen: Akademisk Forlag.

1987   Commercial Networks in the Ancient Near East. In *Centre and Periphery in the Ancient World,* edited by M. Rowlands, M. T. Larsen, and K. Kristiansen, pp. 47–56. Cambridge: Cambridge University Press.

Lebeau, M.

2000   Stratified Archaeological Evidence and Compared Periodizations in the Syrian Jezirah during the Third Millennium B.C. In *Chronologies des Pays du Caucase et de L'Euphrate aux Ive–IIIe Millenaires,* edited by C. Marro and H. Hauptmann, pp. 167–92. Paris: DeBoccard.

Le Breton, L.

1957   The Early Periods at Susa: Mesopotamian Relations. *Iraq* 19:79–124.

Le Brun, A.

1971   Récherches stratigraphique á l'Acropole de Suse. *Cahiers de la Délégation Archéologique Française en Iran (DAFI)* 1:163–216.

1978   Le Niveau 17B de l'Acropole de Susa. *Cahiers de la Délégation Archéologique Française en Iran (DAFI)* 9:57–154.

Le Brun, A., and F. Vallat

1978   L'origine de l'écriture à Suse. *Cahiers de la Délégation Archéologique Française en Iran (DAFI)* 8:11–60.

Lechtman, H.

1977   Style in Technology—Some Early Thoughts. In *Material Culture Styles, Organization, and Dynamics of Technology. Proceedings of the 1975 American Ethnological Society,* edited by H. Lechtman and R. S. Merrill, pp. 3–20. St. Paul: West.

Leemans, W. F.

1950   *The Old Babylonian Merchant.* Leiden: E.J. Brill.

1960   *Foreign Trade in the Old Babylonian Period.* Leiden: E.J. Brill.

Lenzen, H.

1958   Liste der Funde aus dem Riemchengebäude. *Vorläufiger Bericht über die von dem Deutschen Archäologischen Institut und der Deutschen Orient-Gesellschaft aus Mitteln der Deutschen Forschungsgemeinschaft in Uruk-Warka unternommenen Ausgrabungen* 14:30–35.

1959   Die Grabungen der Westecke von E-anna. *Vorläufiger Bericht über die von dem Deutschen Archäologischen Institut und der Deutschen Orient-Gesellschaft aus Mitteln der Deutschen Forschungsgemeinschaft in Uruk-Warka unternommenen Ausgrabungen* 15:8–19.

1961   Die Klenfunde. D. Siegelabrollungen auf Tontafeln und Krugverschlussen. *Vorlaufiger Bericht uber die von dem Deutschen Archaologischen Institut und der Deutschen Orient-Gesellschaft aus Mitteln der Deutschen der Deutschen Forschungsgemeinschaft in Uruk Warka unternommenen Ausgrabungen* 17:29–36.

Levine, L., and T. C. Young Jr.

1987   A Summary of Ceramic Assemblages of the Central Western Zagros from the Middle Neolithic to the Late Third Millennium B.C. In *Préhistoire de la Mésopotamie,* edited by J.-L. Hout, pp. 15–54. Paris: Centre National de la Récherche Scientifique.

LeVine, T. Y.

1987   Inka Labor Service at the Regional Level: The Functional Reality. *Ethnohistory* 34:14–46.

Lindemeyer, E., and L. Martin

1993   *Uruk: Kleinfunde III.* Mainz: von Zabern.

Linick, T. W.

1984   La Jolla Radiocarbon Measurements X. *Radiocarbon* 26(1):75–110.

Liverani, M.

1983   Fragments of Possible Counting and Recording Devices. *Origini*
[1988]   12:511–21.

1998   *Uruk, la prima citta.* Roma-Bari: Laterza.

Liverani, M. (editor)

1993   *Akkad: The First World Empire.* Padua: Sargon srl.

Lloyd, S.

1940   Iraqi Government Soundings at Sinjar. *Iraq* 6:13–21.

Lloyd, S., and F. Safar

1943   Tell Uqair: Excavations by the Iraq Government Directorate of Antiquities in 1940 and 1941. *Journal of Near Eastern Studies* 2:131–58.

Lupton, A.

1996   *Stability and Change. Socio-political Development in North Mesopotamia and South-East Anatolia, 4000–2700 B.C.* BAR International Series 627. Oxford.

Lüthy, H.

1961   Colonization and the Making of Mankind. *Journal of Economic History* 21:483–95.

Lyonnet, B.

1997   Questions sur l'origine des porteurs de pots en Haute-Mésopotamie du VIe au milieu du IIe Millénaire. *Florilegium marianum* 3:133–44.

Machiavelli, N.

1532   *The Prince,* translated by L. Ricci and E. R. P. Vincent. New York: Random
[1940]   House.

Maekawa, K.

1980   Female Weavers and Their Children in Lagash—Presargonic and Ur III. *Acta Sumerologica* 2:81–125.

Mair, L.

1962   *Primitive Government: A Study of Traditional Political Systems in Eastern Africa.* Glouster, Massachusetts: Peter Smith.

Malinowski, B.

1961   *Argonauts of the Western Pacific.* New York: Dutton.

Mallowan, M.

1933   The Prehistoric Sondage of Nineveh, 1931–32. *Annals of Archaeology and Anthropology* 20:127–77.

1947   Excavations at Tell Brak and Chagar Bazar. *Iraq* 9:1–259.

1970   The Development of Cities from Al 'Ubaid to the End of Uruk 5. *Cambridge Ancient History* I(1):327–462.

Mallowan, M. E. L., and J. C. Rose

1935   Excavations at Tell Arpachiyah. *Iraq* 2:1–178.

Marcus, J.

1992   Dynamic Cycles of Mesoamerican States. *National Geographic Research and Exploration* 8:392–411.

1998   The Peaks and Valleys of Ancient States: An Extension of the Dynamic Model. In *Archaic States,* edited by G. Feinman and J. Marcus, pp. 59–94. Santa Fe: School of American Research Press.

Marcus, J., and K. V. Flannery

1992   Ancient Zapotec Ritual and Religion: An Application of the Direct Historical Method. In *The Ancient Mind,* edited by C. Renfrew and E. B. W. Zubrow, pp. 55–74. Cambridge: Cambridge University Press.

Marcus, M.

1990a   Centre, Province, and Periphery: A New Paradigm from Iron Age Iran. *Art History* 13(2):129–50.

1990b   Emblems of Authority: The Seals and Sealings from Hasanlu IVB. *Expedition* 31(2–3):53–63.

Margueron, J.

1992   Les bois dans l'architecture: premier essai pour une éstimation des besoins dans le bassin mésopotamienne. *Bulletin on Sumerian Architecture* 6:79–96.

Marro, C., and B. Helwing

1995   Vers une chronologie des cultures du Haut-Euphrate au troisième millé-naire. Untersuchungen zur bemalten Keramik des 3. Jt. am oberen und mittleren Euphrat. In *Beiträge zur Kulturgeschichte Vorderasiens: Festschrift für Rainer Michael Boehmer,* edited by U. Finkbeiner, R. Dittmann, and H. Hauptmann, pp. 341–83. Mainz: von Zabern.

Marschner, R. F., and H. T. Wright

1978   Asphalts from Middle Eastern Archeological Sites. In *Archaeological Chemistry 2,* edited by Giles F. Carter, pp. 150–71. Advances in Chemistry, Series 171. Washington, D.C.: American Society of Chemistry.

Matthews, D. M.

1997   *The Early Glyptic of Tell Brak: Cylinder Seals of Third Millennium Syria.* Orbis
        Biblicus et Orientalis 15. Series Archaeologica. Freiburg, Switzerland:
        University Press, and Göttingen, Germany: Vandenhoeck and Ruprecht.

Matthews, R. J.

1990   Excavations at Jemdet Nasr, 1989. *Iraq* 52:25–39.

1995   Excavations at Tell Brak, 1995. *Iraq* 57:87–112.

1996   Excavations at Tell Brak, 1996. *Iraq* 58:65–77.

2000   Fourth and Third Millennia Chronologies: The View from Tell Brak. In
        Chronologies des pays du Caucase et de l'Euphrate aux IVe–IIIe millenaires, edited
        by C. Marro and H. Hauptman, pp. 65–72. Istanbul: French Institute of
        Anatolian Studies.

Matthews, R. J., W. Matthews, and H. McDonald

1994   Excavations at Tell Brak, 1994. *Iraq* 56:177–94.

Matthiae, P.

1977   *Ebla: un impero retrovato.* Turin: Einaudi.

Maxwell-Hyslop, R., J. du Plat Taylor, M. V. Seton-Williams, and J. Waechter

1942–43   An Archaeological Survey of the Plain of Jabbul, 1939. *Palestine Exploration
          Quarterly* 74:8–40.

Mayo, D., and H. Weiss

1998   The Beginning of the Ninevite 5 Sequence at Tell Leilan. Paper presented
        at a conference on the Origins of North Mesopotamian Civilization,
        December 15–19, Yale University.

Mazzoni, S.

1994   Afis. In Archaeology in Syria, edited by H. Weiss. *American Journal of
        Archaeology* 98:146–49.

McCorriston, J.

1997   The Fiber Revolution: Textile Extensification, Alienation, and Social
        Stratification in Ancient Mesopotamia. *Current Anthropology* 38:517–49.

Meijer, D.

1986   *A Survey of Northeastern Syria.* Leiden: Nederlands Historisch-Archeologisch
        Instituut te Istanbul.

Mellaart, J.

1981   The Prehistoric Pottery from the Neolithic to the Beginning of E.B. IV. In
        The River Qoueiq, Northern Syria, and Its Catchment, edited by J. Matthers, pp.
        131–326. BAR International Series 98. Oxford.

Miller, A.

1981   Straw Tempered Wares. In *An Early Town on the Deh Luran Plain:
        Excavations at Tepe Farukhabad,* edited by H. T. Wright, pp. 126–29.
        Memoirs of the Museum of Anthropology, no. 13. Ann Arbor: University
        of Michigan.

Miller, N.

1981   The Plant Remains. In *An Early Town on the Deh Luran Plain: Excavations at Tepe Farukhabad*, edited by H. T. Wright, pp. 227–32. Memoirs of the Museum of Anthropology, no. 13. Ann Arbor: University of Michigan.

1984   The Use of Dung as Fuel: An Ethnographic Example and an Archaeological Application. *Paléorient* 10(2):71–79.

1991   The Near East. In *Progress in Old World Palaeoethnobotany*, edited by Wilhelm Van Zeist, Krystyna Wasylikowa, and Karl-Ernst Behre, pp. 133–60. Rotterdam: A.A. Balekema.

1996   Hacınebi 1993: Archaeobotanical Report. In *Uruk Colonies and Anatolian Communities: An Interim Report on the 1992–93 Excavations at Hacınebi, Turkey*, by G. Stein et al. American Journal of Archaeology 100:205–60.

Millett, M.

1990   *The Romanization of Britain.* Cambridge: Cambridge University Press.

Miroschedji, P. de

1976   Un Four de Potier du IVème Millénaire sur le Tell de l'Apadana de Suse. *Cahiers de la Délégation Archéologique Française en Iran (DAFI)* 6:13–23.

1981   Prospections archeologique au Khuzestan en 1977. In *Cahiers de la Délégation Archéologique Française en Iran (DAFI)* 12:169–92. Paris: Association Paléorient.

Moon, J., and M. Roaf

1984   The Pottery from Tell Madhur. *Sumer* 43(1–2):128–58.

Moore, J.

1996   *Architecture and Power in the Ancient Andes.* Cambridge: Cambridge University Press.

Moore, S. F.

1958   *Power and Property in Inca Peru.* Westport, Connecticut: Greenwood.

Moorey, P. R. S.

1977   What Do We Know about the People in the Royal Cemetery? *Expedition* 20:24–40.

1990   From Gulf to Delta in the Fourth Millennium B.C.E.: The Syrian Connection. In *Eretz-Israel: Archaeological, Historical, and Geographical Studies*, vol. 21, edited by A. Eitan, R. Gophna, and M. Kochavi, pp. 62–69. Jerusalem: Israel Exploration Society.

Moortgat, A.

1945   *Die Entstehung der sumerischen Hochkultur.* Der Alte Orient 43. Leipzig: Hinrichs.

1957   *Archäologische Forschungen der Max Freiherr von Oppenheim-Stiftung im nördlichen Mesopotamien 1956.* Köln und Opladen: Westdeutsche.

1967   *Die Kunst des Alten Mesopotamien.* Köln: DuMont.

Morandi B., D.

1998   The Beginning of the Early Bronze Age at Tell Shiukh Fawqani in the Upper Syrian Euphrates. Paper presented at the First International Conference on the Archaeology of the Ancient Near East. Rome.

Morris, I.

1997   An Archaeology of Equalities? The Greek City-States. In *The Archaeology of City-States: Cross-Cultural Approaches,* edited by Deborah L. Nichols and Thomas H. Charlton, pp. 91–106. Washington, D.C.: Smithsonian Institution Press.

Morrison, K., and M. Lycett

1994   Centralized Power, Centralized Authority? Ideological Claims and Archaeological Patterns. *Asian Perspectives* 33:327–50.

Moseley, M. E.

1975   *The Maritime Foundations of Andean Civilization.* Menlo Park, California: Cummings.

Murra, J. V.

1980   *The Economic Organization of the Inka State.* Greenwich, Connecticut:
[1956]   JAI Press.

Murúa, Fray M.

1986   *Historia general del Perú,* edited by M. Ballesteros. Crónicas de América 35.
[ca. 1605] Madrid: Historia 16.

Nadel, S. F.

1940   The Kede: A Riverain State in Northern Nigeria. In *African Political Systems,* edited by M. Fortes and E. E. Evans Pritchard, pp. 164–95. Oxford: Oxford University Press.

Neely, J. A., and H. T. Wright

1994   *Early Settlement and Irrigation on the Deh Luran Plain: Village and Early State Societies in Southwestern Iran.* Technical Report of the Museum of Anthropology 26. Ann Arbor: University of Michigan.

Neumann, H.

1999   Ur-Dumuzida and Ur-DUN. Reflections on the Relationship between State-Initiated Foreign Trade and Private Economic Activity in Mesopotamia towards the End of the Third Millennium B.C. In *Trade and Finance in Ancient Mesopotamia,* edited by J. G. Derksen, pp. 43–54. Leiden: Nederlands Historisch-Archeologisch Instituut te Istanbul.

Nichols, D. L., and T. H. Charlton

1997   *The Archaeology of City-States: Cross-Cultural Approaches.* Washington, D.C.: Smithsonian Institution Press.

Nishiaki, Y.

1999   Tell Kosak Shamali: Preliminary Report of the Excavations. In *Archaeology of the Upper Syrian Euphrates: The Tishreen Dam Area,* edited by G. Del Olmo Lete and J.-L. Montero Fenollós, pp. 71–82. Barcelona: Editorial Ausa.

Nishiaki, Y., T. Koizumi, M. le Mière, and T. Oguchi

2000   Prehistoric Occupations at Tell Kosak Shamali, the Upper Euphrates, Syria. *Akkadica* 113:13–68.

Nissen, H-J.

1970   Grabung in den Planquadraten K/L XII in Uruk-Warka. *Baghdader Mitteilungen* 5:101–92.

1972   The City Wall of Uruk. In *Man, Settlement and Urbanism,* edited by P. J. Ucko et al., pp. 793–98. London: Duckworth.

1974   Zur Frage der Arbeitsorganisation in Babylonien während der Späturuk-Zeit. In *Wirtschaft und Gesellschaft in Alten Vorderasien,* edited by J. Harmatta and G. Komaróoczy, pp. 5–14. Acta Antiqua Academiae Scientiarum Hungaricae 22. Budapest: Akadémia Kiadó.

1977   Aspects of the Development of Early Cylinder Seals. In *Seals and Sealings in the Ancient Near East,* edited by McG. Gibson and R. Biggs, pp. 15–24. Malibu, California: Undena Press.

1983   Political Organization and Settled Zone. In *The Hilly Flanks and Beyond,* edited by T. C. Young, P. E. L. Smith, and P. Mortensen, pp. 335–46. Chicago: Oriental Institute.

1985a   The Emergence of Writing in the Ancient Near East. *Interdisciplinary Science Reviews* 10:349–61.

1985b   Problems of the Uruk Period in Susiana, Viewed from Uruk. *Paléorient* 11(2):39–40.

1985c   Ortsnamen in den archaischen Texten aus Uruk. *Orientalia* 54:226–33.

1986a   The Development of Writing and of Glyptic Art. In *Ğamdat Naṣr: Period or Regional Style?* edited by U. Finkbeiner and W. Rollig, pp. 316–31. Wiesbaden: Beihefte zum Tübinger Atlas des Vorderen Orients, Reihe B, no. 62.

1986b   The Archaic Texts from Uruk. *World Archaeology* 17:317–34.

1987   The Chronology of the Proto- and Early Historic Periods in Mesopotamia and Susiana. In *Chronologies du Proche Orient,* edited by O. Aurenche, J. Evin, and F. Hours, pp. 607–14. Oxford: BAR International.

1988   *The Early History of the Ancient Near East.* Chicago: University of Chicago Press.

1989   The Ubaid Period in the Context of the Early History of the Ancient Near East. In *Upon This Foundation,* edited by E. F. Henrickson and I. Thuesen, pp. 245–55. Copenhagen: Carsten Niebuhr Institute.

1993a   The Context of the Emergence of Writing in Mesopotamia and Iran. In *Early Mesopotamia and Iran: Contact and Conflict 3500–1600 B.C.,* edited by J. Curtis, pp. 54–71. London: British Museum.

1993b   The Early Uruk Period, A Sketch. In *Between the Rivers and over the Mountains,* edited by M. Frangipane, H. Hauptmann, M. Liverani, P. Matthiae, and M. Mellink, pp. 123–32. Università di Roma "La Sapienza."

1993c   Settlement Patterns and Material Culture of the Akkadian Period: Continuity and Discontinuity. In *Akkad, The First World Empire*, edited by M. Liverani, pp. 91–106. Padova: Sargon srl.

1998   Uruk: Key Site of the Period and Key Site of the Problem. Paper presented at the conference on "Artefacts of Complexity: Tracking the Uruk in the Near East," November 6–7, Manchester.

1999   *Geschichte Alt-Vorderasiens*. München: Oldenbourg.

Nissen, H-J., P. Damerow, and R. K. Englund

1993   *Archaic Bookkeeping*. Chicago: University of Chicago Press.

Numoto, H.

1991   Painted Designs of the Ninevite 5 Pottery. *Al-Rafidan* 12:85–155.

1993   Incised and Excised Designs of the Ninevite 5 Pottery. *Al-Rafidan* 14:69–108.

Nützel, W.

1976   The Climate Changes of Mesopotamia and Bordering Areas. *Sumer* 32:11–25.

Oates, D.

1982   Excavations at Tell Brak, 1978–81. *Iraq* 44:187–219.

Oates, D., and J. Oates

1976   Early Irrigation Agriculture in Mesopotamia. In *Problems in Economic and Social Archaeology*, edited by G. Sieveking, I. Longworth, and K. Wilson, pp. 109–35. London: Duckworth.

1991   Excavations at Tell Brak 1990–91. *Iraq* 53:127–45.

1993a   Excavations at Tell Brak 1992–93. *Iraq* 55:155–99.

1993b   Excavations at Tell Brak, Northeast Syria, 1992. *Cambridge Archaeological Journal* 3:129–40.

1994   Tell Brak: A Stratigraphic Summary, 1976–93. *Iraq* 56:152–79.

Oates, J.

1960   Ur and Eridu, The Prehistory. *Iraq* 22:32–50.

1983   Ubaid Mesopotamia Reconsidered. In *The Hilly Flanks and Beyond*, pp. 251–82. Studies in Ancient Oriental Civilization 36. Chicago: Oriental Institute.

1987   A Note on Ubaid and Mitanni Pottery from Tell Brak. *Iraq* 49:193–98.

1993   Trade and Power in the Fifth and Fourth Millennia B.C.: New Evidence from Northern Mesopotamia. *World Archaeology* 24:403–22.

Oates, J., and D. Oates

1997   An Open Gate: Cities of the Fourth Millennium B.C. (Tell Brak 1997). *Cambridge Archaeological Journal* 7:287–307.

Oguchi, H.

1987   Tell Musharifa. In *Researches on the Antiquities of Saddam Dam Basin Salvage and Other Researches*, pp. 49–54. Baghdad: Republic of Iraq Ministry of Culture and Information.

Oldenburg, E.

1991   *Sukas IX: The Chalcolithic and Early Bronze Periods.* Copenhagen: Munksgaard.

Oppenheim, A. L.

1977   *Ancient Mesopotamia.* Chicago: University of Chicago Press.

Ortiz de Zúñiga, I.

1967   *Visita de la Provincia de León de Huánuco en 1562,* edited by J. V. Murra,
[1562]   vol. 1: Huánuco. Perú: Universidad Nacional Hermilio Valdizán.

1972   *Visita de la Provincia de León de Huánuco en 1562,* edited by J. V. Murra,
[1562]   vol. 2: Huánuco. Perú: Universidad Nacional Hermilio Valdizán.

Özbal, H.

1996   Chemical Analysis of a Copper Chisel from Hacınebi Tepe. *Anatolica* 22:109–10.

1997   Early Metal Technology at Hacınebi Tepe. In Excavations at Hacınebi, Turkey, 1996: Preliminary Report, by G. Stein, K. Boden, C. Edens, J. Edens, K. Keith, A. McMahon, and H. Özbal. *Anatolica* 23:139–43.

Özbal, H., A. Adriaens, and B. Earl

1999   Hacınebi Metal Production and Exchange. *Paléorient* 25(1):57–65.

Özbal, H., B. Earl, and M. Adriaens

1998   Early Fourth Millennium Copper Metallurgy at Hacınebi. In Excavations at Hacınebi, Turkey, 1996: Preliminary Report, by G. Stein, K. Boden, C. Edens, J. Edens, K. Keith, A. McMahon, and H. Özbal. *Anatolica* 24:167–70.

Özdogan, M.

1977   *Lower Euphrates Basin Survey, 1977.* Istanbul: Middle Eastern Technical University.

Özguç, N.

1992   The Uruk Culture at Samsat. In *Von Uruk nach Tuttul,* edited by B. Hrouda, S. Kroll, and P. Spanos, pp. 151–65. München: Profil.

Özten, A.

1984   Two Pots Recovered in the Excavations at Samsat belonging to the Late Chalcolithic Period. *Anadolu* 20:261–69.

Palmieri, A.

1985   Eastern Anatolia and Early Mesopotamian Urbanization: Remarks on Changing Relations. In *Studi di Paletnologia in Onore di Salvatore,* edited by M. Puglisi, M. Liverani, A. Palmieri, and R. Peroni, pp. 191–213. Università di Roma "La Sapienza."

1989   Storage and Distribution at Arslantepe-Malatya in the Late Uruk Period. In *Anatolia and the Ancient Near East: Studies in Honor of Tahsin Özgüç,* edited by K. Emre, M. Mellink, B. Hrouda, and N. Özguç, pp. 419–29. Ankara: Türk Tarih Kurumu.

Palmieri, A., and M. Frangipane

1989   The 1988 Campaign at Arslantepe, Malatya. *Kazı Sonuçları Toplantısı* 11:191–201.

Palmieri, A., and K. Sertok

1993   Minerals in and around Arslantepe. *Arkeometri Sonuçları Toplantısı* 9:119–36.

Palmieri, A., K. Sertok, and E. Chernykh

1993   From Arslantepe Metalwork to Arsenical Copper Technology in Eastern Anatolia. In *Between the Rivers and over the Mountains,* edited by M. Frangipane, H. Hauptmann, M. Liverani, P. Matthiae, and M. Mellink, pp. 573–99. Università di Roma "La Sapienza."

Palmieri, A., A. Hauptmann, K. Hess, and K. Sertok

1995   Archaeometallurgical Survey in 1994 at Malatya-Arslantepe and Its Surroundings. *Arkeometri Sonuçları Toplantısı* 11:105–15.

Patterson, T. C.

1991   The Huaca La Florida, Rimac Valley, Peru. In *Early Ceremonial Architecture in the Andes,* edited by C. B. Donnan, pp. 59–70. Washington, D.C.: Dumbarton Oaks.

Payne, S.

1988   The Animal Bones from Tell Rubeidheh. In *Tell Rubeidheh: An Uruk Village in the Jebel Hamrin,* edited by R. J. Killick, pp. 98–135. Warminster: Aris & Phillips.

Paynter, R.

1981   Social Complexity in Peripheries: Problems and Models. In *Archaeological Approaches to the Study of Complexity,* edited by S. E. van der Leeuw, pp. 118–43. Amsterdam: University of Amsterdam.

Pearce, J.

1996   Phase B Ceramics. In Hacınebi, Turkey: Preliminary Report on the 1995 Excavations, by Gil J. Stein, Christopher Edens, Hadi Özbal, Julie Pearce, and Holly Pittman. *Anatolica* 22:100–4.

Pearsall, D., and D. Piperno (editors)

1993   *Current Research in Phytolith Analysis.* MASCA Research Papers in Science and Archaeology 10. Philadelphia: University of Pennsylvania Museum.

Pease, F.

1982   The Formation of Tawantisuyu: Mechanisms of Colonization and Relationship with Ethnic Groups. In *The Inca and Aztec States, 1400–1800,* edited by G. Collier, R. Rosaldo, and J. Wirth, pp. 173–198. New York: Academic Press.

Peasnall, B.

n.d.   Burials from Tepe Gawra. In *Tepe Gawra: The Evolution of a Small, Prehistoric Center in Northern Iraq,* by M. Rothman, Appendix. Philadelphia: University of Pennsylvania Museum. In press.

Peebles, C., and S. Kus

1977   Some Archaeological Correlates of Ranked Societies. *American Antiquity* 42:421–48.

Peltenburg, E.

1999   Tell Jerablus Tahtani 1992–96: A Summary. In *Archaeology of the Upper Syrian Euphrates: The Tishrin Dam Area. Proceedings of a Symposium Held at Barcelona, January 28–30, 1998,* edited by G. del Olmo Lete and J.-L. Montero Fenollós, pp. 97–105. Barcelona: Editorial AUSA.

Peltenburg, E., D. Bolger, S. Campbell, M. Murray, and R. Tipping

1996   Jerablus Tahtani, Syria, 1995: Preliminary Report. *Levant* 28:1–25.

Peltenburg, E., S. Campbell, P. Croft, D. Lunt, M. Murray, and M. Watt

1995   Jerablus Tahtani, Syria, 1992–94: Preliminary Report. *Levant* 27:1–28.

Peregrine, P.

1996   Introduction: World-Systems Theory and Archaeology. In *Pre-Columbian World Systems,* edited by P. Peregrine and G. Feinman, pp. 1–10. Madison, Wisconsin: Prehistory Press.

Pernicka, E., T. Rehren, and I. Schmitt-Strecker

1998   Late Uruk Silver Production by Cupellation at Habuba Kabira, Syria. In *Metallurgica Antiqua,* in Honor of G.-G. Bachmann and R. Maddin, pp. 123–34. Bochum: Deutsches Bergbau-Museum.

Pettinato, G.

1972   Il commercio con l'estero della Mesopotamia meridionale nel 3 millennio av. Cr. alla luce delle fonti letterarie e lessicali sumeriche. *Mesopotamia* 7:43–166.

1979   *Un impero inciso nell'argilla.* Mailand: Mondadori.

Pfälzner, P.

1984   Eine archäologische Geländebegehung in Gebiet des Wadi 'Agig/Ost Syrien. *Archiv für Orientforschung* 31:178–84.

1990   Tell Bderi, The Development of a Bronze Age Town. In *The Near East in Antiquity I,* edited by S. Kerner, pp. 63–80. German Contributions to the Archaeology of Jordan, Palestine, Syria, Lebanon and Egypt. Amman: Goethe-Institut, Al Kutba Publishers.

1997   Wandel und Kontinuität im Urbanisierungsprozess des 3 Jtsds. v. Chr. in Nordmesopotamien. In *Die Orientalische Stadt: Kontinuität, Wandel, Bruch,* edited by G. Wilhelm, pp. 239–65. Internationales Colloquium der Deutschen Orient-Gesellschaft, 9–10 Mai 1996, in Halle/Saale. Saarbrücken: Saarbrücker Druckerei und Verlag.

Pittman, H.

1993   Pictures of an Administration: The Late Uruk Scribe at Work. In *Between the Rivers and over the Mountains,* edited by M. Frangipane, H. Hauptmann, M. Liverani, P. Matthiae, and M. Mellink, pp. 235–46. Università di Roma "La Sapienza."

1994a   Towards an Understanding of the Role of Glyptic Imagery in the Administrative Systems of Proto-literate Greater Mesopotamia. In *Archives before Writing*, edited by P. Ferioli, E. Fiandra, G. Fissore, and M. Frangipane, pp. 177–204. Università di Roma "La Sapienza."

1994b   *The Glazed Steatite Glyptic Style.* Berliner Beitr. zum Vorderen Orient 15. Berlin: Reimer.

1996a   Preliminary Report on the Administrative Artifacts: Hacınebi Tepe 1995 Season. In Hacınebi, Turkey: Preliminary Report on the 1995 Excavations, by Gil J. Stein, Christopher Edens, Hadi Özbal, Julie Pearce, and Holly Pittman. *Anatolica* 22:98–100.

1996b   Preliminary Report on the Glyptic Art: Hacınebi, 1993. In Uruk Colonies and Mesopotamian Communities: An Interim Report on the 1992–93 Excavations at Hacınebi, Turkey, by Gil Stein et al. *American Journal of Archaeology* 100:230–33.

1998   Preliminary Comments on the Glyptic Found in the 1997 Season at Hacınebi Tepe. In Southeast Anatolia before the Uruk Expansion: Preliminary Report on the 1997 Excavations at Hacınebi, Turkey, by G. Stein, C. Edens, J. Edens, K. Boden, H. Özbal, B. Earl, M. Adriaens, and H. Pittman. *Anatolica* 24:170–73.

Pliny
1931   *Natural History,* translated by John Bostock and H. T. Riley. London: Henry G. Bohn.

Polanyi, K.
1957   The Economy as Instituted Process. In *Trade and Market in the Early Empires,* edited by K. Polanyi, C. Arensberg, and H. W. Pearson, pp. 243–69. Chicago: Henry Regnery.

Pollock, S.
1983   *The Symbolism of Prestige: An Archaeological Example from the Royal Cemetery of Ur.* Doctoral dissertation, University of Michigan. Ann Arbor: University Microfilms.

1987   Abu Salabikh, The Uruk Mound, 1985–86. *Iraq* 49:121–41.

1990   Archaeological Investigations on the Uruk Mound, Abu Salabikh, Iraq. *Iraq* 52:85–93.

1992   Bureaucrats and Managers, Peasants and Pastoralists, Imperialists and Traders: Research on the Uruk and Jemdet Nasr Periods in Mesopotamia. *Journal of World Prehistory* 6:297–336.

1994   Review of G. Algaze's "The Uruk World System—The Dynamics of Expansion of Early Mesopotamian Civilization." *Science* 264:1481–82.

1999   *Ancient Mesopotamia.* Cambridge: Cambridge University Press.

Pollock, S., and R. Bernbeck
2000   And They Said, Let Us Make Gods in Our Image: Gendered Ideologies in Ancient Mesopotamia. In *Reading the Body: Representations and Remains in the Archaeological Record,* edited by Alison Rautman, pp. 150–64. Philadelphia: University of Pennsylvania Press.

Pollock, S., and C. Coursey

1995   Ceramics from Hacınebi Tepe: Chronology and Connections. *Anatolica* 21:101–41.

1996   Hacınebi Uruk Pottery: Preliminary Report. In Uruk Colonies and Mesopotamian Communities: An Interim Report on the 1992–3 Excavations at Hacınebi, Turkey, by G. J. Stein et al., pp. 233–39. *American Journal of Archaeology* 100:205–60.

Pollock, S., M. Pope, and C. Coursey

1996   Household Production at the Uruk Mound: Abu Salabikh. Iraq. *American Journal of Archaeology* 100:683–98.

Pollock, S., C. Steele, and M. Pope

1991   Investigations on the Uruk Mound, Abu Salabikh, 1990. *Iraq* 53:59–68.

Polo de Ondegardo, J.

1916   Relación de los fundamentos acerca del notable daño que resulta de no

[1571]   guardar a los indios sus fueros. In *Collección de Libros y Documentos Referentes a la Historia de Perú,* edited by H. H. Urteaga, vol. 3, pp. 45–188. Lima: Sanmartí.

Pool, C.

1992   Strangers in a Strange Land: Ethnicity and Ideology at an Enclave Community in Middle Classic Mesoamerica. In *Ancient Images, Ancient Thought: The Archaeology of Ideology,* edited by A. S. Goldsmith, pp. 41–55. Calgary: University of Calgary.

Pope, M., and S. Pollock

1995   Trade, Tools, and Tasks: A Study of Uruk Chipped Stone Industries. In *Research in Economic Anthropology,* vol. 16, edited by Barry Isaac, pp. 227–65. Greenwich, Connecticut: JAI Press.

Porada, E.

1965   The Relative Chronology of Mesopotamia, Part I. Seals and Trade (6000–1600 B.C.). In *Chronologies in Old World Archaeology,* edited by Robert Ehrich, pp. 133–81. Chicago: University of Chicago Press.

Porada, E., D. Hansen, S. Dunham, and S. Babcock

1992   Mesopotamian Chronologies, 7000–1600 B.C. In *Chronologies in Old World Archaeology,* third ed., edited by Robert W. Ehrich, pp. 77–121. Chicago: University of Chicago Press.

Postgate, J. N.

1983   *The West Mound Surface Clearance.* Abu Salabikh Excavations 1. London: British School of Archaeology in Iraq.

1986   The Transition from Uruk to Early Dynastic: Continuities and Discontinuities in the Record of Settlement. In *Ğamdat Naṣr: Period or Regional Style?* edited by U. Finkbeiner and W. Röllig, pp. 90–106. Wiesbaden: Ludwig Reichert.

1988   A View from down the Euphrates. In *Wirstchaft und Gessellschaft von Ebla*, edited by H. Waetzoldt and H. Hauptmann, pp. 111–20. Heidelberg: Orientverlag.

1994   How Many Sumerians per Hectare? Probing the Anatomy of an Early City. Cambridge *Archaeological Journal* 4:47–65.

Postgate, J. N., and J. Moon

1982   Excavations at Abu Salabikh, 1981. *Iraq* 44:103–36.

Potts, D. T.

1975   *The Late Fourth Millennium Universe of a Highland Community in Iran: Problems of Proto-Elam and Jamdat Nasr Mesopotamia.* Doctoral dissertation, Harvard University. Ann Arbor: University Microfilms.

1990   *The Arabian Gulf in Antiquity.* Oxford: Clarendon Press.

1997   *Mesopotamian Civilization: The Material Foundations.* Ithaca: Cornell University Press.

Powell, M.

1985   Salt, Seed, and Yields in Sumerian Agriculture. A Critique of the Theory of Progressive Salinization. *Zeitschrift für Assyriologie* 75:7–38.

Pozorski, S., and T. Pozorski

1991   Storage, Access Control, and Bureaucratic Proliferation: Understanding the Initial Period Economy at Pampa de las Llamas-Moxeke, Casma Valley, Peru. *Research in Economic Anthropology* 13:341–71.

1993   Early Complex Society and Ceremonialism on the Peruvian North Coast. In *El Mundo Ceremonial Andino,* edited by L. Millones and Y. Onuki, pp. 45–68. Senri Ethnological Studies, no. 37. Osaka, Japan: National Museum of Ethnology.

Prag, K.

1978   Silver in the Levant in the Fourth Millennium B.C. In *Archaeology in the Levant,* edited by P. R. S. Moorey and P. J. Parr, pp. 36–45. Warminster: Aris and Phillips.

1986   Byblos and Egypt in the Fourth Millennium B.C. *Levant* 18:59–74.

Price, B. J.

1984   Competition, Productive Intensification, and Ranked Society: Speculations from Evolutionary Theory. In *Warfare, Culture, and Environment,* edited by B. J. Ferguson, pp. 209–40. New York: Academic Press.

Rashad, M.

1990   Die Entwicklung der vor- und frühgeschichtlichen Stempelsiegel. In *Iran: im Vergleich mit Mesopotamien, Syrien und Kleinasien, von ihren Anfängen bis zum Beginn des 3. Jahrtausends v. Chr.* Archäologische Mitteilungen aus Iran, Ergänzungsband 13. Berlin: D. Reimer.

Ray, A.

1978   History and Archaeology of the Northern Fur Trade. *American Antiquity* 43:26–34.

Redman, C. L.

1978   *The Rise of Civilization: From Early Farmer to Urban Society in the Ancient Near East.* San Francisco: W.H. Freeman.

Renfrew, C.

1986   Introduction: Peer Polity Interaction and Socio-political Change. In *Peer Polity Interaction and Socio-political Change*, edited by C. Renfrew and J. F. Cherry, pp. 1–18. Cambridge: Cambridge University Press.

Rieth, A.

1960   *5000 Jahre Töpferscheibe.* Konstanz: Thorbecke.

Roaf, M.

1984   The Stratigraphy and Architecture of Tell Madhur. *Sumer* 43:110–26.

1990   *Cultural Atlas of Mesopotamia and the Ancient Near East.* New York: Facts-on-File.

Roaf, M.

1998   A Group of Pottery from Mohammad Arab Period I. In *About Subartu* VI(1), edited by M. LeBreu, pp. 131–49. Turnhout, Belgium: Brepolis.

Rogers, J. D.

1990   *Objects of Change: The Archaeology and History of Arikara Contact with Europeans.* Washington, D.C.: Smithsonian Institution Press.

Röllig, W., and H. Kühne

1978–79 The Lower Habur: A Preliminary Report on a Survey Conducted by the Tübinger Atlas des Vorderen Orients in 1975. *Annales archéologiques arabes syriennes* 27–28:115–40.

Rosen, A. M.

1989   Environmental Change at the End of the Early Bronze Age in Palestine. In L'urbanisation de la Palestine à l'age du Bronze ancien, edited by Pierre de Miroschedji, pp. 247–55. Oxford: British Archaeological Reports.

1997   Geoarchaeology of Holocene Environments and Land-Use at Kazane Höyük, Southeast Turkey. *Geoarcheology* 12:395–416.

Rossmann, D.

1976   A Site Catchment Analysis of San Lorenzo, Veracruz. In *The Early Mesoamerican Village*, edited by Kent Flannery, pp. 95–103. New York: Academic Press.

Rostovtzeff, M. I.

1938   *Dura Europos and Its Art.* Oxford: Oxford University Press.

Rothman, M. S.

1987   Graph Theory and the Interpretation of Regional Survey Data. *Paléorient* 13(2):73–92.

1988   *Centralization, Administration and Function at Fourth Millennium B.C. Tepe Gawra, Northern Iraq.* Doctoral dissertation, University of Pennsylvania.

1993   Another Look at the Uruk Expansion from the Zagros Piedmont. In *Between the Rivers and over the Mountains,* edited by M. Frangipane, H. Hauptmann, M. Liverani, P. Matthiae, and M. Mellink, pp. 163–76. Università di Roma "La Sapienza."

1994a   Seal and Sealing Findspot, Design Audience, and Function: Monitoring Changes in Administrative Oversight and Structure at Tepe Gawra during the Fourth Millennium B.C. In *Archives before Writing,* edited by P. Ferioli, E. Fiandra, G. Fissore, and M. Frangipane, pp. 97–119. Rome: Scriptorium.

1994b   Sealings as a Control Mechanism in Prehistory. In *Chiefdoms and Early States in the Near East,* edited by G. Stein and M. Rothman, pp. 103–20. Madison, Wisconsin: Prehistory Press.

1994c   Palace and Private Agricultural Decision-making in the Early 2nd Millennium B.C. City-State of Larsa, Iraq. In *The Economic Anthropology of the State,* edited by E. Brumfiel, pp. 149–67. Monographs in Economic Anthropology, no. 11. Lanham, Maryland: University Press of America.

2000   The Commoditization of Goods and the Rise of the State in Mesopotamia. In *Commodities and Globalization,* edited by A. Haugerud, P. Stone, and P. Little, pp. 163–78. Lanham, Maryland: University Press of America.

n.d.   *Tepe Gawra: The Evolution of a Small, Prehistoric Center in Northern Iraq.* Philadelphia: University of Pennsylvania Museum. In press.

Rothman, M., and M. J. Blackman

1990   Monitoring Administrative Spheres of Action in Late Prehistoric Northern Mesopotamia with the Aid of Chemical Characterization (INAA) of Sealing Clays. In *Economy and Settlement in the Near East: Analyses of Ancient Sites and Materials,* edited by Naomi Miller, pp. 19–45. MASCA Research Papers in Science and Archaeology 7 (supplement). Philadelphia: University of Pennsylvania Museum.

Rothman, M. (editor)

1989   Out of the Heartland: The Evolution of Complexity in Peripheral Mesopotamia during the Uruk Period. *Paléorient* 15(1):279–90.

Rothman, M., and B. Peasnall

1999   Societal Evolution of Small, Pre-State Centers and Polities: The Example of Tepe Gawra in Northern Mesopotamia. In The Uruk Expansion: Northern Perspectives from Hacınebi, Hassek Höyük, and Gawra, edited by G. Stein, pp. 101–14. *Paléorient* 25(1).

Rothman, M., R. Ergeç, M. Miller, J. Weber, and G. Kozbe

1998   Yarım Höyük and the Uruk Expansion, Part I. *Anatolica* 24:65–99.

Rothschild, N. A.

1990   *New York City Neighborhoods: The 18th Century.* San Diego: Academic Press.

Rouault, O., and M. Grazia Masetti-Rouault (editors)

1993   *L'Eufrate e il Tempo: La Civiltà del Medio Eufrate e della Gezira Siriana.* Milan: Electa.

Roux, V., and M.-A. Courty

1997   Les bols elaborées au tour d'Abou Hamid: rupture technique au 4e millénaire avant J.-C. dans le Levant-Sud. *Paléorient* 23(1):25–43.

Rova, E.

1988   *Distribution and Chronology of the Nineveh 5 Pottery and of Its Culture.* Rome:
Contributi e Materiali di Archeologia Orientale 2. Università degli Studi di
Roma "La Sapienza."

1996   Ceramic Provinces along the Middle and Upper Euphrates: Late
Chalcolithic–Early Bronze Age, A Diachronic View. *Baghdader
Mitteilungen* 27:13–37.

n.d.   A Tentative Synchronization of the Local Late Chalcolithic Ceramic
Horizons of Northern Syro-Mesopotamia. *Mesopotamia.* In press.

Rowe, J.

1982   Inca Policies and Institutions Relating to the Cultural Unification of the
Empire. In *The Inca and Aztec States, 1400–1800: Anthropology and History,*
edited by G. A. Collier, R. I. Rosaldo, and J. D. Wirth, pp. 93–118. New
York: Academic Press.

Rowe, J. H.

1946   Inca Culture at the Time of the Spanish Conquest. In *Handbook of South
American Indians,* edited by Julian Steward. Bureau of American Ethnology
Bulletin 143, vol. 2, pp. 183–330. Washington, D.C.

Sabloff, J. A.

1990   *The New Archaeology and the Ancient Maya.* New York: W.H. Freeman.

Safar, F., M. A. Mustafa, and S. Lloyd

1981   *Eridu.* Baghdad: State Organization of Antiquities and Heritage.

Saggs, H. W.

1962   *The Greatness That Was Babylon.* New York: New American Library.

Sahlins, M.

1990   The Political Economy of Grandeur in Hawaii from 1810 to 1830. In
Culture through Time: Anthropological Approaches, edited by E. Ohnuki-
Tierney, pp. 26–56. Stanford: Stanford University Press.

Sanlaville, P.

1989   Considérations sur l'évolution de la Basse Mesopotamie. *Paléorient*
15(2):5–27.

Santillán, H. de

1927   Historia de los Incas y relación de su gobierno. In *Colección de libros y*
[1563]   *documentos referentes a la historia del Perú,* edited by H. H. Urteaga, Tome IX
(2ª serie). Lima: Sanmartí y cia.

Santley, R., C. Yarborough, and B. Hall

1987   Enclaves, Ethnicity, and the Archaeological Record at Matacapan. In
Ethnicity and Culture, edited by R. Auger, M. Glass, S. MacEachern, and P.
NacCartney, pp. 85–100. Calgary: Archaeology Association of the
University of Calgary.

Santley, R. S., and R. Alexander
1992   The Political Economy of Core Periphery Systems. In *Resources, Power, and Interregional Interaction*, edited by E. M. Shortman and P. A. Urban, pp. 23–50. New York: Plenum.

Sauren, H.
1966   *Topographie der Provinz Umma nach der Urkunden der Zeit III. Dynastie von Ur, I: Kanale und Bewässerunsanlagen*. Bamberg: K. Urlaub.

Scammell, G. V.
1989   *The First Imperial Age*. London: Unwin Hyman.

Schacht, R.
1976   Some Notes on the Development of Rural Settlement on the Susiana Plain. *Proceedings of the 4th Annual Symposium on Archaeological Research in Iran, 1975*, pp. 446–62. Teheran: Iranian Center for Archaeological Research.

1981   Estimating Past Population Trends. *Annual Review of Anthropology* 10:119–40.

1984   The Contemporaneity Problem. *American Antiquity* 49:678–95.

Schmandt-Besserat, D.
1978   The Earliest Precursor of Writing. In *Hunters, Farmers, and Civilizations: Old World Archaeology*, edited by C. C. Lamberg-Karlovsky, pp. 152–61. San Francisco: W.H. Freeman.

1981   From Tokens to Tablets: A Re-evaluation of the So-called Numerical Tablets. *Visible Language* 15:321–44.

1993   Images of Enship. In *Between the Rivers and over the Mountains*, edited by M. Frangipane, H. Hauptmann, M. Liverani, P. Matthiae, and M. Mellink, pp. 201–20. Universitá di Roma "La Sapienza."

Schmid, J. G.
1980   *Die Madrasa des Kalifen al-Mustansir in Baghdad*. Bagh. Forschungen 4. Mainz: von Zabern.

1992   Zur inneren Organisation früher mesopotamischer Palastbauten. In *Von Uruk nach Tuttul*, edited by B. Hrouda, S. Kroll, P. Z. Spanos, pp. 185–92. München: Profil.

Schmidt, H.
1943   *Tell Halaf I: Die prähistorischen Funde*. Berlin: de Gruyter.

Schneider, J.
1977   Was There a Pre-Capitalist World-System? *Peasant Studies* 6:20–29.

Schortman, E., and P. Urban
1994   Living on the Edge: Core-Periphery Relations in Ancient Southeastern Mesoamerica. *Current Anthropology* 35:401–30.

Schwartz, G.
1985   The Ninevite V Period and Current Research. *Paléorient* 11:53–70.

1987   The Ninevite V Period and the Development of Complex Society in Northern Mesopotamia. *Paléorient* 13:93–100.

1988a   *A Ceramic Chronology from Tell Leilan: Operation 1.* Yale Tell Leilan Research, vol. 1. New Haven and London: Yale University Press.

1988b   Excavations at Karatut Mevkii and Perspectives on the Uruk/Jemdet Nasr Expansion. *Akkadica* 56:1–41.

1989   Comment on The Uruk Expansion: Cross-Cultural Exchange in Early Mesopotamian Civilization. *Current Anthropology* 30:596–7.

1994a   Before Ebla: Models of Pre-State Political Organization in Syria and Northern Mesopotamia. In *Chiefdoms and Early States in the Near East: The Organizational Dynamics of Complexity,* edited by G. Stein and M. Rothman, pp. 153–74. Madison, Wisconsin: Prehistory Press.

1994b   Rural Economic Specialization and Early Urbanization in the Khabur Valley, Syria. In *Archaeological Views from the Countryside,* edited by G. Schwartz and S. Falconer, pp. 19–36. Washington, D.C.: Smithsonian Institution Press.

Schwartz, G. M., and H. H. Curvers

1992   Tell al-Raqa'i 1989 and 1990: Further Investigations at a Small Rural Site of Early Urban Northern Mesopotamia. *American Journal of Archaeology* 96:397–419.

Schwartz, G. M., and S. Falconer

1994   Rural Approaches to Social Complexity. In *Archaeological Views from the Countryside,* edited by G. M. Schwartz and S. E. Falconer, pp. 1–9. Washington, D.C.: Smithsonian Institution Press.

Schwartz, G., H. Curvers, F. Gerritsen, J. MacCormack, N. Miller, and J. Weber

2000   Excavation and Regional Analysis in the Jabbul Plain, Western Syria: The Umm el-Marra Project, 1996–97. *American Journal of Archaeology* 104:419–62.

Schwartz, M., D. Hollander, and G. Stein

1999   Reconstructing Mesopotamian Exchange Networks in the 4th Millennium B.C.: Geochemical and Archaeological Analyses of Bitumen Artifacts from Hacınebi, Turkey. *Paléorient* 25(1):67–82.

Seeden, H.

1991   Nustell, Zaghan, Hwesh. In Archaeology in Syria, edited by H. Weiss. *American Journal of Archaeology* 95:692–95.

Seeliger, T. C., E. Pernicka, G. A. Wagner, F. Begemann, S. Schmit Strecker, C. Eibner, Ö. Öztunali, and Istvan Beranyi

1985   Archäometallurgische Untersuchungen in Nord- und Ostanatolien. *Jahrbuch des Römisch-Germanischen Zentralmuseums Mainz* 32:597–659.

Sherratt, S., and A. Sherratt

1993   The Growth of the Mediterranean Economy in the Early First Millennium B.C. *World Archaeology* 24:361–78.

Shimada, I.

1994   *Pampa Grande and the Mochica Culture.* University of Texas Press, Austin.

n.d.   Organizational Significance of Marked Bricks and Associated Features on the North Peruvian Coast. In *Arquitectura y civilizaciones en los Andes prehispánicos,* edited by Elisabeth Bonnier. Lima: Instituto Francés de Estudios Andinos. In press.

Simpson, K.

1988   *Qraya Modular Reports, no. 1: Early Soundings.* Malibu, California: Undena Press.

Sinopoli, C. M.

1994   Archaeology of Empires. *Annual Review of Anthropology* 23:159–80.

Small, D.

1997   City-State Dynamics through a Greek Lens. In *The Archaeology of City-States: Cross-Cultural Approaches,* edited by Deborah L. Nichols and Thomas H. Charlton, pp. 107–18. Washington, D.C.: Smithsonian Institution Press.

Smith, C. A.

1974   Economics of Marketing Systems: Models from Economic Geography. *Annual Review of Anthropology* 3:167–201.

1976   *Regional Analysis,* 2 vols. New York: Academic Press.

Smith, M.

1996   *The Aztecs.* Oxford: Blackwell.

Snarskis, M.

1987   The Archaeological Evidence for Chiefdoms in Eastern and Central Costa Rica. In *Chiefdoms in the Americas,* edited by R. Drennan and C. Uribe, pp. 105–18. Lanham, Maryland: University Press of America.

Soden, W. Frh. von (editor)

1982   *Das Gilgamesch-Epos.* Stuttgart: Reclam.

Solecki, R. and R. Solecki

1970   Grooved Stones from Zawi Chemi Shanidar, a Proto-Neolithic Site in Northern Iraq. *American Anthropologist* 72:831–41.

Southall, A.

1988   The Segmentary State in Africa and Asia. *Comparative Studies in Society and History* 30:52–82.

Speiser, E. A.

1935   *Excavations at Tepe Gawra,* vol. 1. Philadelphia: University of Pennsylvania Press.

Spence, M.

1993   Tlailotlacan, a Zapotec Enclave in Teotihuacan. In *Art, Ideology, and the City of Teotihuacan,* edited by J. C. Berlo, pp. 59–88. Washington, D.C.: Dumbarton Oaks.

1996   A Comparative Analysis of Ethnic Enclaves. In *Arqueología Mesoamericana. Homenaje a William Sanders,* edited by A. G. Mastache, J. Parsons, R. Santley, and M. C. S. Puche, pp. 333–53. Mexico City: INAH.

Spencer, C.

1987   Rethinking the Chiefdom. In *Chiefdoms in the Americas,* edited by R. Drennan and C. Uribe, pp. 369–90. Lanham, Maryland: University Press of America.

1998   A Mathematical Model of Primary State Formation. *Cultural Dynamics* 10:5–20.

Spurling, G.

1992   *The Organization of Craft Production in the Inka State: The Potters and Weavers of Milliraya (Peru).* Ann Arbor: University Microfilms.

Stark, B.

1990   The Central Gulf Coast and the Central Highlands of Mexico: Alternative Models for Interaction. In *Research in Economic Anthropology,* vol. 12, edited by B. L. Isaac, pp. 243–85. Connecticut: JAI Press.

Starr, R.

1937–39   *Nuzi: Report on the Excavation at Yorgan Tepa near Kirkuk, Iraq, Conducted by Harvard University in Conjunction with the American Schools of Oriental Research and the University Museum of Philadelphia, 1927–31.* 2 vols. Cambridge, Massachusetts: Harvard University Press.

Steier, P., and W. Rom

2000   The Use of Bayesian Statistics for ^{14}C Dates of Chronologically Ordered Samples: A Critical Analysis. *Radiocarbon* 42(2):183–98.

Stein, G.

1990   Comments on G. Algaze, "The Uruk Expansion: Cross Cultural Exchange in Early Mesopotamian Civilization." *Current Anthropology* 31:66–67.

1993   Power and Distance in the Uruk Mesopotamian Colonial System. Paper presented at the Annual Meeting of the American Anthropological Association, November 21, Washington, D.C.

1994a   The Organizational Dynamics of Complexity. In *Chiefdoms and Early States in the Near East: The Organizational Dynamics of Complexity,* edited by G. Stein and M. S. Rothman, pp. 11–22. Monographs in World Prehistory 18. Madison, Wisconsin: Prehistory Press.

1994b   Economy, Ritual, and Power in Ubaid Mesopotamia. In *Chiefdoms and Early States in the Near East: The Organizational Dynamics of Complexity,* edited by G. Stein and M. S. Rothman, pp. 35–46. Monographs in World Prehistory 18. Madison, Wisconsin: Prehistory Press.

1994c   Segmentary States and Organizational Variation in Early Complex Societies: A Rural Perspective. In *Archaeological Views from the Countryside,* edited by G. Schwartz and S. Falconer, pp. 10–18. Washington, D.C.: Smithsonian Institution Press.

1997   Mesopotamian Metizaje: Interaction, Identity, and Gender in a 4th
        Millennium B.C. Uruk Colony. Paper presented at the Annual Meeting of
        the Society for American Archaeology, April 4, Nashville.

1998   World Systems Theory and Alternative Modes of Interaction in the
        Archaeology of Culture Contact. In *Studies in Culture Contact: Interaction,*
        Culture Change, and Archaeology, edited by James Cusick, pp. 220–55.
        Occasional Paper 25. Carbondale, Illinois: Center for Archaeological
        Investigations.

1999   *Rethinking World Systems: Diasporas, Colonies, and Interaction in Uruk*
        Mesopotamia. Tucson: University of Arizona Press.

2000   Material Culture and Social Identity: The Evidence for a Fourth
        Millennium B.C. Mesopotamian Uruk Colony at Hacınebi, Turkey.
        Paléorient 25(1):11–22.

Stein, G. (editor)

1999   The Uruk Expansion: Northern Perspectives from Hacınebi. Hassek,
        Höyük, and Gawra. *Paléorient* 25(1).

Stein, G., and A. Mısır

1994   Mesopotamian-Anatolian Interaction at Hacınebi, Turkey: Preliminary
        Report on the 1992 Excavations. *Anatolica* 20:145–89.

1995   Excavations at Hacınebi Tepe, 1993. In *XVI Kazı Sonuçları Toplantısı,* pp.
        121–40. Ankara: Ministry of Culture, General Directorate of Monuments
        and Museums.

1996   1994 Excavations at Hacınebi Tepe. In *XVII Kazı Sonuçları Toplantısı,* pp.
        109–28. Ankara: Ministry of Culture, General Directorate of Monuments
        and Museums.

Stein, G., and J. Nicola

1996   Late Chalcolithic Faunal Remains from Hacınebi. In Uruk Colonies and
        Mesopotamian Communities: An Interim Report on the 1992–93
        Excavations at Hacınebi, Turkey, by G. J. Stein et al., pp. 257–60. *American*
        Journal of Archaeology 100:205–60.

Stein, G., and P. Wattenmaker

1990   The 1987 Tell Leilan Regional Survey: Preliminary Report. In *Economy and*
        Settlement in the Near East: Analyses of Ancient Sites and Materials, edited by
        Naomi Miller, pp. 8–18. MASCA Research Papers in Science and Archaeology
        7 (supplement). Philadelphia: University of Pennsylvania Museum.

Stein, G., R. Bernbeck, C. Coursey, A. McMahon, N. Miller, A. Mısır, J. Nicola,
H. Pittman, S. Pollock, and H. T. Wright

1996   Uruk Colonies and Anatolian Communities: An Interim Report on the
        1992–93 Excavations at Hacınebi, Turkey. *American Journal of Archaeology*
        100:205–60.

Stein, G., K. Boden, C. Edens, J. Pierce Edens, K. Keith, A. McMahon, and H. Özbal

1997   Excavations at Hacınebi, Turkey: 1996 Preliminary Report. *Anatolica* 23:111–71.

Stein, G., C. Edens, N. Miller, H. Özbal, J. Pearce, and H. Pittman

1996   Hacınebi, Turkey: Preliminary Report on the 1995 Excavations. *Anatolica* 22:85–128.

Stein, G., C. Edens, J. Pearce Edens, K. Boden, N. Laneri, H. Özbal, B. Earl, M. Adriaens, and H. Pittman

1998   Southeast Anatolia before the Uruk Expansion: Preliminary Report on the 1997 Excavations at Hacınebi, Turkey. *Anatolica* 24:143–93.

Steinkeller, P.

1993   Early Political Development in Mesopotamia and the Origins of the Sargonic Empire. In *Akkad: The First World Empire*, edited by M. Liverani, pp. 107–30. Padua: Sargon srl.

1999   Archaic City Seals and the Question of Early Babylonian Unity. In *Thorkild Jacobsen Memorial Volume*, edited by Tzvi Abusch, pp. 1–12. New Haven: American Oriental Society.

Steponaitis, V.

1978   Location Theory and Complex Chiefdoms: A Mississippian Example. In *Mississippian Settlement Patterns*, edited by Bruce Smith, pp. 417–53. New York: Academic Press.

1981   Settlement Hierarchies and Political Complexity in Nonmarket Societies: The Formative Period of the Valley of Mexico. *American Anthropologist* 83:320–63.

1982   Settlement Hierarchies and Political Complexity. *American Anthropologist* 83:320–63.

Steward, J. H.

1955   *Irrigation Civilizations.* Washington, D.C.: Pan American Union.

1973   *Theory of Culture Change.* Urbana: University of Illinois Press.

Stone, E.

1986   Comment on A. Zagarell, "Trade, Women, Class, and Society in Ancient Western Asia." *Current Anthropology* 27:415–30.

1987   *Nippur Neighborhoods.* Chicago: Oriental Institute.

1997   City-States and Their Centers: The Mesopotamian Example. In *The Archaeology of City-States: Cross-Cultural Approaches*, edited by D. L. Nichols and T. H. Charlton, pp. 15–26. Washington, D.C.: Smithsonian Institution Press.

Strommenger, E.

1963   Archaische Siedlung. In *19. vorl. Bericht über die in Uruk-Warka unternommenen Ausgrabungen*, edited by H. J. Lenzen, pp. 45–55. Berlin: Gebr. Mann.

1980   *Habuba Kabira, eine Stadt vor 5000 Jahren.* Mainz: von Zabern.

Stronach, D.

1994   Village to Metropolis: Nineveh and the Beginnings of Urbanism in
Northern Mesopotamia. In *Nuovo Fondazione nel Vicino Oriente Antico: Realtà
ed Ideologia,* edited by S. Mazzoni, pp. 85–108. Pisa: Giardini.

Suleiman, A., and A. Taraqji

1993   Tell Kashkashouk III. *Syria* 72:172–83.

Sumner, W. M.

1986   Proto-Elamite Civilization in Fars. In *Gamdat Naṣr: Period or Regional Style?*
edited by U. Finkbeiner and W. Röllig, pp. 199–211. Wiesbaden: Ludwig
Reichert.

Sürenhagen, D.

1974–75 Untersuchungen zur Keramikproduktion innerhalb der Spät-
Urukzeitlichen Siedlung Habuba Kabira Sud in Nordsyrien. *Acta Prehistoria
et Archaeologia* 5–6:43–164.

1986a   The Dry Farming Belt: The Uruk Period and Subsequent Developments.
In *The Origins of Cities in Dry-Farming Syria and Mesopotamia in the Third
Millennium B.C.,* edited by H. Weiss, pp. 7–43. Guilford, Connecticut: Four
Quarters.

1986b   Archaische Keramik aus Uruk Warka, Teil 1. *Baghdader Mitteilungen*
17:1–95.

1990   Ausgrabungen in Tall Mulla Matar 1989. *Mitteilungen der Deutschen Orient-
Gesellschaft* 122:125–52.

1993   Relative Chronology of the Uruk Period: New Evidence from Uruk/Warka
and Northern Syria. *Bulletin of the Canadian Society for Mesopotamian Studies*
25:57–70.

Tallon, F.

1987   *Métallurgie Susienne I: de la Fondation de Suse au XVIIIe avant J.-C. Paris:
Ministère de la culture et de la communication,* Éditions de la Réunion des
Musées Nationaux.

Thomas, N.

1991   *Entangled Objects.* Cambridge, Massachusetts: Harvard University Press.

Thuesen, I.

1988   *Hama, The Pre- and Protohistoric Periods.* Copenhagen: Nationalmuseet.

Tobler, A.

1950   *Excavations at Tepe Gawra,* vol. 2. Philadelphia: University of Pennsylvania
Press.

Tomita, T.

1998a   Phases 2–4: Later Periods, Pottery. In *Excavations at Tell Umm Qseir in
Middle Khabur Valley, North Syria: Report of the 1996 Season,* edited by A.
Tsuneki and Y. Miyake, pp. 141–60. Tsukuba: Institute of History and
Anthropology, University of Tsukuba.

1998b   Late Chalcolithic Chronology in Syria and Northern Mesopotamia. In *Excavations at Tell Umm Qseir in Middle Khabur Valley, North Syria: Report of the 1996 Season,* edited by A. Tsuneki and Y. Miyake, pp. 197–201. Tsukuba: Institute of History and Anthropology, University of Tsukuba.

Trentin, M. G.

1993   The Early Reserved Slip Wares Horizon of the Upper Euphrates Basin and Western Syria. In *Between the Rivers and over the Mountains,* edited by M. Frangipane, H. Hauptmann, M. Liverani, M. Matthiae, and M. Mellinck, pp. 177–99. Università di Roma "La Sapienza."

Trufelli, F.

1997   Ceramic Correlations and Cultural Relations in IVth Millennium Eastern Anatolia and Syro-Mesopotamia. *Studi Micenei de Egeo-Anatolici* 39:5–33.

Tsetskhladze, G., and F. De Angelis (editors)

1994   *The Archaeology of Greek Colonisation: Essays Dedicated to Sir John Boardman.* Oxford University Committee for Archaeology Monograph 40. Oxford: Oxbow Books.

Tsuneki, A., and Y. Miyake

1998   *Excavations at Tell Umm Qseir in the Middle Khabur Valley, North Syria.* University of Tsukuba: Department of Archaeology.

Uceda, S., and E. Mujica (editors)

1994   *Moche: Propuestas y Perspectivas.* Travaux de l'Institut Français d'Etudes Andines 79. Lima.

Vallat, F.

1986   The Most Ancient Scripts of Iran: The Current Situation. *World Archaeology* 17:336–47.

Vallet, R.

1997   Habuba Kabire ou la naissance de l'Urbanisme. Paléorient 22(2):45–76.

1998   L'urbanisme colonial urukien, l'example de Djebel Aruda. *Subartu* 4:53–87.

Van Buren, M.

1996   Rethinking the Vertical Archipelago: Ethnicity, Exchange, and History in the South American Andes. *American Anthropologist* 98:338–51.

Van de Mieroop, M.

1993   *Society and Enterprise in Old Babylonian Ur.* Berlin: Dietrich Reimer.

1997   *The Ancient Mesopotamian City.* Oxford: Clarendon.

Van der Leeuw, S.

1994   *The Pottery from a Middle-Uruk Pit at Tepe Sharafabad.* Terre Cuite et Société. Juna-de Pins: Éditions APDCA.

Van Driel, G.

1982   Tablets from Jebel Aruda. In *Zikir Šumim, F. R. Kraus Festschrift,* edited by G. Van Driel et al., pp. 12–25. Leiden: E.J. Brill.

1983   Seals and Sealings from Jebel Aruda, 1974–78. *Akkadica* 33:34–62.

1998   Jebel Aruda: Collapsing Aspirations? Paper presented at the Artefacts of Complexity Conference, Manchester, England.

Van Driel, G., and C. Van Driel-Murray

1979   Jebel Aruda 1977–78. *Akkadica* 12:2–28.

1983   Jebel Aruda, the 1982 Season of Excavations. *Akkadica* 33:1–26.

Van Loon, M.

1978   Architecture and Stratigraphy. In *Korucutepe*, vol. 2, edited by M. Van Loon, pp. 3–46. Amsterdam: North Holland.

1967   *The Tabqa Reservoir Survey, 1964.* Damascus: Direction Générale des Antiquités et des Musées.

Van Loon, M. (editor)

1978   *Korucutepe.* Amsterdam: North Holland Press.

1988   *Hammam et-Turkman I.* Leiden: Nederlands Historisch-Archeologisch Instituut te Istanbul.

Van Zeist, W.

1978   Prehistoric and Early Historic Plant Use in the Altınovan Plain, Southeastern Turkey. In *Korucutepe*, vol. 1, edited by M. Van Loon, pp. 221–57. Amsterdam: North Holland Press.

1994   Some Notes on Second Millennium B.C.. Plant Cultivation in the Syrian Jazira. In *Cinquante-deux reflexions sur le Proche-Orient ancien: offertes en hommage à Léon de Meyer*, edited by H. Gasche, pp. 541–53. Leeuven: Peeters.

1998   The Plant Remains from Fatmalı-Kaleclk. In *Karatepe'deki I?ik (Light on the Top of the Black Hill): Studies Presented to Halet Çambel*, edited by G. Arsebük, M. J. Mellink, and W. Schirmer, p. 781. Istanbul: Ege Yayınları.

Van Zeist, W., and S. Bottema

1977   Palynological Investigations in Western Iran. *Palaeohistoria* 19:19–95.

Venkatesan, M. I., T. W. Linick, H. E. Suess, and G. Buccellati

1982   Asphalt in Carbon-14-Date Archaeological Samples from Terqa, Syria. *Nature* 295:517–19.

Vertesálji, P. P.

1984   *Babylonien zur Steinkupferzeit.* Beihefte zum TAVO B. 53. Wiesbaden: Ludwig Reichert.

Vita-Finzi, C., and E. Higgs

1970   Prehistoric Economy in the Mount Carmel Area of Palestine: Site Catchment Analysis. *Proceedings of the Prehistoric Society* 36:1–37.

von der Way, T.

1987   Tell el-Fara'in, Buto. 2. Bericht. *Mitteilungen des Deutschen Archäologischen Instituts Abteilung Kairo* 43:250–57.

von Wickede, A.

1990   *Prähistorische Stempelglyptik in Vorderasien.* München: Profil.

Voorrips, A.

1981   To Tailor the Inflected Tail: Reflections on Rank-Size Relationships. In *Archaeological Approaches to the Study of Complexity,* edited by Sander van der Leeuw, pp. 189–96. Amsterdam: University of Amsterdam.

Waetzoldt, H.

1972   *Untersuchungen zur neusumerischen Textilindustrie.* Rome: Centro per le Antichità e la Storia dell'Arte del Vicino Oriente.

Wallerstein, I.

1974   *The Modern World System,* vol. 1. New York: Academic Press.

1995   Hold the Tiller Firm: On Method and the Unit of Analysis. In *Civilizations and World Systems,* edited by S. K. Sanderson, pp. 239–47. Walnut Creek, California: Altamira Press.

Wartke, R.

1997   Kneidig. In *Archaeology in Syria,* edited by H. Weiss. American Journal of Archaeology 101:123–26.

Waterbolk, H. T.

1971   Working with Radiocarbon Dates. *Proceedings of the Prehistoric Society* 37(2):15–33.

Watson, P. J.

1979   *Archaeological Ethnography in Western Iran.* Viking Fund Publications in Anthropology 57. New York.

Wattenmaker, P.

1990   Comment on G. Algaze, "The Uruk Expansion: Cross-Cultural Exchange in Early Mesopotamian Civilization." *Current Anthropology* 31:67–69.

Wattenmaker, P., and G. Stein

1989   Leilan 1987 Survey: Uruk Summary. In Out of the Heartland: The Evolution of Complexity in Peripheral Mesopotamia during the Uruk Period, edited by Mitchell Rothman. *Paléorient* 15(1):283–84.

Weiss, H.

1977   Periodization, Population, and Early State Formation in Khuzistan. In *Mountains and Lowlands: Essays in the Archaeology of Greater Mesopotamia,* edited by Louis Levine and T. Cuyler Young, pp. 347–70. Malibu, California: Undena Press.

1985   *Ebla to Damascus: Art and Archaeology of Ancient Syria.* Washington, D.C.: Smithsonian Institution Exhibits.

1986   The Origins of Tell Leilan and the Conquest of Space in Third Millennium North Mesopotamia. In *The Origins of Cities in Dry-Farming Syria and Mesopotamia in the Third Millennium B.C.,* edited by H. Weiss, pp. 71–108. Guilford, Connecticut: Four Quarters.

1989a   Comment on G. Algaze, "The Uruk Expansion: Cross-cultural Exchange in Early Mesopotamian Civilization." *Current Anthropology* 30:597–98.

1989b   Tell Leilan 1989: New Data for Mid-Third Millennium Urbanization and
         State Formation. *Mitteilungen der deutschen Orient-Gesellschaft* 122:193–218.

Weiss, H., and T. C. Young
1975   The Merchants of Susa: Godin V and Plateau-Lowland Relations in the
         Late Fourth Millennium B.C. *Iran* 13:1–17.

Weiss, H., M.-A. Courty, W. Wetterstrom, F. Guichard, L. Senior, R. Meadow,
and A. Curnow
1993   The Genesis and Collapse of Third Millennium North Mesopotamian
         Civilization. *Science* 261:995–1004.

Wells, P.
1992   Tradition, Identity, and Change beyond the Roman Frontier. In *Resources,*
         Power, and Interregional Interaction, edited by E. Schortman and P. Urban,
         pp. 175–88. New York: Plenum.

Wenke, R. J.
1975–76 Imperial Investments and Agricultural Development in Parthian and
         Sasanian Khuzestan: 150 B.C. to A.D. 640. *Mesopotamia* 10–11:31–217.

Westenholz, A.
1979   The Old Akkadian Empire in Contemporary Opinion. In *Power and*
         Propaganda, edited by M. T. Larsen, pp. 107–24. Copenhagen: Akademisk
         Forlag.

Whallon, R.
1979   *An Archaeological Survey of the Keban Reservoir Area of East Central Turkey.*
         Memoir of the Museum of Anthropology, no. 11. Ann Arbor: University of
         Michigan.

White, R.
1991   *The Middle Ground: Indians, Empires, and Republics in the Great Lakes Region,*
         1650–1815. Cambridge: Cambridge University Press.

Wilkinson, T. J.
1990a   Town and Country in Southeastern Anatolia. vol. 1: *Settlement and Land Use*
         at Kurban Höyük and Other Sites in the Lower Karababa Basin. Chicago:
         Oriental Institute.
1990b   Early Channels and Landscape Development around Abu Salabikh: A
         Preliminary Report. *Iraq* 52:75–84.
1990c   The Development of Settlement in the North Jazira between the 7th and
         1st Millennia B.C. *Iraq* 52:49–62.
1994   The Structure and Dynamics of Dry Farming States in Upper
         Mesopotamia. *Current Anthropology* 35:483–520.
1998   Archaeological Survey of the Tell Beydar Region, Syria, 1997: A
         Preliminary Report. Subartu Series, no. 4. Turnhout, Belgium: Brepolis.
n.d.a   Holocene Valley Fills of Southern Turkey and Northwestern Syria:
         Geoarchaeological Contributions. *Quaternary Science Review.* In press.

n.d.b   The Long-Term Limit of Rainfed Cultivation in Northern Syria:
         Proceedings of the International Colloquium on "The Syrian Djezireh:
         Cultural Heritage and Interrelations," April 1996. Deir-ez-Zor, Syria. In
         press.

Wilkinson, T. J., and D. Tucker
1995   *Settlement Development in the North Jazira, Iraq.* Warminster: Aris and Phillips.

Willey, G.
1953   *Prehistoric Settlement Patterns in the Virú Valley, Peru.* Bureau of American
        Ethnology Bulletin 155. Washington, D.C.: Smithsonian Institution.

Williams, C.
1991   A Scheme for the Early Monumental Architecture of the Central Coast of
        Peru. In *Early Ceremonial Architecture in the Andes,* edited by Christopher B.
        Donnan, pp. 227–40. Washington, D.C.: Dumbarton Oaks.

Williams, V. I., and A. M. Lorandi
1986   Evidencias funcionales de un establecimiento incaico del Noroeste
        argentino. In *Comechingonia, Vol. Homenaje al 45°,* pp. 133–49. Córdoba,
        Argentina: Congreso Internacional de Americanistas (Bógota).

Willkomm, H.
1992   Radiokohlenstoffdatierungen. In *Hassek Höyük: Naturwissenschaftliche
        Untersuchungen und lithische Industrie,* edited by M. Behm-Blanke, pp.
        135–39. Istanbuler Forschungen, vol. 38. Tübingen: Ernst Wasmuth.

Wilson, D. J.
1997   Early State Formation on the North Coast of Peru: A Critique of the City-
        State Model. In *The Archaeology of City-States: Cross-Cultural Approaches,* edit-
        ed by D. L. Nichols and T. H. Charlton, pp. 229–44. Washington, D.C.:
        Smithsonian Institution Press.

Wilson, K.
1986   Nippur: The Definition of a Mesopotamian Ǧamdat Naṣr Assemblage. In
        Ǧamdat Naṣr: Period or Regional Style? edited by U. Finkbeiner and W. Röllig,
        pp. 57–89. Wiesbaden: Ludwig Reichert.

Winter, I.
1977   Perspective on the "Local Style" of Hasanlu IVB: A Study in Receptivity. In
        Mountains and Lowlands, edited by L. D. Levine and T. C. Young, Jr., pp.
        371–86. Malibu, California: Undena Press.

Wolf, E.
1982   *Europe and the People without History.* Berkley: University of California Press.

Woolley, C. L.
1955a   *Alalakh.* Oxford: Society of Antiquities.
1955b   *Ur Excavations,* vol. 4: The Early Periods. London and Philadelphia: British
        Museum and University Museum.

Wright, G.
1969   *Obsidian Analyses and Prehistoric Near Eastern Trade: 7500 to 3500 B.C.* Papers of the Museum of Anthropology, no. 37. Ann Arbor: University of Michigan.

Wright, H. T.
1977a   Recent Research on the Origin of the State. *Annual Review of Anthropology* 6:379–97.

1977b   Toward an Explanation of the Origin of the State. In *Explanation of Prehistoric Change,* edited by James Hill, pp. 215–30. Albuquerque: University of New Mexico Press.

1978   Toward an Explanation of the Origin of the State. In *The Origin of the State: The Anthropology of Political Evolution,* edited by R. Cohen and E. Service, pp. 49–68. Philadelphia: Institute for the Study of Human Issues.

1981   The Southern Margins of Sumer: Archaeological Survey of the Area of Eridu and Ur. In *Heartland of Cities,* edited by Robert McC. Adams, pp. 295–345. Chicago: University of Chicago Press.

1984   Prestate Political Formations. In *On the Evolution of Complex Societies: Essays in Honor of Harry Hoijer,* edited by W. Sanders, H. T. Wright, and R. McC. Adams, pp. 41–77. Malibu, California: Undena Press.

1987   The Susiana Hinterlands during the Era of Primary State Formation. In *The Archaeology of Western Iran,* edited by F. Hole, pp. 141–55. Washington, D.C.: Smithsonian Institution Press.

1994   Prestate Political Formations. In *Chiefdoms and Early States in the Near East,* edited by G. Stein and M. Rothman, pp. 67–84. Madison, Wisconsin: Prehistory Press.

1995   Review of G. Algaze, "The Uruk World System." *American Anthropologist* 97:151–52.

1998   Uruk States in Southwestern Iran. In *Archaic States,* edited by Gary Feinman and Joyce Marcus, pp. 173–92. Santa Fe: SAR Press.

Wright, H. T. (editor)
1969   *The Administration of Rural Production in an Early Mesopotamian Town.* Papers of the Museum of Anthropology, no. 38. Ann Arbor: University of Michigan.

1981   *An Early Town on the Deh Luran Plain: Excavations at Tepe Farukhabad.* Memoirs of the Museum of Anthropology, no. 13. Ann Arbor: University of Michigan.

Wright, H. T., and R. Bernbeck
1996   Flaked Stone Assemblages from Hacınebi Tepe. In *Uruk Colonies and Mesopotamian Communities: An Interim Report on the 1992–93 Excavations at Hacınebi, Turkey,* edited by G. J. Stein et al., pp. 239–47. American Journal of Archaeology 100:205–60.

Wright, H. T., and G. A. Johnson

1975 Population, Exchange, and Early State Formation in Southwestern Iran. *American Anthropologist* 77:267–89.

1985 Regional Perspectives on Southwest Iranian State Development. *Paléorient* 11(2):25–30.

Wright, H. T., N. Miller, and R. Redding

1980 Time and Process in an Uruk Rural Center. In *Colloques internationaux du CNRS, L'Archeologie de L'Iraq,* pp. 265–84. Paris: Éditions CNRS.

Wright, H. T., R. Redding, and S. Pollock

1989 Monitoring Interannual Variability: An Example from the Period of Early State Development in Southwestern Iran. In *Bad Year Economics: Cultural Responses to Risk and Uncertainty,* edited by P. Halstead and J. O'Shea, pp. 106–13. Cambridge: Cambridge University Press.

Wright, H. T., R. Whallon, A. Hauptmann, R. Redding, and W. van Zeist

1998 Investigations at Fatmalı-Kaleclk: A Chalcolithic Hamlet in the Upper Euphrates Valley. In *Karatepe'deki Işik (Light on the Top of the Black Hill): Studies Presented to Halet Çambel,* edited by G. Arsebük, M. J. Mellink, and W. Schirmer, pp. 775–809. Istanbul: Ege Yayınları.

Wright, Rita

1989 Comment on G. Algaze, "The Uruk Expansion: Cross-cultural Exchange in Early Mesopotamian Civilization." *Current Anthropology* 30:599–600.

Wright, Robert

2000 *Nonzero: The Logic of Human Destiny.* New York: Pantheon Books.

Yamazaki, Y.

1999 Excavations at Tell al-'Abr. In *Archaeology of the Upper Syrian Euphrates: The Tishreen Dam Area,* edited by G. Del Olmo Lete and J.-L. Montero Fenollós, pp. 83–96. Barcelona: Editorial Ausa.

Yener, K. A.

2000 *The Domestication of Metals: The Rise of Complex Metal Industries in Anatolia.* Leiden: E.J. Brill.

Yener, K. A., H. Özbal, and E. Kaptan

1989 Kestel: An Early Bronze Age Source of Tin Ore in the Taurus Mountains, Turkey. *Science* 244:200–203.

Yener, K. A., and P. B. Vandiver

1993 Tin Processing at Goltepe, An Early Bronze Age Site in Anatolia. *American Journal of Archaeology* 97:207–38.

Yoffee, N.

1981 *Explaining Trade in the Ancient Near East.* Monographs on the Ancient Near East 2(2). Malibu, California: Undena Press.

1991 Maya Elite Interaction: Through a Glass Darkly. In *Classic Maya Political History,* edited by T. P. Culbert, pp. 285–310. Cambridge: Cambridge University Press.

1993   Too Many Chiefs? (Or, Safe Texts for the 90s). In *Archaeological Theory: Who Sets the Agenda?* edited by N. Yoffee and A. Sherratt, pp. 60–78. Cambridge: Cambridge University Press.

1995   Political Economy in Early Mesopotamian States. *Annual Review of Anthropology* 24:281–311.

Young, T. C., Jr.
1986   Godin Tepe Period VI/V and Central Western Iran at the End of the Fourth Millennium. In *Ğamdat Naṣr: Period or Regional Style?* edited by U. Finkbeiner and W. Röllig, pp. 212–28. Wiesbaden: Ludwig Reichert.

Zagarell, A.
1986   Trade, Women, Class, and Society in Ancient Western Asia. *Current Anthropology* 27:415–30.

Zeder, M.
1988   Understanding Urban Process through the Study of Specialized Subsistence Economy in the Near East. *Journal of Anthropological Archaeology* 7:1–55.

1991   *Feeding Cities.* Washington, D.C.: Smithsonian Institution Press.

1994   After the Revolution: Post-Neolithic Subsistence in North Mesopotamia. *American Anthropologist* 96:97–126.

1998   Environment, Economy and Subsistence in Northern Mesopotamia. In *Espace naturel, espace habité en Syrie du Nord (10ᵉ–2ᵉ millénaires av. J-C.),* edited by M. Fortin and O. Aurenche, pp. 55–67. Bulletin of the Canadian Society for Mesopotamian Studies 33. Lyon: Maison de l'Orient.

Zettler, R.
1987   Sealings as Artifacts of Institutional Administration in Ancient Mesopotamia. *Journal of Cuneiform Studies* 39:197–240.

Zettler, R., et al.
1996   Tell es-Sweyhat, 1989–95: A City in Northern Mesopotamia in the Third Millennium B.C. *Expedition* 38:14–36.

Index

School of American Research
Advanced Seminar Series

PUBLISHED BY SAR PRESS

RECONSTRUCTING PREHISTORIC PUEBLO
SOCIETIES
William A. Longacre, ed.

NEW PERSPECTIVES ON THE PUEBLOS
Alfonso Ortiz, ed.

STRUCTURE AND PROCESS IN LATIN
AMERICA
Arnold Strickon &
Sidney M. Greenfield, eds.

THE CLASSIC MAYA COLLAPSE
T. Patrick Culbert, ed.

METHODS AND THEORIES OF
ANTHROPOLOGICAL GENETICS
M. H. Crawford & P. L. Workman, eds.

SIXTEENTH-CENTURY MEXICO:
THE WORK OF SAHAGUN
Munro S. Edmonson, ed.

ANCIENT CIVILIZATION AND TRADE
Jeremy A. Sabloff &
C. C. Lamberg-Karlovsky, eds.

PHOTOGRAPHY IN ARCHAEOLOGICAL
RESEARCH
Elmer Harp, Jr. ed.

MEANING IN ANTHROPOLOGY
Keith H. Basso & Henry A. Selby, eds.

THE VALLEY OF MEXICO: STUDIES IN
PRE-HISPANIC ECOLOGY AND SOCIETY
Eric R. Wolf, ed.

DEMOGRAPHIC ANTHROPOLOGY:
QUANTITATIVE APPROACHES
Ezra B. W. Zubrow, ed.

THE ORIGINS OF MAYA CIVILIZATION
Richard E. W. Adams, ed.

EXPLANATION OF PREHISTORIC CHANGE
James N. Hill, ed.

EXPLORATIONS IN ETHNOARCHAEOLOGY
Richard A. Gould, ed.

ENTREPRENEURS IN CULTURAL CONTEXT
Sidney M. Greenfield, Arnold Strickon,
& Robert T. Aubey, eds.

THE DYING COMMUNITY
Art Gallaher, Jr., &
Harlan Padfield, eds.

SOUTHWESTERN INDIAN RITUAL DRAMA
Charlotte J. Frisbie, ed.

LOWLAND MAYA SETTLEMENT PATTERNS
Wendy Ashmore, ed.

SIMULATIONS IN ARCHAEOLOGY
Jeremy A. Sabloff, ed.

CHAN CHAN: ANDEAN DESERT CITY
Michael E. Moseley & Kent C. Day, eds.

SHIPWRECK ANTHROPOLOGY
Richard A. Gould, ed.

ELITES: ETHNOGRAPHIC ISSUES
George E. Marcus, ed.

THE ARCHAEOLOGY OF LOWER CENTRAL
AMERICA
Frederick W. Lange &
Doris Z. Stone, eds.

LATE LOWLAND MAYA CIVILIZATION:
CLASSIC TO POSTCLASSIC
Jeremy A. Sabloff &
E. Wyllys Andrews V, eds.

Participants in the School of American Research advanced seminar "Mesopotamia in the Era of State Formation," Santa Fe, New Mexico, March 1998. From left: Hans J. Nissen, Guillermo Algaze, Mitchell S. Rothman, Henry T. Wright, Holly Pittman, Terence N. D'Altroy, Susan Pollock, Marcella Frangipane, Glenn M. Schwartz, Gil J. Stein.